WORKS ISSUED BY
THE HAKLUYT SOCIETY

———————

THE ORIGINS OF THE GRAND TOUR

THIRD SERIES
NO. 14

THE ORIGINS

OF THE

GRAND TOUR

THE TRAVELS OF
Robert Montagu, Lord Mandeville (1649–1654)
William Hammond (1655–1658)
Banaster Maynard (1660–1663)

Edited by
MICHAEL G. BRENNAN

THE HAKLUYT SOCIETY
LONDON
2004

Published by The Hakluyt Society
c/o Map Library
The British Library, 96 Euston Road,
London NW1 2DB

SERIES EDITORS
W. F. RYAN
MICHAEL BRENNAN

ISBN 0 904180 85 9
ISSN 0072 9396

British Library Cataloguing-in-Publication Data
A catalogue record for this book is
available from the British Library

Typeset by Waveney Typesetters, Wymondham, Norfolk
Printed in Great Britain at
the University Press, Cambridge

'Remember'

Revd Thomas Brennan RN
(1913–1944)

Hugo Brennan RN
(1916–1989)

John Brennan RN
(1948–1973)

CONTENTS

ILLUSTRATIONS

ABBREVIATIONS, CONVENTIONS AND ACKNOWLEDGEMENTS

BL   British Library, London
Bodl.   Bodleian Library, Oxford
CSPD *Calendar of State Papers Domestic*
HMC   Historical Manuscripts Commission
PRO   The National Archive, Public Record Office, Kew
STC   *A Short-Title Catalogue of Books Printed in England, Scotland, & Ireland ... 1475–1640*, completed by A. W. Pollard and G. R. Redgrave, 2nd edn, revised & enlarged by W. A. Jackson, F. Ferguson, and K. F. Pantzer, Vol. I, A–H, 1986, Vol. II, I–Z, 1976, Vol. III, 1991.
Wing   *Short-Title Catalogue of Books Printed in England, Scotland, Ireland, Wales, and British America and of English Books Printed in Other Countries 1641–1700*, compiled by D. Wing, 3 vols, New York, 1945–51; revised edn, New York, 1972–88.

Full titles of all other works cited are given in the Bibliography, with the title also cited in full in the notes for the first reference, with abbreviated titles thereafter. For works printed in Britain before 1700, *Short-Title Catalogue* references (i.e. *STC* and Wing) are also supplied in the Bibliography. When a pre-1700 travel source is cited for comparative purposes with the edited texts, approximate dates of composition and/or publication for this source are also supplied – e.g. 'Evelyn (1644)' or 'Raymond (1648)'.

When abroad at this period, English travellers generally used the new-style (NS) Gregorian calendar of 1582, as opposed to the old-style (OS) Julian calendar, still followed in Protestant Britain (except Scotland). The new-style continental system, adopted by all other European countries (except Russia), was ten days in advance of the old-style. Under the Julian calendar, 25 March (Lady Day) was regarded as the first day of the new year. The Gregorian calendar was not formally adopted in Britain until 1753. In this edition I describe the most commonly traversed regions during this kind of tour as, variously, 'Western Europe', 'Continental Europe', or the 'continent', although some of the individuals discussed also travelled further east into central and eastern Europe. For the convenience of the reader, in the introductions and annotations I also generally use modern-day geographical delineations of specific regions (eg. Germany, Austria, Switzerland, etc.) rather than the less familiar seventeenth-century territorial divisions.

In the edited texts, the spellings, accenting of foreign words, and proper names in the original manuscripts have generally been retained, although the use of 'i'/'j', 'i'/'y', 'u'/'v', and long 's' has been standardized. Similarly, the use of 'y^e', 'y^t', and 'y^ese' has been standardized to '*the*', '*that*', and '*these*'. Other standard contractions have been expanded, such as 'w^ch'/'which', 'y^r'/'your', and 'Hon^d:'/'Honoured'. In all three manuscripts the use of capital letters is often problematic as it is not always clear (especially with such letters as 's', 'p', 'm', and 'n') whether a capital letter was intended by the scribe. In other cases capital letters are regularly or randomly deployed within sentences (such as the habitual use of capital 'C' in the Hammond manuscript). Apart from ambiguous cases, where it has been necessary to make an editorial decision, the original capitalization of the manuscripts has been generally retained. Some other individual idiosyncrasies of the scribes (such as the habitual use of 'we say' for 'we saw' in the Montagu manuscript) have been retained since the meaning is usually clear from the context. On other occasions (such as the irregular use of 'the' for 'they' in the Montagu manuscript) a missing letter has been supplied within square brackets to avoid unnecessary confusion.

To assist the modern reader the punctuation and paragraphing of all three manuscripts – which sometimes range from the erratic to the non-existent – have been modernized where appropriate. However, this kind of editorial intervention has been cautiously applied. In the case of the Hammond manuscript, for example, although its punctuation does not always equate to modern practice (especially in its use of semi-colons rather than full points), it has generally been retained since it is both clear and standardized within its own conventions. Catchwords at the foot of the pages have been omitted since they are used irregularly. Hyphens in the manuscripts, sometimes indicated by a double dash '=', have been standardized to a single hyphen '-'. Folio references contained in square brackets within the text indicate the folios of the original manuscripts. All marginal annotations included by the compilers and copyists have been recorded in the footnotes; and in the Hammond manuscript the copyist's habit of numbering the letters in the right-hand margin has been standardized by placing the number in square brackets at the head of each letter. Square brackets are employed in the conventional manner to enclose editorial comments or additions and all other substantive matters of scribal commission and omission are recorded in the footnotes. Throughout this edition I have referred to Charles Stuart (later King Charles II) in references before 1660 as 'Charles II' and after the restoration in 1660 as 'King Charles II'.

For personal advice and guidance during the compilation of this volume, I am grateful to Sonia Anderson (formerly Historical Manuscripts Commission), Peter Beal (Sotheby's), Geraldine Brennan (Leeds), Michael Broers (University of Oxford), Deborah Clark (Francis Edwards Booksellers), Geoffrey Forster (Leeds Library), Antony Griffiths (British Museum), Paul Grinke (Bernard Quaritch Ltd.), Paul Hammond (University of Leeds), Margaret P. Hannay (Siena College, New York), Noel J. Kinnamon (Mars Hill, North Carolina), Desmond McTernan (British Library), Reinhard Mast (Reusten, Ammerbuch), and Jill Winder (Brotherton Library). It is also proper for me to acknowledge here my considerable debt to two other individuals, Esmond de Beer and John Walter Stoye, whose writings originally formed the foundation and stimulus for my own interest in English travellers in Western Europe during the sixteenth and seventeenth centuries.

I am grateful to Viscount De L'Isle, MBE, DL, for permission to quote from his family papers (now at the Centre for Kentish Studies, Maidstone). I am also grateful to the Bodleian Library, Oxford, both for permission to consult and edit MS Rawlinson D 76 and MS Rawlinson D 84 and to reproduce illustrations from these manuscripts. During the last decade and a half my ongoing interest in English travel writing has depended heavily upon the extensive holdings in this subject area of the Brotherton Library, University of Leeds. The letters of William Hammond have been edited from one of the library's manuscripts

(MS Trv 2); and the majority of the illustrations included in this volume have been selected from the Brotherton Library's collections. My greatest debt in writing about the experiences, observations, and records of English travellers from this period is to Christopher D. W. Sheppard, Head of Special Collections (Brotherton Library, University of Leeds), whose guidance and assistance have been both invaluable and generously given. I am also happy to acknowledge the support of my own department at Leeds, the School of English, and that of the University of Leeds for a Study Leave in the Humanities Award during the compilation of this volume. Finally, I am once again especially indebted to Professor Will Ryan, joint series editor for the Hakluyt Society, and to Stephen Easton, printing adviser, and Barrie Fairhead, typesetter, for their meticulous and expert advice on the editing and production of this volume.

INTRODUCTION

ROBERT MONTAGU, WILLIAM HAMMOND, AND BANASTER MAYNARD

> let him [the traveller] carefully note all rare observations; for hee lesse offends that writes many toyes, then he that omits one serious thing, and after when his judgement is more ripe, he shall distill Gold (as the Proverbe is) out of this dung of Ennius. Let him write these notes each day, at morne and at even in his Inne, within writing Tables carried about him, and after at leasure into a paper booke, that many yeers after he may looke over them at his pleasure.
>
> (Fynes Moryson, *An Itinerary*, 1617)[1]

This volume publishes for the first time fully annotated, old-spelling texts of three separate manuscript accounts of travels within Western Europe, describing journeys made through France, Italy, Austria, Germany, Hungary, Switzerland, Belgium, and Holland by three young English travellers, Robert Montagu, William Hammond, and Banaster Maynard, between 1649 and 1663 (respectively MSS Oxford, Bodleian Library, Rawlinson D 76; Leeds, Brotherton Collection, Trv 2; Oxford, Bodleian Library, Rawlinson D 84). The three accounts were compiled in markedly different formats and for very different purposes. When viewed together as a progressive historical narrative, they offer an enlightening perspective into the views and aspirations of certain kinds of young Englishmen who were sent abroad by their families during a tumultuous period of English domestic politics and international relations.

One of the most telling aspects of the historical context to these three records of continental itineraries – covering the period from the execution of Charles I in January 1649, through the Commonwealth and Protectorate of Oliver Cromwell, until three years after the Restoration of King Charles II – lies in the personal backgrounds of the three travellers themselves. Each of their families, like so many others of their generation, encompassed a complex series of personal associations with royalist circles and Parliament.[2] Although the Montagus, Hammonds, and Maynards generally thrived after the Restoration, the wanderings abroad of these young men, especially when viewed within the context of the politically conflicting activities of some of their closest relatives, implicitly convey a broader sense of the huge social and familial dislocation occasioned by the constitutional upheavals of the

---

[1] *An Itinerary … Written by Fynes Moryson Gent.*, London: J. Beale, 1617 (rpt. 4 vols, Glasgow, 1907–8), III, pp. 373–4.

[2] For more detailed accounts of each of their family backgrounds, see, for Robert Montagu, pp. 57–60, 69–77; for William Hammond, pp. 147–58; and for Banaster Maynard, pp. 227–34.

1640s and 1650s. As these three manuscript accounts suggest, a young man sent abroad at this time could be viewed either as a student in search of scholarly or cultural enlightenment, or as a wealthy and highly privileged tourist, or as a pragmatic escapee from an increasingly problematic domestic context, or even as a publicly disaffected political or religious dissident (or as a combination of some or all of these elements). Such a traveller might even flatteringly envisage himself as a kind of indomitable exile from his own native land and rightful inheritance, enduring the same vicissitudes as his dispossessed monarch Charles II, who was at this period wandering, variously, from The Hague, Breda, Saint-Germain, St Helier on Jersey, Scotland (and after the Battle of Worcester in September 1651), to Rouen, Paris, Spa, Aachen, Cologne, Düsseldorf, Frankfurt, Brussels, Bruges, Antwerp (and back again to Brussels), Breda, and The Hague (see Fig. 1).

The first account (Bodl. MS Rawlinson D 76), was begun by the fourteen-years-old ROBERT MONTAGU (1634–83), Lord Mandeville and later 3rd Earl of Manchester, but then carried on (from fol. 27ᵛ) by another hand, perhaps that of his travelling tutor, Mr Hainhofer (see p. 64). In describing Montagu's experiences abroad between May 1649 and October 1652 (he finally returned to England in April 1654 but the Bodleian manuscript is incomplete, see pp. 67–8), the writers followed the usual conventions of manuscript travel diaries, dutifully compiling a wealth of geographical, historical, and architectural observations on major locations and landmarks, interlaced with Montagu's own youthful observations and opinions.[1]

Robert Montagu was the grandson of James I's Lord High Treasurer, Henry Montagu (c. 1563–1642), who had been knighted and raised to the barony by King James and created 1st Earl of Manchester three days after the coronation of Charles I. However, Henry's eldest son Edward (1602–71), later the 2nd Earl (see Fig. 16, p. 59), grew increasingly hostile towards the Charles's autocratic behaviour during the early 1640s and became a general in the parliamentary army. But, as the political tensions mounted during the late 1640s, he sought to distance himself from the prosecution of direct military engagements and he certainly opposed both the trial and execution of the king. It seems likely, then, that his eldest surviving son and heir, our diarist Robert Montagu, was sent abroad in May 1649 (the Rump Parliament had abolished the monarchy and the House of Lords in the preceding April and a free commonwealth was declared in May) as much to avoid the possible consequences for his family of these constitutional changes as to broaden his education. This withdrawal of the heir to the Manchester earldom proved tactically astute and enabled Robert Montagu later to present himself as an ardent royalist driven into a youthful exile during the 1650s. This strategy was successful enough to justify his selection in May 1660 as one of the six ambassadors who were sent to The Hague where they formally invited Charles II to return to England. Robert's father, the 2nd Earl, was also deemed a loyal royalist at the Restoration and carried the sword of state at Charles II's coronation on 28 April 1661 (see Fig. 17, p. 72).

As is already evident from his father's difficult political position during the 1640s, the young Robert Montagu grew up within a distinctly tangled web of personal loyalties. His grandfather's elder brother Edward (1562–1644), 1st Baron Montagu of Boughton, was a

---

[1] Francis Bacon (1561–1626), for example, in his essay 'Of Travel' underlined the need for young men to maintain written records of their travels abroad: '*Travaile*, in the younger Sort, is a Part of Education; In the Elder, a Part of Experience … Men should make Diaries; But in *Land-Travaile*, wherein so much is to be observed, for the most part, they omit it; As if Chance, were fitter to be registred, then Observation. Let Diaries, therefore, be brought in use': *The Essayes or Counsels, Civill and Morall*, ed. M. Kiernan, Oxford, 1985, p. 56.

Fig. 1. Anonymous royalist engraving of King Charles II, dating the beginning of his reign as from 30 January 1648 [1649].

3

trusted personal ally of Charles I and was imprisoned by Parliament in 1642 for his vocal opposition to its burgeoning powers. But his own son, Edward (1616–84), 2nd Baron Montagu of Boughton (our diarist's uncle), was for a time closely associated with Parliament; so much so that in May 1646 he was one of those appointed to receive the king from the Scots and to watch over him at Holmby. However, like Henry Montagu, 1st Earl of Manchester, the 2nd Baron Montagu firmly opposed Parliament's civil prosecution of the king; and his son, also named Edward (1635–65), became one of Charles II's most trusted confidants in exile, often acting as a covert liaison for his communications with active royalists back home in England. Another of our diarist's uncles was the exiled Catholic Abbé Walter Montagu (c. 1603–77), an intimate friend of Queen Henrietta Maria and the Catholic Sir Kenelm Digby during their respective residences abroad. He was also the cousin of the talented and politically supple General-at-Sea Edward Montagu, 1st Earl of Sandwich (1625–72), a close personal friend of Oliver Cromwell and, as the times changed, a prominent and influential support of Charles II (see Fig. 18, p. 73, and pp. 73-7, for further biographical details on the Montagus).

The second traveller, WILLIAM HAMMOND (c. 1635–c.1685), was about twenty years old when he set out for the continent in December 1655. In contrast to Montagu's elevated social status, Hammond was descended from a branch of a reasonably well-off, but far from wealthy, gentry family who were then prominent in Cambridgeshire and Kent. His father's main intention in sending him abroad, it seems, was to assist him in finalizing his choice of profession for later life. William Hammond's experiences as a travelling student were recorded, however, not in the traditional form of a travel diary or journal, but rather in a series of thirty-seven entertaining letters sent to his parents at the family seat, Wilberton House, near Ely.[1] Although the originals are now lost, two complete copies of them were made later: one, as stated on its title-page, in 1695 (Leeds, Brotherton Collection, MS Trv 2), from which the text in this edition has been taken; and a second copy (BL Additional MS 59785), which was transcribed at some date between 1739 and the early 1750s (see pp. 159–60).

It is clear from the general tenor of Hammond's chatty and eloquent letters that the family was keen on him becoming a doctor. To that end, his father had agreed to the significant financial outlay involved in enabling his son to study at one of the major centres of medical learning such as Paris, Montpellier or Padua. As the series of letters home progress William Hammond was himself sometimes passionately enthusiastic about pursuing a career in medicine. But, on other occasions, he honestly admits to his parents that he was troubled by the kind of uncertainties and self-doubts which plague so many young people who have attained an age when crucial decisions about their future employment must be reached. Although he provides a vivid impression of English emigré life at Paris, along with interesting accounts of daily news and affairs at Nîmes, La Flèche, Lyons, Montpellier, Florence, and Amsterdam during the mid-1650s, the true focus of Hammond's letters home (as befits missives intended only as private correspondence) is always his own feelings, contemplations, and plans for the future. In this respect, Hammond's fluently written and often amusing letters prefigure, on a relatively modest level, the tendency of many eighteenth-century travellers and writers – most famously Laurence Sterne in *A Sentimental Journey Through France and Italy* (1768) – to regard travel writing not primarily as an

---

[1] From references made in these letters it is apparent that several others have been lost or never arrived back home at Wilberton. Hammond's last letter was written from Amsterdam and dated 28 May 1658 (a clear slip of either his or the copyist's pen, given the 1659 dating of the previous letters). It is possible that some later letters have been lost, although it may be that Hammond headed home a few days or weeks after writing this letter.

exercise in geographical, historical, and cultural documentation but rather as a means of recording and validating the impressions and sensibilities of the individual traveller himself.

William Hammond's father, Anthony Hammond (1608–61) and his mother Anne (née Digges) Hammond, of Wilberton House, near Ely, were well connected in both royalist and literary circles. Anthony's mother, Elizabeth Aucher (or Archer), was the granddaughter of Edwin Sandys (c. 1516–88), Archbishop of York, who had himself spent most of Queen Mary's reign in exile on the continent. His son George (1578–1644) became one of the most famous English travellers of his generation, publishing a popular and often reprinted memoir of his experiences in Italy, Turkey, Egypt, and Palestine, *A Relation of a Journey Begun An: Dom: 1610. Four Books. Containing a Description of the Turkish Empire, of Ægypt* (1615). Another of the Archbishop's older sons, Sir Edwin Sandys (1561–1629), also travelled extensively as a young man in France, Italy, and Germany and compiled an authoritative survey of continental religious affairs, *Europæ Speculum* (1605).[1] In his later years, he became prominent in both the East India and Virginia Companies, being a notably shrewd and successful treasurer of the latter during the last years of James I's reign. (See also pp. 147–8 for the Sandys brothers.)

It is seems very likely that William Hammond's family would have had copies of the Sandys brothers' publications in their well-stocked library at Wilberton (see p. 148), which our letter writer might well have browsed through as a youth. The distinguished reputations of George and Sir Edwin Sandys as travel writers may even have prompted either William Hammond himself or another family member to collect together and preserve for posterity this intimate epistolary record of his continental peregrinations between December 1655 and the summer of 1658. Certainly, the Hammonds were very much conscious of their family associations with several other noted literary men of the period. Our letter writer's father, Anthony Hammond, was a cousin through his mother's line of the cavalier poet, Richard Lovelace (1618–58); and Anthony's overtly Catholic sister, Mary Hammond, had married the royalist, Sir Thomas Stanley, who decamped to Paris with his whole family after the outbreak of the Civil War. Their son, Thomas Stanley (1625–78), was acclaimed from the late 1640s onwards as a poet, philosopher, and translator and he became a close friend of Anthony Hammond's younger brother, William (1614–c.1655), himself a published poet.

The Hammonds were also extensively involved in both domestic and international trade. Much of William's travels abroad were supported by a network of friendly English merchants, as well as by the Catholic divine and ardent royalist, Dr Henry Holden, who was a close friend of Lady Stanley and based at Paris from the 1630s onwards. On his mother's side, William Hammond was also the grandson of Sir Dudley Digges (1583–1639), who had been involved both in searching out a trade route to the east (via a supposed north-west passage) and with the East India Company. Although perhaps now historically insignificant in themselves, the Hammonds are eloquently representative of an important kind of English mercantile family, whose commercial and intellectual interests from the mid-sixteenth until the mid-seventeenth centuries rapidly expanded from the parochial, land-based economies of their home counties to incorporate the lucrative potential of both continental and New World trade, cultural exchange, and colonization. It is noticeable, for example, that Hammond's letters are preoccupied on a number of occasions

---

[1] *A Relation of the State of Religion* (1605), best known as *Europae speculum* from the revised title-page of the 1629 edition.

with his attempts to search out information in France on the cultivation of silkworms for one of his Digges uncles, who was planning to establish silk worm production in the West Indies (see pp. 201, 206).

The third traveller, BANASTER MAYNARD (c. 1642–1718), who succeeded his father as 3rd Baron Maynard in 1689, was still in his teens when he left England in 1660 with his tutor, Mr Henchman, and a trusty manservant called Robert Moody, who was (as we learn from his own narrative) a highly resourceful individual and already an experienced continental traveller. Whether Maynard himself ever compiled a written record of his travels is unknown. Instead, at some later date (probably after 1681, see pp. 230–31), Moody put together a selective and retrospective record of his master's youthful experiences in an attractive presentation manuscript, laid out in its first few pages in imitation of printed-book format with a striking pen-and-ink representation of a printed title-page (see Fig. 38, p. 238). Moody's ostensible purpose in compiling his manuscript (Bodl. MS Rawlinson D 84) seems to have been twofold: to commemorate the impressive geographical extent and educational diversity of Banaster Maynard's travels between the spring of 1660 and April 1663; and, thereby, to reaffirm the social distinction of both his master and the whole Maynard family. Moody's account, for example, entirely ignores the mundanely familiar details of their party's Channel crossing from England (the usual starting point for most continental travel diaries of the period), in favour of a far grander opening to his narrative, describing his master's invited attendance at the spectacular wedding ceremonials in June 1660 at Paris of King Louis XIV and Marie Thérèse of Austria.

Setting out on their travels probably just before the formal restoration of Charles II (who acceded to the throne on 29 May 1660), Moody was careful to make conspicuous and repeated references to the Maynard family's strong royalist credentials. Through the public prestige of his father, Sir William, 2nd Baron Maynard (c. 1623–99), who was appointed as a Privy Councillor and Comptrollor of the royal household by Charles II (see p. 228), Banaster Maynard was able to obtain a personal audience with the Queen Mother of France (the Spanish Anne of Austria), who informed him that 'she was very well satisfy'd with his Father's Loyalty in the whole time of Cromwels Rebellion' (fol. 4ᵛ). So pleased was she with the Maynard family that she generously initiated for Banaster Maynard an impressively elevated chain of patronage. The Queen Mother supplied him with a warm letter of recommendation to her sister, the Duchess of Savoy, who in turn commended Maynard to her daughter, the Duchess of Parma. This latter duchess then wrote a letter of introduction for Maynard to her brother, the Grand Duke of Tuscany, who maintained this exceptionally privileged form of assistance for a young English traveller by recommending Maynard to no less a personage than Pope Alexander VII (who himself sought to assist the young man's subsequent travels by providing him with a letter of recommendation for the Viceroy of Naples).

Throughout Robert Moody's fast moving and selective narrative, the purveying of historical and geographical detail remains secondary to his main concern, which was to exploit the travel diary genre as a means of emphasizing the detailed continental knowledge and social prestige of his master. Even though this account of Banaster Maynard's progress through Western Europe can certainly be read, on one level, as an informative guidebook for continental travellers – it is packed with the names of cities, towns and villages, major roads and rivers, details of the best routes, and kinds of accommodation available – in Moody's skilful hands the travel writing mode is also utilized as a calculated form of *curriculum vitae* for his master. Through the deft stylistic touch of a literally minded servant drafting the diary (and Moody is always careful to represent himself as an honest but simply educated and unsophisticated observer of his master's distinguished conduct at some of the greatest courts of Western Europe), Banaster Maynard emerges from the diary as a courtly and confident young man, consistently charming members of royalty, aristocracy, and high-ranking churchmen with his personal presence, sense of etiquette, and the distinction of his personal lineage. It is easy to suspect that Moody's diary may have been intended not only as a private documentary record of his master's travels but also, more publicly, as an eloquent statement of his suitability for employment by King Charles II (who clearly trusted his father) in continental diplomatic affairs.

Although the full flowering of the 'Age of the Grand Tour' properly belongs to the eighteenth century, the travellers considered in this Hakluyt volume were themselves following in the already well-trodden steps of an established English tradition of Western European peregrination. So as to provide a clearer historical view of this context, the annotated texts of the surviving travel records of Robert Montagu, William Hammond, Banaster Maynard, and Robert Moody are preceded in Section One of this edition by a selective survey of the earlier development of English travel and tourism on the continent from the mid-sixteenth century until the outbreak of the English Civil War. Throughout this period three major and recurrent reasons prompted a diverse selection of Englishmen to cross the Channel and head off into foreign territories, especially those of France, the Holy Roman Empire, and Italy. These three reasons may be summarized briefly here as, firstly, the practical needs of diplomacy (or training for such duties); secondly, the aesthetic allure of cultural tourism; and, thirdly, the expediencies of political or religious exile. To find out how and why these three motivations still very much held true for most English travellers during the 1650s, it is first necessary to look back over the preceding hundred years to the 1550s and the reign of King Edward VI.

SECTION ONE

ENGLISH TRAVELLERS AND THE ORIGINS OF THE GRAND TOUR

1. The Mid-Tudor Origins of the Grand Tour

> And after I had taried a yere sometime in Padoa and somtime in Venice, and obtayned some understanding of the tung, I thowght yt behouffull to travaile into the middes of Italy, as well to have a better knowleg of the tung, as to see the countrey of Tuscane, so much renowned in all places ...
>
> (Thomas Hoby in 1549)[1]

While for centuries Englishmen had travelled on the continent for a wide variety of religious, diplomatic, military, and mercantile reasons, the history of English exploration of Western Europe for specifically educational and cultural purposes begins in earnest during the reign of King Edward VI (1547–53). Italy, with its disparate assembly of aristocratic and republican city-states, began to exert a powerful hold over the minds of the English ruling classes; and its unique geographical identity as the motherland of the new humanist learning and the enduring focus of ancient imperial civilization, rendered it of central importance to scholars and statesmen alike. One man, the linguist and historian William Thomas (d. 1554), perhaps did more than any other to make the intellectual and physical landscapes of Italy accessible to his fellow citizens. But, at first sight, Thomas seems the unlikeliest of individuals for such an important cultural role since he had first made his way to Venice in 1545 as a bankrupt gambler, fleeing an embezzlement charge. After imprisonment there until his debts were repaid, he made his way to Padua, Bologna, Florence, and Rome, all the time polishing his knowledge of the Italian language and familiarizing himself with the history and constitutions of the Italian states. While still in Italy he began to put together a pioneering English/Italian grammar and dictionary.[2] He also drafted parts of his most famous work, *The History of Italy* (1549), which was completed and printed on his return to England, with a fulsome dedication to John Dudley (1502–53), Earl of Warwick (from 1547) and Duke of Northumberland (from 1551), then one of the most influential figures at court.[3]

Thomas's *The History of Italy* offered its English readers a wealth of information on the constitutions and civic life of the great city states, including Venice, Naples, Florence, Genoa, and Milan. The republican constitution of Venice, in particular, with its elections,

---

[1] 'A Booke of the Travaile and Lief of Me Thomas Hoby, with Diverse Things Woorth the Notinge', ed. Edgar Powell, *The Camden Miscellany*, 10, 1902, p. 17.

[2] William Thomas, *Principal Rules of the Italian Grammar, with a Dictionary*, 1550.

[3] *The Historie of Italy ... [which] Intreateth of the Astate of Many and Divers Common Weales*, 1549.

9

ballots, and interdependent relationship between the doge and his councils, both fascinated and impressed Thomas. He also recounted the more problematic histories of Florence, Genoa, and Milan, tracing their constitutional oscillation during the preceding century between liberty and tyranny. Through Thomas's meticulous historical expositions, an English reader back home could rapidly familiarize himself (and, in conversation, even claim some level of intellectual expertise) with the achievements of Italian civic humanism and the attractions of alternative continental modes of government.[1]

The fostering in England of the concept of touring Western European locations as a mode of education during the second half of the sixteenth century also owed much to the well-established practices of international diplomacy. An English emissary or ambassador sent abroad traditionally travelled with a large entourage of civil servants, scholars, chaplains, and servants. Doubtless, among their ranks were many individuals who found themselves abroad only through the necessity of their employment and for whom the attractions of unfamiliar landscapes, alien environments, and foreign languages were minimal. But for others, participation in a diplomatic mission offered, alongside the efficient expediting of required business, enviable opportunities (otherwise impossible for financial reasons alone) for a uniquely challenging form of personal and intellectual development.[2] William Thomas was clearly just the kind of individual to be attracted to such ventures and in 1551 he joined the Marquis of Northampton's grand embassy to France to present King Henri II with the Order of the Garter. Following his return home to England, the success of first printed edition of *The History of Italy* had gained for Thomas the personal interest of its nominal patron, John Dudley, who facilitated his appointment to the prestigious position of Clerk to the Privy Council. Dudley had been the main instigator of Northampton's mission, which also sought to explore the possibility of a match between Edward VI and the king of France's daughter. If this bold but now largely forgotten diplomatic initiative had come to fruition, the dynastic and cultural implications of an harmonious Anglo-French unification could well have changed not only the course of England's relationship with France but also the very nature and ease of access for English travellers to the rest of Catholic Western Europe.

For an educated Englishman of the 1550s, the landscapes of France were by no means entirely unknown territories. For generations, pilgrims, clerics, merchants, diplomats, messengers, and numerous other kinds of travellers had followed one of the three major routes through France and into other parts of Western Europe: down the Rhône Valley to Marseilles and then by sea to Italy; from Paris to Lyons and then across the Alps; or, most commonly, from the Seine to Etaples, and then via the great chain of monastic abbeys and hospices as far as Besançon and then on through Switzerland. In addition to this reassuring level of geographical familiarity, the vitality of the long and culturally fruitful reign of François I (1515–47), in sharp contrast to the iconoclastic desecrations of post-Reformation England, had fostered alluring landscapes of architectural and artistic riches. It would have been difficult for a post-Reformation English traveller in France during the 1550s to avoid making comparisons between the intellectual and cultural wealth of its Catholic religious

---

[1] See Andrew Hadfield, *Literature, Travel, and Colonial Writing in the English Renaissance 1545–1625*, Oxford, 1998, pp. 24–32; and Edward Chaney, *The Evolution of the Grand Tour. Anglo-Italian Cultural Relations Since the Renaissance*, London and Portland, Oreg., 1998, pp. 69–78, 95.

[2] See John Walter Stoye, *English Travellers Abroad 1604–1667. Their Influence in English Society and Politics*, London, 1952 (rpt. New Haven and London, 1989), pp. 91–116, for a detailed analysis of this kind of entourage and the English embassies at Venice and Turin.

institutions as compared with the visually purged and starkly redefined devotional world of Protestant England under Edward VI. In similar fashion, English travellers and exiles during the 1650s, as they gazed upon the visual splendours of Paris and the glories of the French monarchy, might ponder their own loss of the royal art collections, lavish court entertainments, and sheer creative vitality of the court of Charles I.[1]

In his explorations of northern France, William Thomas was accompanied by another member of Northampton's diplomatic entourage, Thomas Hoby (1530–66), the translator of Castiglione's *The Courtier* and, like Thomas, an enthusiastic student of Italianate state-craft and civil cultures. Hoby's earlier career exemplifies another vital element in the grad-ual mid-sixteenth century English formulation of continental touring as a valued form of pedagogic development. In his youth he was representative of the kind of privileged itiner-ant scholar who, usually after a period of study at either Oxford or Cambridge, deliberately sought out excellence in learning from institutions outside his own native land. Hoby first went to Strasbourg as a young man, where he heard the lectures of Martin Bucer and the Florentine exile Peter Martyr Vermigli. He also studied at the University of Padua and was resident for a time, variously, at Siena, Rome and Naples before heading south as far as Sicily in early 1550. Soon afterwards, he made another brief tour of Italy and in about 1564 wrote up his memoirs in a lively manuscript account, entitled 'Book of the Travel and Life of Me Thomas Hoby'.[2]

The purpose of such studies abroad, which could only be undertaken by a highly moti-vated, resourceful, and socially adaptable individual (and one who could also call upon the continuing financial resources of either his own family or other sponsors), was usually entirely clear. A young scholar might have headed to France, Germany or Italy initially because of religious or political problems relating to his immediate personal circle, but once abroad his studies were usually overtly geared to the acquisition of skills which would open up opportunities for him in later life in either public service or in the employ of a powerful patron. (The remarkable trajectory of William Thomas's upwardly mobile self-transforma-tion from a felon and wandering scholar in Italy to a trusted personal servant of the Duke of Northumberland and Clerk to the Privy Council comes to mind here). In this sense, the sharp-eyed careerism and personal drive of young men who had often risen to scholarly attainment from relatively humble social backgrounds (thanks to the mid-Tudor commit-ment to grammar and free schools), also played a major role in opening up the English consciousness to the intellectual attractions of continental Europe.

Frequently (and unsurprisingly given the high costs involved in sending a young man abroad to study), the kind of ambitious, career-focused young English scholar who made his way to Paris, Strasbourg or Padua was often from a family which was already heav-ily involved in either public service or diplomacy (or both). This was certainly the case with Thomas Hoby himself, whose half-brother, Sir Philip Hoby (1505–58), enjoyed a prestigious diplomatic career, including an embassy to the Emperor Charles V from Edward VI, acting as an intermediary in the marital negotiations between Queen Mary and Philip of Spain. Through these kinds of duties, he was able to make the personal acquaintance of the likes of Holbein, Titian, and Aretino. Thomas Hoby was also a for-mer pupil and friend of the renowned Greek scholar, Sir John Cheke (1514–57), who

[1] See Figs 12–13, pp. 50–51, for the visually powerful commemoration of French monarchic grandeur in the mid-17th-century engravings (widely purchased by English tourists) of Israel Henriet and Israel Silvestre.

[2] BL MS Egerton 2148, ed. E. Powell in *Camden Miscellany*, X, 1902. See also Chaney, *Grand Tour*, pp. 6–7, 64–5, 97.

during Mary's reign served a period of exile of his own at Padua and contributed a warm prefatory epistle to Hoby's translation of *The Courtier*. Hoby's other friends included Peter Whitethorne, who had accompanied him on his 1550 Italian itinerary and later translated Machiavelli's *Art of War* (1560); and Henry Fitzalan (1512–80), 12th Earl of Arundel, who made his own tour of Italy in 1566/67. The long-desired fruition of this intense immersion in continental affairs and extended period of career preparation came with Thomas Hoby's appointment as Queen Elizabeth's ambassador to France in 1566 (but, unexpectedly, he died some months later).

The literary efforts of Thomas and Hoby, however, would probably have achieved very little within a broader social context without the sympathetic involvement of more influential figures at the English court. Undoubtedly, the most significant of such patrons during Edward VI's reign was the dedicatee of Thomas's *The History of Italy*, John Dudley, Earl of Warwick and Duke of Northumberland. His personal sponsorship of those who sought to obtain first hand knowledge of continental cultures speaks eloquently of his desire to reverse England's post-reformation cultural exclusion from the rest of Western Europe. In this desire, John Dudley was almost certainly wishing to emulate the examples of King Henry VII (who had been served by his own father, Edmund Dudley (d. 1510), in matters of taxation) and the youthful King Henry VIII in offering employment to highly qualified, multi-lingual scholars, craftsmen, and artists from the continent, such as Desiderius Erasmus, Heinrich Cornelius Agrippa, and Hans Holbein the Younger.

At the heart of this early Tudor development of a growing belief in the educational and career enhancing efficacy of scholarly peregrination and tourism lay a recognition of the direct links between political power and ostentatious cultural fecundity. This was an aspect of national life in which England now lagged far behind the lavish displays of artistry and scholarship at the Florence of the Medicis, the royal court of François I, the grand châteaux of the French nobility, and the great cities of the German and Spanish Habsburgs.[1] Although in no way directly comparable to the sheer scope and grandeur of the most prolific continental princely and ducal patrons, John Dudley's relatively modest range of interests in the arts are at least indicative of a burgeoning English desire to observe and understand the public function of centralized cultural sponsorship and its vigorous display. To this end, Dudley dispatched the architect and artist John Shute on a kind of scholarly fact-finding trip to Italy, with a special brief to examine contemporary Italian interest in classical antiquity and its impact upon continental architectural design. The madrigalist Thomas Whythorne, who was employed in Dudley's household before his fall, also later travelled extensively in Italy and brought back home a wealth of knowledge concerning continental modes of composition and performance. Similarly, the early career of Queen Elizabeth's Secretary of State, Thomas Wilson (c. 1525–81), who lived in exile on the continent between 1555 and 1560, also owed much to the direct sponsorship of the Dudley family.[2]

The imaginative potential of a Protestant England integrated more closely with Western Europe, as posited by John Dudley's diplomacy and cultural vision, was largely neutralized by Dudley's catastrophic downfall and execution, following his unsuccessful attempt to

---

[1] See *The Courts of Europe. Politics, Patronage and Royalty 1400–1800*, ed. A. G. Dickens, London, 1977, pp. 77–146.

[2] Wilson's tract on the English vernacular, the *Art of Rhetoric* had been first suggested to him by Dudley's son, John Dudley, Jr. (c. 1528–54). See *Thomas Wilson. The Art of Rhetoric (1560)*, ed. Peter E. Medine, University Park, Pa., 1994, 5–6.

place his daughter-in-law Lady Jane Grey on the throne of England.[1] The Catholic reign of Queen Mary immediately created a sharp sectarian redefinition of English perspectives on continental travel. Replacing the outward Protestant gaze of John Dudley and his followers upon Italian cultures and civic constitutions, a new (and no less enlightened) vision of Italy was supplied by the returning English Catholic emigrés, led by Cardinal Pole (1500–58). By 1555 Pole's personal conception of the role of England within Western European politics and scholarship had been tempered by his own prolonged residence abroad. As a young man he had studied at Padua and visited Rome between 1521 and 1527. He continued his education at Paris in 1529/30 and then chose to live as a voluntary exile at Padua from 1532 when he refused to accept royal supremacy over the English Church. Pole and his associates brought back to the English court a richly informed knowledge of Italian humanism and civic statecraft. But as they returned to London from Padua (which would always remain Pole's true spiritual and intellectual home), so Queen Mary's accession created yet another new generation of English exiles to Italy, including, for example, the Protestant Francis Walsingham (c. 1530–90), who fled England to study at the University of Padua – a period which stood him in very good stead in later years when he served, effectively, as the head of Queen Elizabeth's foreign intelligence-gathering service.

During the reigns of Henry VIII and Edward VI, as Catholic emigrés fled to safer havens in Western Europe, and then returned home on the accession of Queen Mary, so their Protestant counterparts established a counter-trend, absenting themselves from England during the reign of a Catholic queen but triumphantly returning soon after the coronation of the Protestant Elizabeth (just as many of their Catholic counterparts were once again crossing the Channel in the other direction). It may be surmised, then, that the educational principle of study and travel abroad at this period would have been permeated for many of its practitioners and observers with a strong and poignant concept of both 'exile' and 'return' – concepts which would prove one hundred years later to be no less relevant for English travellers on the continent during the constitutional upheavals and military conflicts of the late 1640s and 1650s.

2. Elizabethan Educational Travellers on the Continent

> It is good that you make a booke of paper, Wherein you may dayly or at least weekly insert, all thyngs occurrent to you
> (William Cecil, Lord Burghley, advising the Earl of Rutland, 1571)

> He is young and raw, and no doubt shall find those countries and the demeanours of the people somewhat strange unto him.
> (Robert Dudley, Earl of Leicester, about Philip Sidney, 1572)[2]

In the January preceding Queen Elizabeth's accession on 17 November 1558 François de Lorraine, duc de Guise, with a force of some 30,000 troops had expelled the English garrison

---

[1] William Thomas was executed a year later for his involvement in the Wyatt Rebellion (February 1554) which opposed the marriage of Queen Mary and Philip of Spain.

[2] William Cecil thus advised the young Edward Manners (1549–87), Earl of Rutland, as he was about to depart for a continental tour: *CSPD, 1547–80*, p. 406, item 6. Robert Dudley, Earl of Leicester, described his nephew, Philip Sidney, as 'young and raw' in a letter to Sir Francis Walsingham at Paris, when asking for his guidance for Philip at the beginning of his continental tour: BL MS Lansdowne 117, f. 159ᵛ.

from Calais. The town had been in English hands since its capture by Edward III in 1347 and the humiliation of its loss for Queen Mary was huge. (She reputedly claimed that 'Calais' would be found graven on her heart after her death.) The 'Calaisis' region was pointedly renamed 'Pays reconquis' by the local French inhabitants; and the new English queen was the first Tudor monarch not to own any land possessions east of the Channel. From a wider perspective, the political dynamics of the rest of France were also changing. The Peace of Cateau-Cambrésis on 3 April 1559 effectively drew to a close the lengthy struggle which had been rumbling on since 1494 between France and Spain for control of Italy. Following the defeats of the French at Saint-Quentin (1557) and Gravelines (1558), the Spanish Habsburgs began a dominance over Italy which was to last for the next 150 years. Savoy and Piedmont were also restored by Henri II to Spain's ally, Emmanuel-Philibert of Savoy.

The newly peaceful political conditions across large stretches of France and Italy engendered far easier access and travelling conditions under François II (1559–60) and during the first half of the reign of Charles IX (1560–74). The vast majority of English travellers during these years, however, have left no surviving written records of their experiences, although the state papers of the period indicate that the usual reasons of diplomacy, church affairs, and trade ensured a steady flow of Englishmen through French and Italian territories.

Fortunately, one singularly illuminating account was compiled by a serving-man called Richard Smith, who in 1563 made his way in the entourage of Sir Edward Unton, via Antwerp, Cologne, Augsburg, Innsbruck, Venice, Padua, and Florence, as far as Rome. Smith presents himself as a keenly observant servant who is genuinely fascinated by the wonderful new sights surrounding him. (A similar narrative persona was adopted a century later by the third writer in this volume, the serving-man Robert Moody, as he described the progress of his master, Banaster Maynard through Europe from 1660 until 1663.) Although a literal and generally unquestioning recorder of whatever he saw – be it the conspicuous wealth of Antwerp, the quaint national dress of German women, or the spectacular landscapes of the Alps – Smith's diary offers what amounts to a very early example of an enthusiastically compiled tourist's record of a 'peregrination' or 'grand tour' through France, Germany, and Italy. Arriving at Rome and armed with a copy of William Thomas's *The History of Italy*, for example, Smith honestly expresses both his enthusiasm for Pope Pius IV's ambitious building programmes at Rome and his disappointment with the general tattiness of the city's eagerly anticipated antiquities. Smith's narrative, unfortunately, is incomplete and breaks off just as his party had reached Mainz on the way home. Nevertheless, it remains a rare and informative example of how an early-Elizabethan English tourist on the continent set about exploring new geographical environments and recording his experiences.[1]

This brief period of relatively unrestricted opportunities for Englishmen to travel in France and Italy was dramatically brought to an end by the publication in 1567 of Pope Pius V's Bull *In coena domini*, which sought to exclude all heretics, especially English Protestants, from entering the Italian states. Inevitably, this gesture evoked a strong reaction from English commentators, who retaliated by depicting Italy as a hotbed of political intrigue and sexual corruption.[2] English isolationism from Catholic Western Europe hardened

---

[1] BL MS Sloane 1813; edited in A. H. S. Yeames, 'The Grand Tour of an Elizabethan', *Papers of the British School at Rome* 7, 1914, pp. 92–113.

[2] See, for example, the stridently polemical condemnation of Italian 'filthy living' in the posthumously published *The Schoolmaster (1570) by Roger Ascham*, ed. Lawrence V. Ryan, Ithaca, NY, 1967, pp. 60–75.

further with the Northern Rebellion (1569), in which several prominent English Catholics were implicated; and then with the irrevocable breach created between England and Italy by the papal excommunication of Queen Elizabeth (1570).[1] Henceforth, the Italian states were systematically represented in Protestant polemical literature as dangerous, and often formally forbidden, territories for young impressionable travellers, with Venice formulaically condemned for its licentiousness, Florence for its Machiavellian intrigue, and Rome for its papist seductions. Although in many ways this was a carefully fabricated and illusory image of Italy, it remained a potent one for the next thirty years.

The signing of the Treaty of Blois in the spring of 1572 significantly reconfigured England's relationship with the rest of Western Europe. In effect, this treaty sought to terminate the traditional English emnity with France and implicitly acknowledged that the escalating military and colonial power of Spain was a far greater threat to Queen Elizabeth's absolute authority. Consequently, the long-familiar trade and pilgrimage routes through France seemed to be opening up once more to English travellers, especially those with an active interest in continental statecraft and politics. One of the very first families to take advantage of this renewed from of career training was the Sidneys of Kent. During the 1570s the Sidneys were headed by Sir Henry Sidney (1529–86), the son-in-law of John Dudley, Duke of Northumberland who, as we have seen, was the leading patron of Italianate interests during the reign of Edward VI.

In the early summer of 1572 Sir Henry found a place for his eldest son, Philip Sidney (1554–86), along with a trusted family servant of Italian extraction called Lodowick Bryskett, on a diplomatic mission led by Edward Fiennes de Clinton, Earl of Lincoln, for the formal signing of the Treaty of Blois. The English determination to engender long-term peaceable relations with France was also indicated by Lincoln's tacit briefing for this mission, which required him to explore the possibilities of a marriage between the thirty-nine years old queen of England and the eighteen years old duc d'Alençon. (This was a diplomatic strategy which, for the Sidneys at least, would certainly have recalled the Duke of Northumberland's plan in 1551 to explore the potential for a match between Edward VI and the daughter of Henri II of France, see p. 10). Philip Sidney's official travel licence has fortuitously survived and it clearly suggests that his presence on this diplomatic mission was to enable him to gain experience in international diplomacy. He was allowed to travel within certain regions of continental Europe specifically 'for his attaining to the knowledge of foreign languages' but he was also sternly ordered not to 'haunt nor repair into the territories or countries of any prince or potentate not being with us in amity or league' (i.e. Spain and Italy).[2]

On his arrival at Paris, Philip Sidney lodged with Sir Francis Walsingham, who was then the resident English ambassador there (and who we last heard of as an exile at Padua during Queen Mary's reign, see p. 13). Hopes for a more peaceful Western Europe following the Treaty of Blois were further raised when in July the Spanish army, under the leadership of the Duke of Alva, effectively terminated French military intervention in the Low Countries by defeating a combined force of French, Dutch, and English soldiers at Mons. For almost three months the young Philip Sidney happily busied himself at Paris, familiarizing himself

---

[1] Other crises with an 'Italian' or Catholic association at this period, such as the Ridolfi Plot (1571), and the execution of England's premier Catholic peer, the Duke of Norfolk (1572), served to harden further English hostility towards Italy.

[2] John Buxton and Bent Juel-Jensen, 'Sir Philip Sidney's First Passport Rediscovered', *The Library*, 5 ser., 25, 1970, pp. 42–6. See Stoye, *English Travellers Abroad*, p. 5, for examples of other licences.

with the French royal court and and planning the next stage of his journey (which probably would have involved exploring other regions of France). But on the night of 24/25 October 1572 yet another major reversal of conditions for foreign travellers came about when thousands of Huguenots were slaughtered at Paris and elsewhere in France during the notorious St Bartholomew's Day Massacre. Overnight, the newly welcoming territories of France had turned into a far more dangerous environment for their youthful English visitors. Probably with Walsingham's assistance, Philip made a decision not to return home to England (as the Privy Council had immediately ordered on hearing of this catastrophe) but to relocate himself in Germany, where he spent the rest of the year on a tour which took him through Strasbourg, Heidelberg, and Frankfurt.

Although Philip Sidney is not known to have compiled a daily diary of his travels, the fortunate survival of many of his letters to family, friends, and newly made acquaintances makes it possible to trace the range and purpose of his itinerary in some detail. Remaining at Frankfurt for the winter and New Year of 1572/73, he continued his exploration of the German states during the spring and then moved on to imperial city of Vienna for the summer. For a young man of nineteen, Sidney was a remarkably adventurous individual and he even made an impromptu excursion from Vienna into Hungary during the following September. But, despite the clear prohibition of his licence, the attractions of Italy were simply too great to resist for this grandson of the Duke of Northumberland and by early November he had found suitable lodgings at Venice. Sidney remained in Italy, basing himself alternately at Venice and Padua, until about August 1574 when he began to consider possible routes for his journey home. Heading north to Verona and crossing the Alps via the Brenner Pass, he visited Vienna again before taking another brief diversion later in the year into Poland. Early in 1575 he then moved on to the imperial court at Prague in Czechoslovakia before crossing Germany westwards in a broad sweep, passing rapidly through the Low Countries, and catching a ferry for England in early March 1575.

Philip Sidney's extensive continental travels from 1572 until 1575 form what may be regarded as the first fully fledged 'Grand Tour' by an Englishman for which we have substantial documentary records. In addition to the impressive geographical extent of his itinerary (and his letters reveal that his route was being carefully planned stage by stage as he travelled), his experiences abroad were clearly intended to provide him with the requisite knowledge of international scholarship, statecraft, and diplomacy now deemed necessary for a prominent public career in later life. In fact, Sidney only had to wait slightly less than two years before being employed by the queen on a diplomatic mission of his own. Still aged only twenty-two, he was chosen in February 1577 to lead an official embassy, via Ostend, Brussels, Louvain, and Heidelberg, to the court of Emperor Rudolph II at Prague to offer English condolences on the death of his father, the late emperor. By the late 1570s, it seems, the essential concept of educational tourism for highly privileged young Englishmen was firmly established as a means of training a self-selecting court élite in international affairs and cosmopolitan culture.[1]

With the key components of the 'Grand Tour' already well defined by the mid-point of Queen Elizabeth's reign, attempts to trace systematically how this educational practice was developed and refined over subsequent decades are hampered by a severe lack of primary

---

[1] For more detailed accounts of Philip Sidney's continental travels, see James M. Osborn, *Young Philip Sidney, 1572–1577*, New Haven, 1972; Katherine Duncan-Jones, *Sir Philip Sidney. Courtier Poet*, London, 1991, pp. 63–85; and Alan Stewart, *Philip Sidney. A Double Life*, London, 2000, pp. 68–138.

evidence. Only a scattering of travel diaries has survived and, in any case, it is likely that many of the young English travellers on the continent from the 1570s onwards never maintained (or even started to keep) a regular written record of their experiences. The very few diaries, memoirs and other written records of individual travellers which have been preserved, however, do at least provide some clues as to how the concept of the 'Grand Tour' remained very much in vogue during the latter half of the Elizabethan period. For example, the gentleman-scholar Sir John North (c. 1551–97), who later fought with Philip Sidney in the Low Countries campaign of 1585/86, undertook an extended itinerary through Flanders, Germany, and Switzerland before residing in Italy from 1575 until 1577. These travels clearly exerted a major educational influence over North, as is demonstrated by his habit in later life of recording his own accounts and ordinary business trips within East Anglia and the Midlands in competent Italian.[1]

Another individual who regularly committed to paper a variety of fascinating records of his experiences abroad was Stephen Powle (c. 1553–1630), who visited Geneva, Basle, and Strasbourg between 1579 and 1581 and was later utilized by Sir Francis Walsingham at Venice in 1587 to report on growing rumours of a Spanish invasion of England.[2] But it is now, more often than not, an almost impossible task – due to sheer lack of primary evidence – to reconstruct in detail the routes and experiences of the majority of English travellers who are known to have been on the continent during at this period. Furthermore, from the late 1570s the growing French civil unrest during the reign of Henri III (1574–89), who was implicated in the murder at Blois of the Catholic duc de Guise (a plot which in turn led to Henri III's own assassination at St-Cloud in 1589), resulted a steady diminution in English eyes of the attractions of travels in France (and, of course, onwards into Germany and Italy).

A few other significant records have survived of English travellers' experiences abroad from the mid-1570s onwards. By far the most substantial is the diary, sometimes kept on a daily basis, of Arthur Throckmorton's experiences in the Low Countries, Germany, Czechoslovakia, Italy, and France. Throckmorton's family, like the Sidneys, prized the educational value of continental travel and regarded it as an integral part of their son's linguistic, cultural, and political education. Also, they could claim a first-hand knowledge of Western European travel stretching back to the beginning of the sixteenth century. Arthur's grandfather, Sir Robert Throckmorton, had died in Italy in 1519 on his way to the Holy Land; and his uncle, Michael Throckmorton (d. 1558), had served at Padua as Cardinal Pole's personal secretary. His father, Sir Nicholas Throckmoreton (1515–71), had been caught up in the Wyatt Rebellion against Queen Mary's proposed Spanish marriage and had fled to France where he fought at St-Quentin. Soon after the accession of Queen Elizabeth, Sir Nicholas was appointed as her resident ambassador at Paris. Clearly, Arthur Throckmorton's travels abroad were, like Philip Sidney's, aimed at furthering his later career options at court.

Between 1576 and 1582 Arthur Throckmorton made two separate trips abroad. The first, accompanying the diplomatic entourage of Sir Amyas Paulet in September 1576, took him to France, and then on to the Low Countries for some valuable military experience in the regiment of Sir John Norris. Having returned safely home in 1578 he set out once again in July 1580, via the Low Countries and Germany before spending the

---

[1] Bodl. Add. MS C 173. Stoye, *English Travellers Abroad*, p. 138.

[2] Bodl. MS Tanner 309. See also Antoni Mączak, *Travel in Early Modern Europe*, translated by Ursula Phillips, Oxford and Cambridge, 1995, p. 244; Chaney, *Grand Tour*, p. 66; and Virginia F. Stern, *Sir Stephen Powle of Court and Country*, London and Toronto, 1992.

winter and New Year season at Prague. Following an itinerary similiar to Philip Sidney's in the previous decade, he also visited Vienna and then traversed the Alps, to take up an alternating residence, as Sidney had done, at both Padua and Venice. Having moved on to Florence by September 1581 (where he took singing lessons from Galileo's father, Vincenzo), he unwittingly became entangled in the perilous affairs of a suspected English intelligence-gatherer, John Pickering, who had been imprisoned as a spy at Rome. Sensibly, Throckmorton decided that it was necessary to extricate himself from these complications and he headed rapidly home through Italy and France, arriving back in England early in 1582. Despite the obvious range of personal dangers which Arthur must have faced as a traveller, his family's commitment to the efficacy of continental peregrination remained such that his younger brother, Nicholas, undertook a comparable tour during the late 1580s.[1]

Throckmorton's diary makes regular reference to meeting a wide range of his fellow nationals while abroad, although none of these young men is now known to have left any written records.[2] In early 1579 Philip Sidney's younger brother, Robert (1563–1626), later Earl of Leicester, was planning his own continental itinerary; and more is known about his experiences abroad because he travelled from Strasbourg to Paris in the company of Stephen Powle who recorded their friendship and shared observations in his diary.[3] In about November 1580 Robert Sidney was at Prague and wrote a dutiful letter to his father, Sir Henry Sidney, about his future plans which included prospective trips through both Italy and France. Sir Henry's eloquent but inconclusive reply well illustrates the potential political problems and personal dangers facing a young man in search of educational enlightenment in the Western Europe of the early 1580s:

> I lyke very well of your beyng at Prage, & of your Intentyon to go to Vienna. I wysh you should curyusly looke upon the fortyfycatyon of that; and consyderyng the Estate of Chrsytendom, I cannot tell hou to desygne your travell into Italy. I would not have you to go spetyally for that thear is perpetuall War betwyne the Pope & us. I thynk the Pryncxes & Potentates of that Regyon, are Confederated wyth hym, and for sum other respects, I would not have you go thyther. Yet from Spayne, we are as it wear under an Inhybytyon; France in endles Troubles; the Low Cuntre in Irrecoverable mysery. So I leave *that* to your brother & your self. Whether Vyenna beyng sean, you will return into Ingland, or spend the next Somer in those partes; whych If you do, I thynk best (you being satysfyed wyth Vienna) you se the Pryncypall Cytties of Moravia & Silesia, & so to Cracoua; and if you can, have any Comodyte, to se the Court of the Kyng of that Realm; & from thens thoro Saxon, to Holst, & Pomerland, seyng the Princes Courtes by the way; & then into Denmark, & Sweden, & se those Kyngys Courtes. Aquaynt you sum what wyth the Estate of the Fre Steates; & so at Hamboro & to Imbark, & to wynter wyth me.[4]

During the 1590s the fashion for foreign travel gathered momentum and Sir Thomas Chaloner (1561–1615), who was to play an important role in the promulgation of educational tourism at the Jacobean court (see p. 23), complained that 'Such a rabble of English roam now in Italy', although few of these individuals left any informative records of their

---

[1] A. L. Rowse, *Ralegh and the Throckmortons*, London, 1962, pp. 80–94.

[2] Throckmorton's diary refers to his encounters abroad with members of the Leigh, Ratcliffe, Sentry, Crichton, Carew, Savile, and Spencer families.

[3] Stern, *Sir Stephen Powle*, pp. 44–51.

[4] *HMC De Lisle and Dudley*, II, pp. 95–6. CKS U1475 Z53/22/69–70. I am grateful to Viscount De L'Isle MBE, DL, for permission to cite this letter and to Professor Noel Kinnamon for his transcription of it.

time there. A notable exception was the Irishman, Henry Piers, who was a convert to Catholicism and an exile from his homeland. He compiled a very detailed (and, it has to be admitted, somewhat pedantic) record of his observations while travelling in the Low Countries, Germany, and Italy between 1595 and 1598.[1] Sir Henry Wotton, who later served as James I's ambassador to Venice on three separate occasions (1604–12, 1616–19, and 1621–4), was studing in Italy during the early 1590s and revelled in Florence's reputation as 'a paradise inhabited by devils' and the home of Machiavelli.[2] Most usefully perhaps for later travellers, Robert Dallington had been earning his living between 1598 and 1600 as a travelling tutor, accompanying Roger Manners, Earl of Rutland, through France, Italy, and Germany; and a few years later he accompanied the earl's younger brother on a similar tour.[3] Although it is not known how much benefit the Manners brothers personally gained from their travels abroad, Dallington himself was a keen observer of everything he saw and produced two important guidebooks for other travellers which were well used throughout the Jacobean period, *The View of France* (1605), examining culture and society under Henri IV, and *A Survey of the Great Dukes State of Tuscany* (1605), detailing the treasures of Medicean Florence.[4]

3. The Expansion of Western European Travel from 1603 until 1625

> the end of travel is his ripening in knowledge; and the end of his knowledge is the service of his country
>
> (Robert Dallington)

> The people of Great Britain (of all other famous and glorious Nations separated from the maine Continent of the world) are by so much the more interested to become Travellers
>
> (Sir Thomas Palmer)[5]

During the first decade of the seventeenth century, the educational efficacy of continental travel for young Englishmen with high ambitions for public and diplomatic service in later life was firmly established in ways which would remain valid for the next two hundred years. Although the central range of itineraries and intellectual pursuits of these kind of tours had been confirmed a quarter of a century earlier by the likes of the Sidneys and the Throckmortons, the accession of James I gave new hope at the English court for a more outward-looking and collaborative role with the rest of Western Europe. From an English point of view, political conditions in France had always played a key role in dictating the

---

[1] *HMC Salisbury*, VII, p. 10. Thomas Frank, 'An Edition of "A Discourse of HP his Travelles" (MS Rawlinson D. 83)', unpublished University of Oxford B.Litt thesis, 1954.

[2] Wotton claimed to have been involved in the dangerous world of intelligence-gathering and described how he had once disguised himself as an Italian as a means of infiltrating a Spanish plot to displace James VI of Scotland in favour of the Infanta in the English line of succession. See Jonathan Bate, 'The Elizabethans in Italy', in *Travel and Drama in Shakespeare's Time*, ed. Jean-Pierre Maquerlot and Michèle Willems, Cambridge, 1996, pp. 56–8.

[3] The Manners family seemed to have shared the Sidney family's enthusiasm for the educational value of continental peregrinations. Roger Manners later became the son-in-law of Sir Philip Sidney, when he married his only daughter, Elizabeth (1585–1612).

[4] Hadfield, *Literature, Travel, and Colonial Writing*, pp. 34–44.

[5] Dallington, *View*, 1605, sig. B1ʳ; and Sir Thomas Palmer, *An Essay of … Travels into Foreign Countries*, 1606, dedicatory epistle to Prince Henry.

likelihood of young Englishmen being sent abroad by their families. While a minority had crossed directly into the Low Countries and could satisfy themselves with a briefer tour of this region and the Protestant German states, the accessibility of France, as England's closest physical neighbour (and also as the most favoured land route, by which most English travellers progressed to Italy and beyond), was the essential trigger for the popularity or otherwise of the Elizabethan and Jacobean grand tour.[1] The Edict of Nantes (1598), under which the Huguenots of France were allowed freedom of worship, had finally concluded the self-destructive 'Wars of Religion' of La Ligue; and the Treaty of London, signed in August 1604, effectively sought peaceful Anglo-Spanish relations (and it was proposed that James I's heir, Prince Henry, would be married to the Spanish Infanta, Anne, daughter of Philip III). Consequently, the families of young Englishmen could begin to dispatch them abroad again, without the fear of sending them through regions which were, periodically, little better than war zones.

The example set by two of the most powerful families at the English court, the Cecils and the Howards, clearly illustrates the renewed importance attached to the acquisition of first-hand knowledge of Western European courts. James I's Secretary of State, Robert Cecil (1563–1612), the son of William Cecil, Lord Burghley, had himself travelled in France during the mid-1580s and had accompanied the Earl of Derby's mission to the Spanish Netherlands in 1588. He sent his own son, William Lord Cranborne (1591–98), on a tour of France, Italy, and Germany between 1608 and 1610; and a detailed manuscript record of the journey was dutifully compiled in William's best schoolboy French. Another young (and altogether more problematic) Cecil, William Lord Roos, began his Western European travels in 1605 and even ventured as far as Spain in 1610 as part of his extended continental education. As expected by his parents and tutor, he also put together a stolidly descriptive account of his experiences there. But this dutiful little document gives no impression of the range of some of Lord Roos's other activities, which included (according to the horrified reports home from Lord Cranborne's tutor, Thomas Lorkin) gambling and feasting at Antwerp and Brussels, open intimacy with Catholics wherever he went, racist denunciations of the Dutch, and the 'unsavory and obscene discourses which my Lord usually fell into, able to corrupt a very chaste mind'.[2]

The Howards were in advance even of the Cecils in taking advantage of the more peaceful conditions immediately following James I's accession. The Earl of Suffolk, sent his eldest son, Theophilus Lord Howard de Walden (1584–1640), to France in 1603 in the company of Sir Edwin Rich, half-brother to Robert, later Earl of Warwick. Although no personal diary of Theophilus's travels is now known, his social status was such that his movements abroad were regularly reported on by English ambassadors and other intelligence gatherers. One of King James's most active continental agents, Sir Anthony Standen, was on his way home from a mission in Italy when he happened to encounter the young Howard, as he mentioned in a letter to his friend, John Chamberlain (who was expected to pass the news on to the Howards):

> neere Lion I met in his peregrination and left in perfect helthe the Lord Howard of Walden and his company, who wysshed I would signifie to his Lord Father and Lady Mother no less, and so I

---

[1] See Stoye, *English Travellers Abroad*, pp. 169–230, for English visitors to the Low Countries.

[2] *HMC Salisbury*, XXI, pp. 104–13, 137–49; *HMC Rutland*, I, p. 422; and PRO SP 94/17/118–54. Lord Roos was a grandson (b. c. 1590) of Thomas Cecil (1542–1623), Earl of Exeter (the eldest son of Lord Burghley). His tutor, Mr Mole, became notorious for being imprisoned by the Inquisition. See Stoye, *English Travellers Abroad*, pp. 26–7, 33, 77–82, 87, 262–6; and for Lord Roos's flaws, as reported by Lorkin, ibid. 33.

humbly beseche your honor to favour me with the delyvery hereof to hys honorable parents the Earl and Countess; I did assure hym that he should receyve all kindes and courtesies in all parts of Italy wythout exception such ys the love and regard borne to your Prince and Soveraigne there.[1]

In late 1607, soon after the the Earl of Suffolk's daughter Frances had married Robert Devereux (1591–1646), Earl of Essex, Suffolk's new son-in-law was also dispatched abroad to continue his education.[2]

Robert Devereux's travels illustrate how by this period the educational grand tour had grown to be viewed as especially desirable for a newly-married young nobleman. William Lord Cranborne, for example, had married Suffolk's younger daughter, Catherine, on 1 December 1608 immediately before his departure abroad; and in 1610 Henry Lord Clifford, who had previously married Cranborne's sister Frances, was also to be found travelling in France, where he attended the royal court, took riding lessons, and attempted to polish his knowledge of spoken French. As with the case of the first and third Civil War travellers in this volume (Robert Montagu, accompanied by his tutor Mr Hainhofer, and Banaster Maynard with his Mr Henchman, see pp. 61–9 and 241), these young men were invariably escorted around the continent by an academic tutor, who was also charged with looking after their moral wellbeing. Cranborne was accompanied by two experienced travellers, Dr Mathew Lister (who had studied medicine at Basle) and John Finet (who later became a Master of Ceremonies at the court of Charles I); and he later met up at Fontainebleau with a third trusted servant of the Cecil's, William Becher, the son of a London merchant.[3]

Some married Englishmen, however, were obliged to wait several years before being able to head off abroad. A notable example of this category of continental traveller is Edward Lord Herbert of Cherbury (1582–1648), who in 1598 had been married to his older cousin, Mary Herbert, with several children born between 1600 and 1607. Complaining that he had been too young to travel abroad before his marriage, he pleaded with his wife to allow him a period of travel as a more mature man since: 'I thought it noe injust Ambition to attaine the Knowledge off Forraigne Countreys especially since I had in greate part already attained the Languages'. Having made the necessary domestic arrangements, Herbert (later English Ambassador at Paris) then headed off to London in high spirits:

> And now coming to Court I obtayned a License to goe Beyond sea taking with mee for my Companion Mr. Aurelian Townsend, A Gentleman That spake the Languages of Frensh Italian and Spanish, in great Perfection and a man to waite in my Chamber who spake Frensh, two Lackyes and three horses.[4]

The numbers of young Englishmen being sent on an educational peregrination were steadily increasing during the second decade of the seventeenth century; and, correspondingly, there is a slight increase in the number of surviving written travel accounts.[5]

---

[1] *The Letters of John Chamberlain*, ed. N. E. McClure, 2 vols, Philadelphia, 1939, II, p. 255.

[2] Stoye, *English Travellers Abroad*, pp. 23, 27, 188–9.

[3] Becher later joined Sir John Merrick's embassy to Moscow (1614–15), served as English Agent at Paris (1617–19), and attained the Clerkship of the Privy Council (1623–41). See Stoye, *English Travellers Abroad*, pp. 47–54.

[4] *The Life of Edward, First Lord Herbert of Cherbury Written by Himself*, ed. J. M. Shuttleworth, London, New York and Toronto, 1976, p. 41.

[5] As a welcome change from the memoirs of young aristocrats, Sir Thomas Overbury's account of his *Travels* through the Low Countries in 1609 may be consulted, although they were first published only in 1626 and some doubts have been cast on his authorship; see Stoye, *English Travellers Abroad*, p. 200.

While most tend towards the dutifully descriptive and rarely offer insights into the feelings and intellectual development of their youthful writers (they do, however, speak eloquently of the physical hardships and fatigues of prolonged months of travelling), some of the more interesting include the manuscript records compiled by Sir Thomas Berkeley (or by another member of his party) as he made his way through Flanders, Germany, Switzerland, and Italy during 1610; Thomas Wentworth (who had married Henry Lord Clifford's sister, Anne) during his travels in France in 1612; and a brief account of Venice in 1614 written out by Sir Thomas Puckering.[1]

Another distinct category of English traveller on the continent evolved after 1610, and it is one which is of special interest to the development of enforced peregrinations during the Civil War period. On 14 May 1610 King Henri IV was assassinated by a Catholic fanatic, François Ravaillac, thereby opening up the French throne to a Catholic dynasty. Already nervous about Catholic conspiracies from the time of the Gunpowder Plot, James I feared that Ravaillac was not a lone extremist but a member of a well-organized, international band of Catholic terrorists. The English king anxiously insisted that 'their aim was not [Henri] alone but at other princes too, whereof I assure you I was one'. By 2 June a hastily-drafted proclamation was issued, forbidding English Catholics 'to repaire … to our court, or to the Court of our dearest wife the Queene, or of the Prince our Dear Son wheresoever'. Catholics were required to reject publicly the Pope's authority by swearing an oath of allegiance to the English monarch.[2]

For those sons of Catholic families who could afford it, an extended period of travel abroad would have seemed an attractive option in the face of this growing anti-Catholic hysteria at the English court. One such traveller who, fortunately, has left a detailed and thoughtful manuscript account of his experiences, was Charles Somerset (c. 1588–1665), the son of the Earl of Worcester. While his father outwardly acknowledged the authority of the Anglican Church, his mother, Elizabeth Hastings (d. 1621), a daughter of the 2nd Earl of Huntingdon, remained a staunchly and publicly committed Catholic. It seems that most of their children followed this maternal lead. Certainly, Charles's eldest brother, Henry (1577–1646) was reputed to have embraced Catholicism openly during his own tour of France and Italy, and at least two of Henry's own sons were educated abroad by the Jesuits. Another of Charles's brothers, Thomas (c. 1597–c.1650) preserved his commitment to Catholicism by living in Ireland and on the continent for much of his adult life. By the mid-1640s Thomas had taken up residence with the English Catholic community at Rome and was visited there by John Evelyn.

Charles Somerset, who had been educated at Eton and Magdalen College, Oxford (which itself was sometimes under suspicion for sympathy towards crypto-Catholic students), in early 1609 married Elizabeth Powell, the heiress of a rich Welshman. Following the now well-established custom of dispatching young men abroad soon after their marriage (thereby enabling his family to receive both the new bride's dowry and her person into their own household), the Earl of Worcester was probably already planning well before May 1610 to send his son Charles for an extended educational peregrination. But the crisis now faced by English Catholics following Ravaillac's murderous action would have certainly confirmed the wisdom of such a plan. Leaving England in April 1611, Charles

---

[1] BL MS Sloane 682; Sheffield Public Library, MSS Wentworth Woodhouse 21, 30; BL MS Harley 7021.

[2] *Stuart Royal Proclamations*, Vol. I, *Royal Proclamations of King James I, 1603–1625*, ed. J. F. Larkin and P. L. Hughes, Oxford, 1973, pp. 245–50.

travelled extensively through France, Italy, Germany, the Low Countries, and Flanders before returning home in May 1612.

The possible readership for Charles Somerset's richly informative and neatly transcribed travel journal, probably the most comprehensive and carefully assembled such account from the Jacobean period, is also worth considering. In June 1610, along with his brother Edward, Charles had been created a Knight of the Bath at the installation of the king's eldest son, Henry, as Prince of Wales (1594–1612). The young male members of the Somerset family, especially Thomas and Charles, seem to have been highly valued members of the prince's intimate court circle. Although their reputed Catholicism would have required, publicly at least, some temporary distancing, it is entirely possible that Charles's Somerset's politically and culturally astute diary (which reads like a well-informed intelligence report on the major influential figures at various Western European courts, finely blended with a detailed cultural guidebook to the finest architectural and historical sites to be seen by the young tourist) was intended for circulation as an informed reference manual on travel and statecraft among the Prince Henry's own court entourage.[1]

By early 1610 Henry Prince of Wales, although only aged sixteen, had already become a focus for those at the royal court who considered closer contacts with continental powers to be an essential element in England's new and forward-looking foreign policy. In particular, he was envisaged as enthusiastically supporting the educational efficacy (even though he had not as yet found any opportunity to travel abroad himself) of continental peregrinations. The renowned traveller, Thomas Coryat, dedicated to Prince Henry his *Crudities* (1611), which recounted his own extensive travels throughout Western Europe (see Fig. 2, p. 24). Coryat enthusiastically underlined the value of the current vogue among the courtier classes for sending their young sons abroad to complete their education:

> it may perhaps yield some little encouragement to many noble and generous young gallants that follow your Highness's court, and give attendance upon your peerless person, to travel into foreign countries, and enrich themselves partly with the observations, and partly with the languages of outlandish regions, the principal means (in my poor opinion) to grace and adorn those courtly gentlemen, whose noble parentage, ingenious education, and virtuous conversation have made worthy to be admitted into your Highness's court.[2]

Prince Henry's interests in continental travel were perhaps only to be expected since many of his closest advisers and tutors had themselves benefited from this form of educational experience. His childhood governor and lord chamberlain, Sir Thomas Chaloner, had travelled widely in Italy as a young man during the 1580s and had resided at Florence as an intelligence gatherer between 1596 and 1598. The prince's chief secretary, Adam Newton (d. 1630), had lived in France during the 1580s and his comptroller, John Holles (1564–1637), had also travelled extensively in France and Italy.[3] His treasurer, Sir Charles Cornwallis (d. 1629), had previously served as English ambassador to Spain, from where as early as 1605 he sent a series of informative letters on Spanish affairs to the eleven-years-old prince.[4]

---

[1] Leeds, Brotherton MS Trv.q.3; pr. *The Travel Diary (1611–1612) of an English Catholic, Sir Charles Somerset*, ed. M. G. Brennan, Leeds, 1993.

[2] Dedicatory epistle to Prince Henry.

[3] Roy Strong, *Henry Prince of Wales and England's Lost Renaissance*, London, 1986, pp. 27–9.

[4] The custom of young men joining ambassadorial entourages was still prevalent at this period; see, for example, R. Treswell, *A Relation of Such Things as Were Observed to Happen in the Journey of the Earle of Nottingham to Spaine*, 1605.

Fig. 2. Title-page of Thomas Coryat, *Coryats Crudities. Hastily Gobled up in Five Moneths Travells in France, Savoy, Italy, Rhetia … Helvetia … High Germany, and the Netherlands* (1611).

Within Prince Henry's personal court circle, informed knowledge of Western European cultures and politics became both fashionable and highly desirable. He was always keen to receive first-hand reports from travellers at foreign courts. The tutors of his young friends who did undertake such tours were strongly encouraged to ensure that a steady supply of correspondence about court affairs, military and naval matters, religious conflicts, and cultural observations were regularly sent home to the prince. For example, when one of Henry's childhood companions, the sixteen-years-old John Harington, was travelling through the Low Countries, Germany, Switzerland, Italy, and France, he dutifully sent home to him formal letters, in both Italian and Latin, describing his observations on two of the prince's favourite topics, military fortifications and continental architectural designs.[1]

The Europhile perspectives of Prince Henry's court (echoing those of the Duke of Northumberland during the early 1550s), mark the culmination of some sixty years of English inquisitiveness concerning continental political and cultural affairs. Although the prince's unexpected demise in November 1612 effectively disassembled what probably amounted to the most pro-continental grouping at the English court, his interests and those of his closest advisers and followers paved the way for the development of a fresh wave of cultural eclecticism by Englishmen on the continent during the second decade of the seventeenth century. Prince Henry had assiduously cultivated for himself the reputation of a connoisseur of the arts (and thereby acted as a posthumous inspiration for the great royal picture collections assembled by his younger brother, Charles I). To this end, Henry employed the services of several discerning courtiers and diplomats, including Sir Dudley Carleton in Italy and Sir Edward Conway in the Low Countries, to act as agents for him in the acquisition of high quality paintings. Fine arts in themselves became one of the recognized currencies of international diplomacy, as the Grand Duke of Tuscany (who was especially responsive to the ever-shifting trends in the mercantile, military, and cultural exchanges between England and Florence) cultivated and flattered the prince's precocious interests with the magnificent gift of a set of twelve bronzes from the studio of Giambologna. There is ample evidence to suggest that Prince Henry consciously wished in his collecting habits to revitalize the example of a century earlier when Henry VII and the young Henry VIII had warmly welcomed foreign artists, scholars, and skilled artisans to their courts.[2]

A growing commercial interest in travel writing is also discernable at this period. Two bulky printed works, Tom Coryat's *Crudities* (1611) and Fynes Moryson's *An Itinerary* (1617), usefully exemplify the kinds of material now becoming more readily available to a broader range of English readers who previously would not have had access to manuscript travel accounts. Moryson's work, whose travels between 1591 and 1597 seem to have been largely financed through a kind of travelling fellowship by his Cambridge college, Peterhouse, was conceived essentially as a scholarly volume and it came to be recognized as one of the most informative and authoritative English guides to Western Europe of the first half of the seventeenth century. Its chosen methodologies, which prefigure the carefully assembled descriptions of continental locations compiled by John

---

[1] *CSP Domestic 1610*, p. 581; BL MS Harley 7007, ff. 255, 266; Strong, *Henry Prince of Wales*, pp. 72–3, and plates 18–20; Stoye, *English Travellers Abroad*, pp. 51, 125; and Thomas Birch, *The Life of Henry Prince of Wales*, 1760, appendix.

[2] See Graham Parry, *The Golden Age Restor'd: the Culture of the Stuart Court, 1603–1642*, Manchester, 1981, pp. 80–81; Strong, *Henry Prince of Wales*, p. 108; and *CSP Venice, 1611*, pp. 122–3.

Evelyn during the 1640s, were essentially objective and forward-looking in their reliance upon empirical observation and the use of the best available secondary sources. Although published as a large folio volume which was not readily portable (suggesting that Moryson's target audience lay primarily in academic studies and family libraries rather than on the continental post-roads), the *Itinerary* anticipates in its descriptions the wealth of historical and cultural detail increasingly required by culturally voracious English tourists. It might even be suggested that the *Itinerary* is one of the early ancestors of modern factually-dense travel publications, such as the authoritative 'Baedeker Guides', 'Murray's Handbooks' and 'Blue Guides', which still satisfy the deep-rooted need of some travellers (whether real or armchair) to understand and categorize whatever they are viewing through a veritable glut of information on its historical, political, and cultural associations.

In contrast to the weighty scholasticism of Moryson's *Itinerary*, Thomas Coryat's earlier *Crudities*, the publication of which was probably self-financed, offered its readers something more comparable with what a modern-day traveller might find in a 'Rough Guide' to various Western European locations. Michael Strachan's pioneering biographical study, *The Life and Adventures of Thomas Coryate* (1962), was the first detailed response to the *Crudities* to underline the importance of Coryat's narrative (which is often deceptively eccentric in its prose style) as confirmation of a broader English acceptance of the now increasingly pervasive concept of the educational 'Grand Tour'. Travelling through Western Europe in what at first appears as little more than a zanily haphazard geographical pattern (Coryat likes to present himself as a traveller driven primarily by whim and mere curiosity, especially since his entire itinerary was reputedly undertaken only because of a bet with a Yeovil linen draper), closer study of the *Crudities* reveals it to be a copiously detailed and discriminating guide to many of the pre-eminent political, religious, and cultural locations of continental Europe. Coryat, it seems certain, deliberately sought to create a divergence between the seriousness of his purpose and the jocularity of his written style. The *Crudities* was proudly dedicated to Prince Henry but its subtitle was almost self-mocking: 'Hastily gobled up in five Moneths travells … Newly digested in the hungry aire of Odcombe in the County of Somerset, & now dispersed to the nourishment of the travelling Members of this Kingdome' (see Fig. 2, p. 24). Surrounding the central panel of the title-page were various comic illustrations of Coryat's progress through Western Europe, variously:

A First, th'Author here glutteth Sea, Haddocke and Whiting
With spring, and after the world with his writing

E Here to his Land-Friggat he's ferried by Charon,
He bords her; a service a hote and a rare one

I See our louse-bitten Travellers ragged device,
Of case, shoes, and stockings, and Canniball lice

The *Crudities* also contained an impressive but bewildering mixture of engravings which usefully characterize the intellectual highs and lows of continental peregrinations at this period. Against a meticulously detailed illustration of the renowned and genuinely intriguing mechanical clock at Strasbourg (see Fig. 3, p. 27) could be held an engraving of the enormous Heidelberg Tun, a subversively comic image in which Coryat, supposedly involved in the serious business of exploring continental societies and cultures, ends up, like

Fig. 3. 'A true figure of the famous Clock of Strasbourg'. From *Coryats Crudities* (1611), p. 452.

Lemuel Gulliver, as a tiny cartoon figure on top of the biggest beer barrel in the world (see Fig. 49, p. 286). At the same time, Coryat's volume also offers various striking and historically important images, such as an informative architectural dissection of the roman amphitheatre at Verona (see Fig. 47, p. 272). He even caters for the tastes of his more salacious readers by providing a visual representation of his personal encounter with the renowned bare-breasted Venetian courtesan, Margarita Emiliana (see Fig. 4, p. 29). In this selection of images are found the familiar blend of intellectual enquiry and casual curiosity so typical of the spirit of cultural tourism from the seventeenth century onwards.

The all-encompassing breadth of the continental interests of Prince Henry's circle is demonstrated by, simultaneously, its attraction of Coryat's dedication of his eccentric volume of travels and by the personal involvement of the greatest English collector and connoisseur of his generation, Thomas Howard (1585–1646), Earl of Arundel, who from about 1607 became one of the prince's major cultural mentors. After Prince Henry's death in November 1612, Arundel cultivated the intellectual friendship of the painter, set designer, and mechanical inventor, Inigo Jones, who had gained considerable acclaim during the previous ten years for his staging of lavish court masques. In April 1613 Arundel was appointed as one of the four royal commissioners to accompany Prince Henry's sister, Princess Elizabeth, back to Heidelberg after her marriage to Frederick, Elector Palatine. With this duty performed, the earl, his wife (Aletheia Talbot, daughter and heir of the extremely wealthy Earl of Shrewsbury), and Jones then headed off into Italy to examine the wonders of its art, antiquities and architecture at Venice, Vicenza, Florence, and Siena.[1] The party wintered at Rome over the Christmas and New Year season of 1613/1614, where Arundel undertook some minor excavations of his own and developed a lifelong passion for Roman statuary and other smaller antiquities – tastes which were rapidly popularized back home in England. After a further excursion to Naples, the Earl was unexpectedly obliged to return to England on the death of his great-uncle, the Earl of Northampton. He headed up through Turin and across the Alps before crossing France to reach Paris and then London in November 1614, while Jones made a final visit to Venice and Vicenza.[2] When Jones also returned to England, they began a collaborative building and collecting programme which effectively set the cultural tone for the concept of the virtuoso during the reign of Charles I.

The passage of the Princess Elizabeth's enormous entourage across France and Germany may be taken as marking the beginning of a new political and cultural phase in Anglo-continental relations. Her marriage also marked the posthumous culmination of many of the broader continental ambitions of the circle of her eldest brother, Prince Henry. Henceforth, the few joys and many more trials and tribulations of Elizabeth of Bohemia and her family (including, most notably from a Civil War perspective, her talented son, Prince Rupert, see Fig. 48, p. 277), along with those of her French sister-in-law, Queen Henrietta Maria, forged for the supporters of the English royal family between 1613 and 1660 an unwavering Western European focus of interest.

[1] Parry, *Golden Age Restor'd*, pp. 95–136. Jones's notes on their travels were added to his own copy of Andrea Palladio's *I quattro libri dell'architettura* (1560), now in the library of Worcester College, Oxford.

[2] See Stoye, *English Travellers Abroad*, pp. 87–9, for Thomas Coke (brother of the more famous John Coke, Secretary of State), who accompanied Arundel and Jones on their Italian explorations and later returned to Italy as the guide and tutor of Arundel's elder sons.

Il Signior Tomaso Odcombiano

Margarita Emiliana bella Cortesana di Venetia

Gu: Hole sculp

Fig. 4. Coryat meets the Venetian courtesan Margarita Emiliana. From *Coryats Crudities* (1611), p. 262.

4. From Education to Exile: Continental Travel from 1625 until 1660

> 'so many of us are doom'd to wander, not like *Cain*
> for drawing blood, but for asking Peace'.
>
> (Sir John Berkenhead)

> 'In this very nick of time comes on the Civil War ...
> to avoid which storm and give myself some convenient education I
> went out of England about 1643 and continued travelling in France,
> Italy, Flanders, Holland, etc. till anno 1649, viz about six years and a
> half, at which time I againe returned after the end of the war and the
> death of the king'.
>
> (Sir Roger Pratt)[1]

During the last ten years of James I's reign, the artistic collections of the Earl of Arundel, along with those of the king's most influential favourite, George Villiers, Duke of Buckingham (who himself had spent some time in France as a young man), laid the foundations for Charles I's ardent desire to project himself among both his own subjects and continental princes as a discriminating intellectual in the vanguard of continental aesthetic taste. As the works of Titian, Veronese, Raphael, and Leonardo found their way into the great royal and aristocratic collections, so English travellers became increasingly aware that the cultural richness of a Western European society was to be viewed as a telling indicator of its political power and social sophistication. Although relations between Arundel and Charles I were not good at the beginning of the reign, it was Arundel who later made one of the most important diplomatic and cultural journeys on the continent during the mid-1630s. In 1636 he led an embassy to the Emperor Ferdinand in an attempt to stall the impending agreement at the Diet of Ratisbon of the Treaty of Prague, involving the Upper Palatinate, formerly the possession of Frederick the Elector Palatine (d. 1632). Hopefully (if not entirely realistically), his widow, Charles's sister, Elizabeth, had been seeking to claim it for her eldest son. The mission was, from a diplomatic perspective, almost entirely pointless but its cultural significance was considerable since at Nuremberg in May 1636 Arundel was able to purchase very cheaply the entire Pirckheimer Library, with its original illustrations and letters by Dürer. (It also contained part of the artist's own diary of a trip through the Low Countries.) On the same trip at Cologne Arundel engaged the services of the talented engraver Wenceslaus Hollar of Prague, who not only dutifully recorded the treasures of the Earl's private collections back home but also produced some of the most important illustrations of the landscapes and cityscapes of seventeenth-century England.[2]

The social prestige of the Earl of Arundel, coupled with the sheer wealth of his collections, has ensured that his travels and collecting habits can still be traced in considerable detail. But of the many other English travellers on the continent during the 1630s and early 1640s far less is generally known about their itineraries and collecting habits (albeit at a more humble level). Nevertheless, the custom of compiling a personal manuscript memoir of continental travels, often written out from diaries and rough notes into a more polished

---

[1] Birkenhead's comment on the exile of English royalists prefaces John Raymond, *An Itinerary Contayning a Voyage Made Through Italy, in the Yeare 1646, and 1647*, 1648, pp. 11–12. Pratt's explanation for his continental travels is quoted in R. T. Gunther, *The Architecture of Sir Roger Pratt*, Oxford, 1928, pp. 3, 10.

[2] Parry, *Golden Age Restor'd*, pp. 122–5. The progress of the embassy was recorded in detail in the personal diary of one of its members, William Crowne; see F. Springell, *Connoisseur and Diplomat ... The Earl of Arundel's Embassy to Germany in 1636 as recounted in William Crowne's Diary*, London, 1963, pp. 54–135.

form once the traveller was either heading homewards or even back home, remained preva-lent. So much so, that conventions for what kind of information should be included were now widely available. The 1625 edition of Francis Bacon's *Essays*, for example, contained a newly published essay, 'Of Travel', advising:

> The Things to be seene and observed are: The Courts of Princes, specially when they give Audience to Ambassadours: The Courts of Justice, while they sit and heare Causes; And so of Consistories Ecclesiasticke: The Churches, and Monasteries, with the Monuments which are therein extant: The Wals and Fortifications of Cities and Townes; And so the Havens and Harbours: Antiquities, and Ruines: Libraries; Colledges, Disputations, and Lectures, where any are: Shipping and Navies; Houses, and Gardens of State, and Pleasure, neare great Cities: Armories: Arsenals: Magazens: Exchanges: Burses: Warehouses: Exercises of Horseman-ship; Fencing; Trayning of Souldiers; and the like: Comedies; Such wherunto the better Sort of persons doe resort; Treasures of Jewels, and Robes; Cabinets, and Rarities: And to conclude, whatsoever is memorable in the Places, where they goe.[1]

Sadly, very few substantial examples of travel records compiled by Englishmen during the 1630s are now known, although one was (probably) assembled by Thomas Abdy, who trav-elled extensively in France, Italy, and Switzerland between 1633 and 1635. He wrote out the first half of his diary in English and then, after wintering at Blois where he studied mathematics, music, dance, and the native tongue, he completed the rest in workmanlike French.[2] Between 1632 and 1637 a member of a very well travelled family network, Thomas Raymond (c. 1610–c. 1681), first arrived on the continent at The Hague with the entourage of his uncle, William Boswell, who had just been appointed English resident there. Raymond then struck out on his own, passing through the Low Countries, Italy, and France, and earning his living, variously, as a soldier in Sir William Pakenham's Dutch contingent, as a personal secretary for almost three years to Basil Lord Fielding, then ambassador at Venice, and as a private tutor at Paris to a young nobleman, Lord Mordaunt.[3] During the mid-1630s George Courthop, the son of a wealthy Sussex landowner, resided in France for some eighteen months, including a year at Loudun where he concentrated on his studies and learned the French language at an academy run by a Scotsman called Mr Strachan. He then headed off southwards, via Geneva, Genoa, Rome, and Naples, before visiting Messina and Constantinople. Courthop had originally crossed the Channel in the company of Lord Dacre, whose tutor persuaded them to travel from Paris down the Loire from Orléans to Tours, Blois, Saumur and Angers, where Dacre decided to stay to further his own studies (while Courthop went on to Loudun).[4] Some travellers, of course, made much briefer visits to the continent. In May 1634 Sir William Brereton, MP for Cheshire in the 1628 Parliament (and later a parliamentary general during the Civil War), crossed to Holland with his whole family for a period of three weeks, purportedly to consult with

---

[1] *The Essayes or Counsels*, p. 56.

[2] Bodl. MS Rawlinson D 1285. Abdy's name on the flyleaf of the manuscript is the only guide to its possible authorship. See Stoye, *English Travellers Abroad*, p. 289.

[3] Thomas Raymond was a relative of John Raymond (see p. 43), Robert Bargrave (see p. 42), and John Bargrave (see p. 43). Thomas Raymond's memoirs, compiled much later, are preserved in Bodl. MS Rawlinson D 1150, pr. *Autobiography of Thomas Raymond and Memoirs of the Family of Guise of Elmore, Gloucestershire*, ed. G. Davies, Camden Society, 3rd ser., 28, 1917; and (unknown to G. Davies) in Bodl. MS Tanner 93, ff. 46–60, which contin-ues the narrative from the previous manuscript. See Stoye, *English Travellers Abroad*, pp. 191, 343.

[4] At Loudun Courthop also made one of the relatively rare references in this period to English women exploring the continent when he met Lady Purbeck, the daughter of Sir Edward Coke. Courthop's travels are detailed in *Camden Miscellany*, 11, 1907. See Stoye, *English Travellers Abroad*, pp. 64, 119, 290.

doctors at Leiden about the health of his children. Taking advantage of this opportunity to undertake what amounted to a 'peregrination in miniature', he also visited the major Dutch cities, had an audience at The Hague with the exiled Elizabeth, Queen of Bohemia, took a keen interest in religious sectarian matters, and purchased some tulip bulbs for his English garden.[1]

Many other travellers at this period would have had little concept of tourism for its own sake since their reasons for being in various parts of Western Europe were primarily commercial. One such individual, who combined his years in foreign trade with a compulsion for meticulously documenting his experiences, was the noted traveller and merchant, Peter Mundy, who crossed to Holland in 1639 before heading to Danzig and beyond, remaining abroad for the next eight years. While in Holland he explored Rotterdam, Delft, and Amsterdam, making voluminous notes on whatever took his fancy, such as Dutch burial customs, architectural designs, marsh drainage, and the works of Rembrandt. Mundy had been living and working abroad for over thirty years and had been spent time in France (1608–10) and Spain (1615, 1621, 1625), Turkey (1617–20), India, Surat, and Japan (1628–39), the Low Countries, Russia, Prussia, and Poland (1639–7), and India (1655).[2] His huge diary (which in terms of its sheer geographical coverage and reliance upon first-hand observation is unrivalled by any other English traveller of the period) gives voice to a rarely heard kind of seventeenth-century Englishman – the intelligent, multi-lingual merchant-trader who roamed Western and Eastern Europe in search of employment, profits, and the sheer challenge of prolonged travel.

These examples of English travellers from the 1630s also exemplify how by now an extended period of travel on the continent was no longer the exclusive prerogative of either the court élite or the spectacularly wealthy. Hugh Popham, financed by a £200 per annum allowance from his father, headed off to Italy in the late 1630s. He had arrived at Rome by February 1639 where he was hospitably entertained, along with several other English visitors, at the English College. In May 1638 the poet John Milton left England for a fifteen-month continental tour, arriving at Florence in June and then travelling on in October, via Siena, to Rome and in December to Naples. By April 1639 he was at Venice, having passed through Bologna and Ferrara, from where he shipped home a large collection of books and other items collected during his travels. He then began his homeward journey, via Verona and Milan, through Lombardy and the Pennine Alps (using either the Simplon or St Bernard Pass) to cross to Geneva and then on westwards through France during the summer of 1639.[3]

This socially broadening trend was markedly accentuated by the first rumblings of the Civil War, although the body of English travellers on the continent during the 1640s and 1650s was by no means largely made up of disgruntled royalist exiles. Instead, as the tensions between royal and parliamentary authority steadily escalated, some individuals simply saw a period of extended travel (like Sir Charles Somerset some thirty years earlier in the wake of James I's anti-papist hysteria) as a tactically wise option to pursue.

---

[1] *Travels in Holland, the United Provinces, England … 1634–1635*, ed. E. Hawkins, Chetham Society, 1, 1844; and Stoye, *English Travellers Abroad*, pp. 174–6, 192–3.

[2] *The Travels of Peter Mundy … 1608–1667*, Volumes I and IV, ed. R. C. Temple, Hakluyt Society, 2nd ser., 17 and 46, 1907 and 1924 (with the fifth and final volume of his travels published in 1936). This edition is based upon Bodl. MS Rawlinson A 315 (Mundy's partly autograph diary) and BL MS Harley 2286 (a scribal transcript given to Sir Paul Pindar). See also Stoye, *English Travellers Abroad*, pp. 181–2, 245.

[3] *CSP Domestic* [1639], p.414; and Gordon Campbell, *A Milton Chronology*, London, 1997, pp. 59–67.

Representative of this kind of traveller was Joseph Colston, who had graduated with a BA degree from Fynes Moryson's Cambridge college, Peterhouse, in 1633 and began his continental peregrinations in September 1641. Colston came from a mercantile London family who derived much of its income from rental properties and small commercial loans. Both of his parents were dead and he depended upon an aunt and a cousin to forward him an allowance while abroad. At first, Colston seems to have been intent merely on enjoying the intellectual and sensory stimulations of an itinerary down through France, before crossing from Marseilles into Italy where he carefully explored Rome, Naples, Loreto, and Venice. He then settled down to a period of medical studies at the University of Padua, from which institution he graduated on 31 December 1642. Although his family seem to have expected him to begin his homeward journey at this point, Colston opted for prolonging his sojourn on the continent, almost certainly as a means of avoiding the growing political uncertainties back home in London. After the Restoration he was enrolled in the Royal College of Physicians and enjoyed a solidly rewarding career in medicine, leading to a knighthood in 1669.[1]

By far the most renowned memoirs of travels on the continent during the 1640s and 1650s are those of the scholar and virtuoso, John Evelyn (1620–1706). Fortunately, his diary has long been accessible to modern readers in E. S. de Beer's monumental six-volume Oxford edition and further comment on its absolute centrality to the history of Western European travel writing is unnecessary here.[2] However, it is important to consider briefly exactly what kind of travel diary Evelyn's account actually provides, since its mode of compilation is indicative of the specific purposes for which these forms of records were envisaged during the second half of the seventeenth century. Evelyn was an intelligent, educated, and keen observer of all he saw and he possessed an enviable access to some of the most prestigious individuals and locations. But, as one reads through his diary (in conjunction with E. S. de Beer's masterly teasing out of Evelyn's silent rephrasing and extensive copyings out *verbatim* from other sources), it becomes apparent that the compilation of an independent, first-hand account of his experiences was never a central purpose of Evelyn as a travel writer.

Instead, even when describing locations which he knew intimately, Evelyn was always careful to prioritize information gleaned from what he regarded as authoritative primary and secondary sources. Only when he had satisfied himself with 'capturing' these nuggets of knowledge did he lace them through with his own comments, which were sometimes genuinely illuminating but on other occasions merely incidental (and often surprisingly brief). Evelyn's description of Paris, for example, was largely written up during his retirement in the 1670s, rather than at the time of his main visit to the city in 1643. He was also was heavily dependent upon the popular guidebook which he had bought there – Claude de Varennes's *Le Voyage de France* (Paris, 1643) – for much of the specific detail of his own description.[3] Citations to this source were not provided in Evelyn's own manuscript account

---

[1] BL MS Sloane 118, a fragmentary diary bound with letters sent from England to Colson while abroad. Stoye, *English Travellers Abroad*, pp. 157–8.

[2] *The Diary of John Evelyn*, 6 vols, Oxford, 1955 (reissued 2000). This edition, with over 12,000 footnotes and 1176 columns of index set a rarely matched standard in editorial procedure for English travel writings. E. S. de Beer served as President of the Hakluyt Society from 1972 until 1978. See also W. G. Hiscock, *John Evelyn and his Family Circle*, London, 1955, and *The Writings of John Evelyn*, ed. Guy de la Bédoyère, Woodbridge, 1995.

[3] *Le Voyage de France, dressé pour l'instruction & commodité tant des François que des estrangers* [translated by Claude de Varennes from the *Itinerarium Galliae* of Justus Zintzerling (Jodocus Sincerus)], Paris, 1643.

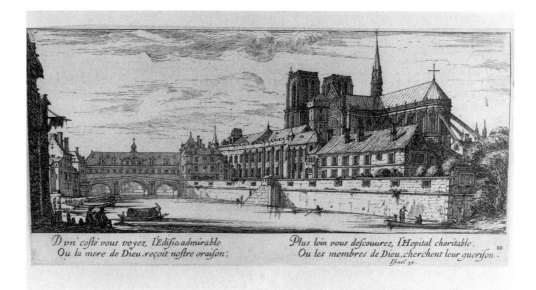

Fig. 5. Paris during the 1650s: 'L'Edifice admirable / Ou la mere de Dieu, reçoit nostre oraison / Plus loin vous descouvrez l'Hopital charitable' (Israel Silvestre).

but this does not mean that as a writer he had any intention to deceive his readers (the chief of whom, of course, remained himself since his diary was intended primarily as a personal record of his travels). For Evelyn, as for many of his contemporaries – and this is a point of particular importance to bear in mind when reading travel diaries of this period, including Montagu's and Maynard's – the compilation of a travel narrative was regarded as the production of an informed personal commentary, filtered through an extensive and expected (but often unacknowledged) use of earlier sources.[1]

From the 1640s onwards, the social diversity of the travellers, coupled with the contrasting purposes for which their written records were compiled, becomes all the more apparent. Robert Bargrave (1628–61), a trainee Levant merchant from a strongly royalist family, made in the summer of 1647 a brief detour during the long sea voyage out to Turkey to examine Leghorn, Siena, and Florence. (His cousin John Bargrave guided him around the latter two cities, see p. 43.) Between September 1652 and March 1653 he crossed overland from east to west on his return journey home from Constantinople, via Bulgaria, Romania, Poland, Germany, and the Low Countries. On a third journey, again as a merchant-trader, made between 1654 and 1656 he visited Spain and then sailed through the Mediterranean to Venice where he conducted further business for a few months, examined the tourist sights, and even found time for a brief excursion to Padua. His final journey homewards took him overland during the spring of 1656 from Venice, via Austria, Germany, and the Low Countries, to England.[2]

[1] Evelyn's techniques for preparing his private, but still monumental, guidebook may be compared with those of Peter Heylin who spent a few weeks in France during the summer of 1625. Many years later notes from his own diary were blended with materials from printed pamphlets and guidebooks to produce his own scholarly guide, published as the *Survey of the Estate of France* (1656).

[2] For further details of Robert Bargrave's travels, see *The Travel Diary of Robert Bargrave (1647–1656)*, ed. Michael G. Brennan, Hakluyt Society, 3rd ser., 3, 1999, pp. 14–33.

Fig. 6. Paris during the 1650s: 'Veuë de l'Hostel de ville de Paris, et de la place de greve' (Israel Silvestre).

In contrast to Robert Bargrave, who began his travels specifically to gain the experience and training for his chosen career in the Levant Company, between 1647 and 1649 Dr Isaac Basire, the expelled Archdeacon of Northumberland, who had formerly served as a personal chaplain to Charles I, undertook an enforced but adventurous itinerary through France and Italy with a small group of youthful pupils from royalist families, including William Ashburnham, Thomas Lambton, John Lawrence, and a Master Ashworth. Under his scrupulous guidance, they examined the antiquities of Rome, Naples, Sicily, and Malta, and collaborated in the compilation of a predictably scholarly summary of their travels.[1] John Finch (1626–82), the son of the Recorder of London, also left England in 1649 for Italy, in the company of his lifelong friend and partner, Thomas Baines (c. 1622–80). They settled in Padua and both enrolled at the medical school, remaining there (apart from some brief tourist excursions in northern Italy) until their joint graduation in 1657, followed by Finch's appointment to the Chair of Anatomy at Pisa in 1659. Although they made a brief return trip home in 1660, Finch and Baines much preferred residence in Italy, where Finch acted between 1665 and 1670 as Charles II's representative at the Grand Duke of Tuscany's court.[2] Other travellers at this period who left informative accounts of their experiences include Robert Bertie, later Lord Willoughby and Earl of Lindsey, who was in France in 1648/9 and sent letters in Latin and French to his father and others; an anonymous traveller through France, Catalonia, and Italy during the same years; the royalist William Edgeman who travelled with Sir

---

[1] Two manuscripts of their memoirs have survived: Durham Cathedral, Dean and Chapter Library, MS Hunter 134; and a slightly abridged version in the anonymous Folger Library MS V.a.428, edited as *Travels Through France and Italy (1647–49)*, ed. Luigi Monga and C. Hassel, Geneva and Turin, 1987. See Chaney, *Grand Tour*, pp. 30, 87.

[2] A. Malloch, *Finch and Baines*, Cambridge, 1917; Edward Chaney, *The Grand Tour and the Great Rebellion*, Geneva, 1985, p. 341; and Stoye, *English Travellers Abroad*, pp. 158–9.

Edward Hyde and Lord Cottington through Flanders, France, and Spain between 1649 and 1651; and Philip Stanhope, Earl of Chesterfield, who made a tour of France and Italy between 1650 and 1652.[1] A sprinkling of printed narratives of individual Western European peregrinations also began to be published, such as pirated editions of Owen Feltham's *Three Months Observations of the Low-Countries* (1648–52), the popularity of which was such that an authorized printing appeared in 1652, with further reprints stretching the public life of his memoirs until 1671.

Two other English travellers of the 1650s merit individual mention. The first, a Yorkshireman and firm royalist called Sir John Reresby (1634–89), travelled on the continent between 1654 and 1658 and compiled (after 1679) a voluminous manuscript of his experiences in a distinctively rumbustious and lively written style. Reresby's narrative, written long after the Restoration of Charles II, is unusual in explaining exactly why and how he decided to withdraw to the continent in the face of the civil upheavals at home:

> I found ther was little means of improvement for a gentleman as to other respects in England, the nobility and gentlemen of the best ranke and estates liveing retired in the country, to avoid the jealousies of the then suspicious government of every act or word that could be construed in favour of the royall familie, wherby to draw them into the dangers and forfitures of delinquencie. And such as lived in town were either such zealots in the rebellious, scismaticall superstitions of thos times, or soe very debauched on the other hand, that it was very hard for a yong man to avoid infection on one side or the other.
>
> These considerations, wrought not only upon me to ask, but upon my mother to allowe me leave to goe to travell. I sett forward for France in Aprill 1654, being then twenty years of age, Cromwell haveing the year before declared his ambition in the dismission of the late Parlament, the calling of another, in the subdueing of Ireland, and makeing the army entirely at his devotion, by which he did as he pleased in the three kingdomes.[2]

The other traveller was Francis Mortoft who left a detailed (but incomplete since it abruptly ceases at Zürich on his return journey home) manuscript account of his travels in France and Italy between 1658 and 1659. Mortoft, it seems, may have been using a bequest left to him by his father of £500 on attaining the age of twenty-one to finance his grand tour. He is a clear and unpretentious recorder of his experiences and his accounts of major cities and towns, including Paris, Orléans, Saumur, Montpellier, Genoa, Pisa, and Rome (where his party spent some three months) are both vivid and historically informative. Although little is known about Mortoft's early life, and nothing whatsoever of his activities after 1659 (it is even possible that he died on the way back to England and his diary was brought then home by one of his travelling companions), his records remain an important example of an itinerant Englishman's first-hand observations of continental societies, religions, and cultures.[3]

---

[1] [Willoughby], *HMC Ancaster MSS*, pp. 341–8; [Anon], Bodl. MS Rawlinson D 120; [Edgeman], Bodl. MS Clarendon 137; and [Stanhope], BL Add. MS 19253.

[2] *Memoirs of Sir John Reresby. The Complete Text and a Selection from his Letters*, ed. Andrew Browning, 2nd edn with a new preface and notes, ed. Mary K. Geiter and W. A. Speck, London, 1991, p. 6. See also *The Memoirs of Sir John Reresby ... 1634–1689*, ed. James J. Cartwright, London, 1875; and *Memoirs & Travels of Sir John Reresby Bart*, ed. Albert Ivatt, London, 1904.

[3] BL MS Sloane 2142. *Francis Mortoft: His Book Being His Travels Through Italy 1658–1659*, ed. Malcolm Letts, Hakluyt Society, 2nd ser., 57, Cambridge, 1925.

5. English Civil War Travellers as Diarists and Collectors

> beasts, fowle, fishes, serpents, wormes (reall, although dead and dryed), pretious stone and other Armes, Coines, shells, fethers, etts. of sundrey Nations, Countries, forme, Coullours; also diverse Curiosities in Carvinge, painteinge, etts., as 80 faces carved on a Cherry stone, Pictures to bee seene by a Celinder which otherwise appeare like confused blotts, Medalls of Sundrey sorts, etts. Moreover, a little garden with divers outlandish herbes and flowers, whereof some that I had not seene elsewhere but in India, being supplyed by Noblemen, Gentlemen, Sea Commaunders, etts. with such Toyes as they could bringe or procure from other parts.
>
> (Peter Mundy on John Tradescant, Sr.'s collections)[1]

At this point, it is necessary to emphasize that the sporadic survival of written diaries and journals of Englishmen in Western Europe during the mid-seventeenth century should be regarded only as partial evidence of how these travellers chose to record their personal experiences abroad. While a travel diary traditionally provided the central framework for remembering and commemorating a period spent on the continent, the young traveller habitually brought home with him numerous other mementos of his experiences, including books, engravings, pictures, antiquities (genuine or specially created forgeries and imitations for the tourist market), and other curiosities. Sadly, these kinds of miscellaneous (and often delicate) items have all too often been dispersed over the centuries by either the families and descendants of the travellers or by the individual literary collectors and institutional libraries which came to own their manuscript journals.

A minority of English travellers (as we have already seen in the case of Inigo Jones) were interested in collecting engravings, statuettes, and architectural plans for professional reasons. Nicholas and Henry Stone, the sons of a funereal monument stonemason, kept a detailed diary of their observations and collecting in Italy between 1638 and 1642. It is clear from Nicholas's accounts that the journey through France was regarded as little more than a means to an end, since his records there are largely concerned with the mundane practicalities of continental travelling. But once they arrived in Italy they sought out, for their father's business, a huge range of illustrative material on Italian statuary, architectural designs, and marble samples. By the time they were about to leave Rome in May 1642, their haul of objects – which included books, plaster statues, mouldings, hundreds of marble samples, prints, and engravings – were packed into smaller boxes and then stowed in an immense chest (specially purchased for the purpose), which was wrapped in stout canvas and secured with ropes. It was then dispatched to two trusted English merchants at Leghorn for shipment back home to their expectant father.[2]

One collection about which a considerable amount of information is still available was assembled by an Essex gentleman of relatively modest means. Richard Symonds, who travelled through France and Italy between 1649 and 1652, was interested in both general sightseeing and the various kinds of trinkets, shells, minor antiquities, and other miscellaneous

---

[1] *Travels of Peter Mundy*, III, pp. 1–3; quoted in Marjorie Swann, *Curiosities and Texts. The Culture of Collecting in Early Modern England*, Philadelphia, 2001, p. 1.

[2] *Diary of Nicholas Stone, Junior, 1638–1640*, ed. W. L. Spiers, Walpole Society, 7, 1919, and Stoye, *English Travellers Abroad*, pp. 139–44, which also examines the artistic education in Italy during the 1640s of Sir Roger Pratt, one of the major English architects of the mid-seventeenth century.

Fig. 7. Venice during the 1650s: 'Veduta del Piaza di S^t. Marco di Venezia vista verso il parto' (Israel Silvestre).

items made available to English travellers by either established curio shops in the major cities or by itinerant hawkers and other private individuals who were well aware of the tourist's insatiable appetite for the new, the rare, and the curious. Symonds, however, devoted most of his finances to the collecting of engravings of the great antiquities, architectural masterpieces, paintings, and sculpture of Italy. His notebooks, albeit at a modest level compared to the Earl of Arundel's fabulous aquisitions, offer a remarkably detailed record of one Englishman's purchases of these kinds of materials. One of his notebooks, for example, contains a detailed list of illustrations bought at Rome in 1650–1 ('Stampe comprate in Roma 1650, 1651'), cataloguing his acquisition at Rome of over 100 engravings of Raphael's works at Rome, five large folios of illustrations of Michelangelo's Sistine Chapel and the 'Day of Judgement', and works by Titian, Caravaggio, and Domenichino. Symonds also purchased over fifty engravings from print vendors in the Piazza of St Mark and the Rialto at Venice.[1] While the Earl of Arundel's immense wealth enabled him to acquire original, precious, and rare works of art, most English travellers of the period, as represented by Symonds, had to satisfy themselves with cheaply produced, but still aesthetically pleasing, engravings of artistic artefacts. Symonds also took detailed notes while attending the studio of Giovanni Angelo Canini, on such practical artistic matters as the mixing of colours, varnishes, perspectives and the equipment required for landscape paintings.[2] Symonds and Arundel were, in purely financial terms, operating in

[1] BL MS Harley 943, ff. 100–110, 114–116.

[2] Symond's copiously illustrated diaries are preserved in BL Egerton MSS 1635, 1636; BL MSS Harley 943, 1278; and Bodl. MS Rawlinson MS D 121. See also M. Ogden, 'A Seventeenth Century Collection of Prints and Drawings', *Art Quarterly*, 2, 1948, pp. 42–73; Mary Beal, *Study of Richard Symonds: his Italian Notebooks and Their Relevance to 17th Century Painting Techniques*, New York, 1984; and Stoye, *English Travellers Abroad*, pp. 145–6, 150.

Fig. 8. Venice during the 1650s: 'Altra veduta della due Piazza di S^t. Marco visto dell. Orloge' (Israel Silvestre).

entirely different environments as travellers, but as collectors they were driven by a very similiar desire to collect, categorize, define, and understand the sheer wealth of the grand expanse of Western European culture.

With regard to two of the travel accounts included in this Hakluyt Society volume, each deriving from uniquely surviving manuscripts at the Bodleian Library, Oxford, it appears that Richard Rawlinson may have obtained Robert Montagu's account of his travels between 1649 and 1652 either directly from the estate of Charles Montagu (1661–1715), 1st Earl of Halifax (who had married Robert's widow), or from one of the later sales initiated by his nephew, George Montagu, Viscount Sunbury and later 2nd Earl of Halifax (see p. 78). Similarly, the account of Banaster Maynard's travels, compiled by his servant, Robert Moody, was acquired for 2s 6^d by Rawlinson from the sale in 1731 of the library of the noted antiquarian, Peter Le Neve (1661–1729) (see pp. 235–6). After Rawlinson's death both manuscripts were then deposited in 1756, according to his bequest, in the Bodleian Library where they have remained until today. But it is this very process of survival – entirely typical of numerous other travel manuscripts once in family ownership and now prerserved in great institutional collections – which causes major problems for historians of seventeenth-century English travel writing.

While we certainly owe today a great debt of gratitude to the likes of Peter Le Neve and Richard Rawlinson (as well as to the Bodleian Library during the mid-eighteenth century) for ensuring the preservation of these manuscripts after they had left the possession of their writers' families, neither Le Neve nor Rawlinson considered it his ostensible role to collect any other artefacts, beyond the purely literary and historical, relating to Robert Montagu and Banaster Maynard. Similarly, while many of the collections deposited in the Bodleian

Library over the generations include such items as coins and medals, these objects were almost always originally catalogued as self-contained, discrete collections rather than being overtly associated with the literary and personal papers of their original owners. While a sixteenth- or seventeenth-century collector might have considered his various accumulations of books, manuscripts, engravings, coins, medals, and other curiosities as forming a unified and, to his eyes, coherent representation of the growth of his personal interests as a collector and traveller, practices of collecting from the early eighteenth century onwards tended to separate out printed and manuscript materials from other more miscellaneous items. Even engravings, woodcuts, and other forms of illustrations, which might well have been originally kept with a traveller's journal of his experiences – those accompanying Robert Montagu's diary, of a performing elephant, the armless woman Magdalena Rudolfs Thuinbuj, and the crest of Ferdinando II (see Fig. 28, p. 133, Fig. 29, p. 139, and Fig. 30, p. 144), are typical of the kind of ephemeral images picked up by mid-seventeenth century travellers in France, Germany, and Italy – tend in major libraries now to be preserved within their own distinct classifications and collections (unless, as in the case of Montagu's account, they were actually stuck into the original manuscript).

Clearly, considerations of finance and space alone have usually prohibited institutional libraries from actively seeking out non-literary items relating to the authors of literary works held in their collections. To compound this problem, the usual practice during the last three centuries of sales rooms in dispersing large family collections (whether the 1731 sale of Peter Le Neve's possessions at the Bedford Coffee House in Covent Garden, see p. 235; or that held at Sotheby's in 1976 at which the British Library acquired their manuscript of William Hammond's travels, see p. 159) has been to divide up the individual lots into distinct classifications, such as 'books and manuscripts', 'works of art', 'miscellaneous collections' (i.e. coins, medals, seals and real or supposed antiquities), 'furnishings', and such like. In effect, then, over the generations the collecting practices of both private individuals and public institutions have ensured that the numerous miscellaneous items which would once have formed an integral collection of one traveller's experiences on the continent have been gradually dispersed into separate collections (often in different institutions or private hands) of books, manuscripts (even these two categories of items are frequently separated from one another), pictures, engravings, coins, antiquities, and other curiosities.[1] This last category of 'curiosities' – which, as the case below of John Bargrave illustrates – can be richly revealing of an individual traveller's intellectual and cultural proclivities. But, sadly, over the passing years such items can often be the most neglected or undervalued, often regarded by the children and grandchildren of the collectors merely as family bric-à-brac, and by later generations (who no longer know what the object once represented) as ephemeral ornaments and oddities.

For modern readers, John Evelyn (along with E. S. de Beer's annotations) still sets the standard in terms of his blending of first-hand observation with factual information gleaned from a variety of secondary sources. Consequently, throughout the textual annotations to this Hakluyt volume frequent reference has been made to Evelyn's own detailed descriptions of locations, buildings, and individuals also described by Robert Montagu, William Hammond, and Robert Moody. Evelyn's diary effectively redefined the genre of English

---

[1] Pertinent to this volume's concerns, is the major and visibly successful attempt from the 1970s onwards to reunite at the British Library many of John Evelyn's printed books with his manuscript collections. See Michael Hunter, 'The British Library and the Library of John Evelyn. With a Checklist of Evelyn Books in the British Library's Holdings', *The Book Collector*, 44, 1995, pp. 218–38.

continental travel writing from the mid-seventeenth century onwards. But during his travels, he was far more than merely a meticulous recorder of what he was seeing, alongside what he learned about these locations either at the time or later from secondary sources. He was, in the best sense of the phrase, a 'cultural tourist', keen to define and understand the essential components of the artistic and cultural life of the countries in which he was travelling. While abroad Evelyn began his scientific and technical studies, and he remained a keen student of anatomy, physiology, medicine, and chemistry (very much the combination of subjects of particular interest to William Hammond during his own travels between 1655 and 1658). Evelyn spent a year at Padua (1645–6) studying anatomy; at Paris (1646/7) he heard lectures on chemistry by Annibal Barlet and Nicasius Le Fèvre; and he also attended various hospitals and several human dissections. His experiences abroad ultimately played a large part in his role as a founder member of the Royal Society.

Of all his scientific interests, Evelyn was most committed to horticulture and forestry. He was expert in every aspect of gardening, from history and theory to the design and maintenance of his own garden at Sayes Court, Deptford, which had been the family home of his wife, Mary Browne, the daughter of Sir Richard Browne (1605–83), English Ambassador at Paris from 1641 until 1660. Evelyn became a close friend of Samuel Pepys at the Navy Office and, for example, wrote his *Sylva* (1664) to encourage the planting of trees suitable for shipbuilding. Among his manuscripts (now at the British Library) is his 'Hortus Hyemalis', an album of dried herbs and flowers collected for Evelyn in 1645 from the Botanic Gardens at Padua. The acquisition of this volume is described in Evelyn's diary for 30/31 July 1645:

> Next morning I went to see the Garden of Simples, rarely furnishd with plants, and gave order to the Gardner to make me a Collection of them for an *hortus hyemalis*, by permission of the Cavalier Dr. Vestlingius their Præfect, & Botanic Professor, as well as *Anatomie*.[1]

From the point of view of the development of the cultural 'Grand Tour', it is interesting to note that Evelyn met up the next morning with the most prolific of all English collectors, Thomas Howard, Earl of Arundel, to examine the garden of the Palace of Mantoa at Padua (situated near the Eremitani). They spent the rest of the day together, examining various other sites of artistic interest. A volume of Evelyn's chemistry lectures notes (MS 32), made at Paris in 1646 has also survived; and it is clear that he made extensive book acquisitions at Paris between 1649 and 1651.[2]

Despite the wide range of Evelyn's intellectual interests while on the continent, as well as the large bulk of his surviving papers now at the British Library, within these collections there is still a noticeable absence of the more miscellaneous objects and trinkets of the kind usually brought home from the continent by English travellers. But it is impossible to imagine that Evelyn, like so many of his contemporaries, did not pick up such items on his travels whenever the opportunity arose. Indeed, he often makes reference in his diary to his active interest in 'curiosities', sketches, maps, engravings, and his purchase of various minor mementoes of his travels. On 24 August 1641, for example, Evelyn was at Amsterdam and noted:

---

[1] Evelyn, *Diary* (1645), II, p. 466. Johann Vesling (1598–1649), was professor of anatomy at Padua (1631–49), professor of surgery (1631–8), and prefect of the botanic garden (1638–49). In 1665 Samuel Pepys recorded examining with Evelyn this volume of samples from the Botanic Gardens at Padua. See also *The Book Collector*, 1995, pp. 165–6.

[2] Evelyn, *Diary* (1645), II, pp. 166, 218–19.

Upon St. Bartholomews-day I went to Hundius's shop to buy some Mapps, greately pleasd with the designes of that indefatigable Person: Mr Bleaw, the setter-forth of the Atlas's & other Workes of that kind is worthy seeing: At another shop I furnish'd my selfe with some shells, & Indian Curiosities'.[1]

Similarly, at Paris in early February 1644, Evelyn described an especially interesting shop of the north bank of the Seine:

... here is a shop cal'd Noahs-Arke, where are to be had for mony all the Curiosities naturall or artificall imaginable, Indian or Europan, for luxury or Use, as Cabinets, Shells, Ivorys, Purselan, Dried fishes, rare Insects, Birds, Pictures, & a thousand exotic extravagances'.

By February 1645 he had moved from France to Italy and was exploring the Phlegraean Fields on his way from Mount Vesuvius to Naples. Near Pozzuoli, he enjoyed a good dinner and then 'bought divers Medailes & other curiosities, Antiquities &c of the Country people, who daily find such things amongst the very old ruines of those places'. It is easy to imagine the locals' delight in the gullibility of passing travellers, as is evidenced by the number of fakes included in the collections of John Bargrave (see pp. 43–5). Later in the same month, Evelyn had arrived at Rome and on the 20th he recorded in his diary: 'I went (as was my usual Costome) & spent an Afternoone in *Piazza Navona*, as well to see what Antiquities I could purchase among the people, who hold Mercat there for Medaills, Pictures, & such Curiosities'.[2]

But many of these items have long since been separated from Evelyn's more prized (at least from the point of view of modern collectors and scholars) manuscripts and books. Fortunately, however, one such collection from the period, combining a rich mixture of manuscript papers with curiosities and minor antiquities collected while abroad, has survived virtually intact. It is this collection, assembled by John Bargrave and now preserved at Canterbury Cathedral Archives, which represents – perhaps more than any other assembly of items from the period – how an ordinary Englishman abroad during the 1640s and 1650s drew together a collection of written reminiscences and, on a very limited financial budget, an accompanying selection of miscellaneous 'antiquities' and 'curiosities' as a means of remembering and commemorating his time away from his home country.

John Bargrave (c. 1610–80), was the son of John Bargrave (d. 1625) of Patrixbourne and the nephew of Isaac Bargrave (1586–1643), Dean of Canterbury Cathedral, who had earlier served as chaplain to the English Ambassador at Venice, Sir Thomas Wotton, between 1616 and 1618, and then as a personal chaplain to Prince Charles. After studying at the King's School, Canterbury, the younger John had matriculated at Cambridge from St Peter's College (Peterhouse) on 8 July 1629 and was awarded BA (1633) and MA (1636) before being elected a fellow of his college (1637). He was ejected from his fellowship in 1643 and by May 1645 had commenced his travels on the continent. Unlike numerous other members of the English gentry who withdrew – either discreetly or in more perilous flight – from England to Western Europe during the 1640s and 1650s, John Bargrave left unusually extensive written records of his experiences abroad. In addition to travels in France, and later in the Low Countries, Poland, and Germany, John Bargrave also made at least four separate perambulations through Italy: in 1646–1647 as tutor to two young Kentish men, Alexander Chapman and John Richards (or Rycaut), who were also accompanied by

---

[1] Ibid, (1641), II, p. 49. The map shop was then owned by Hendrick Hundius the second (c. 1597–1644) and Evelyn's purchases were of maps by the most important cartographer of his generation, Joan Blaeu (1596–1673).
[2] Evelyn, *Diary* (1644–5), II, pp. 100, 343, 368.

Bargrave's young nephew, John Raymond; in 1650 as tutor to Philip Stanhope (later 2nd Earl of Chesterfield) and William Swan; in 1655 with William Juxon, the nephew of William Juxon, then Bishop of London and (from 1660) Archbishop of Canterbury; and again in 1659–1660 with unknown companions for a final visit to Rome.[1]

During this entire period, John Bargrave was an avid collector of small antiquities and other travel mementoes. He compiled in 1676 an extensive catalogue of his cabinet of curiosities (Lit MS E 16), laced through with various anecdotes of his travels both in Italy and in other locations such as Leiden, Utrecht, Paris, Nuremberg, Augsburg, Vienna, Prague, and Innsbruck.[2] On his last visit to Italy, John also purchased at Rome 'The Pope, and Colledge, or Conclave of Cardinalls' (Lit MS E39a-c), an extensive set of prints of Pope Alexander VII and his cardinals. He then heavily annotated these portraits with his own comments on both the individuals represented and papal history, as well as with numerous incidental and fragmentary memoirs of his own travels abroad – thus rendering them as another kind of sporadic and disordered travel diary.[3] In addition to these surviving manuscript collections, Anthony à Wood first suggested (and recent scholarship has tended to agree) that John Bargrave also played a major (and perhaps predominant) role in the compilation of the most famous English guidebook to Italy of the Civil War period, *An Itinerary Contayning a Voyage Made Through Italy, in the Yeare 1646, and 1647* (1648) (see Fig. 9, p. 44). Although this slim volume bore on its title-page the initials of John Raymond (who was, as already noted, Bargrave's nephew and one of his young charges during his 1646/7 residence in Italy), it seems likely that Raymond's manuscript was compiled with full access to John Bargrave's own notes. Furthermore, John Bargrave's own manuscript diary of his travels through France from May 1645 until February 1646 with John Raymond and Alexander Chapman, crammed with his incidental observations, jottings, sketches and reminiscences, has also recently surfaced in Canterbury Cathedral Archives (U11/8).

John Bargrave was an habitual purchaser of antiquities and curiosities on his various travels and the bulk of his collections are still preserved at Canterbury in their purpose-built case and drawers. David Sturdy and Martin Henig have compiled an informative handlist of Bargrave's collections of souvenirs and specimens and they define its range and quality as follows:

> This small private museum, unique in its completeness, has remained almost intact since his death in 1680 and his widow's handing over of it to the Cathedral Library in 1685. The whole collection is essentially Italian with a fairly small number of objects from other countries.
>
> Dr Bargrave's standards as a collector were rather mixed. He was not well off and he was steadily on the move, so that small and readily portable items had to be preferred, with the notable exception of the large and very heavy marble table. Bargrave was sometimes indifferent to perfection and authenticity alike; his antique figurines are all either damaged or false. But they serve as intriguing examples of the interests of the time, with almost no exemplars of the types most in vogue later, the classic themes of the 18th century.[4]

[1] See my 'The Exile of Two Kentish Royalists During the English Civil War', *Archaeologia Cantiana*, 120, 2000, pp. 77–105; and 'John Bargrave and the Jesuits', *Catholic Historical Review*, 88, 2002, pp. 655–76.

[2] See Stephen Bann, *Under the Sign. John Bargrave as Collector, Traveler, and Witness*, Ann Arbor, 1994, for an analysis of Bargrave's habits and purposes as a collector.

[3] *Pope Alexander the Seventh and the College of Cardinals*, ed. James Craigie Robertson, Camden Society, 92, 1867.

[4] *The Gentle Traveller. John Bargrave, Canon of Canterbury, and his Collection*, Abingdon, 1985, p. [1]. See also Stoye, *English Travellers Abroad*, pp. 161–3, for Bargrave's collections.

Fig. 9. Title-page of John Raymond [with the collaboration of John Bargrave], *Il Mercurio Italico* [usually known as] *An Itinerary Communicating a Voyage Made Through Italy in the Yeare 1646, and 1647* (1648).

Bargrave's own catalogue of the collection details such items as a small collection of Roman bronze figures, including 'An infant Romulus … digd out of Quirinus his temple, on the Quirinal hill, when those ruins were removed to make way for the very fine, pretty, rich church of S*ta* Maria della Vittoria' (B1); 'two old Roman sacrificing priests' (B5i); and a 'maymed Mercury with one arm and one legg; ancient, dugg out of his temple' (B7).[1] Other statuettes, such as a drunken and urinating Hercules Mingens, 'dugg our of his temple near the Tyber, at the foot of the Aventine Hill at Rome' (B3); and 'A Roman aegle, in brass' (B18) were almost certainly modern forgeries, specifically cast for the seventeenth-century tourist market. Bargrave was clearly well aware of such risks as a collector and he described an apparently very well preserved bronze stylus as: 'Stylus Romanus. The antiquarian that sold it me avowed it to be truly ancient; but thousands may daily be made' (B36). He also purchased some items which were overtly sold as modern copies, such as a bronze phallic pendant which he described as: 'Two Priapisms, in brass, being votes or offerings to that absurd heathen deity – modern, from ancient' (B17ii). Other forgeries, however, were probably sold to him as genuine antiquities, such as a small bronze dolphin, which he proudly catalogued as: 'An ancient brass Dolphin, dedicated to Venus, and dug out of her temple. Nam Venus orta mari' (B8); and a coral relief, described as: 'The River of Tyber, carved on a piece of coral, ancient' (B16).

Along with these antiquities (both real and modern), Bargrave delighted in acquiring, probably at no great cost, an impressive variety of both intact and fragmentary Roman gemstones, including attractive settings made from cornelian, chalcedony, bloodstone, garnet, sard, and coloured glass. An especially prized oval garnet stone was, according to Bargrave's own records, given to him by one of his young charges, Philip Lord Stanhope, and he was so touched by this gesture that in 1650 he had it set into a sturdy gold ring. Other items were entirely typical of the casual acquisitions of minor mementoes made by successive generations of tourists. Within this category may be placed his small collection of geological and antiquarian stone samples. Some loose cinders in a small oval wooden box with a female figure painted on the lid were labelled: 'Ashes and materialls / of the burning Moun / taine of Vesuvius, near Naples / John Bargrave …' (B26). Another oval box labelled, 'Confetti di Tivoli', contained samples of 'The sand of Teverone that Entereth in / to the Tiber not farr fro*m* Rome / John Bargrave … They seem to be so like sugar plums that they will deceive any man' (B30). Yet another oval wooden box with a female figure painted on the lid (Bargrave probably acquired these boxes as a job-lot specifically for items in his collection), contained a selection of stones wrapped in their original labels. Their titles are worth quoting in full since they speak so eloquently of the kind of scholarly tourist that Bargrave clearly was, carefully picking his way around Italian antiquities with a keen eye for pocketable and easily portable momentoes:

[1] 'Of Constantines Arch / Triumphal at Rome / J Bargrave 1647'

[2] 'A peece of the ruines of Septimus / Severus his Arch Triumphall / at Rome / Bargrave / 1647'

[3] 'A peece of Titus Vespas. / Arch Triumphall at Rome / for taking Jerusale*m*. / Bargrave 1647'

[4] 'This stone / brough fro*m* the Amphitheatre or Colosseum at Rome / 1647 / Bargrave'

[5] 'From the / Piscina mirabili / neere Naples'

[6] 'From the Cuman / Sybells Grotto neere / Puteoli or Puzzulo / neere Naples' [and another label] 'Sybilla / Cumana'

---

[1] The references cited in brackets are from Bargrave's own manuscript catalogue (1676), printed in *Pope Alexander*, ed. Robertson, pp. 113–40.

[7] 'I brought this from the grotta / del cane where anything /that is put in dyeth, and being / throughen in to a lake hard by, it / reviveth. which I saw by a dog, it is in the Kingdom of Naples' [and another label] 'grotta / del / cane'

[8] 'Of the Mosaik worke of / St. Marks Church in / Venice 1647 / Bargrave' [and another label] 'Venice' [comprising 14 mosaic cubes][1]

It is noticeable how frequently John Bargrave attaches his own name to the labelled items in his collection, as though the items were not so much assembled for their own intrinsic interest alone but also for their accumulative and lasting testament to his experiences while abroad. At the very centre and heart of these collections stands the figure of John Bargrave himself, as the traveller, antiquarian, connoisseur, and diarist.

Some items tended towards the macabre, most notably: 'the finger of a Frenchman, which I brought from Tholouse' (B44), when he was given a guided tour of a Franciscan vault. (Although he accepted the finger, Bargrave graciously declined his host's offer of the well-preserved body of a baby.) He also carefully packaged away some small insect remains, bearing the label: 'That within a silke worme / with which she maketh silke' (no catalogue number, see pp. 201, 206 for William Hammond's interest in silkworms); and 'A sea-horse tooth, specific against poison' (probably narwhal, see p. 103, n. 3 below) (B37). Other items were simple but attractive tourist trinkets, such as 'a pretty kind of nun's work purse, made of greenish silk, and carved work mother of pearl shell, presented me likewise by a nun' (B40); 'a pretty little padlock and key of guilt mettle' (B39i) given to him by another nun; and various optical lenses and gadgets (B45–B51), most of which, sadly, have now been lost.

Like many of his contemporary travellers, Bargrave also relished purchasing both individual artistic images, maps, and engravings. Two attractive portraits of him still survive which were painted while he was on the continent. The first is an anonymous oval, half-length portrait in oil on copper of Bargrave alone, painted at Rome in 1650 when he was tutor to Philip Lord Stanhope. The second and earlier three-quarter length portrait is by a named Italian artist, Mattio Bolognini. Understandably, maps were also of considerable importance to Bargrave while abroad and, although they are now lost, his catalogue refers expansively to 'All my Large and lesser Mapps of Italy, Ould Roome and New, in sheets at large very fayre'. (Perhaps the one at the centre of the Bolognini portrait was one of Bargrave's 'lesser' maps.)

His collections of engravings included J. de Rossi's *Effigies nomina et cognomina S.D.N. Alexandri Papae VII* (Rome, 1658), comprising portraits of the pope and sixty-six cardinals (already referred to as 'The Pope, and Colledge, or Conclave of Cardinalls', Lit MS E39a-c); and another set of portraits of various cardinals from the 13th to the early 17th century, published in about 1621 and purchased by Bargrave at Rome in 1660.[2] When he drafted his will in 1670, Bargrave bequeathed to the cathedral library: 'all the Cutts (in my trunks) Of all the Ancient Ruines, the Pallaces, Statues, Fountaines, the Cardinalls, Souldiers, Phylosophers, &c' (now L-8-16). This large volume contained 216 engravings, comprising two unique items and ten discreet sets purchased by Bargrave during his travels on the continent.

The survival together since the mid-seventeenth century of such a large collection of

[1] I have followed the transcription of these labels as given in *The Gentle Traveller*, p. [8].

[2] This latter collection, containing an index and annotations in Bargrave's hand, seems to have become separated from his other papers at some point but was later purchased and added to his bequest to Canterbury Cathedral as Lit. MS.E.39: see *The Gentle Traveller*, p. [11].

European engravings is very rare, but Bargrave's collection may be regarded as not untypical of the kinds of images purchased by travellers at this period as they made their way around Western Europe. When viewed as a whole, the Bargrave archive at Canterbury Cathedral – with its manuscript accounts, catalogues, antiquities, semi-precious stones, paintings, maps, and engravings – well illustrates how, for an itinerant Englishmen during the Civil War period, the compilation of a travel diary was just one aspect of the recording of his experiences abroad. As we go on to consider in this volume, the written records of the travels of Robert Montagu, William Hammond, and Banaster Maynard, we should always bear in mind that far more evidence about their time abroad has probably been lost over the generations than can be deduced from their written records alone. In this sense, a manuscript travel diary, even if complete and written in the traveller's own hand, can only ever be regarded as providing a partial, even fragmentary, insight into how that individual would have planned to present his travels to family and friends on his return to England. Without the accompanying objects collected while abroad, a travel diary or series of letters home can only partly communicate the educational and cultural significance of a period spent in travel through France, Italy, the Low Countries and the Holy Roman Empire between the 1640s and 1660s.[1]

6. The Engravings of Israel Silvestre and Israel Henriet

> He shew'd us a world of landscips & prospects very rarely painted in miniature, some with the Pen & Crayon, with divers antiquities & Relievos of Rome, above all that of the inside of the *Amphitheater* of Titus incomparable drawne by Monsieur *Linclere* himselfe, two boys, & 3 *Sceletons* moulded by *Fiamingo*, a Booke of Statues with the *pen* made for *Hen* the 4th rarely executed, & by which one may discover many errours in that of *Perriere*, who has added divers conceits of his owne that are not in the Originalls.
>
> (John Evelyn at Paris, 1650)[2]

The visual images of notable buildings, antiquities, and individuals brought home by English travellers have usually long since been separated from any written records of their experiences made by their collectors. But it seems likely that travellers of the relative wealth of Robert Montagu and Banaster Maynard (and probably even William Hammond from a gentry background) would have frequently availed themselves, like Evelyn and Bargrave, of the usual opportunities to pick up attractive but reasonably priced engravings of the localities through which they were passing. Unfortunately, any engravings, small antiquities, and other curiosities purchased by Montagu, Hammond, and Maynard have long since disappeared (apart from the few illustrations fortuitously stuck into Montagu's diary – see p. 40).

---

[1] William Hammond, the second traveller in this volume, concluded a letter to his mother, dated 6 September 1658, with the promise: 'What I can hoard up of my scanty allowance, I'le lay out upon some Raritys worthy presenting you, & bring them home with me next Spring': see p. 220.

[2] Evelyn, *Diary* (1650), III, pp. 10–11. Some of the etchings by Louis Lincler (d. c. 1651) of Rome were used by Israel Silvestre as the basis for his own engravings. Evelyn's '*Fiamingo*' is probably François Duquesnoy. His '*Perriere*' is François Perrier (1590–1650), a copy of whose album of engravings, *Icones et segmenta illustrium e marmore tabularum quae Romae adhuc extant* (1645), was presented by Evelyn to the Bodleian Library, Oxford.

Liure de diuerfes Perfpectiues, et Paifages faits fur le naturel, mis en lumiere par Ifrael.
A Paris Chez Ifrael Henriet, rue de l'arbre fec, au logis de Monfieur le Mercier Orfeure de la Royne, proche la croix du Tiroir. Auec priuilege du Rey. 1650.

Fig. 10. Frontispiece to a collection of engravings published by Israel Henriet, *Livre de diverses Perspectives, et Paisages faits sur le naturel, mis en lumiere par Israel* (1650).

In order to exemplify the kinds of engravings readily available to the mid-seventeenth century English traveller on the continent (and other copies were also shipped over for sale by London booksellers), this Hakluyt volume includes a wide selection of illustrations from the studios of two of the most notable engravers at the court of King Louis XIV, Israel Silvestre and Israel Henriet. Because of the ephemeral nature of such images, very few integral collections of their work have survived together.[1] Fortuitously, one of the largest collections of their prints – perhaps the most comprehensive still surviving in this country – has only recently come to light in the Brotherton Collection, University of Leeds, and a wide selection has been included in this edition.[2]

Originally of Scottish origin, the Silvestre family had resided in Lorraine since the

[1] Predictably, the largest collections of Silvestre's and Henriet's engravings are to be found in the Bibliothèque nationale de France at Paris and the Musée Carnavalet, although smaller and usually disparate collections are held by numerous other museums and libraries. See Charles Le Blanc, *Manuel de l'amateur d'estampes 1550–1820*, 4 vols, Paris, 1854–89; and L. E. Faucheux, *Catalogue raisonné de toutes les estampes qui forment l'oeuvre d'Israel Silvestre, précedé d'une notice sur sa vie*, 1857 (rpt. Paris, 1969). I am grateful to Antony Griffiths, Keeper of Prints at the British Museum, for his advice on these engravings.

[2] These engravings, along with many others from the 17th to the late 19th centuries, have been inserted into an 'extra illustrated' edition of *The Letters of Madame de Sévigné* (1862–1876), now in 25 lavishly bound volumes (vol. 24 in 2; vol. 25 in 3), and accompanied by two volumes of 'Lexique', one volume of 'Appendice', and one volume entitled 'Album'. These volumes were acquired by Lord Brotherton before his bequest to the university library at Leeds and no conclusive records are now known about where he obtained them. However, other 'extra illustrated' volumes in Lord Brotherton's collections came from the estate of Alexander Meyrick Broadley (1847–1916), a barrister and journalist, whose library was sold by auction in 1916. It seems very likely the *The Letters of Madame de Sévigné* volumes were also acquired by Lord Brotherton at this sale. I am grateful to Christopher D. W. Sheppard, Head of Special Collections, Brotherton Library, for this information.

Fig. 11. Frontispiece to a collection of engravings published by Israel Silvestre, *Les Lieux les Plus Remarquables de Paris et des Environs Faicts Par Israel Silvestre* (before 1655).

beginning of the sixteenth century. Israel, the son of Gilles Silvestre and his wife Elisabeth Henriet, was born at Nancy on 13 or 15 August 1621. His early training as an artist was from his father who specialized in stained and painted glass windows. During the 1630s his home region was devastated by a series of outbreaks of the plague which claimed his father. Fortunately, he was taken into the care of his godfather and uncle, Israel Henriet (d. 1661), a skilled engraver and former pupil of the renowned Jacques Callot (c. 1592–1635), who had worked for a long period (c. 1609–21) in Italy under the patronage of the Medici family, producing exquisite engravings of their *feste*, or quasi-dramatic pageants.[1] Silvestre was particularly fortunate in this family connection because Henriet was appointed as drawing master to Louis XIII and provided his nephew with ready access to the royal court. Their productive partnership, with Henriet (who also owned the editorial rights to Callot's engravings) acting as the editor and business manager of Silvestre's artistic output, lasted for the rest of Henriet's life.

Silvestre lived with his uncle in his house at Paris from the age of ten until his departure for a tour of Italy from 1639/40 until 1642. (He returned to Italy in 1643/4 and again in 1653). During the early 1640s he also met at his uncle's studio another noted Florentine artist and engraver, Stefano della Bella, who lived in France from 1639 and with whom Silvestre worked closely in collaboration for a number of years.[2] But from the late 1640s, Silvestre was developing his own distinctive artistic style, characterized by a meticulous level of detailed observation and a striking ability to convey the architectural grandeur and aesthetics of power of the French monarchy. Working throughout the periods of the Regency and La Fronde, Silvestre's engravings, which were packaged and sold as sets under

[1] Callot was based in Lorraine from 1621 until his death. He also illustrated religious books and produced a series of engravings depicting the sieges of La Rochelle and the Ile de Ré. He is now best known for his two remarkable series of etchings on the horrors of the Thirty Years' War, the 'small' (1632) and the 'large' (1633), both entitled the 'Miseries of War'.

[2] See F. Viatte, *Dessins de Stefano della Bella*, Paris, 1974.

Fig. 12. Israel Silvestre's 'Profil de la ville de Paris' (c. 1650), showing (from left to right) the church of Saint-Eustache, the dome of the Assumption, the Tuileries Palace, the Tour de Bois, and the Tour Saint-Jacques, as well as the churches of Saint-Gervais, Notre-Dame, Saint-Germain-des-Prés, the dome of the Sorbonne, Saint-Etienne-du-Mont, and the Tour de Clovis.

Fig. 13. Israel Silvestre's 'Profil de la Ville de S. Denis' (c. 1650).

royal patronage, were essentially artistic and political propaganda for the triumphant potency of the French monarchy. For English travellers in France during the 1650s – and these albums were especially popular with foreign tourists – Silvestre's collections of views offered a poignant and sombre reminder of how contrasting the political landscapes of England and France had become.

When Silvestre finally settled at Paris in 1659, Henriet named him as his sole heir; and he inherited his studio when his uncle died on 24 April 1661. During the 1660s the trade in illustrations grew to an extraordinary level, and Silvestre secured a royal licence to edit the engravings of Callot, as well as those of his uncle Henriet. His own output was increasingly prolific at this period and his prosperity grew rapidly. Following his uncle's inheritance and the success of his own business, Silvestre married the eighteen year old daughter of a local merchant, Henriette Selincourt (d. 1680).[1] On 20 March 1663 Silvestre was formally appointed as the official engraver to the king, a post which confirmed his artistic status as the purveyor (both to the inhabitants of France and to the rest of Western Europe) of an approved centralized vision of the French monarchy and society.[2]

One of Silvestre's most famous views, a panorama of the city of Paris (see Fig. 12, p. 50) powerfully exemplifies the strongly nationalistic intention behind his commemoration of the royal splendours of Paris and other notable French locations. His engravings effectively provided young English travellers with a crash course in the sheer cultural richness and political potency of French monarchic society. Silvestre deftly places a crouching rustic figure in the bottom left-hand corner of the engraving, peeping wonderously (like perhaps many of the English travellers first arriving at the outskirts of the French capital) at the sheer magnificence of the Paris skyline. The words accompanying this engraving then forcefully direct the foreign traveller towards an appropriate level of respect and wonder at the grandeur of the architectural landscapes of the French monarchy: 'Est-ce Rome que je voy'. An impressionable English traveller, someone like Robert Montagu or William Hammond perhaps, might then move on to the imposing royal mausoleum of the abbey-church of St-Denis, a sombre and dynastically powerful reminder of the absolute and God-given authority of the French monarchy (see Fig. 13, p. 51). Silvestre's readily available engravings (sold as a kind of up-market seventeenth-century postcard-set) rapidly sensitized many young English travellers, whose previous geographical horizons rarely stretched east of Dieppe and Boulogne, to the political and cultural importance of Western Europe.

Drawing upon knowledge from his own travels during the 1640s, Silvestre also published various collections of views of both the ancient and modern landscapes of Italy. These sets of engravings could be purchased alongside the French ones and must have often tempted young travellers at Paris to dream of heading off across Western Europe to examine the wonders of Rome and Venice for themselves. Selected examples of these Italian landscapes have also been included in this edition (see Figs 7–8, 40–42, 44–6).

---

[1] Of their six children, four followed their father's trade: Charles-François, Louis l'Aîné, Alexandre, and Louis le Jeune.

[2] See, for example, Silvestre's collection known as the *Cabinet du Roi*, a series of engravings of fortified towns and plans and views of palaces, published in 1666. Further important commissions and honours followed during the 1660s and 1670s, leading to Silvestre's nomination for the Academy of Painting and Sculpture in 1670 and his appointment as drawing-master to the Grand Dauphin in 1673. In addition to his own work and that of his uncle Henriet, he also owned the rights to most of the engravings of Jacques Callot and Stefano della Bella; and both his reputation and profits from his sales remained high until his death on 11 October 1691.

This fascination among mid-seventeenth century travellers with the blending of antiquity with modern neo-classicism takes us back to the cultural eclecticism of John Evelyn. Although Evelyn was travelling on the continent throughout most of the 1640s and 1650s, it is important to remember, as already noted, that much of his huge diary was compiled many years later from a rich variety of primary materials.[1] This heavy dependence upon other authoritative sources provides an important clue to Evelyn's intentions in compiling such detailed records of his continental travels during the early years of the English Civil War. As is evident from Figures 14–15, illustrating details from 'the Bathes of Diocletian' and 'Trajans Column', in conjunction with recording his own European travels, Evelyn was also very much concerned with the importation of classical and continental architectural traditions into England. In these meticulously detailed architectural drawings from Roland Fréart's renowned volume (which Evelyn edited for an English readership, as its title-page indicates, specifically 'for the Benefit of Builders'), Evelyn hinted at his own vision of a post-Restoration England which was to be reconstructed in no small measure by those who had travelled widely on the continent, especially in Italy, during the English Civil War.[2] Evelyn, it seems, envisioned in the architectural landscapes of ancient Rome a template and inspiration for England's own nascent concepts of global imperialism and Empire which had been developing since the mid-Elizabethan period. Post-Restoration England was, in the eyes of returning royalist emigrés, in the process of re-assembling itself; and Evelyn's view of how to do this was clear. England should remake itself, under the guidance of that obvious Europhile Charles II, in the image and likeness of the ancient Roman empire and its modern continental adaptations. When viewed retrospectively, this concept may now seem little more than a hopelessly idealized fantasy for the new Caroline reign of the early 1660s. But for those Englishmen who had actually experienced the grandeurs of France and Italy at first hand during the 1640s and 1650s – including Robert Montagu, William Hammond, and Banaster Maynard – the concept of the restoration of Charles II meant not just the re-attainment of his father's monarchic authority but perhaps also a genuine hope for the role of a resurgent and politically confident England on the global stage.

[1] See Theodore Hofman, Joan Winterkorn, Francis Harris and Hilton Kelliher, 'John Evelyn's Archive at the British Library', in *John Evelyn in the British Library*, London, 1995, pp. 11–73, 15–16.

[2] Roland Fréart de Chambray, *A Parallel of the Antient Architecture with the Modern … Made English for the Benefit of Builders … by John Evelyn*, London, 1664, pp. 71, 92.

Of the Bathes of Diocletian

f: 71.

Fig. 14. Detail from 'Of the Bathes of Diocletian'. From Roland Fréart, *A Parallel of the Antient Architecture with the Modern … Made English for the Benefit of Builders. In Which is Added an Account of Architects and Architecture … With Leon Baptista Alberti's Treatise of Statues*, translated by John Evelyn (1664), p. 71.

Fig. 15. Detail from 'Trajans Column'. From Fréart, *A Parallel*, p. 92.

SECTION TWO

THE TRAVELS OF ROBERT MONTAGU,
LORD MANDEVILLE
(May 1649–April 1654)

1. The Family and Early Life of Robert Montagu

The author of this travel diary, Robert Montagu (1634–83), styled Viscount Mandeville (from 1642–71) and later 3rd Earl of Manchester (from 1671), was born in the parish of St Margaret's, Westminster, and baptized on 25 April 1634. He was the eldest surviving son of Edward Montagu, 2nd Earl of Manchester, by his second wife, Anne, daughter of Robert Rich, 2nd Earl of Warwick, Lord Admiral of the Long Parliament.[1] Robert Montagu also had two sisters, Frances, who married Henry, son of Robert Sanderson (or Saunderson), Bishop of Lincoln; and Anne, who married her cousin Robert Rich, 2nd Earl of Holland and 5th Earl of Warwick.[2] Robert's mother, Lady Anne, died in February 1642 and was buried at the family seat, Kimbolton Castle in Huntingdonshire. Edward Montagu took as his third wife, Essex, the widow of Sir Thomas Bevil (d. 1640) and a daughter of Sir Thomas Cheke by his wife Essex Rich, daughter of Robert, 1st Earl of Warwick. This marriage brought our Robert six additional step-brothers and two step-sisters.[3] Two detailed inventories of the major rooms, chambers and Long Gallery at Kimbolton Castle, compiled in 1642 and 1645, when Robert Montagu was eight and eleven years old, provide a vivid impression of his luxurious childhood environment.[4]

Richard Ollard has noted: 'Few families have managed to engross more peerages than the Montagus or Mountagus as they generally styled themselves in the seventeenth century'.[5] The origins of this pre-eminence may be traced back to Robert Montagu's great-great-grandfather, Sir Edward Montagu (d. 1557) of Boughton, Northamptonshire, who had made considerable gains through the dissolution of the monasteries and served as Chief Justice of the King's Bench from 1539. Under duress from John Dudley, Duke of Northumberland (see pp. 9–13), he had been largely responsible for the redrafting of King Edward VI's will in favour of Lady Jane Grey and was briefly incarcerated in the Tower after Queen Mary's accession. He was, however, able to secure his freedom in return for heavy

---

[1] The 2nd Earl of Manchester had married in February 1623 his first wife Susanna Hill of Honily, Warwickshire, who died in January 1625 without issue. He married Anne Rich on 1 July 1626 at Newington Church, London.

[2] See William Drogo Montagu, 7th Duke of Manchester, *Court and Society from Elizabeth to Anne, edited from the papers at Kimbolton*, 2 vols, London, 1864, I, pp. 377–8, for a letter to 'Frank' (Frances) Montagu, from her grandfather the Earl of Warwick.

[3] These step-brothers included Edward, Henry, Charles, and Thomas Montagu (all of whom attended Corpus Christi College, Cambridge) and a step-sister named Essex (b. 1644).

[4] Manchester, *Court and Society*, II, pp. 367–74.

[5] *Cromwell's Earl. A Life of Edward Mountagu 1st Earl of Sandwich*, London, 1994, p. 14.

fines and the loss of some of his estates, spending the rest of his life in retirement at his manor house at Boughton, Northamptonshire.

Sir Edward married as his third wife, Ellen Roper, the daughter of King Henry VIII's Attorney-General. Their eldest son, Edward Montagu (1532–1602), was the father of Edward Montagu (1562–1644), 1st Baron Montagu of Boughton (see p. 74); Sir Henry Montagu (c. 1563–1642), 1st Earl of Manchester (grandfather of our author Robert Montagu); James Montagu (c. 1568–1618), Bishop of Winchester; and Sidney Montagu (father of Edward Montagu, 1st Earl of Sandwich, see p. 76). Inevitably, this plethora of titles sometimes makes it challenging to differentiate the various members of the Montagu family during the seventeenth-century. This introduction, however, will seek to place the life of our diarist Robert Montagu within the broader context of his family's personal and political affiliations from the reign of Elizabeth I until the restoration of King Charles II. In particular, the sheer diversity of the Montagu's public careers and personal involvments during the Civil War, as supporters of both the king and parliament, make them a fascinating example of how a prominent English family negotiated not only the political challenges of the 1640s and 1650s but also those of the Restoration itself.

2. The Montagus, Earls of Manchester

Henry Montagu (c. 1563–1642), 1st Earl of Manchester, was the younger brother of Edward, 1st Baron Montagu of Boughton. After studies at Christ's College, Cambridge (matriculated, 1583) and the Middle Temple (reader, 1606), he began a successful career as a lawyer. He was appointed Recorder of London and in 1620 became, in succession to the disgraced Earl of Suffolk, Lord High Treasurer of England. At this period he purchased Kimbolton Castle (formerly owned by the Mandevilles and Wingfields and also renowned as the place where Queen Catherine of Aragon had died in January 1536) and was created Baron Montagu of Kimbolton and Viscount Mandeville (19 December 1620).[1] Charles I created him 1st Earl of Manchester on 5 February 1626 and he remained one of the king's most trusted and loyal advisers. During Charles I's absence in Scotland in August 1641, for example, he was appointed as one of the guardians of the realm and as a commissioner for granting royal assent to bills.[2]

His eldest son, Edward, the father of our diarist Robert, had more complex dealings with both the king and parliament. Edward Montagu (1602–71), 2nd Earl of Manchester (styled Viscount Mandeville from 1602–42), was educated at Sidney Sussex College, Cambridge (matriculated, 1618), and sat as MP for Huntingdon during the last year's of James I's reign (1623–6). In 1623 he accompanied Prince Charles and the Duke of Buckingham to Spain during their marriage negotiations. As an intimate friend and adviser of the heir to the throne, Edward Montagu was created a Knight of the Bath at the coronation on 1 February 1626 and on 22 May of the same year he was raised to the title of Baron Montagu of Kimbolton. However, by early 1640 Edward Montagu was increasingly at odds with Charles I's autocratic exercising of his monarchic authority. During the Short Parliament (April 1640) he voted (along with his uncle Edward Montagu, 1st Baron Montagu of Boughton, see p. 74) against the king on the precedency of supply; and he signed the petition of August 1640, demanding that a parliament should be called.

[1] See Manchester, *Court and Society*, I, pp. 184–7, 196–202, for the early history of Kimbolton.
[2] Henry Montagu was also the author of *Contemplatio mortis, et immortalis* (1631); and *Manchester al mondo* (1635).

EDWARD MONTAGU, EARL OF MANCHESTER.

OB. 1671.

FROM THE ORIGINAL OF LELY, IN THE COLLECTION OF

HIS GRACE, THE DUKE OF BEDFORD.

Fig. 16. Edward Montagu (1602–71), 2nd Earl of Manchester (Robert Montagu's father).

This Edward Montagu's name was added to those of the five members impeached for high treason on 3 Janaury 1642 but he had been cleared of all such charges by March. In August 1642 he took command of a regiment of foot in the Earl of Essex's army and was active in raising funds for the Parliamentary army.[1] In August 1643 he was appointed major-general of the eastern associated counties and was thereby brought into close association with Cromwell. Between 28 August-16 September 1643 Montagu besieged Lynn-Regis in Norfolk; and on 9 October he joined Cromwell and Fairfax who were then besieging Bolingbroke Castle. On 20 October Lincoln surrendered to Montagu and henceforth he was regarded by Cromwell as an efficient and reliable supporter of Parliament, becoming in February 1644 a member of the new Committee of Both Kingdoms. His greatest military success was to secure Lincolnshire in May 1644 against the incursions of Prince Rupert; and at Marston Moor (1 July) Cromwell commanded Manchester's horse while he himself exercised control as a field officer. After the surrender of York on 16 July, he was ordered to lead a parliamentarian army to Doncaster (23 July).

By this time, however, it seems that Edward Montagu was growing both battle-weary and increasingly sceptical over the direction of the military conflicts. In early August he declined a direction from the committee of Both Kingdoms to march against Prince Rupert since his men were too depleted and fatigued. At the Battle of Newbury (28 October) he was accused of inaction and at a council of war on 10 November he openly expressed his distaste for further military conflicts. By 25 November Cromwell was accusing him to the House of Commons of neglect and incompetence. He attempted to defend himself in the House of Lords but on 25 April Edward Montagu, 2nd Earl of Manchester, resigned his commission from the army.[2]

The 2nd Earl of Manchester's position grew increasingly ambiguous. On 26 December 1645 he was one of those to whom Charles I was willing to entrust the militia in accordance with the Uxbridge proposals. He strongly opposed the ordinance for the king's trial in the House of Lords on 2 January 1649 and retired from public life when the formation of a commonwealth seemed inevitable. Following Cromwell's death, he was known as a keen supporter of the Restoration and, as Speaker of the House of Lords, it fell to him on 29 May 1660 formally to welcome King Charles II on his back arrival in England. He was restored as Chancellor of the University of Cambridge (which he had previously been from 1649–51), appointed Lord Chamberlain of the royal household (30 May), and chosen as a Privy Councillor (1 June). From 9–19 October he served in the trial of the regicides, generally leaning towards the side of leniency. The Montagu's high favour with the new king was confirmed on 28 April 1661 when he bore the sword of state at King Charles II's coronation and was made a Knight of the Garter.[3]

3. Robert Montagu's Continental Travels (May 1649–April 1654)

Robert Montagu's continental travels were probably already being formulated by his family in early 1649, even perhaps as an immediate response to the execution of Charles I on 30

---

[1] In 1626 Edward Montagu had married as his second wife, Anne, daughter of Robert Rich (d. 1658), 2nd Earl of Warwick. Since 1640 he had been prominent in raising military forces for parliament and was appointed Lord High Admiral in 1643. Although he withdrew from public life during the Commonwealth, he remained intimate with Cromwell and his son married the Protector's daughter.

[2] See *The Quarrel Between the Earl of Manchester and Oliver Cromwell: an Episode of the English Civil War* [documents collected by John Bruce], ed. David Masson, Camden Society, n.s., 12, 1875, pp. 78–95.

[3] See *The Earl of Manchester's speech to His Majesty … at his arrival at White-Hall, the 29th May 1660* (1660).

January. By late April all the necessary arrangements were in hand and on 23 the Admiralty Committee sent instructions to the Admirals of the Fleet (or the Commander-in-Chief in the Downs), informing them:

> Lord Mandeville, having a pass from the Speaker for travelling beyond sea, and desiring a passage in some vessel of the State, you are to order some vessel to receive him, his governor, wife, servants, and baggage, at Dover, and transport them to some port near to France, and then commander of the ship is to give him the respect fit for a person of his rank.[1]

Montagu's diary records that these orders were followed to the letter. He was taken in a biscay sloop to Admiral and General-at-Sea Richard Dean, who inspected his licence to travel over the seas from the Speaker of Parliament and arranged for Montagu to sail across the Channel on the frigate *Nonsuch* under the command of Captain Mildmay. The fifteen-years old Montagu was then accorded the required honour, as he passed Walmer Castle, of having a five-gun salute fired in his honour. About two miles from Dieppe his party transferred to a French sloop which dropped them safely at the harbour (having ensured that Montagu's party was protected from the Dunkirk and Ostend privateers which were then frequently stopping and robbing the Channel ferry boats as they approached the French coast), firing another salute in his honour as it returned out to sea (f. 1ᵛ).[2]

Moving on quickly from Dieppe, where he readily admired the shops filled with tourist trinkets made from 'Whalebones Ivory, Tortoisshells and the like', he headed towards Rouen, dining at Tôtes which was the usual stopping point for travellers on the post road. At Rouen he spent two days examining many of the usual tourist sights, including the cathedral with its great bell called the Georges D'Amboise and its treasury; the 'bridge made of boates over the river of Seine'; the old stone bridge which had been partially ruined during the French civil wars; the 'Parliament house'; the mint; and the 'place where the maide of Orleans was burnt by the English' (ff. 2ʳ⁻ᵛ). His party then hired a boat to head up the Seine to Paris, passing Pont-de-l'Arche and its strong fort which had been of considerable strategic importance during the recent troubles of the Fronde; and Gaillon, where the Archbishop of Rouen's palace was a famous tourist spot. By sailing on through a clear, moonlight night they were able to dine at Vernon and about five leagues further up the river they saw the marquis of Rosny's grand palace and park. That night they slept at Mantes and then passed by Meulan before leaving the river at Poissy to catch a coach into Paris where they arrived on 11/21 May 1649 and took lodgings 'in the street of Anjou at the signe of the Angel at one Madam Turgis her house a protestant widow' (f. 3ᵛ).

Although Robert Montagu was clearly at pains to be a diligent travel diarist (doubtless at the insistence of his tutor, Mr Hainhofer), recording all the usual elements required in the delineation of a great capital city, his excitement and sheer sense of boyish wonder is also readily communicated by his fulsome descriptions of Paris, St-Germain, St-Denis, and the great palaces within easy reach of the city. 'Paris the Capitall towne of france and seate of the kings', Montagu explains, 'is for its bignes call'd a little world'. He begins in traditional fashion by recording its geographical position, its three divisions of City, Town and University, its numerous districts and suburbs, its bridges and its gates. With these familiar factual preliminaries dealt with, he then launches into a far more interesting narration of his own, recounting his visits to such famous landmarks as the Pont Neuf, the Samaritaine

---

[1] *CSP Domestic, 1649–50*, pp. 105–6.

[2] See Stoye, *English Travellers Abroad*, p. 284, for examples of these privateering raids, some of which were conducted by ships sailing under the flag of Charles II.

hydraulic water pump, the Louvre Palace, the Palais-Royal, the Palais du Luxembourg, the Place des Vosges, the Grand Châtalet, the Hôtel de Ville, the Palais de Justice, and the university (ff. 4ʳ–8ʳ).

As previously noted (see pp. 33–4), John Evelyn's description of Paris, compiled retrospectively during the 1670s, was heavily dependent upon the guidebook which he had bought when he was touring the city during the 1640s, Claude de Varennes's *Le Voyage de France* (Paris, 1643). Montagu almost certainly also had a copy of this invaluable work to hand as he wrote, suggesting that, like Evelyn, he viewed travel writing as essentially a process of studious compilation, in which authoritative secondary sources were to be selectively combined with first-hand observations. In fact, it seems likely from the systematic and regimented way in which Montagu's lengthy description of Paris is set out in his diary that his tutor, Mr Hainhofer, would have specifically required him (perhaps even standing over his shoulder in classroom mode) to consult and copy from carefully recommended secondary sources like Varennes's guidebook. While Montagu's manuscript is certainly, on one level, a genuine and intimate record of a young man's first-hand observations of continental Europe it is also, like Evelyn's monumental diary, very much a scholastic exercise, compiled as a means of training a potential young courtier in how to lay out cogently his observations and information within specified geographical and historical contexts. Even if a travel diary was probably only going to be read by the youthful traveller's immediate family and friends, it was still expected to possess the clarity and selective organizational qualities of a good official report or council briefing paper – qualities which for many modern readers now seem distinctly alien to the highly subjective forms of travel writing widely favoured since the early years of the twentieth century.

A comparison of Montagu's and Evelyn's respective descriptions of the cathedral of Notre-Dame (both drawing heavily from Varennes, pp. 180–82) clearly illustrates their working methods:

> The foundation are layed uppon pyles, this great body is sustained by 120 great pillars, which makes 5 great allyes. The lenght of it is 174 paces, its breath of 60, and its hight of a 100. The Quire is built all of stone upon the which are graved the Histories both of the old and new Testament. This church hath 45 chappells and 11 gates. Over the the 3 greatest of its frontispeece are in stone the statues of 26 kings from Childebert until Phillipp Augustus ... (Montagu, (1649) f. 8ᵛ)

> It consists of a Gotique fabrique sustayned with 120 pillars which make two allys in the Church round about the Quire, without comprehending the Chapells, long 174 paces, large 60: high 100: The Quire is enclosd with stone worke, graven with the Sacred History, and containes 45 Chapells cancelld with yron: At the front of the chiefe entrance are statues in relievo of the Kings 28 in number from Childebert unto Philip the founder ... (Evelyn (1644 but written c. 1670), pp. 95–6)

It is clear that the compilation of Montagu's account of Paris was also regarded as a conveniently useful schoolboy exercise in French translation and paraphrase. Using sources very similar to Evelyn's, Montagu then goes on to describe in more detail the other major churches of the city, including such still well known edifices as the church of the Sorbonne and the 11th century church of St-Germain-des-Près (see Fig. 22, p. 93), as well as various places of worship which had long since been lost, such as the abbey church of Ste-Geneviève (demolished in the early nineteenth century) and the abbey-church of St-Victor (dispersed in 1790 and later demolished) (ff. 9ʳ–10ᵛ).

After a comprehensive tour of the major churches, basilicas and convents at Paris, Montagu's attention shifted to an examination of its renowned hospitals (ff. 14^{r-v}), various cabinets of curiosities collected by gentlemen of the city, and the royal Jardin des Plantes founded by Louis XIII in 1626 for the cultivation of medicinal herbs (ff. 14^v–16^r). It seems that Montagu was diligently writing to a systematic set of rules since his diary then moves on to discuss both the general civic qualities of Paris ('this famous towne, which is esteemed one of the greatest and finest of the world') and 'the most remarkable places about this towne' (f. 16^{r-v}). These nearby destinations included the village of St-Denis and its abbey church, where Montagu spent a great deal of time exploring its renowned treasures and royal tombs (ff. 17^r–23^v). Later pleasantly rural excursions took him to the Richelieu family's grand Château de Val and water gardens at Rueil-Malmaison; René de Longueil's château at Maisons-Laffite; the Protestant church at Charenton; and the royal park and hunting ground at the Bois de Vincennes (ff. 23^v–25^v). John Stoye usefully summarizes the educational value of Montagu's experiences and mode of recording them up to this point in his diary:

> They [his party] remained a month [at Paris], obediently visiting everything that guides and guidebooks prescribed. So did most of the early travellers and their sightseeing had one extremely important result. Montagu, and he was one of many, learnt a great deal of French history by this Parisian pilgrimage. In accordance with the historical approach of his age, he studied the subject in a piecemeal fashion but as thoroughly as any English history that would have come his way earlier in life, or even later on. A branch of knowledge which is so evident in the appraisals of a good intellect like John Evelyn's, or illustrated on every page of Richard Symonds' exquisite Paris sketch-book [see p. 38], can be watched growing the very immature mind of Robert Montagu Lord Mandeville. It is a process worth observation. The monuments of French history stood before his eyes, covering an immense span of past history and he surveyed them one by one, laboriously copying into his journal the appropriate historical detail borrowed from his tutor or his books.[1]

The idea that Montagu envisaged himself compiling not a daily diary of his itinerary but a more formally arranged report on his travels is confirmed by his handling of the frequently described rural landscapes between Paris and Orléans. The purely visual aspects of the next stage of his itinerary or, for that matter, the minor hardships of long-distance coach and boat travel at this period, were simply of no interest to him as a diarist. While other travellers regularly commented on the excellent stone surface of the road from Paris or the dense forests with their wolves and bandits as Orléans drew nearer, Montagu hastens his readers from Paris (which he left on 8 June 1649) to Orléans two days later in under thirty flatly descriptive words:

> From Paris I tooke my journey for Orleans and passed by Long-Jumeaux, Linas, Chatres la Valleé de Tour fourt, Estampes, Angerville, Artenay and soe came to Orleans. (f. 25^v)

But once he is back in a city with genuine historical associations, his interests are rekindled by its churches, its town house and a famous fifteenth-century memorial on its bridge to Joan of Arc (ff. 25^v–26^r). The purpose of Montagu's travels, however, was not just historical sightseeing since it had always been planned that he would take up residence in some suitable location for an extended period of study. Saumur was this chosen destination and after only five days at Orléans Mr Hainhofer pressed on with his young charge down the

---

[1] Ibid, pp. 286–7.

Loire in a hired boat. On the way, they took in many of the landmarks and sights already familiar to generations of English tourists from the mid-16th century onwards. These included the dominating castle at Amboise, the churches and Pall Mall of Tours, the great abbey church at Marmoustier and the caves near Savonnières on the south bank of the River Cher (ff.26^{r-v}). On 18 June Montagu and his party arrived at Saumur where he was to be based for over a year at the house of a Madame Michon. Mr Hainhofer engaged the services of tutors in fencing, singing, the guitar, dancing, and Latin; and ensured that his young charge also made regular healthy excursions into the surrounding countryside.

Montagu began recording his residence at Saumur in the requisite fashion by describing his visit to its famous pilgrimage church of Notre-Dame des Ardilliers, where, as his attention wandered, he became absorbed not so much in its historic architecture but rather in the numerous cheap devotional tokens, including 'images of armes, hands, leags; and such parts of the body as have been healed after pilgrimages', left there by grateful supplicants. In his second paragraph, he enthusiastically proceeds to compile a detailed account of the miscellaneous natural history curiosities on display in the cabinet of a local gentleman called Monsieur Legier, concluding with a rather macabre exhibit which was bound to appeal to the idle curiosity of the youthful Montagu:

> a little child borne as is thought six weekes after his Conception formed of all his membres, about a spang long and the which there is 2 years that it is kept in a glasse bottle full of strong water which does preserve it intire … (f. 27^r)

But the third paragraph of Montagu's account of Saumur conjures up an image perhaps of the stern Mr Hainhofer coming into the room and glancing over his pupil's shoulder as he wrote, immediately disapproving of this preoccupation with the trivialities of an idle tourist. The diary pointedly shifts into a far more formal written mode: 'I forgott to speake first something of the situation of the towne', and, predictably, then provides a dull little account of the town's geographical situation and civic aspects (which only leaves the reader wishing for more tittle-tattle about cabinets of curiosities and pilgrimage tokens).

It should also be noted that the phrase beginning: 'I forgott to speake first …' is written in a distinctly neater and more precise hand than that of the first 27 folios of the diary. Given Montagu's youth, which is very much in evidence in the larger and more immature hand of the earlier section, it seems unlikely that he was able at this point instantaneously to formalize both his handwriting and his thoughts as a travel diary compiler. The hands seem those of two distinct individuals, although some of the similiarities in letter formation (especially capitals) may suggest that the younger hand was schooled by the writer of the more mature script. If this is the case, then it seems most likely that from folio 27^v Mr Hainhofer, although still writing in the first person as adopted by Montagu in the earlier section of the diary, personally took over the drafting of the account. Certainly, from this point onwards, the diary seems rather more functional and conformist to traditional standards of travel memoir compilation.

It immediately busies itself with a highly informative account of the town of Richelieu, in phrasing which seems more polished than the earlier section of the diary. In fact, the description of Richelieu's palace may be cited as a text-book example of how to lay out a description of a major historical and architectural building. It begins with a general visual impression of the town as one rides towards it, followed by a vivid sketch of the dominating presence within the town of the palace itself: 'As soone as one is out of one of the gates the stately Palace of the Cardinal of Richelieu appeares like to an earthly Paridis, it being built fowre square like the towne having the water running by it' (ff. 28^{r-v}). Passing through the courtyard with its ornamental displays of 'curious marble statues in niches in the wall of very great prise', the visitors enter into the building itself and begin a systematic description of the grand central staircase and first floor rooms, ensuring that a wealth of incidental detail is provided concerning the decoration and furnishing of each salon, study and bedroom visited. In contrast, moving outside again, the cultivated gardens, parks and stables are dealt with in a surprising perfunctory manner: 'the gardens they are very large and pleasant with severall chanels that runne through having a fine parke at the end thereof' (f. 29^r), is all that can be offered to the reader before the writer seems to run out of things to say. Perhaps Mr Hainhofer compiled the description of the house and its interior before, hopefully, leaving the gardens to his young pupil. Or, if Montagu was responsible for the whole description (and perhaps dictated it to Hainhofer), he could well have had to hand an informative guidebook to the aesthetic riches of the house but was obliged to fall back on his own more limited resources for the gardens, parks and stables.

The diary proceeds in similar stylistic fashion to detail brief visits to Loudun, Oiron, Thours, Coulonges-Thouarsais, and Fontenay-le-Comte (ff. 29^{r-v}), followed by a more substantial account of a location of special interest to the English from the time of the Duke of Buckingham's ill-fated expedition there, La Rochelle (ff. 29^v–30^r). Little is actually said about Montagu's daily studies at Saumur, almost certainly because Mr. Hainhofer was also sending home detailed reports on his pupil's education and regular expenses to his father, the 2nd Earl of Manchester (see below). It is interesting to note, however, that Montagu also stayed for a while at the country house near Saumur of 'Mr Brousse a Scotshman, brother in law to Mr Hainhofer and heretofore governour to the Duke of Trimoille' (f. 37^r). Clearly, Mr Hainhofer had some useful connections as a tutor and may well himself have formerly been in the service of the Duke. Having eventually made his way back to Saumur after this mini tour of the region ('I made about 130 French leagues having passed therough severall Provinces of France', f. 33^v), Montagu and his tutor headed off in November 1649 on another four-day trip to see La Flèche, with its 'famous colledge the Jesuites have there'; and then another in early 1650 to Angers (ff. 33^v–36^v).

From this point onwards, Montagu's diary becomes much more of a factual and practical record of his actual itinerary and meetings with important dignitaries than either a considered historical survey of the major cities, towns, and institutions of France (which seems to have been a clear aim of the first part of his diary), or a record of his own impressions as a first-time traveller in the country. By November 1650 he had travelled up through Artenay, Etampes, Linas, and Bourg-la-Reine to take up residence once more at Paris in the rue Dauphine which ran directly from the Pont Neuf on the Left Bank (f. 37^v). After eight days there, Montagu and Hainhofer were on the road again, this time to visit Lyons which was described in the same detailed way as Montagu's earlier analysis of the geographical, historical and social importance of Paris (ff. 40^v–43^v).

On 31 January 1651, Mr Hainhofer, wrote to Robert's father, the 2nd Earl of Manchester, to describe their current educational activities and somewhat perilous financial state:

To the Right Honourable the Earl of Manchester, these present at Kimbolton.

My Lord, – Having already given you to understand by my last letter how the severity of the season, the excessive flooding from the rivers, and the bad conditions of the roads, had induced me to come to the resolution of remaining in this city till the spring, with God's help, and this indeed for the further reason that Monsieur your son, among other studies followed by him here, applies himself so energetically to logic, to the mathematics, and especially to geography, that I make it a matter of conscience not to remove him, nor to separate him from his masters so soon, the more particularly as I find these are amiable and diligent, and, at all events, not to interrupt his studies till he has well grasped and comprehended the principles of those sciences, and made such progress in them as to render the perfecting of the remainder the more easy elsewhere.

And now as to our stock of money, it is now altogether consumed; for, seeing that we have paid what we owed at Saumur, defrayed the expenses of our journey thence to this city, have lived in our present quarters for more than six months, not to mention other expenses, we have nothing left. For this reason, my lord, I now venture to present my most humble request that you will give such order that the sumes of money of which you have made mention in your two last letters be promptly forwarded either to Paris or to this place, lest otherwise we should be exposed to the same inconveniences which, have heretofore befallen us; or even greater, for lack of such resources.

At present, little credit is allowed to anyone, still less to foreigners and Englishmen, who are not looked upon with a favourable eye, if they fail to regularly pay the ordinary professors, and the expenses of board and lodgings, at the termination of each month; otherwise, one is very ill-served and very much despised by all parties. If at the same time you would do me the honour to take into consideration what particularly concerns yourself, and what I have advanced for your service, much having been required for living and other great necessities, you would confer on me a very particular favour.

Assuring myself of the same, and awaiting it as an act of your especial kindness, I conclude, praying God to continue to confer on you and all yours His most chosen benedictions, and on them the distinction of worthily meriting the title which I appropriate to myself, of your lord-ship's very humble and very faithful servant,

Hainhofer

Monsieur your son offers you his humble submission. He wrote to you by the last ordinary, and, please God, designs to pay the same duty to you next week.
From Lyons, this 31st of January
(st. n.), of the year 1651.[1]

This uniquely surviving letter from Robert Montagu's continental tour is of considerable importance, not only for its specific information on how he was spending his time at Lyon but also as a timely reminder of just how much material has probably been lost relating to Robert's whole experience of a continental tour. No trace is now known of any books, maps, guides, curiosities, and other trinkets or works of art which he may have brought home with him. (Given his undiminishing fascination throughout his diary for cabinets of curiosities, it seems unlikely that he would not have been tempted to form his own small collection).[2] Also, Hainhofer's comments indicate that both he and Robert Montagu were regularly sending informal but detailed descriptions of their localities and activities to his parents at the Montagu's family residence at Kimbolton. Hence, Robert Montagu's travel diary as now preserved in Bodl. MS Rawlinson D 76 should be regarded as being compiled not as a comprehensive record of his time abroad but merely as a formal framework for (and supple-ment to) these other kinds of important family records. It might well be suggested that to gain a complete impression of the kinds of records of Montagu's travels which, say, his parents and siblings might have been able to browse through at Kimbolton during the late

[1] Manchester, *Court and Society*, I, pp. 375–7, translated from Hainhofer's idiosyncratic French.
[2] See, for example, Montagu's comments on the cabinets displayed by M. Fedeaux, a canon of Notre Dame at Paris (f. 14ᵛ); another by M. Tribourg at Paris (f. 14ᵛ); M. Flanc's at La Rochelle (f. 30ʳ); and four other sets of cabinets at Lyons (ff. 42ʳ–43ʳ).

1650s, it would be necessary to combine his diary with other now long-since lost documents and objects similar to William Hammond's letters, the collections and curiosities of John Bargrave, and the reminiscences of Banaster Maynard's servant, Robert Moody.

After a six-month's stay at Lyons, with occasional excursions to other locations such as Vienne, pupil and tutor headed off for Geneva, where they resided in the house of a 'Mr Volk'. Montagu continued there his formal educational pursuits, including the study of Latin and dancing, the latter being taught to him by a Mr Denis who, fortuitously, had once instructed him as a young child back home in England (ff. 44r–46r). After three months at Geneva, he set out on 17 August 1651 for Switzerland and Germany, passing rapidly through Versoix, Nyon, Lausanne, Avenches, and Morat before arriving at Berne and Zürich (ff. 46r–49v). The importance of Montagu's family was clearly recognized here and he proudly recorded in his diary:

> The Senat presented mee with 12 great pottes of wine at my arrival and sent to of the Senaturs to dine with mee, who in comeing in made mee a speech in German form the Senat' (f. 49v).

Pressing on through Switzerland, he reached St Gallen and Rorschach but his diary is most memorable at this point for the miscellaneous insertion of a folded illustration of a performing elephant (see Fig. 28, p. 133). Yet again, we are reminded through the survival of this ephemeral representation that Montagu probably collected other (now lost) examples of woodcuts and engravings to add to his collections of materials brought home from his Grand Tour (see also Figs 29–30, pp. 139, 144). Entering Germany, his party made for Augsburg where he remained until 17 September 1651. He then made a brief excursion to Münich and decided to stay there, doubtless at Mr Hainhofer's recommendation, for the coming winter at the house of a Mr Roberts, kin of 'my Lord of Winchester's' (ff. 54r–57v). In the new year of 1652 (the diary does not specify exactly when, perhaps suggesting that it was being compiled retrospectively), he headed off through Horgau, Auerbach, and Burgau to visit Ulm ('a most famous citty for its richnesse and strenth being extremely well fortified a la moderne'). Although he dutifully described its considerable fortifications and cathedral, once again, Montagu's imagination as a diarist was most readily fired by the three chambers of curiosities displayed by a 'Mr Fourtenbach' (who may, in fact, have been the engineer, 'one Furtenback', responsible for the recent strengthening of the city walls).

Moving on through Reutlingen, Tübingen and Calw, he reached the spas of Dörnach where he enjoyed a welcome rest of some six weeks, a sojourn which also gave him the opportunity to go out hunting regularly with a Prince of Württemberg (f. 59r). Stuttgart was his next major destination, where he was granted a personal guided tour of the Altes Schloss by some of its resident courtiers. The remaining pages of his diary (ff. 61r–64v) record Montagu's steady progress through Esslingen, Leipheim, Burgau, Haunstetten, Landsberg, and Oberammergau towards Mittenwald and Seefeld where, in the midst of narrating a story about a local Catholic miracle, the diary suddenly breaks off. No other account of Montagu's travels is known to complete the narrative of his continental itinerary. However, it is clear from comments made on 8 October 1652, just after Montagu had left Augsburg for the second time (f. 61r), that he and his tutor, Mr Hainhofter planned a peregrination of Italy:

> At my returne of the waters I begun a nother journey which was that of Italie and to that end tooke a german messenger by name Simler for to goe straight to Venice; and wee payed for each on[e] 20 ducats for horse and diet and tooke this following way (f. 63r).

Although incomplete, Montagu's diary remains of significance not least because it so meticulously and conventionally records the locations, buildings and other familiar focal points favoured by seventeenth century English tourists. Its informative descriptions of major locations for travellers, such as Dieppe (ff. 1^v–2^r), Paris (ff. 3^v–17^r), St-Denis (ff. 17^r–21^r), Orléans (f. 25^v), Saumur (ff. 27^v–37^r), Lyons (ff. 42^r–43^v), Geneva (ff. 44^r–46^r), Augsburg (ff. 51^v–54^r) and Stuttgart (ff. 59^v–60^v) offer a kind of modest reference manual for any other youthful members of his family who might subsequently be expected to undertake a similar tour. Probably written in the first instance to confirm that his father's money had been wisely spent and that Mr Hainhofer had guided his charge responsibly, Montagu's diary has come down to modern readers not only as a record of one individual's typical experiences abroad but also as a very rare survival of this kind of document. Probably only a minority of young travellers ever bothered to compile such a meticulous diary of their activities; and over the years an even smaller number of such manuscripts have survived.

Montagu's diary is probably representative of the kinds of activities followed by an unremarkable member of the English nobility. Well aware of his privileged position, Montagu is always visibly concerned (no doubt with Mr Hainhofer's encouragement) with recording exactly what a dutiful son should be doing during his travels abroad. Hence, he (or Mr Hainhofer, if his is the second hand in the diary) carefully records even the names of his various tutors at Saumur (f. 36^v) and Geneva (f. 46^r); and he carefully emphasizes how the enforced sojourn at Münich during the freezing winter months was industriously occupied with the study of the German language and geometry (f. 57^r).

As well as confirming Robert Montagu's diligent studentship while abroad, the diary also implicitly serves to reassure his father, the 2nd Earl of Manchester, that the Montagu name was highly regarded throughout Western Europe. Throughout his travels abroad, Montagu's ease of passage was greatly assisted by the current prestige of the Montagus back home in England and his presence was both welcomed and actively sought out by the scions of similarly elevated continental families. While staying at La Flèche, for example, he undertook a brief itinerary with a noble German travelling acquaintance, John George, Prince of Mecklenburg (f. 34^r); and at St Florent he was granted an audience with Cardinal Grimaldi, the uncle of the Prince of Monaco (f. 36^v). One of the social highlights of Robert's tour occurred at Notre-Dame de Cléry (f. 37^v) when, with great pride and delight, his social status allowed him to join briefly the royal entourage of the youthful Louis XIV (1638–1715). While in Switzerland he readily made friends with the Marquess of Baden and various other German nobles; and on the way to Stuttgart he derived plentiful hospitality from a sheaf of letters of recommendation provided by various German dignitaries (ff. 59^v–60^v). He also exploited some useful invitations previously set up for him before his departure from England in April 1649. At Geneva Montagu visited the widowed sister of Sir Theodore Mayerne (1573–1655), formerly physican to the English royal family (f. 46^r); and at Zürich he paid his compliments to one 'Lady Smith', whose son had provided a letter of recommendation (f. 49^v). As his father would surely have expected, this diary acts as a kind of informal *curriculum vitae* for Robert youthful training in mixing with foreign dignitaries and observing the courtesies and practices of international diplomacy.[1]

---

[1] Hence, Montagu endeavours to show, at least spasmodically, a boyish interest in political affairs, recording at Paris in November 1650 how effigies of Cardinal Mazarin were paraded through the streets; and that the dukes de Condé, Conti, and Longueville were all then imprisoned (f. 38^r). Similarly, he makes some basic observations on the republican government of the cantons around Geneva (f. 45^v).

At Thouars, through Mr Hainhofer's connections, he met with Henri, Duke of Trémouille (f. 36ᵛ), who, as previously noted, had once had Hainhofer's brother-in-law as his governor. The Duke had especially close connections with England through the marriage of his sister, Charlotte de la Trémouille (1602–64), with James Stanley (1607–1651), Earl of Derby, known as the 'Martyr Earl' on account of his unwavering loyalty to the royal family. As one of Charles I's most active generals, he was reputed to have mustered some 60,000 loyal men from Lancashire and Cheshire and had attempted to recover Manchester for the king in 1642. He served with Prince Rupert in the north of England in 1644 and lead the assault on Bolton after the royalist defeat at Marston Moor. Although he then withdrew to the safety of the Isle of Man for the next six years, he returned to the English mainland in 1651 and, after the Battle of Worcester in September, he personally escorted Charles II to the safety of Boscobel wood. Soon afterwards he was captured, condemned as a traitor by court martial and executed in October 1651. Robert Montagu was understandably pleased to be able to meet the 'Martyr Earl's' son, Lord Strange, at Thouars (f. 29ᵛ).

The next time we can pick up Montagu's itinerary is on the very final stage of his journey home. On 9 April 1654 a Captain Abraham Algate wrote to the Admiralty Committee:

> I received Rob. Rich and his servants on board the Drake, and embarked for the second time at Dover on the 5th, and landed him on the 6th at Dieppe. He acquainted the Earl of Bolingbroke and Lord Mandeville of our attendance upon them by your order, and next day they with their servants came on board, and were all put on shore at Rye this day, Sunday.[1]

Montagu's distinguished travelling companion was Oliver St John (1634–88), who had succeeded to the earldom of Bolingbroke on the death of his grandfather, the Parliamentarian Lord-Lieutenant of Bedfordshire, Oliver St John (d. 1646), 4th Baron St John of Bletsho and 1st Earl of Bolingbroke. The father of Montagu's travelling companion, Oliver St John (1603–42), had served with distinction in the Parliamentarian army but died from wounds received at the Battle of Edgehill. Robert Montagu was returning in high favour to the England of Oliver Cromwell. It also seems entirely characteristic of the Montagus' political suppleness at this period that the young Robert could mix freely at Thouars with the family of one of the most renowned hero-martyrs of the royalist cause and yet happily travel home in the company of the son of one of Cromwell's most respected soldiers.

4. The Later Life of Robert Montagu, 3rd Earl of Manchester

After Robert Montagu returned home from his continental travels in April 1654, his family began to consider finding a suitable wife for him. His grandfather, the Earl of Warwick, for a time favoured the (considerable) financial and (acceptable) personal attractions of a Miss Massingberd ('Truly, son, 10,000 *l.* is not to be had every day down and on the nail, with a reasonable handsome maid') but these proposals came to nothing.[2] Instead, in early 1654 Robert's family turned their attention to another promising candidate, Anne (d. 1698),

---

[1] *CSP Domestic, 1654*, p. 86. On 14 April Captain Benjamin Sacheverell offered his apologies to the Admiralty Committee for not responding to the Protector's order to pick up the Earl of Bolingbroke and Lord Mandeville because he had been windbound at Dunkirk for several days: ibid, p. 101.

[2] Manchester, *Court and Society*, II, pp. 380–81. A daughter and co-heir (perhaps this same lady) of John Massingberd married Lord George (later Earl) Berkeley, and resided at Berkeley House, Clerkenwell.

daughter of Sir Christopher Yelverton (d. c. 1655) of Easton Mauduit in Northampton-shire, by his wife Anne, daughter of Sir William Twisden.[1]

A series of letters from Sir Christopher Yelverton to Robert Montagu's father has sur-vived, detailing the specifics of their marital negotiations. The first letter courteously acknowledges Sir Christopher's gratitude for Manchester's good opinion 'both of me and my family' and tactfully lets it be known that he has already received suits from other high-ranking families for the hand of his daughter: 'She is my jewel. I have but one daughter, which makes me desirous to settle her so that I may place her in a contented condition, and so as that she may be a comfort and satisfaction unto me in the closure of my days'. It appears, however, that Yelverton was in too frail health to conduct the negotiations in person ('If my strength or condition would admit of it, I should in any place attend upon you, but I stir not from home'). But at this stage in the negotiations, Yelverton was also baulking at the settlement on his daughter which had been proposed by the Earl of Manchester, via his brother who was acting as intermediary. His letter bluntly concluded:

> If yours will not admit of a less supply than your brother did seem to intimate, I must deal clearly with you. I shall not be able any ways to come up to it, being resolved, howsoever my affection may be to my daughter, not to destroy my family, and to pull down my own house about mine ears, with my own hands'.[2]

The correspondence continued for a while in similiar mode, with the Earl clearly seeking out a guaranteed and substantial settlement and Yelverton hoping for a greater jointure to be granted by Robert's father to the couple on their marriage. Both sides, it seems, were tough negotiators and Yelverton was not averse to reminding Manchester that his daughter was of interest to other noblemen: 'My Lord, I do assure you that I have had the like offer from one of your own degree and quality'. As Manchester continued to hold out for a large settlement from the bride's father, he was sharply reminded by Yelverton in July 1654: 'Such a portion as you expect you must either have out of the nobility or the city, for from amongst the gentry it is hardly to be expected'. Yelverton was clearly concerned that, if the Earl did not endow his son with a substantial income, then the young wedded couple would be obliged to borrow money to set themselves up in the state which their rank in society demanded. Robert's grandfather, the Earl of Warwick, also became involved in the negoti-ations and held a meeting with Yelverton; and Lady Cheke, the mother of the Earl of Manchester's third wife, also contributed to the debate in a firm letter of 19 October to her son-in-law:

> My Lord, – Since I wrote my other letter I have been fully informed of all particulars concern-ing Lord Mandeville's business. Truly, my Lord, Sir C. Yelverton hath done his part exceed-ingly well, therefore let me earnestly entreat your Lordship not to stand so strictly upon the 3,000 *l.* but be satisfied with 1,500 *l.* ... I would not have it said this match breaks off from such a partiality in your Lordship as that you should be thought mean to your son'.

The interchanges of letters proceeded in similar fashion for some time long until, finally, articles of agreement were drafted with lands to the value of £4,000 settled upon Robert

---

[1] Sir Christopher was the son of Sir Henry Yelverton (1566–1629), who was appointed as Attorney-General in succession to Francis Bacon and as Judge of the Common Pleas by Charles I. Through subsequent marriages, the Yelvertons succeeded to the barony of Ruthyn and the viscountship of Longueville. In 1717 Talbot Yelverton was raised by King George I to the peerage as the Earl of Sussex (with the title becoming extinct in 1799).

[2] Manchester, *Court and Society*, II, pp. 382–3.

Montagu, with a jointure of £1,300 for Anne Yelverton and an allowance of £1,100 per annum for his son.[1]

With these protracted negotiations brought to a satisfactory resolution, Robert Montagu married Anne Yelverton on 27 June 1655 at St Giles's-in-the-Fields. They had five sons and four daughters. His two eldest sons, Edward and Henry, died young and Robert was succeeded after his death in 1683 as Earl of Manchester by his third son, Charles (c. 1662–1722), who was elevated to the rank of lst Duke of Manchester in 1719. According to Robert Montagu's will, his younger surviving sons were called Robert and Heneage; and three of his daughters were Elizabeth, Katherine, and Eleanor. His other daughter, Anne (d. 1720), made the best family marriage of all of them when in May 1682 she became the third wife of James Howard (1619–88), 3rd Earl of Sussex.

On 28 September 1658 Robert Montagu's step-mother, Essex, Countess of Manchester, died and in July 1659 his father took as his fourth wife, Ellinor, daughter of Richard Wortley of Yorkshire. This lady had already been widowed three times and possessed an impressive marriage pedigree (and, presumably, had also accrued an increasing personal wealth through these unions). Her first husband, had been Sir Henry Lee (d. 1631) of Ditchley, Oxfordshire; her second, Edward Radcliffe (d. 1641), 6th Earl of Sussex; and her third was Robert Rich (d. 1658), 2nd Earl of Warwick – whom our Robert Montagu would have already known well as his own grandfather.

Robert Montagu's public career prospered from the time of the Restoration. He served as MP for Huntingdonshire in the Convention Parliament of April 1660 and remained its MP until 1671. On 7 May 1660 he was sent to The Hague as one of the six ambassadors chosen to attend King Charles II and to escort him back to his kingdom. He was prominent in the ceremony of the coronation as a train-bearer on 23 April 1661 and became one of the lords of the king's bedchamber with an annuity of £1,000 per year.[2] In May 1663 he was chosen by Charles II to lead an embassy to France during the illness of Louis XIII.[3] He was honoured by the University of Oxford with an honorary MA degree on 8 September 1665; and he later served as High Steward of the University of Cambridge (1677–83). In February 1666 he was appointed as a Gentleman of the Bedchamber, a post which he retained until 1681. In 1666/7 he commanded a troop of horse in the Duke of Monmouth's regiment when the Dutch navy was thought to be threatening the eastern counties.[4] He served as Lord Lieutenant of Huntingdonshire (18 June 1671–1681) and took his seat in the House of Lords as the 3rd Earl of Manchester on 4 February 1673. It seems that during much of his married life Robert Montagu, known until 1673 as Lord Mandeville, was well known as a 'rather wild spark about court'. He seems, for example, to have pursued the noted beauty, Mrs Stewart, and even presented her with a ring worth £300.[5] Robert Montagu died on 14 March 1683, aged 48, at Montpellier where he had gone after the weddings of three of his daughters.[6]

[1] Ibid, I, pp. 382–92.

[2] Manchester, *Court and Society*, II, p. 25. See p. 2 for his father's role at the coronation.

[3] *HMC Harley MSS*, I, p. 273.

[4] See BL Add. MS 21425/273, Robert Montagu's letter to W. Love (1667). For other items of his correspondence, see BL Add. MS 29557/162 (1679) and MS 29558/455–65 (1681) letters to Lord Hatton; BL Add. MS 34723, accounts of Richard Simpson of Nether Dean, Bedfordshire, 1681–95, including 'an accompt of money received for Robert Montagu, Earl of Manchester, 1681'.

[5] Manchester, *Court and Society*, II, p. 392.

[6] *HMC Rutland*, II, p. 72. He was buried at Kimbolton.

Fig. 17. King Charles II arrives back in England in 1660, accompanied Robert Montagu and five other English representatives.

Robert Montagu, was succeeded by his third and eldest surviving son, Charles (c. 1662–1722), who was educated at St Paul's School, London, and Trinity College, Cambridge (matriculated, 1678; MA, 1680). He served as Lord Carver to the queen at the coronation of King James II on 23 April 1685. He went abroad early in 1686 (with his cousin, Peregrine Bertie, and was in Venice in February 1687) in disgust at the revival of arbitrary power and became a supporter of the Prince of Orange. He raised a troop of horse in Nottinghamshire for the prince and carried St Edward's staff at King William's coronation on 11 April 1689. In the winter 1697/8 he returned to Venice on an unsuccessful mission to secure the release of English seamen sent to the galleys in the Venetian navy.[1] He served from August 1699–September 1701 as English Ambassador to France; and from April 1707–September 1708 he went via Vienna again as ambassador extraordinary to Venice to ensure the support of the republic for the Grand Alliance. He was admitted to George I's Privy Council in June 1698 and created Duke of Manchester on 30 April 1719.

Robert Montagu's widow, Anne Yelverton Montagu (then aged about 60), married shortly before 18 February 1689 his younger relative Charles Montagu (1661–1715), of Channel Row, Westminster, then 'aged under 24'.[2] This individual was the fourth son of George Montagu of Horton and grandson of Henry Montagu, 1st Earl of Manchester. His younger brother, James (1666–1723) became a noted judge and Solicitor-General. He had studied at Trinity College, Cambridge, from where he took an MA and was elected a fellow. During this period he also formed a friendship with Isaac Newton. After the death of his wife, Anne in 1698, he formed a close liaison with Newton's niece, Catherine Barton.[3] From the early 1690s he enjoyed a highly successful career at court and, as a lord of the treasury, formulated proposals for the national debt and introduced the bill establishing the Bank of England. He also served as First Lord of the Treasury and Chancellor of the Exchequer. He was created Baron Halifax of Halifax in 1700 and raised to the peerage as Viscount Sunbury and Earl of Halifax in October 1714.

5. The Other Montagus

In order to maintain a clear picture of Robert Montagu's extensive and complex family relationships during the Civil War period, it is also necessary to consider briefly the careers of several other family members. The most important among these is perhaps his father's younger brother, Walter Montagu (c. 1603/4–77). After studying at Sidney Sussex College, Cambridge, Walter Montagu went abroad in about 1620 to acquire foreign languages. On his return to England the Duke of Buckingham sent him on a secret mission to France in 1624, concerning the proposed royal marriage with Henrietta Maria, and Walter Montagu became her trusted and life-long friend. He was again in France in 1626, negotiating over seized English vessels. In 1627 he was sent to Lorraine and Italy to stir up discontent against France but he reported to Charles I that such an uprising would gain little support on the continent. He was arrested and placed in the Bastille but was freed and returned to England. He was in France again in 1628, negotiating for the release of some English prisoners, and he did not return permanently to England until 1633.[4]

[1] Manchester, *Court and Society*, II, pp. 31–7.

[2] MS News-sheets, MS Sloane 3929, f. 30. Charles Montagu was created Earl of Halifax in February 1688. Some of Anne Yelverton Montagu's letters are in BL Add. MS 29569/215–256.

[3] Anne Yelverton Montagu was buried on 28 July 1698 at St James's Church, Westminster.

[4] See also Manchester, *Court and Society*, II, pp. 1–9; and Stoye, *English Travellers Abroad*, pp. 312–15.

When later residing in Paris as an attaché to the British embassy, he went to Loudun (see p. 111) to witness the exorcisms of the Ursuline nuns, then notorious throughout France. But in July 1635 he arrived in London to announce his departure for Rome to join the fathers of the Oratory.[1] He returned to England in the late 1630s and remained close to Henrietta Maria. He also regularly assisted Sir Kenelm Digby (whom William Hammond, our second traveller in this volume, also met while abroad, see p. 185) in raising funds from Catholics to support the royalist army. In 1641 Walter Montagu again withdrew to France, with warm letters of recommendation from the queen. He was arrested and imprisoned in England in October 1643 and remained in the Tower until 1647. On 31 August 1649 he and Digby were expelled from England by order of the House of Commons and forbidden to return, on pain of confiscation of their property and execution (see p. 186). Through the support of the queen-dowager of France, Walter Montagu was appointed abbot of the Benedictine monastery of Nanteuil in Metz diocese; and subsequently transferred to the rich abbey of St Martin at Pontoise. He was trusted by the queen dowager of France (Marie de Médicis), Henrietta Maria, and Henrietta's daughter, the Duchess of Orleans. In 1654 Charles I's son, Henry, Duke of Gloucester, was committed to his care at Pontoise. Towards the end of 1660 he made a secret visit to England to see his brother, the 2nd Earl of Manchester (our traveller's father).[2]

Another important branch of the Montagu family was headed by Edward Montagu (1562–1644), 1st Baron Montagu of Boughton, the elder brother of our diarist's grand-father. This Edward Montagu had been educated at Oxford as a companion of Robert Sidney, 1st Earl of Leicester. He was created Baron Montagu on 29 June 1621 by James I and was prominent during the 1630s in Charles I's Ship Money assessments. He was with the king at York in 1639 but voted against him in April 1640 on the question of precedency of supply. In September 1640 he supported the petition demanding that the king should call a new parliament but was not afraid to criticize MPs for their 'usury' in March 1642. By August of that year, Parliament was issuing an order for his arrest and he was imprisoned briefly from September 1642. His failing health necessitated a move, still under house-arrest, to his residence in the Savoy where he died on 15 June 1644. Regarded by his family as a firm royalist, his daughter, Elizabeth (d. 1654), married Robert Bertie, Lord Willoughby of Eresby, 1st Earl of Lindsey, who was killed at the Battle of Edgehill.[3]

Edward Montagu (1616–84), 2nd Baron Montagu of Boughton (the 1st Baron's eldest son), was much more closely associated with the Parliamentary cause. In May 1646, along with the Earls of Pembroke and Denbigh, he received the king from the Scots and accompanied him to Holmby; and he was in close contact with him until Charles I's escape in 1647. He was careful to take no part in the king's trial and he was a keen sup-porter of the Restoration. His eldest son, Edward Montagu (1635–65) – who was approx-imately the same age as our diarist and would have been well known to him – was close to Charles II during the late 1650s and acted as an agent for communcations between him and other supporters of the king's return to England. Although Edward was killed

---

[1] A copy of the 2nd Earl of Manchester's letter to his son on his conversion to Catholicism is in BL MS Harley 1506/8. Walter Montagu was travelling in Italy at this period with the playwright and theatre-manager, Thomas Killigrew: Stoye, *English Travellers Abroad*, p. 159.

[2] Manchester, *Court and Society*, II, pp. 18–19. See also *Miscellanea spiritualia: or, Devout essayes ... by the honorable Walter Montagu* (1648).

[3] See p. 35 for Robert Bertie's letters home from his own continental tour (1648/9).

EDWARD MONTAGU, EARL OF SANDWICH.

OB. 1672.

FROM THE ORIGINAL OF SIR PETER LELY, IN THE COLLECTION OF

THE RIGHT HON^{BLE} THE COUNTESS OF SANDWICH.

London Published Decr 1 1827 by Harding & Lepard Pall Mall East.

Fig. 18. Admiral and General-at-Sea Edward Montagu (1625–72), 1st Earl of Sandwich (the cousin of Robert Montagu's father).

at Bergen in Norway in August 1665 during an attack on the Dutch East India Fleet, his younger brother, Ralph Montagu (c. 1638–1709), continued his branch of the family's prominence at the court of Charles II.[1] During the early 1660s Ralph served as Master of the Horse to the Duke of York; and he succeeded to his brother's post as Master of the Horse to the Queen in December 1665. He remained close to the royal family and was chosen to serve as ambassador extraordinary to the court of Louis XIV in January 1669. He succeeded his father as 3rd Baron Montagu of Boughton on 10 January 1684; and he was elevated to the peerage by King William III on 9 April 1689 as the 1st Earl Montagu (and became Duke of Montagu on 12 April 1705).

The final branch of the Montagu family to be mentioned her is that of Admiral and General at Sea Edward Montagu (1625–72), 1st Earl of Sandwich. He was the only surviving son of Sir Sidney Montagu (d. 1644), younger brother of Edward, 1st Lord Montagu of Boughton (d. 1644) and Sir Henry, 1st Earl of Manchester (d. 1642). His father, Sir Sidney, was expelled as an MP from the Long Parliament in 1642 as a royalist but Edward supported the Parliamentarians. This decision was probably due, in no small measure, to the views of his cousin, Edward Montagu, 2nd Earl of Manchester, and of his father-in-law, Lord Crew of Stene, whose daughter, Jemimah, he married in November 1642. In November 1643 Edward Montagu joined Manchester's army and in 1644 took part in the storming of Lincoln (6 May) and the Battle of Marston Moor (2 July). In 1645 he commanded a regiment in the New Model Army and fought at Naseby (14 June) and the storming of Bristol (10 September). Like his cousin, Edward, 2nd Earl of Manchester, he played no part in the second civil war or in the trial of the king.

Despite his youth, Edward Montagu was greatly admired and trusted by Cromwell who appointed him in January 1656 without any prior experience of seafaring (but jointly with the renowned Admiral Blake), as his general at sea. His (minimal) personal role in the taking of Spanish treasure ships from the West Indies was celebrated by Waller's panegyric poem, 'Of a War with Spain and Fight at Sea by General Montagu in the year 1656'. During 1657 and 1658 Montagu was in command of the English fleet in the Downs, operating against Dunkirk. He attended Cromwell's installation as Protector on 26 June 1657 and offered his support to his son's regime.

However, as has already been noted (see p. 74), another of his cousins, Edward (1616–84), son of the 1st Lord Montagu, was acting as an intermediary for King Charles II and he persuaded Montagu actively to support the Restoration. In February 1660 he was reappointed, jointly with George Monck (later Duke of Albermarle) as general of the fleet. His cousin Edward (1616–84) was sent to Holland to prepare for the king's return. On 8 May Charles II was proclaimed king and two days later Admiral Montagu was ordered to set sail to bring him back to England. On 23 May the king embarked at Scheveling on Montagu's flagship, formerly the *Naseby* (and hastily renamed the *Royal Charles*) and landed at Dover 25 May. Montagu was rewarded by being invested as a Knight of the Garter and on 12 July 1660 was created Earl of Sandwich. As Admiral of the Narrow Seas he was responsible for transporting various members of the royal family back to England, including the Princess Royal from Holland and the Queen Dowager from France; and in January 1661 he took both of them back to France. He carried the sceptre at the king's coronation on 23 April 1661 and on 19 June 1661 Admiral Montagu set sail as commander of the Mediterranean

---

[1] See Manchester, *Court and Society*, I, pp. 273–4, for Edward Montagu's problems at court in 1664, relating to his position as Master of the Horse to Queen Catherine, which prompted him to join the fleet at Bergen.

fleet to negotiate with the Algerines and to bring home the young queen, Catherine of Braganza.[1]

6. The Manuscript of Robert Montagu's Travels

The partly(?) autograph manuscript of Robert Montagu's travels bears on the verso of its cover the bookplate of the noted collector, Richard Rawlinson (1690–1755), and is now Bodleian Library, Oxford, MS Rawlinson D 76. To the top right of the bookplate is written and circled 'MSS.Rawl. Miscell. 76'; and in the top left corner is written (in another hand) '(12894)'[= Madan's Additional MS catalogue number]. The manuscript contains sixty-five folio leaves of which sixty-four bear handwritten text (leaf 48 is blank). Engravings, probably purchased during Montagu's travels, are inserted before folio 50 (a folded engraving of a performing elephant), f. 56 (the armless woman, 'Magdalena Rudolfs Thuinbuj von Stockholm'), and f. 63 (the arms of Ferdinando II). The diary appears to be written up to f. 27[r] in a large, and probably youthful, hand, which is very likely that of Robert Montagu himself. The sometimes awkward sentence-structure, repetitions and numerous minor corrections seem compatible with the written style of a fourteen-years old boy. However, at f. 27[v] the hand entirely changes to a smaller and noticeably more fluent script. Since the manuscript gives no indication as to the identity of this latter writer, no absolutely firm conclusions can be reached over the identity of this second hand. It could well be that of Mr Hainhofer, Montagu's travelling tutor, took over the daily recording of the journey.[2] Alternatively, if this diary was a fair copy compiled at some point after Montagu returned home, then this hand could be that of either a secretary, family member, or tutor. Overall, the manuscript is generally very neat in its compilation and it is possible that Bodl. MS Rawlinson D 76, rather than being the actual document compiled by Montagu during his itinerary, was a fair copy written out (partly by Montagu and then by a tutor or secretary) some time after his return to England from his rough papers and notes for his own reference or for ciculation among family and friends.[3]

There is no evidence on the manuscript itself as to the source from where (or when) the collector Richard Rawlinson originally obtained it. The bulk of the Rawlinson bequest came to the Bodleian Library in 1756 and it seems certain that MS Rawlinson D 76 was among these manuscripts.[4] The miscellaneous group of documents drawn together under 'Rawlinson D' were first arranged up to MS number 407 by Dr Philip Bliss, who formally left the library in 1828 but continued to live in Oxford. Other Rawlinson manuscripts, including 'Rawlinson C' and perhaps also some of 'Rawlinson D', were then catalogued by Stephen Reay, a sub-librarian from 1828 until 1861. Unfortunately, it is not known whether either Bliss or Reay followed Rawlinson's ordering of his own manuscripts (if any such

---

[1] The Earl of Sandwich died at sea on 28 May 1672 at the Battle of Solebay during the Third Anglo-Dutch War when a fireship destroyed his vessel, the *Royal James*. He had four daughters and six sons; the eldest, Edward, succeeded him as 2nd Earl of Sandwich.

[2] See p. 119 for Mr Hainhofer.

[3] The supposition that the manuscript was being compiled as a fair copy, either at home or towards the end of the journey, is supported by the fact that it suddenly breaks off in October 1652, halfway through a page and in mid-sentence, just after Montagu's visits to Augsburg and Seefeld. Since further space was available in the manuscript, it seems that the writer (i.e. the second hand in the manuscript) paused in the task of transcription, with the intention of returning to it later.

[4] Ian Philip, *The Bodleian Library in the Seventeenth and Eighteenth Centuries. The Lyell Lectures, Oxford 1980–81*, Oxford, 1983, pp. 94–8.

ordering was apparent to them when he began this large task), or if they simply imposed their own random ordering upon the 'Rawlinson C' and 'Rawlinson D' manuscripts.[1]

Since the Montagu family have continued in an unbroken line as the Earls and Dukes of Manchester until the present day, it might have been expected that this manuscript would have remained among their family papers at Kimbolton Castle. However, it is clear that MS Rawlinson D 76 was already in Richard Rawlinson's possession before 1755 and, therefore, an alternative provenance may be hypothesized. As already detailed (see p. 73), when the author of this travel diary, Robert Montagu, 3rd Earl of Manchester, died in 1683, his widow, Anne Yelverton Montagu, although then aged about sixty years, married shortly before 18 February 1689 her much younger relative by marriage, Charles Montagu (1661–1715), later Earl of Halifax. If she had retained in her personal possession her first husband's youthful travel diary (rather than giving it to one of their children), then it would have probably remained in Charles Montagu's own library after her death in 1698. It is very likely that Robert Montagu's account of his travels would have been of genuine interest to her second husband, who was of an ostentatiously intellectual bent. He was President of the Royal Society from November 1695 until November 1698 and he publicly cultivated various prominent literary figures, including Joseph Addison, William Congreve, and Matthew Prior. He chaired a committee of the House of Lords which periodically surveyed the state of the nation's official records; and the idea of purchasing the manuscript collections of Sir Robert Cotton to form a public library has been attributed to him. He was also an assiduous amateur poet and many of his verses were collected together in a posthumous edition, *The Works and Life of the Right Hon. Charles, late Earl of Halifax* (1715).

Although Charles Montagu, Earl of Halifax, had no legitimate children (and his earldom and viscounty became extinct upon his death), his barony of Halifax devolved unto his nephew, George Montagu, who was then created Viscount Sunbury and Earl of Halifax on 14 June 1715. This individual would have inherited many of his uncle's personal possessions and papers, including (probably) his library. He died in 1739 and there then ensued a major dispersal of his uncle's estate.[2] Charles Montagu's huge collection of prints, medals, and coins, for example, were sold off in 1740 and his papers and manuscripts relating to public affairs were auctioned in 1760, with other, smaller dispersals occurring between this period. It is possible, then, that Richard Rawlinson may have acquired the manuscript of Robert Montagu's travels, either directly from Halifax's estate, since he is known to have made various purchases at the sales of his books and papers, or via an intermediary, at some point after 1740.[3]

Certainly, Montagu's journal would have been of considerable interest to Richard Rawlinson who, after studies at St Paul's School, Eton, and St John's College, Oxford, had himself travelled between 1719 and 1726 through Holland, France, Germany, and Italy. Rawlinson made two distinct continental tours. He had only just crossed the Channel for

---

[1] Falconer Madan, *A Summary Catalogue of Western Manuscripts in the Bodleian Library at Oxford. Volume III (Collections received during the 18th Century)*, Oxford, 1895, III, pp. 177–9. Madan notes of the Rawlinson manuscripts: 'This comprehensive bequest overwhelmed the small staff of the library, and when the bulk came, in 1756, no attempt was made to set them in order'. See also William Dunn Macray, *Catalogi Codicum Manuscriptorum Bibliothecae Bodleianae*, Oxford, 1893.

[2] This George Montagu was the father of George Montagu Dunk, 2nd Earl of Halifax of the second creation. However, it seems that little of the 1st Earl of Halifax's personal estate, in terms of political papers and books from his library, came into the possession of this 2nd Earl of the second creation.

[3] William Dunn Macray, *Annals of the Bodleian Library, Oxford A.D. 1598–A.D. 1867*, London, Oxford, and Cambridge, 1868, p. 184.

the first time and was at Rouen when he learned in 1719 that he had been awarded an honorary DCL by the University of Oxford. He received the degree there by diploma on 30 June and then headed north to the Low Countries, being admitted to the universities of Utrecht and Leiden in the following September. He returned home to England in November. In June 1620 he set out once more on a much longer itinerary, which over the next six years took in much of Holland, France, Germany, Italy, Sicily, and Malta. He only returned home in 1726 after receiving news of the death of his brother, Thomas. Richard Rawlinson kept a series of small notebooks of his own journeys, in which he jotted down epitaphs, inscriptions, and accounts of places visited, and which are still preserved with his own manuscript collections at the Bodleian Library.[1] During the next thirty years, as he steadily increased the holdings of his own collections, Rawlinson was always keen to acquire manuscript accounts of the experiences of other English travellers, such as the two manuscripts of the travels of Robert Montagu (MS Rawlinson D 76) and Banaster Maynard (MS Rawlinson D 83) edited in this Hakluyt volume, as well as the diary of Robert Bargrave (MS Rawlinson C 799), who travelled widely in Turkey and Western Europe between 1647 and 1656 (published by the Hakluyt Society in 1999).

[1] Macray, *Annals*, 1868, pp. 168–9; Madan, *Summary Catalogue*, 1895, III, p. 177. See also Rawlinson's own diaries, MS Rawlinson D 1180–7.

EDITED TEXT

THE TRAVELS OF ROBERT MONTAGU, LORD MANDEVILLE
(April 1649–April 1654)

[f. 1ʳ]   A*nn*o   1649

The 3ᵈ of May in the name of God I beganne my journy for France, from London, and came that night to Sittyborne[1] at the post house. The next day I din'd at Canterberry at the 3ᵈ Kings.[2] After diner we went to see the fine Cathedrall Church in the which are several monuments of Bishops, Deans and others ecclesiasticall men that are buried there. There is also a fine glasse window now broken since these last troubles of Ingland for the which the french Embasadour ofered a great summe of money to transport it into france but could not obtaine it.[3] Under which church there is another where the french[4] preach. From thence wee came to Dover where wee lay'd at the George neare the sea side,[5] and the next morning we saw the Castel, which contains 30 akers of ground.[6] It hath 60 greate gunns amongst which there is one of 24 foate long, made at Utrecht in Holland in the yeare 1544 given to king Henry the eight by Charles the 5ᵗʰ Emperour of Germany. Its ordinary charge, as they told us, was eighteene pound of pouder and ten pound of lead, it weighes 9000 pound. There wee saw likewise the king's lodgings, a very deepe well which cannot be taken from them and in the chappele not farr of, a fine monument of marble where my Lord of Southamton governour of the sinke ports lies buried there. From which castel in a cleere morning or evening one may see Callés, Buline, Dunquerke, Graveling, also the shipps lying in the Downes.[7]

   [f. 1ᵛ] The next day following wee went in a biscay shaloop[8] to the Admirall in the

---

[1] 'May 3 London Sittyborne 4 Canterbery' in left-hand margin. Sittingbourne.

[2] Originally written 'Cantorberry' with the 'o' revised to 'e'.

[3] On 30 April 1649, a few days before Montagu's departure, a parliamentary ordinance abolished deans and chapters, eight years after Parliament had first proposed doing so. Evelyn (1641), II, p. 76: 'I visited the Cathedrall, now in greatest splendor, those famous Windoes being intire, since demolish'd by the Phanatiques'. See Richard Culmer, *Cathedral News from Canterbury* (1644). Culmer himself scaled a 60-foot ladder to smash sections of the windows with his pike. See *A History of Canterbury Cathedral*, ed. Patrick Collinson, Nigel Ramsay, and Margaret Sparks, Oxford, 1995, pp. 194–203.

[4] 'french' added above.

[5] 'Dover 5' in left-hand margin.

[6] See William Darell, *The History of Dover Castle* (1786).

[7] Calais, Boulogne, Dunkirk, Gravelines, and the Downs.

[8] 'biscay shaloop', biscay sloop, a small one-masted fore-and-aft-rigged vessel with mainsail and jib, especially useful in the rough seas of the Bay of Biscay. A 'sloop-of-war' was a small warship with about 20 guns on the upper deck only, comparable to a modern-day cutter.

Downes which was Colonel Deane[1] then commander in cheefe; to whome after having delivered our order from the parl*i*ament, for a convoy into france, wee went[2] for Deale[3] to the post house in which place there is 3 strong castels neare the sea side equally distant one from the other where of wee saw two, Deale and Wamouth castell, in the seconde of which I had 5 gunns given mee by the governour of the castel as my coming out.[4] After having din'd in the said towne the Admiral sent a boat to fetch us a board the Nonesuch frigat[5] apointed by him for to transport us to Diepe, commanded by Captaine Mildmay[6] having 36 peeces of ordonance and a 150 men in it. The next day morning about two of the clock being sunday wee set saile, with a very prosperous wind and faire weather, and coming within a mile of Diepe wee tooke our leaves of the Captaine, who after wee had entred into a french shalop which came to fetch us a shoare, he tooke his farwell of us by letting loose several gunns, and so wee[7] happily landed about 5 of the clock at Diepe[8] being the 7 of May old stile or else the 27 according to the[9] new and french account,[10] where wee lay at the signe of the Prince of Orange.

Where having made noe stay at all because of my going againe away the next morning for company sake to Rouan[11] I saw but little, [f. 2ʳ] onely at my entrance I observed the towne to bee seated betweene very narrow hills almost at the entrance of the sea, whereof it is beaten on the north-side. Its haven is very suer[12] but withall narrow and closse. The marriners of this towne are held to bee the best and most venturous of any part in france and the inhabitants thereof likewise renowned for their navigations in very farre countryes.[13] Here are also

---

[1] Richard Dean (1610–53), Admiral and General-at-Sea, had commanded Parliamentary artillery at Naseby (1645) and served as a commissioner for the trial of King Charles I (1649). In the same year he was appointed as General-at-Sea and was responsible for the protection of the coast from Portsmouth to Milford Haven. He served as a Major-General at the Battle of Worcester (1651) and was Commander-in-Chief of the Parliamentary army in Scotland (1652). He was involved with Admiral Blake in the Battle off Portland (1653) but was killed in action off Solebay in the same year.

[2] 'went' added above.

[3] 'Deale 6' in left-hand margin.

[4] Montagu is referring here to the three castles of Deal, Sandown, and Walmer, all built by King Henry VIII within the modern town of Deal. Sandown Castle was later destroyed by the sea. The five-gun salute granted to Montagu would have been in recognition of his father's status.

[5] The first *Nonsuch* had been built for Queen Elizabeth's fleet in 1584 and was still in service in 1636. The second *Nonsuch*, on which Montagu sailed, was built in 1646 (389 tons, 98 feet long, 34 guns). The Summer and Winter Guard lists of 1647 record its captains as, respectively, William Thomas and Richard Willoughby. Most famously, in July 1649 the *Nonsuch* and the *Garland* captured the royalist vessel *Santa Theresa*. In July 1653, under the command of Thomas Penrose, it also saw action in the Battle of Lowestoft. The *Nonsuch* was wrecked in the Bay of Gibraltar in 1665. J. R. Powell, *The Navy in the English Civil War*, 1962, pp. 215–17.

[6] Captain Mildmay was a highly experienced captain in the parliamentarian fleet, having previously commanded a small vessel called the *Revenge* (1643), the 6th-rate *Kentish* (1646), the 6th-rate *Peter*, and the 4th-rate *Providence* (1647–8). Powell, *Navy*, pp. 199–221.

[7] 'wee' added above.

[8] 'Diepe 7' in left-hand margin.

[9] 'the' added above.

[10] Although Montagu refers to the date as 7 May (Old Style) or 27 May (New Style), he was clearly confused since there was only ten days difference between the two calendars in the seventeenth century. He probably meant 7 (OS) and 17 (NS).

[11] Rouen.

[12] 'suer', sure.

[13] The seafaring tradition of Dieppe is examined in detail in Michel C. Guibert, *Mémoires pour servir à l'histoire de la ville de Dieppe*, 2 vols, Dieppe, Paris, and Rouen, 1878 [written 1761–4].

Fig. 19. Anonymous 17th-century engraving of Dieppe.

to bee seene divers shops fil'd with great variety of rare turning workes of Whalebones, Ivory, Tortoisshells and the like.[1]

Munday 8 of may I went to dine at Totes[2] a little village standing alone in large fildes with great trees round about being half way to Rowan; and soe passing through another little village caled Malaune[3] where I found very deepe and fowle way. I arrived at Rowan at the signe of the quadran de mer or sea compasse at one M[r] Gilloting.[4] From Deipe to this place they count it 12 french leages or a daye's journy.

[f. 2[v]] I saw at Rowan[5] first the chiefe church which is caled our Ladyes, very faire and strongly built both within and without. It is all covered with lead, having 3 severall towers[6] the biggest is call'd the butter tower built by the Cardinal of Amboise of the impost which was layd uppon butter and eggs by the Pope to have leave to eate them dyring lent, in the which is the biggest bell in all france 13 foote hight, 32 foote broad, 11 foote in diameter and wighes 40000 pound and is called Amboises because of George of Amboise, Cardinal and Archbishops of Rowan.[7] The highest is caled the Pyramid having 600 steps up and it is covered with guilt lead very artificially done upon which there is the word

[1] The trade in carving ivory and tortoise shells is examined in Guibert, *Dieppe*, I, pp. 218–26; and it was praised by John Evelyn (1644), II, p. 124: 'This place exceedingly abounds in workemen that make and sell curiosities of Ivory and Tortoise shells, in which they turne, and make many rare toyes; & indeed whatever the East Indys afford of Cabinets, Purcelan, natural & exotic rarities are here to be had with abundant choyce'. For the collection of such items by English travellers, see p. 37ff.

[2] 'Totes 8' in left-hand margin. Tôtes, although a small and drab town, was a regular post stop on the route between Dieppe and Rouen.

[3] 'Malaune' in left-hand margin. Malaunay.

[4] Evelyn (1644), II, p. 124, stayed at the White Cross. Other inns popular with English visitors included the Ville D'Anvers and the Bon Pasteur. See Stoye, *English Travellers Abroad*, p. 284.

[5] 'Rowan 9' in left-hand margin.

[6] The gothic cathedral church of Notre-Dame. See André Chastel et al., *Histoire générale des églises de France*, 5 vols, Paris, 1966–71, IV.B, pp. 136–42; and Evelyn (1644), II, p. 122.

[7] The Tour de Beurre was built from the sale of indulgences to eat butter during Lent and was completed in 1507. See Somerset (1611), p. 61. The 'Georges d'Amboise' bell, cast by Jean le Machon, was thirty feet in circumference, ten feet high, and weighed 36,000 pounds. It fractured in 1586. It was also described by Heylin (1656), p. 21, and Mortoft (1658), p. 2. In 1793 the Revolutionaries melted it down into cannon. Fragments were made into commemorative medals, bearing the inscription: 'Monument de Vanité / Détruit pour l'utilité; / L'an 2 de égalité'.

God written in ancient carecters which shews that the english built it.[1] I saw likeuise the treasury and church ornaments which where very richly embrodered with pearles and pretious stones; alsoe a stately tabernacle of silver guilt, 2 candlestickes of christal of rock set in gold with diamonds round about them, in the midle two clocks, also a miter of pearles and diamonds.[2] From thenc I went to see the bridge made of boates over the river of Seine which runes closse by this city.[3] Upon which river ships of very great burdens come up to the towne which makes this city being the cheifest of all Normandy very commodious for trading though not hansomely built, the houses being for the most part covered with slate which makes it looke soe darke and melancoly. [f. 3ʳ] I saw the Parliament house, the mint and the place where the maide of Orleans was burnt by the English.[4]

This citty, because it is an Archbishoprick and seat of one of *the* Parliaments of france, as also for its bignes and great trafick, holdes the ranck of one of the cheifest in the kingdome. It is seated on one side on the river Siene. On the east it hath some other little rivers which entring into it doe water certaine streets upon which are severall mills and doe discharge themselfes into the Seine. It hath a bridg upheld by 13 arches which was one of the finest in France but now is broken, where the ships which comes from the occean doe land on the one side of it and boates coming from Paris, on the other.[5] On the east and south side the city is commanded by neighbouring mountaines.

[f. 3ᵛ] The 10/20 may I parted from Rouan by water up the river Seine in a great boate which I hier'd to goe to Paris and coming to Pont de l'Arche,[6] I shott the bridge where there is a strong fort which commands the river soe that noething can passe neither up nor downe without its leave; which place was very considerable in these late stirrs during the seige of

[1] Evelyn (1644), II, pp. 122–3: 'The Cathedrall of the Citty is Nostre Dame, built as they acknowledge by the English, and indeed some English words graven in Gotic Characters upon the Front seeme to confirm it'. Montagu's reference to the tower called the 'Pyramid' echoes Evelyn (1644), II, p. 123: 'It has 3 steeples with a Pyramid', which is a mistranslation from Claude de Varenne's popular guidebook, *Le Voyage de France* (1643 edition), describing 'la tour de Beurre & la pyramide'. The so-called 'pyramid', built c. 1514–44, was replaced in the 1820s by a metal spire. Evelyn based much of his own account of his travels in France upon Varenne's descriptions (which, in turn, were heavily dependent upon an earlier guidebook, *Itinerarium Galliae* by Jodocus Sincerus, also known as Justus Zinzerling). This verbal echo, along with other close parallels to Evelyn's account of his 1644 visit, suggests that Montagu also had a copy of *Le Voyage de France* to hand. See also p. 62.

[2] Francis Mortoft was also given a tour of the church's treasures and was especially struck by the lavish vestments: 'There wee saw many Priest Garments, al laid about with Jewels and Pearles, one whereof is esteemed to be worth 50,000 Crownes, and A Mitre which the Bishop weares on great Feast dayes, that is so full of al manner of precious stones that it is esteemed inestimable' (1658), pp. 2–3.

[3] Evelyn (1644), II, p. 122: 'There stand yet the ruines of a magnificent bridge of stone now supplyd by one of boates onely'.

[4] Le Palais de Justice was the seat of the exchequer and parliament of Normandy. Parts of the building were destroyed by bombing in 1944. See G. de Stabenrath, *Le Palais de Justice de Rouen*, Rouen, 1895; Evelyn (1644), II, pp. 123–4; and Heylyn (1656), pp. 23–4. The place du Vieux-Marché, where Jeanne d'Arc was burnt at the stake on 30 May 1431, is now the site of the Église Jeanne d'Arc (completed in 1979), built in the shape of an upturned boat with early 16th-century stained glass from the former church of St-Vincent.

[5] On the site of the present day Pont Boïeldieu (at the south end of the rue Grand Pont) was a large stone bridge known as the 'Pont Mathildé' in honour of the Empress Mathilde, with thirteen arches and houses on top. It was seriously damaged in March 1564 and although it remained a major local landmark, another wooden structure was erected between 1626 and 1630. See Somerset (1611), p. 60; Evelyn (1644), II, p. 122; Reresby (1654), p. 2; and Heylyn (1656), p. 20.

[6] 'Ponte de l'Arche 10' in left-hand margin. Pont-de-l'Arche, so named after a bridge built there in the 9th century by Charles le Chauvre.

Paris.[1] From thence I past by Gallion where the Archbishop of Rouan hath a fine house.[2] Soe going all night by moone light, I din'd the next day att Vernon,[3] where I shott another bridge and 5 leagues off I saw the Marquis of Rhosnis his fine house, his garden and parke hard by the river side.[4] And I came that night to lie at Mante where I saw the cheife church which is big but built after the old fashon.[5] The next day morning passing by another towne called Meulan, I came and din'd at Poissy[6] being six leagues off of Paris, from which place in the afternoone I took coach and after having past 4 severall bridges over the river Seine, came to Paris being friday the 11/21 may. I lay in the street of Aniou at the signe of the Angel at one Madam Turgis her house a protestant widow. [f. 4ʳ]

Paris[7] the Capitall towne of france and seate of the kings is for its bignes call'd a little world. It stands in the Ile of France and is devided into 3 parts towit, the City, the Towne and the University, separed one from another by the river of Seine which deviding it selfe in two parts makes two Ilands, in the midle of its channel, one call'd the Ile of our Lady, the other of the Palace.[8] And these 3 are joyned together by several bridges, that part which is caled the Towne is the greatest of the 3, towards the east and north it hath the shape of a half moone, having the river Seine of one side and its walles and diches on the other. It hath seven gates to witt Sᵗ. Honorè, Sᵗ. Anthony, Sᵗ. Martin, Sᵗ. Denis, Montmartir, the neue gate and that of the Temple. There are also 5 subbourbs towit Sᵗ. Anthony, Sᵗ. Martin, Sᵗ. Denis, Sᵗ. Honorè, of the Temple; 4 of which gates are lead into the principall streets of the towne,[9]

The City is betwixt the towne and the University inclosed by the river Seine in the forme of an Iland which is the most ancient part of Paris and is as the hart of the City.[10]

The University is the hiest part of it, and seemes to cover the rest in the shape of a hatt,

---

[1] Montagu is referring here to the outbreak of the civil disturbances or Frondes (1648–53; the *fronde* was a Parisian toy sling for pellets, used by the rebels for breaking windows), which broke out during the minority of King Louis XIII as an attempt to check the growing power of royal government and, more specifically, as an expression of resistance to the policies of the queen regent, Anne of Austria, and her chief minister, Cardinal Jules Mazarin (and prior to him, Cardinal Richelieu). The first civil war, known as the Fronde of the Parlement, stemmed from the Parlement of Paris's refusal to approve proposed royal revenue measures in the spring of 1648. Following fraught negotations throughout the summer the Queen and Mazarin ordered on 26 August the arrest of two outspoken members of the parliament but an immediate uprising in Paris ensured their release. Conflict flared up again in January 1649, leading to a total blockade of Paris. The Parlement, however, refused to surrender and hostilities were temporarily ceased with the Peace of Rueil (1 April 1649), which made considerable concessions to Parlement. The second civil war, known as the Fronde of the Princes, was headed by the Great Condé and lasted from January 1650 until September 1653.

[2] 'Gallion' in left-hand margin. Gaillon, where Cardinal Georges d'Amboise had built a huge château during the first decade of the 16th century (largely demolished in 1798). See Stoye, *English Travellers Abroad*, p. 286.

[3] 'Vernon 11' in left-hand margin. Vernon.

[4] Maximilien de Béthune, baron de Rosny and duc de Sully (1560–1641), was born at nearby Rosny and built a large château there between 1595 and 1610.

[5] 'Mante' in left-hand margin. Mantes. The town's church of Notre-Dame bears some striking similarities to Notre-Dame at Paris and dates from the same period (under construction from late 12th until early 13th centuries.

[6] 'Meulan' and 'Poissy 12' in left-hand margin. Meulan and Poissy.

[7] 'Paris 13.' in left-hand margin.

[8] Evelyn (1644), II, p. 92: 'The City is divided into thre Parts, whereof the Towne is greatest: The City lyes betwixt it and the University in forme of an Iland', translated from Varennes, pp. 176–7. The two islands are usually known as L'Ile de Saint-Louis and L'Ile de la Cité (or L'Isle du Palais). See Fig. 5, p. 34, and Fig. 12, p. 50.

[9] Montagu's incomplete account of the city gates and suburbs of Paris is carelessly derived from Varennes. Using the same source, Evelyn (1644), II, p. 94, notes: 'The Suburbs are those of St. Denys, Honoré, St. Marcel, Jaques, St. Michel, St. Victoire, and St. Germaines which last is the largest and where the nobility and Persons of best quality are seated'. However, even Evelyn's summary of Varennes is heavily selective and imprecise.

[10] 'The Citty' in left-hand margin. This description is translated directly from Varennes, pp. 176–7.

towards the south and west and is the least part of Paris. It is seated in the river Seine compryhending in it all the colledges, which are 63, and most ancient Abyes, Monesteries, alsoe bookesellers, printers, and bookebinders.[1]

[f. 4ᵛ] In it there are 8 gates,[2] Sᵗ. Bernard, Sᵗ. Victor, Sᵗ. Marcel, Sᵗ. James, Sᵗ. Michel, Sᵗ. Germain, of Bussy, and of Nesle, 5 suburbs Sᵗ. James Sᵗ. Marcel, Sᵗ. Victor, Sᵗ. Michel, Sᵗ. Germing where the fairest buildings are.

In that part which is caled the towne, I saw first the new bridge[3] in the midle of which is erected King Henry the 4ᵗʰ. his statue, a horse-back of brasse workt with as much art as the peices of antiquity, of the which Rome bragues. It was sent by Ferdinand the first, Great Duke of Florence, and Cosmus his son. On the foure corners are graved on the brasse, the victories of this Great Prince with lattin inscriptions.[4] At the end towards the Louver there is a poump that raiseth up the water of the river into a fountaine, which is called the Samaritan,[5] where the Samaritain woman powers out water to our Saviour. Over it there is a very fine clock, which showes the houres of the day in the forenoone by going up, and those of the afternoone by going downe, with the course of the Sunne and Moone uppon our Horizon by an apple of ebony; also the moneth of the[6] years and the 12 signes of the zodiack, within the house there is a fine grott made of all kind of sheles, through the which the water runnes making a very great noise, it is conveyed to the Louver, [f. 5ʳ] to the Palace Royall and to the garden of the Thuilleries. There is likewise a fine chamber adorned with curious pictures and greate basings and potts of Italian earth, rare for their bignes. There is below also a very neate cabynett of rarityes, which consist of many pretious orientall stones, severall shels and pieces of corrall both white and black, one of white, that hath severall branches and is 23 thumbs high.

The next which I saw was the Louvre,[7] the building is very faire and great, Philipp Augustus who invironned Paris, with walls[8] gave it its foundation, severall of his successors did both increse and augment it. Henery the 4ᵗʰ did build the gallerie which joynes this Palace to the Thuilleries, which is 59 paces loung, the half of it is finely carved and painted,

---

[1] 'The University' in left-hand margin. Yet again, Montagu bases his description on Varennes, 180, although he is more accurate than Evelyn who mistakenly states that there are 65 colleges (rather than the 63 cited by Varennes).

[2] 'Gates' in left-hand margin.

[3] 'New bridge' in left-hand margin. Evelyn (1644), II, p. 92: 'Over the river Seine is built a stately bridg (call'd Pont Neuf) by Hen 3d 1578, finished [c.1606] by Hen: 4th his Successor'. See F. Boucher, *Le Pont Neuf*, Paris, 1925. It was the first bridge in Paris to be built without houses. It is also described by Coryat (1608), I, p. 171; Heylyn (1656), p. 91; and Mortoft (1658), p. 4.

[4] Evelyn (1644), II, pp. 192–3: 'On the Middle of this stately bridge upon one side stands that famous statue of Henry le grand on horse-back … The statue and horse is of Copper, being the Worke of the greate John di Bolognia, & sent from Florence by Ferdinando the first, and Cosimo the second, Unkle & Cousin to Mary di Medices wife of Henry, whose statue it represents'. Although Giovanni Bologna (d. 1608) began the statue it was completed by Pietro Tacca (d. 1640). It was erected in 1614 but destroyed in 1792.

[5] 'Fountaine Samaritan' in left-hand margin. La Samaritaine was originally situated in the Place Dauphine. It was one of the earliest hydraulic pumps, designed by Lintlaër for Henri IV to supply water to the Louvre and Tuileries. It was demolished in 1813. Evelyn (1644), II, p. 93: 'At foote of this Bridge is a water-house, at the front whereof a great height is the Story of our B: Saviour and the Woman of Samaria powring Water out of a bucket; above a very rare dyal of severall motions with a chime'.

[6] 'the' added above.

[7] 'Louvre' in left-hand margin.

[8] 'gave walls to' deleted and 'invironned' and 'with walls' added above. Most of the walls of Paris at this period dated from the mid-16th century but the late-12th-century wall of Philippe II Auguste (1179–1223) was still largely intact on the Left Bank.

Fig. 20. 'Veüe et Perspective de la Galerie du Louvre, dans laquelle sont les Portrans des Royes des Reynes et des plus Illustres du Royaume' (c. 1650–55) (Israel Silvestre).

the other is yet unfinished.[1] Here[2] I saw likewise the haule of Antiquities, which is all of marble and jasper, where there are 9 peeces very considerable for theire antiquity and workemanship.[3] The first and in most esteeme for antiquity sake is the Diana of Ephesus, the same which the Ephesians worshiped and through the which the Divill spake, which stands at the upper end of the haule made of exquisite marble, and soe rarely done that nothing can surpasse it.[4] The next is an More worshiped by the Ethiopians, also a Mercury worshiped [f. 5ᵛ] by the ancient Gaules upon the hill Montmartir. The 4th. is a Venus of Medicis, sent by the Greate Duke of Florence to his sister Queene Mary of Medicis. After folowes an Appollo very finely done. At the end of the haulle are 2 statues of Henery the 4th next is that of David with the head of Goliath at his feete. In the middle of the haule are tow other excellent peices, one on a pedistall where there is Time, Thruth, Envie and Strenth. Thruth is represen[ted] by a man, time by a woman having an houer glasse in hir hand, envie likewise by a woman with tow faces and strenth by a satyre. The other is a sphere, of brasse guilded, made at blois of and immense bignes, all these statues are of marble.[5]

[1] François I had demolished the medieval fortress, the Château du Louvre, and began plans in 1541 for his own palace. The buildings were significantly extended by Henri IV and Louis XIII and the quadrangle was completed during the minority of Louis XIV. Sir Charles Somerset visited the Louvre during the building of Henri IV's additions and left a detailed description of its then incomplete state (Somerset (1611), pp. 70–72, 88, 91). It is also described by Evelyn (1644), II, pp. 103–7 (unusually offering his first-hand observations rather than relying upon Varennes); Symonds (1649), p. 225; and Mortoft (1658), pp. 5–6. See Figs 20–21.

[2] 'here' added above.

[3] Evelyn also describes the 'Hall of Antiquities' (now the 'Salle d'Auguste'): 'descending hence we were let into a lower very large roome call'd the Sale des Antiques, which is a Vaulted Cimelia destin'd onely to set statues in' (1644), II, p. 104–5.

[4] This 'Diana of Ephesus' is now in the Louvre. Evelyn (1644), II, p. 105, also particularly admired this carving: 'that so celebrated Dian of the Ephesians said to be the same which utterd Oracles in that renowned Temple'.

[5] This sphere may be the 'the huge Globe which is hung up in Chaynes', described by Evelyn (1644), II, p. 105.

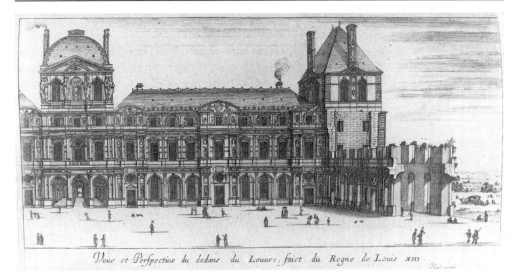

Fig. 21. 'Veue et Perspective du dedans du Louvre, faict du Regne de Louis XIII' (c. 1650–55) (Israel Silvestre).

From thence I went to the Palace Royall which was built by the Cardinall of Richelieu. The building is foure square and round about it are ships, carved very finely because hee built it when he was Admirall.[1] Almost all the chambers are guilt, especially the Queene great chamber which is richly guilt and rarely painted by Italian masters. The seeleling cannot be anouf admired[2] for its excellent carving. In the king's gallery are the pictures of all the famous men in France which governed during the time of the Cardinall. In the midle of it is a dore into the Chappel which is little but very pretty and richly guilt having on [f. 6ʳ] one side of the Alter the picture of John the Baptist and on the other, that of the Virgin Mary with our savior in her armes, made of exquisite marble soe lively done that every body does admire them. These tow peeces were given by the Pope Urban the 8ᵗʰ. to the Cardinal of Richlieu for a new yeares guift.

Luxembourgs house[3] was built by Queene Mary of Medicis.[4] This stately building together with its large court, neat gardens and fountaines doe showe indeed the ingenuity of this great Princesse. The roomes are in generall large, richly guilt, and adorned with fine pictures. Her closett excells the others for its painting and plentifull guilding, round about is represented the history of her marriage, together with her landing at Marseilles. A little

[1] 'Palais Cardinal' in left-hand margin. The Palais-Royal (the name is often applied to the surrounding area as well as to the palace itself) was originally known as the Palais-Cardinal, having been built between 1624 and 1639 for Cardinal Richelieu (who died there in 1642). It was bequeathed to Louis XIII and was first called the Palais-Royal when the queen regent, Anne of Austria (d. 1666), resided there from 1643.

[2] 'The seeleling cannot be anouf admired' offers a characteristic example of the phonetic eccentricities of Montagu's schoolboy spelling habits. Evelyn (1644), II, p. 134: 'The Gallerys, paintings there of the most illustrious Persons of both Sexes, the Queenes Bathes, Presence (in which the rich carved and gilded roofe) Theater, & large Garden, in which is an ample Fountaine, Grove, & Maille; are all worthy of remarke'.

[3] 'Luxembourg' in left-hand margin.

[4] The Palais du Luxembourg was built between 1615 and 1627 by Salomon de Brosse, for Queen Marie de Médicis, who is reputed to have wished for a palace which would remind her of her birthplace, the Pitti Palace at Florence. In 1612 she acquired the adjacent mansion of the duc de Tingry-Luxembourg (the 'Petit Luxembourg'), from which the name of the new palace was derived. See also Mundy (1620), p. 126.

lower are severall cabinets lined with velvet, where shee ust to put her private things, on the one side[1] are nothing but windowes all of christall. The ground is of Ciprus wood cutt in severall roses, none like the other and inlaide with silver. There is a dore out of it which goes into the gallery which is large, rarely guilded, a top, and round about the History[2] of the cheefe action in her life, rarely painted by Itilian masters.[3]

The Place Royall is foure square, where in the midle is Lewis the 13 a horse-back in the fashon of a conquerour. It is of brasse rarely done, and putt uppon a pedistall of fine marble.[4] In this place was the Palace of Turnell built by Charles the 5th [f. 6v] and pul'd downe by the command of Queene Cathrin of Medicis after the death of Henery the 2d. her husband, who died there of a wound which he received of the Earle of Mountgommery, runing a tilt together in the street of St Anthony; and at this present the Kings have such kind of sports uppon extraordinary occations,[5]

The great Chastelet remarkable for its antiquity was built, by Julian the Apostat Governour of the Gaulles to serve him for a Castell where he gathered his tributes. It is now the ordinary seat of the Provost of Paris, who is cheefe administrator of the Justice of this great towne, and ordinary judge of all the differences betwene the Citticens, and all others that reside within the jurisdiction of this presidiall Court of the Chastellet.[6]

The towne house was first founded and built in the raigne of Francis the first in the yeare 1535.[7] Henry the 4th did repare it from the bottom to the topp. The forepart of it is of a very fine structure, and in nothing inferiour to that of the Louver, where Henery the 4th is on horse back. Here the Provost of the Marchants and the 4 Echevins[8] have theirs seat. To these 5 grave men, Philipp the 2d surnamed for his glorious actions Augustus,[9] as he prepared himself for to goe to the holy Land [f. 7r] gave the goverment of his towne of Paris, the which are changed every tow years and others substituted in their place. These are nobly desended and when theire office is finished they are made knights. They have 26

[1] 'side' added above.

[2] 'History' added above.

[3] Evelyn (1644), II, p. 128: 'The Gallery is of the Painting of P: Rubens, being the history of the Foundresses life, rarely designed and greate'. This pictorial series is now in the Louvre.

[4] 'Place Royall' in left-hand margin. The Place Royal was laid out in its present form for Henri IV and opened in 1605. The equestrian statue of Louis XIII (dating from 1825) replaced the one viewed by Montagu, which was destroyed in 1792. The Place Royal was renamed the Place des Vosges in 1799.

[5] The square of the Place des Vosges is built upon the site of the gardens of the Palais des Tournelles, the residence of the Duke of Bedford (d. 1435), Regent of France (and the third son of King Henry IV), after the death of King Henry V (d. 1422). On 10 July 1559 King Henri II of France died after being accidentally hit on the head by the lance of Gabriel, comte de Montgomery, while watching a tournament there, celebrating the marriages of his daughters, Elizabeth and Margaret, to Philip II of Spain and Emmanuel Philibert of Savoy. The palace was then abandoned by his widow, Catherine de' Medici.

[6] 'Chaselet' in left-hand margin. On the Place du Châtelet, at the northern side of the Pont au Change, once stood the Grand Châtelet, a fortress gateway to the Cité. It was formerly the headquarters of the Provost of Paris and the Guild of Notaries. Dating originally from the 12th century, it was extensively rebuilt in 1509 and 1684 and was finally demolished during the first decade of the 19th century. The Petit Châtelet stood at the southern approach of the Petit Pont and was demolished in 1782.

[7] 'Towne house' in left-hand margin. The Hôtel de Ville was built during the 1530s and extensively renovated between 1608 and 1610. It was burned down by the Communards in 1871.

[8] Échevins, municipal functionaries or town councillors of the highest rank in French and Belgian towns. They were royal appointees at Paris and, elsewhere, the equivalent to English aldermen.

[9] Philippe II Auguste (1179–1223). In 1095 Pope Urban II preached the First Crusade at Clermont and Philippe II was a major figure in the Third Crusade against Saladin in the Holy Land in 1191. Montagu is referring here to his 'Testament' of 1190, which provided for the government of his kingdom during his absence.

counsellours, and 10 sergents, which doth assist them. To these are joyn'd the 16 Quarteniers, devided among so many Quarturs of the towne,[1] which doth embrasse all the old Pariches, which are 33 in number. Every one of these quarters have a certain number of Commissioners, The Quarteniers have under them, the Cinquenteniers, which are ordained and appointed over the Dizeniers, all for the police, rest and tranquillity of the Inhabitants, against all seditious men. These officers doe judge of the differences which arise in selling of corne, wine, wood, hay, and uppon all other things[2] which come both by Land and by water and sett a certain prise uppon them.

Within the Citty is the Palace[3] where the antients kings were use to dwel, rebuilt a new and much augmented by Enquirrand of Marigny, superintendant of the King's revenew,[4] or Finances in the raigne of Phillip the 4th. otherwise called the Bel,[5] who first did setle and establish his Parliament there in the yeare 1302 being afore ambulatory and following the kings where soever they went. This Parlement is compos'd of the great chamber, of 5 chambers [f. 7ᵛ] of Inquest, of 2 of Request, of that of the Tournelle and of the Royall chamber. It is in the great chamber that the king hath his List de Justice, having on both sides of him his Peers both Ecclesiasticall and Secular. In this court are admitted all the Archbishops and Bishops, but have noe deliberative voice except the Archbishop of Paris and the Abbot of St Denis which two are Counsellours in Parliament as all the Princes Duckes and Peers of france.[6]

The Chamber call'd les Stydes, was instituted by Charles the 4th. after[7] that the kingdome of France was in peace and that he had introduced severall taxes which he call'd Aydes or Subsides, for to maintain his revenues.[8]

The Chamber call'd des Comptes is over against the Holy Chappel which was instituted by Philipp the Bel.

The chamber call'd of[9] the Felict was instituted by Henry the 4th. in favour of the Protestants to doe them justice without any suspition or hatred. It is composed of a President and of 16 counsellours of the Parliament. All these chambers mentioned are inclosed in the circuit of this pallace.

[f. 8ʳ] The Haule call'd the Procurator's Haule is large and spatious. The roofe is upheld with a ranck of pillers in the midle. It was burnt in the yeare 1618 and since rebuilt. There was a table of marble, esteemed one of the finest peices of Europe which was burnt by the

---

[1] The *quarteniers* were responsible for the quarters or administrative wards of the city.

[2] 'things' added above.

[3] 'Palace' in left-hand margin. The Palais de Justice on the 'Île de la Cité, the royal, legal, and administrative centre of Paris. Louis IX (1226–70) renovated an earlier palace on the same site. From 1431 the Palais was the exclusive seat of the Parlement. This Old Palace was significantly damaged by major fires in 1618, 1737, and 1776.

[4] Enguerrand de Marigny (1260–1315), chamberlain and foreign policy adviser to Philippe IV, le Bel. In 1313/14 he was appointed in charge of the royal treasury and the king's auditing department, the *chambre de comptes*. Later charged with corruption and hated for his ruthless levying of taxes, he was executed soon after the accession of Louis X.

[5] Philippe IV, le Bel (1285–1314).

[6] Evelyn (1644), II, p. 98: 'At one of the Ends stands an Alter were daily Masse is sayd, within are severall Chambers, Courts, Treasures &c above that most rich and glorious Sale de L'Audiens; the Chamber of St. Lewes, and other Superior Courts where the Parliament sits richly guilt on Embossed carvings & fretts guilt with gold & exceedingly beautified'.

[7] 'after' added above.

[8] 'Cour des stydes' in left-hand margin. Charles IV, le Bel (1322–28). For this and other courts, see Henri Stein, *Le Palais de Justice et la Sainte-Chapelle de Paris*, Paris, 1912.

[9] 'of' added above.

fier, about which the Constable, the Marshalls and the Admiral had their Jurisdiction, and where the kings came to keepe the festival day of their mariage and of their first entry into this citty. Within the Haule are divers booksellers, and round about the pallace are galleries with shopes on both sides of them, which is like the Echange att London.[1]

For the University it was heretofore spread all over Paris until that the Queene Joane of Navarra wife to Phillipp the 4th. had caused to bee built the sumpteous Colledge of Navarra; then all the Doctors did chuse together this part of the towne as being the highest and fittest for learning.[2] I saw the Colledge of Sorbonne which is the ancientest built by Robert of Serbonne and since rebuilt after the moderne fashion by Cardinall of Richelieu, I likewise saw severall others. [f. 8ᵛ] For the Churches[3] in general there be 69, the most famous is that of our Lady, which is in that part call'd the Citty. It was designed and contrived by King Robert and was brought to its perfection by Phillipp Augustus.[4] The foundation are layed uppon pyles, this great body is sustained by 120 great pillars, which makes 5 great allyes. The lenght of it is 174 paces, its breath of 60, and its hight of a 100. The Quire is built all of stone uppon the which are graved the Histories both of the old and new Testament. This church hath 45 chappells and 11 gates. Over the the 3 greatest of its frontispeece are[5] in stone the statues of 26 kings from Childebert until Phillipp Augustus. The tow great towers where wee went up to oversee this large city have[6] 389 stepps, where there is 8 great bells and 8 other lesser ones in the litle steepel. As this church is the first in dignity in all the king-dome soe it is honoured with many fine dignityes of Arch-Deacons, great vicars, and served by a great number of Canons priest and chappellains in all a 127.[7] The Holy chapel which is within the pallace was built in the yeare 1242 by Saint Lewis king of france.[8] The low [f. 9ʳ]

[1] Evelyn (1644), II, pp. 98, drawing much of his historical material from Varennes: 'The Palais (as they call it above) was built in the time of Philip the faire, noble and spacious; and the great Hall annex'd to it bravely arch'd with stone having a range of Pillars in the middle, round which, and at the sides, are shops of all kinds; especialy bookesellers; the other side is full of pewes for the Clearkes of the Advocates, which (as ours at Westminster) swarme here'.

[2] 'University' in left-hand margin. Montagu's description is heavily reliant upon Varennes, pp. 183–4, as is Evelyn (1644), II, p. 97: 'The next day we went into the University, and enter'd into the College of Navarre, which is well-built spacious Quadrangle, having a very noble Library; Thenc to the Sorbonne, an antient fabrique built by one Robert de Sorbonne whose name it retaynes; but the restauration which the late Cardinal de Richlieu has made to it of most excellent modern building, together with the sumptuous Church of admirable Architecture is far superior to the rest'. See also Heylyn (1656), pp. 80–89; and John Lough, *France Observed in the Seventeenth Century by British Travellers*, Stocksfield, 1984, pp. 216–19.

[3] 'Churches' in left-hand margin.

[4] 'Our Ladyes' in left-hand margin. Evelyn (1644), II, p. 95: 'it was built by Philip August, but begun by K: Robert son of Hugh Capet'. Notre-Dame, the metropolitan cathedral of Paris, was founded in 1163 and completed between the 13th and 14th centuries. See Chastel, *Églises de France*, IV.C, pp. 15–32.

[5] 'are' added above.

[6] 'have' added above.

[7] Deriving most of his details from Varennes, pp. 180–2, Evelyn (1644), pp. 95–6, echoes much of Montagu's description: 'It consists of a Gotique fabrique [an original observation by Evelyn] sustayned with 120 pillars which make two allys in the Church round about the Quire, without comprehending the Chapells, long 174 paces, large 60: high 100: The Quire is enclosd with stone worke, graven with the Sacred History, and containes 45 Chapells cancelld with yron: At the front of the chiefe entrance are statues in relievo of the Kings 28 in number from Childebert unto Philip the founder, and above them two high towers square built … This is the prime church of France for dignity, having Archdeacons, Vicaries, Cannons, Priests and Chaplaines good store, to the number of 127'.

[8] The Sainte Chapelle was built in 1243–8 by Louis IX, primarily as a shrine for the royal collection of relics. It was deliberately constructed with two superimposed chapels, with the upper chapel used by the royal family and the court and the lower by servants and the populace.

and high chappel are one uppon another upholden by pillars on the sides onely, without any support or stay in the midle, which causes the Architects of our time to admire its building, which is counted the stoutest in france.[1] The glasiers which have contemplated its fine glasse windows say absolutely that the use and custome of it is lost and forgotten.[2] It is famous for its Relicks, as the Crowne of thornes and severall others, a great peece of the Crosse of our Savior, his swadling clothes, some[3] blood which did spring miraculously from an image of his when it was[4] struck by an infidel, the chaine and bond of iron with which he was tied, the reede which the Jews put into his hand instead of a septer, and the spunge which they gave him vinegar with.[5]

The Channons have the same priviledge as them of our Ladys-Church depending onely[6] on the Pope.

Within the University I saw the stately church of Sorbonne built by Cardinall of Richelieu after the Italian fashion.[7] There is a very fine altar with marble pillars; within the Cuppollo above are the pictures of the 4 Doctors of the Church, a little lower the foure Evangelist; and a gaine lower up [f. 9ᵛ] and downe the church the 12 apostles and within in a cave the Cardinall of Richlieu lies buried.[8]

I saw likewise the Abby church of Sᵗᵉ. Geneviefue[9] which was founded by Clovis the first christian king and dedicated to Sᵗ Peter and Sᵗ. Paul. This holy woman is buried in the Cave of the church where her tombe is in great veneration; and because she had much oblidge the Parisians during her life and after her Death continued the same love and care towards them.[10] This church which was call'd Sᵗ. Peter and Sᵗ. Paul was in honour of her call'd Sᵗᵉ Geneviefue. Clovis is buried there in the midle of the Quiry afore the Alter and uppon his tombe there is this Epitaph, Cy gist le cinquiesme Roy de france

---

[1] Evelyn (1644), II, p. 99: 'St. Chapelle, which is a Church built by St. Lewes 1242 after the Gotique manner; what is most observable, is, that it stands upon another church which is under it, sustained by pillars at the sides which seeme to be very weake, which makes it appeare somewhat extraordinary in the Artist: This Chapell is wonderfull famous for its Reliques'.

[2] A considerable amount of the stained glass seen by Montagu still survives, including the spectacular depiction of the Apocalypse in 86 panels in the rose-window, endowed by Charles VIII (1483–98).

[3] 'some' added above.

[4] 'it was' added above.

[5] The relics were traditionally exhibited on Good Friday but most were destroyed at the Revolution. The few surviving ones are now in the treasury of Notre Dame.

[6] 'onely' added above.

[7] 'Sorbonne' in left-hand margin. The Sorbonne, originally a theological college, was entirely rebuilt by Jacques Le Mercier for Cardinal Richelieu from 1629 onwards but most of the present buildings, except for the church, date from the end of the 19th century.

[8] The impressive white marble tomb of Cardinal Richelieu (1585–1642) was designed by Le Brun and carved by Girardon (1694) and is in the church of Ste-Ursule de la Sorbonne (rebuilt at the Cardinal's expense in 1635–9). When the chapel was renamed as the Temple of Reason in 1794, the tombs of the Richelieu family were violated and the Cardinal's monument was eventually moved to the Musée des Monuments Français. It was returned to its original location in 1971.

[9] 'St Geneviefua' in left-hand margin. The abbey of Ste-Geneviève was demolished during the first decade of the 19th century. Its name is recalled in the present-day Bibliothèque Ste-Geneviève, near the Sorbonne, which originated from the abbey's library; and its tower is now incorporated into the Lycée Henri-IV in the Rue Clovis. Evelyn (1644), II, pp. 100–101: 'From hence we went to St. Genevefe a Church of greate devotion, and another of their Amazons [i.e. St Geneviève and Joan of Arc], sayd to have deliver'd the Citty on a tyme from the English; for which she is esteem'd the Tutelary saint of Paris'. St Geneviève reputedly saved Paris from the Huns in 451 by persuading its residents to repent of their sins.

[10] 'that' deleted.

premier Roy Christien, dit Clovis avant son baptesme, que St Remy Archvesque de Rheims baptza et nomma Louis: et a qui un Ange apporta du Ciel une Ampoulle pleine du chresme dont il fut oinct et dont ses successeurs sont pareillement oincts au jour de leur couronnement.[1] The Abbot of this place hath been indowed with many priviledges both by the [f. 10[r]] Popes and kings of france. He depends onely on his Holines. At the publick processions he goes on the side of the Arch-bishop of Paris. He hath his apos-tolical chamber equal in power with that of the Primats, of the which any appel goes immediatly to the court of Rome. When a Pope makes his entry into Paris himself onely hath the honour to recive him. The Arch-Bishop of Paris having beene consecrated in the church of S[t] Victor according to the antient custome,[2] he is oblidge to present him-selfe into this church afore he be received by the canon of our Lady's-church; and at the procession on Palme Sunday where his Maiesty assist with the chapter of this church, he caryes in his hand onely a branch of box which is blessed by the Abbot.

The Abby church of S[t] Germain was founded by Childebert sonne to Clovis, for to putt in the coat of S[t] Vincent which he had brought out of Spaine, with a golden Crosse of massy gold. He is buried behind the great alter.[3] It[4] changed hir name of S[t] Vincent into that of S[t] Germain in the raigne of King Pepin,[5] when he commanded that the body of this holy man should bee brought here. The Pope Alexander the 3[d]., [f. 10[v]] persecuted by the Emperour, came into france who did blesse this church and freed it of the jurisdiction of bishops.[6] This church is very stately built with the Abbot's House all inclosed with walles: who must be one of the King's brothers. He is Lord of the subbourb and hath there his Bailif and court of justice.

In the towne I saw the church of S[t] Germain L'Auxerrois which[7] was founded by Clovis in honour of this *Saint* which was of Auxerre. It is the parishe church of the kings since they dwell at the Louver.[8]

The church of S[t] Innocent was built in the raigne of Philipp Augustus of the confiscation of the goods of the Jews, who were bannish out of france for having crucified a litle child. Its

---

[1] Clovis I (c. 466–511) was the Merovingian founder of the Frankish kingdom who converted to christianity after his marriage to the Burgundian princess Clotilda (later St Clotilda). He built a church at Paris, originally dedicated to the Apostles (which later became the church of Ste-Geneviève) where he was buried. His epitaph reads: 'Here lies the fifth king of France, its first christian king, called Clovis before his baptism, whom St Remy, Archbishop of Reims, baptized and named Louis; and to whom an angel brought from heaven an ampoule full of chrism with which he was anointed, and with which his successors were similarly anointed on the day of their coro-nation'.

[2] The Abbaye de St-Victor was dispersed in 1790 and demolished. Its library, where Rabelais once studied, was especially popular with tourists (see Somerset (1611), pp. 88, 90). The bonded warehouses of the Halles aux Vins later stood on its site and have themselves been replaced by university buildings (Paris-VI and Paris-VII).

[3] 'St Germa' in left-hand margin. The 11th-century church of St-Germain-des-Près, the oldest church in Paris, was by the 17th century the chief house of the Congregation of Saint-Maur (a reformed branch of the Bene-dictines). It was suppressed in 1790 and its renowned library was burned in 1794. See Chastel, *Églises de France*, IV.B, pp. 71–4.

[4] deletion 'it' added above.

[5] deletion.

[6] St Germanicus (d. 576), Bishop of Auxerre, was buried in the St Symphorien Chapel. The rebuilt church was consecrated by Pope Alexander III in 1163, the year after his flight to France in the face of imperial opposition.

[7] 'which' added above.

[8] The original church had been dedicated to St Germanicus but was turned into a fortress in the 9th century by Norman invaders. The gothic church of St-Germain-l'Auxerrois (13th-16th centuries) served as the church of the Louvre and parish church of the court and was where members of the royal family were usually baptized. During the Revolution it was used as a store-house for animal fodder, a printing works, and as a 'Temple of Gratitude'.

Fig. 22. 'Veuë de l'Abbaye sainct Germain des prez les Paris' (c. 1650–55) (Israel Silvestre).

church yard is much remarkable where dead bodyes are consumed in 48 houres.[1] I saw severall others, as St Eustache, St Paul which was the parish church of the kings when they dwelt in the Pallace, that of St John, that of St Gervais, with severall others.[2]

[f. 11^r] For the Monasteries,[3] I saw in the Subourb of St Germain that of the Carthusians fryers the which were[4] brought from Gentilly by S^t. Lewis at the desire of the Prior of the great Carthusians,[5] for to inhabite themselves in this place, where the pallace of Dauvert stood; which was soe troubled and infested with ghost and Divels that noe body could dwel in it. That which is most remarkable here is the tombes of divers Lords, Arch-bishops, and Bishops, and round about uppon the walls of the little cloister is represented the History of that Doctor whose damnation as they say hath been the saluation of many, and which was the very motives that causd St Bruno the Institutor of this order to retire himself with 8 young men of his friends into that fearefull desert hard by Grenoble where he built a litel Chappell and since cast the foundation of that famous Monastery which is the first and Metropolitaine over all the rest which are dispersed abroad in Europe.[6]

[1] 'St Innocent' in left-hand margin. Both the church and the cemetery were demolished in the late 1780s. Evelyn (1644), II, p. 131: 'Henc I tooke a turne in St. Inocents Church-yard where the story of the devouring quality of the ground (consuming Bodys in 24 houres), the Vast Charnells of Bones, Tombs, Piramids and sepultures tooke up much of my time'.

[2] The churches of St-Eustache; St-Paul-des-Champs (demolished 1797), the name of which is still commemorated in the Jesuit church of St-Paul-St-Louis (1627–41); St Jacques-la-Boucherie (demolished 1797), of which only its Tour St-Jacques now survives; and St-Gervais-Saint Protais.

[3] 'Monasteries' in left-hand margin.

[4] 'were' added above.

[5] 'Carthusians' in left-hand margin.

[6] The Order of Carthusians was founded by St Bruno of Cologne (c. 1030–1101) in 1084, in the Chartreuse valley, north of Grenoble and is still renowned for its 'Grande Chartreuse' liqueur. Their communal monastic life was characterized by its frugality, solitary devotions, and ascetic rules. See Lough, *France Observed*, pp. 200–202.

[fol. 11ᵛ] I went next to the Augustins¹ where I saw the Chappell where Henry the 3ᵈ. did institute the order of the Knights of the Holy Ghost, in the yeare 1578,² in acknowledgement of two³ notable favours sent to him from god, which happened both uppon whitsunday in the revolution of one year; to wit, his Election to the crowne of Poland by the states of that Kingdome, in the yeare 1573, and his succession to the Crowne of France (by the death of his brother Charles the 9 who died without any Lawfull children) in the yeare 1574.

The number of the Knights, are, or should bee a hundred, without the Ecclesiasticall, which are 4 Cardinalls, the great Almer of france, and 4 other Prelates, with the officers of the same order, as the Chancellour, the great Provost, master of the ceremonies, the great Thresurer, and the Registers, who have been all instituted to bee commanders of the order. There is likewise [f. 12ʳ] a Herauld of armes, and an Usher, who weare a black Riban as the other weare it blew. The King cheefe of the order makes a vow to live and dye in the Catholicke religion, to maintaine the order with all his power, and not to suffer it in any wayes to be diminish'd, never to change or alter the statuts, nor never to dispence or free the Knights of it, especially of that obligation which bindes them to receive the precious body of christ in the Communion, the first day of the yeare and at Whitsunday: nor of the statut which sayes they must be Catholicks, and gentlemen of three descents. The Knights, and Commanders, makes likewise a vow to live and dye in the Catholicke Religion, to render a most faithfull and ready obedience to the king; to deffend his Maiesty's honour, his rights and quarrells: to serve him in time of warre in the Equipage and furniture of knights, and every time his Maiesty shall send for them to come and never to forsake his person nor the place where they shall have any command to serve his Maiesty; without an expresse commission signed by his hand: not to take [f. 12ᵛ] any wages nor guifts or to except of any Condition from another Prince or oblidge themselves to any body in the world without his Maiesty's leave: to weare a crosse of silver sowed in their clothes and one of gold a bout their necke. The Coller of the order is of gold interlaced of flammes and Cyphers of the King. The Image of the Holy Ghost represented by the figure of a dove is in the midle of the Crosse, the which belongs to the Coller.

The Carmes⁴ have a very fine Convent hard by the place Maubert. They take theire name from Mont Carmel in Judea from whence Sᵗ. Lewis brought them into france in the yeare 1252 being the first that came into Europe.

---

¹ 'Augustins' in left-hand margin. The term 'Augustinian' encompasses various orders following the Rule of St Augustine. Montagu is referring here to the Augustinian Canons who combined their religious observances with a full involvement in secular life.

² The Order of the Knights of the Holy Ghost (L'Ordre du Saint-Esprit) was founded by King Henri III (1551–89) to commemorate his accession to the thrones of Poland and France. He had been elected to the throne of Poland in May 1573 but, following the death of his brother, King Charles IX (d. 30 May 1574), he accepted the French throne and was crowned at Reims on 13 February 1575. The Order was suspended in 1789 and finally suppressed in 1830.

³ deletion 'two' added above.

⁴ 'Carmes' in left-hand margin. The Carmelites were one of the 'Four Orders' (the others being Franciscans, Dominicans, and Augustinians) of mendicant or begging friars and were originally named after Mount Carmel in Palestine. They had arrived in France during the mid-13th century. The Reformed (or Discalced, barefooted) Carmelites became a separate order by a Papal Act of 1593. See Lough, *France Observed*, pp. 204–5. The Carmelites had moved their monastery in 1313 from a site near the Arsenal (then taken over by the Celestines) to the Place Maubert, formerly a notorious place of torture and execution for heretics and other religious nonconformists.

The Celestins[1] hard by the Arsenal was founded by Charles the 5th. It is a fine church with a pretty Cloister and very fine gardens; that which is counted the finest ornement of this place is the Chappell of Orleans, where in the middle of the tombe [f. 13ʳ] of Lewis of Orleans its founder, and that of his wife as also those of his two sonns Charles Ducke of Orleans and Phillipp of Orleans all soe extra ordinary well done that nothing can resemble more its original. This Charles was father to Lewis the 12th. whoe was surnamed father of the people. It is reported of him that he was wont every friday to make a dinner to 13 poore men and washe their feet a fore he satt himself to his owne table.[2] One should never have done to rehearse the Epitaphes, armors,[3] Cyphers, and the Emblemes of the Princes whoe are buried in this church. I will onely relate a few of the chiefest, and begin with that of Lewis the 12th. whoe had for his coat a Porcupine which was his father's order, and the which he did abolish; but reserved it for an Embleme with these words (Cominus et eminus), meaning he would defend himselfe both neare and a farre off against all them that would invade and set uppon his kingdome.

Likewise the Embleme of Francis the first, which was a Salamander in the fire, with these words (Nutriser et extingur) because this animal, as it is reported is of soe cold a nature that he goes through the fire without burning himselfe and sometimes by reason of its coldnessse puts it out, which was a badge [f. 13ᵛ] and signe of this great Prince in all his enterprises. Next that of Henry the second and that of his wife, he had a halfe moone with these words (Donei totum impleat orbem) to signifie that as the moone increases allwayes untill shee be at the full soe he[4] proposed to himselfe noe other resting place but the end of the world to be the limits of his Conquests. The Queen had a Raine-bow with greeck words, the meaning was that they did promise light and quietnesse in the most obscure and intangled busines of the kingdome.

That of Francis the 2ᵈ. which was a Pillar of fire, with these words (lumen rectis) signifying that god sends allways his light to vertuous men for to be a guide to them; as he gave the Pillar of fire to the Children of Israel to conduct them in the Land of Promise. All about the church one sees nothing but tombes of Kings, and Queens, and severall Princes of France which are worthy of observation.

The Minims behind the place Royall have a very fine church and stately Alter.[5]

[1] 'Celestins' in left-hand margin. The Celestines were founded by St Celestine V (d. 1296), a Benedictine monk who became a hermit. He was elected pope in 1294, although he resigned within the same year. The order, which was committed to rigorous asceticism, was later incorporated into the Benedictine order. The present-day Celestine Barracks, located on the Boulevard Henri IV near the Arsenal, was erected in the 19th century on the site of the old Celestine convent (which itself had replaced a Carmelite convent). The huge convent was mostly razed during the Revolution but its memory is still preserved in the Quai des Célestins (so named in 1868), situated on the right bank between the Pont Sully and the Pont Marie.

[2] King Louis XII (1462–1515), 'Père du Peuple', was the son of the soldier and courtly poet, Charles, duc d'Orléans (1394–1465), and Marie de Clèves. His father was Louis, duc d'Orléans (1372–1407), the brother of King Charles VI of France. Charles duc d'Orléans held high command in the French army and, following their defeat at Agincourt, spent some 25 years in England as a prisoner of King Henry V before his release in 1440. This Charles should be distinguished from the more renowned Charles, duc d'Orlèans (1522–45), the favourite son of King François I of France. All of these tombs, and their various inscriptions and emblems as described by Montagu, were destroyed following the Revolution.

[3] 'and' deleted.

[4] 'he' added above.

[5] 'Minims' in left-hand margin. The Minims were an order of mendicant friars, founded in 1435 by St Francis of Paola, the patron saint of seafarers. See G. Roberti, *Disegno storico dell'ordine dei Minimi*, 3 vols, Rome, 1902–22. The Minims had a major house at Chaillot (suppressed in 1790), just outside Paris, and were known locally as 'les minimes de Nigeon' (the old name for Chaillot). The Place Royale was built in 1606–11 and was later renamed Place des Vosges. The nearby Rue des Minimes recalls the location of the 17th-century convent, on the site of which now stands a police barracks.

[f. 14ʳ] The Feuillans of the order of Sᵗ Bernard in the subbourb of Sᵗ Honoré have a fine church and Convent which is held to be the handsomest in Paris.[1]

The Jesuits in the street of Sᵗ Anthony is a stately church. The roofe is most exquisitely done with great galleries round about the church. Its fine pillars, rare pictures, the great Altars and stately frontispeece, can not be enough admired and considered.[2]

The Piquepuces without this subourb deserves to be seene, whoe have a handsome Convent, faire gardens with very prety grottes.[3]

I have here set downe all the cheefe churches and monasteries which I saw. There be severall others, and such a number of fryers, that I have ben assured, that upon any extraordinary occasion the Arch Bishop of this place may set out an army of 10000: of them and not to have the Church service in any wise diminished.

For the Hospitalls I saw that of l'Hostel-Dieu founded by St Lewis in the yeare 1253[4] and since much augmented by Anthony du Prat, Chancellour of france, whoe was afterwards Cardinal and[5] the Pope's Legat in this kingdome, whose gave great [f. 14ᵛ] revenue to this place, both for the maintenance of the sick folks as also for the entertainement of the religious women whoe have the care of them. It is counted one of the richest and finest Hospitalls in france. At Easter the Gold-smiths' wifes doe come and serve heere the sicke people all in silver diches.

That of the Priests de la Charité in the subbourb of Sᵗ Germain is the best governed and the cleanest kept of any in Paris, by Prists soe called.[6] The beds are very handsome all with curtins, the halls extreame cleane and every thing[7] in very good order. Although noe women comes there, the Queen and the greatest Ladys of the Court doe offten come with their traine to serve the sicke people heere for humility sake.

At Monsieur Fedeaux, Canon of our Lady's church, I saw a very fine Rock, of all kind of

---

[1] 'Feuillans' in left-hand margin. The present-day Terrasse des Feuillants adjoined the convent of the Feuillant order (endowed by Anne of Austria in 1622), which was dissolved in 1791. The Feuillants were a reformed branch of the Cistercians, founded by Jean de la Barrière in 1577. In 1592 Pope Clement VIII approved the Feuillants as an autonomous order.

[2] 'Jesuits' in left-hand margin. The church of Saint-Paul-Saint-Louis was built between 1627 and 1641 through the support of King Louis XIII and was designed by members of the order themselves. Cardinal Richelieu celebrated the first mass there on 9 May 1641. The church thrived until the expulsion of the Jesuits from France in 1762. The altars and decorations noted by Montagu were all dispersed during the Revolution when the church was utilized as a repository for books taken from other monasteries. See also Evelyn (1644), II, p. 96.

[3] 'Pique-puces' in left-hand margin. There were several religious institutions on the Rue de Picpus (Pique-Puce) at this period and it is not clear as to which order Montagu is referring. A community of the Canonesses of St Augustine was installed there in 1647 (suppressed 1790) by Cardinal de Retz; and their buildings were taken over in 1805 by the Sisters of the Perpetual Adoration of the Sacred Heart who still occupy them. Most famously, their convent shelters the Picpus Cemetery for the 'graves of the nobility' executed by the guillotine sited at the Barrière du Trône.

[4] 'Hospitals' in left-hand margin. The Hôtel-Dieu, the oldest hospital in Paris and situated near the Place du Parvis Notre-Dame, had been enlarged by King Henri IV. The present buildings date from about 1868–78 but those examined by Montagu reputedly dated from the time St Louis IX (1226–70). See Lough, *France Observed*, pp. 82–6.

[5] deletion.

[6] 'La charité' in left-hand margin. The Hôpital de la Charité stood near the Rue des Saints-Pères from 1605 until 1937 but now only its chapel of St-Pierre survives. Evelyn (1644), II, p. 101: 'That of the Cahrite neere my Lodging is another, built by Q: Mary di Medicees, where I have taken greate satisfaction to see how decently and Christianly the sick People are tended, yea even to delicacy; being sometymes (as I have seene them) served by noble Persons men and Women'.

[7] 'thing' added above.

shells and precious stones, which are all naturall and of all colours.[1] This Rocke is call'd the vision of S[t] Anthony, whoe [f. 15[r]] is represented in the midle in the habit of an Hermit in the wildernes, as he was when the Divel came to tempt him, the which is also represented in the shape of severall beasts; all soe extraordinarily well done and[2] the which cast such a glittering and shining in ones eyes that it doth ravish the sight and causes admiration in the spectators.[3] In this rocke are 400 divels represent all after severall fachons with pretious stones.[4]

Hee is about making of another in the which there will be 60 kindes of beasts, which will be done all of shells and pretious stones of all sortes of colours. I saw a Cow and some sheeps which were allready most rarely done. The designe is the separation of Lot from Abraham, drawen from the 13 of Genesis, when their heardmen fell out; because the Land was not able to hold them, that they might dwell together, by reason of the increase of their cattell; and that Abraham told Lot, "let there be no strife, I pray thee, betweene thee, and mee, for wee are brethren. Is not the hold Land before thee? Seperate thy self, I pray thee, from mee. If thou wilt take the left hand, I will take the right; and if thow departs to the right hand, then will I goe to the left". [f. 15[v]] Hee showed us severall peeces of Agathe and Orientall Jasper and other precious stones which are to helpe to make it.

There I saw likewise a very prety Cabinet of Rarities,[5] which consist of severall shells and pretious stones, divers peeces of Cupps of Agathe which the Emperour's souldiers broke and spoiled after the taking of the Castel of Mantua,[6] the 12 Romaines Emperours in agathe, many peeces of Christall of Rock, of Corall, some Topase and such other precious orientall stones. There is also the Picture of Henry the 4th king of France whoe is after the Mosaique fashon, done of very small stones without any painting, whoe resembles much its Originall. It was sent by the Great Ducke of Florence to his sister Queen Mary of Medicis.

I saw also the cabinett of Mr Tribourg[7] which consists of all sortes of out Landish armes and knives, with rare Italian statues of wax, severall works of ivory. There is also our Savior's tombe all of mother of pearle curiously done, fine pictures and all sortes of feather of birdes. [f. 16[r]]

I saw in the suburb of S[t] Victor the king's Garden of simples where there is betwixt 3 or 4000 severall sortes of physicall Herbes. The king's first Physitian hath the direction and overseeing of it.[8]

---

[1] 'M[r] Fedeaux Cabinat' in left-hand margin.

[2] 'and' added above.

[3] St Anthony of Egypt (d. 356), a religious hermit and one of the earliest monks, was celebrated in Christian iconography for his legendary resistance to the temptations of the Devil, who appeared to him in a variety of shapes.

[4] 'in this Rocke … with pretious stones' added in the hand that completes the diary from f. 27[v].

[5] Evelyn also examined an extensive cabinet of rarities, owned by a M. de Richaumont: 'The next day I was carried to see a curious Collection of a French Gent: which abounded in faire & rich jewels of all sorts of precious stones imaginable; most of them of greate sizes, & invaluable price; besides the most perfect for their bignesse that ever I beheld; he had also a number of Achates & Onixes, I veryly believe neere a bushell, amongst which some admirably colour'd & antique; nor inferior was his collection of Landskips form the best hands, most of which he had caus'd to be copy'd in miniature' (1644, II, p. 132).

[6] The city of Mantua was sacked by the imperial forces in 1630. At the same period (1627–30) King Charles I had been steadily acquiring a large part of the spectacular art collections of the Gonzaga princes of Mantua, following the deaths of Ferdinando (d. 1626) and Vincenzo (d. 1627) and the city state's rapid decline into disorder.

[7] 'M[r] Tribourg' in left-hand margin.

[8] The royal Jardin des Plantes was founded in 1626 by King Louis XIII as a physic garden for the cultivation of medicinal herbs. It was placed under the supervision of the royal physician, Guy de la Brosse, and was only opened to the public in about 1650. Montagu would have been allowed a private visit in view of his social status; as was Evelyn (1644), II, p. 102, who based his account upon Varennes, p. 188, but also expanded it with personal observations.

Now that I have set downe what I have observed in particular, I must say some thing in generall of this famous towne, which is esteemed one of the greatest and finest of the world. It is all built of free stone, all the houses most commonly foure storyes high which were counted some two years agoe because of some new taxes, they would impose uppon the people, and were found to be twenty two thousands eight hundred body of houses. The streets are most of them large & above six hundred in number. The Emperour Sigismond[1] having been in France after he was returned into his owne Countrey sayd hee had seen in France, a World, a Towne, and a Village, meaning Poictiers by the Village, Orleans by the Towne and Paris by the World. In a word it hath been and is now more then ever so well peopled that it is reported, when Lewis the 11th was desirous to know how many men Paris [f. 16ᵛ] could make fit to beare armes there went presently out of it seventy thousand all stout men and well armed. There is againe some Histories which sayes that Charles the 6th, returning from Chartres to Paris, the Inhabitants came to meete him in the number of two hundred thousand both men and women.

I went likewise while I stayed heere to see the most remarkable places about this Towne and first to Sᵗ. Denis which is 2 litle leagues off of this place. Soe soone as I was out of Paris in the way to Sᵗ. Denis, I saw[2] Montmartre or the Hill of the martyrs where the Parisians did worship the Image of Mercury before Sᵗ. Denis the Areopagite came into France, whoe refusing to doe the same was by them put to death and[3] which after his head was cut off carryed it between his hands (as they say) soe farre as the place where there is a church dedicated to[4] his name.[5] By the way there be severall [f. 17ʳ] Crosses where they say he rested himselfe, and at the kings of France's Funeralls, when they carry their bodyes from Paris to Sᵗ Denis, ever since they have taken a custome, to make a station at every one of them.

The plaster of the which they build Houses at Paris comes from thence, therefore they have a proverb which sayes, Il y a plus de Montmartre a Paris que de Paris a Montmartre.[6]

The towne of Sᵗ. Denis was at first but a little ferme called Catulliacus,[7] of a vertuous woman whose name was Catulle; whoe buried there Sᵗ. Denis and his companions Eleuthere and Rustique after they had their heads cut off uppon Montmartre because they[8] would not worship the Idol of Mercury.[9] It did increase by little and litle until the raigne of

---

[1] Montagu is probably referring here to Sigismund I of Hungary (1368–1437), who was elected Holy Roman Emperor in 1411 rather than to one of the more famous three king Sigismunds of Poland: Sigismund I, 'the Old' (1467–1548); Sigismund II Augustus (1520–72); and Sigismund III Vasa (1566–1632).

[2] 'Sᵗ Denis' and 'Mont marter' in left-hand margin. The church of St-Pierre-de-Montmartre replaced an earlier church which had been erected to commemorate the martyrdom of St Denis.

[3] The text is smudged here.

[4] 'to' repeated.

[5] St Denis (d. c. 250) was Bishop of Paris and is patron of France. According to legend, St Denis carried his own head to this spot after his execution.

[6] 'There is more of Montmartre in Paris than Paris in Montmartre'. Plaster of Paris, or calcinated gypsum, was so called because it was originally prepared from the gypsums of Montmartre.

[7] 'Sᵗ Denis' in left-hand margin. The village of St-Denis was founded on the reputed site of Catolacus, the burial place of the missionary apostle of Lutetia (the pre-Roman site of Paris which was named from the 4th century onwards after its once dominant Gallic tribe, the Parisii).

[8] 'had' deleted.

[9] The crypt of the abbey church of St-Denis was constructed around the original Carolingian *martryium*, the site of the graves of St Denis and his companions, Rusticus and Eleutherius, who were beheaded with him.

King Dagobert,[1] whoe in[2] acknowlidgment of the favours he had receaved by the intercession of S[t]. Denis Apostle and patron of the Gaules caused here to bee built a sta[t]ly church covered of silver over the place where the relicks of this S[t]. were kept in a Chasse of gold set with perles. [f. 17ᵛ] The which was given by S[t]. Eloy Bishop[3] of Noyon, soe this Church after it was finished came to be the most famous and richest in france and men began to build presently a Towne, of the which King Dagobert gave such an absolute power to the Abbot over the goods, bodys and lives of the Inhabitans that they were meere slaves to the Abbot.

And further to increase his dominions hee instituted heere a[4] yearely Faire which was to last a moneth[5] during the which, it was forbiden to the Marchants of Paris to oppen their shopps or to sell any weare, with a command to all other Merchants from all parts of the kingdome to bee at it.[6]

Charles the Great[7] gave an order that the Bishopps of France should obey to the Abbot and that the Kings should not be crowned nor the Bishops Consecrated without his consent. He likewise made Hommage of his Kingdome to S[t]. Denis and obliged all his subjects to pay him yearely a certain Tribut for every house of theirs and ordained that all slaves that would willingly [f. 18ʳ] acquit themselves of it should be set at liberty and call'd (the free men of S[t]. Denis).

Charles le Chauve[8] did not onely confirme these prerogatives but also did augment them by new authoritys and revenews. Hee gave to this Church the Towne of Ruel[9] with all the appartenancies belonging there unto and granted the Abbott all kind of Justice, ordaining his Jurisdiction should extend nine leagues long a bout the River Seine which Justice he call'd (the Court of S[t]. Denis).

King Rupert[10] confirmed also the rights and priviledges granted to the Church by King Dagobert and gived her some new ones but above all did much inrish it.

And Lewis the 6ᵗʰ. otherwise call'd le Gros,[11] having done as much permited never the lesse to Sugger the 2ᵈ Abbot[12] to quit to the inhabitants his subjects the grievous taxes and tributs they payd him, according to the ordinances of its founder.

It remaines now to say in few words the greatnesses, authorityes, preheminenses and

---

[1] The abbey of St-Denis is thought to have been founded c. 475 and rebuilt in 630–8 by the Frankish King Dagobert of the Merovingian dynasty, who also founded a Benedictine monastery there. See Chastel, *Églises de France*, IV.C, pp. 137–40. See Fig. 13, p. 51.

[2] 'the' deleted.

[3] St Eloi, Bishop of Noyon-Tournai, who evangelized Bruges in the 7th century.

[4] 'heere a' in left-hand margin.

[5] deletion.

[6] Various fairs took place at St-Denis but Montagu is perhaps referring here to the *Lendit*, a medieval fair held in the region.

[7] Charlemagne, Holy Roman Emperor (c. 742–814).

[8] King Charles I, 'le Chauve' (840–77).

[9] Rueil, near St-Germain-en-laye. See Fig. 23, p. 104.

[10] Montagu's 'King Rupert', probably derived from either an unidentified written source or a guide to the abbey church, is probably a confusion for King Robert 'le Pieux' (996–1031).

[11] King Louis VI, 'le Gros' (1108–37).

[12] Following Dagobert's 7th-century church, another edifice was built by Abbot Fulrad in the mid-8th century, which was itself replaced by a magnificent structure, incorporating parts of Fulrad's structure, built (1136–47) by Abbot Suger (1081–1151), a childhood friend and later adviser of King Louis VI. Suger's church is widely regarded as a landmark in western gothic architecture, of which the west porch and apse still survive. See Sumner McKnight Crosby, *The Royal Abbey of Saint-Denis from Its Beginnings to the Death of Suger, 475–1151*, ed. Pamela Z. Blum, New Haven and London, 1987, pp. 121–277.

prerogatives the [f. 18ᵛ] antients Kings of France gave particularly to the Abbots of Sᵗ. Denis, which are of high esteeme and most worthy observation. For antiently they were Masters of their Chappell and great Almners of their Maiestyes, and yet at this present whosoever is Abbot of Sᵗ. Denis is also Counsellour to the Parliament of Paris and hath there deliberative voice as all the other Counsellours and Peeres of France. The which priviledge hath been granted to them by Phillipp the Long,[1] whoe did exclude all other Prelats of it.[2]

The Arch-bishop of Paris, as I have said some where, he onely injoys at this day the same pre-rogative. They are alsoe exempted from subjection of all Bishopps and particularly of that of the Arch-Bishopps of Paris, this was yeelded to them by Sᵗ. Landry at the instance of Clovis the 2ᵈ.[3]

The Popes have likewise granted the same Abbots the power to conferre any order and to blesse the ornaments of the Altars, which prerogatives onely they and Bishopps have, and which is more can commit the same authority [f. 19ʳ] to one of their fryers for the like func-tions. Among others the Pope Steephen the 3ᵈ.,[4] at the request of Charles the great, gave them power to build Abby Churches in what place soever they would in the kindome of France, to chuse a Bishopp for to be over the priests, and that their abby church of Sᵗ. Denis should depend onely on his Holines.

They have thirteene rich Prior-shipps, 50 or 60 Curates and other Parishes in their owne disposing.

It was in this Church that the Auriflamme was kept, which was a Banner of a vermillion colour all covered of golden floure de Lews, the which as the History sayes,[5] was sent from Heaven to Clovis the first.[6] The antient Kings of France had a custome to goe take this stan-dart off the great altar of Sᵗ. Denis[7] when they undertook any warre against strangers or infidells. It was in the end lost in a batle they had with the Low-Country-men and was never heard of after.

This Church then as it is to be seene at this day was rebuilt by the Abbot Suggere but as it is reported much inferior to the other built by King Dagobert. [f. 19ᵛ]

In its frontispeece are two great high square towers upheld by foure great pillars in the which are the bells of pure mettle, the three great gates are of brasse exellently wrought, which have been guilt. King Dagobert caused them to bee brought from Sᵗ. Hillarys Church of Poictiers.[8]

---

[1] King Philippe V, 'le Long' (1316–22).

[2] About 2 cm of space is left at this point in this line, probably to indicate a paragraph break.

[3] Clovis II (c. 634–657), the son of Dagobert I and Merovingian Frankish king of Neustria and Burgundy. St Landry (Landerieus), Bishop of Paris (650–61), was one of the twenty-three bishops who signed the foundation charter for the Abbey of St-Denis in 653. He was buried in the church of Saint-Germain-des-Prés (then called Saint-Vincent).

[4] Pope Stephen III of Rome (752–757), the successor of Pope St Zacharias (d. 752), is sometimes called Stephen II because Zacharias's nominated successor, Stephen II, died before his consecration could take place. Hence, Pope Stephen IV (768–72) is also sometimes called Stephen III. Montagu is almost certainly referring to the latter pope since 'Charles the great' became King of the Franks in 768.

[5] 'is' deleted.

[6] King Clovis I (c. 466–511), the Merovingian founder of the Frankish kingdom and the first barbarian king to convert to Christianity. The Oriflamme was the banner of St Denis which was usually kept alongside his relics in the abbey. When in 1124 the Holy Roman Emperor Henry V invaded territories belonging to Louis VI, the French king rode into battle with the Oriflamme, thereby confirming its legendary status among the French nobil-ity and militia.

[7] deletion.

[8] The church of St-Hilaire-le-Grande was rebuilt in the 11th-12th centuries on the site of a Gallo-Roman edifice. This detail is derived from Varennes, pp. 192–4.

This Church hath 390 foote of lenght, a 100 of breadth and 80 of hight; the very body of it is 130 foot long and[1] the roof[2] upheld by 60 pillers.[3]

The Quiry is devided in three. The first where the Priest's chaires are is 68. foot long and 35 broad, the second is 45 foot long and 35 broad, and the third hath onely 25 foot of lenght, but is as broad as the others.

In the first Quiry are the Tombes of Charles le Chauve, of Dagobert, of Charles Martel, of Hugues Capet, and of Eude whoe made himselfe King by usurpation.[4]

In the second there is yet to bee seene some markes of the Toumbs of Phillipp Augustus, of Lewis the 8th. of the house of Mont-pensier, and of his [f. 20[r]] sonne S[t] Lewis whoe have been cover'd of silver and the which were plundered and demolisht by the Inglish in the raigne of Charles the 6.th.[5] In the same Quiry are likewise the Toumbes of Phillipp Le Hardy, and close by, that of Phillip le Bel, with those of Elizabeth of Arragon, wife to Phillipp the Hardy, of Pepin and of Berthe his wife, of Carloman and of Lewis sonne to Lewis le Begue. At the right hand are those of Lewis Hutin, of Joane Queene of Navarra, of Rupert and of his wife Constance and of his sonne Henry, of Lewis le Pros, and of his sonne Phillipp; of Carloman sonne to Pepin, of Hermintrude wife to Charles le Chauve, and of Charles the 8.th made of Copper and guilt over with his statue upon his tombe kneeling, with this Epitaph, which shows his victoryes over the Duck of Bretagne, his Triomphes in Italy, his Conquest of the Kingdome of Naples, and the succour hee gave to Henry King of England.

Hic octave iaces Francorum Carole Regum,
Cui victa est forti Britonis ora manu,
Parthenope illustrem tribuit captiva triumphum
Claraque Fornovio pugna per acta solo,
Cæpit et Henricus regno depulsus avito,
Bellare auspiciis sceptra Britanna tuis,
O plures longiqua dies si fata dedissent,
Te nullus toto maior in orbe foret.[6]

[f. 20[v]]

---

[1] 'and' added above.   [2] 'is' deleted.

[3] Evelyn (1644), II, p. 86 (from Varennes, pp. 192–4), supplies similar details: 'The Church was built by K. Dagobert, but since much enlarged; being now no lesse then 390 foote long & 100 in bredth: 80 in height without comprehending the cover; it has also a very high shaft of stone, and the gates are of brasse'.

[4] Montagu's descriptions of the tombs and relics at St-Denis are exceptionally detailed for an English account at this period. Evelyn (1644), II, pp. 86–7, merely paraphrases a few select details from Varennes, pp. 192–4. In 1793 it was agreed at the revolutionary Convention to destroy the royal tombs at the abbey. The coffins were opened, the lead reused for bullets, and the bones discarded in pits. The treasury was looted and despoiled at the same period but most of its contents in the mid-17th century can been reconstructed from detailed lists in J. Doublet, *Histoire de l'abbaye de S. Denys en France*, Paris, 1625; Paris, Bibliothèque nationale MSS 4611 and 18765 (both 1634); S. G. Millet, *Le Trésor sacré … de S. Denis*, Paris, 1645 edn, which Montagu consulted, see note 174; and M. Félibien, *Histoire de l'abbaye royale de Saint-Denys en France*, Paris, 1706 (rpt. Paris, 1973). See also Blaise de Montesquiou-Fezensac (with Danielle Gaborit-Chopin), *Le Trésor de Saint-Denis*, 3 vols, Paris, 1973–7.

[5] Evelyn (1644), II, p. 86: 'Here whiles the Monke conducted us, we were shew'd the antient, and moderne Sepulchers of their Kings beginning from the founder to Lewes his son; with Charles Martel, Pepin his son, & father of Charlemagne, these lye in the Quire, & without more then as many more'.

[6] 'Here you lie Charles the eighth king of the Franks, by whose powerful hand the coast of Brittany was conquered; captive Naples granted you a famous triumph, the renowned Battle of Fornovo [against the League of Venice in 1495] through your actions alone began; and Henry [King Henry VII of England], driven away from his ancestral kingdom, to make war for his British sceptre under your auspices. O, if the Fates had given you many and long days, no one in the world would have been greater than you.' This panegyrical inscription offers a remarkably deceptive and (at times inaccurate) perspective on several key conflicts during Charles VIII's largely unsuccessful and expensively belligerent reign (1483–1498).

In the 3.ᵈ Quiry are the Toumbes of Phillipp le Long, of Charles le Bel, & of Queene Joane his wife, of Phillipp de Valois, of his first wife Joane of Burgundy, and of his sonne John, and of the Queene Marguerit wife to Sᵗ Lewis.

Theese 3 Quiryes have 3 Altars, to wit, that call'd le Matinal, the Great, where there is a table and crosse all of gold inrished with several perles and pretious stones; and the 3.ᵈ over the which are the Chasses of St. Denis, Patron of France, of Eleucthere and Rustic his companions, of St. Denis Bishopp of Corinth, and of St. Denis King [f. 21ʳ] of France.[1] On the side of the great Altar are steares which leades behind the Church, where there is several Chappells, in the which there be many stately Toumbes, and Chasses of Saincts, in the which their relicks are, as of Sᵗ. Hypollite, of Sᵗ. Eustache, of 3 of the eleven thousand virgins and divers others.

There is also heere a very fine Cuve or bassin of Porphyre, of an extraordinary bignes, and all of one peece the which King Dagobert brought from Sᵗ. Hillarye's church of Poictiers, where they say it was a fount, where they Chrishtned children. The use they put it too is onely to make Holy water on Easter and whitsunday even.

Out of the Quiry at the right hand is to bee seene the stately Toumbe of Francis the first, of Queene Claude his wife, and of francis and Charles their sonns; upon the sides of it are graved the warres, victoryes and Trophies of this great Prince.

Closse by the chappell of Sᵗ. Hyppollite, is the sumpteous Toumbe of Lewis the 12 surnamed (father of the people) and of Anne of Bretaigne his Queene; over it they are represented kneeling, and praying; and under it laying [f. 21ᵛ] dead, and as[2] it were halfe wratten, with the figures of the Cardinall vertues at the foure corners of it; to witt, Wisdome, Justice, Fortitude and Temperance, the 12 Apostles round about and a little lower the Victoryes of this good Prince.[3]

The Bodyes of Henry the 4ᵗʰ. and of Lewis the 13ᵗʰ.are under Canopyes covered of black velvet. There be here several other Tombes and riches the which would be to tedious for mee to rehearse seeing there is a whole booke that treates onely of the singularities of this church intituled Le Thresor sacrè de Sᵗ. Denis.[4]

For the Threasure of Sᵗ. Denis, it is very famous both for its rishes and for divers Relicks which are kept there, although several changes of time and fortune have much diminished it.[5]

For of the 6 great tables of gold which were all covered of pretious stones, where of one was given by King Dagobert, this church its founder, the 2.ᵈ by Charles le Chauve, and the other foure by the Abbot Juggere, there is only one remaining which is, as [f. 22ʳ] I have said, in the table of the great Altar inrish'd with many pretious stones and so well wrought that the fashion is esteem'd to bee worth above 4000. tournois. The Images of gold given by

---

[1] Somerset (1611), p. 75: 'And at the upper ende of the high altar in the Abbye *St. Dennis* his bodie and *St. Eleutherius*, and *St. Rusticus* are buried both his Companions'.

[2] 'as' added above.

[3] Montagu may be confused here since his description seems more relevant to the disturbingly realistic tomb of Henri II (d. 1559) and Queen Catherine de' Medici (d. 1589) by Pierre Lescot (1510–71) and Germain Pilon (1564–83), representing them alive and kneeling in bronze above, dead and nude in marble below. See Coryate (1608), I, p. 183.

[4] Montagu is referring here to S. G. Millet, *Le Trésor sacré … de S. Denis*, Paris, 1636 (rpt. 1645).

[5] 'Treasure' in left-hand margin. See Michael G. Brennan and Veronica Ortenberg, 'Deux visiteurs anglais au trésor de l'abbaye de Saint-Denis au dix-septième siècle', *Paris et Ile-de-France Mémoires*, 42, 1991, pp. 261–71, for specific references to Montesquiou-Fezensac's individual identifications and descriptions of items from the treasury as described by Montagu.

King Pepin. The Image of the Trinity, and the fine golden Candelsticks given by Lewis le Gros, were taken by the Inglish. There was also a fine great Crucifix of gold given by the Abbot Juggere which was taken during the troubles de la ligue, by the Ligueurs themselves

The cheefest peeces then, which doth compose it, are, first, a rich crosse of massy gold within the which is set a great peece of the crosse of our Saviour, which is a foote and halfe long, about the bignes of a thomb, and halfe a foote crosse. A naile of the same crosse set in a case of silver guilt. A Crosse of silver guilt, with[1] a Crucifix raised in the midle set uppon a table of the same. A great Crosse of gold inrisht with a great Amethist, of many saphirs, Esmeraulds, and perles. An other Crosse of massy gold call'd the Crosse of S[t]. Laurens because there is with in it, a peece of the Gridiron upon the which this saint was broyled. Two other silver Crosses where of one of them is guilt. A Case or Box of gold [f. 22v] upheld by the foure corners of foure pillars allso of gold, within the which there is a Crucifix of the Crosse of our saviour set uppon a Crosse of gold; which was made by the Pope Clement the 3[d]. his owne hands. A Chasse or shrine of silver guilt, which is call'd the Holy Chappell, by reason of its shape; filled of 12 litle glasses of Cristall full of Relicks, as of the blood of our saviour, of the Cloath hee was cloathed with in his Child-hood, of the milk of the Virgin Mary and such others. An other fine Shrine of silver made upon the paterne of our Lady's Church of Paris, with its Towers, steepel, gates, and all the rest extraordinarily well repre-sented. An Image of the Virgin Mary holding our saviour in her armes, of silver guilt; 3 other Images of the same virgin, one of silver guilt, an other of Ivory, and the 3[d]. of very fine Amber. A curious cristal of rock cut in an Ovall fashion. A Chest of silver guilt where there is some Relicks of the Prophet Isaiah. An Image of S[t]. John Baptist. The head of S[t]. Denis of pure gold upholden by two Angels of silver.[2] His image of silver, his drinking cup, [f. 23r] with his two bottles of christall, his Pontificall ring, his Inck-horne after the Greecke fash-ion, his pilgrim stafe, and many other fine Images.

A Shrine of silver where in there is a shoulder of S[t]. John Baptist, with many other curious shrines to keepe relicks. The great challice or drinking cup of silver guilt, which is only used at the Alter upon some great Holy-dayes. Divers others Challice and among others 2 which are of Agathe. Some Miters, Bishopps staffes, severall Claspes, some Censors or perfuming pannes, some Copes or hoods for Bishopps and many other church ornaments given by sev-eral Kings and Princes. Also the drinking cup of King Solomon, the sword of Turpin, that of the maid of Orleans, the Hunting horne of Roland, the Chess boord of Charles the greate, Judas lanterne, An Unicorne's Horne,[3] Virgils looking glasse. Heere is alsoe King Henry the 4th. in his Maiesticall Robes, and the Royal Ornements of their maiestyes of France, the Crowne, the Scepter, the Hand of Justice, the Royal Cloak, the Dalmatique, and the Bottine, the which the Abbot is bound to have cary'd in the places where the Kings are Crowned, with divers pretious [f. 23v] stones, as some Onyx, Agathes, Chrysollits, cut in severall fashions. The particularities of all which Threasure would bee to tedious heere to insert and must bee seene in the booke forenamed *which* treates on all the rarities of this church.

---

[1] deletion 'with' added above.

[2] Coryate (1608), I, p. 185, was disappointed to find that the reliquary of St Denis revealed very little of his skull. See also Moryson (1595), I, 4p. 17; Somerset (1611), p. 74; Evelyn (1644), II, pp. 85–91; Heylin (1656), p. 54.

[3] A tusk of a male narwhal, supposedly sent to Charlemagne by Aaron, King of Persia. Coryate (1608), I, p. 184, describes the same tusk: 'an Unicornes horne valued at one hundred thousand crownes, being about three yardes high, even so high that I could hardly reach to the top of it'. 'Unicorn horn' was a highly prized and enormously expensive antidote to poison. By the 17th century the term was widely used to denote narwhal (or 'sea unicorn') tusk as a trade commodity.

Fig. 23. 'Veuë de la Cascade de Ruel' (c. 1650–55) (Israel Silvestre).

From hence I went to Ruel to see the fine House belonging to the Ducke of Richelieu built by the Cardinal his Uncle.[1] There is a handsome Haule adorned with fine pictures. I saw two other roomes which are very pretily painted and guilt, with a neat garden above staires and was deprived of the rest by reason the Ducke was there. The Gardens are very curious and large where there is many stately walkes and other curiosityes. As first a fountaing which spurst up water a great height. In the midle of it stands a Hercules of brasse cuting off one of Hydras head and seven others coming in its place.[2] The Emperour Julian's Triompheal Arck is counted a rare peece painted in a perspective with soe much art that it many times deceave [f. 24ʳ] the birds flying in the aire whoe taking it[3] for the skyes doe hit themselves against it, as a swallow did not long agoe which killed her self in this manner.[4]

Ther is alsoe a fine grotte but some of the pipes being broken I could not see the water-works. A fore it, is the great Fountaine which is very deepe, wall'd round and paved in the bottome. It is of a great bignes more long then broad. There is round a bout it 50 great leaden bassins and within it soe many fountaines the which springs up water above the

[1] 'Ruel' in left-hand margin. Montagu is describing the Richelieu family's Château de Val at Rueil-Malmaison (as Rueil has been known since 1928) rather than the renowned Château de Malmaison there, now a Napoleonic museum. Evelyn (1644), II, p. 108: 'From hence about a leage farther, we went to the Cardinal Richlieus Villa at Ruell; the House is but small, but fairely built in forme of a Castle, moated about'. The Peace of Rueil, between the Court of France and the Parlement de Paris was ratified on 1 April 1649.

[2] Evelyn (1644), II, p. 109: 'But though the House be not of the greatest, the Gardens about it are so magnificent, as I much doubt whither Italy have any exceeding it for all varietyes of Pleasure: That which is neerest the Pavillion is a Parterre, having in the middst divers noble brasse statues perpetualy spouting Water into an ample Bassin, with other figures of the same metall'.

[3] 'it' added above.

[4] Evelyn (1644), II, pp. 109–10, tells the same tale about the arch: 'The skie, and hills which seeme to be betweene the Arches, are so naturall, that swallows & other birds, thinking to fly through, have dash'd themselves to pieces aginst the Walls. I was infinitely taken with this agreable cheate'.

height of a man and falling into 2 other roes of great leaden shells which are in the side of the fountaine one under an other makes a most pleasant noise. In each roe of the shells there be alsoe 50; soe that there be 150 bassings & shells.

For the Cascade or falling of waters it is divided into the midle by a roe of Cypres Trees between each of which stands a great bassin & in every one of them a fountaine which are eight in number. There is on both sides 50 steps and at their ends also two other roes of Cypres Trees. There is also a dragon which casts out water a great way.

S^t. Clou is a fine House painted on the outside belonging to the Archbishop of Paris where there is fine Gardens and fountaines with curious perspectives.[1] I saw also the [f. 24^v] chamber in the which Henry the 3d was kill'd by a Jacobin fryer presenting him a letter from the first president of Paris. Some drops of his blood are yet to be seene a'fore the Chimney which can never be rubbed out.[2]

St Germain is 5 leagues off of Paris. The old House was founded by Charles the 5th and rebuilt by Francis the 1st. as appeares by the crowned F. f. which are painted over the Chimneyes. Henry the 4th. built the new house upon the top of a hill, where the king and Queene have their lodgings separed one from another.[3] Among other roomes I saw the chamber where Lewis the 13 died.[4] In the King's gallery are the plat formes of all the antientest Townes of the world, and in that of the Queene severall rare peeces of Ovid's Metamorphoses. But that which was most worthy to bee seene heere was the water works now almost all spoilt and broken. I saw the 2 lower most which are in a gallery, that called the Haule of[5] Orpheus is the finest, whoe playin upon his Harpe brings forth divers kinds of wild beasts which dance all about him. At the other end of the gallery is to be seene Perseus whoe comes to deliver Adromeda from a sea Mounster, the which he strikes with [f. 25^r] his sword.[6] Maisons is 2 leagues off of this place and 5 from Paris. It is a most stately House which the President de Maisons is a bout building.[7] All the roomes are large; the seeldings of some extraordinarily well carved, which are to bee finely painted and richly guilt. I saw below staires a very pretty Cabinet all done round about with christall and its pavement curiously painted. Above staires are handsome Tarraces with very fine prospects. There is alsoe lovely gardens where there is severall fine Orange and lemons trees.

I went likewise to Charenton where the Protestants have their church which is 2 Leagues from Paris; which place was famous for an Eccho esteemed the wonderfullest

---

[1] 'St Clou' in left-hand margin. The palace at St-Cloud was erected in 1572 by a wealthy citizen and was entirely destroyed by fire in 1870. Evelyn (1644), II, pp. 107–8, provides a fuller description of the building and its gardens.

[2] King Henri III was assassinated on 1 August 1589 by a Dominican friar, Jacques Clément.

[3] 'St Germaine' in left-hand margin. A royal château was first built on the site in the 12th century by Louis VI and entirely rebuilt by François I between 1539 and 1548. The Château-Neuf, below the original castle, was begun by Philibert de l'Orme for Henri II and completed by Henri IV between 1599 and 1610. It was assigned to the exiled James II in 1688 and demolished between 1776 and 1782, except for the Pavillion-Henri IV and Pavillon-Sully. See Evelyn (644), II, pp. 110–11.

[4] Louis XIII had died of tuberculosis at Saint-Germain-en-Laye on 14 May 1643, where his son Louis XIV had been born on 5 September 1638.

[5] 'or' written but then the name 'Orpheus' given in full on the next line.

[6] These waterworks are analysed by A. Duchesne, *Les Antiquitez et recherches des villes, chasteaux, et places plus remarquables de toute la France*, Paris, 1614. See also Somerset (1611), pp. 82–4; Evelyn (1644), II, p. 11; and Heylyn (1656), pp. 61–3.

[7] 'Maisons' in left-hand margin. The château at Maisons-Laffitte was built by François Mansart between 1642 and 1651 for René de Longueil, Marquis de Maisons, who was Surintendant des Finances. Maisons was renamed Maisons-Laffitte after the financier Jacques Laffitte (1767–1844) who purchased the château in 1818.

Fig. 24. 'Veue de Sainct Germain en Laye' (c. 1651–55) (Israel Silvestre).

in Europe. It answeared untill 10 or 12 times and is now lost since the Carmes have built their Convent.[1]

Returning back to Paris I passed by le Bois de Vincennes which is the Course of Paris where in the summer at the evening the nobility goes to take the aire.[2]

At the end of the other Course call'd le Course de [f. 25ᵛ] la Reine hard by the Louvre, I saw Chaliot[3] an other fine House, where among other roomes I observed a lovely gallery adorned with severall curious picturs. At one end of it stands Lewis the 13 a horse back done with plaster, there is alsoe a pretty parke and fine walls.

From Paris I tooke my journey for Orleans[4] and passed by Long-Jumeaux, Linas, Chatres la Vallée de Tour fourt, Estampes, Angerville, Artenay[5] and soe came to Orleans.

In this Towne,[6] which is seated uppon the river Loire, I saw first the Church of Sᵗᵉ Croix

---

[1] 'Charenton' in left-hand margin. Evelyn (1644), II, p. 115: 'I went to Charenton 2 leagues from Paris, to heare & see the manner of the French-Protestant Churches service: The place of meeting they call the Temple … In this passage we went by that famous bridge over the Marne where that renown'd Eccho returnes the Voice 9 or 10 times being provoked with a good singer'. The church was built in the mid-1620s and demolished in 1685. Both Evelyn and Montagu seem to be taking their description of the echo from Varennes, 175.

[2] 'Bois de Vincennes' in left-hand margin. The park, a royal hunting ground, was first walled in the 12th century and became a public park in the 1730s under Louis XV. The Château de Vincennes (14th–16th centuries) was a popular royal retreat until the completion of Versailles in the early 1680s.

[3] The Chaillot district stretches along the Right Bank. The present-day Palais de Chaillot, erected for the 1937 Paris Exhibition, stands on the site of a country house built by Marie de Médicis, later owned by Marshal François de Bassompierre (1579–1646). In 1651 his heirs sold the château to Queen Henrietta-Maria of England, who founded the Convent of the Visitation there (razed by Napoleon).

[4] 'June 8' in left-hand margin.

[5] Longjumeau, Linas, Etampes, Angerville, and Artenay. Montagu's 'Chatres la Vallée de Tour fourt' probably refers to the very steep hill known as the 'Côte de Torfou' and the 'le Bas de Torfu' (to the north-west of the village of Torfou), on the present-day N20 road between Linas and Etampes.

[6] 'Orleans 10' in left-hand margin.

Fig. 25. 'Veües et Perspective du Pont, et du Temple de Charenton' (1645) (Israel Silvestre's drawing engraved by Claude Goyran).

which is the cheefest,[1] next that of the[2] Jesuits whoe have here a fine Colledge, that of St Aignam, les Peres de L'oratoire, that of S[t]. Steephen, that of St Samson and others.[3] Upon the bridge stands a crucifix at the foot of which there is the Virgin Mary holding our saviour in her armes and at each end Charles the 9 and the maid of Orleans kneeling, done of brasse and armed from top to toe.[4] In honor of her they make yearely a generall procession the eight of May, which is the day shee [f. 26ʳ] raised the seege of the english, where all the orders of the towne doth assist, which goes as farre as the bridge where there is a Masse said.[5] I went alsoe to the towne house where off of a hight Tower I vewed the towne.

Here I inbarked my selfe upon the River Loire for Saumur and saw[6] these Townes by the way. First Blois, where I layd at the Gally.[7] I saw here the Castle and the garden of simples,[8] in the which there is severall kinde of phisicall herbes brought from most parts of Europe. This garden is devided in two by a fine Long Gallery built by Henry the 4th.[9]

[1] The 12th-century Cathedral of Ste-Croix had been vandalized in 1568 by the Huguenots. As part of his absolution and supposed conversion to Catholicism, Henri IV was obliged by the Pope to begin its reconstruction. At the time of Montagu's visit, building work was still in hand. See R. G. Chenesseau, *Saincte-Croix d'Orléans*, Paris, 1921.

[2] 'the' added above.

[3] Much of old Orléans was destroyed in the Revolutionary period and by bombing by the Italians in 1940 and by the Allies in 1944. Of the churches visited by Montagu, only St-Aignan (named after the 5th century bishop of Aurelianis now survives (unless his 'Peres de L'oratoire' is a mishearing for the 16th-century church of St-Pierre-du-Martroi).

[4] This bridge was ruined in 1746. The monument (1468) to Jeanne d'Arc was vandalized by the Huguenots but restored in the 17th century. It was completely destroyed in 1792.

[5] On 8 May an annual procession was made to the statue near the bridge, followed by a mass. This custom was described by Varennes, 27. See also Somerset (1611), p. 99; Evelyn (1644), II, p. 137; and Heylyn (1656), p. 140.

[6] 'that' deleted 'saw' added above.

[7] 'Blois 15' in left-hand margin.

[8] 'the' repeated.

[9] The Château or Castle, and the Garden of Simples are described in Varennes, pp. 51–3, and by Evelyn (1644), II, pp. 140–41, who noted in particular the life-size equestrian statue of Louis XII (destroyed 1791) at the entrance to the castle; 'a very wide payre of Gates nailed full of Wolves heads & Wild Boares'; and a 'longe Gallery full of antient Statues & Inscriptions both of Marble and Brasse'. He was also impressed by the 'large Garden, esteemed for its furniture one of the rarest in Europ, especialy for simples and exotic plants'.

Next Amboise where I saw the Castle which hath a way for a Coach with six horses to goe up.[1] In the Chappell there is a paire of Stagg's Hornes of a Mounstrous bignes.

And Lastly Tours.[2] S[t] Gratian is its cheefest Church, after which I went to see S[t] Martin and some Monasteryes, both of men and women especially that of S[t]. Francois or of the Minimes whoe have a hansome Church with very neat altars.[3]

The Palle Maille is count'd the finest in France. It is a thousand paces long and hath six roes of high trees on both sides.[4] The Abby Church of Marmoustier is a bout a quater of a league from the Towne upon the river side,[5] where I saw the [f. 26[v]] Barrill of S[t] Martin[6] which is soe bigge that a man can goe in a horse-back. Closse by there is alsoe a fountaine that cures the Ague.

I went also to see the Caves Goutiers which are 2 leagues off of this place where the water is is soe cold in summer that as it dropps downe from above it is turned into stones that resemble sugar candy.[7]

From hence I cam to Saumur where I saw our Ladys-church des Ardilliers,[8] famous for the many pilgrimages which are made there[9] by sicke people.[10] In this church there is a fine Threasure where I observed first a crowned hatt with an L. upon it, given by Lewis the 14 at present King of France; a paire of silver candlesticks given by Lewis the 13 his father which are foure foot high and are esteemed to be worth 14000 [ll] tournois, with other little ones; some Crosses and children made of silver; a Crowne of silver given by the Duchesse of Savoye; a little drinking cup of Agathe all of one peece esteemed at 7000 [ll] tournois; a Wolfe of silver given by a Gentle-woman which was used of such a disease by the Intecession of the Good Lady, after shee had visited this church.

Severall images of armes, hands, leags; and such parts of the body as have been healed after pilgrimages and devotions made in this church, &. The Image of the [f. 27[r]] Good Lady, the same which works miracles.

---

[1] 'Amboise 16' in left-hand margin. Amboise is dominated by its Château. Evelyn (1644), II, pp. 143–4, also notes: 'It is full of halls, & spacious Chambers, and one Stayre Case large enough and sufficiently commodious to receive a Coach and land it on the very towre … that which is most prodigious & observable is in that antient Chapell a staggs head, or branches hung up in chaynes'. The stag's horns were, in fact, made of wood and fell apart in 1870/1 when a Prussian soldier attempted to loot them.

[2] 'Tours 17' in left-hand margin. Much of the centre of the old town was destroyed in 1940.

[3] St Gatien (or Gratian) had introduced Christianity to Tours, and St Martin was its third bishop. The Cathedral Saint-Gatien was built between 1220 and 1547. Part of the cloister of the 12th-century church of Saint-Martin (largely destroyed in 1802) is now incorporated into the Couvent de Petit-Saint-Martin. The crypt containing the saint's tomb lies under the present-day basilica built from the 1880s until the 1920s. See Evelyn (1644), II, pp. 144–5, for his descriptions of these churches.

[4] Evelyn (1644), II, p. 145: 'From hence we walk'd to the Mall, which is without comparison the noblest for length, & shade the bst in Europ, having 7 rowes of the talest & goodliest Elmes I had ever beheld'.

[5] The abbey at Marmoustier had been founded by St Martin in 372 and was suppressed in 1792. See Evelyn (1644), II, pp. 146–7 (largely from Varennes, p. 58).

[6] Evelyn (1644), II, p. 147: 'Hence ascending many stepps we went into the Abbots Palac, where we were shew'd a monstrous vast Tunn (as big as that at Heidelberg) which they report St. Martine (as I remember) did fill with one cluster of Grapes growing there'.

[7] These caves near Savonnières, on the south bank of the River Cher, are described in more detail by Evelyn (1644), II, p. 148 (largely from Varennes, p. 59).

[8] 'Saumur 18' in left-hand margin. The church of Notre-Dame-des Ardilliers at Saumur was significantly redeveloped during the 17th century, including additions made in the 1640s by Cardinal Richelieu and a rotunda started in the mid-1650s (but not completed until 1695). It was so named after a statue of the Virgin Mary found in 1454 in 'un terrain argileux' (clayey soil), from which the name 'ardilliers' was derived.

[9] 'there' added above.

[10] 'there' deleted.

At Monsieur Legier I saw a Cabinet of Rarities which consist[1] of severall things, as, first a Cane of the reed papyrus of the which Philadelphus invented the way to write upon it;[2] some serpents among others one of 9 foot long, a Crocodill, a sea Hogge, some sea dogges, a sea calfe, an Orbis and some other strange fishes which lives in the river Nylus;[3] several becks of birds, the foote of an Elke, the foote of a Caribou – a beast of Canada at least as big as a stagge, of the which it is reported that because of its nimblenesse he can run uppon the snow and not sinke in it; some Ostrigges egges; some Bowes of the Bresilians which are done with some certain fishes teeth poysoned, in stead of iron of the which if one be wounded it is present death with out an antidote; the back and belly of a Tortue; divers sorts of sea shells, some minerall stones; some serpents toungs; the back bone of a Wheale; a Cameleon; a little child borne as is[4] thought six weekes after his Conception formed of all his membres, about a spang long and the which there is 2 years that it is kept in a glasse bottle full of strong water which does preserve it intire and other rarityes.[5]

[f. 27ᵛ] I forgott to speake first something of the situation of the towne, the which I found very pleasant being seated at the foote of a little montaigne and having the fine river of Loire running by it, with also a curious pleane and medowes. As for the place of it selfe, it is very little but alwayes full of strangers of all kind of Nations, because of the cheapness of the pensions and exercises of the body, the goodnes of the Language, as also because the Protestans have a church and colledge in the towne the which is something rare in France.[6]

As for the Castel[7] it is on a high hill but noe more soe stronge as formerly, those of the towne having digged caves all under it, soe that it is easie to bee blowne up.

Having stayed heere the three moneths of the summer, I begun my journey to Richelieu the 18 of September,[8] and to that purpose wee tooke horses of Le Roux Messenger of Rochelle, and went first to Monsereau a little towne upon the Loire about a League from Saumur,[9] and in the way I saw great stone querries being about [f. 28ʳ] 4 miles long under ground. From thence I went to

Chinon a little towne and dwelling place of Charles .7.[10] as also the birthplace of Rabelais a famous Phisician and Professeur at Monspellier.[11] Hence I came to

[1] deletion.

[2] King Ptolemy Philadelphus (285–247BC) attempted, according to legend, to assemble at Alexandria in Egypt a library of all the books then known in the world.

[3] 'sea hogge', porpoise; 'sea dogges' and 'sea calfe', common seals; 'orbis', serpent.

[4] deletion.

[5] After this paragraph in Montagu's diary, the second hand takes over the recording of observations.

[6] The town became a Huguenot stronghold after the reformation and became popular with English Protestants during the mid-17th century. Its privileged status was lost by the revocation of the Edict of Nantes in 1685.

[7] 'The Castel' in left-hand margin. The Castle or Château, extensively rebuilt during the 16th century, commanded the confluence of the Loire and Thouet. It was the residence of the governors of Saumur until Louis XIV converted it into a state prison.

[8] 'September 18' in left-hand margin.

[9] 'Monsereau' in left-hand margin. Montsoreau, situated at the confluence of the Loire and Vienne rivers.

[10] 'Chinon' in left-hand margin. In 1428 King Charles VII united the General States while the English were attacking Orléans and it was at Chinon that Joanne d'Arc persuaded him on 9 March 1429 to assist Orléans.

[11] Little is known about the early life of François Rabelais (1484–1553), the son of a wealthy landowner who deputized for the lieutenant-general of Poitou in 1527. The nearby hamlet of La Devinière, rather than Chinon, has been claimed as his birthplace, although it is known that he did once live at a house (now demolished) on the Rue de la Lamproie. Rabelais studied medicine at the University of Montpellier where he also later lectured on the Greek physicians. From 1631 Chinon had been governed by the Richelieu family.

Champigny[1] where I saw the holy chappel thereof with severall relikes, also the marble tombes of all the familie of the Ducks of Mompensier. And so to

Richelieu[2] 7 Leagues of Saumur, seated in a very great plaine, and it is a very pleasant place tho esteemed very unholsome. At my first entring into it I thought I was rather in a[3] court of some faire Palace then in a towne, for first it is fowre square and all the houses make almost but one, being built all a like of free stone and covered with slate soe that when one is in the midst men see the fowre gates with all the streetes of the whole citty. This place is very little inhabited.

The church is very large and full of curious marble pillars, and rich gilding. It hath two great Pyramides a top in stead of a steeple.[4]

As soone as one is out of one of the gates the stately Palace of the Cardinal of Richelieu appeares [f. 28ᵛ] like to an earthly Paridis, it being built fowre square like the towne having the water running by it; and in the middle is a very faire court and round about it stands nothing but curious marble statues in niches in the wall of very great prise being all sent as presents out of Italie to the Cardinal; and the rarest amongst them are two slaves which stand on the cheefest dore, they are soe well done that nothing but live is wanting to them.

Then entring into the house I saw first a very faire paire of staires all of spotted marble and being come up I saw the hale where the gardes stand. Next is the Cardinal's dining roome curiously guilded with his armes over the chimny held up by fowre angels and under it is this Anagrame uppon his name:

Hardy maine de Hercule.

Then I came into the king's chamber rarely guilt and adorned with exquisite pictures, and by is his closet with other fine chambers for his followers. Next is the Queene lodging where one sees soe much gilding that it daseled ours eyes and especially in the Queene's cabinet where there are the 4 elements in 4 peeces soe rarely done that it causeth admiring in every one that sees them. Hard by are the curious chambers of Moises, Lucretia, of the historyes of Ovid Metamorphosis, and the like; and having passed by these cham[bers] I came to a long gallery[5] very richly gilded having on both sides the representations of all the warlick exploits of the Cardinal of Richelieu done in great; and at the other end it is rounde, caled a cupola, all with marble pavement with a curious [f. 29ʳ] table of Purphire in the midle and a place for the musick a toy all full of niches with Urnes of Purphire in them. Also the roofe of the gallery is very rarely gilded and painted by the rarest maistres in France or Italie.

[1] 'Champigny' in left-hand margin. Champigny-sur-Veude. Its 16th-century château of the Bourbon-Montpensier family was demolished by Richelieu, although its Chapelle St-Louis, containing various Montpensier family tombs, survived.

[2] 'Richelieu 19' in left-hand margin. Richelieu, once an insignificant village, was constructed by the cardinal in his own honour on a regular quadrilateral plan drawn up by Jacques Le Mercier. See Evelyn (1644), II, p. 150. Richelieu's father had begun to rebuild the old château in about the 1580s and the cardinal had originally only intended to complete his father's work, before deciding on a new and more grandiose scheme of his own.

[3] 'towne' deleted.

[4] It seems likely that Montagu was using the same secondary source here as Evelyn (1644), II, p. 150, who writes: 'But since the Cardinals death, it is thinly inhabited, it standing so much out of the way, & in a place not well situated either for health or pleasure … The church is well built, & of a well orderd Architecture, within handsomly pav'd & adorn'd'.

[5] Evelyn (1644), II, p. 151: 'The long Gallery is paynted with the famous Acts of the Founder; the roofe with the life of Julius Caesar; at the end of it, is a Cupola or singing theater, supported with very stately pillars of black marble'.

Next is the Cardinal's Lodging the which is not soe sumptious, as the others because he hath not altered it nor built it a new as he hath the rest.

I saw also in a loe chamber a curious table all inlayed with pretious stones having in the midle an agate of an etraordinary bignest, with severall other riche housold stuff.[1] This is all I could observe of the house; and As for the gardens they are very large and pleasant with severall chanels that runne through having a fine parke at the end thereof.

The stables are built more stately then many a nobleman's house and doe hold a hundered horse in them very well. There is also an ecco hard by which answereth 6 times togeather.

The deseased Cardinal soe caled did build this place all at his one charges but since his deathe it is falen to the Duc of Richelieu his neveu.[2]

Having stayed heere two dayes I went to Loudun,[3] little towne in a plane and 5 leages from Richlieu. The castel thereof is demolished soe that there is nothing to bee seene there but fine churches and handsome wenches in great numbre. I saw likewise in the cloister of St Benoist one of the nuns which had written on her hand Jesu maria Joseph, the which shee told us that the divil in going out of her had marqued it so having bin possessed by him almost two yeares, as also she sayed that every eeve of our Ladyes day it goes away and [f. 29^v] next day comes againe.[4] This place is very famous for fine band strings and lace, also for a place where one makes excellent good cheere. As soone as I had dined here at the 3 Kings, being esteemed for one of the best inns in France, I tooke horses and went to

Oiron,[5] dwelling place of the Duke of Roané, 3 leages from Loudun. The cheefest things there are the fine moat, and entri into the house, with a very hight Pavilion all painted with [rare?] kind of picturs of Romances, because the master of the house did not only love them but made them himselfe. And having seene this place wee came that night bak againe to Loudun and the day after arrived at Saumur for the 2 time.

This journey was of 3 dayes long,[6] during the which time I made a bout 27 leages.

Having rest a little[7] wee begane another journey and went with Le Roux horses, to

Touars[8] a little towne 7 leages from Saumur where I saw the stately Pallace of the Duke

---

[1] This table is now in the Louvre Museum.

[2] The Cardinal had arranged for his eldest grand-nephew, Armand-Jean Vignerot (1629–1715), to change his name and arms to those of Richelieu. He was the grandfather of Louis-François-Armand du Plessis, duc de Richelieu (1696–1788), Marshal of France.

[3] 'Loudun 20' in left-hand margin.

[4] Loudun had been notorious since the burning alive of Curé Urbain Grandier in 1634 on a charge of instigating the demonic possession of the nuns and Mother Superior (Jeanne des Anges) of its Ursuline convent, see Evelyn (1670), III, pp. 557–8. A number of associated miracles were also claimed and the conversion to Catholicism of Walter Montagu (the son of the first Earl of Manchester and our traveller's uncle) was supposed to have been instigated by one of them. Walter may even have been the source of Robert Montagu's knowledge of these affairs, although they were widely reported in England. See Lough, *France Observed*, pp. 192–200, for other accounts, including that by the playwright Thomas Killigrew, who visited the convent in the company of Walter Montagu in December 1635 and witnessed the exorcism of several nuns, see p. 74.

[5] 'Oiron' in left-hand margin. The village was under the control of the Gouffier family during the 16th century. The building of its château was begun in about 1518 by Artus Gouffier and completed in the late 1540s by his son, Claude. The pavilion described by Montagu also dated from this period. The château was acquired in 1667 by the duc de Feuillade who greatly enlarged it.

[6] '21 Saumur' in left-hand margin.

[7] 'Octobre 4' in left-hand margin.

[8] 'Touars' in left-hand margin. The ancient fortress of Thouars had been under the control of the La Trémouille family since the reign of Charles VIII.

of Trimoille[1] et Pere de France, built in the top of a rock having a fearefull precipis on one side and the towne on the other. There are three very remarcable things in this house, as first that all the offices are under grounde and looking out of the windowe one sees the[re] againe the precipis. These offices are held for the fairest in all france. Next is the balconie and the curious prospect.

After having visited my Lord strange[2] I went to my Lodging at the wilde man where I lay that night [f. 30^r] and next morning went for Rochelle and came to Le Chaume a village.[3] Then to

Coulonges[4] another village 4 leagues from Touars where I dined and came that night 5 leages farther to

Bressiure[5] little marquet towne next morning to

Ponsange[6] where I dined having mad 8 leages then I advanced 4 leagues farther and lay at

Mouilleron a little village,[7] so passing therough a very dangerous place for robing caled La Chastaign erraye,[8] I went to

Vounant village[9] and at last to

Fontenay Le Conté[10] a little towne in Poictow where I dined and the Protestans having in the towne a church I heard a peece of a sermon it being on a sunday. This towne is full of Protestants, and 7 leages from the place where wee lay. Having made 3 leagues more I arrived at

Gue de Velile[11] where I lay that night and put my selfe the next morning on a chanel made by some Hollanders to hinder the drowning of the countrey there about, and therefore is caled the Little Hollande and it caried us as far as

Marans[12] which is 2 leagues and half soe wee tooke againe our horses and having made 5 leagues more wee came to

Rochelle[13] principale towne of a little countrey caled Le Pays d'Onis.[14] This citty is not very ancient and at first was built by raison of the comodiousnesse of the port that [f. 30^v] is there, but the inhabitants there of groing rich by the great trading begun to fortify it and made it soe strong that it was held for impreniable. The which reason made that most of the Protestans retired them selves thether being a place of security for them, till at last the Papists and Protestants making war one against another, Louys 13 layed the seege before it and being not able to take it by force he environned it by land with his army; and with the Cardinal's of Richelieu's help he made a dig or casey thoe a thing thought impossible to bee done in the sea,

---

[1] This château, replacing an earlier structure, had only been completed in the mid-1630s. It was sited upon a plateau at the top of an amphitheatre of terraces rising up from the River Thouet.

[2] This Lord Strange was probably Charles Stanley (1628–72), the son of Charlotte de la Trémouille, Countess of Derby. He later became the 8th Earl of Derby.

[3] 'Le Chaume' in left-hand margin. Montagu may be referring to St-Germain de Longue Chaume.

[4] 'Coulonges' in left-hand margin. Coulonges-Thouarsais.

[5] 'Bressiure .6.' in left-hand margin. Bressuire.

[6] 'Ponsange' in left-hand margin. Pouzauges.

[7] 'Mouilleron 7.' in left-hand margin. Mouilleron-en-Pareds.

[8] La Châtaigneraie.

[9] 'Vounant' in left-hand margin. Vouvant.

[10] 'Fontenay le Conte' in left-hand margin. Fontenay-le-Comte remained staunchly Protestant, although it was besieged eight times between 1568 and 1621.

[11] 'Gue de Velile' in left-hand margin. Le Gue-de-Velluire, where Montagu traversed the Marais Poitevin with its extensive network of canals and dykes.

[12] 'Marans' in left-hand margin. Marans.

[13] 'Rochelle 9' in left-hand margin. La Rochelle.

[14] La Rochelle was the capital of the old province of Aunis.

by the which he hindered any provitions to come in other by sea or by land. And soe having tooke it by hunger he caused the walles to bee rased so that now it is more like a village then a towne having noe defense at all and almost desert.[1]

There are here severall fine churches and especially that which the protestans had heretofore being made without any piller and in ovalle forme.

At M[r] Flanc's house a Minister I saw a cabinet of rarityes and amongst other things he shoed us a bird of Paradis which had two strings instead of feet, with a cameleon which lives by the aire, as also bread made of old bootes the which they did eat in the last seege.

Then I went to the refining house where the [f. 31[r]] suc[2] is boiled and refined in great quantitie, it being the only place in all france for that. As for the aire it is something thik because of the neibouring sea. The Earle of Ognon is gouverneur thereof as well as of the isle of Re and Oleron,[3] which are not far from thence abondant in corne and vines. Heere having stayed a day I went and passed the river of Charente where wee were like to bee drowned. At that night came and layed at

Brouage[4] stronge fortresse built by the deceased Cardinal of Richelieu. The fortifications are very well worth the seeing, having round about it triple bastions, with every one his dich full of water, it standing in the sea having but one gate and a few houses in it. It is 6 leagues from Rochelle, then going 3 leagues farther I came by

Marennes,[5] famous for its greatnes it being one of the largest marquet towne in all France. There is a faire church built by the Inglish, which the Papists have at present. The Protestans have also another pretty church in the towne that night I lay at

Xaintes[6] 9 leagues farther it is the Capitalle citty of Xaintonge province; and layed at S[t] John Baptist head where wee were very well treated. As soone as it was day wee walked about to see the towne then which I found pretty pleasant having the river of Charante running by it, and curious gardens and [f. 31[v]] medowes on both sides it. That which I saw there was, first an old triumphat Arche built by the Romans,[7] the ruines of an Amphithiatre,[8] old buildings of Churches and the like ancient things. Having employed the hole morning of seeing this place I advanced farther to

S[t] Jean d'Angely[9] where wee refresshed our selves a little because of the heat and there being nothing here to bee seene, it having much suffered in the last warres, I went to

Moze[10] a village 10 leagues of Xaintes where I lay and next morning I dined 5 leagues farther at

---

[1] In 1627 Louis XIII and Cardinal Richelieu besieged the town by constructing a blockade across the harbour mouth to cut off supplies by sea. Two English relief expeditions (July–October 1627 and September 1628) failed and on 28 October 1628 the mayor, Jean Guiton, and the garrison were forced to capitulate.

[2] *sucre*, sugar.

[3] The barons d'Oignon had risen to prominence at the French court from the time of Artus de la Fontaine, baron d'Oignon, Master of Ceremonies under François II (1559–60), Charles IX (1560–74), and Henri III (1574–89).

[4] 'Brouage 20' in left-hand margin. Richelieu had based his operations at Brouage during the siege of La Rochelle and built its ramparts between 1630 and 1640.

[5] 'Marennes 21' in left-hand margin. Marennes.

[6] 'Xaintes 22' in left-hand margin. Saintes, formerly written 'Xaintes', was situated on the River Charante and was once the capital of Saintonge province.

[7] written 'and old triumphat Arche'. The Arc de Germanicus, erected in honour of Tiberius and Drusus Germanicus in 21 AD, stood by the Roman bridge (demolished in 1845).

[8] The Arenes, or small Roman amphitheatre, at Saintes dates from the 1st or 2nd century AD.

[9] '23 St Jean d'Angely' in left-hand margin. St-Jean-d'Angely.

[10] 'Moze' in left-hand margin. Mauzé-sur-le-Mignon.

Fontenay[1] la batu a little towne which stands in a plaine and I was told that the inhabitans thereof speake the worst Frence in all France. Two leagues farther I saw

Niort first towne of Poictou[2] on that side. I dined at the white horse which is putt in the number of one of the best innes in France. This towne is famous for nothing then for the two faires which are held here every yeare. From thence I went 4 leagues farther and lay at a village but the next morning having made a quarter of a Frence league I came to [f. 32r] La Mailleray[3] dwelling place of a Mareschal of France soe caled, where at first coming in I saw the statelynes of the house, having a great court before it where round about are the stables filled with fine horses of divers countries. A little lower are tow great ponds all paved with stone and railed round about made to water or wash the horses in and are seperated by a causie which goes strat to the house which stands a little lower. The building is not very big but never the lesse hath very fine chambers in it and well gilded, the cheefest thing is the Orange garden containing about 500 orange trees, the which gives a very curious sent in to the other gardens which are very spatious and pleasant. Soe having seen the master of the house wee went to

St Mairant[4] 2 leagues of where wee dined and so to

Poictiers[5] that night being 9 leagues farther and the next day I went about the towne the which I found very great. The reason thereof is because that there are severall gardens, vinyards, and filds inclosed in it.

The cheefest things I saw there are, the Churches as

The Cathedral of St Peeter[6] built with very great stone by Henry the second Duc of Normandie and King of England.[7] They keepe severall reliques of St Peeter.

Our Ladyes church is a very ancient and little.

St Hilary's church[8] is the fairest of all in the which I saw the tumbe of Godfroy le grand which is very [f. 32v] well worth remarquing because it consumes all bodyes in 24 houres and when you take a knife and scrape it there comes out an odious stink. The[y] showed us also the cradel of St Hilary's being a great peece of wood vary holow within, and it is much esteemed because of its vertu being able to make a foule become a wise man if he lies in it 8 dayes. And by it is an alter where the[y] say masse for him. There are very many which goe thether in Pilgremage to that purpose. I saw other relikes and rich adornements of Alters.

The colledge[9] is large and full of scolars of all nations but above all of Irish.

---

[1] 'Fontenay la Batu' in left-hand margin. Now Frontenay-Rohan-Rohan (to be distinguished from Fontenay-le-Comte, north-west of Niort.

[2] 'Niort 24' in left-hand margin. Niort.

[3] 'Mailleray 25' in left-hand margin.

[4] 'St Mairant' in left-hand margin. St-Maixent-l'Ecole on the right bank of the Sèvre-Niortaise Valley.

[5] 'Poictiers 26' in left-hand margin. Poitiers.

[6] 'The Cathedrale church' in left-hand margin. The Cathedral of Saint-Pierre (12th–14th centuries), with two dissimilar and still unfinished towers.

[7] King Henry I (1068–1135) was the son of King William I and Matilda of Flanders, and grandson of Robert I, duke of Normandy. His elder brother, King William II, succeeded his father only in England; Normandy passed to his elder brother, Robert. From 1096 until 1100 William II held the duchy of Normandy as a pledge but was never its duke. However, Henry I annexed the duchy of Normandy after the battle of Tinchebray in September 1106.

[8] 'St Hilarys' in left-hand margin. The 11th–12th-century Romanesque churches of Notre-Dame-la-Grande and St-Hilaire-le-Grand.

[9] 'colledge' in left-hand margin.

The cheefest nunnery is that of the holy crosse[1] where none but those of Royal blood can bee Abesse and the nunnes are all Ladyes in[2] numbre 200.

The nunnery of S[t] Rhodegonde[3] is hard by where wee saw her tombe and the[y] told us that in that place shee was wont to talke with our Savior.

Wee could not come to see the cabinet of M[r] de la brunetiere[4] because he was out of towne.

The[y] turne heere in Ivory and in wood the best of any place in France.

Half a league from hence is La Pierre Levee,[5] the which is a stone of treescore [f. 33[r]] foot a bout being hold up by 5 other great stones after a very strange maner. And having seene these things in a day I went the next morning 8 leagues farther to

Chastellerault[6] a little towne in the way having a very fine bridge of 9 arches and is a 130 steps long and 60 broade. The towne is famous for the excellent good knives and sisers which are made there. Thens I came againe to

Loudun[7] 10 leagues from thence and having seene it before I will say nothing of it only that I lay that night at the 3 Kings and next morning came to

Monstreuil,[8] little towne 6 leagues of belon[g]ing to the Duke of Longueville and that night safely arrived againe at

Saumur[9] 3 leagues farther where being returned to our dwelling place I went to our pension at Madame Michon's house. [f. 33[v]] This journey lasted about 13 days in the which time I made about 130 French leagues having passed therough severall Provinces of France as

Therough Aniou[10] a Duché the which tho it bee the least province in France yet it is of great revenu to the king because of its fruitfullnesse both in wines and Fruicts. It is also very pleasant being watered with 40 little rivers and is full of fine woods.

Poictou[11] which is devided into high and low, is one of the greatest and finest provinces in

[1] 'St Croix' in left-hand margin. The abbey was founded by Sainte Radegonde, who is regarded as the patron saint of Poitiers.

[2] 'the' deleted.

[3] 'S[t] Rhodegonde' in left-hand margin. The church of Ste-Radegonde, where the saint of that name, the wife of King Lothair (Clotaire) I, was buried in the crypt in 587. The black marble sarcophagus has been empty since 1562 when the Huguenots burnt its contents.

[4] 'cabinet' in left-hand margin.

[5] 'Pierre Levee' in left-hand margin. La Pierre Levée, probably the dolmen of raised stones near Brantôme.

[6] 'Chastellerault 27' in left-hand margin. Châtellerault. Its Henri IV Bridge was built in 1565.

[7] 'Loudun 28' in left-hand margin. Loudun.

[8] 'Monstreuil' in left-hand margin. Montreuil-Bellay. This duc de Longueville is now best remembered as the husband of Anne-Geneviève de Bourbon-Condé, duchesse de Longueville (1619–79). In 1642 she married Henri II d'Orléans, duc de Longueville (1595–1663), Governor of Normandy and a widower twice her age. The marriage was unhappy and in 1646 she formed a liaison with the duc de la Rochefoucauld, author of the *Maximes*. She was born in the prison of Vincennes, where her parents had been incarcerated because of their opposition to Marie de Médicis' favourite, the Marshal d'Ancre. After the death of Louis XIII, her father became chief of the Council of Regency during the minority of Louis XIV. She was heavily involved in the first Fronde and brought over her second brother, Armand, prince of Conti, to their side (although she failed to attract her other brother, the 'Great Condé', who remained loyal to the king). The second Fronde was largely her work.

[9] 'Saumur 29' in left-hand margin.

[10] 'Aniou' in left-hand margin, encompassing the *département* of Maine-et-Loire and coextensive with the former province of Anjou. Following the death in 1480 of its last independent ruler, René I, Anjou was returned to the Crown of France.

[11] 'Poictou' in left-hand margin, encompassing the *départements* of Vendée, Deux-Sèvres, and Vienne, and co-extensive with the former province of Poitou.

France, tho something melancolie for traveling because of the continuall woods one sees in it. It is very plentifull in corne woolle, etc.

The nobilitye are pretty civil but the comon people mighty rude and the language is very bad.

Xaintonge[1] is another little province the cheefest things it produces are, vines, salt, and safran.[2] In passing therough this province I came by a plene of 30 leagues long.

Pays d'Aulnis[3] is a little countrey in the which Rochelle stands and is not very fruictfull. [f. 34r][4]

Having rested againe here till the 1 of November I made a little journey with the Prince of Mahlebourg,[5] and the first place wee came by was[6] Longué a little village, then to

Beaufort[7] a little towne, so to

Baugé[8] a very pretty towne where wee dined and saw an old castel with other old buildings, and that night wee lay 13 leagues of at

La Fleche,[9] a pleasant towne in Aniou and renowned for the famous colledge the Jesuites have there. The which as soon as it was day wee went to see and found it very stately, having 3 great courts one with in another and as many bodies of lodgings soe that a king and all his court might very well lie in it.

The classes are very well built one by another and distingueshed with marble frontispieces.

The library is also very faire full of all kind of bookes, and rare globes.

There is also a very fine play house with a theatre of 3 stories hight where the scholars play twice a yeare in Latin.

The church is very great and richly guilded and in it lyes the hart of Henry the 4.[10]

The gardens are large and pleasant like the rest and it is held for the statelyest colledge in all France.

Thence wee went and walked about the towne and saw the Gouverner's fine house and gardens. [f. 34v] The morning being spent about seeing these things wee went and lay at a village 5 leages of and hard by Angers.[11] The next wee came to

Verger house of Prince of Gymené,[12] the which is both strong and pleasant thoe very ancient, and so wee dined the next day at

---

[1] 'Xaintonge' in left-hand margin. Saintonge district, encompassing most of the *département* of Charente-Maritime.

[2] saffron: the purple-flowered saffron crocus, the stigma of which is used as a dye and to flavour and colour food.

[3] 'Pays d'Aulnis' in left-hand margin. The ancient province of Aunis encompassed the northern part of the *département* of Charente-Maritime and the southern part of Deux-Sèvres.

[4] 'November 1' in left-hand margin.

[5] The counts of Nassau-Saarbrüchen were also princes of Mahlberg from 1629.

[6] 'Longué' in left-hand margin. Longué-Jumelles.

[7] 'Beaufort' in left-hand margin. Beaufort-en-Vallée.

[8] 'Baugé' in left-hand margin. Baugé. The castle had been largely rebuilt in the 1430s.

[9] 'La Fleche 2 Colledge of the Jesuites' in left-hand margin. La Flèche. Henri IV had originally granted the Château de la Flèche, south of Le Mans, to the Jesuits in memory of his parents. The Jesuit College officially opened in 1607 and then moved to new buildings in 1622.

[10] The hearts of Henri IV and Marie de Médicis were burnt by the Republicans in 1793 but their ashes are now housed in a niche above the gallery in the north transept of the Chapel (1622).

[11] Angers.

[12] 'Verger 3' in left-hand margin. The Château du Verger was built in the 15th century by Pierre de Rohan, seigneur de Gyé, and was partly demolished in 1776 by Cardinal de Rohan.

Pont de Lé[1] which is so much as Cæsar's bridge, having bin built by him when he conquered the Gaules. They are very long and made after the Roman fashion but much broken because of its antiquity. Then wee lay that night at

Brissac[2] the pleasant dwelling of the Duke soe caled. It is 4 leagues from Angers. It hath very deepe diches round about it and also curious terraces to walke there on. As for the house there is but 3 chambers finely gilded in it which are the kings and Queenes, the gardens are the pleasentest of all. Wee went next to

Doué[3] 7 leagues of a marquet towne, where wee saw an Amphithiatre, which is a building in forme rounde and in are tow Theatres made like tow half moones one against another, where the peeple in time of the heathens did gather them selves together to see the fithing of wild beasts [f. 35ʳ] with men which were condemned to die. And if they could kill the wild beast there lives were saved and because one could see from all places of the building what was done below, it is caled in Greeck Amphitheatron, from Amphi, which signifies in greeck round a bout, and Theaomai, I behold. This which I saw is something little thoe entire and walking into very greate caves under ground wee found several serpents tongues and the like. Then againe to

Saumur[4] 4 leages of Doué.

This journey was of 4 dayes long during the which I made 36 leagues.

While I lived heere att Saumur I went 4 Leagues of to Bourgeil[5] a countery house of the Arch Bishop of Rhiems, the which I saw with much pleasure because of its fine gardens and water works, they being the cheefest for the house is something little with ordinairy chambers in it. And because the Arch Bischop is reported to bee a very great eater wee went downe into the kitchin and into the places where they keepe the provision and there wee found very great quantity of foules of all kindes and dainty bits which come from a far of, as birds out of Languedoc, Capons from Geneva and the like sufficient for a hundered persons, and the servants told us that it was his ordenairy cheere [f. 35ᵛ]

1650

Having rested heere a little I went to

Angers[6] the capitale towne of that Province soe caled where wee employed the tow first days of seeing the towne and the most remarquable things in it.

The towne is seated on the rivers of Maine and Loire, tho very uneven soe that one must still goe up and downe.

The Castel[7] is very strong tho old, in the which wee saw severall fine peeces of ordonance and a cage of iron, wherein René king of Sicily loked up his wife up for many yeares

---

[1] 'Pont de Lé 4' in left-hand margin. Probably Les-Ponts-de-Cé.

[2] 'Brissac 5' in left-hand margin. The Château de Brissac at Brissac-Quincé, the seat of the Brissac family since 1611. The château was built by Charles de Cossé, the first duc de Brissac, who claimed to have opened the gates of Paris to Henri IV in 1594.

[3] 'Doué' in left-hand margin. Doué-la-Fontaine. Its Arènes were supposed to be of Roman origin, although they seem to have been constructed in the 15th to 17th centuries.

[4] 'Saumur' in left-hand margin.

[5] 'Bourgeil' in left-hand margin. Bourgueil.

[6] 'June 7 Angers' in left-hand margin. Angers was the ancient capital of the duchy of Anjou and préfecture of Maine-et-Loire.

[7] 'Castel [June] 8' in left-hand margin. The castle, completed in 1238 in the shape of an irregular pentagon, dominates the town.

together as being jalous of her. It is still kept in a chamber and showed to strangers when they come there.[1]

The cheefest church is caled St Maurice[2] being very great with 3 fine tours. The midlemust is up held by those of the both sides having an Arche under it. There are severall relikues kept there as a picher of Cananea, the sword of St Maurice and others.

There are severall fine churches here to bee seene.

The palle maille[3] is very pleasant[4] and in summer much frequented by the Ladyes of the countrey which are generaly faire in that province.

Butt the 4 day[5] did I see the cheefest thing of all which is caled La Feste de Dieu or festum Corporis Christi, in the which did I observe [f. 36^r] very many superstitious ceremonies. And the procession goes according to this order as

First marche all the trades men every one in his company having a Great torche in his hand with his booke and beades, and soe goes singing.

Then comes all the marchants in the same posture with candels in there hands and musicians mingled amongst them which play as the others sing.

Then followes 24 severall histories of the Bible made of the purest white ware every one on his basis of wood and must have 44 or 20 men to carry one alone. All the cittycens both Catholike and Protestant must contribute to the making of them only, for the ware is given to those which makes them, who having melted them sell it againe.

Next goes all the orders of Friers, as Capucins, Gray friers, Recoles, Carmes, Augustins, Minimes, et^c., every order having its crosse before it.

Then comes all the priests with rare musick and singing boyes which sing all in Latin.

And next goes the Arch Bishchop with the hostia or sacrement in his hand being inchased in a gold handel and fowre other priests goes on both sides which holdes a very rich canapy over his head.

Then comes the governour and chiefest of the towne with his gardes on both sides.

Next goes all the young Lawers with curious flowers in there hands and are caled the Basoches.

All this company goes in the cheefest churches and streets praying untill noone. It is held for the cheefest ceremonie of that nature in all France [f. 36^v] and I found it finer and statelyer then that of Paris. Soe having seene all wee came againe to

Saumur[6] having seene in the way the quarries of sleat with the which all the houses of the towne are covered. Angers is 12 leagues of this place.

---

[1] René I of Anjou (1409–80), was titular King of Naples from 1435–42; but Montagu may mean here Roger I (1031–1101), who was Count of Sicily from 1072, or his son Roger II (1095–1154), who was crowned King of the Norman Kingdom of Sicily on Christmas Day 1130.

[2] 'St Maurice [June] 9' in left-hand margin. The 12th-13th-century Cathedral of St-Maurice, with an incongruous central tower of 1540 set between two earlier ones. The vaults of the interior are set on stilts to give the impression of domed bays.

[3] '[June] 10' in left-hand margin.

[4] 'pleasant' added above.

[5] '11 [June]' in left-hand margin. The Feast of Corpus Christi was observed on the Thursday after Trinity Sunday and by the 15th century it was regarded as a major church observance, lavishly celebrated by local and civic communities. Its procession, in which rulers, nobility, magistrates, local dignitaries, and the general populace took part, became the feast's most renowned feature. English visitors were especially impressed by its pageant and procession because the feast had been suppressed in Protestant countries, following the rejection of the doctrine of transubstantiation during the Reformation. For other accounts by English travellers of the celebration of Corpus Christi in France, see Somerset (1611), p. 92; Evelyn (1651), III, p. 35; and Lough, *France Observed*, pp. 216–19.

[6] 'Saumur [June] 12' in left-hand margin.

While I stayed heere I made severall visites to the Cardinal Grimaldy, Uncle of the Prince of Monaco[1] when he lived at S[t] Florent,[2] the which used mee very courtiously and permitted mee to hunt in his woodes when I would tho it is a thing not usyall but an extraordinairy favour; and having leave I killed in the summer that I was at Saumur 8 very great staggs and 4 young ones in his woods, the which I still presented him but he would never take none sending them stil to my Lodging.

The second time that I was at Touars[3] the Duke of Trimoille receaved mee with great courtesy, making mee to lye in his owne house and to eat with him, as also I had long conference with him in the which he offererd to doe me very many favours especially if he did goe into Italie as Ambasadour and in parting permitted mee to hunt in his warren which is 5 leagues long, the which permission he gives to very few. I saw also Madame La Duchesse his wife who asked mee many questions concerning Ingland. I spock with the Prince of Tarante and with the Earle of Leval his two sonnes, with La Princesse of Tarante and madamoiselle the Dukes onely daughter.[4] And having stayed heere two dayes [f. 37r]

I came againe to Saumur[5] and during that yeare I stayed heere I made more particulier acquaintance with the Prince of Meckbourg his name being Jean Gorge, also with two German Earles of Levenstrine with the Baron of Trawn and two other German Barons and with severall other gentlemen of divers nations.

As for the masters[6] I had there were first, old M[r] Hubert for fencing, M[r] du Bres for singing, M[r] Nelloin for the Gittar, M[r] Oldeberg for the Latin tongue and Du Puis for dancing.

Having stayed heere a yeare[7] I went into the country to the

Terra house[8] of M[r] Brusse a Scotshman, brother in law to M[r] Hainhofer[9] and heretofore governour to the Duke of Trimoille, where I spent the rest of the summer and made acquaintance with severall gentlemen there round about, as with M[r] de La Pierre, M[r] de Boisset, M[r] de S[t] Cir governour of Touars, and others. Having stayed[10] heere 4 months I begun my journey to Paris with M[r] Brusse and his sonne and so came to

---

[1] The Grimaldi family, who had controlled Monaco since 1297, were closely allied to France, except for the period 1524 until 1641, when they fell under the protection of Spain. This Cardinal Grimaldi was also Archbishop of Aix from 1655–85.

[2] 'St Florent' in left-hand margin. St-Florent-le-Vieil.

[3] 'Touars' in left-hand margin. Thouars.

[4] Henri, duc de La Trimouille or Trémouille (1598/9–1674), was the son of Claude, duc de La Trimouille (1566–1604), and Charlotte-Brabantine (d. 1631), daughter of William the Silent. He had married in 1619 Marie de la Tour (1599–1665) and their eldest son, Henri-Charles (1621–72), was known as the prince of Tarente.

[5] 'Saumur' in left-hand margin.

[6] 'July' in left-hand margin.

[7] '22' in left-hand margin.

[8] 'Terra' in left-hand margin: i.e. country house.

[9] This Mr Hainhofer, Montagu's tutor, was probably a son or nephew of the renowned musician and connoisseur Philip Hainhofer (1578–1647), whose father Melchior had been a silk and velvet merchant at Augsburg. After studies at Ulm and Padua (where he registered in the legal faculty with his younger brother Hieronymous), Philip returned to Augsburg where, in addition to his musical interests, he became a trader in clocks, Asiatica and exotica, and works of art. He was employed by several notable patrons, including Duke William IV of Bavaria, as an agent to supply them with works of art and other curiosities and he was also active in garden design. A Jerome Hainhofer, perhaps Montagu's tutor, produced an English translation of Jacques Du Bosc, *The Secretary of Ladies. Or, A New Collection of Letters and Answers* (1638). See Hans-Olof Boström, 'Philipp Hainhofer and Gustavus Adolphus's *Kunstschrank* in Uppsala', in *The Origins of Museums. The Cabinet of Curiosities in Sixteenth- and Seventeenth-Century Europe*, ed. Oliver Impey and Arthur Macgregor, Oxford, 1985 (rpt. 1986), pp. 90–101.

[10] 'November [1650]' in left-hand margin.

Saumurs againe,[1] 5 Leagues of where wee lay that night and next day tooke a coach and went to

Trois Volans[2] where wee dined and came to

Langé[3] 10 Leagues of where wee lay for that night and next morning dined at

Tours[4] 5 leagues of an lay againe at

Amboise[5] 10 leagues farther and next day dined at Blois 18 leagues from thence. So lay at [f. 37ᵛ] Sᵗ Laurent[6] 4 leagues of and dined next day 6 leagues farther at

Nostre dame de Clary[7] where I mett the king of France coming from the siege of Bordeaux[8] and wee went along with his followers that night 7 leagues farther to

Orleans[9] where wee lay and visited the Prince of Meclebourg[10] that night the next morning being on a sunday wee continued our journey to Paris and wen[t] to

Artanay[11] 9 leagues of where wee lay, then to

Angerville[12] village 10. to

Estampes[13] little towne 9 leagues of where wee dined and lay at

Chastres[14] 5 leagues from thence next morning passed tharough

Lineas[15] village

Longumeaux[16] another village so to

Bourg de la Reine[17] where I dined and in the afternoone I arrived at

Paris,[18] 10 leagues of Chastres and had our lodging in the Dauphine's street.[19] The day I came heere some of the inhabitants did hange up the Cardinall Mazarin's effigies with a rope about his neake in sevall places of the citty with these following verses at it [f. 38ʳ]

> Voicy une Harpie, habilé en Cardinal
> Qu'on depende la copie, pour pendre l'original.[20]

[1] 'Saumurs 1 [November]' in left-hand margin.

[2] 'Trois Volans 3' in left-hand margin. Les Trois Volets.

[3] 'Langé' in left-hand margin. Langeais.

[4] 'Tours' in left-hand margin. Tours.

[5] 'Amboise 4 Blois' in left-hand margin. Amboise and Blois.

[6] 'Sᵗ Laurent 5' in left-hand margin. St-Laurent-Nouan.

[7] 'Nostre Dame de Clery' in left-hand margin. Cléry-St-André.

[8] Bordeaux enthusiastically supported the Fronde and the city had openly opposed the royal authority since September 1649. Louis XIV and Mazarin laid siege to it in September 1650 and the city accepted their terms on 29 September. Evelyn (1650), III, p. 23, recorded the arrival of the king back at Paris on 15 November 1650.

[9] 'Orleans 6 [November 1650]' in left-hand margin. Orléans.

[10] This is possibly a reference to Adolf Frederick I, duke of Mecklenburg-Schwerin (d. 1658), whose territories lay along the Baltic Sea coastal plain. He had been ousted by Albrecht Weuzel von Wallenstein in 1627–31 for siding with Christian IV of Denmark (although was later restored by the Swedes who gained Wismar and its environs under the Peace of Westphalia in 1648).

[11] 'Artenay' in left-hand margin. Artenay.

[12] 'Angerville' in left-hand margin. Angerville.

[13] 'Estampes' in left-hand margin. Etampes.

[14] 'Chastres' in left-hand margin. Châtres, the name of which was changed to Arpajon in 1720. See Somerset (1611), pp. 93–4.

[15] 'Lineas' in left-hand margin. Linas.

[16] 'Longumeaux' in left-hand margin. Longjumeau.

[17] 'Bourg de la Reine' in left-hand margin. Bourg-la-Reine.

[18] 'Paris 9 [November]' in left-hand margin.

[19] The Rue Dauphine runs directly from the Pont Neuf on the Left Bank.

[20] 'Here is a harpy, dressed as a Cardinal / Oh to take down the copy to hang the original'.

The three Princes that of Condé, Conty, and Longueville, being in Prison,[1] Au bois de Vincennes[2] there were severall jeering verses made on them.

From Saumur to Paris[3] are rekoned a 100 leagues and because I had bin heere a fore I say nothing but what I had the first time seene, and stayed heere but 8 dayes. So parted from M[r] Brusse and his sonne heere and began our journey to Lyons comeing first to

Ville Neuve[4] where wee met the king againe comeing from Fontainbleau wee lay that night at

Pont thierry[5] 9 leagues from Paris being a little market towne and dined next day 6 leagues farther at

Fontainbleau[6] soe caled because of the curious waters which are there round about. It is a little marquet towne tho famous because of the stately Palace belonging to the king which is there, the which I saw as soone as I arrived.

As for the house[7] it is built fowre square having 3 greate courts one within another and as many bodies of Lodging, the which are very stately tho' something ancient being first built by S[t] Louis and enlarged by Henry the 4[e]. There are very many faire galleries and fine chambers in number 704. In the cheefest gallery are represented the victories of [f. 38[v]]

Henr[y] the 4[e].

The Queenes gallerie is also very faire and adorned with curious picters.[8]

In the hall[9] where the feasts are heald there is on the chimney Henry the 4[e] a horseback made of white marble and is esteemed 18000 crounes because of the skilfull making of it. There is on both sides the meekenesse and peace represented in the like marble.[10]

There are severall other halles as that of the bales and the like.

The king['s] two chapels[11] are most richly guilded and adorned with rare pictours.

The Queene hath a very little chapel with picturs round a bout it made after the Mosaic fashion.

There are several faire courts as that of the whitehorse, of the Fontaine and others.

The gardens[12] are very large and pleasant because of the rare water workes and fine fontaines which are there in abondance, in the midst of king's garden is a very great fountaine made of Corinthian brasse and is caled Le Tibre, there being a woulfe in the midst

---

[1] Louis II de Bourbon, 4th prince of Condé (1621–86), was prominent in the Fronde uprisings (1648–53). He had been earlier known as the duc d'Enghien and later as the 'Great Condé'. Armand I de Bourbon, prince de Conti (1629–66) was Condé's brother. Henri II d'Orléans, duc de Longueville (1595–1663), had been the husband since 1642 of their sister, Anne-Geneviève de Bourbon-Condé, duchesse de Longueville (1619–79). They had been arrested on 18 January 1650 on Mazarin's orders and were imprisoned for thirteen months. They incarceration prompted the Second War of the Fronde.

[2] The Bois de Vincennes, a royal hunting ground and from 1731 a public park for the citizens of Paris.

[3] '16 [November]' in left-hand margin.

[4] 'Ville Neuve' in left-hand margin. Villeneuve-St-Georges.

[5] 'Pont thierry 17' in left-hand margin. St-Fargeau-Ponthierry.

[6] 'Fontainebleau 18' in left-hand margin. Fontainebleau, a royal hunting ground since the 12th century, was extensively redeveloped by François I, Henri II, and Henri IV. Louis XIII was born there.

[7] 'the Palace' in left-hand margin.

[8] Evelyn (1644), II, p. 117 (from Varennes, pp. 172–3): 'It abounds with very faire Halls, Chambers & Gallerys: In the longest which is 360 foote long & 18 broad is paynted with the Victoryes of that greate Prince Grandfather to the present [Henri IV]'.

[9] 'The hale' in left-hand margin.

[10] Evelyn (1644), II, p. 118: 'In the Sale des Festines, is a rare Chimny-piece, and Hen: 4th on horse-back of White-marble esteemed worth 18000 Crownes: Clementia and Pax nobly don'.

[11] 'the Capel' in left-hand margin.

[12] 'Gardens' in left-hand margin.

Fig. 26. 'Veuë du grand Jardin et de la Fontaine du Tibre de Fontaine bel eau' (c. 1650) (Israel Silvestre's drawing engraved by Adam Perelle).

which gives suc to Romulus and Remus,[1] and round a bout it are other stately statues of brasse. At the 4 corners of the gardens are fowre other fontaines of Corinthian brasse which run continually.

In the other gardens are the fish ponds which have an infinit deale of fish in them, the [f. 39ʳ] king taking very great delight in feeding them himself. The rest is nothing but woods, gardens, and walks and in them are fruicts of all kinds in number 6000 trees.

Soe having seene all I advanced that night 4 leagues farther to

Nemours[2] little towne hard by Fontainbleau in the which there is nothing to bee seene of note. Next day I dined 5 leagues of at Pont Agasson[3] another little towne and lay at

Ferrieres[4] 4 leagues of, a Marquet towne. The next day wee dined 4 leagues of at

Montargis[5] a little towne having a Castel which makes a great show a far of but neere hand it is nothing so that in France when they will jeere one the[y] say, 'c'est le chateau de Montargis beau en apparence mais rien en effect'.[6] I came that night to

Nogent[7] 5 leagues of and next morning passed thorough

La Bruissiere village[8] and dined at

Gien[9] a little towne 6 leagues of Nogent and I lay againe at

---

[1] Evelyn (1644), II, pp. 118–19 (from Varennes, 174): 'The Greate Garden being 180 thoises long and 154 wide has in the Center the Fountayne of Tyber in a Colossean figure of brasse, with the Wolfe over Romulus & Rhemus: also at each corner of the Garden rises a fountaine'.

[2] 'Nemours 19' in left-hand margin. Nemours.

[3] 'Pont Agasson' in left-hand margin. Unidentified but the name implies that Montagu was travelling along the banks of the Loing Valley and, from the stated distances covered, he was probably in the vicinity of Souppes-sur-Loing.

[4] 'Ferrieres 20' in left-hand margin. Ferrières-en-Gâtinais.

[5] 'Montargis' in left-hand margin. Montargis.

[6] 'The château of Montargis, fine in appearance but nothing in reality'.

[7] 'Nogent 21' in left-hand margin. Nogent-sur-Vernisson.

[8] 'La Bruissiere 22' in left-hand margin. La Bussière.

[9] 'Gien' in left-hand margin. Gien.

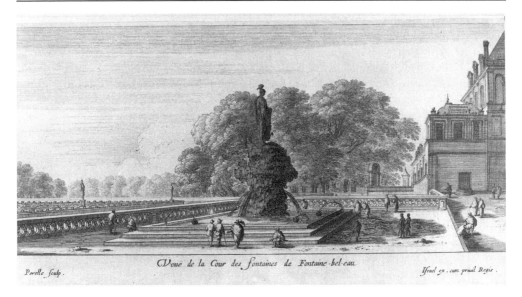

Fig. 27. 'Veuë de la Cour des fontaines de Fontaine-bel-eau' (c. 1650) (Israel Silvestre).

Briare[1] 4 leagues of a marquet towne and next day I dined at

[f. 39ᵛ] Cosne[2] 9 leagues of a village and lay at

Pouilly[3] 4 leagues farther. It is a little towne seated on the Loire and next day dined at

La Charité[4] another towne seated on the Loire, famous for the sieges which it hath endured and after diner I passed therough

Pouges[5] a little marquet towne tho very famous for its rare[6] minerall waters which are there and for that reason the cheefest nobilité of France come there in summer to drink them and thoes that cannot come have them sent in bottels to them with a certaine marque on them, but they have not that vertu when they are transported. That night I lay at

Nevers[7] 8 leagues from La Charité being the capitale citty of the Nivernois, it is of a pretty bigness and is seated on the Loire.

The castel is as yet hansome tho very old.[8] The Duke so caled had a fine cabinet in it but it is of late removed elce where.

The Jesuites have also a fine colledge[9] there. Next day I dined at

St Pierre le Moustier[10] 7 leagues of a very ancient citty and I lay 5 leagues farther at

[f. 40ʳ] Ville neuve[11] a little towne and dined next day 4 leagues of at

---

[1] 'Briare 23' in left-hand margin. Briare.

[2] 'Cosne' in left-hand margin. Cosne-Cours-sur-Loire.

[3] 'Pouilly 24' in left-hand margin. Pouilly-sur-Loire.

[4] 'La Charité' in left-hand margin. La Charité-sur-Loire.

[5] 'Pouges' in left-hand margin.

[6] 'waters' deleted.

[7] 'Nevers 25' in left-hand margin. Nevers.

[8] Montagu is referring to the Palais Ducal, built in the late 15th century by Jean de Clamecy, duc de Nevers, and much altered in the 16th and 17th centuries by the Gonzague dukes of Nevers. Building work was continuing when the palais was visited by Sir Charles Somerset (1611), p. 105.

[9] Evelyn (1646), II, p. 533, also visited the Jesuit College.

[10] 'St Pierre Le Moustier' in left-hand margin. St-Pierre-le-Môutier.

[11] 'Ville neuve 26' in left-hand margin. Villeneuve-sur-Allier.

Moulins[1] Capital of the Province of Bourbonois. The citty is little but pleasant because of the fine houses and walkes there about. It is famous for excellent good knives and sisars which are made there.

The Castel of the Duke of Burbon is very stately and pleasant having very fine water works and gardens round about it; and because the Duke comes never there the house keeper hath leave to take strangers in pension into the Castel, yet seldome does the strangers stay there because that there is no exercises to bee had there.[2] I lay that night at

Varrennes[3] 8 leagues of a village next day dined at

La Palisse[4] 6 leagues farther and lay at

La Paveodiere[5] a village 5 leagues of and next day dined at

Roane[6] one of the greatest marquet townes in all France and lay that night at

St Saforin[7] 4 leagues of a vilage and next day dined at

Tarrare[8] after having passed a montaing so caled being 5 leagues from St Saforin and lay at [f. 40ᵛ] La Bresse[9] 4 leagues of a little towne and dined 3 leagues of at

Lyon[10] the Capital of the Lyonais is a very very bigh and extreamely well seated, having the river of Saone which devided the citty in two and the Rhosne washes its walles. The[y] have two very fine stone bridges over them.[11] The reason that this place is so spatious is because it hath two montaines inclosed in it that of St Sebastien and of St Just.[12] The inhabitans there of are very rich because of the comodiousnes of its trading. For by the Rhosne one can goe into Italie, Spaine Africque and other places. La Saone fals from certaine montaines in the Duché of Bourgondy and is not so large nor so deepe. A dayes journey and half one is goeing to Roane where man may take a boat and goe into the midst of France, into Ingland, and Flandres.

The cornes are very plentifull here they comeing from Bourgondy. They have heere of all kinds of good fruicts and wines which come out of Provence. The best wines are thoes of Frontiniac and of Condrié, the last is holsomer tho not so delicious. The[y] say commonly this verse of Lyons.

Lyon deux villes, deux ponts, deux rivieres et deux monts[13]

[f. 41ʳ] The Cathedral church[14] is that of St Jean very spatious and stately built; tho'

---

[1] 'Moulins' in left-hand margin. Moulins was renowned for its cutlery. Evelyn (1644), II, p. 155: 'After dinner came manny who offer'd knives & Cisars to sell, it being a Towne famous for those trifles'. See also Reresby (1656), p. 33.

[2] The 13th-century ducal castle was the principal seat of the dukes of Bourbon from the late 14th century until the confiscation of the duchy in 1521. It was almost entirely destroyed by fire in 1755. See Evelyn (1644), II, pp. 154–5.

[3] Varennes 27' in left-hand margin. Varennes-sur-Allier.

[4] 'La Palisse' in left-hand margin. Lapalisse.

[5] 'La Paveodiere' in left-hand margin. La Pacaudière.

[6] 'Roane' in left-hand margin. Roanne.

[7] 'St Saforin' in left-hand margin. St-Symphorien-de-Lay.

[8] 'Tarrare' in left-hand margin. Tarare.

[9] 'La Bresse 30' in left-hand margin. Probably l'Arbresle.

[10] 'Lyon' in left-hand margin. Lyons.

[11] The Pont du Change is the older bridge over the Saône; and the Pont de la Guillotière is the oldest over the Rhône.

[12] Evelyn (1644), II, p. 157: 'But what appears most extravagant, & very stately are the two high Cliffs, cal'd St. Just & St. Sebastian, upon one of which stands a strong fort, guarisond'.

[13] 'Lyons, two towns, two bridges, two rivers, and two mountains'.

[14] 'The Cathedrall.' in left-hand margin. The cathedral of St-Jean. Following Caesar's conquest of Gaul the Roman colony of Lugdunum (the forerunner of Lyons) was founded in 43 BC. The spread of Christianity was evident in the area in the 2nd century and St Pothin, the founder of the church at Lyons, was martyred in 177. Like Evelyn, Montagu derived most of his historical information about the cathedral from Varennes, p. 161.

ancient it is reported to bee built of the ruines of an old temple dedicated to the Emperour August[us].

St Just[1] is a very old church having within great quantité of reliques which are showen on very great holy dayes. On the day of the innocent children there is a ceremony wort[h] seeing. The childeren goeing in procession in rich cloathes and cheanes.

Nostre dame de Fourniere[2] is extreme old and very little having bin dedicated in time of the heathens to the Godesse Venus.

L'Observance convent of the cordeliers,[3] [there] are two rare peeces to bee seene and especially that of the descent of our savior from the crosse.

The colledge and church of the Jesuites[4] are very stately built. The church hath bin rarely guilt by one of theire order.

The Library is very great filled up with curious bookes of all sortes and in the wale is a dove so well painted that one would thinke that it comes from the skies. A little higher is a fine perspective of a Jesuite opening a dore. Here is the best musick to bee hard in all the towne tho still after one manner a Jesuite saying this verse in Latin to prove it

Ecclæsia Lugdunensis non admittit novitates[5]

In the Novitiat is a sun diall which marques alle the victories of Henry 4 by the cours of the soone [f. 41[v]] and a dove with an olive branche markes all the holy dayes of our Lady.

The church of confort being the convent of the Jacobins[6] hath its quire all of white marble as also the Luthariens of the Empire have liberty to bee buryed therein.

The Nunnes of St Ursel[7] sing most rarely well at vespres every holy day and especially when the Cardinal of Lyons comes to heere them.

The Abaye of Aisnay[8] is very ancient and here to fore was caled Athenæum, and also there was in old time an alter before the which the learned man did prononce there speeches and gave them also in writing; and he that had made the worst of all was faint to take that which he had writ and seeke it out with his tongue or else they throwed him into the Soane, on the which a learned man made these following verses:

---

[1] 'St Just' in left-hand margin. The St-Just area is near the two Roman theatres and the body of the saint was buried in the church of the Seven Martyrs at Lyons.

[2] 'Nostre dame de Fourniere' in left-hand margin. The present basilica of Notre-Dame de Fourvière is a 19th-century construction but a chapel dedicated to the Virgin had stood at this site from the 12th century. After 1643, when Lyons was striken by the plague, the aldermen used to process each year on 8 September to pray for the Virgin's protection for the town.

[3] 'L'observance' in left-hand margin. Coryat (1611), I, p. 209, refers to the church of the 'Observantines' and 'S. Justus'.

[4] 'Colledge of Jesuites' in left-hand margin. Coryat (1611), I, pp. 209–10: 'I was at the Colledge of the Jesuites, wherein are to be observed many goodly things. The severall Schooles wherein the seven liberall sciences are professed, and lectures thereof publiquely read'. He also describes his tour of the library.

[5] 'The church of Lyons does not admit the new' (or 'novelties').

[6] 'Confort' in left-hand margin. This church of the Jacobins was destroyed during the Revolution, see Evelyn (1644), II, p. 157, n. 8.

[7] 'St Ursel' in left-hand margin. The Society of the Sisters of St Ursula of the Blessed Virgin had been founded in 1606 at Döle in France by the Venerable Anne de Xainctonge (1587–1612). The order sought to educate girls along lines established for boys by the Jesuits. They had recently been formally approved by Pope Innocent X in 1648.

[8] 'Abaye d'Aisnay' in left-hand margin. St-Martin-d'Ainay, the oldest church in Lyons, is a remnant of a former Benedictine abbey.

Paluit ut nudis pressit qui calcibus anguem
Aut Lugdunensem Rhetor dicturus ad aram[1]

La Charité[2] is a very great building appointed for the poore, thay being about 1000 in number in that house, as also the orphelins and unlawfull children are kept there where the[y] learne what what the[y] have a minde to. On the soone- [f. 42ʳ] diall are writt these verses:

L'heure ne Paroise point, si le soleil n'esclaire,
L'homme sans charité, a Dieu ne scauroyt complaire.[3]

The Towne house[4] is very old and little but of late they have begung to build a very stately one which is neere hand finished.

Belle cour[5] is a very fine walking place in the towne and in summer is continually full with coaches and excellent good company which come there to recreate themselves.

In a church caled Ilse barbe[6] lies burried Sᵗ Longius which piersed our Saviour with his speare whilst he was at the Crosse.[7]

The Penitans blanc[8] which wheepe themselves every good friday and then goe with naked fiere in a long white habit like a sheete having two holes in it for the eyes, into the cheefest churches and pray all night long. They have a very fine chapel by the gray friars. There are also blake ones of that order.

There are severall other ceremonies towards Christmas here to bee seene.

The cabinet of Mʳ Gaspard de Monconys Seigneur de Liorques[9] and the king's Lieutenant Général[10] hath a cabinet curious for all kind of medals of gold, silver, brasse and the like in number 4000. He hath also a curious head peece and boucler made after the ancient fashon with gold flowers on it. [f. 42ᵛ] Mr Dumé[11] the gouvernour's secretary hath a fine cabinet of picturs in his house.

---

[1] 'Just as the man went pale who crushed a serpent with his bare heels / So does an orator about to speak before the altar at Lyons'.

[2] 'La Charité' in left-hand margin. See Evelyn (1644), II, p. 157, n. 9.

[3] 'The hour will not appear at all, if the sun does not shine, / The man without charity, will never know how to please God'.

[4] 'Towne house' in left-hand margin. The Hôtel-Dieu, originally a medieval hospital, was extensively redeveloped from the early 17th century onwards.

[5] 'Belle cour' in left-hand margin. Evelyn (1644), II, p. 158: 'The place of the Belle Court is very spacious, especialy observable for the view it affords, so various & agreable, of hills, rocks, Vineyards, gardens, Precipes, & other extravagant & incomparable advantages abounding in this Citty'.

[6] A monastery had been founded in about 440 on L'Ile Barbe 6km to the north-west of Lyons on the Saône.

[7] I.e. the martyr St Longinus, the centurion at the Crucifixion who had pierced Christ's side with a lance and acknowledged him as the Son of God.

[8] 'Penitans' in left-hand margin. Montagu's reference to their white garb probably indicates the Carmelites, although the Carthusians also traditionally wore white. The order of Friars Minor Conventual (Franciscans) were known as Grey Friars or Cordeliers; and the Dominican Friars were known as Jacobins or Black Friars.

[9] 'Cabinet of Mʳ Gaspard de Monconys Seignʳ de Liorques' in left-hand margin. Perhaps a relative of the traveller and writer Balthasar de Monconys, whom Evelyn cited as one of his sources when writing about the nuns of Loudun (1670), III, p. 557–8. Evelyn drew extensively upon his *Journal des Voyages* (1665/6) for his own accounts of Italy.

[10] This word is written indistinctly and may be the result of a confusion at the moment of writing between 'general' and 'colonel'.

[11] 'of Mʳ Dumé' in left-hand margin.

Hard by the bridge of the Rhosne in a widowe's house caled Madame Marc Antoine. One sees all the kings of France curiously done in box all of one peece in a frame of ebeny. Also the passion of our Saviour done in wood like a Pyramide, with a dead man's head cutt in wood, the which all together she esteemes at 300 pistols and not under.

The Library of Mr Henry Gras Doctour in Physick is the fairest in all Lyons containing 1200 great volumes in folio and 4000 lesse ones.

The Cabinet of Mr de Cerviere heretofore Lieutenant Collonel d'un Regiment is compounded of three cabinets full of curiosites.

And in the first I saw severall peeces of Ivery turned one with in a nother; also two doores for to set in a court of guard which as you open one the other shuts by holpe of an iron which is hidden in the wood. Then I saw the entry of a fortresse with his draw bridge and its doore which opens fowre severall wayes, so that as you open it on one side it shuts on the other. Then a wheele which brings up what booke one will with out letting it fal. Severall pompes very nessessary.

[f. 43^r] In the second cabinet, the cheefe peece is a watch which goes by the help of water which filling a little bouket of water it emptieth its self and so make a minute and still beginning finishes a houre. The fore part of it is made of ebony with much Ivery inlayed.

There are divers bridges to passe en arme over a river in a little time. One is compounded of half barils with boards over them, having every one two wheels and being made to fold one horse can draw two at a time.

Another made of 4 or 5 boates and more easy then the first.

Another of boards only.

After that he showed us a cabinet with glasses representing a faire house the which was changed by the turning of a lok into a table covered with gold and silver and was changed into a garden of fine flowers and last of all into a feast where all kind of meats.

There where severall Machines of that nature.

An other instrument to make water come up from a low place into a fountaine made in a higher place that one may make use of it more commodiously.

Also severall fontaines having instruments which makes them cast the water in severall figures and fashions. Also an instrument with the which one man can beat more corne in a day then six after the common fashon of treshing.

A new invention to beat the Lames.

Another for to make golden thread.

Severall fontaines with statues in them which walke up and downe by the artifice of the water.

[f. 43^v]   1652

A cheare in the which one goes up and downe into what chamber of the house on[e] desire and that is by the help of some springs in it which are hiden. The Cardinal Mazarin hath one in his house, as also Madame La Duchesse de La Trimoille.

While I stayed heere I went and saw Vienne, little towne in Dauphiné.[1] There are severall antiquites to bee seene, as the tour of Pilate where he was kept, the lac and abisme

---

[1] 'Vienne' in left-hand margin. Pilate had been associated with Vienne since at least the 9th century by St Ado in his *Chronicles*. Evelyn (1644), II, p. 159 describes the castle at Ponsas, near St-Vallier, forty miles down the Rhône, supposedly inhabited by Pilate. Varennes (1643), 158, notes the house in Vienne traditionally associated with Pilate.

wherein hee precipitated him selfe in, and other such ancient things.[1] I saw the place where the[y] make blades of swords in great abondance as also the paper mills.

Having stayed heere 6 months[2] I parted for Geneva and passed thorough these following places as

St Crestofle[3] to which place Mr Cæsar Gras a great lover of the English brought us a going. Wee dined that day at

Monluel[4] and lay at

Chateau galliard.[5] Next day wee dined at

Sardon[6] a little towne having a montain by it so caled. I came by

Nantua[7] a pretty citty having a fine lac at [f. 44r] one end of it. And I lay that night at

Chatillon[8] another little towne and in the morning wee went a league farther and saw the place where the river of Rosne looseth itself running under great stones into the ground and so lies hid for half a league then comeing out runnes downe to Lyons. This is very well worth remarquing so I advanced and came therough.

L'escluse[9] a strong fortresse of the king of France on the borders of Savoye. This place with 20 men can defend its self against 2000, so I came to

Collonges[10] where wee refreshed our selves by reason of the extreme heat. Then came to

Chancy[11] a village where wee passed the saied river of Rhosne and 3 leagues farther arrived at

Geneva[12] being 18 great leagues from Lyons. This place is seated betwixt France, Suisse and Savoy. The river of Rhosne devides the citty in two and fales from the mountaines or Alpes which are towards Suisserland, so runs thorough the Lake of Geneva without mingling his swift waters with the sleeping ones of the sayed Lake so that one may very well perceave the difference betwixt the Rhosne water and that [f. 44v] of the lake. There are three bridges of wood and on the cheefest are houses of artisans built on both sides and most of gunsmits which worthe very well. Harby the bridge is an Iland having a very old tour which the[y] say was built by Julius Cæsar.[13] The Republike puts their amunitions of warr in it.

As for the gates they are in number three and by the New gate one goes into France, by that of Rive one goes into Savoy, and by Cornevine one goes into Suisserland.

The citty is devided in high and low, in the upper lives the councellors and the cheefest of the towne as also most strangers take pension in it. In the Lower lives all kind of tradesmen and In keepers.

---

[1] 'May 1651' in left-hand margin.
[2] '29' in left-hand margin.
[3] 'St Cristofle 30' in left-hand margin. Montagu was probably travelling at this point on the Villeurbanne-Miribel-Montluel road.
[4] 'Monluel' in left-hand margin. Montluel.
[5] 'Chateau galliard' in left-hand margin. Château-Gaillard.
[6] '31 Sardon' in left-hand margin. Cerdon.
[7] 'Nantua' in left-hand margin. Nantua.
[8] 'Chatillon June 1' in left-hand margin. Châtillon-en-Michaille.
[9] 'L'escluse' in left-hand margin. Fort de l'Ecluse.
[10] 'Collonges' in left-hand margin. Collonges.
[11] 'Chancy' in left-hand margin. Chancy.
[12] 'Geneva 2.' in left-hand margin. Geneva.
[13] Evelyn (1646), II, pp. 528–9: 'On Two Wooden bridges that go Crosse the river, are severall water Mills, & shops of Trades, especialy Smiths & Curttlers, & betweene the bridges an Iland, in the midst of which a very ancient Tower, said to be built by *Julius Caesar*' (from Varennes, p. 220).

There are fowre churches in the citty. The cheefest is that of S[t] Peeter hertofore a Cathedral. It hath 4 steepels but the cheefest is filled with canons and soldiers in time of warr.[1] The ancient inscriptions which the learned men find heere makes them juge that it hath been heretofe dedicated to Apollon or to some other god of the heathens and the Eagle with two heads showes it hath bin an[2] Imperiale citty.

The towne house[3] is a new building being adorned with 4 greate pillars of blanc[4] [f. 45[r]] marble. The goeing up is paved with very little stones so neatly that one may goe up with a coach and six horses to the very top having a nother way to come downe. One sees in a hale there severall Urnes with deads men's ashes in them, they having been found when the diches of the citty were inlarged.

In the chamber where the juges assemble themselves one sees 7 juges painted without hands except he which is in the midst which hath but one.[5]

The Arsenal[6] is joining the towne house and is three stories hight. In the first are the canons and other warlike instruments. In the second are armes for a good number of men and in the third are the Laders tooken from the Savoyards in the time of L'escalade, also other prises tooke on the ennemies.

The colledge[7] is of a fine building, having a curious aspect on the Lake.

The hospital is hard by being nearly built.[8]

This towne is very well fortified having severall good bastions, and every night the[y] shut up the portes of the Lake with great iron cheanes.

Hard by are the places where they keepe the [f. 45[v]] the fairest troutes all the yeare long to make presents to great persons when they come thorough Geneva.

The greatest trafike of this place is of bookes, silke stuffs, watches and fat capons which are sent as dantyes to other places.[9]

This Republike comands to sevarall villages in France, Savoy, and Suisse. There Bischop was temporall Prince of this place but the Inhabitans changing of theire religion drove him out and made alliance with the 4 cantons of Zurich, Berne, Basle and Shaffusen.

At present this state is governed in a Democracie mingled with Aristocracie. For the common people having all the power doe resigne it over to 25 Senateurs of the which the 4 Syndics are the cheefest. They carrying 4 black steekes with sliver ends as a marke of Seigneurie, the first hath the generall government of the common-wealth and the three

---

[1] The cathedral of St-Pierre, dating from the 12th-13th centuries. Evelyn (1646), II, pp. 527–8: 'This was in St. *Peters*, heretofore a Cathedral, & a reverend pile: It has 4 Turrets, on which stands a continual Sentinel, on another Cannons mounted'.

[2] written 'and'.

[3] 'Towne house' in left-hand margin. The Hôtel de Ville was built mainly during the second half of the 16th century.

[4] Montagu writes 'blanc' (white) here but Evelyn (1646), II, p. 525, notes: 'The *Portico* has foure black-marble Columns' (both taking much of their description from Varennes, p. 222).

[5] Evelyn (1646), II, p. 529: 'against the wall of one of the Chambers seaven *Judges* painted without hands, all excepting one in the middle who has but one; I know not the storie' (from Varennes, pp. 222–3). This painting, in the Salle du Conseil, refers to Exodus 23:8.

[6] 'Arsenal' in left-hand margin. The Arsenal, dating from the 15th-17th centuries, has been heavily restored and it now used as an archive.

[7] 'College' in left-hand margin. The university was founded in 1559 and the buildings examined by Montagu were completed by 1562. See Evelyn (1646), II, pp. 529–30.

[8] Evelyn (1646), II, p. 530, mentions: 'I also went to see the *Hospital*, which is very commodious', implying that Montagu witnessed ongoing structural developments.

[9] Ibid (1646), II, p. 524, also details the commerce of Geneva.

others have offices a part. The Syndics are chosen every yeare anew so that one stayes in his charge but a yeare.

[f. 46^r] The counsel of 25 choose the counsel of 200, and all the inhabitans to gether choose the Syndics and other officiers.

I lay at one Mr Volks house in pension and during the 3 months that I stayed heere I made more particulier acquaintance, with the Marquis of Baden et de Durlach,[1] a German and souverain prince, with Barons one of Vindishrats, of Baytisaux and of Drucxes, as also with severall gentilmen of all nations.

While I was heere I continued only the Latin tongue with Mr Tridon and dancing with one Mr Denis who hath taught mee in Ingland when I was yet very young.

I went also to Aubone[2] Barronie and dwelling place of My Lady Biondy a widow and sister to Sr Theodore Myerne,[3] and visiting her shee showed mee very many civilites together with her neece M^s Vindsor.

Having stayed heere the 3 months of the summer[4] I begun my journey for Germany passing thorough Swisserland and other places. I parted the 17 of August and came by these places, as

Versay village.[5]

Copet[6] little towne, so to

[f. 46^v] Nion[7] another towne, and I dined at

Rolle[8] a marquet towne one the Lake of Geneva being 8 leagues thence, and that night lay at

Aubone[9] 2 leagues of where I visite againe My Lady Biondy who lodged mee in the castal. And taking my leave of her the next day after dinner I went and lay at

Morges[10] a little towne belonging to M^{es}. de Barne, it is 2 leagues of Aubone. Heere wee first entered into Suisser Land and saw these following places of that countrey. I dined next day at

Lausanne[11] 4 leagues of a very neat citty and because it is seated betwixt two little rivers caled Laus and the other Anna this following verse was made on it.

Inter Laus et Annum fuit fondata Lausanna[12]

I saw heere a fine church the which as they report was splitt in two by an earth quake and shut up againe by another. One sees still the krack in the wale.

[1] Probably the Marquis Frederick V of Baden-Dorlach (1594–1659).

[2] 'Aubone' in left-hand margin. Aubonne, with spectacular views over the Lake of Geneva.

[3] Sir Theodore Turquet de Mayerne (1573–1655) studied at Montpellier and was a royal physician at Paris before coming to England in 1603 as Queen Anne's doctor and remained in England, treating members of the royal family and the nobility. His wife was a sister of Sir Giovanni Francesco Biondi (1572–1644), secretary to the Venetian ambassador at Paris, who came to England in 1609 and served James I as a representative at the Calvinist Assembly at Grenoble. He died at Aubonne where his widow remained.

[4] 'August 14' in left-hand margin.

[5] 'Versay' in left-hand margin. Versoix.

[6] 'Copet' in left-hand margin. Coppet.

[7] 'Nion' in left-hand margin. Nyon.

[8] 'Rolle' in left-hand margin. Rolle.

[9] 'Aubone 18' in left-hand margin. The château at Aubonne was, successively, the residence of the traveller in Asia and the Orient, Baron Jean-Baptiste Tavernier (1605–89), and Admiral Duquesne (1610–86).

[10] 'Morges 19' in left-hand margin. Morges.

[11] 'Lausanne' in left-hand margin. Lausanne, overlooking Lac Léman. Two streams, the Flon and the Louve, which formerly flowed through the centre of the city have now been filled in.

[12] 'between Laus and Anna was founded Lausanne'.

The colledge and Library are very faire.[1] Heere we mett our company which were a German Baron caled Mr Truchses and Mr Volke [f. 47^r] our hoste with his wife. And continuing our journey wee lay that night at

Moudon[2] 5 leagues of a little towne. And next morning passing therough

Payerne[3] wee dined at

Avanches[4] 7 leagues further, marquet towne so passing by

Morat[5] a little citty having a great lake at one end of it. I saw in the high way harby the towne a house filled up with dead men's heades and the Latin inscription over the dore showes that Charles the Last, Duke of Bourgondy, being utterly defeated in that place by the Suissers the[y] caused all the heades to bee gathered together and put in that house for a remembrance.[6] I lay that night at

Pont de Giminé[7] 5 leagues farther. And next day I dined 3 leagues of at

Berne[8] the head citty of a Canton so caled and comes from the word Ber which signifies a Beare in theire Language and for that reason they keepe still beares in a foure squared place made like a dich.

[ff. 47^v–48^r blank]

[f. 48^v] This towne is very faire having greate stately buildings in it. On both sides of the streets are arches under the which one may walke dry altho' it raines never so fast. The towne[9] is as well strong as pleasant having very fine bullwarks raised a new round about it. The streets are very Cleanely, having its chanel of cleare water running thorought it so that it washes every thing away.

As for the Ursenal it is very faire and great.[10]

The cheefest church is very faire within and in its steeple hath a bell of an extra-ordinary bigness and weigth.[11] After diner we advanced further and lay at

Weiningen[12] a village 5 leagues of then dined at

Arbourg[13] 8 leagues of. So lay at

Araw[14] 3 leagues of, a village taking its name from the river which runs by it. And next day dined at

Baden[15] 4 leagues of, where wee saw the hott bathes which are very famous over all

[1] Montagu is referring here to the buildings of the old Academy (dating from 1587), to the north of the Cathedral. A School of Theology was founded at Lausanne in 1537.

[2] 'Moudon 20' in left-hand margin. Moudon.

[3] 'Payerne' in left-hand margin. Payerne.

[4] 'Avanches' in left-hand margin. Avenches.

[5] 'Morat' in left-hand margin. Morat.

[6] Charles, Duke of Burgundy (1433–77), known as 'Charles the Bold' or 'Charles le Téméraire'. After besieging the town of Morat for thirteen days, Charles suffered a heavy defeat at the hands of the Swiss forces under Adrian of Bubenberg on 22 June 1476, in which some 10,000 of his Burgundian soldiers were thought to have been killed. He was himself killed in a battle near Nancy in January 1577.

[7] 'Pont de Giminé 21' in left-hand margin. Probably Gummenen (Pont).

[8] 'Berne' in left-hand margin. Berne. The name is traditionally claimed to be derived from the German *bär* (bear) and the bear forms the city's heraldic device. The *Bärengraben* (Bear Pit) dates from at least the early 16th century, in which several bears are traditionally maintained at the city's expense.

[9] Many of these buttressed *lauben*, or arcades still survive in the old centre of the city.

[10] The Grosse Schanse was the main bastion of the city's fortifications between the 1620s and 1840.

[11] The Münster at Berne was begun in the 14th century and completed in the 16th.

[12] 'Weiningen 22' in left-hand margin. Probably Wangen an der Aare or (farther to the east) Aarwangen.

[13] 'Arbourg' in left-hand margin. Aarburg.

[14] 'Araw 29' in left-hand margin. Aarau, situated by the River Aare.

[15] 'Baden' in left-hand margin. Baden, renowned for its saline and sulphur baths.

germany so that that there are still great[1] number of people which come there to bee cured. I washed my handes in the place where it riseth but it was so hott that it did almost burne my hands. The water [f. 49r] smels much after brimstone and the like. I lay againe that night at

Alstetten[2] a village 5 leagues of and dined at

Zurich[3] 2 leagues farther, Capitall of the Canton so caled and is one of the Ancients Citty in all Suisser Land, being built 16 yeares after that of Treuves which was built during the time of the Patriarche Abrahan. At one end is a fine lake caled after the cittye's name, having very fine countrey landes and villages on both sides it. The river of Limat[4] runs thorough the towne. As for the fortifications the[y] are begun but as yett not finished.

The Arsenal[5] is of a large extent and is 4 stories high. In the first are the Canons, morter-peeces, Granades and the like warlicke instruments. In the second are the armes belonging to horse men in great number. In the third are the muskets, pikes, and other armes belonging to the foote soldiers. In the third[6] are the maches, and spades to dig with all as also other instruments.

The church is very ancient but very faire within.[7]

The colledge hath a very fine Library filled with rare books and curious manuscripts. I saw in it a little cabinet of rarites having in it mummy and severall stranger birds as also a deads man sknine.

[f. 49v] The Senat presented mee with 12 great pottes of wine at my arrival and sent to of the Senaturs to dine with mee, who in comeing in made mee a speech in German from the Senat.

I visited My Lady Smith[8] having a lettre of recomendation from her Sonnes. And having stayed heere a day I went next morning and dined at

Vinterthurne[9] a marquet towne 4 leagues of where wee saw an Elephant which played all maner of triks, as is to bee seene by the picture. Wee lay that night at

Rekebach[10] 5 leagues of a village and dined next day at

St Gall[11] 4 leagues farther, a little citty in Suisserland. It takes its name from one Gallus a scottch man. They trade much heere with Linnen.

The Abbaye[12] is very stately being seperated from the towne by a wale and two greate gates. In it lives the Abut which is a souverent Prince. The church is very richly gilded. Next day I went to the port of

[f. 50r]

[1] 'quantitie' deleted 'number of people' added above.

[2] 'Alstetten 24' in left-hand margin. Alstetten.

[3] 'Zirich' in left-hand margin. Zürich.

[4] The city stands at the north-west end of the Zürichsee, on either side of the River Limmat.

[5] 'Arsenal' in left-hand margin.

[6] 'fourth' presumably intended.

[7] Montagu is probably referring here to the Grossmünster (12th-13th centuries) on the east bank of the River Limmat.

[8] Unidentified.

[9] 'Vinterthurne 25' in left-hand margin. Winterthur.

[10] 'Rekebach 26' in left-hand margin. Rickenbach (to the south of Wil, the usual stopping place on the route to St Gallen).

[11] 'St Gall 27' in left-hand margin. St Gallen, named after the 7th-century Irish missionary, St Gallus or Gall, who also founded the hermitage (later an abbey) there.

[12] 'Abaye' in left-hand margin. The old abbey was seriously damaged in 1712 and deprived of its temporal powers in 1798, with spinning wheels being set up in its empty buildings. The Cathedral, formerly the abbey church, dates from the mid-18th century.

Fig. 28. A performing elephant, a print inserted in the travel diary of Robert Montagu, Lord Mandeville. Bodl. MS Rawlinson D 76, f. 50.

133

[f. 50ᵛ – blank]

[f. 51ʳ] Roschak[1] 2 leagues of. And there wee embarqued our selves and passed the lake of Lindaw in 4 houres time and dined at

The sayed Lindaw[2] being the first towne of high Germanye on that side. It is very stronge and stands half in the Lake and on the other side are double bastions with double diches so that it is a very considerable place tho little.

Heere I left Swisserland and entred into Germany. The Suissers are very rich and good soldiers but extreme rude and heavy. As for the countrey it is very fruictfull and full of rivers, Lakes and woods. Having dined heere I went and lay at

Ravenspourg[3] a village 5 leagues of. And dined next day at

Laykirch[4] 6 leagues of. And lay againe at

Memmingen[5] 8 leagues farther, an Imperial citty. In the Protestans church are curious organs to bee seene. And I dined at

Mindelheim[6] 7 leagues of. And lay againe at

Erlingen[7] 5 leagues farther. And next morning having made 5 leagues more I arrived at Augspourg[8]

[f. 51ᵛ] Augspourg is one of the cheefest Imperiall cittyes of Germany and is caled in Latin Augusta Vindelicorum because of two little rivers which run by it, one caled in Latin Vinda, and the other Licus. This citty is very pleasantly seated and is the cheefest in Schaabe Land. The houses are very stately built, most of them being painted by Italian masters; and above all 3 great tours most curiously well done although the[y] begin now to decay. And because I was resolved to stay heare till I had learned something of the german tongue I lodged my selfe at Mʳ Hainhofer's Uncle's house[9] and to say things at Leasure.

The towne House[10] is one of the statelyest buildings in all Germany. It is built after an Italian fashion and hath 5 stories one upon the other. The frontespeece is very faire, having great marble stones in severall places of it. The entry is all paved with marble and hath 4 great marble Pillars in the midst of it. In one I saw the resemblance of a little childe in a cradle and by it a lopster the which although growne in it yet is very naturally done. In the entry are severall peeces of ordenance and the citty garde watches there day, and night, goeing up a stately paire of staires. Wee say a very fine hall of marble stone but a bove that is the great hall where they are wonte to feaste the Ambassadours. [f. 52ʳ] This banqueting hall is most rarely built and hath very much guilding and painting in it. One both sides are the counsell chambers and other primate lodgings. Above

---

[1] 'Roschak' in left-hand margin. Rorschach.

[2] 'Lindaw' in left-hand margin. Lindau, despite its small size in the 1650s, had been heavily fortified in the 13th century as a free imperial town.

[3] 'Ravenspourg 28' in left-hand margin. Ravensburg.

[4] 'Laykirch' in left-hand margin. Leutkirch.

[5] 'Memmingen 29' in left-hand margin. Memmingen.

[6] 'Mindelheim' in left-hand margin. Mindelheim.

[7] 'Ertingen 30' in left-hand margin. Ettringen.

[8] 'Augspourg' in left-hand margin. Augsburg (the Roman encampment of Augusta Vindelicorum) is situated where the River Lech meets the River Wertach.

[9] See p. 119.

[10] Montagu is probably referring to the Fuggerhaus (1512–15), south of the church of St Moritz, the town house of the princes Fugger von Babenhausen. The Habsburg's banker Jakob Fugger (1459–1525) resided at Augburg and in 1519 he founded the Fuggerei, a small community of dwellings for the poor of the city.

is a very fine terrace to walke on, having in each corner a pine aple made of brasse representing the citty's armes.[1]

The Indas or Secret entrie found out by the Emperor Maximilion .1. is very woorthy to bee seene.[2] It is an way to lett in any one by the night without opening the citty gates and it is made after this fashon. On the wall of the citty is a very thike toure built, and in this towre are severall engins of iron soe that the man which is in it, he hearing one ring a bell, letts downe a drawebridge with two doors before, soe that as he opens the farther he shoutes the t'other. Then being all come in, he shuttes the first two doores and drawes the brigde up againe to hinder any more from comeing up againe. Then lifting up a iron hammer another dore opens of it self and shuttes another. Then he letts doune a candel to see how many you are and what you will, soe if he likes you and does not suspect you he lets you out into the citty.

The water tour is so well and artificially contrived that it furnisches the whole citty with waters;[3] and that by the help of severall pumps and mathematicall Instuements and is held for one of the fairest waterworks in Germany.

[f. 52ᵛ] As for the government of the citty it is Aristo [   ][4] it being ruled by 31 of the Patricians and to them are added 14 marchans or of the common people. These together make up a counsell of 45 and the cheefest amongst them are the tow Governers and next to them[5] the Bourgemasters which are 6, half of them Lutherans and the other half Papists.

This place is likewise much spoken of for the many rare and skillfull artists but especially for joyners, turners, silversmiths and the like which daily invent new devices and subtilities; and above all in choise cabinets of all sorts and prices both for use and pleasure, *which* with great cost and charge are sent into divers parts of the world.[6] And of this city which for the neatur of its buildings, streets, fountaines, and other things one made these Latin verses.

> Augusta sunt hic omnia, et inclyta
> Quæcunq cernis: templa, domus, fora,
> Turres et horti, porticusque.
> Menia et hospitia, et tabernæ.
> 2. Augustior Respublica nobilis,
> Virtute præstans et sapientia:
> Formis puellarum, virum*que*
> Miribus ingeniis abundans, etc[7]

---

[1] Rather than a pineapple, both Sir Charles Somerset (1612), p. 268, and Robert Bargrave (1656), p. 246, describe the city's arms as a bunch of grapes. They also both stayed an inn of that name.

[2] Maximilian I (1459–1519), Holy Roman Emperor, established the dominance of his family, the Habsburgs, in sixteenth-century Europe. In 1500 the imperial princes at the Reichstag (Imperial Diet) at Augsburg withdrew their support from Maximilian but, as detailed by Montagu, his response was effective.

[3] Bargrave (1656), p. 245: 'theyr Water mills, which from the river, mount the water, in quantity to serve the whole City, up into two high towers, with Engine-pumps, of sundry sorts, made with great Cost, art and Industry'.

[4] space left in text. Somerset (1612), pp. 265–6, also describes the constitution and government of the city.

[5] 'Governers and next to them' in left-hand margin.

[6] Bargrave (1656), pp. 245–6, provides an interesting account of the craftsmen of Augsburg, with particular reference to their ingenuity in clockwork devices.

[7] 'All things here are majestic [i.e. a play on the name of Augusta] wherever you look: temples, houses, market places, towers, gardens, porticoes, balconies, inns, and taverns. 2. Even more majestic is the noble republic, outstanding in virtue and wisdom, abundant in the beauty of its maidens and men and in its wondrous inventions.'

[f. 53ʳ] The Procession of the Papists on good friday[1] at Augspourg is the most famous in all Europe for the statelynesse and great number of persons which whippe themselves. They begin this Procession at nine a clock at night, and in it acte the whole History of the passion of our Savior, after this manner.

First comes a man which blowes very sadly a strange kind of horne. Next to him comes about 3 Capucins which carye our Savior on a great wooden crosse. And then comes the read whippers, soe caled because they have a long read garment which covers them from head to foot, having only two little eyes holes therough they which they see to goe, and behinde on the back it is all cutt open that it may not hinder their whipping. Of this sort came at first a hunderd and many of them did most cruelly whippe themselves on the back with whipps made of smale knotted cordes and in every one are 8 or 9 needles. And those who had much sinned did whippe themselves with two one in eache hand, and every one of them did whippe themselves according to the imposition layed uppon them by theire priests. And on both sides did goe a great many common fellowes with torches and others with wine and taking the wine in mothes did spitt into the wounds of the whippers to hinder the swelling of them. After these whas caried a figur representing our Savior praying on the mont of olives and after followed a great many prests and singin boyes with severall musicians. [f. 53ᵛ] Then came about 50 more read whippers in the same posture as the former, accompanied with 70 persons in such read gownes and every one with extended armes where tied on a great wooden crosse. This is heald for far more dangerous and cruell then whipping and this punishment is layd only on the greatest sinners, and as they told mee 3 or 4 of thoese which are bunden on the croses doe die every yeare in the Procession. And I saw many which were ready to sounde for the great paine the[y] endured. After these came another image with this inscription, 'Ecce homo', and in it is our Saviour with a crowne of thornes on his head and Pilate and another standing by him. And after this goes 60 more read whippers which beat themselves like the formers. Then came a Image how the Jues mocked our Savior in putting a crowne of thornes on his head. Then comes about 60 which carie crosses on their shoilders of a very great bignesse. After these comes a great company of foot men in Jewes' cloathes, some with swordes, some with steekes and other weapons. In the midst of these fellowes, where they theeves leade their hands being bounded next to them, came our Savior lead by two hangmen and carring his crosse on his shoilders; and close by him [f. 54ʳ] was Simon of Cyrene which helped him to carrye his crosse. He which represented our Savior was most cruelly beated by the Jewes and for his paines he hath 3 or 4 crownes given him by the Jesuites. Next came Pilate and his sholdiers in armer from head to foote, every one his pistol coct in his hand and of these horse men are about a 100. Then came severall other images as our savior's imbalming, then his tombe and others. These where accompagnied with whippers, with thoes on crosses and in a manner crucified, and with thoes that caried crosses. Also with more horsemen and footmen, so that this Procession lasted 5 houres a going up and downe the citty and all together did make about a thousand persons.

[1] The Peace of Augsburg, promulgated on 25 September 1555, had established in the imperial cities the relatively harmonious co-existence of Catholicism and Lutheranism who were both free to pursue their own religious worship. They were also, supposedly, to share the governance of the city. But as Somerset (1612), p. 266, noted of the magistrates: 'there are some 14. or 15. that are Lutherans; but none of them be of the privie Counsell; for the towne is governed chiefly by Catholikes'. Over fifty years after Montagu's visit, Blainville (1705), I, p. 290, commented: 'The Magistrates of Augsburg are half Catholics, half Lutherans ... Though the Senate of Augsburg be half Catholic, half Lutheran, yet the former have four Times as many Churches as the latter'.

The 7 of September[1] I made a little journey into Bavaria and passed by these following places

Kissingen little village where wee lay that night, and the next morning to

Mittelstetten and dined at

Bruck[2] a little market towne and towards evening came to

Menchen[3] the cheefest citty in Bavaria and residence of the Duke of that name. This [f. 54ᵛ] towne is very well fortified and its situation is very pleasant. It being towards the evening I saw that day nothing but the churches, as first the

Cathedrall of our Lady[4] which hath two great tours from the which one may very well veeue the citty. The church is very anchient but hath very good painting in it. In a little chappell are severall reliques of St Paul sett in gold and silver, as also severall pretious stones which have bin presented unto our Lady working miracles. Next I saw

The Jesuites church and colledge,[5] the which is very magnifick as for the first it hath a very faire frontispec adorned with the statues of severall Dukes of Bavaria. The church is very large and built without any piller, having great white statues round about it. There are three altars very richly guilded and under that the Jesuites have their tresor. In the milde of the church stands a [?] with reliques [?] have a cristal covering over it.[6] The pavement of the church is of white and black marble.

[f. 55ʳ] The colledge of it selfe is so great and stately that a king may very well keepe his court there. Whithein it are severall fine roomes to walk in and it hath about 800 great windowes so that it is held for one of the greatest colleges in Europe.[7]

Next day I saw the Duke's Palace,[8] the which is more then a kingly building and if it bee not statlyer then the Italien buildings yet none goes before it. The entry is a very long court made in a perspectivish manner. In going up of the left hand is the chappell where the Duke heares mass every day but above is a very little one having Sᵗ. George a horse back on the alter. The body of the horse is of massy gold covered with diamants and other pretious stones for the vally of 12000 quart escus. The chambers are very comodius built every one having his little closett by it. Their pavement are of white and blacke marble stone and after severall kinds of fachon as alsoe guilding and rare painting are there in great abondans. In the dining halle is a paire of organs which playes of it self while the Duke sitts at table. For thence I went into the other champers the which wee found to bee very stately guilded in all places, and adorned with pretious marble and iaspir stones. Wee say 3 great galleries paved

---

[1] 'September 17' in left-hand margin.

[2] Kissing, Mittelstetten, and Fürstenfeldbruck (also known as Bruck).

[3] '19' in left-hand margin. München. The duke was the Catholic Elector Maximilian I (1573–1651).

[4] The 15th century Frauenkirche, or Cathedral of Our Lady, was severed damaged by allied bombing in 1944/45. The two towers (99m and 100m high) were completed in 1525.

[5] The church of St Michael was built by the Jesuits between 1583 and 1590. See Misson (1687), I, p. 139. The gable bears a sculpture of Christ guiding the victory of Otto I, the Great (912–73), at Lech in 955 over the Magyars, with portraits of successive emperors and dukes of Bavaria.

[6] The first '[?]' indicates an illegible word, and the second '[?]' a missing word.

[7] The college, now the Alte Akademie, was built by the Jesuits between 1585 and 1597 as a seminary and school. It was later used as the university and city library. It was severely damaged in 1944 but has been restored. Somerset (1612), p. 264: 'this Colledge of the Jesuites is so statelie a building that I may say both for the beautie of the Colledge and the church, the richnes of the high altar and all the rest of the altars, and the richnesse of the stuffe and furniture belonging unto them, it hath not his fellowe in Europe'.

[8] A Residenz, or ducal palace, was first built on this site by the Wittelbachs in the late 14th century. The Old Residenz, Banqueting Hall, Antiquarium, and the Old Court Chapel have survived from this period. Between 1611 and 1619 Elector Maximilian I built the Maximilianische, or Alte Residenz, adjoyning the Residenzstrasse.

137

with blake and white marble, in one are all kind of strange [f. 55ᵛ] hornes of staggs and other beasts.

Belowe ist the Antiquarium,[1] so caled because of the ancient statues and rare Antiquites which are kept there; and it is built like a halle all of marble from top to the very bottome, having the foresaid statues on the walle. And the ancients is La Dea de la natura, or Godesse of nature having bin here to fore worshipped by the heathens. At one end is a most curious table made of inlayed stones as agatts and the like. This peece is worthy to bee seene. Hard by is the Duches hur privie grarden with a little walke covered against the raine. Heere are most admirable peeces to bee seene. In steade of the wale are great perspectives made of in layd stones but soe naturaly as if it was painted. There is a dog and a catt which are ready to fite to gether soe well made that one is ready to seperate them. At the first coming in in the mids of the gardan is another such table with inlayed stones and in the beades are very curi-ous flowers.

The great garten[2] is devided in severall parts as the fisicque garten, the mathematicshe garten, the geometrish garten, the water werke garten and the like round a bout these gartens is a coverd walke wherein hang the pictures of all the deeds and great exploits which the Dukes of Baviars have done.

[f. 56ʳ]

[f. 56ᵛ – *blank*]

[f. 57ʳ] Heere I receaved much civilitie from an Inglish gentelman by name Mʳ Roberts, akinde to my Lord of Winchester's.[3] Hee went with mee round about the house to see the rarities of the Pallace, for that court makes much difficulty to lett strangers come in without they are know to bee men of very great quallity.

The second day I returned again to this towne and stayed heere the hole winter, imploy-ing my time to learne the language of Geometrye.

[f. 57ᵛ]   1652

At this time[4] I begun to make my journey to the minerall waters of Dynach[5] and tooke this way following. Having hired 3 horses and a man to looke to them giving a crowne a day besides the nurriture, thus from Augspourg to

Krieshauer a village,[6]

Steppe. Biberach, Horgaw, Aurebach.[7]

Susmerhausen a market towne[8] where wee dined that night, it being 3 miles from Augspourg to wit german ones. After diner road by

---

[1] Reresby (1657), pp. 97–8, describes in detail the hall, long gallery, and the Antiquarium, which was built for Albrecht V between 1569 and 1571. It was the oldest German museum of supposed Greek antiquities (although many are Roman or Renaissance copies) and was also used as a banqueting hall in the 17th century.

[2] The Hofgarten was laid out after 1613 in the French style by Heinrich Schön.

[3] John Paulet, Marquis of Winchester (c. 1598–1675) was a noted royalist. His chief seat, Basing House, had been a regular meeting place for Queen Henrietta Maria and her friends. During the Civil War he fortified the house and held it for the king until it was stormed by Cromwell in October 1645. Known henceforth as 'the great loyalist', he was then committed to the Tower of London on a charge of high treason, where he remained impris-oned and his property was sequestrated.

[4] 'July 2' in left-hand margin.

[5] See p. 141, n. 10.

[6] Montagu seems to have travelled from Münich to Augsburg, and then on to Kriegshaber (now virtually a north-west suburb of Augsburg).

[7] Steppach, Biburg, Horgau, and Auerbach.

[8] Zusmarshausen.

Fig. 29. 'Magdalena Rudolfs Thuinbuj von Stockholm', a print inserted in the travel diary of Robert Montagu, Lord Mandeville. Bodl. MS Rawlinson D 76, f. 56.

Burgau a little citty and Capital of a province soe called, then by Kneringan a village[1] and attained that evening to

Genspourg[2] 3 german miles farther where wee lay at the golden crosse, this place takes its name from a river caled Gens. From hence wee advanced to Ulme in the morning free, it beeing but 3 german miles farther.

Ulme[3] this is a most famous citty for its richesse and strenth being extremely well fortified a la moderne; and was it not for a little hill which lies neare it, it would bee Imprenable, but they are about to digg it a way. Its situation is on the Danubius one of the Famous rivers of Europe. Thereuppon Ovid sayes

> In numerique alii quos inter maximus omnes
> cedere Danubius se tibi Nile negat.[4]

[f. 58ʳ] The cheefest things heere to bee seene are.

The fortifications and bullwarks newly made by one Furtenback an engenire. In time of peace they serve for walks to the inhabitans.[5]

The Cathedrale church is much esteemed for a huge old tower it hath. In it are a most rare paire of Organs of such a bignesse that the[y] dare not sound them all at one time for feare of breaking of the church windowes, the holl body of it trembing when they play.[6]

The waterworks are worthe seeing but not like them of Augspourg.

Cabinet of Mʳ Fourtenbach[7] is a most rare peece and consits of 3 chambers of rarieties. In the first was of rare picters and Coup fersteeken[8] most done by him and his sonn. In the next were all kind of warlick instruments and of architecture, a pretty invention for to trie pouder whether it bee good and how stronge it is, severall models howe to make a comodius bilding, also how to fortifie with advantage any citty. He showed mee a stick with the which hee could measure any thing as well as with any instryment. In the other chamber was models of all kind of fier-works and belowe he hath a little garden in the which is a pretty grott which cast water in what fachon hee will. He hath severall wayes how to make a place imrenable; also he said he would under take to make a ship like unto the Arck of Noab for to hold all beasts every one having his particular chamber.

[f. 58ᵛ] After diner I advanced to a little place caled Helstet.[9] From thence to

Bleaubiren[10] a little citty 4 german miles distante. Here is a rich convent and in the church is an Alter that man much esteemes both for its antiquitye and rich gilding. It opens

---

[1] Burgau and (perhaps) Unter-Knöringen Ober.

[2] '3' in left-hand margin. Günzburg.

[3] Ulm.

[4] 'The Danube refuses to give way to you the Nile / as the greatest of all the other rivers': Ovid, *Epistulae ex Ponto*, lib.IV.10

[5] Ulm has a double set of town walls. Much of the city explored by Montagu was totally destroyed during World War II. This 'Furtenback an engenire' may be either Joseph Furtenbach, who wrote about stage-lighting for plays in *Sciena d'Comoedia* (1628), or a member of his family.

[6] The Cathedral at Ulm, begun in the 14th century, is renowned for its high tower, originally built by Matthäus Böbinger. (It now stands some 161m high, including 19th century additions).

[7] Presumably, this 'Mr Fourtenbach' is the same individual who, according to Montagu, built the town's fortifications.

[8] 'Coup fersteeken', perhaps from '*stechen*', to prick or pierce; '*stechkunst*', engraving.

[9] 'Helstet', unidentified. The usual stopping place between Ulm and Blaubeuren would have been Klingenstein, Herrlingen, or Blaustein.

[10] '4' in left-hand margin. Blaubeuren.

4 times where uppon are severall histories out of the bible. Wee lay here at the golden crowne. Next day dined at

Aurach a little citty in the Duchy of Virtemberg.[1] By it is a strong castel. Heere wee dined 3 miles from our Lodgings. We went heere to the [Castell?] then that afternoone made 4 miles more and came to

Rittlingen[2] a free citty. It was of a Sunday night and thereby wee saw most of the inhabitans a broade and I observed the women were very handsome generaly. Next day wee went a little out of our way to see the Ab[bo]t of

Bebenhousen[3] one of the Learneds men in germany and his name is Doctor Andreas. The place of its self is but little and not worthe seeing but this gentleman is extreame kind to strangers. That night wee went to

Tubingen[4] and lay at the golden sheepe where the hoste used very skurvely.[5] This place belongs to the Duke of Wirtemberg and is famous for its Universitie.[6] Also the exercises as riding and the like are very well up held by the Duke. The Castel was heretofore worthe seeing but by the warrs is ruinated.[7]

[f. 59ʳ] There is also a faire Librerary to bee seene. The next morning I departed from hence to a little towne caled Aerenberg, Isingen, Boldringen, Altingen, Soamme.[8]

Calb,[9] heere wee dined, a little towne ruinated by the warrs. A houre from hence are the waters from Tibigen are 5 miles.

Dynacke the drinking place.[10] It is a village lying in a very deepe vally having nothing but woods round about it, a very melancoly place was it not for the good company which still comes in summer thether to drinke. I remained here the space of six weekes, waiting uppon the Prince of Wirtemberg[11] who showed mee many faveurs in taking mee a hunting where I observed it was far differed to the inglish fachen for as wee don hunt with doggs only till a stagg bee runn down, the[y] doe it with farr more paine and ceremony. For the day afore a Prince will hunt he sends word to his hunstmen there upon the[y] goe with a master [and] 200 countrey fellowe[s] to a certaine forest, they having noe Parke, and there drive severall staggs and sometimes wilde Boares in a peece of ground which they have before incompaced with netts and [?]ches, and soe shutt them in till the next day for the Duke to hunt soe that he is assured to finde some thing or other. This is a very chargeble businesse for I have seene at the taking of two poore staggs a matter of 3 or 4 hunder country fellow[es], 10 or 12 waggons full of netts and instruments belonging to it, of a 30 cupple of doggs and

---

[1] Bad Urach.

[2] Reutlingen.

[3] Montagu presumably visited the Cistercian monastery at Bebenhausen, to the north of Tübingen.

[4] '5' in left-hand margin. Tübingen was the capital of the dukes of Württemberg.

[5] 'in' deleted.

[6] The university at Tübingen was founded in 1477 by Eberhard the Bearded, with various buildings situated along the Bursagasse and Neckargasse, including the Bursa (1479), formerly the university's faculty of philosophy.

[7] Montagu is probably referring to the Burg Hohenzollern, located on the top of a 850m peak. Its 15th-century buildings, however, have now largely been replaced by a mid-19th-century structure.

[8] Herrenberg, Unterjesingen, Poltringen, Altingen, and (perhaps) Stammheim (which may have sounded like 'Stamme' in the local Swabian accent).

[9] Calw.

[10] Montagu's reference to 'Dynacke' probably refers to Teinach, a village in the Black Forest still renowned for its springs. His description of it as a 'drinking place' makes it unlikely that Montagu is referring to Dörnach, situated to the north-east of Tübingen (just north of Pliezhausen).

[11] This prince of Württemberg may have been a son of Eberhard III, who was duke from 1628 until 1674.

besides the followers of the Prince, soe it seemes to bee some little armee. This last a hole day [f. 59ᵛ] and sometimes longer for the Prince his two waggens still with him of provisions, soe that wee were many times treated in the woods as well as if wee had bin in his pallace.

Our company was the two Princes of Turlech, one being maried to the Brother of Gustave Adolpho Marquis of Baden.

The eldest sister of the Duc of Wirtemberg called die Freline Antoni, also a Countesse of Stollenberg [now?] kept herr companie.[1]

A German Earle caled Forbenius Maria de Firstember whose company I much esteemed being mych familier with him. There where also more as die Freti von Rachonis, and mistres Besserer, Mr im Tour, Baron from Tacis and his lady. With this company wee had much pastime and without forgetting madame Widerhold who made us dance almost every evening.[2]

From hence beeing honoured with a letter from the Prince himself I tooke my way for Stuggart to see his court and deliver my above said Letter to the Duchesse his Lady.

Calb,[3] a citty named above. Then to a little place caled

Wilerstat[4] this towne was before 2 or 3 worthe seeing for its strenthe but since the Marchell of Turrenne with his armie burnt it all downe because it held for the Emperor, soe that now there remaines only two or 3 houses and the walls. At then to [f. 60ʳ] Leon Berk another such place,[5] where wee dined and after dinner advanced to

Stugart[6] the cheefest cittyes of Virtemburger-land and 7 miles from the waters. Its situation is very low having nothing but little hills about it and upon them does groe a very good sort of wind and in great quantitie. Heere having been honored with the company of the Duchesse and dined at her table being splendedly treated, I tooke my leave of her, although shee much desired to have mee stay a day or two longer. And before my taking horse I was acompanyed by severall of the courtiers about the Pallace and veued all things with leasure.[7] As for the new bilding it is very stately and worthy of a Princes dwelling. Hard by is the garden very well adorned with statues and waterworks, also flowers. There is on[e] place that when on[e] lays any thing upon a table and sayes "take it a way", in the meanetime fals a great quantitie of water on your head, soe that one is well wetted for his pains. In the garden is a very faire bancqueting house in german caled Die Lusthouse. The hale is one of the biggest that every I saw, having noe pillar at all and I went a topp of it to see the

---

[1] The text here is carelessly written and probably confused. It seems that either 'Princes' should read 'Princesses' or 'Brother' should read 'sister'.

[2] The details and erratic spellings supplied in this list are too scanty to allow individual identifications, although several of the names (such as the margravates of Baden-Baden and/or Baden-Durlach, and the Taxis (or Tassis) family whose members held various high positions in Germany and the Spanish Netherlands) were presumably associated with prominent families of the period.

[3] '6' in left-hand margin.

[4] Weil Der Stadt. Henri de La Tour d'Auvergne, vicomte de Turenne (1611–75), was Marshal of France from 1643. He commanded the royal armies during the Fronde (1648–53). Following the defeat of the French Army of Germany in the Black Forest in late 1643, Turenne's counter-campaigns steadily devastated large parts of the Rhineland, in military combinations with Louis II de Bourbon, duc d'Enghien and prince de Condé (1644) and the Swedish army (1646–7).

[5] Leonberg.

[6] Stuttgart. The city had been the seat of the counts (later dukes) of Württemberg since 1321.

[7] The Altes Schloss dates from the 16th century (and was heavily restored after World War II) and the Nues Schoss from the 18th century.

skill of it and I found it was made in fachon of a barrell with bands of iron and great quantity of wood. Within it is painted and guilded richly, representing all the persons which served this Duke's Father when he went a hunting, and soe exactly done that all the beasts which were taken are there represented [f. 60ᵛ] with the doggs which were at there to take them and severall other sircomstances.

A nother rarity in this hall is that one sitting at each corner of the hall, the[y] can discours together or heare all which is said in the rome, but the doors must bee shutt or elce the voice goes out. Under this banqueting house are fountaines which runn in summer for to rafresh the place and if one will one may bathe there.

The Ursenal is worthe seene. Therein are severall representations of maskes held by the Ancestors of this Prin[c]e, also old kind of weapons and the like. After all this they leade downe into the seller for to taste the severall sorts of winne which are there. Here they presented mee first a glasse called the Welcome which is in fachon of a little barrell about it are written severall [lines?] in verses *with* golden letters and armes of the Prince. Here are hogheads which resemble more houses then vessels, having for their frontespeeces the Armes of the Princes; and a little belowe them are verses which containe the yeare when the hogshead were filled and what for wine, and in quantity so much. Wee drunke of some which was above 100 yeares old, others of 60, 50, 30, 20, 10, 2 and the like. From thence wee were conducted to the butterey and there the courtiers did strive againe to fondle one acording to there customes, being a right mark of afection and love, for Diem noctemque continuare, potando nulli opprobium.[1]

[f. 61ʳ]

[f. 61ᵛ – blank]

[f. 62ʳ] From hence I parted late in the evening and came that night only to

Etrlingen two houres riding an Imperiall citty but not much considerable. Wee lay at the black eagle and parted next morning betimes for

Boberslingen, Richeback, Ebersbach,[2] and dined at

Geppingen[3] a little citty and by it are minerall waters like them of Dynach. It is 4 miles from the place where wee lay. After dinner Genge, Seele, Coucken, Altenstat and lay at Geitlingen[4] [?] miles. This place is famous for the rare tourners whome live here. Next day at

Ursprin.[5]

Ulme 3 miles but I have spoken of this towne before. Soe next day to

Leibheime a little towne 3 miles.

Genspourg 1 mile

Burgau[6] 4 miles

Susmerhausen, Horgaw, Krieshauer[7] and to

Augspurg any ancient dwelling place. Heere wee tooke a passe for the journey of Italie, as it to bee seene in the next leafe.

---

[1] 'To continue drinking through day and night is no disgrace', Tacitus, *Germania*, ch. 22.

[2] Esslingen, Plochingen, Reichenbach, and Ebersbach.

[3] Göppingen.

[4] Gingen and Salach (but in reverse order), Kuchen, Altenstadt, and Geislingen. The number of miles following Geislingen has been deleted.

[5] Ursprung.

[6] Leipheim, Günzburg, and Burgau.

[7] Zusmarshausen, Horgau, and Kriegshaber.

Fig. 30. The crest of Ferdinand II, a print inserted in the travel diary of Robert Montagu, Lord Mandeville. Bodl. MS Rawlinson D 76, f. 61.

[f. 62ᵛ – blank]

[f. 63ʳ][1] At my returne of the waters I begun a nother journey which was that of Italie and to that end tooke a german messenger by name Simler for to goe straight to Venice; and wee payed for each on[e] 20 ducats for horse and diet and tooke this following way.

Hausteten[2] a little village and place of recreation of those of Augepourg. That night wee came thoe late and in very ill weather to

Maria Hilf[3] a market towne where there is great pillgramage to it by cause of a good Lady who woorks miracles there. This night was passed very merrily by the good company which wee had being of gentle-women who came those sixe miles with us. Yett notwithstanding the next morning wee were forced to seperate ourselves, they returning home and wee advancing our journey passed by

Landsberg a little towne in Bavaria situated on the river of Lech. The Jesuites have there a very fine colledge and church.[4] This is 2 miles from Maria Hilf, so passing farther came and dined about 3 miles farther at a place caled

Raumakesielt. After diner rod by Shongaw[5] a pretty little towne on a hill which in these last warrs hath oft bin beseeged. It belongs to the Duc of Bavaria. Here not staying wee advanced that night 4 miles farther and lay at

Beütingen[6] a village. Here the rugged way of the Tirolish montaines begun. Nere 4 morning wee came by [f. 63ᵛ] Soya, Reitabach, Wourmesoie[7] all poore villages agree to theire dwelling place which is very barren producing nothing but firr trees. That day dined at

Unde Amingan[8] a village 5 houres riding from the place where wee lay, for they count not by miles nor Leagues but by houres. This place is poore to the apperance but when wee were in the Inn wee made great cheere, and had especially, a fish caled Forellen the best that every I eat.[9] After diner passed thorough

Upper Amingen[10] a village half a mile of and then to

Eskal a very stately Monastery of Benedictins;[11] and in the church is a little image to bee seene which hath that vertu (as they report) that it showes whether one hath yett his maid-enhead or not. And after this manner: if one can lift this image up from the ground then hath on[e] it but if not then the person hath lost it. Here wee stayed not but so to

Borchheim[12] a village and passing the River of Loise[13] came to

[1] 'Octobre 8' in left-hand margin.

[2] Haunstetten.

[3] Montagu's 'Maria Hilf' (Maria's Help) may be in the vicinity of Klosterlechfeld which had an early 17th-century Franciscan monastery, next to which was a cylindrical pilgrims' church, imitating the Pantheon at Rome, built by Elias Holl.

[4] Landsberg. The Jesuit monastery there was founded in 1576 and had attached to it the Church of the Holy Cross.

[5] 'Raumakesielt', unidentified, and Schongau.

[6] Peiting.

[7] 'Soya', unidentified, Rottenbuch, and Wurmansau.

[8] Unterammergau.

[9] 'Forelle', trout.

[10] Oberammergau.

[11] Ettal. Its Benedictine monastery was founded by Emperor Ludwig the Bavarian in 1330 but the present buildings date mainly from the 18th century.

[12] 'Borchheim', unidentified.

[13] The River Loisach.

Partenkirch[1] where wee lay a fine place and is almost worth the naime of a citty. It lies [f. 64ʳ] in a countrey caled Freisingish. It is 3 miles. Next morning very early wee roade by

Mittenwaldt[2] a little towne and the last in our way of the Ducke of Bavaria. Farther came wee therough the passe of

Sheidniz[3] where wee showed our paseport or Fede which wee had from Augsprug. Here is a little fortresse built for to hinder the comming in of an enemis into the domi[ni]ons of the Arch Duc of Insprug. We riding up a light montaine wee came to a place caled Sthosberg.[4] So 6 hours riding to

Seefeld[5] a village a top of this hill. Here is not to bee seene much only two church one of Augustins friers[6] where is a very great wonder to bee seene which happened 1384. To this end wee went to a Prist to desire him for to showe us the miracle and relate the histore which he did after this manner.

There was was a gentleman, who living not farr of this convent, came on a holy day to receave the sacrement and being at the altar ready to receave it the Prist offered to give him a little Hostia according to the Papists custome. But this gentleman grue angry and said he would have one like thoese that the prists doe take themselves which are bigger and there-fore [f. 64ᵛ] ordained only for their holy bodyes. Yett not withstanding this Prist out of curtesie gave him one, but as he will swaloe it the alter sinkes with the Gentleman and he holding him selfe on the hard stone his hands remained out of great miracle printed in the alter and his feet about an ell deepe in the stone. There uppon the Prist goes to him and takes the Hostia out of his mouthe reserving it for a miracle to this very day in a cristall incased in gold, which wee say allso the hole [as he?] suncke downe. His name was Mʳ Ostwald Miller, but the servant went presently and told this his mistris who was very angry and said it could bee as little true as that roses should growe uppon a drie peece of wood, which day before here dore and immediately apeared 3 roses uppon[7]

---

[1] Partenkirchen, which was combined with Garmisch in 1935.

[2] Mittenwald.

[3] The Scharnitzpass at the Austrian frontier. Claudia de' Medici, the widow of Archduke Leopold V, built a fortress here (known as the Porta Claudia) to defend the pass from Swedish forces during the Thirty Years's War.

[4] 'Sthosberg', unidentified.

[5] Seefeld.

[6] Montagu's two churches may be the Pfarrkirche (early 14th century), dedicated to St Oswald of Northumber-land; and the Seekapelle (1628), a church erected by Leopold V and his wife Claudia.

[7] Montagu's carelessly written narrative breaks off here without completing the story.

SECTION THREE

THE TRAVELS OF WILLIAM HAMMOND
(December 1655–May 1658)

1. The Family and Early Life of William Hammond

The travels of William Hammond (c. 1635–c. 1685), the author of the letters contained in Brotherton Library MS Trv.2 and British Library Additional MS 59785, provide an illuminating perspective on how a well-educated mercantile gentry family from the south-eastern counties of England would have viewed continental travel during the mid-seventeenth century. At the same time, these letters also offer a convenient framework for assessing how the development of the English Civil War during the 1640s and its constitutional aftermath during the 1650s impacted upon various Hammond family members and their relatives. William was probably so named after his paternal grandfather, Sir William Hammond (d. 1615), who resided at St Alban's Court, Nonnington, near Dover.[1] He married Elizabeth Aucher (or Archer) of Bishopsbourne and their eldest son, Anthony (1608–61), married Anne, daughter of the ambassador and diplomat Sir Dudley Digges (1583–1639).[2] This Anthony and Anne were the parents of our letter writer, William, and resided at Wilberton, near Ely in Cambridgeshire.

Through family stories and reminiscences, William Hammond could have learned as a child and young man about his relative's earlier activities in continental and overseas travel. His grandfather, Sir Dudley Digges, had founded in 1612 a company which sought to develop trade links to the East via a supposed North-West Passage; and he had also been extensively involved in the affairs of the East India Company later in the same decade. William's grandmother, Elizabeth Aucher (Archer), was the granddaughter, through the line of her mother Margaret, of Edwin Sandys (c. 1516–88), Archbishop of York, and a niece of the writer and translator George Sandys (1578–1644).[3] In 1553 Edwin Sandys, then vice-chancellor of Cambridge University, had supported the plans of John Dudley, Duke of Northumberland (see pp. 12–13), for the succession of Lady Jane Grey but he was imprisoned in the Tower of London and the Marshalsea prison when this plot failed. Escaping this detention, he fled to the continent where he remained in exile at Antwerp, Augsburg, Strasburg, and Zürich until his return to England in 1559, when he was made Bishop of Worcester by Queen Elizabeth. Although Edwin Sandys does not seem to have left any written account of his time abroad, his six-year exile would have well known within

---

[1] See William Berry, *Pedigrees of the Families in the County of Kent*, London, 1830, pp. 94–5; and the introduction to *The Poems and Translations of Thomas Stanley*, ed. Galbraith Miller Crump, Oxford, 1962, pp. xxi–xxxiv.

[2] This Anthony Hammond may have been the author of *The Gentleman's Exercise* (1661).

[3] After Sir William Hammond's death in 1615, his widow Elizabeth married Walter Balcanquall who became Dean of Durham in 1639. His brother, Samuel, was President of Pembroke College, Cambridge, where both William Hammond (1614–c.1655) and Thomas Stanley (1625–78) studied.

Hammond family circles, not least because their home, at Wilberton near Ely, had formerly been the residence of the Sandys family.[1]

Probably motivated by his father's recollections of such experiences, Archbishop Edwin Sandys's son, George Sandys (1578–1644) – William Hammond's great-uncle – proved to be one of the most renowned English travellers of his generation. After studying at St Mary's Hall, Oxford, he travelled to Italy and then on through Turkey, Egypt, and Palestine. His account of these experiences was first published in 1615, and regularly reprinted, as *A Relation of a Journey Begun An: Dom: 1610. Four Books. Containing a Description of the Turkish Empire, of Ægypt*. George Sandys was also a competent classical scholar and translated from the Latin *The First Five Books of Ovid's Metamorphosis* (1621) and Hugo Grotius's *Christ's Passion. A Tragedy* (1640).[2] Given the wealth of references to books in Hammond's letters home to his parents, it seems likely that at least some of the works of George Sandys would also have been familiar to him from the family's well-stocked library at Wilberton.[3]

Another of Archbishop Sandys's sons, Sir Edwin (1561–1629), would have provided an no less interesting precedent for Western European travel to our William Hammond. With his close friend, George Cranmer (1563–1600), he made an extensive tour of France, Italy, and Germany, remaining abroad until at least April 1599, from where he dated his major survey of continental religious affairs, *Europae Speculum*.[4] During the second and third decades of the seventeenth century Sandys was an active member of the East India and Virginia Companies. He served as a member of the latter's council from 1607; and he was a notably effective treasurer from 1619 onwards in resolving problems occasioned under his predecessor (the renowned colonialist Sir Thomas Smythe), and in drafting the forms of government of the colony which enabled it to thrive during the 1620s. One of the colonialists who sailed for America in 1621 was Sir Edwin's younger brother, George, who stayed there as a planter until the early 1630s. He also finished the remaining books of his translation of Ovid on the outward transatlantic voyage and at the colony, with the completed volume sent back to England and printed, with a dedication to King Charles I in 1626. On his return to England, a new, revised edition was printed under his supervision at Oxford in 1632.

On William Hammond's father's side, several members of the family also had either significant experience of continental travel or some claim to fame as writers. His father, Anthony (1608–61) was a cousin, again through the line of his mother, Elizabeth Aucher (Archer), of the royalist poet, Richard Lovelace (1618–58). Lovelace was imprisoned in 1642 in the Gatehouse at Westminster for his support of the 'Kentish Petition' (during which time he wrote his celebrated poem 'Stone Walls do not a Prison Make'). After being freed in 1645 he rejoined King Charles I and was with him at the surrender of Oxford in

---

[1] Several of Archbishop Edwin Sandy's children were born at Wilberton, including Sir Miles (baptized 29 March 1563–1645), Margaret (baptized 22 December 1566), and Thomas (baptized 3 December 1568). After he became Bishop of London in 1570, Sandys younger children were usually born there (for example, Henry was baptized on 30 September 1572 at Woolwich). It is not known whether Wilberton came to Anthony Hammond (1608–61) directly from the Sandys family or through intermediaries.

[2] During the early 1630s George Sandys also compiled *A Paraphrase upon the Psalms of David* (1636) and obtained a lucrative patent for the sole rights to publish this edition for fourteen years.

[3] William Hammond's aunt, Margaret, (his father's sister) married another member of the Sandys family, Henry.

[4] *Europae Speculum* or *A Relation of the State of Religion*, was printed in an unauthorized (and rapidly withdrawn) edition in 1605 and then again in 1629, in an edition which claimed to be printed at The Hague but was really published by the Londoner stationer, M. Sharpe. This edition bore a note: 'From Paris, IX° Aprill. 1599 … and finished, 2. Octob. An. M.DC.XVIII'.

1646. He then left England, probably with Prince Rupert's entourage (see Fig. 48, p. 277), and served as a colonel in the army of King Louis XIII against Spain before returning to England in 1648 and being imprisoned again (until December 1649). His renowned poetic collection, *Lucasta, Epodes, Odes, Sonnets, Songs, etc.* (1649) was prepared for publication during this latter period of incarceration and dedicated to Anne Lovelace, the wife of his distant relative, the staunch royalist John, second Baron Lovelace of Hurley (1616–70), who had also been with the king at Oxford. The second Baron's son, John (c. 1638–93), was probably well known by our William Hammond since he had matriculated at his Oxford college, Wadham, on 25 July 1655. He also travelled in France and the Low Countries during the late 1650s, although it is not known whether he and William Hammond ever met on their respective travels.

William Hammond aunt, Elizabeth (1612–89) a younger sister of his father, married Sir John Marsham (1602–85) of Whorn Place, Cuxton, in Kent. Sir John was another well-travelled member of Hammond's inner family circle, having been at Paris during the winter of 1625/6, before travelling on through France, Italy, and Germany until his return home in 1627 when he became a member of the Middle Temple. He was abroad again in 1629 when he passed through the Low Countries to the siege of Bois-le-Duc. From there he joined the embassy of Sir Thomas Edmondes, ambassador extraordinary to the court of King Louis XIII, which travelled from Flushing to Boulogne and Paris. Marsham sided with the king at the outbreak of the Civil War and was at Oxford with him. In 1638 he had been appointed one of the six clerks in chancery but was deprived on this position by Parliament. After the surrender of Oxford in 1646 he withdrew from public life to his estate of Whorn Place at Cuxton, Kent. After this period he became a prolific collector of Egyptian antiquities and published a notable volume on chronology, *Chronicus Canon* (1672).[1] There is no doubt that William Hammond would have known all about Sir John Marsham's travels and writings since he married their daughter, Elizabeth (his first cousin), after returning home from his own continental itinerary.

2. The Hammonds and the Stanleys

William Hammond's paternal uncle, also named William (1614–c.1655), was another member of our author's family with literary ambitions. In 1633 he was a Greek scholar at Pembroke College, Cambridge, and elected as Fellow Commoner of the college on 13 December 1639. This elder William Hammond personally encouraged his another of his nephews, Thomas Stanley (1625–78), to come to Cambridge in June 1639 and to matriculate at his own college as a Fellow Commoner on 13 December 1640. This link between the Hammonds and the Stanleys was probably the most important of all of our author's immediate family connections with literary figures.

His aunt, Mary Hammond (his father's elder sister), had married at Bishopsbourne on 15 October 1621 (as his second wife), Thomas Stanley of Cumberlow Green in Hertfordshire

---

[1] After the Restoration Sir John Marsham regained his position in chancery, was knighted, and raised to the baronetcy on 12 August 1663. He died at Bushey Hall, Hertfordshire, on 25 May 1685. His son, John, became the 2nd Baronet, followed by his son, John (d. 1696). Since this latter John had no legitimate children, the baronetcy reverted to his uncle Robert (d. 1703), the brother of the 2nd baronet. Robert's son, Robert (d. 1724), succeeded him and was created Lord Romney on 25 June 1716. Some of Sir John Marsham's miscellaneous correspondence and papers are now preserved at the Centre for Kentish Studies, Maidstone (U1121); and his annals are in the Bodleian Library, Oxford (MS Don c 60).

and Leytonstone in Essex.[1] Thomas was the grandson of Thomas Stanley (d. 1584), the natural son of Edward Stanley (1509–72), 3rd Earl of Derby; and he was knighted by King Charles I at Whitehall on 5 January 1622.[2] As a youth their eldest son, Thomas (1625–78), was tutored by William Fairfax, whose father, Edward, had translated Tasso's *Gerusalemme liberata*. Their teacher-pupil relationship developed into a warm and longlasting friendship. Stanley also clearly appreciated the companionship and advice of his uncle, William Hammond, while studying at Cambridge.[3] In 1641 William Hammond and Thomas Stanley undertook a trip together to the north of England and visited Durham where William's mother (and Thomas's grand-mother), Elizabeth Aucher Hammond, now resided with her second husband, Walter Balcanquall (c. 1586–1645), who was Dean of Durham from 1639.[4]

Following the outbreak of the Civil War, Thomas Stanley provided yet another family example of a tactical withdrawal to the continent for several years for political reasons, this time mainly in France. It seems very probable that his experiences there played a significant part in prompting the decision of our William Hammond's parents to send their own son to study abroad in late December 1655. Certainly, once he had arrived at Paris by 1 January 1656, William Hammond was in regular and intimate communciation with his uncle and aunt, Sir Thomas and Lady Mary Stanley, who themselves had quietly withdrawn to France as the Civil War hostilities escalated. William Hammond attended their daughter Elizabeth's entry into a convent at Dieppe (letters 12 and 36); and also consoled them when their younger son, Steward, died there in early March 1657 (see letter 10). It is not known exactly when their son, Thomas Stanley, returned to England but Anthony Wood suggests that he had established himself in the Middle Temple by the mid-1640s, which was well known as a haven for young men and academics ejected from Oxford for their royalist views after the city's surrender in June 1646.[5] At the Middle Temple Thomas Stanley met another of his kinsman who would have been familiar at least in name (and probably in person) to our William Hammond, namely, Sir Edward Sherburne (1618–1702), who had served King Charles I as commissary-general of artillery at the Battle of Edgehill in 1642.

By late 1646 Thomas Stanley was beginning to earn a notable reputation on the metropolitan literary scene. He contributed commendatory verses to the *Horae Vacivae, or Essays* of John Hall (1627–56) – whom he had probably met at Durham on his northern itinerary with William Hammond – and to James Shirley's *Poems* and John Suckling's *Fragmenta Aurea*. It seems likely that Stanley's literary circle at this period also included Thomas Herrick, Richard Lovelace, and John Denham.[6] To William Hammond, our young letter writer, Thomas Stanley would have offered a stirring example (like Richard Lovelace's) of

---

[1] Thomas Stanley's first wife was Mary Apulton of South Benfleet, Essex, but their three sons all died in childhood.

[2] See Matthew Carter, *Honor Redivivus: or, an Analysis of Honour* (1655); and *The Visitations of Essex* [1552–1634], ed. W. C. Metcalfe, Harleian Society, 13, 1878, p. 493.

[3] Thomas Stanley was incorporated into the University of Oxford on 14 July 1640. He received his MA at Cambridge in March 1642, in the company of Prince Charles and George Villiers (1628–87), Duke of Buckingham.

[4] Stanley, *Poems and Translations*, ed. Crump, pp. xxiii–xxiv.

[5] Anthony à Wood: [he] 'lived somewhile in the Middle Temple, then newly returned from his Travells in France, where He entred into a near Communication of Friendship & Studies, with his, till then, unknowne, but afterward most intimate and dear Kinsman, Edward Sherburne Esquire': Bodl. MS Wood F.44, f. 244ᵛ, quoted in Stanley, *Poems and Translations*, ed. Crump, p. xxv.

[6] See Stanley, *Poems and Translations*, ed. Crump, p. xxv.

the loyal ultra-royalist, utterly committed to the king's cause. In Stanley's case (he, unlike Lovelace, was of a delicate constitution and unable to serve on the battlefield), this involved a more symbolic kind of service as a founding light of a secret royalist order, denoted by a black twist of fabric worn around the arm as a symbol of their sympathy with King Charles I's increasingly beleaguered position.[1]

Poetry also became a potent political tool in the hands of Thomas Stanley. The earliest printed volume of his lyric verse, *Poems and Translations*, was privately published (perhaps in a print-run of only fifty copies) in 1647, and was intended for circulation only among his own intimate circle of family and friends.[2] Given the literary interests of our author's family, it seeks likely that a copy may well have once been in Wilberton library. Certainly, when Thomas Stanley married on 8 May 1648 Dorothy Enyon of Flower, Northampton, William Hammond (our author's uncle), along with Shirley, Sherburne, and Fairfax, were among friends who contributed epithalamiums, included in a revised and expanded edition of the *Poems* in 1651.[3] But the lyric love poetry, for which Stanley is now best remembered, was only a relatively minor part of his poetic output at this period.

Following the king's execution in January 1649, Stanley retired from London society to Cumberlow Green, where he began a powerful translation of John Gauden's *Eikon Basilike*, published as the *Psalterium Carolinum* (1657). These verses offered a sombre record for its readers of the late 1650s of the King Charles I's mounting problems and personal dangers during the 1640s. A series of twenty-seven odes traced the tragic progress of the king's affairs from the Earl of Strafford's execution in May 1641 (Ode II), up to the time of his imprisonment in November 1648 at Carisbrooke Castle on the Isle of Wight (Ode XXVII). The intervening odes covered such subjects as 'Upon the Queen's departure and absence out of England' (Ode VII), 'Upon the Covenant' (Ode XIV), 'Upon his Majesties leaving Oxford, and going to the Scots (Ode XXII), and 'Penitentiall Meditations and Vowes in the Kings solitude at Holmeby' (Ode XXV).[4] Given the time our William Hammond spent with Thomas Stanley's parents on the continent, it seems probable that he would have followed with interest the transformation of his cousin from the time before his own departure abroad as a lushly lyrical poet (in the 1647 and 1651 volumes of *Poems and Translations*) to a strident and defiant voice of political dissent (in his *Psalterium Carolinum* of 1657).

Despite his deliberately low profile during the 1650s, Thomas Stanley enjoyed a high public reputation among other writers and he maintained close contacts with his family circle, including the Hammonds. Sir John Marsham (the husband of his mother's sister, Elizabeth, and our letter writer's father-in-law, see p. 156) suggested that he should compile a history of philosophy (published in four volumes in 1656). He also still relied heavily in his literary pursuits upon the advice and companionship of his former tutor, William Fairfax and his uncle, William Hammond, who addressed several friendly verses to him. But by

---

[1] Shirley appears to refer to this order in his poem, 'On a Black Ribband'; as does Herrick in 'Upon a black Twist, rounding the Arme of the Countesse of Carlile'.

[2] 'Printed for the Author, and his Friends' (title-page). The Bodleian Library copy of *Poems* (1647) has the initials 'W. F.' in gilt on its binding, possibly indicating that it was a copy given to his former tutor and friend, William Fairfax.

[3] The 1651 edition was published by Humphrey Moseley, who also produced the first collected edition of John Milton's *Poems* (1645). See G. E. Bentley, 'James Shirley and a Group of Unnoted Poems on the Wedding of Thomas Stanley', *Huntington Library Quarterly*, 2, 1938–9, pp. 219–32. As a wedding present, Sir Thomas Stanley presented Rushden Manor to the couple. Their son, Thomas, was born in 1650 and matriculated at Pembroke College, Cambridge, on 6 April 1665. They had eight other children, *Poems and Translations*, p. xxviii.

[4] *Poems and Translations*, ed. Crump, pp. 270–318.

1655 both Fairfax and Hammond were dead and Stanley's own health was increasingly frag-
ile. (It is thought that he was suffering from diabetes). He took solace in posthumously editing the verses of his uncle, William Hammond, publishing them in a collection of *Poems* in
1655. Stanley celebrated their friendship in a warm poetic epistle, 'To Mr. W. Hammond'.
Stanley's state of mind (and his thoughts doubtless reflected how many members of the
Hammond family viewed these difficult times) was poignantly suggested in a lament he
wrote following William Hammond's death, addressed to: 'Hammond, dear Uncle, of so
sweet a fame!'. Recalling their travels in 1641 northwards to Durham, he recalled their
happy departure from Cambridge before the gathering political storm:

> From thence we to the North together went:
> Happy those hours! how sweet! how innocent!
> But oh! the halcion-dayes we there convers'd
> Presag'd a storm, by which too soon dispers'd
> With equall grief, then, under different climes
> We wail'd the fury of unruly Times;
> Which weather'd out, at last I liv'd to see
> My native soil once more, and dearer Thee.
> Thee dearer? vain comparison! alas!
> Thou wert the same, she far from what she was;
> Her face, disfigur'd so by Civill Wars,
> Cou'd scarce be known, through those dishonour'd scars.
> Wars, which in such a slavish peace did cloze
> As Eastern Monarch's grant to Captiv'd foes,
> To servitude so miserable led
> That who remain'd alive envy'd the Dead. (lines 11–26)[1]

Another of Thomas Stanley's formerly close friends, John Hall, died in 1656. The trajectory of Hall's career well illustrates how complex the tensions between personal loyalties
and public politics had become during the 1650s for the Hammond family; and it demonstrates why the Hammonds of Wilberton may well have found it expedient to pack their son
off safely abroad during the mid-1650s. As an associate of the philosopher Thomas Hobbes
and the educationalist and continental emigré Samuel Hartlib (who was also a friend of
John Milton, see p. 32), John Hall had provided valued access for Thomas Stanley to their
exciting intellectual activities. But in 1650 Hall accompanied Cromwell to Scotland and, as
the author of the notorious *The Grounds and Reasons of Monarchy*, became one of his most
potent anti-royalist pamphleteers.[2] In 1660 Stanley signed the pledge, along with John
Dryden, Thomas Sprat, John Aubrey, Sir Kenelm Digby (whom our William Hammond
met at Paris in March 1658, see letter 27), and John Evelyn for the Royal Society. He was
elected a Charter Member in 1661 and a Fellow of the Society in 1663.[3]

For our author, William Hammond, his cousin Thomas Stanley would have offered an
inspiring model for intellectual and literary pursuits, although it is noticeable that in his

---

[1] Ibid., pp. 61–2, 356–7.

[2] Stanley also knew John Evelyn who noted on 26 November 1659: 'I was introduced into the acquaintance of
divers learned & worthy perons, Mr. *Massham* [i.e. Marsham], Mr. *Dugdale*, Mr. *Stanley*, &c'. Evelyn (1659), III, p.
237. See also J. M. Osborn, 'Thomas Stanley's Lost "Register of Friends"', *Yale University Library Gazette*, April
1958, pp. 1–26.

[3] Stanley died on 12 April 1678 at Suffolk Street, Strand, and was buried at St Martin-in-the-Fields, London.
Poems and Translations, ed. Crump, pp. xxxiii–xiv.

letters he always carefully avoided any forthright expression of his own political views. A young man abroad in the mid-1650s could, in theory at least, either present himself as loyally exiled royalist or as an enthusiastic republican. But, more pragmatically, most chose the stance of a keenly interested but neutral observer of English politics. For William Hammond, this last option was clearly preferred and in his many references to Cromwell as Lord Protector he is always careful to avoid any form of judgmental comment. After all, letters home to family and friends from the notoriously Catholic environment of France and Italy could be easily intercepted and secretly perused for disloyal sentiments. Indeed, there are several references in Hammond's correspondence to missing letters (see p. 170, n. 1) and neither he nor his parents could guess what might have happened to them. Hence, studied political neutrality was a distinctive and carefully maintained epistolary tone for William Hammond.

3. William Hammond's Continental Travels (December 1655–May 1658)

In keeping with this sophisticated and cultured family background, William Hammond's letters are characterized by their stylistic fluency and perceptive use of incidental detail. Ostensibly sent abroad by his family to study physic at Paris and Padua, William Hammond's letters provide an intriguing insight into the often uncertain thoughts and experiences of a young man whose stated purpose in travelling was to gain the necessary expertise to launch himself into a professional career and to set up as a medical practitioner back home in England. Hammond's letters effectively offer an ongoing debate with his father over this major life-decision: 'there is no greater Advantage towards the Study of Physick than Travelling', Hammond reassures his father, noting that 'the Protector's Physician Dᴿ Bates was ten or 12. years abroad'. He also provides a detailed account of the training of French physicians and concludes: 'a French Physician is made up of a little read-ing & a very great deal of Experience' (letter 3). Occasionally, however, Hammond himself doubts the wisdom of seeking to acquire his medical training abroad: 'my strong resolutions to improve my Profession: yet it may be, at the year's end, I may think more might be got in a Study, than in Rambling abroad' (letter 5). The Grand Tour, Hammond concludes on one occasion, can sometimes equate to little more than an indulgence in 'the Gadding humour' (letter 4). Unexpectedly disappointed by the poor quality of the medical school at Montpellier (letter 22), his enthusiasm for physic is fired up again by personally tending his cousin Bowyer at Nîmes during an outbreak of the smallpox (letters 17–20), and by the high quality of the public lectures on medicine at Paris (letter 24). Confident again in his own vocation, he enthuses: 'the first thing to be look't after at my returne to England must be a greater house in London, whose bulke may be apparent enough, to save me the Labor of hanging out an Urinall from the Window. I know my Sisters will be glad to hear of that, since living there with me, they will be more in the eye of *the* World, & likelier to meet with husbands' (letter 25).

The surviving thirty-seven letters (some were clearly lost in the post) indicate that Hammond and his travelling companion (a cousin called Bowyer) stayed at Paris from January to mid-summer 1656 (letters 1–6), and then moved to Florence for the month of June, before returning to La Flèche in France in late July (letters 7–8). By February 1657 he was back in Paris again (letters 9–13), before transferring to Lyons in the following June (letters 14–16). His party moved on to Nîmes in September 1657 and then on to Montpellier in December (letter 22), before returning to Paris where he resided until the end of April 1658 (letters 23–29). Heading south to Lyons in May (letter 30) he once more visited Florence from June to September 1658 (letters 32–35), before returning to Paris in the following October (letter 36). The last letter in the collection (letter 37) was written from Amsterdam and describes a succesful expedition into Germany and the Spanish Netherlands.

Hammond earnestly portrays himself in his letters as a diligent, shrewd and serious-minded student, keenly seeking to fulfil his family's ambitions. Nevertheless, as one reads through his correspondence, another image also gradually forms of the young man behind the pen. By his own admission, he was a corpulent and easy-going sort of individual (letter 11); and he also appears to have been rather too easily swayed on occasions by the enthusiasms of his present company. Throughout the correspondence, he regularly seems to be on the point of departing for some new destination with a recently acquired set of friends – plans which invariably come to nothing (letters 3, 4, 16, 30). He was certainly no great linguist and he struggled with even the basics of French: 'this Crabbed Tongue, which is so contrary both in Syntaxe & Pronunciation to our English' (letter 2), although he fared much better at Florence in soon acquiring a working knowledge of Italian (letter 34).

In view of his family connections with various men of letters (including Richard Lovelace, Thomas Stanley, and his uncle William Hammond), it is not surprising that Hammond demonstrates himself to be an accomplished literary stylist. He provides a memorable account, during the severe winter of 1649/1650 at Paris, of how his chemistry tutor discovered that the raging frost had 'Cooagulated all his Dissolutions: his Spirits, Essences, Baums & Quintessences' (letter 3). In another fluent letter (letter 26) he details his genuine fascination with chemical research. He also gives an elegant spin to his not infrequent distractions from study. At Florence, for example, he explains to his father: 'I might be reckon'd amongst the Swine, if I shou'd not bestow some time, in Viewing & Considering the Grand Duke of Tuscany's Pearls & Raritys' (letter 7). In other letters, with the self-conscious eye of a proto-medical man, he compares the essays of Jean-Louis Guez de Balzac (1597–1654) to the sermons of John Donne, Dean of St Paul's: 'they are both so Copious & witty in describing their own Torments & Diseases, as if Nature by a painfull Screwing up their Nerves, had tuned their Brains to such a Melodious Facility of Expressing itself' (letter 8). In similarly literary vein, he also filters his description of the French countryside around the River Loire through John Denham's renowned pastoral poem in praise of the Thames, 'Cooper's Hill' (letter 10).

As a young traveller, financial considerations were never far from Hammond's mind; and he provides detailed information on the 'bills of exchange' system used widely by European travellers. At Paris, for example, his financial transactions were handled by a merchant, Mr Wildigo, who received payments from Hammond's family via a Mr Skinner (letter 1). His skill with the pen frequently adds a certain wistful grace to his persistent pleas to his father for more money: 'an Empty Purse is a dolefull Companion to a Traveller' (letter 17); or 'I now begin to see the Efficacious Virtue of Mony & may be easily perswaded, that bodily health & strength will never keep us upon the Center of content, without the Counterpoise of an Heavy Purse' (letter 21).

Throughout his travels, Hammond greatly benefited from the hospitality of the renowned Catholic royalist Dr Henry Holden, who had resided at Paris since the 1630s and was a close friend of Hammond's aunt, Lady Mary Stanley: 'a man that has seen so much of this World, & made so good use of what he has seen' (letter 9). Dr Holden provided advice on accommodation in Paris, organized Hammond's bills of exchange, wrote to 'one D[r.] Kirton, a Doctor of Physick at Florence, in my behalfe' (letter 5); and introduced him to the once noted (but now old and lonely) virtuoso, Sir Kenelm Digby (1603–65) (letters 14, 27, 37). Hammond's letters are also invaluable for the specific information they supply on the time it took letters to and from England to be delivered to various European destinations (about a week from London to Paris but a month or more to La Flèche and Florence). For most of his travels, his post was sent first either to Dr Holden in Paris or to some suitable merchant friend of the family and then forwarded by carrier to Hammond's current locale.

This collection of letters also provides a wealth of first-hand detail about numerous locations, individuals and topics of popular interest during the mid-1650s. At Paris Hammond enrolled in one of the best riding academies (letter 2); and, through the influence of Dr Holden, attended the Louvre Palace and the French ballet to see the young Louis XIV dance (letters 9, 26). At Florence he wondered at the spectacular stage effects of the opera: 'A little Rhetorick wou'd perswade me, that I have been a spectator to the reall sports of the Poeticall Gods in the Clouds; & to the Noble Actions of the old Greeks in their famous City of Argos' (letters 7, 34). Various famous individuals also flit through his correspondence, most notably the itinerant Christina, Queen of Sweden (letters 7, 12, 24, 26, 32), whom Hammond memorably caricatures for her 'Manlike behaviour' and her 'Hermophrodite's Habit' (letter 16).

Political conditions back home are never far from Hammond's mind. Soon after his arrival in France, he compares the 'Rascall Beggerlyness' of the French infantry to the 'Substantiallness of my Lord Protector's Souldiers', deeming the French militia 'much liker the Scoth, than English Army' (letter 1). He relishes recounting to his father in July 1657 the recent English naval victory at Tenerife as reported in the Lyons Gazette (letter 15). He was not always able, however, to hide entirely his anxieties over the gradual disintegration of democratic government in late 1650s England. On 2 March 1658 at Paris he commented to his father: 'We hear the Protector plays the Chymist with his Parliament, & turns it into as many shapes, as my Master does his Quicksilver' (letter 26); and the concluding comment in his last letter, posted from Amsterdam on 6 May 1658, picks up on the aftermath of the bitterly contentious second session of the Second Protectorate Parliament: 'We heard some buzing of new Troubles in England, but I suppose the dissolving of the Parliament, has quieted all' (letter 37). On a domestic level, Hammond's thoughts from abroad were often focused upon his happy home life. He is concerned by news of his mother's illness (letter 21) but later delighted by her safe confinement with a new baby brother (letter 28). Similarly, he is interested in news (letter 25) of the plans of his uncle, Edward Digges, to retire to the West Indies and, as requested, supplies him with information on the French silkworm industry (letter 26). He also makes numerous other references to family members and friends involved in trade abroad (letters 4, 6, 7, 10, 12, 13).

4. William Hammond's Later Life and the Other Hammonds

At the time when he set out on his travels in December 1655, our author, William Hammond (c. 1635–c.1685), had a younger brother, named Anthony (1641–80), later of Somersham Place, Huntingdonshire. In one letter William Hammond jokingly suggests to his father that he might become a merchant, 'since my Brother flyes from all Professions' (letter 15). This Anthony married Amy Browne (d. 1693) of Gloucestershire, and had a son, also called Anthony (1668–1738), MP for the county of Huntingdon (1695), for the

University of Cambridge (1698–1701, until defeated by Isaac Newton), and for Huntingdon (1702). He was known in Parliament as 'silver-tongued Hammond' and became a minor poet and pamphleteer.[1]

It is uncertain whether William Hammond had any other living brothers; and the evidence provided by his letters is inconclusive. He ends one missive home (letter 8) with greetings to 'my Brother and Sisters'; and in another (letter 11) he again remembers his 'Brother, Sisters, etc.'. Elsewhere he refers to one of these sisters as 'Dear Sister Nan' (letter 13); but he does not provide the names of the others.[2] In another letter, dated 6 April 1658, Hammond also records his pleasure at the news of the birth of a new (as yet unnamed) brother (letter 28).

Before undertaking his travels on the continent, William had matriculated at Wadham College, Oxford, on 14 November 1650. His family, presumably, were even then intent upon him laying the educational foundations for some suitable profession, although there seems to be no evidence to suggest that after his return to England he pursued, as expected, a medical career. Instead, he may be the William Hammond named as a barrister at law in 1663.[3] Certainly, his letters suggest that, although intelligent, genial and of a deft literary turn of mind, William Hammond was never destined in later life for great things.

According to a pencil note, added by an unknown hand facing the title-page of the Brotherton Collection manuscript of William Hammond's letters, he married his first cousin, Elizabeth, daughter of Sir John Marsham (1602–85) and his father's sister, Elizabeth Hammond Marsham (1612–89). Their son, William (12 August 1664–1717), matriculated at University College, Oxford, on 7 May 1680.[4] Apart from these scant details, nothing else is known about William Hammond's (probably entirely unremarkable) life after his return from his continental travels.

Finally, when considering the the activities and personal connections of William Hammond's immediate relatives during the Civil War, it needs to be emphasized that his family should be differentiated from two other prominent Hammonds of the period, whose families also originated from the south-east of England and occasionally interacted with his own. The first individual was the Rev. Henry Hammond (1605–60), the youngest son of John Hammond, MD (c. 1565–1617), and grandson of John Hammond, LL.D (1542–89). This Henry Hammond was educated at Eton and Magdalen College, Oxford (1621), before ordination in 1629. He preached at court in 1633 and so impressed Robert Sidney, 2nd Earl

---

[1] See Bodl. MS Rawlinson A 245 for this Anthony Hammond's 'Collections and Extracts relating to the Affairs of the Nation, with an Autobiographical Diary'. He contributed a preface to *A New Miscellany of Original Poems, Translations and Imitations* (1720), which included poems by Matthew Prior, Alexander Pope, and Lady Mary Wortley Montagu. See also Stanley, *Poems and Translations*, ed. Crump, p. xxiii. One of Anthony's pocket books (1717–34) is now BL Add. MS 22584.

Anthony married in 1694 at Tunbridge Wells Jane Clarges (d. 1749), and had at least two sons: Thomas (d. c. 1758) and his younger brother, James (1710–42). Due to his debts Anthony Hammond died in 1738 in the Fleet prison and his estate was not administered until April 1749 (after which his son, Thomas (d. c. 1758), was obliged to sell the family seat of Somersham Place to the Duke of Manchester. Coincidentally, Robert Montagu (1634–83), 3rd Earl of Manchester, the author of the first travel diary included in this volume, was the father of Charles Montagu (c. 1662–1722), created the first Duke of Manchester in 1719.

[2] At the end of one letter (23) William Hammond uniquely refers to 'my brothers'.

[3] See Joseph Foster, *Men at the Bar: a Biographical Hand List of the Members of the Various Inns of Court, Including Her Majesty's Judges*, 2nd edn, London, 1885.

[4] *Alumni Oxonienses: the Members of the University of Oxford, 1500–1714*, 4 vols, Oxford and London, 1891–2, ed. Joseph Foster, II, p. 640.

of Leicester, that he was appointed as his personal chaplain at Penshurst Place, Kent. Having raised a troop of horse in July 1643 to assist Charles I, he was obliged to flee Penshurst and took up residence at Oxford where he was appointed as a royal chaplain. From a reference in William Hammond's letters to books recommended to his uncle William Hammond by a 'Dr Hammond' ('My Morality & Civil Law-books, from the Note, D[r]. Hammond was pleas'd to leave my Uncle William', letter 29), it seems that Henry Hammond may have been on friendly terms with our branch of the Hammonds. Henry Hammond was also the uncle of Robert Hammond, Governor of the Isle of Wight; and Henry was instrumental in the king's flight there to Carisbrooke Castle in November 1647 (as commemorated in Thomas Stanley's translation, Ode XXVII, 'Meditations upon Death after the votes of Non-Addresses, and his Majesty's closer Imprisonment in Carisbrook Castle').[1]

After Charles I's execution, Henry Hammond (now deprived of a living) was generously supported by the Worcestershire royalist, Sir John Pakington. But in 1655 an ordinance was issued forbidding ejected clergy from serving even as private chaplains or tutors, thereby effectively depriving them of any means of supporting themselves. In defiance of these regulations, the Pakingtons bravely continued to support him tacitly until his death on 25 April 1660, the day on which Parliament voted to support the return of King Charles II to England. If he had lived, his first biographer reported, he would have been appointed as Bishop of Worcester. Hammond was a prolific writer and publisher of biblical commentaries (most famously of his *Practical Catechism* in 1644); and tracts of a firmly political nature (including *Of Resisting the Lawful Magistrate under Colour of Religion* in 1644; *Humble Address to the Lord Fairfax and the Council of War, 15 January 1648, to Prevent the King's Murder in 1648*; and *The Christian's Obligation to Peace and Charity*, dedicated to King Charles I, in 1649).[2] If, as previously noted, this Henry Hammond was on friendly terms with the Hammonds of Wilberton, then it seems entirely possible that our William Hammond would have been familiar with Henry Hammond's controversial writings and prominent loyalty to the royalist cause.

The second prominent Hammond at this period, was Henry Hammond's nephew, the Parliamentarian soldier, Robert Hammond (1621–54). It seems likely that the Hammonds of Wilberton would also have at least known of (and were perhaps personally intimate with) this Robert Hammond. Furthermore, the idea of our letter writer pursuing his medical studies abroad could well have been inspired by the illustrious example of Robert's grandfather, John Hammond MD (c. 1565–1617), who had served as personal physician to King James I and was one of the court doctors appointed to undertake the sombre task of performing a post-mortem examination on Prince Henry after his sudden and unexpected death, probably from typhoid fever, in November 1612 (see p. 25).

After studies during the late 1630s at Magdalen College, Oxford, Robert Hammond served as a lieutenant in 1642 in the English forces sent to Ireland. He was appointed in 1643 a captain in the Earl of Essex's regiment of cuirassiers and by 1645 had secured the command of a regiment of the foot in the New Model Army. He served for Parliament at Naseby, the storming of Bristol and Dartmouth, the Battle of Torrington, and the siege of Basing House. He was appointed Governor of the Isle of Wight in September 1647. This sinecure became extremely difficult for Hammond when, partly through the offices of his

---

[1] *Poems and Translations*, ed. Crump, pp. 315–18.
[2] See John Fell, *Life of Hammond*, 1661 (rpt. 1662); and *The Workes of Henry Hammond*, 4 vols, 1684.

uncle Henry Hammond, Charles I decided in November 1647 to withdraw there voluntarily. Robert Hammond immediately wrote to Parliament to inform them of what had happened and he was issued with instructions to set a guard on the king and to prevent him from leaving without parliamentary permission. He, therefore, found himself not Charles I's protector but his gaoler.

At first, Robert Hammond's relations with the king were friendly but they became more strained when he was required by Parliament to search his possessions; and an unfounded rumour that he and Charles had fallen to blows circulated in a quarto pamphlet: *The Fatal Blow, or the Most Impious and Treasonable Fact of Hammond in Offering Force unto and Hurting his Most Sacred Majesty Discussed* (1647). Hammond's relations with his king continued to deteriorate during 1648 and he earnestly sought to be relieved of his unwelcome guardianship. But the breach in November 1648 between the army and parliament only served to complicate his position further, eventually leading to the seizure of the king against his orders on 29 November 1648. He was eventually awarded a pension by Parliament of £400 per annum in recognition of his services, which was commuted for lands in Ireland to the value of £600. Hammond withdrew from public life for the next few years, although his friendship with Cromwell seems to have remained strong. Certainly, once he had become Protector, Cromwell was keen to utilize Hammond's services again; and he was appointed a member of the Irish Council in August 1654 (although he died in Dublin in the following October from a fever).[1]

If, as seems likely, the Hammonds of Wilberton knew both Henry Hammond and his nephew, Robert, they would have readily appreciated the challenges, tribulations, and sheer complexity of their respective services to king and parliament. Under such prevailing conditions, the quiet withdrawal in December 1655 of their son, William, for an extended and educationally worthwhile sojourn on the continent would have doubtless appeared to other members of their family circle as a wise and expedient measure.

5. The Manuscripts of William Hammond's Letters

(i) University of Leeds, Brotherton Collection, MS Trv.2

This manuscript copy of William Hammond's letters, according to its title-page, was transcribed from the originals ('Inserted & Transcrib'd after the same Copys, as they were written by him') in the year '1695'. It comprises 128 pages, measuring 183mm x 149mm, and is in an eighteenth-century (?) binding of panelled calf gilt, with gilt roses in the compartments of the spine.[2]

It was purchased from the booksellers, Grinke and Rodgers, for the Brotherton Collection, and entered in the library's acquisition's book on 18 December 1969. The manuscript had previously been in the private collection of Sir Bruce Ingram but was not

---

[1] This Robert Hammond has also sometimes been confused with his uncle, Thomas Hammond, lieutenant-general of the ordnance in the New Model Army. Thomas Hammond served as one of the judges at the trial of King Charles I, although he did not sign the death warrant. He died before 1652 and was one of twenty dead regicides exempted from the Act of Indemnity and forfeiture of lands at the Restoration.

[2] Either this manuscript, or a copy, is described in John Burke, *A Genealogical and Heraldic History of the Commoners of Great Britain and Ireland*, 4 vols, London, 1834–8, II, p. 131, in an account of the Hammond family: 'Mr. Hammond having been bred a physician, went abroad in pursuit of professional knowledge, and a very curious account of his travels written by himself, is still preserved among the family papers'.

among his travel journals sold at Sotheby's on 16 December 1963.[1] However, lot 214 in this sale was described as:

> Commonplace Book kept by various members of the Hammond family, including detailed household accounts covering the period 1650–69 (c. 65 *pp. in all*) and a 90–page section of medical and cookery recipes, etc., Manuscript on paper, c. 157 *pp. plus blanks, written in several hands, some waterstains, contemporary calf gilt (worn)*, g.e.
> *4to* [England, 17*th century*]

Although Sotheby's records show that this volume was sold to the book dealer Francis Edwards, its present location is unknown.[2]

(ii) British Library Additional MS 59785

This manuscript is an eighteenth-century copy of either the original letters or a later copy. It was purchased from Sotheby's, 12 August 1976, lot 349. It comprises ii + 90 pages, measuring 254 x 190mm, and is in a late eighteenth-century gilt-stamped binding. The earliest date when it was transcribed may be deduced from various bibliographical annotations made by the transcriber, referring the reader (letter 4) to 'Dr Birch's Life of M^r: John Greaves Professor of Astronomy at [?] London. 1737'; and (letter 27) to the 1739 edition of Humphrey's translation of *Spectacle de La Nature*. The transcriber also makes a reference (letter 19) to 'Philip the 5th. now King of Spain', who reigned from 1700 until 1746. This last reference seems to imply that the anonymous transcriber of BL Additional MS 59785 began his or her work on the manuscript at some point between 1739 and 1746.

However, in the annotations to letter 4, the transcriber also notes: 'See Life of D^r. John Wilkins Bishop of Chester annex'd to his Mathematical Works: London 1708. pa: iii. appointed Warden of Wadham College Oxford April .13th. 1648'. Immediately below this reference to John Wilkins is added yet an apparently hastily jotted note: 'D^r. Birch's Life of [?] Tillotson .... pa. [?]'. This clearly refers to Thomas Birch's *The Life of the Most Reverend Dr John Tillotson*, which prefaced his monumental and immensely popular three-volume edition of *The Works of the Most Reverend Dr. John Tillotson, Lord Archbishop of Canterbury*. But this collection was first published in 1752 (with a revised edition in 1753). If the reference in letter 19 to 'Philip the 5th. now King of Spain' (d. 1746) is accurate, then this additional reference to Birch's life of Tillotson suggests that the transcriber of BL Additional MS 59785 continued to compile his or her proposed annotations to the manuscript during the early 1750s.

A single clue to the transcriber's identity is provided in BL Additional MS 59785. On f. 62^v, the following note glosses William Hammond's comments on the silk mills of Lyons:

> If the writer had Lived to see the Surpriseing Silk Mill, created by Sir Thomas Lombe K? (& alderman of London & Sheriff 1722) in the Seventeenth Century, he wou'd not have been surprised, at this at Paris; & as I have here, an opportunity of Communicating the whole apparatus, of that at Derby, I shall here, added it, as a very valuable Remark, at the same time observeing, this, was not generaly known, to ev'ry one; & was communicated, to me, by his

---

[1] I am grateful to Paul Grinke, now of Bernard Quaritch Ltd, for this information.

[2] I am grateful to Sonia Anderson, formerly of the Historical Manuscripts Commission, for drawing my attention to this Sotheby's sale; to Peter Beal for providing me with a photocopy of the entry for lot 214; and to Deborah Clark, manager of Francis Edwards (now of 13 Great Newport Street, Charing Cross Road, and The Old Cinema, Hay-on-Wye), for confirming that Edwards's records do not survive from the early 1960s.

Widow, my First Cousin. If I swell the Note, too Longe, Believe me, Reader, it is done entirely to please you, & entertain you, &, in order, to prevent so extrodinary, an occurence, to Dye with me, which wou'd have been a Great Fault.

The transcriber is referring here to Sir Thomas Lombe (1685–1739), who introduced silk-throwing machinery into England and in 1718 patented it as his new invention. He served as sheriff of London and was knighted in 1727. His half-brother, John Lombe (c. 1693–1722) was sent to Italy to familiarize himself with the silk-throwing process but, according to popular (but unsubstantiated) rumours, was poisoned back home in Derby over a period two or three years by a women sent to him by jealous Italian workmen. After Sir Thomas Lombe's death on 3 January 1739, which was announced in the *Gentleman's Magazine* of that year, his huge fortune of £120,000 was left to his widow and his two daughters, Hannah Lombe and Mary Turner Lombe. The death of his widow on 18 November 1753 was announced in the same magazine, although in both cases, frustratingly, her name is given only as 'Lady Lombe'. However, the naming of her second daughter, Mary Turner Lombe, may well indicate that her maiden name had been Turner.

The hand in BL Additional MS 59785 is a large and uneven one. As regards the writer's age, all that can be said is that Lady Lombe (who died as a mature women in 1753) is described as a 'first cousin'. Whatever the age (or sex) of the transcriber, it seems likely that this manuscript was copied either from the original letters or from an intermediate copy, rather than from the Brotherton Collection manuscript itself. Although it diverges from the text of Brotherton MS Trv.2 in various minor aspects of transcription and spelling, it contains no substantive additions or variations to the texts of the letters themselves. It is clear that the transcriber planned to provide a detailed annotation of Hammond's letters (perhaps even for eventual publication), identifying individuals and explaining historical circumstances. However, many spaces are left at the bottom of pages (with the symbols '*', '[ ]' or '[ ]' corresponding to notes added in the body of the text), indicating that this task was only partially completed. All completed, or partially completed, notes (other than minor cross-references to undrafted notes) are recorded by the notation '*' within the footnotes to this edition, along with any significant textual divergences from the Brotherton manuscript text of the letters.

EDITED TEXT

THE TRAVELS OF WILLIAM HAMMOND
(December 1655–May 1658)

[f. 1ʳ]

Several
Letters of Mʳ William Hammond[1]
during
His three years Travells abroad,
in France, Italy, Germany, & Holland,
Written by him
Unto his Father Anthony Hammond
Esquire, of Wilberton near Ely,
herein
Inserted & Transcrib'd after the
same Copys, as they were written
by him. –
1695.[2]

[f. 1ᵛ–blank][3]

[1]

[f. 2ʳ] Most Honoured Father, & Mother,

Being now at Length safely arriv'd at Paris, I shall obey your Commands in giving you
an Account of myself ever since my Removall from London. The first Week I bestowd
in Kent, where I tooke my Leave of as many of my Friends, as the Scarcity of my time
wou'd permit. I cannot but mention, how kindly Wellcome my Cosin Richards[4] made
me, & tho' he himself was almost bed-ridd by the Gout, yet thorow the help of his son,
I make no Question, but my first Bill is sufficient: For Mʳ Skinner[5] undertooke it, & he

---

[1] '.A.' [= 'Author'] has been added next to 'Hammond' in the right-hand margin, in another hand, referring the
reader to a pencil note, in the same hand, added on the preceding page: '.A[uthor]. Son of Anthony Hammond
Esq and Ann his wife daughter of Mr Dudley Digges of Chilham Castle (or 'Cartte'). He married his first cousin
Eliza*be*th Marsham daughter of Si*r John* Marsham'.

[2] * No title-page is present in BL Additional MS 59,785.

[3] Seven lines of badly faded and now largely illegible pencil notes have been added to this page, in a later
(perhaps 19th-century) hand. They appear to relate to a female member of the Hammond family, [Charlotte?],
but only the words 'Daughter of [Revd?] Anthony [?] Hammond [?] married Benjamin [?]' are (tentatively) deci-
pherable.

[4] 'Cosin Richards'. Letter 29 reveals his first name to be Gabriel.

[5] 'Mʳ Skinner', unidentified.

161

was never found other wise, than very Punctuall. The Summe we brought to Dover was but Twenty Pounds Sterling, of which I chang'd four Pound for Pistoles & some Lewisses;[1] & for the Sixteen Pound remaining M[r] Skinner gave me a Bill to M[r] Wildigo's, Merchant in Paris, whereby I am to receive 207 Livres, which is after the rate of 55, a very gaining Exchange, Insomuch that if I cou'd have return'd my Hundred Pound Sterling, it wou'd have been better worth to me here, than a Hundred & Thirty Pounds.[2] Last Munday I shew'd [f. 2[v]] my Merchant his Bill, & this Afternoon appointed to come & receive it. My Cosin & I are both in very good health, not finding any great Difference betwixt the London & the Paris Air, only that this is much the Clearer, as being void of all Sea-coal smoaks,[3] & Strange Sights of Brew-houses, &c. We were both sufficiently purged, by the Narrow seas of Dover, for tho we were but 4 hours passing to Callis; yet I do verily believe, it gave me hourly Vomitts, & him half as many. Neither were the French Water-men less Cruell in Purging our Purses; It Costing us rather more than less, a Pistole from the Packet-boat, which I discharged at Dover to our Inn. The rest of our Journey was after the common rate by the Messengers, with whom we were four days travelling thorow Bolognia & Picardie;[4] Countrys so like to East Kent, that a few Arguments wou'd make me believe, they have been formerly Contiguous. We had the Luck to find all the Souldiers in their Winter-Quarters, but they are since Marcht into *th*e Champain;[5] So that there is no passing that way again this Summer, without being certainly rob'd. We [f. 3[r]] found so much difference betwixt the Substantiallness of my Lord[6] Protector's Souldiers, & the Rascall Beggerlyness of *th*ese French Foot, that we tooke them rather for boys, than Men; & I think them much liker the Scoth, than English Army. Since our Coming to Paris We have been Extremely oblidg'd to my Aunt Stanly's[7] Friend D[r.] Holden,[8] who sent us to the Pension, where we now are, which tho it be none of the best in Town, yet 'tis tolerable, & by much the Cheapest: He bids us

---

[1] 'Pistoles', foreign gold coins, most commonly a Spanish coin worth about 16s 6[d] to 18s. The name was also used in France for the *louis d'or* (or Hammond's 'lewisses') of Louis XIII, first issued in 1640 and minted until the time of Louis XVI.

[2] Hammond's account of his financial transactions with 'M[r] Wildigo', a merchant at Paris, illustrates how English travellers of this period commonly obtained cash while abroad, via transfers from England to known merchants on the continent who were prepared to give them credit.

[3] 'Sea-coal smoaks', the pungent smell of sea-colewort, also known as sea-kale or sea-bindweed.

[4] The area immediately south of Boulogne-sur-Mer (formerly Bononia) and the province of Picardy (which was frequently invaded from the Spanish Netherlands until France acquired Artois and southern Hainaut in 1659.

[5] 'Champain', open countryside. In addition to incursions from the Spanish Netherlands, Hammond was travelling in the militarily active period immediately following the civil disputes, known as the Frondes (1648–1653), which culminated in the triumphal entry of Louis XIII into Paris on 21 October 1652, and that of Cardinal Mazarin on 3 February 1653.

[6] * BL Add. MS 59785, f. 1[v]: 'I shall here take the Liberty & in the future opportunitys that occur to explain some Circumstances by Notes – This was Oliver Cromwell'.

[7] Lady Mary Hammond Stanley, the elder sister of William Hammond's father, Anthony. The transcriber of BL Add. MS 59785, f. 2[r], marked both Lady Mary Stanley's name, and that of Henry Holden, for annotation, but left the bottom of the page blank where the note would have been placed. I have not attempted to record the numerous other places where this transcriber identified the need for a note but did not ultimately provide one.

[8] The Catholic divine Henry Holden (1596–1662), a professor at the Sorbonne and one of the vicars-general of the diocese of Paris, was an influential and hospitable figure for English exiles (especially, but not exclusively, Catholic ones) at Paris during the 1650s. See letter 9 for Hammond's detailed consideration of Holden's life and career.

get all our Lettres to be directed to him, & so they shall come Safe to us in what parts of France soever we be.[1] Thus begging your Blessings, I rest

Paris January }
2. 1656. }

Your most Dutifull Child
William Hammond. –

[2]

Most Honoured Father,

If my last, which pretended to speake nothing but French,[2] had the good Fortune to find the way to Wilberton;[3] I hope it had so much of true French in it, as to express the chief part of his Errand, which was to Present my Duty, & humbly to begg the Blessing; as for its Enlargements, tho the Languague [f. 3ᵛ] might be so broken, as not to let them be understood, they might at worst shew you my Proficiency in this Crabbed Tongue, which is so contrary both in Syntaxe & Pronunciation to our English, that it may well goe hand in hand with the Latine for matter of difficulty. And it Cost me above tenn Year's time, before I cou'd obtain so much Mastery in the Latine, as I have done in Eight Months of the French: Yet the much greater Proficiency I see others have made in as little time (by having the Advantage over me in Loquocity & in Totally abandoning themselves to French Conversation) makes me very far from thinking my time so much as Indifferently well spent. I hope you'l please to indulge so far to the slowness of my Capacity, as to let me obtain that Improvement by Length of time; which Quicker Witts make more haste in getting: & be pleas'd to Consider that two years spent in France with an English Companion, is but Equivalent to one year, spent entirely amongst none but French. Since my last We have remov'd our Quarters from a Pension into a Chamber-Garny,[4] nigh one of the best Academys in Town, wherein [f. 4ʳ] I have now been enter'd a whole Week, this being the fifth Morning that I come from Mounting three Horses every day. The first day it Cost me six Pistolls Entrance to the Master, & his Creats,[5] a Crown to his Porter, another to his Palfrenier, three Crowns my stirrups, four Crowns my Little Boots, a Crown my Spurrs; & I have advanct for three Months. Vid: from the Ninth of January to the Ninth of Aprill, after the Rate of four Pistolls a month, having thereby the Advantage of running at the ring every day, which otherwise I shou'd have done but once a Week. The Charge in all comes to above Twenty Pistolls, a summe that has made so great a Gapp in my Purse, that without a speedy supply of tithes Twenty Pounds, t'will be an hard matter to avoid a Vacuum: & I humbly desire, you'le please to let either My Cosin Richards or my Cosin Dawson[6] return me it at the best Exchange, which must be at least 27 Pistolls, or 270 Livres for Twenty

[1] Hammond's account illustrates how letters from England could be efficiently distributed to English travellers, via well-established postal systems, as they proceeded through France and beyond. For the times taken to deliveries, see letter 8. Letter 32 details how the friendly assistance of local English merchant at Leghorn, Mr Brown, was also utilized as a reasonably reliable means for Hammond to receive his post while in Italy. But letter 39 traces how this system could result in chaos when the same Brown confused Hammond's letters received as letters to be posted out to England.

[2] This letter, with Hammond's first attempts at writing in French, has been lost.

[3] *BL Add. MS 59785, f. 2ᵛ: 'Wilberton The Seat of Anthony Hammond, Esq: Father to The Writer of these Letters'.

[4] 'Chamber-Garny': *chambre-garnie*, furnished room.

[5] 'Creats': perhaps 'creat[ure]s', i.e. horses.

[6] 'Cosin Dawson', unidentified.

Pound sterling; For my last Exchange was exactly after that rate. Dr. Holden kisses your hand & sends this Enclos'd: I humbly beg *your* Blessing on

Paris Jan*uary* ⎫
13. 1656. ⎭

Sir, *your* most Dutifull Child
William Hammond. –

[3]

[f. 4ᵛ] Most Hon*oured* Father,
The Lettres, which I sent to Wilberton by the two¹ former Posts, have left me so barren a subject for this Present, that I am afraid, it will hardly Usherr me to the bottome of my Page. Really, Sir, for this month it has been so cold here in Paris, that I think the French Witts are absolutely Frozen; otherwise 'twere impossible, so much of their Carnivall cou'd be spent with so little Variety. My Chymist Master takes himself to be utterly undone, the raging Frost has Coogulated all his Dissolutions: his Spirits, Essences, Baums & Quintessences freize & breake all his hard-namd Glasses. I hope if it be Equally cold in England, 'twill fright à way all the Agues, Especially those that are at Wilberton. I am very glad, that Dr. Broome² getts such Credit in London. I hope to play the Ren & rise upon the Eagle's shoulders,³ for he is a man that I know has a Particular good will for me, & did me the Favour to give me severall Visitts at my Chamber in Gray Inn. But indeed, Sir, there is no greater Advantage towards the Study of Physick, than Travelling, & without doubt he that knows the ways of the French, Italian, Dutch & English Docto*rs* will be [f. 5ʳ] better able to shift, than an English one, that lives Hood-wink't in London. The Protector's Physician Dr. Bates⁴ was ten or 12. years abroad, and a great while retaind Physician to the German Army: And there is hardly any of the Upper-forme Physicians in London, that have not either travelld, or got some other ways notable Experience, by Armys, or having their nigh Kindreds great Docto*rs* before them. I find that a French Physician is made up of a little reading & a very great deal of Experience; their Usuall Study goes noe farther than having been at Courses of the severall Parts of Physick, as a Course of Chyrurgery, a Course of Herbalizing, Physiology, & Courses of all Apothecarys Businesses: by the means of w*hich* they get a thorow Superficiall Knowledge of all things Necessary to Physick, & afterwards perfect it by running to publick Hospitalls, & many private Operations, that they help one

---

¹ * BL Add. MS 59785, f. 4ʳ: 'I presume The writer means the Two first Letters of This Collection Dated January .2ᵈ. & .13ᵈ. 1656'.

² 'Dr. Broome', unidentified.

³ * BL Add. MS 59785, f. 4ᵛ: 'The Writer aludes to a Fable of the Wren & Eagle'. This is Aesop's fable in which a competition takes place to decide which bird is supreme. It is decided that he that flies highest will be the monarch. The wren craftily hitches a ride on the back of the eagle and wins.

⁴ Dr George Bate (1608–68), graduated as MD from St Edmund Hall, Oxford, in 1637. He served as physician to King Charles I during his residence at Oxford and after the king's execution was employed by Cromwell as one of his doctors. He treated him for gallstones during the winter of 1655 and throughout his last illness in 1658. He also attended the autopsy and left a detailed account of its findings. After the Restoration, Bate served as a court physician to King Charles II. It was even rumoured that he had claimed to have administered a poison to Cromwell that caused his demise. Bate also sometimes worked during the early 1650s alongside another of Cromwell's physicians, Dr Laurence Wright (1590–1657), who took a BA from Cambridge in 1609 and then matriculated at Padua on 22 August 1612. Wright became a Fellow of the Royal College of Physicians in 1622 and served as physician-in-ordinary to Cromwell and the London Charterhouse from 1624 until 1643. See Antonia Fraser, *Cromwell Our Chief of Men*, 1973 (rpt. 1974), pp. 381, 577, 672–5, 681; and Stoye, *English Travallers Abroad*, pp. 338–9, n. 21.

another to. I am at present engag'd in some of their Courses, where I have lighted upon a Knot of very Ingenuous English Gentlemen, *that* are put upon the Same Profession; who having been about two years in France are this Spring going to Padua,[1] where they will study out *the* next Summer, & spend the Winter following in [f. 5ᵛ] Rome; with intent to be in England Easter come Twelve-month. They proposing me so short a time to be so well spent, endeavour to tempt me; but I dare not so much as propose any such thing, 'till my Mother's danger be passt:[2] & tho' I cou'd be very much pleas'd with one year more to be spent in Italy, yet above & beyond all my greatest desires are to be, Sir

Paris, Febru*ary* ⎫
2. 1656 ⎭

Your most Dutifull Son
William Hammond.

[4]

Most Hon*oure*d Father,

Having now at length spent this long & tedious Winter here in Paris, I was yesterday Casting, how I shou'd spend the Following summer to my best Advantage. And Really, Sir, tho' the Gadding humour be much abated in me, yet seeing myself at this time in a Wandering kind of Life, I had resolved to have Presented up one more Petition to you: Which was, upon supposition my time of Travell was Expiring, that I might fetch a little Tour down the River Rhine into Holland, & from thence into England. I know not what Planet reign'd yesterday, but if ever I turne Astrologer, I'le mark him as my Patron: For I had no Sooner [f. 6ʳ] Embarkt myself in those rambling thoughts but I receiv'd your Lettre of the 29 of March, for w*h*ich I return my most humble Thanks. The Season it comes in makes me chiefly take notice of your Goodness, in being pleas'd to enlarge my Travells a year longer; & granting me leave to tend towards those Noble Countrys of the South. I am almost asham'd to confess what an Unsettleness of thoughts, it has for the present engender'd in me: A young man subject to strong desires, must have long Convert in the Vanitys, & have seen thorow the Emptiness of this World, before he can promise himself the Mastery of such Unruly Passions. Really, Sir, You may Imagine with what Eagerness I embrace such a Motion, as may bring me into Italy. Yes I dare not let this Paper be the Messenger of my Resolutions: what comes from me now, must necessarily appear as Confus'd, as I have confesst my thoughts are; that which troubles me most, is to see the Spring so far advanc't, & that my Compaignons are already gathering towards their Rendevous at Geneva, from whence they intend to pass the Alps in a Caravan.[3] I am afraid

---

[1] Throughout the Tudor and Stuart periods the Medical School at the University of Padua attracted many notable Englishmen, including Thomas Linacre (1492) and John Caius (1539). Vesalius (1540) and Fallopius (1561) were medical professors there. The Anatomical Theatre (1594) was built by the surgeon Fabricius, tutor of William Harvey (graduated 1602), the author of *De Motu Cordis* (1628). For the medical studies there of Joseph Colston (1641–2), Edward Browne (1661), and the companions John Finch and Thomas Baines (1653–1659), see Stoye, *English Travellers Abroad*, pp. 157–8, 338–9, notes 19–21; and J. M. Woolfson, 'English Students at Padua 1480–1580', unpublished PhD dissertation, University of London, 1994. For a manuscript register (eventually used as a kind of informal 'visitor's book') of English visitors to the University of Padua between 1618 and 1765, see Horatio Brown, *Inglesi e Scozzesi all'Università di Padova*, Venice, 1922, and Chaney, *Evolution of the Grand Tour*, pp. 368–70.

[2] As later correspondence reveals (see letters 7 and 23), Hammond's mother was pregnant.

[3] See Stoye, *English Travellers Abroad*, pp. 94, 132, for the usual routes taken by travellers from Geneva into Italy (most frequently via the Simplon Pass, a well-established trade route).

the Considerable Distance between Paris and Wilberton, will require so much time in Con-
[f. 6^v] veying my Lettres, that before I can receive a Reinforcing of your Commands I shall
be overtaken by the Summer's Scorching heat, & go nigh to miss of all sorts of Company. If
I go down to Marselles[1] & embarke there, Company will not be so very necessary, as in passing the horrid Hills of Switzerland & the Valteline:[2] but 'twill be much the longer &
tediouser Voyage for me, who resolve to set up my Summer's rest in Padua: & where I'le
faithfully promise to improve myself in my Profession, as much as the Place & Opportunity
will give me leave.

And if you shall not think it a fit place for me to receive my D*octor*'s degree in: I dare almost
presume so far upon Dr Wilkin's[3] (Our Warden's) Goodness & Civility, as to reckon upon my
time running on in Wadham Colledge, as much & sure, as if I had been always resident, &
cannot so much as make the least doubt of it; if you wou'd please to propose it to him, or in
his stead to Mr Rooke,[4] or Dr Ward:[5] Tho' I believe, there are some small Fees, annext to the
Continuing one's Name in the Colledge books, which cannot amount to above a Crown a
year. My Cosin Dawson has, according to your Orders, sent [f. 7^r] me a Bill of Exchange for
the value of twenty five Pounds Sterling, tho' indeed I might have left out the word value; For
his Merchant is so far from letting me gaine any thing, that after the rate of this Bill, I have
but 26 Pistolls, in the hundred; allowing me but 105 French Crowns for Twenty five Pounds
English: And there is ne're a Mint in France, that will deny to give me 13 Livres[6] for twenty

[1] Marseilles.

[2] 'horrid hills': the Alps. 'Valteline': the Valtellina region around the upper region of the Adda River, with its four major Alpine passes: the Stelvio, Bernina, Aprica, and Umbrail.

[3] BL Add. MS 59785, f. 6^v: 'See Life of D^r. John Wilkins Bishop of Chester annex'd to his Mathematical Works: London 1708. pa: iii. appointed Warden of Wadham College Oxford April .13th. 1648.'; added below this note 'D^r. Birch's Life of [?] Tillotson [space] pa. [?]'. Thomas Birch's *The Life of the Most Reverend Dr John Tillotson*, prefacing Birch's three-volume edition of *The Works of the Most Reverend Dr. John Tillotson, Lord Archbishop of Canterbury* (1752). See also p. 159. Hammond had matriculated at Wadham College, Oxford, on 14 November 1650. John Wilkins (1614–72) was Warden of Wadham College from 1648–59. Although he had served as private chaplain to Elizabeth of Bohemia's son, Charles Louis (King Charles I's nephew), he supported the Parliamentarians during the English Civil War. (Hammond mentions meeting Charles Louis in letter 37.) He was appointed Master of Trinity College, Cambridge, in 1659 but deprived of this office at the Restoration. He continued, however, to hold various church appointments and became Bishop of Chester in 1668.

[4] BL Add. MS 59785, f. 6^v: 'See D^r. Ward's Lives of the Profession of Gresham College. 17 *added above* page 90. 91. 92. 93. 94. 156. 337'. See John Ward, *The Lives of the Professors of Gresham College* (1740; rpt. 1750). Lawrence Rooke (1622–62) was educated at Eton and King's College, Cambridge, and was elected to a fellowship there in 1643. After gaining an MA in 1647 he migrated to Oxford, where he became a fellow commoner of Wadham College in 1650. He was appointed as Professor of Astronomy (1652–57) and Professor of Geometry (1657–62) at Gresham College, London. Along with John Wilkins, he was involved in the formation of the Royal Society and also published astronomical works.

[5] BL Add. MS 59785, f. 6^v: 'See Popes Life of D^r: Seth Ward Lord Bishop of Salisbury. See D^r *added above* Ward's Lives of Profession of Gresham College 17 *added above* pa: 92. 93. 113. 115. 145. See D^r *added above* Birch's Life of M^r: John Greaves Professor of Astronomy at [?] London. 1737'. See Walter Pope, *The Life of the Right Reverend Father in God Seth Ward, Lord Bishop of Salisbury* (1697) and Thomas Birch (ed.), *Miscellaneous Works of Mr John Greaves, Professor of Astronomy in the University of Oxford ... To the Which is Prefix'd, an Historical and Critical Account of the Life and Writings of the Author* (1737). Seth Ward (1617–89), formerly fellow of Sidney Sussex, Cambridge (1640–43), where he lectured on mathematics. Ejected from his fellowship in 1643 on account of his opposition to the Covenant, he worked as a private tutor at Aspenden (1645–9) and was incorporated as MA at Oxford in 1649, in conjunction with his appointment as Savilian Professor of Astronomy (1649–61). Although he was elected as Principal of Jesus College, Oxford, he was ejected by Cromwell in 1657. After the Restoration he held various church livings, becoming Bishop of Exeter (1662–7) and Salisbury (1667–89).

[6] 'livres', *livre tournois*, (arch.) franc, a gold coin introduced in the 17th century, subdivided into 20 sols.

English Shillings. Really, Sir, I have told him of it so often, that I do now despaire of making him understand it; & I think his best way will be to Change his Marchant often, Lest when his defect of Understanding be known, his Marchant may take an Advantage to Cosen me of more Considerable Summes, than this lost, which comes not to above the value of two or thre Pistolls. Dr Holden returns you his most humble Service: He is a great Advancer of my Journey towards Italy, & withall advises me to set out in the beginning of May, Lest I shou'd be Inconvenienc'd by the melting Snows of Valteline. It shall be with very much regret, if I leave Paris before I receive some more News from Wilberton; yet I humbly beg, you'le please to pardon me, if I shou'd [f. 7^v] lay hold of any great Opportunity or Conveniency,[1] that may happen in the mean time. As long as I stay in Paris, I'le not faile to Present my Duty by every Post that parts: and I shou'd be much joy'd, you wou'd please to impose[2] upon me any of my Uncle's Quæry's,[3] or other Friends, that so I might be sure of Spending some time well in a Country so plentifull of things worth observing. But at present my Paper begins to Check me of my Tediousness. I shall only humbly present my Duty, & heartily begg your Blessing upon, Sir,

Paris, Aprill }   Yours most Dutifull Child,
20. 1656. }   William Hammond. –

[5]

Most Hon*oure*d Father,

I am afraid my last savour'd to much of a Rambling humour; The Newness of designing soe great a Journey, had a little Confus'd me, but I hope you'le please favourably to par-don *th*e slips of your most Dutifull Child. Really, Sir, it is not the Curiosity of Staring upon New Towns & Countrys, that drives me into Italy: yet, 'tis a hard matter, to say positively what it is. I have been already so deceiv'd in my Imaginations, & designs, I for-merly propos'd to my- [f. 8^r] self during my Travells in France; that I am asham'd to entertaine, much less to express any, *that* present themselves concerning Italy. I am sure the reallest & what will savour most of Duty, is my strong resolutions to improve my Profession; yet it may be, at the year's end, I may think more might be got in a Study, than in Rambling abroad. However, Sir, be pleas'd to pardon a young man, that thirstes after Experience; & if I be deceiv'd in my Imaginary hopes, 'tis better by far as a Break'fast,[4] than a Supper. I dare allmost warrant myself cur'd of that humour by this time Twelve-month: Methinks I am already a great Relisher of the Wise man's Text, *that* pronounces all things Vanity:[5] & I believe my mind will hardly be to great a Gainer by this Journey, as my Body, which by accustoming itself to great & powerfull Undertakings in its youth, will easierly slight the Inconveniencys, that accompany Age. My first Step in Physick shall be to understand my own body, & after having Study'd it both in its

[1] written 'conveveniency'.

[2] written 'im=impose' over a line.

[3] Probably a reference either to his uncle 'Ned Diggs' (see letters 5, 15, 25, 27) or to his uncle Marsham (see letter 7). Hammond's mother was Anne, daughter of Sir Dudley Digges; and his father's sister, Elizabeth (1612–89), married Sir John Marsham (1602–85). Hammond later married their daughter, Elizabeth (see p. 156).

[4] BL Add. MS 59785, f. 8^v: 'The Writer seems to imply that an early mistake in Life is hapier remedied than in more advanced years which he pretily calls "the Supper"'.

[5] Ecclesiastes 1:2.

Travells & in its Ease, if I attain not Perfection enough to be Master of my own health, I will never be so Unconscionable, as to practise upon others. There is Nothing I fear so much as travelling in the Scorching [f. 8ᵛ] Sun; it makes me hasten out of Town. & on the Thirtyeth of this Present,[1] I hope to set out with the Messenger of Lyons. My Cosin Bowyer[2] does infinitely multiply his Courtesys upon me; and now at last has oblidg'd me by lending me to *th*e Value of 25 Pound Sterling, my Following Quarteridge; which I humbly beg, you wou'd please to returne him. The parting with such a Summe, tho' it might be Inconsiderable to him, as Heir of Camberwell,[3] yet as a Traveller, may very much inconvenience him, if not suddenly restor'd.

Dʳ Holden has procur'd me a Bill of Exchange to Legorne;[4] whereby for 210 Livres paid here at Paris, I am to receive 67 Peices of Eight there:[5] most of the rest I have Chang'd into Spanish Gold, w*hic*h will best pass in Italy. Since my last I have heard, that my Companions at Geneva are deterrd from their intended Voyage thorow Switzerland & the Valteline, & are since falling down to Marselles, resolving to pass from thence to Legorne, from whence they will Cross over to Padua. I make no Question but to overtake them before they quitt the French Shore; & I hope by the latter end of May to present my Duty unto you in a Lettre Dated at Padua. If I thought the haste I make out of Towne wou'd [f. 9ʳ] displease you any way, really, Sir, it will heartily grieve me to have done it: I hope, you will rather impute it to the Preventive Care, I have of my health, than to any Youthfull Huddle or Rashness in me. Your Blessings upon my Actions must be the Chief Ingredient to their Prosperity; & I humbly begg you wou'd please to impart it proportionably to the sincerity of, Sir

Paris Aprill　}
27. 1656.　}

Your most Dutifull & Obed*ient* Child
William Hammond

The Post script

Sir, I am almost asham'd to present my Duty to my Mother in a Post script; the next Poste I'le endeavour to Expiate my Fault by a long Lettre. When you shall please to returne my Cosin his mony; I hope my Cosin Dawson will remember, that the Value of Twenty five Pounds, Sterling here in France; which the Mints will allow, is 32 Pistolls, & ½ a Pistoll, or 325 Livres, or a 108 Crowns, one Livre: & I hope he will let me gaine a little more than

---

[1] BL Add. MS 59785, f. 8ᵛ: 'April'.

[2] 'My Cosin Bowyer', was presumably a son of Sir Edmund Bowyer (c. 1613–81) whose first wife Hester (d. 1655), daughter of Sir Anthony Aucher, provided the family link with our author (whose paternal grandmother was Elizabeth Aucher).

[3] * BL Add. MS 59785, f. 9ʳ: 'Camberwell the Seat of' followed by a later pencil addition in another hand 'Bowyer (Sir Edmund) 1657'. Bowyer House (demolished 1861), Camberwell Green, was situated on what is now the Camberwell Road. John Evelyn visited the house in September 1657, describing it as the Bowyers's 'melancholy Seate at Camberwell' (1657), III, pp. 196–7.

[4] Leghorn (English) or Livorno (Italian), dated from 1571 when Cosimo I of Florence (1519–74) instigated the building of a new port. Leghorn was a major location for both English traders and travellers. Like many of his contemporaries, Hammond would probably have been aware of the high reputation of the engineer Sir Robert Dudley (d. 1649), the illegitimate son of Queen Elizabeth's favourite, Robert Dudley, Earl of Leicester, who had worked for Ferdinando I (1549–1609) and Cosimo II (1590–1621) as their maritime designer and administrator at Leghorn.

[5] 'Peices of Eight', Spanish *peso*, or piece of eight (i.e. divided into eight *reales*), was also known as a dollar within English speaking contexts.

that, by bargaining with severall Marchants. I wish my Uncle Diggs[1] wou'd give me Recommendations to some of his Acquaintance in Leghorne. D[r.] Holden has written to one D[r.] [f. 9[v]] Kirton, a Doctor of Physick at Florence,[2] in my behalfe.

[6]

Madam,

I have had almost a Fort night's tryall of D[r.] Holden's Civility, & cannot but much admire the Goodness of the man, having done us such reall kindnesses, as we cou'd expect from none but a Father. I hope your Lady ship[3] will please to accept of my base thanks for this, which indeed has been so great a Benefit to us, as makes me Conclude myself altogether incapable of any other Requitall: My Comfort is, that I know your Ladyship to be Compos'd of so much Goodness, as that this Favour (tho' too great for my Expression) may yet be reckon'd among your Works of Charity. On Munday next the D[r.] intends to remove us to a Country Towne of his own Chusing; We neither of us know, where it is or what Name it bears, having so entirely given ourselves over to his Tuition, as that we resolve to follow his Directions without the least Questioning: There is one Accident fallen out, that had I been a Catholick, I shou'd not only have confesst, but have done Penance for it too before [f. 10[r]] this time; & 'tis this, that I have not only my selfe been a sufficient trouble to the Doctor, but have Unluckily brought upon him *th*e trouble of another, whom we unfortunately took up at London, as a Companion to Paris, where he promised to quitt us; but now we find too late, that our Southern heads cannot ridd us of his Northern Craft:[4] For Lodging him, we suppos'd only for the first night, at our Quarters, he has ever since hung upon us, and encroaching upon the Doctor's Civility, has I fear put him to a double trouble: On Munday we shall quitt ourselves of him, but we almost despair of ever ridding the D[r.] of him, who is so extremely Civill, not only to our Persons, but to this stranger for our sakes. I humbly desire, that your Ladyship will be pleas'd to Excuse it to him, & to let him know, that we have thus Unfortunately brought an Inconveniency upon him & ourselves. The Doctor tells me, that my Cosin[5] is to come hither with Humphrey.[6] I wish I knew what time, *tha*t I might wait on her at the Water-side: Madam, my Cosin presents his humble service & thanks, I am

Paris May }
6/16 1656 }

Your most Dut*iful* & Obed*ient* Nephew, William Hammond

---

[1] * BL Add. MS 59785, f. 9[r]: 'Sir Dudley Digges', although Hammond's 'Uncle Diggs' was, in fact, a son of Sir Dudley Digges, whose daughter, Anne, was Hammond's mother. See letter 35.

[2] 'D[r.] Kirton, a Doctor of Physick at Florence', unidentified.

[3] * BL Add. MS 59785, f. 10[v]: 'I take this to be to Lady Bowyer'. The letter is, in fact, addressed to Hammond's aunt, Lady Mary Stanley.

[4] Hammond's comments on this troublesome northerner may be compared with the impression (unintentionally) conveyed by the *Memoirs and Travels* of the brusque Yorkshireman Sir John Reresby (1634–89). Justly characterized by one of his modern editors as 'quarrelsome, addicted to the use of violence, and none too refined in his ideas and manners', Reresby was at Paris in the spring of 1654 and again in January 1658. *Memoirs of Sir John Reresby. The Complete Text and a Selection from his Letters*, ed. Andrew Browning, *Second Edition with a New Preface and Notes*, ed. Mary K. Geiter and W. A. Speck, London, 1991, p. xxiii.

[5] This cousin was Hammond's 'Cosin Betty' (see letter 12), the daughter of Sir Thomas and Lady Stanley, who became a nun at Dieppe (see letter 36). * BL Add. MS 59785, f. 11[r], mistakenly notes: 'Bowyer mentioned in the 5 Lett*er*'.

[6] 'Humphrey' was probably a family servant of the Stanleys.

[7]

[f. 10ᵛ] Most Hon*oure*d Father,

Since my last of the Ninth, I have spent my time in Florence.[1] These Italian Towns, are so much more pleasant, than those of France, that I cannot bring myself to run Poste & in haste thorow them. I might be reckon'd amongst the Swine,[2] if I shou'd not bestow some time, in Viewing & Considering the Grand Duke of Tuscany's Pearls & Raritys.[3] Really, Sir, I am much taken up with the rich Magnificence of this Petty Prince, whose Dominions tho' they hardly equall any one Province of France; yet his Court goes far beyond that Noble Monarch's in Paris. This Week the Town is Cramm'd with a multitude of Strangers from all Parts, who flock hither to the seeing of a famous Opera, made in Congratulation for the Birth of a young Prince in Spain.[4] I may pretend to some Skill in Perspectives; but cou'd never till now believe, 'twas possible so much to deceive my sight, as it has been twice this week by the Machines of this Famous Opera. A little Rhetorick wou'd perswade me, that I have been a spectator to the reall sports of the Poeticall Gods in the Clouds; & to the Noble Actions of the old Greeks in their famous [f. 11ʳ] City of Argos.[5] Here are severall Venetians, Romans, & Neopolitans, who profess that there has never been its like in Italy: & for Voices, whatsoever is choice & rare in these Southern Parts, are won to be Actors on this Glorious Stage; So that all Conclude this World can invent nothing more pleasant to the Eyes, or Melodious to the Ear. Thus the Epicurean[6] Italians wallow in their Pleasures & delights, whilst other Parts of Christendome are over-whelmed with Intestine or Forreign Warrs & Miserys. Really, Sir, 'tis infinitely alter'd in its Genius from what 'twas, during the Old Roman heros; it does not only profess an Enmity to *the* Sword, & an Aversion to all Warlike Actions, but methinks they beginn also to decline in Knowledge & Book-Conversation; it may be the French Armys (now they have found the way into Italy)[7] will in

---

[1] In letter 6, dated 6/16 May 1656 from Paris, Hammond refers to Dr Holden's plan to relocate him and his party in 'a Country Towne of his own Chusing'. This letter, penned 22 June 1656 from Florence, refers to a now missing letter of 9 June which, presumably (and perhaps along with others also lost), provided details of the journey from France to Italy. Within just over one month, it seems, Hammond had either travelled through France and across the Alps or (more likely) had sailed from Marseilles to Leghorn to reach Italy.

[2] * BL Add. MS 59785, f. 11ʳ: 'This aludes to the ungratefull & unthankfull Property of Swine who while they delight themselves with any Gratification never Look up to that Palce whence those Benefitts derive'.

[3] Ferdinando II (1610–70), Grand Duke of Tuscany, a noted patron of the sciences. In addition to his own family wealth and rarities, his estate had gained considerably more treasures through his marriage to the heiress Vittoria della Rovere in 1634.

[4] King Philip IV of Spain and his second wife, Mariana, daughter of Emperor Ferdinand III, had only one surviving son, King Charles II (1661–1700), 'el Mechizado' ('the Mad'), the last of the Spanish Habsburg monarchs. The death in 1646 of Baltasar Carlos, Philip's son and heir from his first marriage to Isabella (the sister of King Louis XIII of France), prompted his marriage in 1649 to Mariana (who had originally been intended as a bride for Baltasar Carlos).

[5] Argos, in the eastern Peloponnesian peninsula, was a traditional enemy of Sparta. In Homer's *Illiad* Argos was the kingdom of Diomedes and, in a wider sense, Agamemnon's empire. According to Herodotus, the Argive king Pheidon seized Olympia and held the Olympic games there.

[6] * BL Add. MS 59785, f. 11ʳ: 'The Followers of Epicurious Philosophy teach in the Schools that …'.

[7] Northern Italy had proved a strategically vital region during the struggles between France and Spain during the latter part of the Thirty Years' War (1618–48; with France involved from 1632). Spanish troops, dispatched via overland routes to the Low Countries, were mustered at Milan and control over this regions became vital for Spain during the Dutch Revolt. These circumstances had led to a renewal of the Franco-Spanish war in Italy during the War of the Mantuan Succession (1629–31), resulting in the victory of Charles Gonzaga, duke of Nevers, who was backed by the French. From 1648–61 the French royalist army countered the more widespread threat of the Fronde (led by the prince of Condé, see p. 121, n. 1). See also letter 10.

time wake them from their Luxurious Lethargy. 'tis reported, the Queen of Swede makes some bustle about her Imprisonment at Rome;[1] that she declares herself for the French & their Interest, upon which score all of that Nation, that are in Rome, beginn to stirr in her behalf: We hear very fresh Accounts of all that's done [f. 11ᵛ] in the Northern parts, but hear seldome of our Neighbouring Army in Mantoua; only it's said, they are not yet resolv'd what shal be their Summer's Enterprise. I have not yet had the good Fortune to light upon a Suitable Companion for me; & really, Sir, the summer is so far come on, that I am a little startled at so long a Journey, as from hence to Padua. But wheresoever I reside, I'le Religiously observe my Duty & Obedience to you in studying Physick. Last Post I Presented my Duty to my Mother; I have but little Enjoyment of my Travells, whilst I remain in this Uncertainty of your Wellfare at Wilberton: I now begin to be very Inquisitive of my Uncle Marsham's[2] Nephew, Mᵣ Browne at Leghorne,[3] whether he have not any Letters for me, Enclos'd in his Correspondents, Mᵣ Mellish his Packets from London.[4] I am forc't to keep up my Courage by Presuming on your Blessings upon, Sir,

Florence   }   Your most Dutifull Child,
June 22. *1656.* }   William Hammond. -

[8]

[f. 12ʳ] Most Honou*re*d Father,
The last You were pleas'd to send me bears date of the Tenth of June, which came to my hands the Fourth of July, together with an Enclosed from my Mother; The second day after their Receipt I sent away a double Packet in Answer to them both. Since which my Cosin & I have chang'd our Quarters of Chasteaudun,[5] to settle ourselves for some time in the famous University of Fleche; wherein we find the Pensions so much Cheaper, than they were in the other place, as will save the Charges of our Removall. We find the Town but small in Bulk, stufft full with Fryars and Jesuits; the last have their Chiefest Colledge here, A Pile Magnificent enough, & yet whose greatest splendor Consists in the Custody of Henry[6] the fourth's heart, which is therein kept, as a Royall Relique to Posterity;[7] & which in time may come to be as Precious, as Julius Cæsar's Ashes, preserv'd in Oxford

---

[1] Queen Christina (Kristina) of Sweden (1626–89) was crowned in 1644 but abdicated in favour of her cousin Charles X Gustav, on 6 June 1654. She immediately left Sweden and in December 1655 Pope Alexander VII welcomed her at Rome. Her presence there, however, soon became problematic when she began to foster a plan, with Cardinal Mazarin and the duke of Modena, to seize the throne of Naples (then in Spanish hands) so that she could become its queen and then leave the throne to a French prince. This wild intrigue collapsed in 1657. See Fig. 33, p. 190.

[2] * BL Add. MS 59785, f. 13ʳ: 'See Birch's Life of Mᵣ: John Greaves Professor of Astronomy at Oxford: pa. XXVI. Sir John Marsham author of the Canon Chronious'.

[3] This particular Mr Browne had not been identified, although he should be differentiated from Sir Richard Browne (1605–83), English Agent at Paris from 1641–60, and Edward Browne (1644–1708), the son of the physician Sir Thomas Browne, was in Italy during the latter half of the 1660s.

[4] 'Mᵣ Mellish', unidentified.

[5] Châteaudun, about 50km south of Chartres. It is probable that Hammond would have been based there only temporarily after his return from Italy.

[6] * BL Add. MS 59785, f. 13ᵛ: 'Henry the 4ᵗʰ. of France stabb'd by Raviliac the Friar, the 14ᵗʰ. of May .1610. his Daughter Henrietta Maria married May the 11ᵗʰ. 1625 King Charles the 1ˢᵗ of England'.

[7] See p. 116, n. 9, for the Jesuit college at La Flèche.

Library.[1] The Genius of the place begins to infect us with a sedentary Bookishness, which does us some good in attaining the Grounds of the French Languague; *the* Syntaxes whereof I think much harder, than [f. 12ᵛ] that either of the Latine or the Greek. I endeavour to get their History & the Country's Geophrophy together with their Languague; & having read the Life of Lewis the 13ᵗʰ,[2] I am now beginning with Serres his Generall Hystory;[3] For variety I have borrow'd Balzac his Lettres,[4] whose Easy & Ingenuous way of writing very much resembles that of our English Dʳ Donne,[5] & they are both so Copious & witty in describing their own Torments & Diseases, as if Nature by a painfull Screwing up their Nerves, had tuned their Brains to such a Melodious Facility of Expressing itself. Since our Coming to this place here we have found a very great Degree of heat, but height of it is passt: The Gazett mentions the Encrease & Spreading of the Sickness begun in Naples, whereof there dyes 1500 dayly in that City; It[s] Continuance will kill the Spaniard more Subjects, than we yet hear the Protector has done in Flanders,[6] or the King of France[7] at Valencienne, whither the Duke of Orleans[8] is sent for;[9] it is thought, to Conclude a Generall Peace betwixt the two Crowns. I present my most humble Duty to my Mother & Uncle; with [f. 13ʳ] my Brother & Sisters, of whose health & Well-fare, 'twou'd very much Joye me to hear. I humbly begg your Blessing on, Sir,

Dè la Fleche   }
Aug: 2. 1656   }

Your most Dutifull Child,
William Hammond. –

[1] The Obeliscus Vaticanus, from Heliopolis, was erected by Caligula on the spina of the Circus Neronis and now stands in front of St Peter's. In the Middle Ages it was called the tomb of Julius Caesar, whose ashes were supposed to be contained in a gilt ball on its top, now in the Museo dei Conservatori. Hammond's reference to ashes at, presumably, the Bodleian Library, Oxford, is unclear.

[2] * BL Add. MS 59785, f. 14ʳ: 'Life of Lewis 13 wrote by.' Perhaps Jean Valdor, *Les Triomphes de Louis le Juste XIII. du nom, roy de France* (1649).

[3] * BL Add. MS 59785, f. 14ʳ: 'Serres General History'. Jean de Serres's *History* was well known in England from the popular translation by E. Grimeston, *A General Inventorie of the History of France* (1607). Hammond was presumably reading one of the numerous French editions of de Serres, such as *Inventaire général de l'histoire de France*.

[4] * BL Add. MS 59785, f. 14ʳ: 'Letters'. Jean-Louis Balzac (1597–1654) was renowned for his *Lettres choisies*, published from 1648 onwards.

[5] * BL Add. MS 59785, f. 14ʳ: 'Dʳ Donne Dean of Sᵗ: Pauls. See his Life by Isaac Walton 16. Sir Richard Baker in his Chronicle Folio. pa: calls him'. John Donne (c. 1572–1631), poet and Dean of St Paul's, London. A volume of his *Letters* was first published in 1651. Hammond may also have been familiar with Donne's tortuous literary style from *Poems by J. D.* (1633); his treatise on suicide, *Biathanatos* (1644); and his *Essayes in Divinity* (1651).

[6] * BL Add. MS 59785, f. 14ᵛ: 'Oliver Cromwell'. From the mid-1550s Cromwell was moving towards a pro-French and anti-Spanish foreign policy, which included attempts to seize control in the West Indies and an alliance with Portugal in 1654. The outbreak of war with Spain necessitated the recall of Parliament on 17 September 1656. In return for sending an expeditionary force to Spanish Flanders to fight in support of the French in 1658 Cromwell gained possession of Dunkirk, which had been captured by the Spanish in 1653.

[7] * BL Add. MS 59785, f. 14ᵛ: 'Lewis XIV. King of France. who Died September 1ˢᵗ. 1715'.

[8] * BL Add. MS 59785, f. 14ᵛ: 'Philip Duke of Orleans youngest Son of Lewis XIII and Brother to Lewis XIV married Henrietta Maria Daughter of Charles the 1ˢᵗ King of England. Died 1705'.

[9] Valenciennes was the scene of various struggles for power in the 16th and 17th centuries, being only finally ceded to France by the Treaty of Nijmegen (1678). Gaston (Jean-Baptiste), duc d'Orléans (1608–60), commonly known as 'Monsieur', was the brother of Louis XIII. Having supported the Fronde, he was exiled in 1652 but reconciled with Louis XIV in 1656.

[9]

Most Honoured Father,

I most humbly thanke you for your last of the 12th of January; & that you were pleased to give so Quick Orders for the Payment of my 20 Pound: This Week I receiv'd a Bill from my Cosin Dawson of Mr Peter Barr[1] on his Correspondent here, who accordingly has paid me 85 Crownes, 42 Sols. I humbly desire, that you will please to see my Cosin better inform'd in our Forreigne Returns, before he sends me another Bill; For certainly if he had but known, that a Crown simply expresst goes but for 3 Livres, & thirteen Livres is the lowest value of 20 shillings sterling, his Arithmetick (tho never so little) might have shewn him, that 85 Crownes, 42 Sols, that is, 257 Livres, & 2 Sols wants full 3 Livres of the Intrinsick value of 20 pound Sterling, after the rate of 30 in the Hundred. Be pleas'd to pardon my Particularizing, for as this present there are so many Out-letts [f. 13ᵛ] in my Purse to one In-lett, that it wou'd have been a certain mark of my ill-hus-bandry, if I had not cry'd out upon the losse of a Crown; Especially when my Cosin Bowyer (who has less need of it) receivd a Bill the same Week, after the rate of 32 in the Hundred.

I shall now endeavour to answer some Particulars in your last, amongst which *the* hardest task you were please to put upon me, was to give you my Opinion of Dr. Holden;[2] a man that has seen so much of this World, & made so good use of what he has seen, as it can be hard for him at this Age, so well to manage his Soul, as to let but what parts of it he please, be seen by so raw & unexperienc'd a Fellow as myself. And you were pleas'd to anticipate me in mentioning those parts, *whi*ch have been most obvious to me, & on which otherwise I shou'd have totally insisted, to wit, his Universall Charity & Particular good Offices to his Countrymen: all else that I can say of him, is that he was born beyond the River of Trent, bred in Flanders, Polisht partly by his 30 Year's abode in France, under the Chiefest Men of Louis 13th. Court, having been Chaplain to Marillac, Keeper of the Seals;[3] [f. 14ʳ] but chiefly by his Travells into Italy, wherein he spent a Considerable time. & the ranke he now bears in the World, is a Doctor of the Sorbonne, a Colledge sufficiently known to all the Princes in Christendome.[4] What Reflections I may make to myself upon this Narrative Knowledge I have of him, must needs be very Childish, in respect of what you may please to deduce from it. The place of his Birth, as being a Northern man, is apt to make me think that his Goodness comes not to him as a Birth-right, & tho' the Name of Dr. may intimate Bookishness; yet I think, his study has rather serv'd him to balance & weigh the Ocurrences & Affaires both of Church &

---

[1] 'Mr Peter Barr', unidentified but presumably a merchant at Paris with whom credit could be arranged.

[2] * BL Add. MS 59785, f. 16ʳ: 'The Writer in this Letter gives a very pretty Account of Dr: Holden'.

[3] Michel de Marillac (1563–1632) was a close ally of Queen Marie de Médicis and through her influence he became finance minister (1624–6) and Keeper of the Seals (1626–30). He fell from power and died in exile follow-ing the queen's unsuccessful attempt to displace Cardinal Richelieu (1630–1). His niece was the renowned Saint Louise de Marillac (1591–1660), co-founder, with St Vincent de Paul, of the Daughters of Charity, a congregation of laywomen dedicated to medical and educational work among the poor.

[4] Henry Holden was born in 1596 near Clitheroe in Lancashire. He was educated at Douai, where he registered on 18 September 1618 (under the name of 'Johnson') and 1623 he graduated as a Doctor of Divinity at the Sorbonne where he was appointed to a chair. He was naturalized and served as confessor to the church of St Nicholas du Chardonnet and as one of the vicars-general of the diocese of Paris. He was also a close associate of Thomas White, Sir Kenelm Digby's friend. See letter 37. Hammond's reference to Holden's 'Travells into Italy' seems to have been unknown to previous biographers.

State, than for Scholasticall Quidditys:[1] And I do not see how a man of Parts, that has spent 30 years in one of the best Kingdomes of Christendome, & the greatest part of those 30 years whilst there sat at the Helm the greatest Headpiece of Europe Cardi*na*ll Richlieu[2] a man of his own Coat, & under whom he had liv'd not so obscurely, as not to see something of his Parts; I cannot see, how such a one can harber other than very Judicious Conceptions of all the present Affairs of Christendome: & indeed the Multiplicity of Lettres, [f. 14ᵛ] & Conferences, that I see he has with Persons of the highest Ranke & Condition, makes me very much inclin'd, to Admire rather, than understand his Abilitys.

My Cosin Bowyer presents his Service; in following his good Example, we have brought about this first Month of our Chambre-Garny for 12 Crowns apiece, including fire & Candle, which is always excepted in[3] Pensions of 20 Crowns a month: This Week Mʳ· Holden procur'd us a sight of the King's Ballet, where we see this Grand Monarch[4] shew his subjects, & all the Forreigne Ambassadors, how much he cou'd command his Leggs; & to speak the truth he dances with so great a Grace, & if he once get but as good a Grace at the head of his Army, all Christendome will be stage little enough for his Warlick Ballets.[5] In his Person[6] he is very proper & of a sanguine look; which sanguiness, added to his Youthfullness, makes him as yet much delight in Courtly Gamings & Pastimes: Last night he came, accompanied with all *the* Nobility, to the fair Sᵗ· Germans (next door to us) where he was pleas'd to spend from 5 till 9 a clock, in playing with his Followers for some of the Pedlars' knick- [f. 15ʳ] knacks. I find that in Paris they have their Winter in three Partitions; the first of which, is all betwixt the King's coming from his Campagne, till Christmass, wherein there is but little Variety either for their own Divertisements, or a stranger's Observation; only the Renewing of the Parliament, which is on Sᵗ Martins day,[7] & some renowned sermons made during the Advent: Their second Partition is, from Christmas till Ash-wednesday, by the Name of Carnivall,[8] wherein they give themselves over to all

---

[1] 'Scholasticall Quidditys': scholarly quibbles or subtleties. By 1656 Holden was already an established theological controversialist, best known for his *Divinae fidei analysis*, Paris, 1652 (rpt. Cologne, 1655; tr. into English by 'W. G.', 1658), on the Catholic articles of faith. In 1656 and early 1657 Holden was heavily involved in a controversy with the Jansenist, Antoine Arnauld; and he was probably drafting *A Letter to a Friend* (Paris, 1657) in defence of the philosopher and controversialist Thomas White, alias Blackloe (1593–1676) whose *Obedience and Government* had been published in 1655.

[2] Armand-Jean du Plessis, cardinal and duc de Richelieu (1585–1642).

[3] * BL Add. MS 59785, f. 17ᵛ, reads for 'in pensions' > 'on pensions' with the following note about 'on': 'Sic originale &c I here take this opportunity to inform the Reader I keep strictly to the Original Orthography'. This minor textual variant tends to suggest that the transcriber of BL Add. MS 59785 was working from copy of Hammond's letters other than Brotherton MS Trv.2, since this manuscript clearly reads 'in pensions'.

[4] * BL Add. MS 59785, f. 17ᵛ: 'Lewis the XIV. He Died Sep: 1*st*. 1715. – He was aged about 17. in 1656/7 which is the era of this Letter'.

[5] Louis XIV (1638–1715), the son of Louis XIII and his queen Anne of Austria, had succeeded to the throne of France on 14 May 1643. Neglected by his parents, the young Louis acquired a love of the arts from his godfather and first minister, Cardinal Jules Mazarin, who was especially keen for the young king to develop his physical condition through dancing and horse-riding. See Ragnhild Hatton, 'Louis XIV At the Court of the Sun King', in *The Courts of Europe. Politics, Patronage and Royalty. 1400–1800*, ed. A. G. Dickens, 1977 (rpt. New York, 1984), pp. 233–62, 234. See also Julia Prest, 'Dancing King: Louis XIV's Roles in Molière's *Comédies-ballets*, from Court to Town', *The Seventeenth Century*, 16, 2001, pp. 283–98.

[6] * BL Add. MS 59785, f. 17ᵛ: 'The Writer in this Lettre Describes the Person of Lewis XIV very particularly'.

[7] * BL Add. MS 59785, f. 18ʳ: 'Sᵗ: Martin's Translation is celebrated according to the Roman Calendar on the 4ᵗʰ. of July'.

[8] * BL Add. MS 59785, f. 18ʳ: 'Carnivall derives its Name from […]'.

94

Fig. 31. A 17th-century Italian portrait of King Louis XIV, as collected by English tourists.

175

Divertisements imaginable, & which amongst the French consists most in Dancing. I have been close tyed to my Exercises this year, as has hinder'd me from seeing any but the Chief which was that of the King's, & for the next year I hope, you'le please to give me leave to send you an Account of the Carnivall at Venice: The third Partition of our Winter will be Lent, a sad time! Of which hereafter. At present I most humbly begg your Blessing on

Paris February ⎫   Your most Duty*ful* Child,
10 1656/7   ⎭   William Hammond.

I humbly present my Duty to my Mother, Brother,[1] Sisters, untill the next Poste.

[10]

[f. 15ᵛ] Most Hon*oure*d Father,
The English Poste having this Week fail'd of his usuall day, I receivd your last of the 26 of February, but on the 8ᵗʰ of March: I wish, I may but intimate how than[k]full I am for it, by endeavouring to write you some small Account of any thing here. If I have shew'd myself too backward in rendring you an Account, of what I see or observe; I humbly entreat, you will favourably interpret *tha*t backwardness: so small a Distance, as Disjoyns France & England, affords but little Variation in the Manners & Customes of either's Inhabitants. Of the Chorography[2] of the Country, & Sictuation of their Towns, *th*e Variety is hardly greater, than what is to be found in a Map; yet as their Considerable Towns are much more Numerous, than Ours; so for the Generality of them, they much Excell them for the Pleasantness of their Scituations, but Especially in Fithness of Buildings & Cleanlyness of their streets; having also this Advantage over Ours, as to have their Bordering Hills & Inclosures Adorn'd & Beautyfied with Vine-Yards & delicious Fruits: & in my Journeys on the River of [f. 16ʳ] Loire, I cou'd not but think that the Pleasure of its Towns & Adjacent Countrys, far exceeded that of our Famous Thames, tho view'd from so advantageous a Place as Mʳ Denham's Cooper's-Hill.[3] The Capitall Citys of each Nation differ much after the same Proportion, yet if Paris have the Advantage in being surrounded by a Country bedeck't with Vine-yards, London may bragg of a much Nobler River. And thus far I am sure they agree, that they are both a Confus'd Harbour of all sorts & all Conditions of Inhabitants; & the same eye, that cou'd from Paul's discern such an Infinity of Counter-working interests, were it plac't in *th*e Tower of Notre-dame, wou'd suspect that the same kind of Objects were represented to it thorow a Mutiplying Glass. I believe a Curious Observer wou'd find those Neigh-bouring Countrys, to differ most in their ways of Government both Civill & Ecclesiasticall. But herein I am so far ignorant as to want so much as a Superficiall Knowledge of them; towards the Understanding of the Civill, I have often been at the Pleadings in Parliament & other Courts of Justice: But this Parliament of Paris is rather to be Compar'd to our upper bench [f. 16ᵛ] in Westminster Hall, than to any higher Instruments of Government; It being the States-Generall of this Kingdome, that bears the fittest Comparison with our London Parliament: The Lawyers are much after the

---

    ¹ * BL Add. MS 59785, f. 18ᵛ: 'he says Brother I suppose his other Brothers were Dead at that Period'.
    ² 'Chorography', the description of regions or districts of size between those involved in topography and in geography.
    ³ *Coopers Hill. A Poeme* (1642; and regularly reprinted) is the chief topographical poem of Sir John Denham (1615–69), combining historical, political, and local references.

same cutt with Ours, & I think 'twere no easy matter, to decide which are the best speakers; yet the French speak with a more Active kind of Eloquence & the Subjects of their Pleadings savours more of the Politer sort of Studys, & Learnings, inasmuch as Justinian excells Littleton.[1] One of the Chiefest Tryalls, that has this Winter been heard in Parliament, tended towards the Conviction of a Chief Magistrate of this Town to have held Secret Intelligence with the Prince of Condè:[2] The Cardinall[3] is very earnest for his Condemnation, but whether thorow Reason of State, or Indulgence of his Judges, his Tryall goes but very slowly & lingringly on. Some Signall Differences there are betwixt these Parliaments, & our Westminster Courts; the chief of which is, that they serve towards the raising of Monys upon the poor Subject; & towards the next Campain, both Clergy & Laity are Sufficiently taxed; yet to what Quarters of the Kingdome the King will march in Person is [f. 17ʳ] not as yet to be ghuest at. Some think 'twill be into Alsatia, there to Rencontre the Emperor's Forces, who with Sword in hand intends to demand the Arrears due to him from this Crown for that part of Alsatia he Conditionally quitted;[4] Those in Piedmont are either very much wrong'd by the Weekly Gazette, or else have but small hopes of their Monarch's Presence there, or indeed of any Considerable & timely Supplys, insomuch that they have almost given over the hopes of keeping Valence[5] from the Early Sparniard; Especially since the Duke of Modena[6] is return'd to them from this Court with but very faint Promises: & I believe, the Irruptions of the Warlike Prince of Condè, will summon his Majesty's Chiefest Forces & Personall Presence into these Northern Parts. For the present, the Carnivall's Jollity being past (which in this Court was something encreast by reason of the Cardinall his Neece with the Count of Soissons)[7] the King is now in Mourning for the death of the King

[1] Hammond is comparing here the 'Code of Justinian' (*Codex Justinianeus* or *Corpus juris civilis*), the collection of laws and legal interpretations drawn up during the reign of the Byzantine emperor Justinian 1 from AD 529–565, with the *Treatise on Tenures* by Sir Thomas Littleton (1422–81), the first important English legal text which was neither written in Latin nor largely dependent upon Roman law. It was the principal authority for English real property law.

[2] Louis II de Bourbon, 4ᵉ prince de Condé (1621–86), also known in his youth as the duc d'Enghien. He was the leader of the aristocratic uprisings known as the Fronde (1648–53). He had left Paris in October 1652 to serve in the Spanish army and a sentence of death had been passed on him on 25 November 1654. He was finally reconciled with Louis XIV in 1660. See also letter 7 and p. 121, n. 1.

[3] * BL Add. MS 59785, f. 20ᵛ: 'Richlieu'.

[4] 'Alsatia': Alsace. Under the Peace of Westphalia (1648) France had incorporated into its possession the cities and bishoprics of Metz, Toul, and Verdun in Lorraine. It also secured (problematically) some less clearly defined rights, previously exercised by the Holy Roman Emperor Ferdinand III (1608–57), over various towns and regions in Alsace. Although, in terms of localities, these gains appeared relatively modest, they rendered southern Germany much more vulnerable to incursions by the French army. The apparently intentional vagueness over the specific clauses relating to cessions in both Lorraine and Alsace provided during the 1650s the supposed legal and nationalistic pretexts for Louis XIV's military aggression towards the emperor's territories.

[5] * BL Add. MS 59785, f. 21ʳ: 'Valence a Town of France, in the Principality of Dauphine, situate at the Confluence of the Rivers Rhone & Isere'. Valence, *préfecture* of the Drôme *département*, overlooking the Rhône.

[6] Francesco I d'Este, duke of Modena (1629–58) had been allied to Spain but then lent his support to France, in the hope that this would support his claims to Ferrara. He later attempted a reconciliation with Spain but died of malaria on the battlefield, fighting the Spaniards.

[7] Louis de Bourbon, comte de Soissons (1604–41) had an illegitimate son, Louis-Henri, known as the Chevalier de Soissons (d. 1703). The count's sister, Marie (1606–92), married in 1625 Thomas de Savoie, prince de Carignan. Their youngest son, Eugène-Maurice de Savoie-Carignan (1633–73) assumed the title comte de Soissons. However, Hammond may be confused here since it was Armand de Bourbon, prince de Conti (1629–66) – the younger brother of Louis II, prince de Condé (1621–86), see letter 10 and p. 115, n. 8 – who married Anne-Marie Martinozzi, the niece of Cardinal Mazarin. (Their first son, who died in infancy, was born in 1658). See p. 182, n. 6.

of Portugall,[1] & towards the keeping of Lent is usually present three times a Week at the Sermon of the Famous Pere le Boux;[2] a man of the most Perswasive Rhetorique, & [f. 17ᵛ] Eloquence, that I ever heard or cou'd imagine, & Generally these French Preachers imploy their Talent, more towards the working on the Passions, than the Reason of their Auditory: whereas I think, the English Veine tends more towards Instruction, than Perswuasion. My Cosin & I keep Lent in nothing (but that towards the benefitting our Languague). We frequent the Lenten Sermons; as for Diet we find Flesh almost as freely as at any other times of the Year: howsoever, I cannot but be very sensible of my Mother's Tenderness & Affection towards me, in sending me her Excellent Receipts. I most humbly beg her Pardon for not returning my humble thanks in a Lettre by this Post; last Week I presented my Duty in a Particular, which I hope, she has receiv'd, & next week I intend another. In the Interim I humbly begg your Blessing on, Sir,

Paris March   }   Your most Dutyfull,
the 10. 1656/7   }   Child William Hammond.

My Cosin Bowyer presents his humble service, & mine attends all my Friends.
My Aunt Stanly has lost my poor Cosin Steward,[3] who dyed at Diepe of a Fever.

[11]

[f. 18ʳ] Most Honoured Father,
I had not the Fortune to receive yours of the 23 of March, untill last Tuesday. I shall endeavour to Express my Gratitude for your Excellent Mementos, by applying myself for the Future towards the attaining Lycurgas[4] his Kind of Improvement: & I wish that, as We yet retain many other of the old Grecian Customes, so we cou'd but imitate their Beneficiall way of Travelling; whose Gentry seldome left their Native Soile, but at their Return they recompenced their Absence, by bringing with them some Observation, that might help to Improve their Civill or Learned Common-wealth. I am afraid in this matter, that it may be truly said, that we have only their Fiddle & want their Fiddle-stick; that we Imitate them indeed, in seeing many Towns, & passing thorow divers Countrys, but that our Observations are very disproportionable. This first year (to follow the Modern rode) I have been forc't to spend, in getting a Superficiall Knowledge in Superficiall things.

---

¹ * BL Add. MS 59785, f. 22ʳ: 'Not observing to Leave room for a Note on the other side [i.e. the previous page] subjoyn it here. John Duke of Braganza was the unanimous voice of the people advanced to the Throne of Portugal, defeated King Philip of Spain's Forces sent against him, & by the assistance of the English & French, drove the Spaniards out of Portugal in 1648 & having reigned from the year 1640 to 1656/7 Died & was succeeded by his Son Alphonsus IV. King of Portugal'. King John IV of Portugal (1604–56), formerly duke of Braganza, had died on 6 November 1656 at Lisbon. Although a supporter of the English royal family during the early 1640s, he had struck a treaty with Cromwell in 1654 which gained English military assistance in exchange for trading privileges. After his death, his queen, Luisa, became regent for their son, Afonso VI (1643–83) until 1662. Their daughter, Catherine of Braganza, married King Charles II of England in 1662.

² Guillaume Le Boux (1621–1693), member of the order of Oratorians (Congregation of the Oratory of St Philip Neri).

³ Lady Stanley's younger son, Steward, died at Dieppe where his sister, Elizabeth, became a nun. See letters 12 and 21. Stanley, *Poems*, ed. Crump, p. xxi.

⁴ Lycurgus (fl. 7th century BC), lawgiver and king of Sparta, who, according to Plutarch, went on extensive travels in search of knowledge.

Henceforward my Aime shall be for things of more Use & Substance. And I humbly begg, you'le please to help me with your Di- [f. 18ᵛ] rections: A Youngster[1] in the wide World without a Guide, like a ship in the Ocean without a Pilot, may make ashift to keep above Water, but is very Uncertaine at what harbour he shall at length arrive at. This last fortnight having left *th*e Academy, I accompany my Cosin every morning to the Palais, where sit all the Upper Courts of Justice & amongst them the Parliament;[2] & it has been our Fortune to beginn with hearing of a Cause of no small Note; Especially of a Private One. It concerns the Old Famous Duke of Rochan,[3] since whose Death his Family has been something Ecclipsed, by reason of a Daughter left sole Heiress, & who married herself very unequally to a Private Gentleman, Mounsier Chabot;[4] The Old Duke's Wife being much offended with her Daughter's Match, endeavour'd in *th*e Year 1641 to have disinherited her by Pretending to have a son bred up in Holland: but this design being voided by the death of the pretended son, she afterwards took another way; which was, seeing her Daughter big & likely to bring Monsier Chabot an Heir, w*hi*ch by the Queen's[5] Goodness was to have succeeded both to the Riches & Title of his Mother's Father; [f. 19ʳ] she Employd her mony & Perswasions so well upon the Mid-wife, that this Crafty woman at *th*e same time *tha*t she deliverd her of a son made her believe, she was brought to bed of nothing, & that so effectually, that she has lived these sixteen years in that Faith. Now at length *th*e old Mid-wife confesses her Cheat, & the son thus long hidden happens to be one of the Dutchess of Chabot's, his now Mother's Page. There are Ladys of great Quality interessed in the Tryall, but the Chief Actors are dead, & the Midwife 80. years old is now in Prison; the youth is handsome, & spritely, & seems not so much mov'd, tho' 'tis now at the stake, whether he shall get his Livelyhood by his sword, or be Heir to 30,000 pounds a year.

  Some of our afternoons we spend in hovering about the Louvre,[6] where we find but very little News stirring; 'tis yet very uncertain what Compagne the King will take, for tho' he has been Provok'd by the Son of St. Ghillain in these Northern Parts, yet his Revenge may be taken in Piedmont; especially if the Turke summon the Emperor to use his Germans in his own Defence. Yet it may be, the Duke of Mantoua's late Revolt from the Alliance of this Crown, may be as Considerable, as the Deffect of Ger- [f. 19ᵛ] mans to the Spanish.[7] 'Tis doubted here whether the Dutch intend a War or Peace with this Crown. We shall quickly know by *th*e stay or Return of an Extraordinary, who is sent, but not yet arrivd there. We

---

[1] * BL Add. MS 59785, f. 23ʳ: 'The Writer Aged (1657.)'. Hammond was approximately twenty-two years old in 1657.

[2] L'Ile de la Cité was the royal, legal, and ecclesiastical centre of Paris. St Louis IX (1226–70) renovated an earlier palace on the site of the Palais de Justice and built the Sainte-Chapelle. From 1431 it became the exclusive seat of the Parlement. Accidental fires in 1618, 1737, and 1776 largely destroyed the Old Palace.

[3] The soldier, writer, and leader of the Huguenots during the French Wars of Religion, Henri I, duc de Rohan (1579–1638), married Marguerite de Béthune (d. 1661), the daughter of the duc de Sully. He received a mortal wound at the Battle of Rheinfelden on 28 February 1638 and died without a legitimate male heir.

[4] The title duc de Rohan (created 1603) was transferred in 1648 to the house of Chabot and thereafter called Rohan-Chabot.

[5] * BL Add. MS 59785, f. 23ʳ: 'She was Infanta Maria Theresa, Eldest D*aughte*r of Philip IV of Spain.

[6] * BL Add. MS 59785, f. 23ᵛ: 'One of the Fine Palaces of the Kings of France'. King François I demolished the medieval fortress, or Château du Louvre, and began plans for his own magnificent palace in 1541. The building was extended by Henri IV and Louis XIII and the quadrangle was completed during the minority of Louis XIV. The buildings were left to decay from 1676 and occupied by squatters until 1754.

[7] One of the Gonzaga dukes of Mantua.

Fig. 32. 'Les Galeries du Louvre' (c. 1650–55) (Israel Silvestre).

hear of a great[1] Battle lately betwixt the Swede & the Polack; 'tis not declared, which has the better; & therefore it may be ghuest, the Swede has the worst.[2] I dare not venture upon any more News, since it most commonly proves but so much Untruth. You were pleas'd in your last to demand an Account of my Health. I have not hitherto ventur'd to Commend the French Air & Diet, nor the Strength of my own Constitution, lest some following Sickness might shamefully disprove me: but now having very nigh passt the four Seasons of the year, without the least Unusuall Distemper, I do verily believe that the same Temperance, that wou'd preserve my health at home, may as easily do it abroad; & Certainly their Drink & Bread far exceeds Ours. For my Corpulency I cannot positively say, whether it be encreast, or decreast, For it has been neither overfedd, nor over-workt. I am afraid, whensoever I fall from Wine to Beer; that that Coole Drink & Natural Phlegme [f. 20ʳ] will make me fatt.

Sir, since you have been pleas'd to shew your Tenderness in enquiring after my health, & that a Traveller's Pulse beats truest in his Purse; I humbly entreat, you'le please to hear something of that. Having now spent a year in travelling the Summer, & Learning Exercises in *th*e Winter, I hope (without the Imputation of Ill husbandry) I may say my Allowance ended w*i*th the Year: Yet having had your Commands of staying till Easter-term for a Recruite, I thought it might prove less displeasing to sollicite my Cosin Richards,[3] who last Friday furnisht me with 20 Pound, for which I receiv'd here 87 Crowns, upon Condition, *tha*t the said 20 Pound be paid within 2 Months to Mᵣ Ashurst, in Throgmorton-Street in London;[4] who is Correspondent to Mᵣ Wildigo's Merchant in this Town.[5] I hope you'le be pleased to Consider, that such a summe in his fullest Extent cannot last three months; & that if you shall think fit, I shou'd leave Paris this Summer. The other Thirty Pound must help to my Removall, which I wish might be to the Southerne Parts of France. Be pleas'd to pardon my boldness, in Urging a [f. 20ᵛ] Second Bill before the first be paid: If I were certain, it wou'd any ways inconvenience you, I shou'd never have mention'd it. For your Pleasure makes up the Will, Wishes, & thoughts of

Paris April }
the 10. 1657. }

Your most Dutyfull Child,
William Hammond. -

I am sorry to be forc't thus in a Post script, to Present my Duty to my Mother. I'le endeavor

---

[1] * BL Add. MS 59785, f. 24ʳ: 'Charles Gustavus, suceeded his Cousin Christina Queen of Sweden, was a very sucessful Prince, & recovered the Swedish Provinces of Schonen, Bleking, & Holland from the Danes, Leaveing his Crown to his son Charles 1660'.

[2] The reign of the last Vasa king of Poland, John II Casimir Vasa (reigned 1648–68) was marked by a series of military disasters. The Ukrainian Cossacks, led by Bohdan Chmielnicki, revolted in 1648 and 1651, leading to the establishment of their own military state (1651–4). With the support of the Cossacks, the Russian tsar Alexei Mikhailovich conquered much of eastern Poland in 1654–5. Taking advantage of these disputes, King Charles X Gustav of Sweden occupied Polish territories in 1655 and was generally recognized as king by the Polish aristocracy, following the flight of John II Casimir to Silesia. However, the sheer barbarity of the Swedish army prompted renewed hostilities. The Poles enjoyed some military successes, under the brilliant command of Stefan Czarniecki, between 1655 and 1657 against both the Swedes and the invading army of Frederick William of Brandenberg. See also letter 36.

[3] 'Cosin Richards', see letter 1.

[4] Throgmorton Street runs north and parallel to Threadneedle Street. Much of this area was badly damaged or destroyed by the Great Fire of London (September 1666).

[5] 'Mᵣ Wildigo', see letter 1.

next Post to make amends. My Cosin returns his humble service; & I to my Uncle, Brother, Sisters, &c. The D^r. kisses your hand.

[12]

Most Honoured Father,

Upon hopes that my Last of Aprill 21.[1] has perform'd his Errand, in humbly presenting my Duty, & rend'ring an Account of your other Commands, I might lighten the burden of this Present Paper; which (barring Repetitions) can add little or nothing, *tha*t may prove pertinent, before it get to Wilberton: I have something overslept the season of taking News to my Aide, & might be thought to Transcribe the English Journall, if I shou'd now mention the Emperor's[2] Death, or the [f. 21^r] Probability of the A. D. Leopold to be his Successor:[3] An Affaire of so great Consequence to all Europe is usually, as quickly seen in a Printed Gazette, as a Private Lettre; Especiall in England where it cannot but be very Acceptable, it being no small hindrance to the Spanish Progress. Yet if the Rumor, that runns about this Town, prove true of the King of Swedes[4] being beaten & taken Prisoner;[5] each Party by that means having Equall Losses, things will be but in Statu Quo. The 23 of Aprill the Prince of Conty[6] set out towards his Generall Rendevous in Piedmont, where this Summer he Commands in Chief; & the sixth of this Current, the King & Court went to Compeigne. Things are yet but in a Preparation, & 'tis hard to say, which Quarter shall endure the Brunt of this Summer's Warr; 'tis thought, the Electors may divert the right down blows of *th*e Two Crowns, by calling them either to part, or side their Differences. The Duke of Longueville,[7] is going down from hence

---

[1] This letter of 21 April 1657 is lost.

[2] * BL Add. MS 59785, f. 25^v: 'Ferdinand the 3^d Died'.

[3] * BL Add. MS 59785, f. 25^v: 'Leopold Emperor of Germany was the only Surviving Son of the Emperor Ferdinand the 3^d was Born 9th. June 1640. He was appointed King of Hungary by his Father The Emperor Ferdinand the 3^d. – on the 27th of June 1655, & King of Bohemia 2^d August 1656 – He was elected Emperor 8th. July 1658 & Croun'd at Franckfort the 22^d of that Month'. Emperor Ferdinand III (1608–57) had died on 2 April and was succeeded by his second son from his first marriage to Maria Anna (daughter of Philip III of Spain), Leopold I (1640–1705). His elder brother, Ferdinand IV had died unexpectedly on 9 July 1654. Leopold I was only elected and crowned emperor at Frankfurt in the summer of 1658 after protracted objections from France.

[4] * BL Add. MS 59785, f. 26^r: 'Charles the XI'.

[5] King Charles X Gustav (1622–60) of Sweden had succeeded the the throne, following the abdication of Queen Christina in 1654. In July 1655 he began the First Northern War (1655–60) against Poland, supposedly because the Polish king, John II Casimir Vasa, had refused to acknowledge him but really in an expansionist attempt to establish a unified northern state. He enjoyed considerable successes in his battles with Polish forces until Russia, Brandenberg, Denmark, and the Netherlands successively joined the struggle to oppose his territorial advances. By the spring of 1657 his progress in Poland had virtually stalled and, instead, Charles X then turned his attention to an attack upon Denmark. The rumour in April 1657 that Charles X had been captured was untrue. See also letter 36.

[6] Armand de Bourbon, prince de Conti (1629–66), the younger brother of Louis II, prince of (the Great) Condé (1621–86). Originally intended for the church, he became a general of the Fronde in 1649 and was arrested with Condé in 1650. In 1652 he commanded Bordeaux but was driven out by government forces in July 1653. Reconciled with Cardinal Mazarin, in 1654 he married his niece, Anne-Marie Martinozzi (1637–72); and was sent by him to military commands in Catalonia (1654) and Italy (1657). See also p. 177, n. 7.

[7] Henri II d'Orléans, duc de Longueville (1595–1663) was drawn into the Fronde by his second wife, Anne-Geneviève de Bourbon-Condé (1619–79), whom he married in 1642. She was the sister of Armand de Bourbon, prince de Conti. He was arrested, along with Conti and Condé, in 1650. His marriage was unhappy (his wife was the lover of the duc de la Rochefoucauld, the author of the *Maximes*) and by the mid-1650s he had largely devoted himself to governing Normandy.

into Germany, to endeavor the hindrance of the succession of the House of Austria, yet *th*e French have generally but small hopes of his speeding. I dare not pretend to the least Judge- [f. 21ᵛ] ment in Propheticall News & I humbly beg your pardon, if this passt News, out of staleness, prove but so much Impertinency. I had not made so great an Intervall betwixt this present Lettre & my last, but that for these three Weeks I have been from Paris, to wait on my Aunt Stanly at Diepe; whither she was pleas'd to invite me to the Clothing of my Cosin Betty, whom we have now left a Sister of the Visitation, an Order lately Erected by Francois Sales Bishop of Geneva.[1] I dare say her Choice of a Nunnery, proceeded wholly from Devotion, for had she entertaind any Worldly Fancys, certainly she never wou'd have chose the worst Town in France, & in that Town, so homely a Cloyster. My Aunt is very much leaner, since her coming into France, she has little mind to returne for England, since my Grand-mother is settled;[2] I rather think, she will shortly Enclose herself in the same Walls with my Cosin Betty. Since our Returne to Paris (*whi*ch was but on the 14ᵗʰ·) we have had Extraordinary hot weather, & the Air having been prepar'd for heat, by the long & Continuall Rains, that fell last Month. My Cosin Bow- [f. 22ʳ] yer presents his Service; we intend *th*e next Week to take the Country Aire, by sending towards Lyons. Dʳ· Holden is very earnest we shou'd spend this Summer at Mountpelier,[3] & I hope we may, if the Early heats do not make us shorten our Journey. I find myself after [*thu*s?] much Travell more settledly dispos'd towards a Profession, than ever: & I hope at my returne to express my Gratitude for your great Goodness in my Education, by setling to whatsoever you shall please to command. In the Interim I humbly beg the Continuance of you[r] Fatherly Tenderness in supplying my wants. In the Southerne Parts of France I shall be far from England, but I hope not from bills of Exchanges: I desire you'le please to make use of Dʳ· Holden, who upon the Receipts of Bills or Lettres of Credit here, will returne me the Value into those Parts; so that either must be sent open to him, with Orders to be receiv'd in this Town by him for my Use. If you shou'd please to trust me with a Lettre of Credit for the rest of this Year's Expences to be receiv'd by me, as Occasion serves; I do believe 'twou'd rather add to, than diminish my Fugality: For Pinches & Wants of supplys [f. 22ᵛ] forces a man some-times to Transgress *th*e Rules of Good Husbandry, by selling at easy rates, or Living at great rates to salve a present want. My last Journey to Diepe, & my summer's Cloths have made a large gap in my 20. Pound; I am afraid the rest will hardly bring me to Lyons. My Cosin is so good, as to proffer me the Community of his Purse. I humbly beg you'le please to prevent, that his Goodness brings him to no Inconveniencys, but that my supplys may be so timely, as to hinder that we both may not want. But I humbly & heartily referre myself to your Goodness; of which I have had so long & great

---

[1] Saint François de Sales (1567–1622), Catholic Bishop of Geneva, was beatified in 1661 and canonized in 1665. At Annecy (where the bishop's see of Geneva had been exiled in 1535) he was a vociferous opponent of Calvinism and in 1610 co-founded, with St Jane Frances de Chantal, the Visitation of the Holy Mary (the V.H.M. or order of Visitation Nuns), which became a noted teaching order. He wrote an *Introduction to a Devout Life* (1608) and was named in 1923 as the patron saint of writers. The V.H.M., which by the 1650s ran several private academies for girls, was especially attractive to well-educated women who wished to enter a convent.

[2] Hammond's reference to 'my grand-mother', in conjunction with his aunt Lady Mary Stanley, suggests that he must be referring to his paternal grandmother, Elizabeth Archer (or Aucher), the wife of his grandfather, Sir William Hammond (d. 1615). Elizabeth was the grand-daughter, though her mother's line, of Edwin Sandys (d. 1588), Archbishop of York. After Sir William's death, she married Walter Balcanquall (c. 1586–1645) and it appears from Hammond's comments that she was still alive in 1657. See p. 150.

[3] Montpellier. See letter 22 for Hammond's opinion of its medical school.

Experience; & Change my Importunity in begging Mony, into that of begging your Blessing, Sir, upon

Paris, May ⎱   Your Most Duty*ful* child,
19. 1657. ⎰   William Hammond –

[13]

Most Hon*oure*d Father,

I have had the good Frtune to receive yours of the 7th of May, whilst I am in Paris. I am now in such a huddle, being to set out towards Lyons to Morrow morning, that I dare not venture upon any Answer, but only my very humble Thanks for your Goodness [f. 23^r] in well receiving my poor Endeavours. I must likewise trespass upon the Patience of my Noble Friend, Mr Knatchbull,[1] & my Dear Sister Nan, my Uncle Marsham &c: I hope to make them amends, by more diligently serving them for the future, in a Country where there will be oft'ner Occasions presented.

    I humbly thank you for the Order, you have been pleas'd to give for the Payment of the other 30. Pound; but whether it be thorow my Cosin's Dawson's delay, or Mr Ashurst's neglect; his Correspondent Mr Wildigo, has yet heard nothing of it. I am extremely beholding to the Goodness of Dr Holden, who out of his own Purse has this morning given me a Bill of Exchange for forty Pistolls, the Value of Thirty Pound Sterling, to Lyons. I shew'd him what you wrot me concerning the Order, Mr Ashurst wou'd give his Correspond*en*t; & Mr Wildigo tells me, that after the Receipt of any such Order, he will restore Dr Holden his Mony in my name. This Lettre was wrot, humbly to desire that *th*e Doctor might not stay for his mony. For it was not thorow the Plentifullness of his own Purse *tha*t he lent it, he was fain to take it up of a Merchant of his Acquaintance. I know that this [f. 23^v] Explanation of the Case needs not to be seconded with farther Pressing. I am very much rejoyct, that my Uncle Diggs will spend this Summer with my Mother. I am afraid, if running News prove true, that he is come over in such a Juncto of Affairs, as may be far from inviting his Transplantation. I hope we shall one day see a settlement & an End of our miserys, which are the Prayers of him, that humbly beggs your Blessing, to make him worthy of the Title of

Paris May ⎱   Your most Dutifull Child,
26. 1657. ⎰   William Hammond. –

I humbly present my Duty to my Mother, hoping she has receiv'd mine of the last Poste. My service attends all your Friends.

[14]

Most Hon*oure*d Father,

On the 27 of May, We left Paris, & on the 10 of June we came to Lyons. My Cosin's apprehension of heat, made our Journy *th*e longer; for to avoid the Tumbling of Coach, or Horse,

---

[1] This 'Mr Knatchbull' cannot be identified with any degree of certainty. However, Sir Norton Knatchbull (1602–85), a prominent royalist, MP for Kent (in 1639; and later New Romney, 1661), an author of *Animadversiones in Libros Novi Testamenti* (1659), could well have known the Hammond family.

we tooke the River Seyne from Paris to Auxerre, which is 40 Leagues, & 5 days' Journy.[1] From Auxerre we passt thorow the heart of Burgoigne, taking in our way, the [f. 24ʳ] Famous Ruines of Cæsar's Alexis,[2] the Capitall City Dijon, & the most remarkable Town of Beaune;[3] whose Adjacent Grounds, are now as Famous for Moderne Wines, as they were anciently for the Egregious Conquest Cæsar had of the Swisses after their three years' Preparation.[4] And indeed the whole Country in Generall is the best, that I have seen yet in France; it being hilly & fill'd with Mountains on its Western sides, & an unbounded Plaine to the Eastern, whose Fruitfullness is wonderfull both in Corn, & Wine. From Beaune we went to Chalons, & thence tooke boate upon the Soan for Lyons;[5] passing by (at our Right hand) a Laughing[6] Country, which at a noble distance, & from an easy sloap of its high Mountains, seem'd to rejoyce in its Naturall Beauty. On our Left, we had the flat and fertile County of Bresse, and Principality de Dombes,[7] which extends allmost to the very Gates of Lyons. This last River kept us but two days; so that our Travell was seven days upon Water, & three upon Horse, the other five days being spent at Fontainbleau,[8] Dijon, & Beaune. My Cosin has chose this Town for his first station in these Southerne Parts, being desirous to [f. 24ᵛ] get some Superficiall Knowledge of a place so Considerable for Merchandise & thorowfares. I imagine myself already[9] amongst the Jealous Italians; in seeing the strict watch & ward, the punctuall Examinations, & Billets & Quarantins of Lyons.[10] One thing I much admire in a Town so full of Traffick & dealing, that they have no Court of Justice amongst them, but being under the Jurisdiction of the Parliament of Paris, are forc't to run an hundred Leagues for the Decision of any Cause that exceeds 50 Crowns; when within four Leagues they have the Parliament of Dombes, & within 18 that of Grenoble, & but 3 days' Journey to that of Dijon. Its Populacy makes things a little cheaper here than at Paris, our bare Pension is 15 Crowns amonth. I am afraid such Rates will not agree long with my Purse. There was almost a Necessity for one's Month's stay, our Bills being not Payable, but at a Month's sight: & Dʳ Holden promises us, Sʳ Kenelm Digby[11] shou'd take us with him in passing for Montpelier. This Advantage we find

---

[1] See Lough, *France Observed*, pp. 24, 26, 141, for English travellers passing through Auxerre at this period; and ibid, pp. 19–23 for their travels through France by river.

[2] * BL Add. MS 59785, f. 30ʳ: 'See Cæsar's Commentaries'. The hill-fortress of the Mandubii at Alésia (Alise-Ste Reine) near Mont Auxois. In 52 BC Caesar besieged and captured Vercingetorix who was put to death in captivity at Rome in 46 BC.

[3] Dijon and Beaune.

[4] The Celtic Helvetii had migrated from southern Germany in about 100 BC to the region between lakes Constance and Geneva, and the Jura and the Alps. Julius Caesar defeated a second migration in 58 BC and sent the survivors back home. After a decade of military conflict, known as the Gallic Wars (58–51 BC) and recorded in his *Commentaries*, Caesar had conquered the whole of Gaul (with the siege of Alésia as one of the most vital moments in this conquest).

[5] Chalon-sur-Saône.

[6] * BL Add. MS 59785, f. 30ᵛ: 'I am well perswaded the writer['s] thoughts were lead to that Beautifull Description in Sacred Writ in the Language of that Inspired Eastern Penman'.

[7] The Plateau de Bresse in the valley of the Saône; and the Plateau de Dombes, containing numerous small lakes and hills, culminating in the south with the escarpment of the Rhône valley.

[8] Queen Christina of Sweden, whose travels through Europe had been mentioned by Hammond in letter 7, retired in 1657 to the royal palace of Fontainebleau (c. 40 miles south of Paris). See Fig. 33, p. 190.

[9] 'allready' deleted.

[10] The rigour of the customs' inspections at Lyons were notorious. See Lough, *France Observed*, p. 75.

[11] Sir Kenelm Digby (1603–65), a renowned naval commander, author, diplomat, and virtuoso, had been a staunch supporter of King Charles I and chancellor to Queen Henrietta Maria. He was banished from England in 1643 and again on 31 August 1649 (following his return to England in the previous May) but was permitted to return in 1654, after which date he worked on the continent on Cromwell's behalf. A Parliamentary broadsheet

here, that there's more certain News from the Italian, & Catalonian Armys; tho' at present they afford but little Noveltys, nei- [25ʳ] ther Army being yet ranged, nor in a Posture to undertake any thing; there's nothing expected from that in Catalonia, but *that* of Piedmont talks high. But I believe the main Faits will be done by the 6000 Red-Coats landed at Bologne. I humbly beg your Pardon for these tædious Nothings. I cannot but perceive myself a little infected, by reading so many Itinerarys, & like them, am apt to fall into Thread-bare Descriptions. I wish I cou'd a little polish them by that of Mʳ de l'Hospitall's, *which* you were pleas'd to mention in your last; but I find, that that's quite out of Print & not to be had.¹ I hope, you'le be pleas'd to bestow your Instructions upon me in these Quarters; that I may at least observe something Pertinent either to my Present or Future Condition, as also your Blessing upon the Endeavours of

Lyons June }
17. 1657. }

Your most Dutifull Child
William Hammond –

[15]

Most Hon*oure*d Father,

My last of June the 17 gave you an Account of my Journey & Arrivall at Lyons. I have since had Leisure to repose myself, & find that tho' there be betwixt three or four Degrees from Paris hence, yet tho' Change of Aire does not [f. 25ᵛ] disturb my body. I wish that this Paper (after so long a Voyage, as from hence to Wilberton) cou'd entertaine you with any Considerable Remarques of this Place or Time: but there are few Travellers have those Opportunitys of observing, their hearts cou'd wish for. I can well tell you, that 'tis a Town thus & thus pleasantly situated, at the meeting of the Grave Soane, and sprightly Rhosne; that these are remaining such & such Ruines of the Roman's noble Structures, be it in Aquæ-ducts, in Amphitheatres, in Bridges, in Baths, in Temples, or the like.² That the Gallantry of the Town are the Merchants & *the* Merchant's Wives; who, as the French Ben Johnson, Cornelius observes, delight in having their Coaches & Lacquies roule about the Streets.³ That instead of a Parliament, there is only a Presidiall Court, whose power is much

---

was published on 31 August 1649, detailing Digby's banishment along with Walter Montagu, the paternal uncle of Robert Montagu, whose diary opens this collection. Digby's wife, Venetia Stanley Digby (d. 1633), painted by Van Dyck in a famous allegorical portrait as Prudence and also in a post-mortem portrait, was the daughter of Sir Edward Stanley of Tonge Castle, Shropshire, and grand-daughter of Thomas Percy, Earl of Northumberland (executed 1572). See Robert Torsten Peterson, *Sir Kenelm Digby, the Ornament of England, 1603–1665*, 1956, pp. 41, 101–5.

¹ Probably the lawyer and writer Michel de L'Hospital (c. 1507–73), whose best known works for English readers were his *Epistolia* (edited by Henri Estienne in 1577) and *Carmina*.

² Hammond playfully declines to enumerate and describe the ruins surviving from Lugdunum (founded 43 BC), the Roman capital of Gallia Lugdunensis. Two Roman theatres still survive at Lyons, the largest being erected by Augustus and doubled in size by Hadrian so that it could hold some 10,000 spectators. The Old Town (Vieux Lyon) is on the west bank of the Saône and modern (or Central) Lyons lies between the Saône and the Rhône on a narrow peninsula.

³ The poet and dramatist Pierre Corneille (1606–84), deemed the creator of French classical tragedy, is aptly compared here to the Ben Jonson (1572–1637), since both wrote plays on classical themes. Hammond, however, is probably referring to Corneille's depiction of polite society in his early comedies, such as *Mélite*, *Clitandre*, *La Veuve*, *La Galerie du palais*, *La Suivante*, and *La Place royale* (all staged between 1620 and 1634). Following the popular failure of his play, *Perharite* in the early 1650s, Corneille had temporarily given up the theatre at the time of Hammond's reference to him, in favour of writing a verse translation of *The Imitation of Christ* by St Thomas à Kempis.

shorter in Nisi prius's,[1] than in matters of Life & Death. And that the Merchants, to their own Inconvenience, chuse rather such a Pedling Court, than (by having a Parliament here) to be outstrutted & over-mastered by the Lawyers.

These & the like, are things, of which Table-talke may informe every Ordinary Passsenger. But to give any rationall Account of the [f. 26ʳ] Politie of Lyons, of the way of Trafficke, & Priviledges, the Marchants have here, above other places, &c. Really, Sir, herein I must confess my Ignorance, & that not for want of will & desire to know it, but for want of knowledge enough, in that kind, to be able to ask pertinent Questions. A Traveller, that wou'd satisfye himself & others, must have a great deal more superficiall Knowledge than a Poet: & the first and maine Step to Learning is to frame an Idea in our heads of what 'tis we aime at. I remember, Dʳ Holden has a story of the Protector's[2] Scout-master-generall, Watson;[3] who in 1647 leaving his places, came over to see France, Italy & other Parts of Europe; This man out of the habit his former Imployment had given him of Comprehending all designs, all Motions, & enfin all businesses he set himself to pry into, in six months time understood Paris, better than most of its Governors, & before two years end gave so rationall & deep an Account of the body of France, & its Interests both within & abroad of all *the* Principality & Governments of Italy especially Rome, Venice & Genoa, that the the Dʳ professes, he never found a map of a greater reach & Fathome, and that which made him more admire him, was *that* [f. 26ᵛ] by vocation (before the warrs) he was but an Ordinary North-Country Farmer, of a plain Rustick Carriage, & far from taking helps from books, or Learning. And in good truth, says the Doctor, if the Protector[4] & all his Councell have but such Head-pieces, 'tis no wonder, they have outwitted a Pllegmaticke & Easy King.[5]

Those that write after the best Copy, have an Advantage over others with an ill one; & tho' books & business worke not the same Effects in mens brains; no Question, but those Effects may be brought into an Equilibrium, by helping out the weaker with Sufficient Councell & Advice. And if you wou'd please to give me heads of the most Materiall things to be observ'd in such like Towns, as this, or other Common-wealths, or Principalitys in Italy: If after the application of diligence & Industry, I fall short of my aime, at least I shall do better than at present. If you shall think it fit, I will venture to begg some Instructions concerning Marchandise from my Uncle Ned Diggs. I wish 'twere my Fortune to do him service & myself Good, whilst I am about the Coasts of the Mediterranean Sea, & since my Brother flyes from all Professions, the Pompe of Lyons almost encourages me to turn Marchant. [f. 27ʳ] This day's Gazette gives us an Account of the Victory of our Ships over the Spanish fleet at the Isle Tenerif;[6] that they have sunk most of them, but left the Riches on Shore; where they hope, neither Partys will be much the better for it. That the Italian Army makes it his business to Clear Valence[7] from the Ports about it, & to that end they

---

[1] 'Nisi prius's': here probably just civil cases.

[2] * BL Add. MS 59785, f. 33ʳ: 'Cromwell'.

[3] * BL Add. MS 59785, f. 33ʳ: 'an Extraordinary Anecdote of Dr: Holden concerning Oliver Cromwell's Scout-Master-General, Watson'.

[4] * BL Add. MS 59785, f. 33ᵛ: 'Cromwell'.

[5] * BL Add. MS 59785, f. 33ᵛ: 'Charles the 2ᵈ. who was uterly immersed in Pleasures & Intreagues & Litle regarded the affairs of this Kingdom'.

[6] On 20 April 1657 the English fleet, under the parliamentarian Admiral and General-at-Sea, Robert Blake (1599–1657), won his last major victory when it attacked and destroyed sixteen Spanish vessels from the West Indies fleet in Santa Cruz despite bombardment from shore batteries. Blake died at sea, on route home to England in August 1657.

[7] * BL Add. MS 59785, f. 34ʳ: 'See my Note (   ) page'.

have lately taken the Castle of Non,[1] & put a relief both of men & Provisions to Valence itself.[2] That the Northern Army is at length set down before Montmedy,[3] one of *the* Considerablest Towns in Luxembourg, & that the Mareshall of Turenne with our 6000 English is tending thither;[4] finding that Don John, & the Prince of Condè[5] esteem it Considerable enough to desire to relieve it. That the Germans on the other Side are as busy in endeavouring to recover Poland, intending with one Army to disturb Transilvania, & with another to regaine Cracovia;[6] & that the 14th of August[7] is appointed for the Chusing a New Emperor at Francfort;[8] that the Warr is not yet declar'd betwixt Swede & Denmarke; & lastly that Holland & France are absolutely reunited. I humbly begg your Pardon for having been thus tedious. I am apt to think, that I can never write enough, when I send to Wil- [f. 27ᵛ] berton. The remembrance of it tempts me unto Verbosity,[9] each thought desiring to be sent to such a Beloved place, & in the interim almost forget the chief Cause of their appearing in Paper, is humbly to begg your Blessing on

Lyons July }
the 6. 1657 }

Your most Dutifull Child
William Hammond. –

My Cosin is desirous to stay here, till the heats be over, which will be in September, & by that time he has great hopes of obtaining leave to spend *the* next Winter in Italy, at least at Venice: he presents his humble service. My last carry'd with it an Inclos'd to my Mother, &

[1] * BL Add. MS 59785, f. 34ʳ: 'Non Cape is a Promentory on the West Coast of Africa opposite to the Canary Islands'.

[2] The town of Valence, capital of Drôme *département*, was built upon a succession of terraces overlooking the Rhône'. Hammond's 'castle of Non' may refer to the nearby ruined castle of Mont Crussol.

[3] * BL Add. MS 59785, f. 34ᵛ: 'A Toun of the Netherlands, in the Principality of Luxemborg Situate about 20 Miles West of Luxemberg Subject to France. [Salmon's Modern Gazetteer]'. Thomas Salmon, *The Modern Gazetteer: or, A Short View of the Several Nations of the World* (1746; with numerous later reprints).

[4] Montmédy was captured in 1656 by Henri de La Tour d'Auvergne, vicomte de Turenne (1611–75), Marshal of France from 1643 and commander of the royalist forces during the Fronde.

[5] Hammond's 'Don John' is Juan José, an illegitimate son (1629–79) known as the second Don John of Austria, of King Philip IV (d. 1665) of Spain by an actress popularly called La Calderona. The first Don John (1547–78) was the illegitimate son of Emperor Charles V and half-brother to King Philip II of Spain. This second Don John was half-brother to the sickly King Charles II of Spain (b.1661; reigned 1665–1700); and much of his ten-year minority was consumed with feuds between Don John and Charles's regent, the Queen Mother Mariana of Austria. Hammond's 'Prince of Condé' is Louis de Bourbon, 4ᵉ prince de Condé (1621–86). See letter 10.

[6] * BL Add. MS 59785, f. 35ʳ: 'Cracow is reckon'd the Capitall City of Poland, Situate in the Principality of Little Poland, & Palatinate of Cracow, in a Fine Plain, near the banke of the Vistula, the best built Town in the Kingdom. It is the See of a Bishop, & a university. Here the Supreme Courts of Justice are held, and the Regalia, kept in the Castle. It stands about 410 Miles East of the Fronteir of Silesia, & 140 South West of Warsaw. [Salmon's Modern Gazetteer:]'. Transylvania, part of Hungary during the 11th-16th centuries, became an autonomous principality within the Ottoman Empire during the 16th-17th centuries. During this period it was ruled by György Rákóczi II (1648–60). Kraków (Cracow), a city and city-province in southern Poland, situated on both sides of the River Vistula. In 1609 King Sigismund III Vasa had moved his capital to Warsaw; and both the Swedish Wars and the plague had a devastating effect on the area during the mid-17th century.

[7] * BL Add. MS 59785, f. 35ᵛ: 'See Note [ ] page. [ ] which is useing the New Stile'.

[8] Hammond's date of 14 August 1657 turned out to be inaccurate. Leopold I had found himself heir apparent when his elder brother Ferdinand IV died unexpectedly on 9 July 1654. In 1655 he was elected and crowned King of Hungary and then of Bohemia in 1656. When his father, Ferdinand III, died on 2 April 1657 the opposition of France to his succession delayed the coronation until 1658.

[9] * BL Add. MS 59785, f. 35ᵛ: 'The Writer seldom uses such words'.

another to my Sister Nan. This beggs respite, till the next Post, when I shall more largely tender my Duty to my Mother, & all the rest of our Wilberton Friends.

[16]

Most Honoured Father,

The third of the present month I presented you my most humble thanks for yours of June 29ᵗʰ, Wherein I also presum'd to enclose one for my Uncle Edward Diggs. The Rarity & Variety of things, incident to a Traveller, that lyes long at the same place, makes this Paper come something tardy after the rest. And since you have thought to Communicate my uncoth [f. 28ʳ] Lettres to my Uncle, I am almost asham'd to write to Wilberton, when I can add nothing *tha*t may send to the Satisfaction, of his Quæries. I hope, before I quitt these Southern parts, to be able to give in a Generall & Cohærent account, which may in some manner expiate the small Progess, I seem to make in the beginning: 'Chi ha tempo, ha vita', says the Italian;[1] & if my Uncle please but to allow me time enough, I need not despair to render a rationall account of a matter of Fact.

The Remarkablest Variety, that this summer has afforded us, is that 'tis now at length our turns to have a sight of the Rambling Queen of Swede,[2] Who lyes incognito at a Marchant's house, about a League from this Town. There have been already sent over so many Ingenuous Descriptions of her, that I dare not venture upon any thing that way; yet I believe the subject wou'd be different enough. For hitherto she has been describd in Princely & Magnificent Entrys & Treatments; now the Relator may search out Expressions of a Royall Poverty, treated by the unmercifull Haughtyness of a Marchandising Towne. Really, Sir, it is a very Sensible & Feeling sight to us Ramblers, to see [f. 28ᵛ] the Queen of Travellers crawle Neglectedly thorow the proud Streets of Lyons, in a Thredbare Coach drawn by six Consumptive horses, that seem to have been kept at the same Rock, with Pharaoh's lean kine.[3] Yet this Cloude makes her quitt neither her Spritely Carriage, Manlike behaviour, nor her Hermaphrodite's Habit. She still retains the humour of despising her own Sex, & takes notice of no Visits or Obeisance that Women do to her. Our Curiosity carried us to'ther day, to the Country-house where she lodg'd. The roome we saw her in was decently spacious, at the farthermost end of which, she was merrily reading a Copy of Verses to a Recollect monke, & two Marchants;[4] the other end was filld *w*ith spectators, most of which were the Chief Dames of Lyon, who had stay'd there almost an hour without the least notice or Nod of the Queen's, & at length were as negligently frighted out by her Majesty's manly Collation brought in, consisting chiefly of Frontinac Wines & Westphalia bacon.

Her Traine was made up of all Quarters of Europe, being in number about 15 or 20 lusty Fellows, some Italians, some Spaniards, [f. 29ʳ] but most Swedes & many French. She keeps but one durty[5] Creature of her own Sex, who has no Office about her Person, but serves

---

¹ 'Where there's time, there's life' (Italian proverb).

² * BL Add. MS 59785, f. 36ᵛ: 'Christina. See Note   '. I.e. The itinerant Queen Christina of Sweden. See letter 7.

³ Hammond refers here to the Pharaoh's dream in which seven fat kine and then seven lean ones came up out of the Nile to graze on its banks, symbolizing years of plenty and famine (Genesis 41:1–4).

⁴ The Recollect Augustinian Order.

⁵ * BL Add. MS 59785, f. 37ᵛ: 'The Great Humour of the Writer in this relation of her Maid flung me into such an immoderate degree of Laughter as hardly to contain myself from Convulsions. I think I never knew a Man enter into the Character of anybody better & writes as the Queen thinks'.

Christine peut donner des Loix
Aux Cœurs des Vainqueurs les plus braues,
Mais la Terre a t'elle des Rois
Qui soient dignes d'en estre Esclaues?
De Scuderi.

Fig. 33. Queen Christina (1626–89) of Sweden.

only to keep keys & looke after Linnen. The Cause of her Stay here, is to wait the King's Answer, of whom she begs leave to spend the rest of her time at Paris. 'Tis thought, she may prevaile, coming in season, now his Majesty is pleas'd with his Victorious reducing of Montmedy.[1]

As I ended this broken Narration, 'twas my good Fortune to receive yours of August 3[d.] together with the Enclosed from my Mother. My heart is yet panting[2] with the deep Impressions your Tenderness workes in me, & the Emotion in me thorow Joye to hear from Wilberton, makes me a little Confus'd in my thoughts: be pleas'd therefore to pardon me, if in this Extempore-answer I commit any defects.

Last Saturday my Cosin Bowyer receiv'd a Positive Command from my Lady his Mother, not to come nigh Italy this Winter: & you being pleas'd to send me the same Orders so soon after his, having Duty to Enjoyne us both, we are Joyntly resolv'd to lay aside that design. And Really, Sir, I begin to feel a sensible Decrease of my rambling humour, & am so quotted[3] with [f. 29ᵛ] the Vanity of spending time in France, that I am far from desiring to see any Country in the World, at so dear a rate,[4] as passing thorow Quarantins, & the Pestilence of an infected Air. The Reflection upon the Cheat of Travelling, & that little improvement, I either have or am like to make by it, has made me resolve to spend *that* remainder you shall think fitt to allow me in a more pertinent kind of life & to that end I have seriously Wedded myself to the study of Physick, intending to make it the subject of my most Considerable thoughts, & to get the Mastery of it so far (whilst I am abroad) as no discouragement may withdraw me from it, when I come home. I am not at all agog[5] of any Particular place to study in, & if you shall think fitt to remove me to Leyden in Holland,[6] it shall be as Equally indifferent to me, as Montpelier or Padua; & this Advantage I may hope for in Holland, above *that* of France or Italy, that being a Country more like our Fenns, I may at spare times get there a more pertinent & Usefull knowledge concerning their husbandry or Improvement of their Lands. That I have stay'd thus long at Lyons, has been meerly out of Complacency to my Cosin, who left Paris in Complacency to me. [f. 30ʳ] In the beginning of September he has resolv'd to goe with me the Tour of the most southern parts, taking in Grenoble. I hope to see Geneva,[7] when I goe down the Rhine, & shall endeavour to make the best remarks I can, in that holy City, which sends forth its sweet streams of Presbiterian Preachers thorowout the whole Land of France.[8]

---

[1] For Montmédy, see letter 15.

[2] * BL Add. MS 59785, f. 38ʳ: 'The writer is very fond of the Eastern Stile, which not only displays his Superior Judgement but also manifests the innate Goodness of his Heart & disposition. The Sacred Penman & Man after God our Heart says Psalm [...]'.

[3] * BL Add. MS 59785, f. 38ᵛ: 'Sic Originale. See my Note [   ] pa: where I declared my keeping up to the Original Orthography. Brotherton MS Trv.2 also has the spelling 'quotted'.

[4] * BL Add. MS 59785, f. 38ᵛ: 'This is agreeable my Note [   ] pa: [   ]. because this expression is also Eastern'.

[5] * BL Add. MS 59785, f. 39ʳ: 'Sic originale'.

[6] Leiden (Leyden) was already renowned for its university's medical faculty, which was later brought into even greater prominence by Hermann Boerhaave (1668–1738), professor of botany, medicine, and chemistry and, ultimately, rector of the university. The English doctor, Sir Thomas Browne studied there. See Stoye, *English Travellers Abroad*, pp. 157, 176–80, 194, 211, 351. See also E. Peacock, *Index to English Speaking Students ... at Leyden University*, London, 1883.

[7] * BL Add. MS 59785, f. 39ᵛ: 'The Place of Calvin's Residence'.

[8] Protestantism was formally adopted at Geneva in 1535, with John Calvin arriving there in the following year. Presbyterianism was specifically developed by Swiss and Rhineland reformers during the 16th century. The influence of Presbyterian preachers in England was at its height during the Civil War period. The Rump Parliament, which tried (1648) and executed (January 1649) King Charles I, had been purged of its Presbyterians (some 140 members), leading to a sharp decline in their political influence.

Be pleas'd to pardon me, if I a little deferr the account of Lyons, which you are pleas'd to demand of me, & my next shall not faile to obey you. The Extraordinary heats of this place lasted not above a month, & we have since had an Extraordinary Wett & mild summer; so that their Vondage¹ will hardly begin till October: We hear that Genoa is almost utterly dispeopled, but that Rome & all other Parts are not much endanger'd. It seems, News (like snow-balls) increase by rowling, for my Lady Bowyer tells us, that there is not so much as a Village in Italy free from the Plague. Our Italian Army comes not so handsomely off, as that of Picardy; for the Spaniard has lately routed them from before Alexandria,² where they were set down in a formal siege. I am much Interess't in the behalf of our 6,000 Red, who have been now above 4 months in France, & not the least mention made of [f. 30ᵛ] them in our Gazetts. I returne my most humble Thanks & Duty to my Mother, & next Post do promise to do it more at large. In the interim, I begg your Blessing upon.

Lyons August ⎫   Your most Duti*full* Child
the 28. 1657 ⎬   William Hammond. –

The latter end of my lettres plead Pescription of presenting my Duty & service thorowout *you*r Family.

[17]

Most Honour*e*d father,

About three Weeks since I presented my humble Duty, in one to my Mother Dated from Avignon.³ Since which time we have run thorow all Provence,⁴ & are now at Nismes in Languedoc.⁵ We arrived here the 22ᵈ of September, & intending to spend a day or two here, in seeing its Reliques of Roman Architecture.⁶ The very next day after our Coming, it pleas'd God to afflict my poor Cosin Bowyer with the small-pox.⁷ I have been much daunted with the severity of the Almighty's punishing us, to lay us in the bed of sickness, not only when we were farthest from all succours of Friends, or Acquaintance, but even in our most Unsettled kind of Life, & one of the most unquiets & thorow-fare Inn of France. 'tis now *th*e Ninth [f. 31ʳ] day of his Sickness, & tho' he has hitherto been in very great danger of his life; yet now I make no Question, but (by the Mercy of God) he will recover. I am now in the Epitome of my travells & my great days' Journeys are reduc't into *th*e small

¹ *vendange*, wine harvest or vintage.

² * BL Add. MS 59785, f. 38ᵛ: 'A Citty in Italy about 40 Miles N: West of Genoa'. Alessandria (north of Genoa).

³ * BL Add. MS 59785, f. 40ᵛ: 'a Large City of Provence. [Salmon's Modern Gazetteer]'.

⁴ * BL Add. MS 59785, f. 40ᵛ: 'a Government of France. [Salmon's Modern Gazetteer]'.

⁵ Hammond had presumably travelled along the familiar southern route from Lyons through Valence, before staying at Avignon and Nîmes.

⁶ * BL Add. MS 59785, f. 40ᵛ: 'a City of France. [Salmon's Modern Gazetteer]'. Nîmes (the Roman colony of Nemausus) was admired by English travellers, almost exclusively, for its impressive Roman remains, including the three-tier Pont du Gard aqueduct which supplied it water, its Amphitheatre, its ramparts, and the Maison Carrée (a Roman temple built in the style of the Parthenon). Francis Mortoft also visited Nîmes at this period (Mortoft (1658), pp. 26–7).

⁷ Smallpox was a common risk for travellers in this region of France. In September 1611 Sir Charles Somerset arrived at Avignon and 'was in this towne verie sick and in great extremitie for a moneth of the small pockes'. (Somerset, 131). See Lough, *France Observed*, pp. 29–30, for other examples. Cousin Bowyer's illness recalls the popular saying: 'Avenio ventosa, sine vento venenosa, cum vento fastidiosa' – 'windy Avignon, pest-ridden when there is no wind, wind-pestered when there is'.

walk betwixt the Chimney corner, & my Cosin's Bed-side, thinking it the part of a Gentleman & true Friend, to give all help & Comfort to my Sick Comerade. And really, Sir, I find so much Virtue & Goodness in him, as I must have been of a strange nature, not to hazard all to save his life. Be pleas'd to pardon me, if (thorow the Unsettledness of my mind, by reason of my Cosin's sickness) I do not at present add Variety to my Lettre, by any of *the* latest Rencounters or Observations. I have sufficiently instructed myself towards the Answering my Uncle's[1] Quærys; and as soon as it pleases God to give me a little repose by restoring my Cosin his health, I will endeavour to range them in a lettre. 'tis now four Months since I made bold to salute my Uncle Marsham with a Lettre, writing others at the same time to M*r*. Knatchbull, & M*r*. Rooke;[2] but as yet I have not had the fortune to know, whether they were receiv'd. Here has for these seven or [f. 31ᵛ] eight days run a strong report of the Surprisall of Barcelona,[3] but it now beginns to be doubted; From Arles[4] hither we came riding over a Country, ready to be drown'd by the swelling Rhosne, which is this Autume more swell'd, than the oldest man alive has hitherto seen it; insomuch that they are faine to boat from house to house in Avignon, Tarason, &c.[5] They impute it not only to the Excessive rains, fallen in the Franche-County,[6] but also to a new Outlett lately made in Switzerland; Insomuch that all this part of the Country are listing themselves towards the draining of these Fenns. I humbly beg you'le please to send to D*r*. Holden an early supply for my use; for really, Sir, an Empty Purse is a dolefull Companion to a Traveller. In the interim I crave your Blessing upon

Nismes October}
the 1ˢᵗ. 1657   }

Your most Dutifull Child
William Hammond. –

My Duty & Service always presents itself to your Friends.

[18]

Most Honoured Mother,

My Last of the first of October, carried my Father the sad news of my dear Cosin Bowyer's sickness of the small-pox. 'tis unexpressible what af- [f. 32ʳ] flictions we have both suffer'd within these fifteen days; he thorow the Torment of a body infinitely fill'd with the Pox, & I thorow the imminent danger I have hitherto apprehended of his death. 'Tis now four days since the Physicians have given him over; yet God be thanked, he Continues still in life, & is rather mended than worse. I now begin experimentally to understand what's meant by an akeing or rather breaking heart; & to my shame be it said,

---

[1] * BL Add. MS 59785, f. 41ʳ: 'Edward Diggs'.

[2] See letter 13 for Mr. Knatchbull and letter 4 for Lawrence Rooke.

[3] * BL Add. MS 59785, f. 41ᵛ: 'in Spain [Salmon's Modern Gazetteer]'.

[4] * BL Add. MS 59785, f. 41ᵛ: 'Famous for the Councils held here [Salmon's Modern Gazetteer]'.

[5] * BL Add. MS 59785, f. 41ᵛ: 'a Town in France. [Salmon's Modern Gazetteer]'. Until a suspension bridge of 1829 the Rhône at Tarascon was crossed by a bridge of boats, from which carts and carriages were not uncommonly lost in stormy weather and at high tides.

[6] The region of Franche-Comté was one of the most ravaged and war-torn regions of France traversed by Hammond on his travels. It had come into the hands of the Spanish Habsburgs following Charles V's partition of his dominions. During Louis XIII's wars against Spain it was repeatedly invaded from 1636 onwards but in 1648 it was included in the Peace of Westphalia. It was conquered by Condé in 1668 during the War of Devolution, ceded back to Spain by the Peace of Aix-la-Chapelle, and finally retaken for France by Condé in 1674.

I was never till now so thorowly sensible of the Affliction my Kentish disease gave you. When I find, that the Danger of a Friend's life gives me so many restless nights, so many fears, sighs, sobs, & heart-akings; it makes me every moment reflect upon the Torments, your Tenderness over me, made you suffer at that time: & I find no greater regrett of Conscience, than for my Insensibility that way, & that I have hitherto liv'd so stupid, as not to have given some signall Marke of my Gratitude for your tender & Motherly Affection. I hope that Angry God who is now Scourging us for our Sins, will at length change his anger into so much mercy, as I may have the opportunity of manifesting my Piety towards you. The state I am now in, makes me Uncapa- [f. 32ᵛ] ble of any but dole-full & Melancholy thoughts; be pleas'd then to pardon the shortness of this Lettre which as it encreases in length, must have also encreast in Sorrow: & far be it from me, to occasion Grief to my Parents, I will rather change my lamenting into Praying & begging, & begin with humbly begging your Blessing upon

Nismes October⎫   Your most Dutifull Child
the 9. 1657 – ⎭   William Hammond. –

My Duty & Service is always ready to my Friends.

[19]

Most Honoured Father,
'Tis now a full month, that I have livd in the Purgatory of Travellers, & instead of going forward in our Grand Tour of France, I have stayd on Assistant to my Cosin, whose greatest day's Journey, for these thirty days past, has been but from[1] one side of his bed to t'other.

The First of this Current month, I gave you an account of the beginning of his Sickness & on the following 9th day, I presented my Duty to my Mother, in a kind of desparing style. The little experience I have had in things of this nature, makes me take all Alarms. Howsoever, I am much joyed to have the Luck of Contradicting myself; & with pleasure falsify my [f. 33ʳ] Last, in sending you (at present) an assurance of his Totall & perfect recovery. I reckon nigh upon four years, since I first began the study of Physick; yet to my shame must I confess, that I have profitted, more, in the industrious, & interessedly observing the Effects of Nature thorowout this my Cosin's Sickness, than in all that former time: which makes me conclude, that a month's Experience is better, than 50 months Contemplation. He is not yet so thorowly recover'd, as to give me an entire repose, my most vacant thoughts are still intermix't with petty fears & Jealousys of his relapse. I am very sensible of the Impertinency, this Lettre is like to be guilty of; if after so long a Journey, it bring you no other account, than what Concerns my Cosin. Really, Sir, I am as yet Capable of no Digression, but what wou'd prove so broken & interrupted, as Respect & shame wou'd hinder its sending. The great affair of Languedoc is at present, their states now sitting at Pezenas;[2] from whence the Country is expecting

---

[1] 'from' inserted above.

[2] Pezenas was at this period the seat of the Estates (or Assembly) of Languedoc, which determined the levels of taxation applied to this region of southern France. During the 1650s Molière and his company regularly performed at Pezenas during the sessions of the Estates.

severall resolutions: the maine must be an Imposition of a Tax towards filling the King's Coffers; amongst the rest, 'tis thought, one will be for the new banking the Rhosne betwixt Avignion & the Sea side with some few necessa- [f. 33ᵛ] ry Draines, to lay dry this Levell, which is on its Western shore. It is said that the oldest man living in this Country never saw greater Floods, than have come down this Autume, which burst their banks, & overflow'd more of their Country than ever. I can wittness, that their Banks are far from being so substantiall, as ours in the Fenns; neither have they the Art of giving such a slope towards the River. I rod on the[1] top of it from Arles to Beaucaire,[2] & I found that it cou'd not be above eight Foot high, having both its outward & inward sides equally of some ten foot slope.

'Tis an Easy matter to give an account of all the Memorable Exploits of these southern Campaignes. For neither the Catalonian, nor Italian Armys will prove this year guilty of any Fame or Credit: *th*e hot report of Barcelona's surprice is now utterly hush't; & from Italy the Prince of Conty, is ordering affairs for his returne to Paris, being at present sick of the Air of Piedmont. The French have their eyes most intent upon their Northern Army, & the Town I am now in, is much joyed to hear any thing that sends to the Renown of our Protector.[3] We hear that the former body of six Thousand English, is now made up of a 11000, & joyn'd with the Mons*ieu*r of Turenne,[4] are sitting down before [f. 34ʳ] Gravelin,[5] having already taken the Fort of Mardike.[6] We have little account of the affairs of Portugall, only 'tis said, that the King of Spaine[7] is drawing of his men towards Catalonia; Mons*ieu*r d'Harcourt has quitted his Government of Alsatia,[8] for that of Anjou,[9] & is lately sent by *th*e King into Portugall.[10]

I am asham'd to run on in this style, being certain the Diurnalls[11] will have made my News stale before this get to Wilberton. This paper might have prov'd more pertinent, if I had had the happyness to have lately heard from you; it is now three months since I receiv'd your last, & tho' upon the Presumption, of sympathys, I perswade myself, that

---

[1] 'the' inserted above.

[2] * BL Add. MS 59785, f. 44ʳ: 'a Toun of Langeudoc about 7 Miles from Arles. [Salmon's Modern Gazetteer]'. Hammond evidently rode along the banks of the Rhône from Arles to Beaucaire.

[3] * BL Add. MS 59785, f. 44ᵛ: 'Oliver Cromwell'.

[4] See letter 15 for Turenne.

[5] * BL Add. MS 59785, f. 44ᵛ: 'A Port Town of the French Netherlands [Salmon's Gazetteer]'. The fortified town and seaport of Gravelines was captured by the French from the Spanish in 1644 but it was then taken by the Austrians in 1652 before finally returning to France in 1658 by the Treaty of the Pyrenees. English travellers were also often interested in the town because on 29 July 1588 the Spanish Armada had been dispersed and routed off Gravelines by the English navy after being driven out of Calais by fire-ships.

[6] * BL Add. MS 59785, f. 44ᵛ: 'A Port Town of French Flanders [Salmon's Gazetteer]'.

[7] * BL Add. MS 59785, f. 44ᵛ: 'Philip the IV. who Dyed 7th. Sep*tember* 1665'.

[8] * BL Add. MS 59785, f. 44ᵛ: 'a Principality of Germany. [Salmon's Modern Gazetteer]'.

[9] * BL Add. MS 59785, f. 44ᵛ: 'This Title was annexed to the 2ᵈ son of the King of Spain & is now enjoyed by Philip the 5th. now King of Spain'. Philip V of Spain reigned from 1700 until 1746.

[10] Henri de Lorraine, comte de Harcourt (1601–66), had served as King Louis XII's Master of the Horse and was one of France's most distinguished military leaders. He gained significant victories against the Spanish during the Fronde (1648–53) and personally accompanied King Louis XIV to Normandy to reassert royal authority. However, considering his efforts during the Fronde to have gone unrewarded, he seized several towns in Alsace and only gave them up when forced to by Henri, duc de La Ferté-Senneterre. He was reconciled to Louis XIV and was appointed Governor of Anjou.

[11] Diurnals: daily newspapers or newsletters.

all is well at Wilberton, yet thorow Ignorance of any Particularitys, I am forc't to write in Generalls. Really, Sir, there is nothing wou'd be more Cordiall to me after this last month's affliction, than to receive a Renewall of your Blessing upon

Nismes October ⎫
the 23. 1657 ⎭

Your most Dutifull Child,
William Hammond. –

I humbly present my Duty to my Mother, Brother & Sisters &c. My Purse is crying for a supply.

[20]

[f. 34ᵛ] Most Honoured Father,
The third of this present month: I receiv'd yours of September the seventh. Really, Sir, it has done me more good, than all the Doctors & Apothecarys did my Cosin; & thorow its Cordiall Virtue, I have all ready conquer'd & broke through all my last 6 weeks Toiles & Vexations. Yesterday we remov'd out of the Inne, where we have hitherto lain, & are now lodg'd in a reasonable Pension, wherein we shall be forct to lye, till we can get recruits of Mony from Paris. I will not complain of the hard usage we have receiv'd from the Protestants of these Countrys here, since the Goodness of one amongst them, has in a manner expiated the Fault of all the rest. I will only say, that after having appeal'd to the Consistory & heads of the Religion, we were forc't to pay down our Hugonot Hostesse,[1] the summe of 400 Livres odd mony for six weeks Diet & Lodging, which had been something more tolerable had she not retracted, & forsworn an Agreement, I had made at the beginning with her for a less summe. I begin to see, that there is no such dreadfull Creature, like a Presbiterian in Prosperity; & how just soever they be, thorowout all other Towns of France, where they are the weaker Party; yet in Nismes & Geneva they [35ʳ] prove the most imperious & unconscionable dealers of the World.

I am but just out of the disturbance of that unjust Action, & this morning is the first of my new Pension; I dare not venture upon any long Lettre; till my mind have taken a little Repose: Animæ sapientiores fiunt quiescendo.[2] It will savour more of that Dutyfull respect I bear you, in that I rather chuse to be short, than Impertinent: & instead of Unconsiderable discourse fall into earnest Prayers for your Blessing upon

Nismes November ⎫
the 6. 1657 – ⎭

Your most Dutyfull Child
William Hammond

My Cosin presents his humble service, & I am allways most mindfull of my Duty to my Dear Mother, Brother & Sisters &c:

---

[1] Under the Edict of Nantes the Huguenots had been granted ten places of safety in Languedoc after the Wars of Religion (1561–98) and their communities had continued there, despite periodic hostilities with national leaders, most notably that of the governor of Languedoc, Henry II de Montmorency against Cardinal Richelieu in 1632.

[2] 'Spirits become wiser by resting'.

[21]

Most Honoured Mother,

The sixth of this Month I sent word to Wilberton of my Cosin's perfect recovery, & of our removall from the Inne to a cheaper Pension. At that time I was in hopes, that this my next, might have been wrot from Montpelier, & that befoe this, we shou'd have chang'd from a Town wherein we have each of us suffer'd our Parts. I now begin to see the Efficacious Virtue of Mony & may be easily perswaded, that bodily health & strength will ne- [f. 35ᵛ] ver keep us upon the Center of Content, without the Counterpoise of an Heavy Purse.

God be thanked; we are both Lusty & very well, but this sickness has so entangled us in Expences and Debts, that there is yet above twenty Pistolls owing, & we have not mony enough left in all our Pocketts to purchase a pair of shoes: The sence of my Poverty has brought me into a very industrious humour, & I may say that I never gave a more resolute onsett upon Physick, than since my coming to Nismes. The Physicians of this Town do me too much honour, & I now find the advantage of having study'd & frequented our London Physicians; *the* account I give of their opinions & Lectures, makes me a Doctor myself, & has bred to good an Opinion of me in these Country Physicians, that one of them has had the Goodness to send me 30 Crowns; perswading himself, that whatsoever I am at present, my Future Practise will quickly make me rich enough to pay him. I shou'd be much joyed, if my Father wou'd look upon this summe, as so much gain'd by the Profession, he has put me upon: & since 'tis the first mony come to me that way, I hope he will be pleas'd liberally to augment it towards the Encouragement of my farther proceedings.

[f. 36ʳ] The Town I am now in yeilds nothing remarkable enough to help out a long Lettre: yet I cannot complaine that time is any thing irksome to me, having the advantage of being able to study away the serious part of the day; & for my Recreation, besides ordinary Conversation, methinks I meet with the old Roman Heros; whilst I walk about the stately Pile of their Amphitheatre[1] & their Flourish'd Temple; both which remaine yet tolerably entire in this Town.[2] 'Tis no small affliction to me, that this great Distance makes me hear so seldome from Wilberton, especially since my Father's last frighted me with the Description of so sickly a time thorowout England. And there is nothing wou'd be more Joyfully wellcome to me, than an assurance of your Wellfare & your Blessings upon

Nismes November }
the 20. 1657   }

Your most Dutifull Child,
William Hammond –

[22]

Most Honoured Father,

Last Poste brought me two of your Lettres together, one concerning mine which I sent from Avignion, the other in answer to that[3] despairing Lettre, which I formerly sent my Mother in the Criticall point of my Cosin's sickness. Really, [f. 36ᵛ] Sir, it cost me many a tear, before I had read it out, being griev'd, to see that my little Discretion had caus'd

---

[1] * BL Add. MS 59785, f. 47ᵛ: 'The Roman Amphiatre at Nismes is reckond the most entire of any in Europe'.

[2] The amphitheatre at Nîmes could seat some 20,000 spectators. In the 11th century it was converted into a Visigothic stronghold, known as the Château des Arènes. See Mortoft (1658), pp. 26–7. Hammond's 'flourish'd temple' probably refers to the Maison Carrée (a Roman temple built in the style of the Parthenon), dating from the Augustan age. See Somerset (1611–12), p. 136.

[3] 'to that' written again and deleted.

so Passionate a sorrow in my Parents for a thing, that has since prov'd Chymæricall. I humbly beg your pardons, & do promise for the Future to be a more Cautelous [?] Messenger of unwellcome News. I have already receiv'd the Fruits of that mony you were pleas'd to send the Doctor, & 'tis now almost a fortnight, since I redeemd myself from Nismes. The considerable stay that I have now made in Languedoc, made me come to Montpelier, rather as one of its Neighbours, than as a Forreign Stranger: having had the opportunitys (during my Cosin's sickness) to informe myself of the Condition & ways of its surrounding Countrys: & doubtless (at my poor Cosin's cost) I have been sufficiently instructed in the manners of these Countrye Physicians' Practise; who, tho' they be not so quick-scented to start new Inventions; as our London Doctors; yet, methinks, the advantage the Country gives them of a more frank & naturall delivery, both of their words & Actions, makes them happyer in getting & preserving their Practise.

I must Confess, my Expectations have been a little deceiv'd in this Towne;[1] not but that the Generalitys of it: Vid: its Buildings, Gardins, & [f. 37ʳ] scituation makes it one of the Prettyest, I have yet seen in France; but when I descend to Particulars, instead of Schools of Physick, Correspondent to ours of London, Oxford or Cambridge; I find an abject, & inferior Corner, whither the Students (as if they were the Dreggs of the Towne) shoud resort.[2] Instead of Lectures, I find their chief Professor dead, & his Chair vacant; insomuch, as they tell me, 'tis above three years, since they have had any Publick Lessons in the Schools. Instead of their Incomparable & Renown'd Jardin du Roy, I find it comes short of the Duke of Orlean's his Blois, by above a 1000 Plants.[3] And which is worst of all, instead of Learned & Edifying Disputes in matters of Physick, all sorts of its Inhabitants are at this time, up to the head & ears in Controversys of Religion, & their dayly Employment is to run from the Tample to the Church to hear the furious disputes betwixt the Ministre & a Capucin. Really, Sir, I am almost asham'd to specify so many defects of a Town, the renown of whose Ancestors makes it still sufficiently admird in our Northern parts. Yet since you were pleas'd to command my Opinion of the place I preferr'd Truth before dissembling, being emboldned by the Generall account of all Stranger-students who after having livd & studied [f. 37ᵛ] here above six or twelve months, give the like Character of this famous place.[4]

The Winter now being well come on, there is but little stirring or Noveltys in these parts,

---

[1] * BL Add. MS 59785, f. 48ᵛ: 'Montpelier, a City of France, County of Nismes – It is said here are a great many Physicians, & 200 Apothecarys. People do not only practice Physick here, but Study it, this being a university designed Chiefly for Students in that Science [Salmon's Modern Gazetteer]'.

[2] The school of Physic at Montpellier had been incorporated in 1221 (prior to the university's incorporation in 1289) and enjoyed a high reputation – despite Hammond's negative views – during the 17th century, attracting students from all over Europe. The writer and doctor Sir Thomas Browne (1605–82) studied there in about 1630; and Thomas Sydenham (1624–89), later an expert on epidemic diseases, in 1659. François Rabelais (c. 1495–1553) had studied there and the faculty possessed an exhibit, known as the 'robe of Rabelais'. See also Somerset (1611–12), p. 137, and Lough, *France Observed*, pp. 201–6.

[3] The Jardin des Plantes, established at the command of Henri IV by Pierre-Richer de Belleval in 1593, is the oldest botanical garden in France. See Mortoft (1658), p. 25. Hammond's unfavourable comparision is to the Château de Blois on the banks of the Loire, owned by the house of Orléans since 1397 and by the crown from 1498 when Louis XII, who had been born there, succeeded to the throne. Gaston-Jean-Baptiste, duc d'Orléans (1608–60), widely known as 'Monsieur', was the brother of Louis XIII.

[4] * BL Add. MS 59785, f. 49ʳ, has the following note at the bottom of the page but no reference to its location within the text: 'is an elegant City. The Natives remarkable for their Politeness, &, Speaking French in Perfection – [Salmon's Modern Gazetteer].

Fig. 34. 'Veue de l'Eglise Sainct Pierre de Montpellier' (c. 1650–55) (Israel Silvestre and Israel Henriet).

our Eyes being generally intent upon the proceedings of our Protector[1] in Flanders:[2] only this I may say, that it has & continues to be the wettest Winter, that has happen'd here any time these twenty years, having drown'd not only the Meadows, but carried away infinite Quantitys of Salt to the value of 100000 Crowns. I pray God, our Fenn-banks may be stronger than these of the Rhosne. I never till now was so sensible of the bigness of France, for being here at the farthest Corner of it, methinks a Lettre is so long a coming over it, as makes my life very unpleasant, by the Incertitude of your Wellfare, this sickly time; & my best comfort is in Praying heartily for it, yet the Efficacy of those Prayers, must proceed from your Blessings upon

Montpelier Dec*ember*
the 11. 1657 –   }

Your most Dutif*ull* Child
William Hammond –

[23]

Most Honoured Mother,

'Twas no Small Joye to me, that y*ou*r Last brought me the good hopes, of having another[3] Brother or Sister. The time which I have now spent [f. 38ʳ] amongst a Forreigne & strange People, has taught me now, how to prize the increase of my Kindred & Friends. And since you were pleas'd to express a desire of having me within Call in time of your Child-bed; my

---

[1] * BL Add. MS 59785, f. 49ᵛ: 'Oliver Cromwell'.

[2] This is presumably a reference to the French campaign supported by English troops in Spanish Flanders which resulted in the ceding of Dunkirk to Cromwell. See letter 8.

[3] 'another' written twice.

Duty has brought me a Journy of four hundred miles nigher, than I was, when I wrot to my Father from Montpelier. I might run an hazard of betraying mine Ignorance in Physick, shou'd I apprehend that you are in any danger after so many former happy Deliverances: & Every good Christian ought to have so much Divinity, as to know that a Goodness so extraordinary as yours, is a sufficient Guard from the hurt of that Punishment of sin. Yet, as I am your most Obedient Child, I wou'd have taken a Journey ten times longer, to have manifested my Duty: & as I am a man, I shou'd have given but little Marks of my Reason, shou'd I not have answer'd the Desires of a great Belly. My Will & Desires are so wholly resignd up into those of my Parents, that I know not how to ask a little longer time of Travell, till I more fully understand your Pleasure. The sweet Conversation I receive from my Reviv'd Cosin Bowyer makes me wish that my time were link't with his; which certainly cannot be long, since my Lady Bowyer's tender Affection is become so Attractive, as to [f. 38ᵛ] Enjoyne how so great an approach as from Nismes to Paris; & that in the heart of Winter after a Disease, that disarmes a man from hardship: 'tis not above two days, that we have been in Paris, I am affraid that my Unsettledness is too visibly seen by this uncoth Lettre. You will please to pardon me, if my Witt be tired, as well as my body after a Journy of three & twenty days Continuance. We were three days on horse-back, six days in a Litter, & thirteen days in the Lyon-Coach. Yesterday Dʳ Holden receiv'd from my Cosin Dawson a Bill of 25 Pound for my use. The Necessity it found me in, makes me extremely sensible of your Goodness, in so timely providing for me; & tho' I have this year been at Extraordinary Charges, yet I will endeavour to Express my Gratitude, by making it hold out till next Quarter day. I humbly begg my Father's Pardon, for not writing this Post; the huddle I am yet in, does make me unfitt to write two Lettres at once: all that I can pertinently do at present, is humbly to present my Duty, & begg your Blessings upon

Paris January
the 5. 1658 }

Your most Duty*full* Child
William Hammond –

I dare never forget a Corner to my Brothers, Sisters, &c. –

[24]

[f. 39ʳ] Most Hon*oure*d Father,
Yesterday Dʳ Holden gave me your Lettre of the 28 of December. I have sav'd it 400 miles Travell by meeting of it here at Paris & 'tis one benefit, that I have got by my long Journey, that the News of your Wellfare at Wilberton, is come ten or twelve days sooner to me, than it wou'd have done, had I been at Montpelier still. Really, Sir, your later Lettres so often & joyntly styl'd my mother's future Child-bed; a Danger that at length they rais'd such an apprehension in me, as has made me run from one End of France to t'other, without ever looking behind me. At my arrivall in Paris, the Doctors grave Councell, & the Regrett to quitt my Cousin, prevail'd so far upon me, as to Consent unto an halt: & having since consider'd, that I am now w*i*thin Call, & not above five days Journey from home; I hope 'twill not savour of Undutifullness to give a look or two, before I leap the Ditch, that separates France from England. Tho' it may be a Mark of my Duty & Piety, to my Mother, yet it may prove Scandalous to my Profession to have quitted my Travells out of apprehension of a danger, that Physicians will call Imaginary. But since the ways of Providence are inscrutable, I cannot but rejoyce, in that I am nigher home [f. 39ᵛ] than I was, & I shall not

have the least thought of stirring farther from England, till I receive the good News of my Mother's happy Deliverance. The Profession I have now undertaken, gathers like a Snow-ball in rowling, & tis apparent that our greatest Doctors in Physick, have been those, who by the advantage of Travelling, have view'd, compar'd, & digested the severall Practises of most of *th*e Europæan Physicians. But I will not be too busy in urging Arguments of that nature. I shall ever Confess it a great Indulgency in you to have bestow'd these two years' Travells upon me, by which I have learnt so far to understand myself, as to know, that your Pleasure shou'd be the Guide of my Actions.

Instead of spending this Winter as idly, as I did *th*e last, the first week of my arrivall, I enter'd my self into their Publique Lectures & it has cost me 12 Crowns of my Cosin Dawson's last mony of 25 Pounds, towards the Learning of Chymistry, which is here, very faithfully & learnedly taught, & whereby I hope to make a great step in the under-standing of the Materia Medica.[1] My Studiousness makes me something ignorant of the Publique Affairs of France, yet since you were pleas'd to mention the sadness of our English Court for the Loss of S^r.   Reynolds;[2] I may describe this [f. 40^r] Court in a greater sorrow, for the death of *th*e Cardinall's second, but most hopefull Nephew, whom he had made Possessor of most of the richest Church-Benefices in France. The young man being a Pensioner in the Jesuit's Colledge, had the misfortune to be toss't in a blan-ket by four of his school fellows, of whom Count d'Harcourt's Nephew was one,[3] who being of too small strength to sustaine his Corner, let the young Mazarin fall with his head foremost, whereon he receiv'd a Mortall wound, & dyed of it, about some eight days since. The Queen of Swede has utterly lost her Credit in France & Italy, since her putting to death the Duke of Parma's kinsman, her Major Domo: & it is said, she is now gone to visitt Madrid.[4]

My Cosin presents his humble service: this long Journey does not agree very well With his body, & I doubt the dreggs of his last sickness, have thorow his own fault been let alone too long, to leave him at an easy rate; he has at present a most terrible Cough, & having been let blood, we find it extraordinaryly Corrupted. Last week I wrot to my Mother, & I have formerly written to my Grand-mother; but next post I intend to re-iterate my Duty. Whilst I stay'd in Languedoc, I found sufficient Opportunitys of informing myself con- [f. 40v] cerning my Uncle's Quærys in Silke,[5] & when you shall think fitt, I will range them & send them you to Wilberton. The Head of our English Travellers here in Paris, is now my

---

[1] 'Materia Medica', i.e. the herbs, minerals, etc., used in medicine; more generally the study of pharmacology.

[2] Hammond is presumably referring here to Sir John Reynolds (1625–57), a soldier in the parliamentarian army who had taken part in the Irish campaigns. Between 1654 and 1646 he served as MP for various Irish seats and was knighted in 1655. He commanded the English forces sent to assist the French in Flanders in 1657 but drowned on the way back home to England.

[3] Henri de Lorraine, comte de Harcourt (1601–66) See letter 19 and p. 195, n. 10.

[4] Queen Christina's plot (supported by Mazarin) to seize Spanish controlled Naples and become its queen had collapsed by 1657. France was scandalized when, while staying at Fontainebleau, she summarily ordered the execu-tion of her equerry, Marchese Gian Rinaldo Monaldeschi, allegedly for betraying this plot to Rome. She refused to justify her actions to the French authorities, claiming it was within her rights as a queen, and thereby also alienated the patronage of Pope Alexander VII.

[5] * BL Add. MS 59785, f. 53^r: 'M^r: Edward Diggs'. Sericulture, the cultivation of silkworms, was popular in both France and Italy and interest had been high in England since the reign of King James I. See Thomas Moffet, *The Silkewormes and their Flies (1599)*, ed. V. Houliston, Medieval & Renaissance Texts & Studies, Binghamton, New York, 1989, p. xi, for James's support for a mulberry-tree planting campaign. Among the most popular publica-tions on the subject was Olivier de Serres, *The Perfect Use of Silk-wormes*, translated by N. Geffe (1607).

Lord S^t. John his son,[1] who is newly arriv'd with his Coach & 6 horses out of England: & indeed our English Court & Courtiers are highly priz'd in Paris; neither is there any Forreign Ambassador more esteem'd, than our Resident, to whose last Child the Cardinall has made himself Godfather.[2]

My Chymistry Lecture begins to call upon me. I humbly beg your Blessing, & if I light upon the Phylosopher's stone, 'twill be easier for me then to shew myself, Sir,

Paris January }   Your most Dutifull Child,
the 16. 1658. }   William Hammond. -

[25]

Most Honoured Mother,

The Sickly time you were pleas'd to mention in your last of the 28 of December has made me sad ever since; & there is nothing I long for more than another Lettre from Wilberton, to assure me that all is well there. In France all is so fickle, that the very Weather is asham'd to be Constant; last month 'twas so extreme cold that many poor people dyed of it in the streets, [f. 41^r] & Messengers dyed upon the road, blown thorow with the peircing wind: & now 'tis so very hot, that all are like to Choke with the misty soultry Air. I hope England is of a more constant temper, otherwise I fear 'twill be ill for my Sister's Quartan agues.[3] I am up to the head and ears in the study of Physick, & the first thing to be look't after at my returne to England must be a great house in London, whose bulke may be apparent enough, to save me the Labor of hanging out an Urinall from the Window. I know my Sisters will be glad to hear of that, since living there with me, they will be more in the eye of the World, & likelier to meet with husbands.

I am sorry to hear my Uncle Ned is retiring into his Indies:[4] I was in good hopes, that he wou'd have settled in our Fenns. But if he resolve to returne, I wish my Sisters have now & then a Silk-Gown from thence. You will please to pardon my Lightness; really 'tis now above two months since I heard from Wilberton; so that 'twere hard for me to write any thing pertinently, not being able to ghuess, in what condition this Lettre may find you at Wilberton. Here is no News, only that the Great Family

---

[1] The St John family were cousins of Oliver Cromwell. Sir Henry St John was elected to 1621 Parliament; and another cousin, Oliver St John (c. 1598–1671) was appointed Chief Justice of Common Pleas in 1647. He also served as a member of the Council of State in 1659–60 and left England in 1662. The St John family of Bletso were also Earls of Bolingbroke, from the time of the first Earl, Oliver Lord St John of Bletso (d. 1646). However, his grandson, Oliver St John (1634–88) had succeeded to the Bolingbroke earldom in 1646. The first traveller in this volume, Robert Montagu, travelled home to England in the company of this Oliver St John. See p. 69.

[2] William Lockhart (1620–75) was English Ambassador at Paris from 1656 until 1658.

[3] 'Quartan agues', a fever recurring every three or four days.

[4] * BL Add. MS 59785, f. 54^v: 'M^r: Edward Diggs'. Edward Digges (1621–75) was the son of Sir Dudley Digges, Master of the Rolls, and his wife Mary Kempe, of Chilham, Kent. After emigrating to North America he settled at Belfield on the York River in Virginia and developed a successful tobacco plantation. He was a Member of the Council of Virginia in 1654 and Governor from 31 March 1655 until 13 March 1657. From Hammond's letters, it appears that he had returned to England for a short visit in 1657/8 but had already determined to go back to his plantation where he was later renowned for his attempts to introduce sericulture. The ancient mulberry of Williamsburg was planted at his order. He served as Auditor General of the colony until his death in 1675. See also p. 155.

[f. 41ᵛ] of the Duke of d'Espernon is newly Extinct, Monsier de Candale being dead at Lyons.[1]

The Chief business of this Lettre, is only to present my Duty & humbly to begg your Blessing upon

Paris February ⎱
the 23. 1658 – ⎰

Your most Duti*full* Child,
William Hammond. –

I humbly present my Duty to my Father, & my Cosin his service to you, he is now Physicking, & gives me Opportunitys of Encreasing my knowledge in Physick.

[26]

Most Hon*oure*d Father,

Yesterday I had the good fortune to receive yours of January 25. The approbation you are pleas'd to give of my studying Chymistry, makes me fall more heartily to it, & tho' my braine be at present so stuff't with Chymical hard words, & strange figur'd Vessels, as I am fitter to mount, than to write a Lettre: yet rather than neglect my Duty, I'le venture the presenting it in Canting terms.[2] I can hardly keep myself from giving in a large[3] account of all those Animals, Vegetables, Mineralls & Mettalls, which so lately I saw Metamorphosed into their Waters, Spirits, Oyles, Balms, Salts, & Magisteres, &c: Really, Sir, [f. 42ʳ] of all men a Scholler is the truest subject, of whom it may be said; that out of the fullness of his heart, his Tongue speaks: The two years Travells, you have been pleas'd to bestow upon me, is not sufficient to Cure me of that Imperfection; & tho' my Notions have been sufficiently toss't & shaken both by the great horses in the Academys, as by the rugged thrusts in Fencing Schools; yet I find such a Resettlement of them, as I fear after all, will make me savour more of the Scholler than of the Genteel Traveller. However, I will endeavor to purge myself of that unsociable scent, & preserve no more of it, than what may become a well-bred Physician. The most remarkable affair of this Town is at present the unmeasurable Inundation of the River Seine; which swoll'n by the sudden Thaw of snow, rushing from the hills of Champain & Bourgogne, is come to Town with such a Violence, as yesternight it broke down one of the chiefest Bridges, which being built over with large & well-built houses, has kill'd many & ruin'd more; but the number of either is yet uncertain.[4] 'Tis above eight days, that a great Part of the Town has lain drown'd, people being forc't to use boats in the streets, instead of horses or Cooches: so that tho' by their stone- [f. 42ᵛ] built houses they have the Advantage of London, it not being so subject to Fires; yet at times

---

[1] Jean-Louis de Nogaret de la Valette, duc d'Épernon (1554–1642) had been a favourite and ruthless minister of King Henri III. Involved in numerous intrigues during the next reign, he was inconclusively implicated in the murder of Henri IV by François Ravaillac (who was in the pay of Épernon's mistress). He facilitated Marie de Médicis' regency for the infant Louis XIII but he was disgraced when the King came into full power in 1617. Richelieu deprived him of the governorship of Guienne in 1638 and he was exiled to Loches in 1641. Hammond is referring here to the death on 27 January 1658 at Lyons of Louis Charles Gaston de Foix, duc de la Valette et de Candale.

[2] 'canting terms', professional jargon or language.

[3] * BL Add. MS 59785, f. 55ᵛ: 'See Lettre [   ] page. [   ] where the Writer speaks of The Effects of the Frost on the Chymical Preparations'.

[4] The water level in the city of Paris is usually about 30 feet below street level but its situation, effectively in a geographical bowl hollowed out by the River Seine, renders the areas around the river highly vulnerable to flooding.

they receive more damage from their boisterous River, than ever London did from fire. But whilst the City at one side lyes thus overwhelm'd with waters; on the other side the King & Court are as full of Mirth, as their Carnivall & *th*eir last Summer's Prosperity require: and that *th*eir Pastimes may not want for noble spectators. The Queen of Sweden (who instead of going south-ward, laid hid at Fontainbleau) is newly arriv'd, who seems much to admire the K*in*g of France his Dancing, tho' the Machines of his Balletts come far short of what she saw in Italy.[1]

We hear the Protector[2] plays the Chymist with his Parliament, & turns it into as many shapes, as my Master does his Quicksilver.[3] His Embassador here, is at present in dispute both w*i*th Pope, & Cardinall[4] concerning my Lord Inchequin's son:[5] who being a young Papist, was last summer at his Father's return to the Warrs in Catalonia, committed to the Custody of an Irish Priest, Rector of one of the University's Colledges. My lady his Mother being a Protestant,[6] & desirous to convert her Son is her husband's absence, prevail'd so far upon his tutor, as to have the [f. 43ʳ] Liberty of fetching her son abroad Conditionally; that she wou'd restore him to his Colledge a'nights. But instead of performing that Condition, at length she carried him, & resign'd him up into our Embassador's Custody; where (the young man professing, that he was violently retain'd both in the Colledge, & in the Popish Religion) she thought him in the best Refuge this Town affords, not Considering that the Scripture supports all places in this World, lyable to be broken up by Thieves, & Consequently accessible unto the Irish.

And indeed by his Tutor's means, he was stolne away at length from our Embassador's doors, & immediately Convey'd to his Father in Catalonia. Upon which the Embassador demands satisfaction for the Affront done him; & the Cardinall in recompence promises him, that either the Child shall be restor'd him, or his Father banisht the Kingdome. My Lord Inchequin is now return'd to Paris, & instead of bringing his son with him, has left him in the Pope's Dominions at Avignon.[7] The dispute grows hotter upon it, & the Father is in great perplexity; sometimes pretending, that his son is violently retain'd from him by *th*e Pope; [f. 43ᵛ] sometimes resolving to quitt the Kingdome, & with it his Charge of 1500 Pistolls de'rent:[8] but the more moderate advise him to resign himself & son into the Cardinall's hands, Charging his Conscience with whatsoever may follow. I have need to

---

[1] See letter 9 and p. 174, n. 5, for Louis XIV's dancing skills. Following the collapse in 1657 of her wild scheme to seize the throne of Naples, Queen Christina was staying at Fontainebleau (see letters 7, 14, and 24).

[2] * BL Add. MS 59785, f. 56ᵛ: 'Oliver Cromwell'.

[3] The Parliaments of the Protectorate sat from (1) 3 September 1654 until 22 January 1655; (2) 20 January until 4 February 1658; and (3) from 27 January until 22 April 1659. Hammond is here referring to news arriving at Paris of the dissolution of Parliament on 4 February 1658.

[4] * BL Add. MS 59785, f. 57ʳ: 'Mazarin'. i.e. Pope Alexander VII and Cardinal Jules Mazarin (1602–61).

[5] Murrogh O'Brien (c. 1614–74), 1st Earl Inchiquin, had left Ireland for France in 1650. He was elevated to the earldom of Inchiquin on 21 October 1654. As Hammond notes, he served during the 1650s in the French army at Catalonia. He was a known Roman Catholic and his eldest son, William (c. 1640–92), later the second Earl, is presumably referred to here. William did indeed later revise his religious allegiance from his father's Catholicism, since in the 1680s he led the Munster Protestants against the Roman Catholics.

[6] Murrogh O'Brien married Elizabeth (d. 1685), daughter of William St Leger, Lord Protector of Munster.

[7] Avignon was purchased by Pope Clement VI from Queen Joanna of Naples (and Countess of Provence) in 1348 and remained in the possession of the papacy until the French Revolution. It became a recognized place of asylum, not only for persecuted Catholics but also for numerous other sorts of exiles, heretics, renegades, and criminals. The 'Avignon Papacy', when the popes were actually resident there, lasted from 1309 until 1377.

[8] 'de'rent', *de rente*, revenue or rent.

pray heartily, that you may not have heard this story before; For else I have Cramm'd my paper with a very tedious impertinencyes. Really, Sir, it is a Mastery over myself, that I can talk so long without interposing some Chymicall Notions; & I had a far great mind to have balk't that Relation, & enlarg'd upon what I know of that French Notary Flammell.[1] His Charitys are yet so visible here in Town, that none dare deny either the Person or his vast Expences, & so prove him a Chymist, he has left severall Hireglyphicks, surrounding his Picture in S[t.] Innocent's Church-yard:[2] yet my Master gives this account of him, that when the Jews were banisht Paris & France, he living at that time, out of the good will they bore him, was entrusted with that hidden Treasure, which they cou'd not either safely, or so speedily convey away; that in their absence resolving to spend their Mony, he took Chymistry for a Cloake, & pretended his Witt found that out by stills, of which his [f. 44ʳ] Knavery cosen'd the poor Jews: but 'tis the Vice of schollers to Calumniate one another.

Be pleas'd to pardon my delay in the silke account; it shall go hard but I'le send it in my next. My Aunt Stanly is coming to keep her Lent in Paris, & has a promise from my Lady Onion,[3] & my Cosin Tom,[4] to meet her next May in Diepe. I humbly present my Duty to my Mother, & begg your Blessings upon, Sir,

Paris March }   Your most Dutifull Child,
the 2. 1658. }   William Hammond. –

[27]

Most Honoured Father,

This week yours of the 22[d.] of February, came to Paris. Really, Sir, I am heartily asham'd to perceive, that my Lettres come so slowly to Wilberton; & I am afraid, the unfortunate stops & delays, they find in these terrible winter ways, may make me seem guilty of an Undutifull Neglect. I have hitherto never fail'd to write every other Saturday, & if these Floods Continue, & the Post do not mend his haste, I am resolv'd to present my Duty, by every Courrier that parts.

Now I venture to send in at length my accounts to my Uncle,[5] I doubt (if you take the pains to survey this Enclosd to him) you will say, that [f. 44ᵛ] I have manag'd my busyness very indiscreetly, & that (if I had foreseen myself incapable of giving in a larger & fuller answer to his Quærys) I shou'd have had the witt, to have done it in time, & not after so great a Crye to have yeilded so little Wool. Yet I hope, you'le please to Consider those great diversions, I had by reason of my dear Cosin's Infirmitys:[6] & for Excuse to the shortness of my answers. Really, Sir, when I weigh the Pithyness, & Artist-like Demands, my Uncle was pleased to send me; methinks the very Aire of them strikes pertinency in me, & makes me

---

[1] * BL Add. MS 59785, f. 58ʳ: 'Anecdote of Flammell the Chymist', i.e. Nicolas Flamel, the famous French alchemist, who had his laboratory at Avignon, was reputedly immensely rich, and made many benefactions there.

[2] The medieval Cimetière des Saints-Innocents, on the site of the present-day square and rue des Innocents, was the major cemetery of Paris until 1785 when the remains were exhumed and placed in the Catacombs.

[3] See p. 113, n. 3.

[4] This 'Cosin Tom' may have been either 'Cosin Bowyer' (see letter 5ff) or 'Cosin Dawson' (see letters, 2, 4, 5, 9ff) to whom Hammond habitually refers without a first name. The other cousin to whom he regularly refers, 'Cosin Richards' (letters 1 and 11), was called Gabriel.

[5] * BL Add. MS 59785, f. 59ʳ: 'Mʳ: Edward Diggs'.

[6] See letters 17–19.

know, that he, that cou'd put such Quærys, is far from standing in need of any Informations an unexperienc'd youth can send him; & that it was rather yours & his Goodness, to imploy me, more for the encreasing of my own knowledge, than his. And indeed before I cou'd be thorowly satisfy'd in the sence of his Quærys, I was forc't to run thorow the whole Body of that knowledge, & bestirr myself lustily, whilst I was in those southerne parts of France. Yet I have had but too much experience to teach me, that book knowledge & base Relations from men's mouths, breed a world[1] of wrong Conceptions, & apprehentions, which are far from jumping with Reall, & [f. 45ʳ] Ocular demonstrations: so that in speaking to a man of my Uncle's Experience, I shall commit fewest faults in my brevity & keeping home to his Questions: & towards the Justifying that 'twas not my Ignorance, but Choice that made me short, be pleas'd to pardon me, if I insist the whole List of my knowledge in that kind.[2]

Not to Pedantize in disputing with the Poetts, whether 'twas Venus, that first invented silke from the Worm-seeds, old Saturn presented her: Or with Pliny, whether 'twas the Daughter of Plato:[3] neither minding Pausanias, or Strabo.[4] But to be more pertinent; Certain it is, that a Syrian was the first that brought it into Italy, & that in the time of the emperors, Justinian, & Heliogabalus:[5] bearing its Latine name serica, from its Country Syria.[6] And tho' schollers make nice disputes; whether this Worm, like others be bred from Putrefaction, or was created in the beginning in its distinct species;[7] Whether it be a living Creature, as well in the seed, as in being a Worm or Flye; & lastly, whether its silke be only its Foame or Spittle. Yet the most usefull knowledge is, that the best Worm-seed is now to be had either in Spain or Italy, & of Italy at the Faire of Nocera besides Naples.[8] That towards the pro- [f. 45ᵛ] ducing silke, when the white Mulberry begins to put out his first & tenderest leaves, they hatch the seed some 5 or 6 days after the New Moon, by folding it into severall parcells in white woolen Cloth, &

---

[1] 'of' deleted.

[2] * BL Add. MS 59785, f. 60ʳ: 'The Writer in this Letter gives on Ingenious Account of the Silk-Worm'.

[3] See letter 24 for Hammond's earlier concern for his uncle's interest in silk production. The two major classical accounts known at this period were from Aristotle's *Historia animalium* (5.97.6), which describes the life cycle of the wild silk moth of Cos in the eastern Agean; and from Pliny's *Naturalis historia* (11.76) which developed Aristotle's account of an Assyrian wild silkmoth. The reference to 'Plato's daughter' is an error – Pliny in fact ascribed the invention to 'Pamphile, a woman of Cos, the daughter of Platea'. Sericulture, utilizing the eggs of the domesticated Chinese silkworm and the white mulberry, was only introduced into the Mediterranean during the mid-6th century. See *The Oxford Classical Dictionary*, 3rd edn, ed. Simon Hornblower and Antony Spawforth, Oxford and New York, 1996, p. 1407.

[4] 'Pausanias', a reference to the most accurate ancient source on China, silk and silkworms: Pausanias, *Description of Greece*, 6.XVI.6–8 (of which there were many Latin editions from 1500 onwards); Strabo's *Geographia* mentions silk at XV.1.20. Hammond may have been familiar with it through the monumental critical edition by Isaac Casaubon (1587; rpt. 1620).

[5] The Eastern Roman Emperor Justinian (AD 527–65) who, according to the Byzantine historian Procopius (*The Gothic War*, IV.17), is supposed to have sent agents to bring silkworms from China, and the Emperor Heliogabalus (AD 218–22) who is reputed to have dressed only in silk. Hammond, as he wrote, had either forgotten or was unaware of the wide chronological disparity in the dates of these two emperors.

[6] In fact, the Latin word *seres* (derived from the Greek) referred to the people of eastern Asia from the area of modern China, renowned for their silken fabrics. *Sericus* = Chinese; *serica* = silken garments. This derivation from Syria seems to be Hammond's own invention, but is a quite plausible popular etymology (*syricus* = Syrian) in view of Syria's position on the Silk Route, and its own fame as a producer of silk fabrics (Pliny mentions Assyrian silk see n. 3 above).

[7] * BL Add. MS 59785, f. 50ᵛ: 'Moses in his History of the Creation [Genesis 4:24(?)] says God Created "Creeping Things" & 4. 25ᵗʰ says "every Creeping thing"'.

[8] From Naples, Nocera (Inferiore) lies on the other side of Vesuvius, on the road to Salerno.

putting them either under *their* Arm-pitts, or into young women's breasts; either of w*hic*h by its Fomenting heat makes the little seeds sprout out into a little black & hairy Maggot: & sometimes it is done by putting them betwixt two Pillows, & laying the pillows by the fire side.

That the first Care of these little Maggots must be, to put them on a smoth & Lukewarm Table, well spred with young white Mulberry leaves, & to nourish them for nine or ten days, about which time they take their first sleep: & in Case here be no Mulberry leaves to be got, they will eat the[1] Leaves of Nettles, Elmes, Lettuces, or Oaks. This their first sleep lasts for some 3 or 4 days, wherein they eat nothing at all: the Italians call it a brown sleep, dormire bruna, & the Gascons la premiere müe.[2] When they wake, they eat for 9 or 10 days more, & fall asleep again, as at first, call'd dormire bianca; là seconde müe: afterwards waking, they eat another 8 days, call'd la Troisième müe: then waking they feed 8 days more, & fall asleep, dormire grossa, [f. 46ʳ] là quatriéme müe; after which, waking they eat like so many little Divells for the space of 8 days, neither sleep they any more, but Encease in bigness. 'Tis now the severall Colours of their bellys, foreshow what Colour'd silk, they will yeild. The Golden belly makes the Yellow silk, & the silver'd makes the White: & after this last terme they eat no more. Their Experienc'd Governour removes them from their table, putting them to climb the branches of Oake,[3] or Chessnut, &c. The Industrious Worm in climbing plays the Spider, & in the space of two days makes a shift to hide himself in his silken bagg, which the French call Coucons, or Pelletons:[4] wherein if they be let alone, in 15 days they will eat their way, & come out a Butter-flye: which Butter-flyes engender & produce the seed. Those Coucons, that are intended to make silk, after having kill'd the Worms within them, are at leisure unravell'd by putting them into a Tubb of hot water,[5] & w*hic*h an Industrious hand making 8 or 10 of those Coucons goe to a Thread, which is wound off upon a Wheel of some five foot Diameter. The Coucons being so reduc't upon this Wheel, are said to be brought into Flakes of silke,[6] which like Flax is sold in Marketts, & by *the* Mills is reduc't into [f. 46ᵛ] Threads. The silk-mills[7] are so common, that 'tis hardly worth while to describe them. The best in France is newly set upon in Lyon:[8] where an Ingenious Marchant (having transplanted seven or eight poor Familys of Bolognia, & with them their Silk Inventions) in a roome of some 78 Foot has erected so ingenious a Manufacture; that at one sight, one may there find in a Rationall method, the whole series of bringing the Flakes of the Coucon to weavable threads. His building is divided into three stories of height; the two lowermost contain nothing extraordinary, being only an addition to *the* simple Mills one over another, for by the help of 9 Cylinders (four on one side of the

---

[1] * BL Add. MS 59785, f. 61ʳ: 'Spectacle de la Nature Translated by Mʳ: Humphreys being universally allowed to be as fine a thing as ever was wrote – I shall therefore here & there intersperce such Remarks as shall arise upon this Subject. The Edition I shall quote from, is that of 1739, Vol .I. page. 39. 40. 41. 42. 43. 44. 45. 46. 47. 48.'.

[2] i.e. the first moulting, or shedding of a skin.

[3] * BL Add. MS 59785, f. 61ᵛ: 'Spectacle de La Nature. vol. 1. pa: 40. Dialogue .3.'.

[4] 'Coucons', cocoons.

[5] * BL Add. MS 59785, f. 61ᵛ: 'Spectacle de La Nature. vol. 1. pa: 49'.

[6] * BL Add. MS 59785, f. 61ᵛ: 'Spectacle de La Nature. vol. 1. pa: 49'.

[7] * BL Add. MS 59785, f. 62ʳ: 'Silk Mills'.

[8] The manufacture of silk at Lyons had been originally introduced from Italy, certainly by the mid-fifteenth century. The modern-day Musée Historique des Tissus (founded 1856 and inaugurated in 1951 in the Hôtel de Villeroy on the rue de la Charité) at Lyons traces the history of its silk manufacture.

roome, & five on to'ther) he has plac't together 46 ordinary Mills;[1] four Cylinders containing each of them four Mills one above another & the other five each of them six. The singularity of his Work-house lyes chiefly in his third story or Garret, where by the motion of those nine Cylinders, his Flakes are wound off from their first wheels upon as many spindles, it will supply his 46 Mills, allowing 120 spindles to each Mill. Really, Sir, 'twas a pleasant sight, to have my Eyes & Ears so filld with the [f. 47ʳ] Industry of man, as they were in that roome. I may well say, that (including wheels, spindles, & Reels) there was above Twenty Thousand Motions[2] at the same time, & that done by the going round of nine men only, (each Cylinder having a man to drive it round). 'Tis true, there were others to prepare the Flakes for their first wheel; & little Children employ'd in the Garret, to knit knots in chance an End of the silke shou'd faile, or a thread break. They told us, that they were in all 140 Persons, the work requiring such a number, which was not much; Considering they work off, nigh upon Forty Thousands Pounds of silke every year.

I am afraid to add any more Particulars in this subject: methinks, it has already taken up too much of my Paper. Only be pleas'd to let me say, that if I have not spoke to any particular points, you have formerly demanded of me, you'le please to impute it to the losing of one of your last summer's Lettres, which being sent to Lyon after my Removall, I cou'd never recover. I suppose that its subject was about Henry the 4th Edict of Silke, Which I translated from du Serres,[3] & sent to Wilberton, but have never since heard so much, as whether 'twas receiv'd nor not.

[f. 47ᵛ] I am sorry, that Jonas Moor[4] shou'd be so mistaken, as to think that after two years laying aside Mathematicks, I shou'd be a fitt Person to receive his intricate Problemes. Howsoever, since you were pleas'd to recommend it, I have since presented it to Sʳ Kenelme Digby,[5] & he has done me the Favour to disperse it since amongst the great Mathematiciens of France; so that Jonas need not doubt, but to receive the honour, that's due to him abroad,

[1] * BL Add. MS 59785, f. 62ʳ, leaves two lines blank at this point, noting: 'I think proper to observe to the Reader that this space in pa: & was not that the Original was defective but occassion'd by an accident in the paper to the Annotator'. This ambiguous comment may indicate that their was either a space in the manuscript from which the transcriber of BL Add. MS 59785 was copying or that there was some fault in the compilation of BL Add. MS 59785. Brotherton MS Trv.2 has no space at this point in letter 27.

[2] * BL Add. MS 59785, f. 62ᵛ: 'If the writer had Lived to see the Surpriseing Silk Mill, created by Sir Thomas Lombe K? (& alderman of London & Sheriff 1722) in the Seventeenth Century, he wou'd not have been surprised, at this at Paris; & as I have here, an opportunity of Communicating the whole apparatus, of that at Derby, I shall here, added it, as a very valuable Remark, at the same time observeing, this, was not generaly known, to ev'ry one; & was communicated, to me, by his Widow, my First Cousin. If I swell the Note, too Longe, Believe me, Reader, it is done entirely to please you, & entertain you, &, in order, to prevent so extrodinary, an occurence, to Dye with me, which wou'd have been a Great Fault'. The transcriber is referring here to Sir Thomas Lombe (1685–1739), who introduced silk-throwing machinery into England and in 1718 patented it as his new invention. He served as sheriff of London and was knighted in 1727. His half-brother, John Lombe (c. 1693–1722) was sent to Italy to familiarize himself with the silk-throwing process but was rumoured to have been poisoned by jealous Italian workmen.

[3] Hammond's source here is probably is Olivier de Serres, either from the original French, La Cueillete de la soye, par la nourriture des vers (Paris, 1599), usually bound with his Le Théâtre d'agriculture, or from the English translation by N. Geffe as The Perfect Use of Silk-Worms (1607).

[4] Sir Jonas Moore (1617–79), a distinguished mathematician whose Arithmetick was published in 1650, had been mathematical tutor to the Duke of York during the late 1640s. He was clearly intimate with the Hammond family, perhaps through some local connection since he compiled a major survey of the Fen drainage system in 1649. After the Restoration, he was knighted and appointed Surveyor-General of the Ordnance in 1663.

[5] See letter 14 for Sir Kenelm Digby.

as well as at home. Sr Kenelme bids me insert his hu*m*ble service to you; really Sir, methinks his old Age finds not that Reception in the World, as a man of his Parts & Learning might have promis'd himself: yet no wonder, if blind fortune mistake & preferr rather those, that Croud next her, than those that are Worthy it. Our Lent affords us very little Variety here in Paris; & a Dutifull Respect forbids my writing ordinary & flying reports, In which I am usually anticipated or Convinc't of Falshood. My Lord Inchequin has his Charge taken from him,[1] & last week, the Protector's[2] kinsman, young Mr Whaly, & Mr Desbrough[3] were like to have been stolne by Irish Officers, but by good fortune they escapt, & the Thieves lye now in the Bastile for [f. 48^r] it. Dr Holden returns his humble service & my Cosin begins to thinke rather, of presenting you his Duty, than his service: be pleas'd to pardon my Tædiousness, & I humbly beg your Blessing upon, Sir,

Paris March ⎫
the 23. 1658. ⎰

Your most Dut*ifull* Child -
William Hammond

I have chosen rather to keep my Uncle's Quærys by me, as a Monument, to be Glory'd of, when Virginia flourishes in silke, than to returne them back agen.

[28]

Most Hon*oure*d Father,
I receiv'd yours of the 15 of March, on *th*e fourth of this present Aprill. I cannot express the Joye it gave me, in telling me of a New-born Brother. I need not say, 'twas unexpected to me, since I did sufficiently discover it in my last to my Mother, where I had the Confidence to Congratulate her safe Delivery of a Daughter. I hope she'll please to Conclude from thence, that whatsoever study I follow, I shall never have Craft enough to be a Conjurer. Really, Sir, methinks the Addition of another Brother adds life to my Industry, & I bestirr myself with a great deal more heartiness, since I see myself seconded by three Brothers, that may joyntly help to the upholding our [f. 48^v] Family.[4] The Country, I now live in, affords Examples enough to fortify my Resolutions for a Profession & the French are so generally Enemys to sloth & Idleness, that both their Gentry & Commonalty count it a disgrace to be destitute either of Offices or a Profession; indeed they have *th*e Advantage over us, in that they can provide for, & Enrich their Children by Church-benefices, when they find them, not like to raise their fortune by any other means. There is hardly a day passes, but I hear some Lecture or other in their Colledges; & tho' I have not books about me, yet I find that the Advantage

---

[1] See letter 26 for Lord Inchiquin's troublesome son.

[2] * BL Add. MS 59785, f. 66^r: 'Oliver Cromwell'.

[3] These references are to the sons of Edward Whalley (d. c. 1677) and John Desborough (1608–80). Whalley had served with distinction as a lieutenant-colonel in Cromwell's horse and in 1648 was a custodian of Charles I at Hampton Court. He sat as a judge and was a signatory of the king's death-warrant. By the mid-1650s he held the rank of major-general over the Midland District and sat in Cromwell's two Parliaments. He escaped to New England in 1660. Desborough served as a major-general in command of Cromwell's horse at the storming of Bristol (1645) and also fought at the Battle of Worcester (1651). He was appointed General of the Fleet in 1653 and sat in Cromwell's Parliaments. He was a strong opponent to Richard Cromwell's succession in 1659. Although he became implicated in a plot to assassinate Charles II and his mother, Henrietta Maria, and was imprisoned in 1660 (and again in 1666 for intrigues in Holland) he was released in 1667.

[4] See letter 13 for Hammond's brothers.

of hearing & frequenting Professors, is Equivalent to them. I hope, you will be pleas'd to pardon me, that I make this kind of talke the ordinary subject of my Lettres. Really, Sir, 'tis almost Impossible for a student to Cultivate himself, & his Actions, whilst his mind is thirsting after Learning, & we have *th*is disadvantage, under men of Parts that never studyed, *th*at whilst we rove after Exterior Notions & things, *th*at are without us, they have the Opportunity of studying themselves, & become Doctors in that most pertinent knowledge of Nosce Teipsum.[1] We every day expect, when *th*e King [f. 49ʳ] shou'd put himself into the Campaine, & the Report is generall, that Hesdin[2] is now at length totally resign'd into the Spaniards hands, by which they will not only recompence their last summer's Losse of Montmedy,[3] but may very probably divert this Crown's designs, in joyning with the Protector[4] towards the Siege of Dunkirke.[5] The Monks in Flanders do much apprehend the Progress of our English; & I thinke they have joyntly lay'd their heads towards the Penning of a Remonstrance, directed to the King of France; wherein after much blaming the Cardinall,[6] they at length fall upon our Protector, & intending to raile at him, they speak much to his advantage: amongst the rest, they plead *th*at Historys can witness France has formerly been too hard for England, in six hundred severall Treatys. And that now at length they are overreach't in this last Treaty betwixt the Protector & Cardinall. But I am asham'd to go on in hear-says; & cannot but thinke it more decent for me, to end in humbly begging *you*r Blessing upon, sir,

Paris Aprill }
the 6. 1658. }

Your most Dutifull Child,
William Hammond. –

I humbly present my Duty to my Mother, Bro*ther* & Sisters, &c: my Aunt Stanly will not come to Paris, till nex[t] summer.

---

[1] Hammond is probably referring here to Sir John Davies's famous philosophical poem, *Nosce Teipsum. This Oracle Expounded in Two Elegies* (1599) and reprinted in his 1622 collected works. The poem comprised two parts: (1) 'Of Human Knowledge' and (2) 'Of the Soul of Man and the Immortality Thereof'. *Nosce Teipsum* was written while Davies himself was a law student, and is preoccupied with a search for the meaning of (and direction in) life. Its sentiments would have been especially appealing to a young man such as Hammond sent abroad in search of a profession, not least the lines:

> Why did my parents send me to the schools
> That I with knowledge might enrich my mind?
> Since the desire to know first made men fools,
> And did corrupt the root of all mankind.

[2] * BL Add. MS 59785, f. 67ᵛ: 'a Toun of the French Netherlands 20 Miles S: W: of Sᵗ: Omer's [Salmon's Modern Gazetteer]'. The 16th-century town of Hesdin, situated midway between St-Omer and Abbeville, had been refounded in 1554 by Charles V, after the entire destruction of the earlier town.

[3] See letter 15.

[4] * BL Add. MS 59785, f. 67ʳ: 'Oliver Cromwell'.

[5] * BL Add. MS 59785, f. 67ʳ: 'This Town being taken from the Spaniards by the united Forces of England & France, was put into the hands of the English, anno 1658, but was sold to France in the Reign of King Charles to 2ᵈ but at the Treaty of Utrecht 1703 Great Britain insisted upon the Harbour & Fortifications being demolish'd which was done accordingly [Salmon's Modern Gazetteer] *and added below* 'Sir William Temple's Memoirs'. Dunkirk was captured in 1658 by the Marshal de Turenne (1611–75) after the Battle of the Dunes. It was then ceded to Cromwell as a reward for assisting the French victors. See also letter 15.

[6] * BL Add. MS 59785, f. 68ʳ: 'Mazareen'.

[29]

[f. 49ᵛ] Most Honoured Father,

I wish I cou'd express, how sensible I am of your Goodness, in being pleas'd to send me so quick an answer to my last of October the 28:[1] by which I am very much joyed to hear of so good a Government, settled in our Fenns; I hope the like Prosperity may attend it, as has for many years accompanied Rumney Marsh.[2] And since you have been pleased to procure my Land to be erected into a Seigniory; the first part of my Profession must be thorowly to understand the Laws of Sewers.[3] But the losse of my books were enough to deterr me from all Future bookishness; for to speak it without any pride, I do verily believe that none of my age, had made a better Collection of authors, it being usually my Custome never to buy any book, without the commendation of those, that were Masters in the subject, of which it treated. Thus my Physick-books came from the directions of Dʳ Scarbrough,[4] & other able Physicians: my Mathematique books had undergone the test of Dʳ Wards,[5] Mʳ Rook's,[6] & Mʳ Wren's Judgements;[7] My Morality & Civil Law-books, from the Note, Dʳ Hammond was pleas'd to leave my Uncle [f. 50ʳ] William;[8] & for my History, besides those Considerable books that came from your study, I had made a Collection of many others, that you had been pleas'd to give some Commendations: & in all, I am much deceiv'd, if by the help of my Catalogue I cou'd not sufficiently prove, that they cost me above Threescore Pounds sterling: most of them coming from the shop of Davis in Oxford, & Martin at the

[1] Hammond's reference to his last letter of 'October the 28' is confusing since the previous surviving letter in this sequence is dated 6 April 1658. Either the transcriber has made a slip or this is a reference to a now lost letter sent 28 October 1657.

[2] Romney Marsh borders the English Channel, from Hythe in the north to the Dungeness promontory in the south.

[3] Hammond's apparently light-hearted meaning is not clear here, although his words imply that his father had allocated some lands in the Fens to him, which would now necessitate him gaining some expertise in drainage systems.

[4] * BL Add. MS 59785, f. 69ʳ: 'Dʳ: Charles Scarborough' [Birch's Life of Greaves, pa: LVIIJ'. The noted physician, Sir Charles Scarburgh (1616–94), had studied at both Cambridge and Oxford during the 1640s (taking an MD from Merton College in 1646) and became a Fellow of the Royal College of Physicians in 1650. He was later appointed personal physician to Charles II, and James II, and Queen Mary. He was knighted in 1669.

[5] * BL Add. MS 59785, f. 69ᵛ: 'Dʳ: Seth Ward afterwards Bishop of Salisbury. [Ward's Lives of Gresham Professors 92. 93. 113. 115. 145. Birch's Life of John Greaves: pa: XXX. XXXI. XXXII'. See letter 4 for Seth Ward (1617–89).

[6]* BL Add. MS 59785, f. 69ᵛ: 'Ward's Lives of Gresham Professors. pa: 90. 91. 92. 93. 94. 137. 156. Birch's Life of John Greaves'. See letter 4 for Lawrence Rooke (1622–62).

[7] * BL Add. MS 59785, f. 69ᵛ: 'afterwards Sir Christopher. Wards Lives. 95. 96. 97. 98. 102. 103. 104. 105. 106. 107. 110. 337. Please to see the next page's notes'. The architect of post-Restoration London, Sir Christopher Wren (1632–1723), took his MA from Wadham College, Oxford, in 1653 and was then a fellow of All Souls College, Oxford, from 1653 until 1661. He was appointed Professor of Astronomy at Gresham College, London, in 1657.

[8] * BL Add. MS 59785, f. 70ʳ: ' Dʳ. Hammond the Celebrated Annotator on the New Testament. See Dean Fell's Life of Dʳ. Hammond'. The formality of Hammond's specific reference here to a 'Dʳ Hammond', alongside the more intimate designation of 'my Uncle William', may imply that the former was not a relative, while the latter is clearly his uncle, William (1614–c. 1655), the third son of Sir William Hammond (d. 1615) of St Alban's Court (our letter-writer's grandfather). This uncle William was a close friend of the poet Thomas Stanley. See pp. 149–52. The first reference to a 'Dʳ Hammond' may indicate Henry Hammond (1605–80), formerly incumbent in the 1630s to the Sidney family, Earls of Leicester, at Penshurst Place, near Tonbridge in Kent and then in 1645 personal chaplain to Charles I. Although he was deprived of his living and imprisoned following the execution of the king, he later lived with Sir Philip Warwick (1609–83) and Sir John Pakington (1620–80). See pp. 156–7.

Bell in Pauls-Churchyard,[1] who (I am Confident) wou'd not have scrupled to have valued or given me Forty Pounds back again for them.

For the repeated Catalogue, I had some books double, but cannot positively say, that they were those contain'd in the scrowle[2] you mention; Especially if Sᵣ Walter Raleigh[3] be amon[g]st them, whom with the Turkish History,[4] & my Collection of our English history, as Herbert's Henry 8ᵗʰ. Cambden's Queen Elizabeth & all Sᵣ Francis Bacon's[95] works[6] &c: I left out in my study for my Brother's reading, putting them into a particular Catalogue. I humbly desire, you'le please to remember my love of Mathematicall instruments, to the value of above three pound, together with many Considerable Maps & Cutts. I am loth to come [f. 50ᵛ] to my greatest loss, which was my papers (if the Fellow had so little mercy, as to rob me of that, which cou'd no ways profit him) amongst which (besides the Legacy of my dying friend at Oxford, who left me all his seven years' Industrious Collections) these were MSS of Dᵣ Ward's, Dᵣ Scarbrough's, with many worthy Memorandums of Mᵣ Wren's, & Mᵣ Rook's: but I hope, the knave has spar'd me these, which otherwise I cou'd not value at too high a rate. For my books if he allow me but forty pound, I must endeavour to make the best of my Losse, which I cannot but look as an rightly applyd Punishment, for my too slow obedience in settling to a Profession according to your Commands. I hope, you'le please to pardon the unsettledness of my younger days, & believe that the more I disperse the thick Clouds of my unexperienc'd mind, the deeper Impressions your Fatherly Tenderness strikes into me: & after Travell has but lac'd a settled Foundation for the Operations of my mind, I vow a sacred Obedience to whatsoever Employment you shall please to put me upon.

[f. 51ʳ] My Cosin presents his humble service to you; we are now settled in our winter Pensions, having chosen a Lodging pleasant & healthy, by reason of the good Air, it looks into. The only fault is, its dearness being after the rate of 50 Pistolls a year; howsoever I make no Question, but to keep within your allowance of an 100. Pound, & learn all Exercises that my Cosin does; only I am afraid my Purse will hardly let me ride so long as he, unless I encroach upon the mony coming to me for the loss of my books. On Saturday last Mᵣ Skinner sent me his Lettre of Credit to Wildigo's, upon which I took up 661 Livres for the value of fifty Pound sterling to be repaid him[7] in London; the rate of the Exchange is by that account 54 ½ or 32 & 2 Livres in the hundred: my Cosin had Ashurst's Bill from London for the same summe, & had but after the rate of 55 ¾, which is less than 30 in the hundred: so that I cannot think my loss was much by returning it from Dover. Yet for the future, if you will please to let my Cosin Dawson[8] lye upon the snap for a good Exchange, it may be my fortune to get after the rate of

[1] Richard Davis traded (1646–88) as a bookseller in Oxford from his shop near Oriel College. He mainly sold classical, scientific, and religious works. John Martin (or Martyn) traded (1649–80) from the 'Bell' in St Paul's Churchyard, London. He formed a partnership with James Allesty and succeeded him as publisher to the Royal Society.

[2] Scroll, presumably used as a personal library catalogue.

[3] * BL Add. MS 59785, f. 70ʳ: 'History of The World and incomparable book'.

[4] * BL Add. MS 59785, f. 70ʳ: 'Sir Paul Ricaut's History of the Turks'.

[5] * BL Add. MS 59785, f. 70ʳ: 'Lord Verulam. who wrote the Life of Henry VII'.

[6] The books mentioned here were probably editions (the first edition of each is cited here) of Sir Walter Raleigh, *The History of the World* (1614); Michel Baudier, *The History of the Imperial Estate of the Grand Seigneurs*, tr. from French by E. Grimeston (1635); Edward Herbert, first Baron Herbert of Cherbury, *The Life and Reign of Henry VIII* (1649), begun in 1632 and modelled upon Bacon's *Henry VII*; William Camden, *Annals. The True and Royal History of Elizabeth Queen of England* (1625); and Sir Francis Bacon, Viscount St Albans, either his *Opera ... tomus primus* (1624), or *Francisci Baconi ... operum moralium et civilium tomus* (1638).

[7] 'him' deleted.

[8] See letter 1 for Mr Skinner and Wildigo and letter 2 for Hammond's cousin Dawson.

40 Pence to the French Crown, which is 150 Pistolls for an hundred pound sterling. I humbly begg [f. 51ᵛ] your pardon, in that I took up so great a summe at once, & please to Consider, that at this my first setting in Pension, to my Exercises, and in Clothing myself, I may have more occasions for mony, than hereafter I shall have. I have now receiv'd in all 10 Pound in London from my Cosin Dawson at my parting, 20 pounds afterwards of my Cosin Gabriell Richards,[1] & now this 50 pound sterling, which comes to 80 Pounds; the other 20 pounds will come time enough in February next, my year beginning again on the 25 of March following. I am very sorry to be so large in my mony storys, knowing wel, how hardly it comes from Wilberton, and how much it behoves me to be Thrifty.

We have here but little News, only that Valence is retaken by the Spaniard,[2] & we see the Regiments dayly marching out of this Towne, towards Poictou, Zaington, & Aunis,[3] to force them to pay their Gabell of salt, which they have so many years escapt, by *the* great summe, they formerly paid to Henry *the* 2ᵈ·. But my paper putt me in mind of an end; I therefore humbly begg your Blessing upon

Paris Aprill
the 18. 1658. }   Sir, Your most Dut*ifull* Child
                                                      William Hammond.

[30]

[f. 52ʳ] Most Hon*oure*d Father,

On the 30ᵗʰ· of Aprill I set out from Paris, & upon the 8ᵗʰ· of this present, I arriv'd (God be thanked) safe & sound to Lyon. The Company, I came with, were all French, who upon a rode are the merryest & most divertizing People in *the* World. Really, Sir, these nine days' Journey, that I have made amongst them has weaned me from all desires of meeting with any of my Country-men; they are usually either too Phlegmatick, or too Melancholy, to add joye to so long & tædious a Voyage. Providence has very seasonably put this Opinion into me, for since my coming to Lyon, I learn that all my Companions are already got into Italy; so that, like the Huntsman, I am forc't to Conclude, they are drye meat. I look upon this year, as one of the most Fortunate of my Life; the very first day of it, I had the good fortune to bring my dearest Cosin into Paris safe & recover'd from that most desperate Small-pox, which was within a hair's bredth of killing him at Nismes:[4] and since I have been enrich'd by the addition of another Brother into our Family; & to encrease my good fortune, you are pleas'd to bestow a year's Travell upon me into Italy.

[f. 52ᵛ] If beginnings be any thing Ominous unto what may follow; I hope this year may some ways answer my Expectations. The very first day that I left Paris, I found that one of our Company was a French Colonell & a Protestant, who with a Companion, & his two Valets de' Chambre, is returning to his Regiment, that's Quarter'd upon the borders of the Venetian State:[5] *the* Gentleman is particularly Civill to me, & professt me the Convenience

---

[1] See letter 1 for this cousin Gabriel Richards.

[2] Valence.

[3] Enforcing the salt tax in the regions of Poitou-Charentes, Saintonge (now Charentes-Maritimes), and Aunis (now Deux-Sèvres).

[4] See letter 17.

[5] French military presence in this area dated back to the renewal of the Franco-Spanish war in Italy during the War of the Mantuan succession (1629–31), in which the French-backed candidate, Charles Gonzaga, Duke of Nevers, was ultimately successful. By the time of the Peace of Westphalia (1648) the Venetian Republic was bounded on the French side by lands under the jurisdiction of the County of Tyrol and the Bishopric of Trent.

213

of passing with him in to Italy. Being arriv'd here at Lyons, I find that he is a Person of no small Quality, and that thorow his Courtesy, I am engag'd into the Company of most of the French Nobility, who are just now going down from hence to Tholone in Provence,[1] there to embarque themselves for Leghorn, from whence they'le cross over into the State of Mantoua, where under the Conduct of Mons*ieu*r de' Modene, & Lieutenancy of Mons*ieu*r de' Navaille, they intend this Campaine, to assault the Eastern Part of the Dutchy of Milan. I will take the Opportunity of accompanying them as far as Leghorn; & there (God willing) I will resolve of what's to come. Really, Sir, I am afraid Heaven has a design to make me change [f. 53ʳ] my Profession: Instead of meeting with my intended Caravan of Physicians, I am her lighted amongst the French Officers, who being pleas'd with the little smattering knowledge they find in me concerning the Art of War, seem to entice me into their Compaigne: but I believe Phoebus[2] will read me another Lecture, before I gett to Leghorn. There is nothing I more admire, *than* the Indefatigability of the French Gentry: they make nothing of running Post from Paris to Lyons, & from thence immediately to take horse for 18 or 20 days, to pass over the horrid Mountains of the Grisons, & Valtoline[3] to Bressia & Mantoua;[4] where instead of refreshing themselves, they undergo the hardships of a following Compaine, which is usually the besieging of some Town or another.

I tell them, that the Life of an English Noble-man is much easier, than theirs. If any of us, once in our lives, chance to run Poste from London to Edinborough, 'tis an Act fitt to be recited by our Children's Children: whereas this very Colonell, I am now with, about a month since came from Bressia to Lyon, from thence immediately took Post to Paris, & is now return'd on horse-back with me to Lyon: from [f. 53ᵛ] whence his Companion (that was all this time in the same Journeys with him) is this very day parted on horse-back to repass the Alps to Bressia. And tho' I instance only him, 'tis every day seen, that the like toyle is undergone by their Barons, Counts, Dukes, & Pairs de' France.[5] 'Tis Custome from their Childhood, that gives them so strong bodys; & since the most part of my time has been spent in Exercises, rather of the mind, than of the body; I shall be much asham'd of myself, till I find I can doe as much in Study & Contemplative things, as they do in bodily Toyles. As soon as I get to Padua, I am resolv'd to ride Post, & mount the Alps in the Study of Physick; after which I'le think it but a pleasure to spend my Campaine in *the* Practise & Cure of Diseases; & it may be, shall do more Execution, & kill more than *the* great Warrior of them all. Be pleas'd to pardon these Impertinencys, & I will end in humbly begging your Blessing upon, Sir,

Lyon May
the 10. 1658. }

Your most Dut*ifull* Child,
William Hammond –

I humbly present my Duty to my Mother, & my love to my Brothers, & Sisters, &c.

---

[1] Toulon, where Henri IV had founded a naval arsenal.

[2] This word has been added in the left-hand margin and in the Brotherton MS only the letters ' …bus' are visible due to the binding. But the word is clearly transcribed as 'Phoebus' in BL Add. MS 59785.

[3] The Alpine canton of the Grisons (Graubünden) is the largest and most easterly in Switzerland and named after the Grauerbund (Gray League) founded in 1395. The Valtellina (Veltlin), situated in the upper valley of the Adda River down to its entry into Lake Como, was disputed by Milan and the Graubünden until it was acquired by the latter in 1639.

[4] Brescia and Mantua.

[5] Presumably 'pères' (fathers, priests) of France.

[31]

[f. 54ʳ] Most Honoured Mother,

In the Second of the Month, I sent away a Packet for Wilberton, & on the 7ᵗʰ· following, it was my good fortune to receive yours of the 14ᵗʰ· of July. Amongst all the various Objects, this Travelling life presents me, there is none more wellcome to my Eyes, than your Lettres from Wilberton: & whatsoever motions of this or other Crowns, my neighbouring Jesuits acquaint me with, my Curiosity is trulyer satisfyed in the relation of the health & well-fare of your Family, & the Settled Government and Fertility of the Fenns. I am therefore more Concern'd in that intended way of Governing our three Levells after the manner of Rumney-Marsh, than either in the Pope's Quarrell, when about a month since besieged by the Spaniards in his Country Castle; or in the Mareshal of Turenn's Cause, who was lately arrested upon suspicion of holding Correspondence with the Prince of Conde, when he gave so great a blow to the French before Valenciennes to the loss of 6000 Persons.[1] 'Tis as pleasing news to me, that the Fenns are this year like to get some reputation by relieving their neighbouring Countrys, as to hear the old Queen [f. 54ᵛ] of Sweden applauded for her hearty Negotiating a Generall Peace, for which purpose she has lain all this Summer in Avignion, & from thence is now coming to Orleans, there to be receiv'd by the Duke of Guise. I am very sorry to hear, that my Father's Crop of Cole-seed[2] is like to prove so slight, knowing that 'tis the Plenty or Scarcity of that, which must supple or stiffen my Joynts towards the Learning of any of my French Exercises. The season here has been very hot & dry all this summer, only in these 7 or 8 last days, we have had a very great deal of rain, which will produce a fertile Vintage. Mʳ· Holden writes me word that Sʳ· Thomas Stanly is dead; my Cosin Betty is at the end of this month to be Cloathed a Nun in the Towne of Diepe; whither she has invited me, but my Purse makes me a sufficient Excuse, since it cannot cost me so little, as 20 Crowns.[3] We have now been six Weeks in this Towne of Là Fleche, where we find accommodations very good, only the Inhabitants are over-zealous Catholicks, & most of them Monks & Jesuits, not a Protestant suffer'd to dwell in the Towne: To strangers for their own Interest they are very Civill & we have [f. 55ʳ] the advantage of the Jesuits' spritely sermons,[4] who for their lively Acting go much beyond any of our Protestants,[5] that I ever heard, and I think Hugh Peters[6] comes nighest them. As soon as our month is out, we intend to draw towards Paris, taking all the Towns of the River Loyre in our way, & we hope to be at Orleans time enough to see the Queen of Sweden's Entry; we fear that some of those pleasant Towns may entice us to spend one month in them, whereby to perfect so much of the Languague, as we have got in these private Country Towns. When I come to Paris, I shall count myself as nigh Wilberton, as if I were at

---

[1] For Henri de La Tour d'Auvergne, vicomte de Turenne see letter 15. Valenciennes changed hands several times during the French civil wars before finally accepting the authority of Louis XIV in 1677.

[2] Cole-seed or rape.

[3] See letters 6, 12, and 31.

[4] See letter 8 for the Jesuit college at La Flèche.

[5] 'any of our Protestants' underlined (by a later hand?).

[6] Probably Hugh Peters (or Peter) (1598–1660) who had been a minister at Salem, Massachusetts, before returning to England in 1641. His powerful preaching style won many recruits to the Parliamentarian forces and he compiled accounts of various civil war battles and sieges. He was appointed as a chaplain to the Council of State in 1650 and regularly preached at Whitehall during the early 1650s. After Cromwell's death he withdrew from public life but was executed at Charing Cross on 16 October 1660 for his support of the murder of King Charles I.

London: & if you'le please to pardon me for presenting my Duty so Seldome, whilst I am so far out of the way, I do promise then to be more diligent, & oft'ner humbly begg *you*r Blessing upon

Là Flech Aug*ust* ⎱
the 27. 1658 – ⎰

                                   Your most Duti*full* Child,
                                   William Hammond

My Duty I must present in this Postscript to my Father, my next shall be a French Lettre, w*hi*ch will require some time to perfect, being destitute of all help. I present my Duty to my Uncle: & love to my Brothers & Sisters, &c:

[32]

[f. 55ᵛ] Most Hon*oure*d Father,
Since my last of the 24 of May, I am gott up as far as Florence, whither I arriv'd on *th*e sixth of this June. The Oblidging Civility of my Uncle Marsham's Nephew, Mʳ Brown forc't me to spend those 15 days about the Sea-coasts in seeing Lucca, Pysa, & Leghorne;[1] where for 5 or 6 days I lodged in his house. Really, Sir, the Town itself is able to tempt a Traveller to spend some days in considering it: which tho' it be but little is so neat & Compacted, & does so swarm with People of all Nations, & that Multitude does so unanimously Consent in an Industrious way of raising their Fortunes; that methinks, my time was not ill-spent in staying there a little to view them.[2] 'Tis now the Shop & Center of *th*e Mediterranean Trade, & by the Conversation I have had with the Marchants & Captains of ships, I fancy myself to understand all the Several Ports of the Streights, & am afraid understand more of Marchandizing than ever my Brother D.[3] will doe; sed ne sutor ultra Crepidam.[4] Be pleas'd to pardon *th*e Physician, that meddles in feeling the Pulse of all sorts of affairs, as well as that of all kind [f. 56ʳ] of bodys. I will promise constancy to *th*e Profession, you have put me upon; for since I have escaped that grand temptation of turning souldier, when in my journy from Lyons to Marselles, I was so Caress'd & allur'd by the French Nobility; 'twill argue but a very low spirit, to become wavering at the baits of any other Profession, since all must truckle[5] to that of Warr. I have not yet been long enough in Florence, to know whether I like it or dislike it; but however I find it, I am resolv'd Padua shall be my Summer's Seat,

---

[1] * BL Add. MS 59785, f. 70ʳ, for 'Lucca the Industrious', Pisa, Leghorn, and 'Florence the Fiar', the transcriber simply refers the reader in each case to '[Salmon's Modern Gazetteer]'. See letter 7 for this Mr Brown, then resident at Leghorn. This tour in his company of Lucca and Pisa provided Hammond with a brief taste of the traditional 'Grand Tour' itinerary of Italy at the period. On a political level, Lucca was also of particular interest to English visitors during the Commonwealth and Protectorate since it preserved its own governmental independence until the time of Napoleon. Francis Mortoft commented in the same year that Lucca was 'one of the Prettyest contrivedst Cittyes in Italy and a free Common wealth' (1658), p. 46.

[2] The commercial prosperity of Leghorn (Livorno) dated from 1571 when the building of a new port was instigated by Cosimo I (1519–74). Ferdinando I (1549–1609) generated an especially cosmopolitan population for Leghorn when he issued a proclamation of religious liberty, stimulating an influx of entrepreneurial exiles, including persecuted Jews, Greeks fleeing Turkish oppression, converted Moors expelled by Philip III from Spain and Portugal, and Roman Catholics from England. See also letter 5.

[3] 'my Brother D.'. If this is a reference to a sibling, Hammond had at least two other adult brothers by 1658, Anthony and another whose name is unknown. In letter 15 he makes a scathing reference to a brother's apparent unwillingness to commit himself to the world of business. See also letter 13.

[4] 'Let the cobbler stick to his last' (Pliny), usually 'ne sutor supra crepidam'.

[5] 'truckle', humbly submit.

that by fullfilling my Promise I may expiate the fault, I committed in making such huddling haste out of Paris. I have not yet had the opportunity of hearing of the Progress of the French army in Mantoua, but when I come to Padua, one of the French Colonells has promis'd to keep Correspondence with me. We hear that the poor Queen of Sweden is secur'd in Rome, & therefore likelyer to end her famous Royall travells in a Prison, than in a Monastery. The reason why is not yet publickly known. Some say, 'tis in revenge of the Murder of her Major Domo in Fontainbleau, but most that she meddled in the Duke of Modena's Interest against the [f. 56ᵛ] Pope,[1] & that at her passage from Modena to Ferrara, she endeavour'd to make Ferrara revolt to its ancient Master the Duke. 'Tis also Confirm'd, that the Venetian have lost their Impregnable Fort on the Isle of Corfu, by an Accident of Gun-powder.[2] These seas are now famous for none, but our English Exploits, & Generall Stokes[3] is now scowring of them with some 15 Men of War; he lately took severall of the Majorcans, & executed some 8. or 10 English at Marsielles, whom he took in those Enemy's Vessells. The Marchants expect him every week at Leghorn, where 'tis thought, he will revenge himself of the Town & Castle, for having shot above two hundred shot at him, when he was last there; upon his seasing upon a Majorcan in their Rode.

Mr. Brown is so industrious & thriving a marchant, as the seeing his indefatigableness, has added spurs to my Intentions: & next unto Secretarys of State, I see none so full of business as Marchants. Really, Sir, I think a man may learn more Geography & Names of chief Towns, from the several superscriptions of their Lettres, than from [f. 57ʳ] Heylin's book.[4] He has proferr'd me the Convenience of his Correspondent in London, by whose means you may please to send me your Commands into Italy. The passing them thorow Dr. Holden's hands will be more Chargeable & uncertain to me; whereas if they come directed to Mr. Brown, his Universall Correpondence will easier find me out, Especially since I receive Credit from him, wheresoever I go;[5] I mean for this summer: having put my 20 Pistolls into his hands, to be return'd me as Occasion serves. His Correspondent in London is Mr. Henery Mellish;[6] & I humbly beg you will please to return me my next & last Travelling mony by him. Really, Sir, Italy does so little answer my Imaginations, as I am afraid I shall hardly have patience to stay out my year; unless Padua prove more tempting, than I hear 'twill do. It may be, 'tis the melancholy Posture I am now in, makes me think so, being as yet destitute of Companions, *that* please me, & out of all hopes of any sudden News of your Wellfare at Wilberton. My greatest support & Comfort, is in constant praying all may be well, & those many proofs I have for- [f. 57ᵛ] merly receiv'd of your Fatherly Tenderness, yet makes me presume on your Blessing upon, sir,

Florence June }
the 9. 1658 – }

Your most Dutif*ull* Child,
William Hammond.

[1] See letter 7 for Queen Christina's intrigues with the duke of Modena and letter 24 for the execution of her major domo.

[2] The Venetians held sovereignty over Corfu from 1401 until 1797 and made it their principal arsenal in Greece. Major and minor explosions inevitably followed, especially at the Byzantine Castel de Mar, which was used as a powder magazine (dating from 1558), and the Venetian fort of San Salvatore (demolished during the 1840s).

[3] 'Generall Stokes', see p. 220, n. 3.

[4] * BL Add. MS 59785, f. 79ʳ: 'Dr: Peter Heylin Sub Dean of Westminster his Cosmography'. Peter Heylin, *A Full Relation of Two Journeys: the One into the Mainland of France* [in 1625]. *The Other* [in 1629] *into Some of the Adjacent Islands* (1656).

[5] See letter 1 for the distribution and delivery of Hammond's mail while he was on his travels abroad.

[6] See letter 7 for Mr Henry Mellish.

[33]

Most Honoured Father,
I now begin to be much afraid, that most of my Lettres, since my coming to Florence, are miscarried. The greatest damage, such an Accident cou'd produce, were to making me Guilty of a seeming Undutifullness. I hope you will please to censure favorably; for really, Sir, there is no Case wanting on my side. I can protest to have sent above a dozen Lettres, yet cannot believe, there is above three of them receiv'd, which were those I sent in my Cosin Brown's Packetts, the others going single by Lyons for Paris, I begin to doubt of their safely, because I receive no Answer from D̲r̲ Holden. I hope every day to receive the good news of your Wellfares at Wilberton; as yet I have heard from nobody, not so much as from my Cosin Bowyer. 'Tis three months, that I have liv'd all alone here in Florence, & really, Sir, can hardly keep myself from Melancholy, to be so long without seeing or hearing from any Friend in England. [f. 58ʳ] This last week I misfortunately fell into the Clutches of the Doctors, & Apothecary, who have pick't my Purse of four Pistolls: The occasion was a very violent Flux joyn'd with a Feaver, & unspeakable Faintness. The Physicians judg'd it from my drinking too much base water, for fruite I eat none at all. God be thanked, by the means of a small Purge or two of Rubarbe they have set me up again, & 'tis now above eight days, that I enjoy my former health. My former Lettres were all so Cramm'd with impertinent Discourses, of what I see & observe in these Countrys, as I cou'd almost wish they were miscarried; yet betwixt good & bad they were so full, that they have left me nothing more to say of this Town or Court. I am resolv'd to Continue here, till I receive your first Lettres from England, & then obey your Commands, in going whither you shall please to direct. The great heats are now passing over, & I don't doubt but in a very short time to have Companions for my Travells, but can never be better accompany'd, than with your Blessing upon, Sir,

Florence August
the 22. 1658
   }

Your most Dutifull Child,
William Hammond. –

[34]

[f. 58ᵛ] Most Honoured Father,
This Summer's Travells seem infinitely different to me from those of France. Whilst I was at the other side of the Alps, the Regularity & Certitude of Posts, made me within reach of home both in Provence & Languedoc. Now, tho' still in the same Climate, the vast mountains make as great a difference, as if I were gone to the Antipodes. I am very sorry, 'tis my Misfortune to be left alone to myself in a Country, which might have afforded me many opportunitys of serving my Friends. Really, Sir, 'tis one of the chiefest Causes, that makes me incapable of giving in a tolerable account, how I have spent this summer. At my first coming to Florence, the Inticement of an Opera made me loyter away so much time, till the great heats were so far come on, as 'twas too late for me to go forwards for Venice. I have since made an end of the Summer in this Town, my most Visible Improvement is in the Language, of which I have enough to carry me thorowout Italy. For other things, either in Architecture, Painting, or Musick, it may be I might have made as good a Progress in Lombardy as here. Yet really, Sir, this Town has this Peculiar, that it is the Asylum of all Virtuosos; there being none, of what [f. 59ʳ]

Country, soever he be, but if he be Excellent in any thing, he may assure himself to obtaine a Competent Pension of the Grand Duke. Two of my Country-men at present, one for his Excellency in the Greek, receives 500 Scudos d'intrata, the other for Hebrew has a Professor's place in Pisa. And I make no Question, if M[r.] Wren[1] were here, he might succeed the famous Galileo[2] in the Mathematick Profession. 'Tis not time altogether lost to have been an Eye-witness to the Regularity & Pomp of this Prince his Court; which 'tis thought is kept at the least Cost, & yet with the most Glory of any Court of Christendome: I am sure, it goes far beyond that of Paris. 'Tis wonder to see him so generally belov'd, & yet so absolute a Tyrant: I don't think the Peasants of France pay nigh those Taxes & Gabells, that the poor Toscan Contadine[3] is Lyable to; yet I remember, as I passt thorow Pisa, going to see the grand Duke's Gardens & Galery,[4] he has there hung up, as a Publick Spectacle, a pair of French Wooden shoes, to intimate the Poverty & misery of *the* people. However the dispute be decided, I am sure, our English Farmer is a Prince in respect of either. I have been far from loosing my time this [f. 59[v]] Summer in matter of Physick; having at times been Student, Doctor & Patient, & really, Sir, I find the last is the worst, & most Chargeable Condition. 'Tis a little too much for a young Student, to preserve the health of his own Crasy body, in such unusuall heats, & so different a Climate. My main Buckler[5] is Temperance, & I find a man may erre in that, if he do not well understand the Temperature of his inwards. I have learnt much by the Conversation of our English Doctor, & having climb'd up one or two hills in Physick, I see I am not as yet at *the* top, but that the top of one hill, is but the seat of another. The Cool weather does now come on so fast, as I can have no Excuse to lye longer in this City. I had resolv'd to have expected your Commands & directions from England; but my Cosin Brown sends me word, that three weeks since he receiv'd your Lettres, & by mistake instead of sending[6] them me to Florence, they were sent back to London. I cannot in likelyhood expect any more these 6 weeks, which time I'le goe & spend at Rome, & from thence directly to Padua, where without faile I intend to be in the month of December. We have no News here, only great Rumors of the [f. 60[r]] French over-running the State of Milan,[7] where

---

[1] * BL Add. MS 59785, f. 82[r]: 'Sir Christopher Wren'. See letter 29 for Hammond's contact with Christopher Wren.

[2] Galileo Galilei (1564–1642), a mathematician, astronomer and physicist, was a native of Pisa where he became a lecturer in mathematics at the age of 25 years. The Venetian Senate later granted him a lifetime appointment as professor of mathematics at the University of Padua. From 1610 he also served the Grand Duke Cosimo II as his 'first philosopher and mathematician'. Tried by the Inquisition for his adherence to the Copernican theory of the universe, he was confined under house-arrest for the last eight years of his life. Hammond's interest in Galileo predates the first English translation of his writings by Thomas Salusbury, *Mathematical Collections and Translations*, 2 vols, 1661–65.

[3] 'Toscan Contadine': Tuscan countryman or peasant.

[4] Florence had taken possession of Pisa in 1509. The Grand Duke during Hammond's visit was Ferdinando II de' Medici (1610–70), who succeeded his father, Cosimo II de' Medici (the student, patron, and employer of Galileo) as Grand Duke of Tuscany in 1621. Hammond is probably referring here to the Palazzo de' Medici, now the Prefettura at Pisa.

[5] 'buckler': literally, a small round shield; figuratively, a defence.

[6] 'of sending' deleted.

[7] * BL Add. MS 59785, f. 83[v]: 'The See of an Archbishop. [Salmon's Gazetteer]'. At the time of Hammond's reference Milan had been a central focus of rivalry between France and Spain for over one hundred and fifty years. Following the enforced replacement in 1450 of the Visconti dynasty with that of the Sforzas, in 1499 the Duchy of Milan came under the authority of King Louis XII of France, was retaken by Ludovico Sforza in 1500, but then almost immediately repossessed by the French who ruled until 1513. The Sforzas retook the city in that year only for the French King Francis I to reconquer it through his famous victory at the Battle of Marignano in 1515

having taken Trin & Mortara;[1] 'tis said, Pavia & Novara[2] begin to mutiny, & talk of Revolting.

Our Admirall Stokes has accorded with those of Tripoli;[3] & the Tumults of Marseilles are quite allay'd. Be pleased to pardon my Impertinency, & I humbly begg your Blessing upon, Sir,

Florence Sept*ember* ⎱
the 6. 1658. – ⎰

Your most Dut*ifull* Child,
William Hammond. –

[35]

Most Honoured Mother,

I am now so well recover'd of that little sickness, I had this summer, that I hope it has Cleansed my body, for all the while that I am to stay abroad. The Extreme heat & drought of this summer, must necessarily work some alterations in an English man's body; & I rather admire, I have escapt so well, than otherwise. There is nothing wanting to the accomplishing my Perfect health, but the assurance of yours at Wilberton. Methinks, I have now been four months out of the World, or at least in a new one, having not had the least Item of News from England. I am afraid to insist long upon it, least I shou'd let slip some marks of my Melancholy, for which I am sure, you wou'd reprove me, & see [f. 60ᵛ] I make little use either of my Learning or Travells, whilst I abandon myself to so deep a Melancholy. My Father (I humbly thank him) has been pleas'd to provide me the chief thing Necessary, so that I cannot at all misdoubt *the* want of mony. I might have spent my time a great deal Chearfuller & more to my advantage, had he been pleas'd to have sent me his advice, & Instructions for my Travells: being left to myself, I must of necessity take what Courses, my unexperienc't youth perswades me to. Providence has secur'd me from keeping any ill Company, having spent this summer all alone, & am afraid am like so to pass some part of the Winter. I hope, 'tis not Self-Conceit, but I have always avoided Companions, by whom there is nothing to be got; & indeed the advantageous Conversation of my lost Cosin, has made me a little more Curious, than I was. If I light upon half a dozen indifferent Ones, I will rather mix with them, than link myself to one bad one. I am sorry to loose the Opportunitys of serving you, whilst I am here abroad; this Town affords so many delicate wearing stuffs, and silks, that I heartily wisht you wou'd have pleas'd to imploy me both for yourself & my [f. 61ʳ] Sisters. What I can hoard up of my scanty allowance, I'le lay out upon some Raritys worthy presenting you, & bring them home w*i*th me next spring. In the mean time, I humbly begg your Blessing upon

Florence Sept*ember* ⎱
the 6. 1658 – ⎰

Your most Dut*ifull* Child,
William Hammond –

(although Milan was returned once more to the Sforzas under a peace treaty of 1529). Through the demise of its duke in 1535 Milan came under the authority of the Holy Roman Emperor Charles V, who in 1540 endowed his son, the future Philip II of Spain, with the Duchy. Milan then effectively remained under Spanish control until 1706 but the treat of French incursions was ever-present.

¹ * BL Add. MS 59785, f. 83ᵛ, glosses 'Trin' as 'not Describ'd by Geographers'; and 'Mortara' as 'a Toun in Italy'. Probably Trino and Mortara, both of which lie on the road from Turin to Milan.

² Pavia and Novara; both glossed in BL Add. MS 59785, f. 83ᵛ as 'a City of Italy'.

³ England first accredited a resident consul at Tripoli in 1658 and concluded five treaties with Tripoli between 1658 and 1694, largely concerned with the regulation of piracy. Admiral Stokes negotiated the first treaty of 1658.

[36]

Most Honoured Father,

Having (since my last from là Fleche been in a Continuall motion from Town to Town) yours of September the 8th. came not to me, till yesterday, the second day of my Arrivall in this Town: where I hope, my Purse will give me Leave to take up my winter Quarters. From là Fleche we passt to Angiers, thence to Saumur, to Richilieu, Tours, Ambois, Blois, Orleans, from whence we came to Paris. We find the Loyre a most goodly water, having rid in this journey, above 60 Leagues upon its banks; the Water is at present very low, but about six weeks since, there was so suddain & great a flood, as is thought to have spoilt to the value of 100,000 Pound in Hemp, from its source in the Auvergnian hills to Nantes: but as it destroy'd their hemp, the rain prov'd very seasonable for their [f. 61v] Vineyards, which the Inhabitants account to have yeilded as plentifull a Vandage[1] this Autume, as at any time these seven years: And thereupon, wou'd begin to think themselves happy (Especially having this summer thriv'd, not only in their Tillages, but also in their Campane, Capelle in Picardy, & Valance in Piedmont,[2] being at last come under this Crown) were they not in hourly fear of the Cardinal's Squeezing them:[3] who having lately brought his King out of the Campane to Paris, begins to fright the Bourgois with future disadvantageous Airs & Proclamations, hoping they will smother them by good round summes of mony. I dare not presume to give any account of Forreigne Affairs, having misst the Gazettes for some Weeks; but I may safely confirm the Report of the Famous Venetian Victory over the Turks:[4] What the Proceedings of the King of Sweden are, is very doubtfully reported; some say, he Carrys all before him, Others that the Russian has fallen upon him, & besieg'd & taken Riga, which makes him leave the thoughts of Dantzick,[5] & take Care of his own Kingdome; the Manly Queen of Swede about six weeks since passt thorow this Town [f. 62r] with great Applause, & visitting the King at Compeigne,[6] is now return'd into Italy. We hear of a Loss, the King of Spain had by sea, in some of his West-India ships, but are as yet very far from a certain Relation of it, farther than

[1] 'vandage': vendange, the wine vintage or harvest.

[2] La Capelle and Valence.

[3] At this period, France was still in a state of some considerable uncertainty along its northern borders, thereby fostering a fear among all levels of the French population that ever more funds would be consumed in defensive military activities. As recently as August 1658 Cardinal Mazarin had managed to conclude a defensive league, known as the League of the Rhine, between France and the German states closest to the French frontier. However, the Franco-Spanish war still rumbled on since the Spanish refused to acknowledge this peace, partly because the Dutch United Provinces (who had signed a separate agreement with France in January 1658) had refused to collaborate in this agreement. A general treaty, ensuring peace with Spain, was not agreed until November 1659.

[4] Hammond is probably referring here to one of the numerous naval engagements in the long struggle (beginning in the mid-1640s) between Venice and the Turks for the island of Crete, which resulted in its fall to the Turks in 1669.

[5] Gustavus II Adolphus of Sweden had captured Riga in 1621 and it was not finally taken by the Russians until their campaign of 1709–10. The Swedish King in 1658, Charles X Gustav (1654–60), dreamt of uniting the whole of Scandinavia under his own rule, leading to Sweden's First Northern War (1655–60) against a coalition which eventually included Poland, Russia, Brandenberg, Denmark, and the United Netherlands. Danzig (Gdansk), ceded to Poland in 1455, was one of the four chief towns of the Hanseatic League and was crucial to Charles X Gustav's plans to strengthen Sweden's hold over the Baltic and to counter a potential Russian threat in Poland.

[6] The old palace at Compiègne.

that they were taken by our English Vessells.[1] But of all Countrys I can hear least of England, & its Affairs; Our Protector's Resident lyes still in Paris; & when I am thorowly settled, I shall endeavour to informe myself from him, or his Followers, being desirous to know the Effects of this lifted Parliament.[2] I heartily wish, that this dry summer may have done no Prejudice to *the* Outfalls of our Fenn-rivers; lest their scowring shou'd Cause new Taxes; which by this time, I hope, may be regulated, by that new form of Government, you were pleas'd to tell me of, to beginn on Michaelmas last; M[r.] Holden is newly come to Town from my Aunt Stanly, & my two Cosins at Diepe, where my Cosin Betty cannot be Cloth'd, till farther security for the Payment of monys be given by my Cosin Tom.[3] On Wednesday next, the first of November, I hope to be settled in my Pension & shall beginn to follow what Exercises, my [f. 62[v]] mony will hold out to; resolving also to obey your Commands, in endeavouring to get a better Character, my Unsettledness having kept me from it all this summer. I am unwilling to trouble you with the account of my mony; hoping that Gabriel Richards[4] will supply me, from whom I have yet receiv'd but Twenty Pound Sterling, having borrowed the rest of my Summer's Charges from my Cosin Bowyer; & now according to your Commands I intended to have Charg'd him w*i*th part of my Lettre of Credit, but my Marchant refusing it, I have this Post wrott unto him to furnish me some other way; & I shall endeavour to husband it to the best Advantage, being very sensible, how ill it can be spared at Wilberton. I humbly present my Duty to my Mother, to whom I shall present it more largely by the next Post: in the interim I humbly begg your Blessing upon

Paris Octob*er*
the 27. 1658 ⎫⎬⎭

Your most Dut*ifull* Child,
William Hammond. -

[37]

[f. 65[r]] Most Hon*oure*d Father,
The last in which I presented my Duty was dated from Francfort. I have since passt thorow Mayence, Cologne, Arneham, Utrecht, & 'tis six days that I have been now in this famous

---

[1] Cromwell's ideological hostility towards the papist threat of Spain culminated in his ordering an English naval expedition against the Spanish Indies in December 1654, which sought to seize and colonize the islands of Hispaniola and Cuba before attacking Spanish strongholds on the mainland of Spanish America. Jamaica was captured in 1655, although it proved of little immediate use to the English, but Hispaniola held firm and the impetus of Cromwell's anti-Spanish colonization plans were effectively stalled in the Americas. These activities were also strongly disapproved of by the English mercantile community of London, which had quietly built up during the early 1650s a range of productive business relationships with metropolitan Spain, and valuable English trade routes and connections were rapidly lost to the Dutch. Cromwell's policy towards the West Indies thereby played a major role in the trade depression of the last years of the Protectorate.

[2] Hammond's news from home was indeed somewhat out of date since the second session of second Parliament of the Protectorate had been dissolved on 4 February 1658. Parliament was not recalled until 27 January 1659.

[3] See letter 12 for cousin Betty's entrance into a convent at Dieppe. On a visit to Dieppe in 1682 one John Herne met the 'sister to Mr. Stanley the famour philosopher' (*HMC Various Collections*, II, p. 1983). Hammond's cousin Tom is presumably Thomas Stanley (1625–78).

[4] For Gabriel Richards see letters 1 and 29.

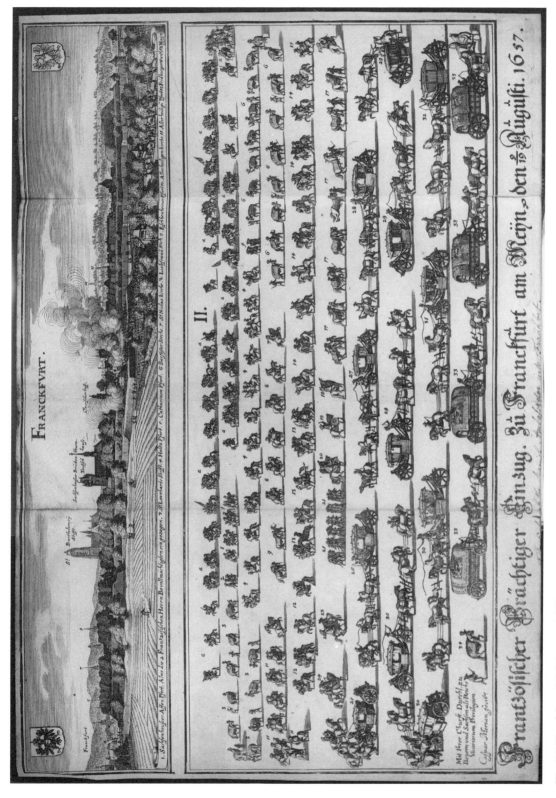

Fig. 35. Frankfurt, 9/19 August 1657.

Fig. 36. Frankfurt, 22 July/1 August 1658.

City of Amsterdam.[1] I suppose, 'tis those that come from the Northern Parts, who chiefly admire this Town; he that comes immediately from the stately Town of Venice, & other Majesticall Citys of Italy, will rather take it for a well rang'd Gang of Seamen's & Marchant's Booths, than any ways Comparable to Venice. For their Riches & Trafficke, Questionless it will vye with any Town in Europe. And really, Sir, 'tis no small pleasure to see a Town thus sictuated in a Bogg & Quagg, that produces nothing like Timber, so surrounded with an Unlimited Wood of Sea-Vessells, whose Masts stand as thick, as the Trees of any Grove. I cannot at all admire their Air, I don't remember that ever I felt so damp a one in my life, 'tis pitty, it has not that drying breath of the Alps, which Clears Venice. To morrow morning I think to Change it for that of Leyden, where I shall at least be sure to be more in my own Element, I mean in respect of *th*e [f. 63ᵛ] University. At Francfort I found S*i*r Kenelm Digby, who commanded me to present his humble service to you; he has lain hid in his study there for these seven months, & intends a Studying Voyage thorow all Germany; Great Witts do not look upon themselves as Prophets in their own Country: his Fellow Traveller Mᵣ White had just then left him, he told me, *tha*t he was gone down to Leyden, to print *th*e Effects of their last Winter's Study, which amounted to no less, than the Exact Squaring of the Circle.[2] I am afraid this Age will not deserve so great a Blessing; However they intend to venture their Credits upon it, & have already assur'd it to most of the Princes of Germany; the Prince Elector told me of it, as I passt at Heydlebourgh.[3] There is nothing tempts my Loytering here in this Country, but the Informing myself a little about *th*eir draining, in reference to which I will make a stop at Leyden, till I can receive your farther Commands. And indeed 'tis but to make a Virtue of Necessity, for at present there is a Generall Embargo, & no stirring from any Port of the United Provinces, which 'tis said, will last till the Fleet set off from the Texelt,[4] [f. 64ᵛ] a time to be limited not only by the

---

[1] Since Hammond's previous surviving letter is dated from Paris 27 October 1658, the dating of this concluding letter, '6 May 1658'[?], in both the Brotherton and British Library manuscripts, needs to be reconsidered. Both of these versions (copied, respectively, in 1695 and in the mid-18th century) probably derived from a (now lost) source, or sources, which gave the date of this letter as '1658'. However, it is clear from letter 30 that Hammond left Paris on 30 April and arrived at Lyons on 8 May 1658. It seems, then, that this concluding letter almost certainly dates from May 1659, when Hammond was probably making his way home to England via a rapid tour of Germany and the Low Countries. At some point after the end of October 1658, he probably travelled from Paris through Germany to Frankfurt (perhaps for the Easter Fair), before visiting Mainz (Mayence), and Cologne. Hammond's references to Arnhem, Utrecht, and Amsterdam suggest that he may have been intending to return home by moving on from Amsterdam to Antwerp and then to Dunkirk, a traditional route for homeward bound English travellers at this period. However, the dismal climate of Amsterdam in the spring prompted him to decamp to Leiden and the company of Sir Kenelm Digby (see letters 14 and 27).

[2] The friend of Digby mentioned here was Thomas White (1593–1676), the Catholic philosopher and controversialist, who adopted the various pseudonyms Albus, Anglus, Blacloe, and Blacklow. Educated at the Catholic colleges of St Omer, Douai, and Valladolid, he taught at Douai and became president of the English College at Lisbon. White's own writings, included the highly controversial *Institutionesa sacrae* (1652) and *Obedience and Government* (1655), which questioned papal infallibility. He assisted Digby with the drafting of his *Institutionum peripateticarum libri quinque* (1651) and other works. See Peterson, *Digby*, pp. 223–6.

[3] This is probably a reference to Charles Louis (1617–80), the son of Elizabeth (daughter of King James I of England) and Frederick V (1596–1632). It is frustating that none of Hammond's letters describing his visit to Heidelberg has survived since during the 1650s it was one of the most important locations for English travellers of a royalist disposition. Robert Bargrave visited Heidelberg in March 1656 and left a detailed account of the warm welcome offered to him by the Palsgrave and his immediate family who clearly sought to offer special hospitality to English visitors (Bargrave (1656), pp. 248–9).

[4] The island of Texel, adjacent to the town Den Helder which was developed in the seventeenth century from a small fishing port into a major naval base.

Winds, but the Runagate humour of their seamen, who are generally unwilling to imbarke upon Men of Warr. Really, Sir, 'tis little to my own Content, to have been thus long, & to think of being longer in an Uncertainty of your health. I shall think every day a year, till I am in England, & tho' your last & my Mother's did almost assure me of your Recovery, yet I shall never be settled, till I receive the full assurance from my own Eyes. We heard some buzing of new Troubles in England, but I suppose the dissolving of the Parliament,[1] has quieted all. I humbly present my Duty to my Mother, & begg your Blessing upon, Sir,

Amsterdam   }
May .6. 1658 – }

Your most Dut*ifull* Child,
William Hammond. –

---

[1] Assuming that this letter was written in May 1659, Hammond is referring to the dissolution of the last Protectorate Parliament on 22 April 1659.

SECTION FOUR

THE TRAVELS OF
THE HONOURABLE BANASTER MAYNARD
(Spring 1660–April 1663)

1. The Family and Early Life of Banaster Maynard

Our third traveller, the honourable Banaster Maynard (c. 1642–1718), as he is described on the title-page of Robert Moody's manuscript (Oxford, Bodleian Library, MS Rawlinson D 84), was the eldest surviving son and heir of Sir William, 2nd Baron Maynard (c. 1623–1689).[1] The latter was the son of Sir William Maynard (c. 1585–1640), 1st Baron Maynard, and grandson of Sir Henry Maynard (d. 1610) of Little Easton (or Easton Parva), Essex, who had served towards the end of Queen Elizabeth's reign as secretary to William Cecil, Lord Burghley and MP of St Albans.[2] In reward for his considerable administrative and personal services to Burghley, Sir Henry was granted an estate at Easton by the queen in 1589. The family mansion, Easton Lodge, was mainly built from the mid-1590s onwards in the traditional Elizabethan style but was considerably enlarged and redesigned by several of its later occupants. Much of the building and its contents was destroyed by a major fire on 31 January 1847, although it was completely restored at a cost of £10,000 in the years following.

Sir William, 1st Baron Maynard, took an MA from St John's College, Cambridge (1608), and was also appointed as a Gentleman of the Privy Chamber at about this time. He was knighted on 7 March 1609 and served as MP for Penrhyn (1610–11) and Chippenham (1614). Following the death of his father on 11 May 1610, he was created a baronet on 14 March 1611. His first wife was Frances (c. 1593–1613), daughter of William, 1st Baron Cavendish of Hardwick (and from 1618 1st Earl of Devonshire). Following her death (without children) on 1 September 1613, he married Anne (d. 1647), daughter and heir of Sir Anthony Everard of Great Waltham, Essex. He was created Baron Maynard of Wicklow on 30 May 1620 and Baron Maynard of Little Easton (or Estaines) on 14 March 1628.[3]

Sir William's eldest son, William, 2nd Baron Maynard – the father of our traveller Banaster Maynard – matriculated as a pensioner on 2 April 1638 from St John's College, Cambridge, and received his MA in 1639.[4] He succeeded to his father's title in December

---

[1] There is a monument to William Lord Maynard in Easton village church. Bourchier's Chapel, on the south side of the chancel, is the burial place of the Maynard family.

[2] See Conyers Read, *Lord Burghley and Queen Elizabeth*, 1960 (rpt. 1965), pp. 376, 431, 477, 506–42 *passim*. Sir Henry Maynard's wife was Susan, daughter and co-heir of Thomas Pierson, an usher of the Star Chamber.

[3] Sir William, 1st Baron Maynard, also served as Lord Lieutenant of Cambridge in 1620. His younger brother John (c. 1592–1658) matriculated from St John's as a fellow commoner at Easter 1612. He served as MP for Chippenham (1624–6), Calne (1628–9), and Lostwithiel (1647–8); and he was created a Knight of the Bath in 1625.

[4] William, 2nd Baron Maynard, married (1) c. 1641 Dorothy Banaster (d. 30 October 1649), who was the mother of our traveller and (2) before 30 May 1662 Margaret Murray (d. 1682), daughter of William Murray, 1st Earl of Dysart.

1640; and he served as Lord Lieutenant of Cambridge from 1640 until 1662. The 2nd Baron was impeached by the leaders of the independent party in the House of Commons in September 1647, although the impeachment was not prosecuted. He firmly opposed the trial of the king and was imprisoned under the Commonwealth for his sympathies towards the idea of a presbyterian-royalist alliance. After Cromwell's death and the fall of Richard Cromwell's protectorate in April 1659 he became known as a supporter of the restoration of Charles II and was involved the rising in Norfolk of August 1659 and the plans to secure Yarmouth as a safe landing point for an invasion by royalist supporters.[1] After the Restoration the 2nd Baron's support was amply rewarded by Charles II who appointed him as a privy councillor and as comptroller of the royal household, a position in which he was reaffirmed after the accession of James II and held until his resignation in 1685.[2] His eldest son William (who predeceased him), had a son, Thomas (c. 1686–1742) who matriculated as a fellow-commoner on 2 June 1702 from Christ's College; and was later MP for Eye (1710–15) and West Looe (1715–22).[3] Thomas's younger brother, Prescot Maynard (b. c. 1688), matriculated as a pensioner from Sidney Sussex College, Cambridge, on 26 April 1705. He was admitted to the Middle Temple on 12 February 1707. During the reigns of Charles II and James II the Maynards enjoyed both prominence and importance at court, largely through the 2nd Baron's office as comptroller.

2. Banaster Maynard's Continental Travels (Spring 1660–April 1663)

Banaster Maynard, who later became 3rd Baron Maynard on the death of his father William in 1689, does not appear, like his father and grandfather, to have studied at either Cambridge or Oxford, probably because of the upheavals of the Civil War. Instead, proba-bly just before the formal Restoration of Charles II, he set out for an extended continental itinerary in the spring of 1660. We only know the specific details of his travels because some years after his return home (see p. 235), his personal servant on the itinerary, Robert Moody, compiled an informative diary of his travels. Unfortunately, nothing else is now known about Moody himself, although from his own accounts he seems to have already been a well-travelled, resourceful and adaptable individual – the ideal travelling companion for the youthful and inexperienced Banaster Maynard.

Moody's manuscript opens with an ornamental title-page, carefully drawn in imitation of a printed book (see Fig. 38, p. 238); and it is followed by 'The Epistle Dedicatory' to Banaster Maynard, in which Moody recounts how he decided:

> to make the best improvement my Capacity would permit which suitable to the weaknesse thereof) I perform'd in as compendious a Manner as I could by making a Diary, As Likewise particular Observations of all such Occurrences which I thought most Remarkable in your Honour's Progresse ... from Paris through the Principle and most pleasant parts of Europe (ff. 2^r–v).

[1] *The Letter-Book of John Viscount Mordant, 1658–1660*, ed. Mary Coate, Camden Society, 3rd ser., 69, 1945, pp. 19, 22. See also pp. xi–xx, for an informative exposition of the background to presbyterian-royalist links and nego-tiations at this period.

[2] *Alumni Cantabrigienses*, pt. I, vol. 3, III, pp. 168–9.

[3] This Thomas Maynard (b. c. 1686–1742) later became a Commissioner for Stores in Minorca (1717) and a Commissioner of the Customs (1723–30). He resided at Hoxton Hall, Suffolk. Another Henry Maynard, described as the son of 'William, Baron of Easton', matriculated from New College, Oxford, on 29 May 1685, aged 16. *Alumni Oxonienses: 1500–1714*, III, p. 994.

Moody goes on to detail their party's travels through 'France, Savoy, Pie-mont, through all Italy, Hungaria, Bohemia, Germany, Holand and the Spanish Netherlands' (f. 4ʳ). He meticulously records the names of all cities, towns, and villages passed through, along with information on the overall mileages, time-scales, traversing Alpine passes, and modes of transport available for each section of their itinerary. He notes how Mr Henchman, a travelling tutor, directed Maynard's general education and choice of destinations (see p. 241), while Moody himself handled such practical matters as the finding of suitable lodgings, the domestic catering for Maynard's group, and the transactions involved in dealing with his bills of exchange. Moody even proudly records how once he was personally able to save the day at Metz when Maynard ran perilously short of funds, only for his trusty servant to produce triumphantly some eighteen golden pistols previously sewn into his trousers at Paris (f. 32ᵛ). Moody seems to have been especially adept at the planning of grand entertainments, such as lavish parties thrown by Maynard for English merchants and residents at Florence (f. 12ʳ) and Leghorn (f. 13ʳ). His account of the Florentine feast also illustrates just how highly Maynard's social status was regarded by foreign princes:

> My Maister being arriv'd at Florence, the next Day after he went to see the great Duke, and haveing kiss'd his Hands deliver'd the before-mention'd Letter which my Maister had from the Old Duches of Parma, the Duke smil'd and bid him welcome to Florence, and two or three dayes after when we dream'd of no such Matter, one Morning about ten of the Cloak their cam into my Maister's Lodging six Porters with large Baskets on their heads Loaded with the Choicest wines Flor*ence* could afford, Turkys, all sorts of wild Fowle, all sorts of sweetmeats and Confitures and severall other things what was Most rare, they enquir'd for Il Signor Maynardo Meaning my Maister and tould him that the Great Duke had sent him that present as a marke of the esteem he had for him. Haveing given two or thre pistols in gould amongst the men for a reward they were all dismist. My Maister and the Governor haveing view'd every particular began to Ruminat how to dispose of so many varieties, and at last concluded to invite all the English that were in Florence to Dinner and to make a mery Day of it and accordinglie they did. And to honnour the feast the more they envited S*ir* Tho*mas* Bendish who was Just arriv'd at Florence from his Ambassy in Constantinople. So haveing ended the Day & most part of the night with Musick and drinking of Healths everyone retir'd to their severall Habitations, and My Maister had severall invitations afterwards while he stay'd their. And when he went to give the Grand Duke thanks and to take his leave, his Highnesse was pleas'd to give him a letter of Recommendation to the Pope (ff. 11ᵛ–13ʳ).

Always alert while abroad to the proper and expected social recognition of his master's elevated status, Moody habitually records the most interesting and amusing acquaintances made by Maynard on his travels, including 'several other English gentleman at Paris (f. 4ᵛ); Mr Allen, an English merchant at Genoa (f. 9ᵛ); an Irish Colonel called Tafft at Milan (f. 10ᵛ); English merchants called Ashby, Sidney, Browne, Dethick, and Kent at Leghorn (f. 13ʳ); the Prince of Brandenburg, with whom Maynard explored Naples and Vesuvius (ff. 17ᵛ); a Scottish Colonel at Utrecht (f. 35ᵛ); and an especially entertaining Englishman called Mr Ogle at Amsterdam (f. 35ᵛ). Of special interest are Moody's account of Maynard's presence at Paris in June 1660 for the marriage of King Louis XIV to Marie-Thérèse of Austria and its accompanying operas, comedies and firework displays (ff. 4ʳ⁻ᵛ); Maynard's audiences with the French Queen Mother (f. 4ᵛ), the Duchess of Savoy at Turin (ff. 8ʳ–9ʳ), the Duchess of Parma at Parma (ff. 10ᵛ–11ʳ), the Grand Duke of Florence (ff. 11ᵛ–12ʳ), Pope Clement IX at Rome (ff. 15ʳ⁻ᵛ) and the Viceroy of Naples (f. 17ʳ⁻ᵛ). He also records Maynard's invitation to dine at the English College at Rome (f. 16ʳ) and their joint impressions of the Ascension

Day ceremonies at Venice (ff. 20^{r-v}). Perhaps most remarkable of all is Moody's detailed account of Maynard's attendance at the wedding (and subsequent entertainments) of the Prince of Tuscany to the daughter of the Duke of Orléans, held at Florence in June 1661:

> A while after their came out frome another Corner an Atlas the most prodigious for bignesse that I think ever was seen with the world on his back. Their was under this Atlas as we were inform'd at least 100 men by whoes help he came a very slow pace till he came to the Midle of the place, and then made a stand for some time. At last the Glob of the world split in fower partes, Resembleing the fower Quarters of the world (that is) Europe, Affrica, Asia, and America: In every Quarter their was at least twenty Persons the best voices that could be had, And their Clothing, Voices, and language according to that part of the world wherin they had been bred. Europe began first to sing intimating that they were come thither to congratulat and wish a happie Successe to that Nuptiall: Africa sung next on the same subject. Asia next, and last of all America: And all such Ravishing voices and all so winning and pleaseing that no man knew who exceeded the other, thus they continu'd till day began to cast light upon the firmament and then broke up and every one retir'd to their severall habitations. (ff. 21^{r}–22^{r}).

Maynard also stayed at 'the Mad Duke of Norfolke's Hous' at Padua (f. 23^{r}) and at the famous Heren Logiament at Amsterdam (f. 35^{r}). He dined with Prince Rupert at The Hague (f. 35^{r}) and with the Dowager Countess of Sussex and her daughter at La Flèche (f. 43^{v}); and, perhaps with most pleasure, he met up with his younger brother, William, at Paris in April 1662 (ff. 42^{v}–46^{r}).

It is possible, since William's arrival at Paris suggests that the educational value of a 'Grand Tour' was highly valued by the 2nd Baron Maynard, that Robert Moody compiled his travel diary not only for his former master, Banaster Maynard, but also for any other members of the family who might be intending a similar trip. Certainly, his accounts sometimes read more like a functional guidebook than a personal memoir.

> So, that proceeding from Paris through the Principle and most pleasant parts of Europe, I have particularized every day's Journey untill your Honor's happy Arrivall in England, with the Names Scituations and Distances of all Capitall Cities, Towns, and most Villages of Note, or Importance (f. 2^{r-v})

On many occasions, his primary focus is clearly upon establishing the route to be followed and he largely ignores specific visual details in favour of compiling a stage-by-stage geographical itinerary of the roads followed by Banaster Maynard. But, on other occasions, he provides rather more information, especially when describing the major cities and towns through which they passed, including Paris, Lyons, Turin, Geneva, Milan, Pavia, Florence, Leghorn, Pisa, Rome (where Moody had previously lived for some three years: 'I knew the language and the Citty as well as if I had been borne in it': f. 14^{v}), Naples, Vienna, Prague, Dresden, Münich, Augsburg, Heidelberg, Frankfurt, Cologne, Amsterdam, The Hague, Dordrecht, and Brussels.

Ultimately, however, the actual reasons why Robert Moody chose to compile such a detailed account of Banaster Maynard's continental travels between 1660 and 1663 can only now be speculated upon. As an individual who seems to have earned a living in personal service, it seems probable that Moody's intentions were, at least partly and entirely reasonably, self-interested and perhaps aimed at securing further employment (see p. 236). It should also be noted at this point that Moody's account (as it is now preserved in Bodl. MS Rawlinson D 84) was probably put together at some considerable period of time after their return to England in April 1663. Towards the end of the diary (see p. 297), Moody refers to their hospitable treatment at Nieuport by a 'M^r. Henry Howard afterwards Duke of Norfolke' (f. 41^r). Since this Henry Howard (1628–84) did not succeed to the dukedom until the death in December 1677 of his unmarried brother, Thomas Howard, this reference determines the earliest date at which Moody could have been writing. It is possible, of course, that he made this reference during that duke's lifetime, or even at some point after his death on 13 January 1684. However, earlier in the diary while describing Strasbourg, Moody mentions that the city 'now belongs to the King of France' (f. 31^r). Traditionally ruled by a guild of its citizens as a free city within the Holy Roman Empire, Strasbourg was seized in 1681 for France by King Louis XIV (see p. 284). Since France was not in control of the city during the early 1660s, this comment tends to suggest that Moody was writing, at least this part of the diary, sometime after 1681. While Moody almost certainly compiled some parts of his diary from contemporaneous notes made during the itinerary, occasionally, his memory seems to have let him down in some minor details. For example, his reference to his master's meeting at Florence with Sir Thomas Bendish, the homeward bound English Ambassador, simply does not fit the known dates for Bendish's movements; and it is likely that Moody had either confused his ambassadors or (more likely) the actual dates when he and Banaster Maynard were themselves at Florence (see p. 252).

Such minor lapses in narrative accuracy, however, should in no way deflect attention from the central importance of Moody's diary as one of the earliest written records of post-Restoration travel on the continent by young Englishmen. The early years of Charles II's reign, and the rise of Francophile fashions at his court, saw a dynamic resurgence in the popularity of educational tourism among not only the nobility and court élite but also the gentry and mercantile families of London and the provinces. In 1660 there also appeared Edmund Warcupp's highly influential translation, as *Italy in its Original Glory*, of Franciscus Schottus's *Itinerario d'Italia*, which had originally been written for the Jubilee Year of 1600. (Warcupp's edition provided a major source of information for many English travellers of the period, not least John Evelyn who used it extensively in the Italian commentaries of his own diary). By the mid-1660s the concept of the 'Grand Tour' as promulgated during the later-seventeenth and early eighteenth century was coherently established, as demonstrated in a wide variety of surviving written accounts relating to such travels, including the commonplace book of Robert Southwell who was in Italy in 1660–61 and later became Secretary of State for Ireland and President of the Royal Society; or the journal and letters home written during the mid-1660s by Edward Browne who, like William Hammond, had been sent abroad to study physic (but, unlike Hammond, he later became a distinguished medical practitioner).[1]

To cite only a few other representative examples of post-Restoration English travellers on the continent, there was William Trumbull (1639–1715), later Chief Secretary of State, who famously opened his autobiography written in old age with the dismissive statement: 'I went abroad and spent about 2 years in France and Italy [1664–6] where I learnt little besides the Languages, partly from my youth and the warmth of my temper, partly from lazynesse and debauchery'. In writing these words, he had apparently forgotten that, in addition to travelling with the likes of Christopher Wren, Edward Browne and Algernon Sidney, he also compiled a meticulously detailed pocket-book of his tourist excursions in

[1] [Southwell], BL Egerton MS 1632 and *HMC Egmont MSS*, I, part II, pp. 603–10. [Browne], *Journal of a Visit to Paris in … 1664*, ed. G. Keynes, 1923, and *Works of Sir Thomas Browne*, 4 vols, ed. S. Wilkin, 1835, I, pp. 70, 89–106. See also Stoye, *English Travellers Abroad*, pp. 122, 157, 163, 172; and *Journal of a Foreign Tour in 1665 and 1666 … by Sir John Lauder*, ed. D. Crawford, Scottish Historical Society, 36, 1900.

Italy, packed with architectural, historical and antiquarian details.[1] The non-conformist naturalist John Ray (1627–1705) led a party of scientifically-minded gentlemen to Italy in 1665, including Francis Willoughby, Phillip Skippon, and Nathaniel Bacon; and Martin Lister and John Downes, two medical men who studied in France in the mid-1660s and enjoyed distinguished careers as physicians in later life, have left informative records of their interests, expenses, social contacts and reading matter while abroad.[2]

By the late 1665, however, a temporary hiatus occurred in the developing English fashion for continental travel and education as it became apparent that Louis XIV was making serious preparations for war. Having assumed personal control of the kingdom following the death of Cardinal Mazarin in 1661, he launched an invasion of the Spanish Netherlands (which he regarded as his wife's inheritance) in 1667. Although he was obliged to retreat in the face of both Dutch and English pressure in 1668, he resumed his campaign, now in alliance with Charles II, in 1672. It was only by the first Treaty of Nijmegen in 1678, with Louis XIV triumphant, that a semblance of Western European peace was temporarily restored. Most of those Englishmen already then abroad for either education or pleasure during the mid-1660s were obliged to made a rapid return home to England. But, even with this enforced pause in its development, it is clear that the attractions of undertaking a continental peregrination for educational or cultural purposes had become firmly rooted in the English social imagination. As we move on into through the reigns of James II and William and Mary, and then perhaps read through Jeremy Black's richly informative account of a later period of English continental travel in his *The British Abroad. The Grand Tour in the Eighteenth Century* (1992), it is clear that the experiences of the likes of Robert Montagu, William Hammond, and Banaster Maynard between 1649 and 1663, along with those of numerous other travellers, effectively laid the foundations in English society for what is now commonly referred to as the eighteenth-century 'Grand Tour'.[3]

3. The Later Life of Banaster Maynard, 3rd Lord Maynard

At some point soon after Banaster Maynard's return home to England, his family were able to agree a particularly advantageous match for him. Henry Grey (1594–1651), who succeeded his father, Anthony, in 1643 as 9th Earl of Kent, had been a prominent supporter of Parliament in Leicestershire, served as Commissioner for the Great Seal on three occasions between 1643 and 1648, and was Speaker of the House of Lords in 1645 and 1647.

---

[1] Oxford, All Souls College, MS 317, f. 1; quoted in Stoye, *English Travellers Abroad*, p. 171. Trumbull's Italian pocket-book is now University of Leeds, Brotherton Library, MS Trv.d.1. See also Ruth Clark, *Sir William Trumbull in Paris 1685–1686*, Cambridge, 1938, pp. 1–6; Margaret Whinney, 'Sir Christopher Wren's Visit to Paris', *Gazette des Beaux-Arts*, 51, 1958, pp. 229–42; and her *Wren*, 1971, pp. 25–33; Harold F. Hutchison, *Sir Christopher Wren*, Newton Abbot, 1976, pp. 57–60.

[2] [Ray], *Observations … Made in a Journey Through Part of the Low Countries, Germany, Italy, and France* (1673); [Lister], Bodleian Library, Oxford, MS Lister 19; [Downes], BL MS Sloane 179. See also Stoye, *English Travellers Abroad*, pp. 95–302; and ibid., pp. 302–8, for the continental education of various young members of the Wharton family.

[3] This Hakluyt volume seeks to trace the development of the Grand Tour only up to Banaster Maynard's return to England in April 1663. The specific activities of the English abroad during the reigns of James II and William and Mary, however, still await a systematic study, although some important research concerning English travellers during this period may be found in Edward Chaney, *The Grand Tour and the Great Rebellion*, Geneva, 1985; John Lough, *France Observed in the Seventeenth Century by British Travellers*, Stocksfield, 1984; and in Jeremy Black's earlier study, *The British and the Grand Tour*, London, Sydney, Dover, New Hampshire, 1985.

He took no part, however, in either the trial or execution of the king. His first wife, Mary Courteen (1609–44), whom he had married in October 1641, died in March 1644, leaving a single son, Henry, who died as an infant three months after his mother. In somewhat rapid and intriguing circumstances, Henry Grey soon remarried, taking a widow, Amabella Benn Fane (1607–98), as his second wife on 1 August 1644.[1] Their first son, Anthony (1645–1702), was born in the following June and later succeeded his father as 10th Earl of Kent, and several other children ensued.[2] The family of the Earl of Kent resided at a grand mansion known as Wrest Park, Silsoe, about ten miles south of Bedford.[3] Henry Grey and his wife, Amabella, also had a daughter called Elizabeth (d. 1714). On 9 November 1665 this young woman, who would not yet have been twenty years old, married our traveller, Banaster Maynard. It seems that the married couple took up residence at the Grey's family home at Wrest Park and then stayed their for most of their married life. They had a daughter (almost certainly their first child) who was named Amabella (1666–1734); and when she married in 1691 or 1692 Sir William Lowther (1663–1729), 1st Baronet of Swillington in Yorkshire, she was described as the daughter of Banaster Maynard of Wrest Park, near Flitton, Bedfordshire.[4] Banaster Maynard would have presumably known his mother-in-law, Amabella, Dowager Countess of Kent, very well since she she probably lived with them at Wrest Park until her death in 1698 at the remarkable age of ninety-two.

Banaster Maynard and his wife Amabella had several other children of which their fourth son, also called Banaster (b. 1676, died before 4 March 1718) matriculated as pensioner from Christ's College, Cambridge, on 19 April 1694.[5] Our traveller was eventually succeeded as 4th Baron Maynard by his eldest surviving son, Henry (c. 1672–1742), who had matriculated from Trinity College, Oxford, on 31 October 1689, aged seventeen. He was awarded his DCL on 16 July 1713 and died on 7 December 1742. Another of our Banaster Maynard's younger sons, Charles (c. 1690–1775), matriculated as a fellow-commoner from Christ's in December 1707. He was awarded an MA in 1711. He succeeded his brother as 6th Baron Maynard (1745) and was created Viscount Maynard of Easton Lodge on 18 October 1766. He served as Recorder of Saffron Walden (1749) and Lord Lieutenant of Suffolk (1763–9).[6] At his death on 30 June 1775, this baronetcy (and those of 1620 and 1628) became extinct, though the Viscountcy remained.[7]

[1] The Gray family mausoleum is at St John the Baptist Church, Flitton, and includes white marble effigies of Henry Grey, 9th Earl of Kent (d. 1651), and his wife Amabella (d. 1698). Amabella Benn was the daughter of Sir Anthony Benn, formerly Recorder of London. She had previously married (1) a Mr Douce of Hampshire and (2) Anthony Fane, a younger son of the Earl of Westmorland.

[2] A licence was issued in 1689/90 for his eldest son, Henry Lord Ruthven, to travel abroad for the purposes of study; see *CSP Domestic 1689–90*, p. 533.

[3] The present house, the third on the site, dates from 1834, with grounds laid out by Capability Brown in the late 1750s.

[4] The first three children (Amabella, William and Henry) of Sir William Lowther and his wife Amabella were baptized at Flitton between November 1692 and April 1695, suggesting that they also remained at Wrest Park in the years immediately following their marriage. However, they then moved in about 1695 to Swillington in Yorkshire, where William built a grand new house on land which his grandfather had purchased in 1656. They had at least two other children (John and Jane) who were both baptized at Swillington. William Lowther served as MP for Pontefract between 1701 and 1708.

[5] This Banaster Maynard built in about 1716 the Almshouses, near the churchyard, as the residences of four poor widows to be selected by his heirs. The bequest was made to meet the terms of the will of his grandmother, Lady Margaret Banaster, who in 1662 left from her personal estate £20 per year for four poor widows of the parish.

[6] *Alumni Cantabrigienses*, pt I, vol. III, pp. 168–9.

[7] His Viscountcy was inherited by Charles (b. 1751) the son of his father's second cousin, Sir William Maynard, 4th Baronet. By this time, Sir William's son had become the 5th Baronet.

It seems that Banaster Maynard's life at Wrest, and then later at Easton Lodge when he succeeded to his father's title in 1669, was largely uneventful. He seems to have maintained a town house in Chelsea since there have survived from the period 1685–1688 a series of legal documents concerning the conveyancing of properties, mortgages, and financial bonds which usually describe him as 'The Hon. Banastre Maynard Esq, of Great Chelsey, Middlesex'.[1] But, despite the great promise of his continental travels (if we accept the grandiose image of them as depicted by Robert Moody), Banaster Maynard left no lasting mark on either the political or cultural life in late seventeenth-century England.

4. The Other Maynards

This line of Maynard baronets should be distinguished from that of another of the younger sons of Sir Henry Maynard (d. 1610), Charles (d. 1665), an auditor of the Exchequer, whose son, William (c. 1640–85), by his wife Susan Corsellis, was created Baron Maynard of Walthamstow on 1 February 1682.[2] William's third but first surviving son, William (c. 1676–1715, matriculated St John's College, Oxford, 7 July 1694), died unmarried and was succeeded by his brother, Henry (d. 1738), a noted Turkey merchant formerly resident at Aleppo. He was succeeded by his son, William (1721–72), who was followed by his son, Charles (b.1752) who also succeeded on 30 June 1775 to the peerage as 2nd Viscount Maynard of Easton Lodge, following the death of his third cousin, Charles Maynard, the 1st Viscount.[3] (As already noted, this Charles Maynard was one of the younger sons of our traveller Banaster Maynard.) The Maynards of Walthamstow's baronetcy was thereby merged into this peerage and both became extinct on 19 May 1865 on the death of Charles's son, the 3rd Viscount and 6th Baronet of Walthamstow.[4]

Two other prominent Maynards of this period belonged to unrelated families. The first individual was Sir John Maynard (1592–1658), the son of Sir Henry Maynard of Estaines Parva, Essex, was active courtier and masquer during James I's reign[5] At the coronation of King Charles I he was created a Knight of the Bath but in 1642 he supported parliament and was active in raising troops in Surrey. However, by 1647 he was increasingly at odds with the army and he was included among the eleven members charged with disaffection by Fairfax on 16 June 1647 and was impeached for High Treason on 1 February 1648. He refused to recognize the jurisdiction of the House and was fined and imprisoned in the Tower until June of that year. His son, John (d. 1664), was knighted on 7 June 1660.

The second individual was the distinguished lawyer and judge Sir John Maynard (1602/4–90). He was one of the principal speakers at Strafford's trial and vigorously defended parliamentary privilege when the king attempted to arrest five members in December/January 1641/2. Although he opposed the deposition of the king, he accepted

---

[1] University of Nottingham, Portland (London) MSS, P1 E9/2/36/1–4 (26 January 1685); P1 E9/2/37/1–2 (31 May 1688).

[2] This William (c. 1640–85) was MP for Essex (1685). He married in 1667 Mary, daughter of William Baynbrigg, a merchant tailor of London.

[3] For the 2nd Viscount's travel journal (1773), see National Register of Archives, MSS Eur. E 292. For 14th-20th century estate papers and miscellaneous family papers relating to the Viscounts Maynard, see NRA 20041 Easton, D/DMg and *HMC Principal Family and Estate Collections A-K* (1996), 45h.

[4] See *Complete Baronetage*, ed. George Edward Cokayne, 5 vols, Exeter, 1900–1909, I (1611–1625), p. 78; and IV (1665–1707), p. 126

[5] See John Nichols, *The Progresses, Procession, and Magnificent Festivities of King James the First*, 4 vols, 1828, III, pp. 521, 941; and Thomas Birch, *The Court and Times of James I*, ed. Robert F. Williams, 2 vols, 1848, II, p. 472.

parliamentary legal work under the Commonwealth and on 1 May 1658 he was appointed as the Protector's Serjeant and acted as Solicitor General under Richard Cromwell. He managed a smooth transition through the Restoration, riding in the king's procession at the coronation on 23 April 1661 and assuming the position of king's Serjeant.[1]

5. The Manuscript of Banaster Maynard's Travels

The manuscript of Banaster Maynard's travels, now Oxford, Bodleian Library, MS Rawlinson D 84, was (with Robert Montagu's account, MS Rawlinson D 76) part of the original bequest of Richard Rawlinson's manuscripts to the library in 1756 (see p. 77). The Rawlinson Catalogue entry notes for MS Rawlinson D 84: Chartaceus. In folio, saec. xviii, ff. 45. In catal. codd. P. Le Neve 433, et exinde emptus pretio 2s 6d.[2]

Peter Le Neve (1661–1729) was a noted antiquarian and collector of genealogical, heraldic and other historical manuscripts, Norroy King of Arms, and the first President of the Society of Antiquaries upon its revival in 1707, as well as being elected a fellow of the Royal Society and appointed in 1704 as Richmond Herald. After his death in 1729, the bulk of his collection of manuscripts passed to his executor, the antiquary Thomas Martin (1697–1771), of Palgrave in Suffolk, and he soon began to disperse them. Le Neve's library, along with various manuscripts, was auctioned at the Bedford Coffee House, Covent Garden, in February 1731, with another sale held on 30 March. Many of Le Neve's other manuscripts were acquired by Richard Rawlinson at these sales and they are now preserved in the collections of the Bodleian Library, Oxford.[3] It has not been possible to establish exactly how Le Neve originally obtained Robert Moody's manuscript account of Banaster Maynard's travels, although it may have come into his possession directly from a member of the Maynard family.

One other possibility should perhaps also be considered here. The finely-drawn title-page of Robert Moody's account of Banaster Maynard's travels, along with its formal dedication and meticulously neat script, suggest that the manuscript was almost certainly intended as a presentation gift for Banaster Maynard himself.

As Moody remarks in 'The Epistle Dedicatory', he had not only recorded the basic geographical facts of Maynard's travels in his diary but also 'intermixing some passages herein, The Recollection of which may peradventure incline you to joyn with the Poet in saying *Hæc olim meminisse juvabit*' (f. 2ᵛ). Furthermore, in its whole conception, Moody's diary was intended, albeit implicitly, as a sustained prose panegyric of his former master:

---

[1] Richard L. Greaves and Robert Zaller, *Biographical Dictionary of British Radicals in the Seventeenth Century*, 3 vols, Brighton, 1982–4, II (G–O), pp. 230–31.

[2] The preceding manuscript, Bodl. MS Rawlinson D 83, is also a travel journal: 'A discourse of HP [i.e. the Irishman Henry Piers (d. 1623)] his travelles written by himself anno IHS 1605', but Rawlinson's own catalogue entry makes clear that he had acquired this item in 1747 from the sale of the library of James Brydges, 1st Duke Chandos (1673–1744), and that this manuscript had previously been in the collections of Sir James Ware (1594–1666). The other contingent Rawlinson D manucripts (Rawlinson D 82 [a 15th-century manuscript of 'The Siege of Thebes', 'The Seige of Troy', and the eighth book of Gower's 'Confessio Amantis']; Rawlinson D 85, 'The life of Andreas Auria, or D'Oria, Prince of Malfi [by Charles Sigonius and translated from the Latin by I.C.]... 1631'; and Rawlinson D 86, 'The Life and death of Sir Thomas More' [a transcription by N(icholas) H(arpsfield)], seem to have no connection with Robert Moody's account of Banaster Maynard's travels (MS Rawlinson D 84).

[3] See *A Catalogue of the ... Library Collected by Peter Le Neve* [with prices and purchasers' names in manuscript], 1731 (BL copy, 270.i.23 (3)).

Nor can I forget the Effects of those Princely Recommendations wherewith your Honour was at all times furnisht, from Persons of the Most Royall, and Illustrious Degree, to others of the like Rank, and Eminency; So that your Reception was ever noble and generous; Your Entertainment at all places highly splendid, but your departure most uneasy; to such particularly who at any time had the honour of your obliging Conversation. (f. 2ᵛ)

However, at the time when Moody was compiling the manuscript, it is not known whether he was merely a former employee of the Maynards or still in the paid service of the family. If the first context is the case, then it is possible that if Robert Moody was overtly attempting to utilize the manuscript as a means of ingratiating himself with his former employer, then Banaster Maynard may have found it an unwelcome gift and may even have refused to accept it. If so, then the young Le Neve could easily have acquired it, no doubt very cheaply, from Moody himself since no other means of raising funds from the manuscript (if its sole intended recipient had turned it down) would have been readily available to Moody. It should be emphasized, however, that there is no evidence, either one way or the other, to suggest how Banaster Maynard responded to this manuscript gift.

Fig. 37. Engraving of King Charles II by Frederik Bouttats, the younger (after Wallerant Vaillant). Published at Antwerp during the 1650s.

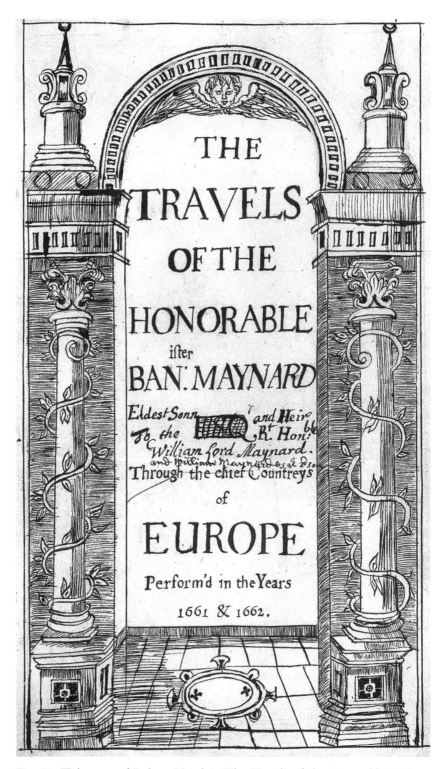

Fig. 38. Title-page of Robert Moody's 'The Travels of the Honorable Banister Maynard'. Bodl. MS Rawlinson D 84.

EDITED TEXT

THE TRAVELS OF
THE HONORABLE BANASTER MAYNARD
(Spring 1660–April 1663)

THE

TRAVELS

OF THE

HONORABLE

BAN.ister MAYNARD

Eldest Sonn and Heir[1]

To the R.t Hon:ble

William Lord Maynard.

and William Maynardes, [?] 2d [?]

Through the chief Countreys

of

EUROPE

Perform'd in the Years

1661 & 1662.

---

[1] 'ESQ' heavily deleted from this line.

[f. 1ᵛ – blank]

[f. 2ʳ]

The Epistle Dedicatory

To
My Honoured Master, Banister Maynard[1]
Eldest Son and Heir to the Right Honourable
my Lord Maynard[2]

Ever Honoured Sir

It's observable in the course of Human Life, *that* Providence frowns not always on the Unfortunate, but sometimes may respit them from their Miseries by a Juncture of Felicity and Satisfaction.

Such then was my happy Circumstance (as with all humble gratitude I am oblig'd to acknowledg) When under your Honour's Protection, and as an Attendant in your former Travells, Providence then fixing me in a station so advantagious and agreeable to my inclination.

What then remain'd but to make the best improvement my Capacity would permit which suitable to *the* weaknesse thereof) I perform'd in as compendious a Manner as I could by making a Diary, As Likewise particular Observations of all such Occurrences which I thought most Remarkable in your Honour's Progresse.

So, that proceeding from Paris through the Principle and most pleasant parts of Europe, I have particularized every day's Journey untill your Honor's happy Arrivall in England, with the Names Scitu- [f. 2ᵛ] ations and Distances of all Capitall Cities, Towns, and most Villages of Note, or Importance; Also intermixing some passages herein, The Recollection of which may peradventure incline you to joyn with the Poet in saying *Hæc olim meminisse iuvabit*.[3]

Nor can I forget the Effects of those Princely Recommendations wherewith your Honour was at all times furnisht, from Persons of the Most Royall, and Illustrious Degree, to others of the like Rank, and Eminency; So that your Reception was ever noble and generous; Your Entertainment at all places highly splendid, but your departure most uneasy; to such particularly who at any time had the honour of your obliging Conversation.

I shall not add further, but in this my chiefest satisfaction will consist, If your Honour at sometimes may peruse the 'nsuing leaves, and have any Diversion thereby then my labour shall be highly recompenc'd, and my self (if 'twere possible) be the more deeply engag'd to continue for ever,

Sir,
Your Honour's most faithfull,
and Obedient Servant.
Robert Moody.

[f. 3ʳ⁻ᵛ – *blank*]

---

[1] 'Esqʳ' heavily deleted after 'Banaster Maynard'.

[2] See pp. 227–8 for Sir William, 2nd Baron Maynard (c. 1623–1689).

[3] 'forsan et haec olim meminisse iuvabit', 'it may be that in the future you will be helped by remembering the past', Virgil, *Aeneid*, I.203.

[f. 4ʳ] The Travells of my Honor'd Maister, Mr. Banister Maynard, Eldest Sonne and Heir to the R*igh*t Hon*our*able my Lord Maynard.

Most faithfully Pen'd and set down by me Rob*er*t Moody who was his servant, and had the honnour to wait on him in his whole Journey through France, Savoy, Pie-mont, through all Italy, Hungaria, Bohemia, Germany, Holand and the Spanish Netherlands.

My Maister haveing seen the Cerimoniall Rites of the French King's Mariage,[1] with the Qwen's entry into Paris which was very Magnificent, the severall Operas, Commedies, Fire-workes, Balles, and other divertisments, too long to particularize; And he being as it were weary with seing so many splendid showes and Rareties, He tooke a full resolution to leave Paris with all its Gaudy Entertainments for a time; and soon after put his Heroick intention in execution.

[f. 4ᵛ] And about thre days before his depart he went to the Pallais Royale to kisse the Qwen-Mother's[2] Hands, and to tell her of his intended Travells. The Qwen understanding whoes Sonne he was, smil'd, and tould him that she was very well satisfy'd with his Father's Loyalty in the whole time of Cromwel's Rebellion,[3] and for a Mark of her favour she would give him a Letter of Recommendation to her sister Madam-Royale the Duchesse[4] of Savoy.[5] And accordinglie caus'd her Secretary Imediatly to write it, And haveing sign'd it with her own Hand, Deliverd it to my Maister wishing him good Successe in his intended Journey, the effects of which letter shall be related as it falls in Course.

Mr Henchman who was my Maister's Governor,[6] Aggreed for a Certain summe of Money with the Messenger to furnishe us with Horses, Meat, Drink, Lodging, and all Other necessarys from Paris to Lyons, and accordinglie we took our Journey in the company of Severall English Gentlemen September
the seventh
1660.

---

[1] King Louis XIV (1638–1715) had been passionately in love with Cardinal Mazarin's niece, Marie Mancini, but in June 1660 he was finally persuaded into marriage with Marie-Thérèse of Austria, as a means of ratifying the peace between the two countries.

[2] King Louis XIII's widow, the Queen Mother, was the Spanish Anne of Austria (1601–66), a daughter of King Philip III and his cousin the Austrian Archduchess Margaret. She had acted as regent during her son's minority (1643–51).

[3] William 2nd Baron Maynard was a staunch royalist during the English Civil War (see p. 228) and was a member of the Sealed Knot Society which from autumn 1653 was actively plotting against Cromwell. Some of the society's early meetings, held at Paris in the Tuileries or the Jardin Renard, had been attended by Charles II. He gave its activities his seal of approval in November 1653. See Antonia Fraser, *Cromwell Our Chief of Men*, London, 1974, p. 479; and her *King Charles II*, London, 1979, pp. 140–41.

[4] 'the Duchesse' inserted above.

[5] Following the death of Victor Amadeus I (1587–1637), Duke of Savoy, his widow Christine de France (the sister of King Louis XIII), also known as Maria Cristina or Madame Royale, became regent for her two sons, Francis Hyacinth (d. 1638) and Charles Emmanuel (1634–75). Challenges to her authority by her son's uncles, Prince Maurice (d. 1657) and Thomas of Carignano (d. 1656), engendered a civil war between the 'Madamisti' and the 'Principisti' (1639–42). The redoubtable Madame Royale saw off these threats and effectively governed long after the majority of her son, Charles Emmanuel. At the time of Maynard's visit, tensions had somewhat diminished through the Peace of the Pyrenees (1659).

[6] Maynard's tutor was possibly a relative of Humphrey Henchman (1592–1675), whom his family may have first known at Cambridge. He took his MA (1616) from Christ's College and was a fellow of Clare Hall (1616–23). After serving as canon and precentor of Salisbury (1623) and rector of the Isle of Portland, he was deprived of his living at the outbreak of the civil war. He assisted Charles II to escape from England after the Battle of Worcester (1651). Immediately following the Restoration he was appointed as Bishop of Salisbury (1660–63) and then Bishop of London (1663–75).

[f. 5ʳ] Every French League makes 3 English Miles.

	Leagues
From Paris to Milly the first night	12
The second Day to Pontgason at Dinner[1]	8
To Montargiers at night good Lodging	4
To Bussier the second Day at Dinner	7
To Briar a pleasant village	3
To Bonny at night indifferent	3
To Conne the 3ᵈ. Day at Dinner	5
To la Charitè at night, Good Lodging & good wine	4
To Nivers the 4th Day at Dinner[2] Here is a most famous Glass-hous	}5
To Sᵗ Pier at night[3]	5
To Moullin the 5th Day at Dinner, Good Schisseurs and good knives mad there	}7
To Veren at night indifferent	6
To Pallis at Dinner a Castle and River	4
To Paquodir at night a very good Lodging	4
To Roana we crost the River Loire	4
To Sᵗ Saffleur on the top of a high Mount at Dinner[4]	3
To Terrara at the foot of the Mountain[5]	3
To Broell the 8th Day at dinner[6] Their growes excellent good Wine	}3
To Lyons at the 3 Kings[7] an Excell- ent good Lodging	}3

[f. 5ᵛ] At Lyons la Maison de ville or Towne Hous is most remarkable, A Rare piece of Architeckture;[8] And goeing up to the top of a Hill where our Lady's Church stands,[9] one may see all Lyons and many Miles round, as also two Rivers the Roan and Soan meet together, on which River they go as farr as Avignon in Provence in Boat.[10]

[1] Moody's 'Milly' is probably Melun. His route from there to Montargis would have taken him either due south, close to the Fontainebleau estate, or slightly to the east, following the River Seine down as far as the River Loing.

[2] Montargis, La Bussière, Briare, Bonny-sur-Loire, Cosne-Cours-sur-Loire, La Charité-sur-Loire, and Nevers.

[3] (Probably) St-Parize-le-Châtel.

[4] Moulins, Varennes-sur-Allier, Lapalisse, La Pacaudière, Roanne, and St-Symphorien-de-Lay.

[5] Tarare. John Evelyn wrote of his journey via St-Symphorien-de-Lay and Tarare in September 1644: 'It being late e're we left this Towne, we rod no farther than Tarrara that night (passing St. Saforin) a little desolate Village, standing in a Vally neere a very pleasant streame encompass'd with fresh meadows, & Vineyards: the Hills, which we rod over before we descended, and after on Lions side, are so high & mountainous, that fir & pine grow frequently on them', Evelyn (1644), II, p. 156.

[6] (Probably) L'Arbresle.

[7] Lyons. The 'Three Kings' or 'King's Arms' had been regarded by English travellers as one of the most fashionable and comfortable inns at Lyons for over sixty years. In 1611 Sir Charles Somerset described it as 'the fayrest Inne of France' and Thomas Coryat also stayed there in 1608. See Somerset (1611), p. 120.

[8] The Hotêl de Ville as noted by Moody was designed by Simon Maupin during the 1650s but has been extensively restored and altered on several occasions since then.

[9] The church of Notre-Dame de Fourvière, situated to the west of the cathedral of St-Jean.

[10] Evelyn (1644), II, pp. 156–7: 'Lions is incomparably situated upon a Confluence of Rivers Saone & Rhodanus, which washes the Walls of the Citty in a very rapid streame. Each of these has its bridg; and that over the Rhone consists of 28 Arches'.

Veuë d'ône partie de la ville de Lion, et de la Riuiere de Sone. Ifrael excudit, cum priuilegio Regis.

Ifrael Silueftre delin. et fc.

Fig. 39. 'Veuë d'une partie de la ville de Lion, et de la Riviere de Sone' (c. 1650–55) (Israel Silvestre).

Here my Maister and[1] the Governour consulting together, thought it not convenient to travell so many in company; tooke their leave of the other Gentlemen, who tooke their way towards Geneva, And so hired fower Horses & a Viturin or Groome[2] to tend them and be our guide frome Lyons to Turin in Pie-mont.

And so we departed frome Lyons the 22th of September in the year of our Lord God –
1660.

From Lyons to Aren – 4 and to Artas at night[3]	
3 Leagues in all	}7
To Scampi and then to la Frett	3
To Rivelle their is Steell Milles	
And also Curious Paper Milles	}2
To Moyran[4] growes excellent good wine	2
To Genoble at night	1

At Genoble the Hugenots' Church[5] and the Parlement Hous[6] is worth seing. Their is also [f. 6ʳ] a River and a curious Ston Bridge.

From Grenoble to the Grand Charereux   4

The Grand Charereux is an extraordinary great convent thre Miles up in a wood and their is a fountain where they say Sᵗ Bruno their Patron[7] lov'd and did penance. My Maister and his Retenue was treated with a noble Dinner and all sorts of delicat wines as all Gentlemen are who have the curiositie to travell up thither.

From the Great Carthusians to Sᵗ Pier where[8] Runs a little River that parts
France & Savoy.   }4

Haveing past the River we went up a great Mountain, and before we arriv'd at the foot of the Mountain night over tooke us in so much that we lost our way. Traveling over Hedges through Brooks and Briers, through watry grounds and sometimes our Horses up to their Bellyes. In this manner we travel'd from 4 in the afternoon till ten at night, and then as God would have it we spi'd a light and soon after arriv'd at a certaine village [f. 6ᵛ] Call'd Nostre Dame de Myan[9] which was but thre Leagues frome St. Pier although we had travel'd six howers by the Cloak.

---

[1] 'our' deleted.

[2] 'Vittorin', an anglicized form of *vetturino*, in Italy one who lets out carriages or horses on hire.

[3] Moody's 'Aren' and 'Artas' are uncertain, unless 'Aren' is his mishearing of Vienne, the next major town due south of Lyons. Alternatively, his party may have headed south-east from Lyons via la Verpillière and Bourgoin-Jallieu before heading due south to Champier.

[4] Champier and La Frette, Rives, and Moirans.

[5] The Hugenots had gained freedom of worship at Grenoble under the Edict of Nantes (1599).

[6] Moody is probably referring here to the Palais de Justice, on the site of the ancient palace of the dauphins, much of which was built in the 16th century; rather than to the Hôtel de Ville, formerly the house of the Constable de Lesdiguières.

[7] The Carthusian monastery of La Grande-Chartreuse, standing high above the right bank of the River Isère, was founded in 1084 by St Bruno. Much of its present buildings date from the 17th century. See Lough, *France Observed*, pp. 201–3, for other 17th-century descriptions.

[8] St-Pierre-de-Chartreuse is situated at the meeting of the Guiers-Morts and other mountain streams.

[9] At this point on their intinerary, Moody's 'Nostre Dame de Myan' is unclear, although heading towards the Granier plateau, his party would have probably passed close by Notre Dame de Casalibus. He may have mistakenly added 'Myan' from the town of Myans (which he was soon to pass through) to the north of the Granier plateau.

About a Mile frome this Town their is a great Mountain nam'd Grenij.[1] Near which Mountain their stood a famous Citty nam'd St. Andrew which in former times was the head Town of Savoy, but in the year 1449 their happen'd a grievous Earthquake which rent the said Mountain and destroy'd the *said* citty, killing to the number of 6,000 soules which was Registrated in French at the same time it hapen'd and fix'd by the Altar in the said Church of Nostre Dame de Myan –[2]

Frome Nostre Dame de Myan we went to Momillan, this Momillian is
the strongest Town in all Savoy and has a Castle Impregnable[3]   } 2
To Ugebell[4] at Dinner, their we saw a hansome woman which is very rare in
those parts   } 4
To Chambery[5] at night a bad Lodging   4
To S[t]. Michael[6] at Dinner excel*lent* good Trouts   } 5
And rare good wine and over the Chimney was writ these Latin Verses which M[r]. Henchman causd me to[7] write down.

> Tollas Lignum foco si vis extinguere flamas
> Si Veneris Motus, Otia vina dapes[8]

[f. 7[r]] To st André at night[9]   2
Here by the Rashnesse of the Governor in setting out too late from S[t]. Michals, Night overtooke us, And haveing Cragie Mountains to passe and some precipieces not two foot broad we were expos'd to great danger; the night being extreame darke we set the Viturin on a white Horse and made him lead the way and we follow'd his trace till we arriv'd about nine a Cloack at S[t]. Andre, where we had a good Lodging and a Roasted Phesant for 18 pence to supper. these Birds being very plenty in that Mountanous Country.

To Modan and then to Bramont, ex*cellent* good wine[10]   3
To Arenberge at the foot of Mountsiny[11] at Din*ner*   2
Here we were forc'd to hire Mulles to go up the Mountain, they being sure footed creatures and will pick out their way very carefully. When we arriv'd at the Top of Montsiny their is a nother Mountain on the top of that as we conjectur'd about a League high whereon as we

[1] The Granier plateau (Col du Granier).
[2] The northern end of the Granier plateau is especially prone to fissures and collapse. The hamlet of St-André still survives, despite the catastrophe of 1449. At this point, Moody is definitely referring to the town of Myans. The nearby Abimes de Myans were formed by another landslide from the Granier in 1248, in which many villages were destroyed with the loss of over 5,000 lives.
[3] Montmélian was an ancient stronghold of the dukes of Savoy. Its enormous fort, famously taken by Henri IV in 1600, was destroyed in the 18th century.
[4] 'Ugebell', unidentified.
[5] Chambéry.
[6] Either the Mt St-Michel or (more likely) St-Michel-de-Maurienne.
[7] 'to' *inserted above*.
[8] 'You must remove the wood from the fire if you wish to extinguish the flames; / if you wish to extinguish the flames of Venus [you must remove] idleness, wine, and banquets.'
[9] St-André.
[0] Modane and Bramans.
[11] (Probably) Lanslebourg-Mont-Cenis.

were tould the snow has lyen over since the Flood of Noah. We travell'd along a pleasan[t] plain the Mountain on our left hand about a league till we came to a good Inne.   4

[f. 7ᵛ] To ride down the Mountain no Man dare Ventur neither on Horse nor Mulle, but their are bare footed fellows stand always ready with bearing Barrows Maid of wood and [?]iths who cary Gentlemen to the foot of the Mountain in an howers time for a halfe Crown.
Which is to Nonvallesse[1] and is   3
As for our horses we threw the bridles over their Necke and left them[2] with the Viturin to pick out their way.
  From Nonvallesse to Zusa[3] a pretty Wall'd Town with a Cittadelle   2
To Jackonir[4]   8
To Sᵗ Ambroise[5]   2
Near[6] on the Top of a high Mountayn their is a Most famous Convent cald St Michæl[7] to whom it is dedicated.
  From Sᵗ Ambroise to Riccole[8] a very pleasan[t] Town and a noble Pallace belonging to the Duke where he keeps Court when he goes a hunting with the Ladyes, for their the Ladys Ride a hunting on Horseback as well as the Men   3
  From Riccole to Tourin[9] head Town of Savoy and the Duke's Court

[f. 8ʳ] Being arrivd at Turine, my Maister haveing refresht and Drest himself, went the same night to Court and deliver'd his letter to the Duchesse Royall of Savoy,[10] and was very favourably receiv'd; The next Morning and every day so long as he stay their, a Coach and two of the Duchesses own footmen was sent to wait, with orders to show him without and within the Citty what was most rare to be seen.
  First we went to see the Duke's Court and Pallace;[11] And next the Cittadell[12] which is very strong and in it the biggest Well in Christendome –
  Next we went to Valentin Hous[13] about two Milles out of Town. A Hous rarely furnish'd

---

[1] Novalesa stands at the end of the old Mont Cenis pass and was usually the place where travellers either left off or picked up their mules used for the crossing.

[2] 'them' added above.

[3] Susa, with an 11th-century castle.

[4] 'Jackonir', unidentifed. Moody seems to be referring to the area in which the modern Bussoleno is the main town.

[5] Sant'Ambrogio di Torino.

[6] 'which' deleted.

[7] The Sacra di San Michele, located high on the ridge of Monte Pirchiriano outside Turin in about 1000 AD, was suppressed in 1622.

[8] Moody's 'Riccole' is possibly Rivoli.

[9] Turin, the capital of the Duchy of Savoy since 1563.

[10] Christine de France, the Duchess Royal of Savoy, who was still immensely influential at Turin, despite her son, Charles Emmanuel (1634–75), having assumed the title of Duke of Savoy in 1638. See p. 241, n. 5.

[11] The recently completed Palazzo Reale at Turin had been built by Amedeo di Castellamonte between 1646 and 1660.

[12] Moody's 'Cittadell' is probably the building now known as the Palazzo Madama, a 15th-century square-shaped castle, built upon the site of 13th-century fortifications. Since 1935 it has housed the Museum of Ancient Art.

[13] The Castello del Valentino, beyond the Ponte Umberto I, was built between 1630 and 1660 in the French style with an extensive botanical garden. It is now occupied by the university.

and adorn'd with all sorts of Picktturs and other rich furnitur. and comeing out on the left hand ther is a Most pleasant Garden with Leamonds, Oranges, Pomgranads and many other sorts of Rich fruite –

From thence we went to Millfiore[1] where their is a vast and pleasant Garden, but the Hous [f. 8ᵛ] has been much Ruin'd in the time of the warr by the souldiours and at that time not repaired.

Next we went to Montquallis[2] a Most pleasant Hous and Garden.

And frome thence to la vigne de Madam[3] which is a Most sumptious Hous[4] with very large Rooms Most nobly furnish'd and a Garden that surpassed all the othe[rs] for beauty and rarety.

At the end of the Bridge their is the Cappucins on a little Hill,[5] the Church is Richly adornd with Rare Picktturs and other furnitur. A very pleasant Garden, and in it many pretty devices of Rocks & shells and watter sprwting out as if they were things naturall –

These good Fathers are never Idle, they are either Reading, Praying Sweping the church, setting out the Altar or workeing in the Garden insomuch that the capucins' convent is always More neat and Clean then any other order and yet thye war neither shirts nor shooes. –

My Maister haveing seen all what was Most rare in and[6] about Turin he went to take his leave of her highnesse

[f. 9ʳ] My Maister went to kisse the Duchess' hands and to give her thanks for her great Civility shewn to him. Her highnesse wish'd him good successe in his Journey and was pleas'd to give him a letter of Recomendation to her Daughter the Duchesse of Parma.[7] And so we parted from Turin the 5ᵗʰ of October, 1660. And here begins Italian Miles which is the same as English Miles

	Miles
From Turin to Cair	5
To Vila-nuova[8]	5
To Ast at night, their growes good wine d'Ast[9]	10
To Philsan,[10] out of Pie-mont into the state of Millan – which belongs to the King of Spain To Allexander a great River and a very fine ston Bridge cover all over like a Hous[11]	10

---

[1] 'Millfiore', unidentified.

[2] Moody's 'Montquallis' may be Moncalieri, about 8km from Turin beyond the River Po. Its 15th-century castle was enlarged in the 17th-century.

[3] Probably the country residence of Madame Royale.

[4] 'Hous' written above.

[5] The Capuchin monastery standing on the Monte dei Cappuccini, which is approached from the city heading south over the Ponta Vitt. Emanuele I.

[6] 'in and' added above.

[7] In 1659 Violante of Savoy had married Ranuccio II Farnese (1630–94), Duke of Parma (acceded 1646). They had no surviving children and in 1664 Ranuccio II secondly married Isabella D'Este, by whom he had Odoardo (1666–93); and in 1669 thirdly married Isabella D'Este, by whom he had Francisco (1678–1727), Duke of Parma; and Antonio (1679–1731), Duke of Parma.

[8] Chieri and Villanova d'Asti.

[9] The city of Asti is capital of the Asti province of the Piedmont region. It is still famed for its fine wines, most notably Asti spumante.

[10] Felizzano.

[11] Alessandria was primarily of importance through being almost equidistant from Turin, Milan, and Genoa.

To Nuova at night, here begins the Repub-
like of Genova[1]   } 12

To Gave a strong Castle   5

To Voltagis an English woman Mary'd
to a Genovese Merchant   } 5

To Moullin[2] at night and then to Genova   15

Genova head Citty of Liguria, situated on the Sea coast, and May be Reckon'd one of the Principall sea Ports of all Italy:

[f. 9ᵛ] The People of Genova enjoy the treasure of liberty and are ruled as a Republick in such a manner[3] that the whole state is content with the Government. Insomuch that those who submit themselves unto her have their life, honnour and goods in safty. The streets are narrow, but the buildings are high and sumptious, strada nuoa or new street is built all of Marble.[4] their are very fine Churches that of Signor [Saulij?] and the Jesú and Sᵗ. Siro[5] are the chiefest except *the* Cathedrall Church of Sᵗ Laurance.[6] But as for Pallaces I think verily there are the finest in Christendome, the Palace of the Prince of Dorio[7] is the Chiefest that of St Pier di Arena and Albara[8] are very rare all richly furnish'd with Gardens and water-workes and other rareties therto belonging. Their are also good store of shipes and Gallyes and an excellent Harbour. My Maister was very civily entertained by[9] the English

---

[1] Novi Ligure. Following domination by the Sforza family (1466–99) and the French (1499–1512), Andrea Doria (1466–1560) had devised in 1528 a new constitution for Genoa which freed it from foreign domination. Through this constitution, political power was placed in the hands of 24 groups of noble families who elected the *dogi biennali*, a new duke every two years. The senate of 400 members also elected the *consiglio minore* of 100 members and a council of 8 members who acted as the doge's advisors.

[2] Gavi, Voltaggio, and Molini.

[3] 'that' deleted.

[4] The Strada Nuova, first laid out in 1558, is now the Via Garibaldi. It was the location for some of the grandest mansions of leading patrician families. Evelyn (1644), II, p. 176: 'We went the next day to see the famous Strada Nova … for statlinesse of the buildings, paving & evenesse of the Streete, certainly far superior to any in Europ for the number of houses' (drawing upon Raymond (1648), pp. 13–14). Genoa was renowned for its picturesque setting, spectacular buildings and immaculate streets. Lassels, *The Voyage of Italy*, 2 vols, Paris, 1670, I, pp. 82–3: 'The common Italian Proverb, calls it, *Genua la Superba* … if ever I saw a towne with its holy day clothes alwayes on, it was *Genua*'.

[5] 'Signor [Saulij?]', unidentified but possibly Moody's confusion with the church of San Siro. The large church of San Siro, near the Via San Luca, had been extensively rebuilt between 1586 and 1613. His reference to 'the Jesú' may mean the Jesuit College on the Via Balbi, built from the mid-1630s and now part of the university. See Evelyn (1644), II, p. 177; and Mortoft (1658), p. 43.

[6] The Romanesque cathedral of San Lorenzo. Evelyn (1644), II, pp. 176–7: 'St. Laurenzo in the navil (as it were of the City) of white and black polish'd stone, the inside wholy incrusted with marble, and other precious materials' (drawn from Pflaumern, pp. 575–6).

[7] The Palazzo or Villa Doria, known as the Palazzo del Principe, situated beyond the Piazza Acquaverede. The palace had been granted to Andrea Doria in 1522 and was largely rebuilt for him by Perin del Vaga (d. 1547) and Giovanni da Montorsoli (d. 1563). See Evelyn (1644), II, pp. 174–5; and Mortoft (1658), p. 41.

[8] This passage describing the palaces of 'St Pier di Arena and Albara' is borrowed from Raymond (1648), p. 10. It was also cited by Evelyn (1644), II, p. 170: 'those pleasant Villas, & fragrant Orchards which are situated on this Coast, full of Princly retirements for the Sumptuousnesse of their buildings & noblenesse of the plantations; especialy those at St. Pietro d'Arena'.

[9] 'by' added above.

Merchants at Genova but especialy one M[r]. Allen who never left him except when he was a sleep.[1]

We departed frome Genova thowards Millan October the 20th 1660. And tooke our way [f. 10[r]]

To Seravala a very pretty Town	28
To Tortona we past a River call'd Scriuia	12
To Pontecorona	5
To Vogere we past the Staffora River	5
To Pancarana we past the R*iver* Poe in Barke[2]	
And soon after we arriv'd at Pavia	} 15

Pavia is a very strong Citty well wall'd, the River Poe runs on one side and the River Tecino on the other. Francis the first King of France had a sad overthrow before this Town: 20,000 kill'd, himselfe taken Prisoner and Carry'd to Madrid in Spain where he was a long time detein'd till Hostages were sent for the payment of his Ransome.[3] We were show'd to a certain Church Yard where all the French Mens' Sones are Pill'd up, Just like Pilles of wood in our wood-wharfs.

About a quarter of an Mile from Pavia we past over the River Tecino on a Bridge

And then went on our Journey To Binasco[4]	10
To Millano	10

At Millan the Dom church build in honor of S[t]. Charles Boromeo.[5] The Great Hospitall The Jesouits Church and the Castle are all worth seing.[6]

[f. 10[v]] Colonell Tafft an Ireish nobleman wh[o] had A Regiment in the spanish service,[7] He was very kind to my Maister. He did not only Cause him to Dine with him every Day while he stay'd their But Carry'd him in his Coach through all that Spacious Citty and show'd him all what was Most Rare.

[1] It was common for English visitors to be guided around the city by English merchants. John Evelyn's guide, for example, was called 'Mr. Thomson' (1644), II, p. 172.

[2] Serravalle Scrivia, Tortona, the River Scrivia, Pontecurone, Voghera, the River Staffora, Bastida Pancarana, and the River Po.

[3] Pavia stands just to the north of the confluence of the Rivers Ticino and Po. The Battle of Pavia was fought on 24 February 1525, at which King François I of France was defeated and taken prisoner by Emperor Charles V.

[4] Binasco.

[5] The huge 14th–18th-century cathedral at Milan was built upon the site of an older church dedicated to Santa Maria Maggiore and was dedicated by St Charles Borromeo (1538–84; canonized 1610).

[6] The Ospedale Maggiore (Great Hospital) was built in the mid-15th century but much of it was destroyed (now restored) during World War II. The buildings are now occupied by the Università degli Studi. Charles Borromeo, Cardinal and Archbishop of Milan, from 1560 established various seminaries at Milan and entrusted a college for lay students to the Jesuits. The Castello Sforzesco was built by Francesco Sforza in 1451–66 on the site of a 14th-century castle. It suffered extensive damage, especially to its archives, during World War II.

[7] This was possibly Theobald Taaffe (d. 1677), second Viscount Taaffe and 1st Earl of Carlingford, an Anglo-Irish Catholic peer, who had acted as Charles II's Chamberlain while exiled at Paris. He had also reputedly shared the favours one of the king's mistresses, Lucy Walter (and was probably the father of her second child, Walter). He was an energetic supporter of the exiled king, negotiating on his behalf with the Pope and various members of the Catholic continental aristocracy. His sons, Nicholas (d. 1690) and Francis (1639–1704), succeeded him as the 2nd and 3rd Earls of Carlingford. Francis entered the service of Charles, Duke of Lorraine, and saw active service in the Austrian army.

We parted frome Millan the 29 of October	} 10
And tooke our way to Marignana	
To Lody a pretty hansome Town at night	10
To Cassall at Dinner	10
To Fonby at night	6
To Piacenza a very pleasant Town belongs	} 9
to the Duke of Parma	
To Fiorenzola[1]	15
We past the Tarro a very dangerous River[2]	} 8
when it Rains and then To S[t] Dionino[3]	
To la Parola[4] another water to passe	2
To Parma Citty wher the Duke keeps Court	13

At Parma my Maister went to court and deliver'd his Letter to the young Duchesse and was Receiv'd with a great deal of respeck,[5] and had A Coach sent to wait on him every day[6] while he stay'd their. And the Old Duchesse[7] was extreamly taken with my Maister, Insomuch that when my Maister [f. 11[r]] Went to take his leave, she gave him a noble Letter of Recommendation to the Great Duke of Tuskany her Brother.[8]

And so we parted from Parma to St Illario[9] Where we past over the River Lonza[10] on a	
brave ston Bridge, and then to Reggio	15
And then we past 2 Rivers more in Barke	} 8
And at last arriv'd at Marzaia	
To Modena Citty where the Duke keeps Court[11]	8

We saw the Duke's Pallace and some of the Best Churches, as for the rest their is not Much remarkable.[12]

To go from Modena to Bolognia we past The Pannaro River in Bark, and the River Amola, Samogia, Canaro, Reno,[13] And then

[1] Melegnano, Lodi Vécchio, Casalpusterlengo, Fómbio, Piacenza, and Fiorenzuola d'Arda.

[2] The River Taro. This reference is misplaced since Moody and his party would have crossed the River Taro after passing through the village of Parola.

[3] 'St Dionino', unidentified. Moody may have meant San Pancrazio, a few miles to the west of Parma.

[4] Parola.

[5] The 'young Duchesse' was Violante of Savoy who in 1659 had married Ranuccio II Farnese (1630–94), Duke of Parma (acceded 1646). See p. 247, n. 7.

[6] 'day' added above.

[7] Moody's reference to 'the Old Duchesse' is not clear since there was no living Dowager Duchess of Parma at this period. Ranuccio II (1630–94) had succeeded as Duke of Parma his uncle Odoardo Farnese (1612–46), who died unmarried. Ranuccio was the son of Odoardo's sister Mary, Duchess of Modena (b.1616) who married Francesco d'Este, Duke of Modena.

[8] Ferdinando II de' Medici (1610–70), had become Grand Duke of Tuscany in 1621.

[9] Sant'Ilário d'Enza.

[10] The River Enza which Moody would have crossed just *before* passing through Sant'Ilário d'Enza.

[11] Reggio Nell'Emilia, Marzaglia, and Modena.

[12] The Este family gained control of the city in 1288 and Borso d'Este was the first duke of Modena in 1452. They remained the dominant family until 1796. Mary of Modena (1658–1718), the future queen of King James II of England, was the daughter of Alfonso IV d'Este, Duke of Modena (from 1658–62) and his duchess Laura Martinozzi. The Palazzo Ducale had been begun in 1634 for Francesco I (1629–58) on the site of an old Este castle.

[13] The modern-day Via Aemilia from Modena to Bologna crosses the Rivers Panaro, 'Amola', unidentified, Samoggia, 'Canaro', unidentified, and Reno.

To Bolognia which makes in all 20

Bolognia[1] is a very great Citty and is in the Pope's Teritorys, The sasseges that's made in Boglognia and wash-Balls are esteem'd all Christendome Over. We parted frome Bolognia the 8th Day of November 1660.

From Bolognia to Scaricalasino[2] at night 20
To Fiorenzola at Dinne 10
To Scarperia, Good Knives Made[3] 10
[f. 11ᵛ]
To Pont Sᵗ. Pier[4] and then to Florence.

We arriv'd at Florence the 10th day of November. Florence is a Most famous Citty and stands in the heart of Tuscany. A noble River runs through the heart of the Citty nam'd Arno, Wheron is built fower Bridges.[5] Their is very fine Churches, the Dom and the Nunciata are Pri[n]cipall.[6] The great Duke's Pallace and Gardens are most worthy to be seen,[7] but that call'd the Great Duke's Gallery is most remarkable, their being in it many curious Raretyes.[8]

My Maister being arriv'd at Florence, the next Day after he went to see the great Duke, and haveing kiss'd his Hands deliver'd the before-mentioned Letter which my Maister had from the Old Duches of Parma, the Duke smil'd and bid him welcome to Florence,[9] and two or thre dayes after when we dream'd of no such Matter, one Morning about ten of the Cloak their cam into my Maister's Lodging six Porters with large Baskets on their heads Loaded with the Choicest wines Florence could afford, Turkys, all sorts of wild Fowle, all sorts of sweetmeats and Confitures and severall other things what was Most rare, they enquir'd [f. 12ʳ] for Il Signor Maynardo, Meaning my Maister and tould him that the Great

---

[1] Bologna. From 1506, when Pope Julius II reconquered the city, Bologna was incorporated into the Papal States. Evelyn (1645), II, p. 426: 'This Citty is famous also for Salsicci [sausages], & sell a World of Parmegiano Cheeze, with Botargo, Caviare &c; which makes some of their shops perfume the streetes with no agreable smell: here we furnish'd ourselves with Wash-balls, the best being made here, and a considerable commodity' (drawing upon Raymond (1648), p. 182).

[2] Scaricalasino. Moody certainly had his copy of Raymond (1648), pp. 176–8, open as he compiled this itinerary, as did Evelyn (1645), II, pp. 419–20, as he described his own journey in the other direction from Florence to Bologna.

[3] Firenzuola and Scarperia.

[4] This bridge spans the River Sieve at S. Piero a Sieve. See Evelyn (1645), II, p. 419, for a vivid impression of the dangers and breath-taking views of this route.

[5] Moody is probably referring to the Ponte Vecchio, Ponte a Santa Trinita, Ponte alle Grazie, and the Ponte S. Niccolò over the River Arno.

[6] The 14th–15th-century cathedral of Santa Maria del Fiore is dedicated to the Madonna of Florence and is distinctive for its white marble from Carrara, green from Prato, and red from the Maremma. The church of the Santissima Annunziata was founded by the Servite Order in 1250, rebuilt in the 15th century, and extensively renovated between 1601 and 1615. It contains the Chapel of the Annunziata, built at the expense of Pietro de' Medici.

[7] The Palazzo Vecchio (old), Palazzo Pitti (new), and either the Boboli Gardens or the geometrically laid out gardens crossing the gardens between the Palazzo Pitti and the Forte di Belvedere, commissioned by Ferdinando I in 1590 and designed by Buontalenti in the shape of a six-pointed star.

[8] The Galleria degli Uffizi was housed on the third floor of the Palazzo Uffizi by roofing in the open terrace on the top storey of the building. A large theatre was added to the Uffizi by Buontalenti between 1586 and 1589. The renowned collections of the Uffizi were founded by Cosimo I (1519–74) and much enlarged by Francesco I (1541–87). Ferdinando I (1549–1609) also transferred scuptures here from the Villa Medici at Rome.

[9] Ferdinando II de' Medici (1610–70), Grand Duke of Tuscany.

Duke had sent him that present as a marke of the esteem he had for him. Haveing given two or thre pistols in gould amongst the men for a reward they were all dismist. My Maister and the Governor haveing view'd every particular began to Ruminat how to dispose of so many varieties, and at last concluded to invite all the English that were in Florence to Dinner and to make a mery Day of it and accordinglie they did.[1] And to honnour the feast the more they envited one Sir Thomas Bendish who was Just arriv'd at Florence from his Ambassy in Constantinople.[2] So haveing ended the Day & most part of the night with Musick and drinking of Healths every one retir'd to their severall Habitations, and My Maister had severall invitations afterwards while he[3] stay'd their. And when he went to give the Grand Duke thanks and to take his leave, his Highnesse was pleas'd to give him a letter of Recomendation to the Pope[4] haveing taken his leave of all the other gentlemen his acquaintances we parted from Florence the the 20th of November 1660

From Florence to Poggio Gayano wher ther
is a most sumptious Pallace belongs to the Grand Duke[5] } 10

[f. 12ᵛ] To Pistoia[6] a good hansome Town   10
To Lucca   25
   Lucca is a very pleasant Citty, situated in a plain but invironed round with Hills and those Hilles all cover'd over with wine and fruite It is rull'd as Common Wealth or free state.[7] We saw the Armory which is able to Arme 30 thousand Men. The great Duke has

---

[1] 'did' added above.

[2] Sir Thomas Bendish (c. 1607–c. 1674) had been appointed in January 1647, under a double commission from both King Charles I and Parliament, as English Ambassador at Constantinople. Having retained his ambassadorial position throughout the Commonwealth and Protectorate, Bendish was honorably recalled from Constantinople in June 1660.

Here, however, some doubt must be cast over either Moody's exact dating of Maynard's movements in Italy or as to which English ambassador Maynard actually met at Florence. Moody claims that their party arrived at Florence on 10 and left on 20 November 1660, meeting Bendish there. But it is known that Bendish only began his return journey home from Constantinople aboard the third-rate ship *Plymouth* on 7 March 1661. This dating is confirmed by the survival of a daily journal kept by the captain, Thomas Allin. See *The Journals of Sir Thomas Allin, 1660–1678*, ed. R. C. Anderson, Navy Records Society, 2 vols, 1939–40. Having picked up Bendish and his party on 7 March 1661 at Constantinople, on the return journey to England the *Plymouth* called at Zante, Messina, Leghorn, Alicante, and Malaga, before finally arriving back in the Downs on 26 August 1661.

Because of the clear evidence supplied by Captain Allin's journal, one of two conclusions seems probable. Either Moody's dates are completely confused (since Bendish arrived at Leghorn – from where he could have made a quick trip to Florence – in early summer 1661); or Moody is confusing his ambassadors since Bendish's replacement, Heneage Finch, Earl of Winchilsea, had travelled to Turkey on the outward voyage from England of the *Plymouth*, which left the Downs on 20 October 1660. Winchilsea's party undertook some brief diplomatic business in Portugal and Algiers during early November 1660 (O.S.) and, allowing for the difference between OS and NS dating as used by Allin and Moody, the *Plymouth* could well have called at Leghorn during Maynard's stay there in mid-November 1660. For further details of Bendish, Winchilsea and Allin's journal, see Bargrave (1647–56), pp. 2–5.

[3] 'he' added above.

[4] This letter of recommendation from the Grand Duke of Tuscany was to Fabio Chigi (1599–1667), Pope Alexander VII, who was pope from 1655 until 1667.

[5] The renowned villa of Poggio a Caiano, situated about 18km from the city centre at the foot of Mount Albano, became the favourite residence of Lorenzo il Magnifico (1449–92).

[6] Pistoia.

[7] Lucca. After a period of subjection to Pisa (1343–69), Lucca had been granted a charter of independence by Emperor Charles IV. Mortoft (1658), p. 46: 'Lucques, some 26 mile form Massa, which is one of the Prettyest contrivedst Cittyes in Italy and a free Common wealth'. See also Evelyn (1645), II, pp. 408–9.

made severall attemp[t]s to surprize Lucca, but the Luchesses were alwayes so cunning to prevent his designs.

From Lucca to Pisa   12

This Pisa is a very hansom Citty and belongs to the Great Duke. It was a Republike in former times, and was a flourrishing people, and able to set out 6 gallyes against the Turks but the Great Duke envieing their prosperitie tooke the Towne by stratageme, and have continu'd in subjection though with an unwilling Mind ever since.[1]

From Pisa to Liggorne   15

Livorno is a very famous Seaport, belongs to the Great Duke. The Inhabitants are frome most parts [of] Europe [f. 13ʳ] And other parts of the World. For their are Turks, Jewes, Armenians, Arabians, Greekes, But I think verily more English then any other Nation, and live more splendid and greater then any.[2] My Maister being arriv'd he went to give his Merchants, Mʳ. Ashby and Mʳ. Sidney a visit, who were to pay him his Bills of Exchange. And was envited by them the next Day to Dinner. And being come thither accordinglie, found a Table Cover'd able to entertain twenty Guests and truely their was not many fewer, for all the most eminent Merchants of English in Town came to welcom my Maister to Livorn. I cannot expresse the Rich entertainment was their and the most exquisit wines the Town could afford and those are rare indeed, Now Mʳ. Ashby, Mʳ. Sidney, Mʳ Browne, Mʳ. Dethick with the help of Joseph Kent had contrivd that every severall Merchant should envite my Maister to Dinner every Day till he had Din'd with each, and all to meet togither at such a Merchant's Hous who gave the Dinner, and truely they were as good as their words for my Maister thought to stay but thre or fower dayes in Ligorn, and by their civill Importunities he was forc'd to stay a whole Month, And so haveing received his Money and taken his leave of all [f. 13ᵛ] those noble Merchants we went frome Livorn back to Pisa not without thre or fower to accompany him thither, we Lodg'd at the thre [D?]onzellas[3] in Pisa the best Lodgin in that Town, where my Maister tooke the liberty to treat them and drink all their healths over and over he left behind.[4] Haveing stay'd a Day & two nights he tooke his leave &[5] he sent his Commendations back by those Gentlemen to the rest. And so we parted, frome Pisa for Rome the 19th of December 1660.

Frome Pisa to Cashino	8
To Pontedano[6]	4
To Scalla a Good Lodging[7]	10
To Castellfiorentino	8

[1] The Florentines had first gained possession of Pisa in 1405. When Emperor Charles VIII entered Italy in 1494 he was expected to grant Pisa its freedom but, instead, the Florentines were able to confirm their hold on the city during the first decade of the sixteenth century, when many of its residents went into exile.

[2] Leghorn (English) or Livorno (Italian). The building of a new port was instigated in 1571 by Cosimo I (1519–74). Ferdinando I (1549–1609) issued a proclamation of religious liberty, creating Leghorn a haven for persecuted Jews, Greeks fleeing from Turkish oppression, converted Moors expelled by Philip III from Spain and Portugal and Roman Catholics from England.

[3] The name of the inn is written indistinctly with some erratic strokes (or alterations) to the first letter but it seems likely that Moody was referring to the three 'Donzellas' (i.e. maidens or damsels).

[4] '15' [miles] added in right-hand margin.

[5] 'tooke his leave &' added above, repeating 'tooke'.

[6] Cascina and Pontedera.

[7] The village of Scala, just to the north of the now much larger San Miniato.

To Poggi-bons	12
To Siena[1]	14

Romulus build Rome, and Remus built Siena but Siena was first finisht so that Siena is the ancientest of the two.[2] Romulus drew a Di*t*ch where he intended to build the city[3] and appointed so many Gates as he intended to have, And Made a law that who ever should go over his Ditch and not go round to the Gate should surely dye: Remus haveing finished [f. 14ʳ] his Citty of Siena, came to se how his Brother's Citty went forward, and seing a Ditch drawen round it in stead of a Wall began to scoff at his high walls, says Romulus: "my Walls are high enough to keep you and all others out, for I have made a Law that non on pain of death presume to come over my Ditch nor enter Rome but at the Gates appointed." "And what if I should transgresse and break this Law", says Remus, "then" says Romulus "thou shalt surely Die." "I'le venter that" sayes Remus and Jumpt over the Di*t*ch, And his Brother Romulus kill'd him dead in the place.[4] Those two Brothers were stollen frome their Mother as soon as borne. and convoy'd away to be kill'd, but were both nourish'd and fed by a Wolfe who preserv'd them[5] frome danger a long time till God was pleas'd to send Other assistance, and were found after to be of Kingly Race: – – –

Siena in former time was a Republick, but now is under Obedience to the Great Duke of Tuscany, but with Regret.

Frome Siena to Torniery we past a River	18
We past another River and then to hala[6]	8
And then we went up a great Mountain till we came to RadicoFany [7]an excellent Lodging	} 8
[f. 14ᵛ]	
To Pontcentino[8] a dangerous River when't rains[9]	7
A little further we past the Paglia River on a Ston-Bridge, and then to Aqua pendente[10] at night	} 7
To Bolsena[11] near which Town their is a Great Lake Call'd the Lake of Bolsena	} 8

---

[1] Castelfiorentino, Poggibonsi, and Siena.

[2] Evelyn (1645), II, p. 202, records that near the Senate House 'stand the statues of Romulus & Rhemus with the Wolfe, all of brasse, plac'd on a Columne of Ophite stone'.

[3] 'city' added above.

[4] According to legend, Romulus and Remus were the sons of Rhea Silvia, daughter of Numitor, king of Alba Longa. Rescued from the Tiber by a wolf and a woodpecker, both sacred to Mars, they were looked after by a herdsman, Faustulus. They eventually founded a town on the site where they had been saved. When Romulus built a city wall, Remus jumped over it and was killed by his brother. Siena had originally been an Etruscan settlement and later became the Roman city of Sena Julia.

[5] 'them' written above.

[6] Torrenieri on the River Asso. The next river would be the River Tuoma but Moody's 'hala' is unidentified. The next stopping place after Torrenieri was usually San Quirico d'Orcia.

[7] Radicófani.

[8] Perhaps a confused combination of Ponte a Rigo and the nearby Centino.

[9] i.e. 'when it rains'.

[10] The River Páglia and Acquapendente.

[11] Bolsena, standing on the north-east side of the Lake of Bolsena formed from the crater of an extinct volcano.

To Montfiascone,[1] their Growes Most excellent Musca- della wheroff a German Noble-man drank him- selfe dead	} 8
To Viterbo, at night. Viterbo Wine is esteem'd through all Italy	} 8
To Rensiglione in the State of Castro	10
To Monte-Rosse di Santa Chiesa	10
To Boccano	7
To la Storta[2]	7
From la Storta to[3] the famous Citty of Rome	8

We enter'd in at the Porta del Popola[4] the 23 of December in the year of our Lord God 1660, and tooke up our Lodgin at the signe of the Gambery in Strada Corso,[5] I haveing liv'd thre years in Rome before, I knew the language and the Citty as well as if I had been borne in it. And on Chrismasse Eve I perswaded my Maister to go to a Church calld the Apolinario near the Piazza Navona[6] where I knew their would be rare Musick, and truely I was [f. 15ʳ] not deceiv'd, for I think my Maister never heard such voyces before nor after where we continu'd till next Morning, and then return'd to our Lodging.

We continu'd at the Gambery or Lobster till after the holy Dayes. And then my Maister with the help of the Governor tooke a Lodgin at a Privat hous near Trinitá del Monte[7] of one Mʳ Pendrich a Scots Gentleman. In which Hous their Lodg'd a worthy Gentleman, one Doctor Gage[8] who was very good company for my Maister the whole winter.

We hir'd an Italian Cooke one Sebastian to dress our Meat, and I my selfe was Caterer to buy all thing that was needfull.

Being thus settled in Our Lodging My Maister began to consider how to deliver his letter to the Pope. He wore a border with a Cape as the fashion was in those Dayes, but was tould he must not appear before his Holynesse in a Cape, and so with Much difficultie we found

---

[1] Montefiascone, meaning literally 'bottle-mountain'. See Somerset (1612), p. 218, and Mortoft (1658), pp. 60–61, for the often-recounted 'Est, est, est' story of a German bishop who drank himself to death on the excellent wines of the region.

[2] Viterbo, Ronciglione, Monterosi, Baccano, and La Storta.

[3] 'to' added above.

[4] The Porta del Populo stands on approximately the same site as the ancient Porta Flaminia. The outer face of the gate had been carved in 1561 after a design by Michelangelo but the inner face had been executed as recently as 1655 to mark the entry into Rome of Queen Christina of Sweden.

[5] The 'Gambery' inn on, presumably, the Via Corsa (usually known as 'Il Corso'), joining the Piazza Venezia and Via Condotti.

[6] The church of S. Apollinaire belonged to the Jesuit Collegio Germanico; and Evelyn (1645), II, p. 290, records attending a sermon there.

[7] The church of the Trinità del Monte was attached to the French Convent of the Minims.

[8] Although this 'Doctor Gage' cannot be identified with certainty, various members of the Catholic Gage family were prominent in Western European affairs during the first half of the 17th century. The individual encountered by Maynard and Moody at Rome may well have been Francis Gage (1621–82), who had studied at Douai and Tournay College in Paris. He was awarded a DD by the Sorbonne in 1654 and appointed agent to the English Chapter at Rome between 1659 and 1661. In 1676 he became president of Douai College. Francis's royalist half-brother, Sir Henry Gage (1597–1645), had been educated in Flanders and Italy. He served the Spanish military forces at Antwerp and Flanders. During the Civil War he gained prominence in the defence of Oxford and relieved Basing House in 1644. In the following year he was killed at Abingdon. Another of Francis's half-brothers, George (fl. 1614–40), was a Catholic agent sent by James I to Rome in 1621 to obtain dispensation for the proposed marriage of Prince Charles with the Spanish Infanta. He stayed at Rome for three years for these (unsuccessful) negotiations.

Graué par Ifrael filueftre

Veüe d'vne partie de la place Nauonne a Rome.

Auec priuilege du Roy

Fig. 40. 'Veuë d'une partie de la place Navonne a Rome' (c. 1643–4) (Israel Silvestre). The Piazza Navone with the fountain del Moro (1574), S. Giacomo degli Spagnoli (1500), the cupola of S. Andrea della Valle (1622–5), and the Palace Torres-Lancellotti (1552–60). From a collection of twelve engravings (published c. 1643–4).

a Periwigg at a French Barbers that was a whole Head. Haveing all things in readynesse my Maister went couragiouslie to give his Holy-nesse a Visit, And was introduc'd by Monsignor Crach the Pope's Confessor who as fortun fell out was an Ireish man. The Pope was so well [f. 15ᵛ] pleas'd with the recommendation the letter gave my Maister that he Imediatly bestow'd on him a Gould Medall – and bid him let him know before he left Rome which way he intended to Travell, a favour which few receives except it be an Ambassador or some Great persone of note.

The rest of the Winter my Maister employ'd to se things the Most rare in Rome both above and under ground, for their is Rome above ground and Rome under ground where the poore Christians did live for thre hundred years time under the Pagan Emperors. They made streets, Churches and Chapells where they met and did their devotion. Their is certain men they call Antiquaries that shewe these places to strangers otherwise it were very dangerous to go down without good guides their haveing many people lost themselves by their Curiosity in ventering too farr.[1] If I should endeavour to mention every particular thing that's rare and worth seing in Rome, T'would make my booke swell too bigg. For brevitys sake, I shall only satisfie the Reader with some few of the Most remarkable.

Churches.

Their is in Rome above thre Hunderd churches [f. 16ʳ] smale and great, seven of which are esteem'd beyond the rest for devotion. The first is S. Peter in Vatican, the second is Sᵗ. Paul about a Mile without the Citty in the way nam'd ostiense,[2] the 3ᵈ. is Sᵗ. Maria Major in the Way call'd Esquilma, Sᵗ. Sebastian without the Gate call'd Capena;[3] the 5ᵗʰ Sᵗ John Lateran in Mont Celio, the 6ᵗʰ is santa Croce or Sᵗ Crosse in Jeruselem, also in Mont Celio, the 7ᵗʰ is Sᵗ. Laurenzo, or S. Laurence without the Gate Esqiuilino.[4] The Campitogla or Town Hous[5] is full of rare antiquities, the same place wher the senat sat above a thousand yeares ago. it is most worthy to be seen, The Pope's Pallace name'd Monte Cavallo,[6] The Pope's Pallace Cal'd Belvedere near Sᵗ Peter in Vaticano,[7] the Castle Sᵗ Angelo,[8] Pallatzo

---

[1] The existence of the catacombs, containing both pagan and christian burials, was gradually forgotten after the 9th century. From 1432 isolated excursions were again made into them and after 1578 those of S. Sebastiano became widely known. The subsequent influx of visitors caused considerable damage. the first systematic examination of them was made by Antonio Bozio (c. 1576–1629). John Evelyn (1645), compiled detailed descriptions of various catacombs, including those of Domitilla (II, pp. 363–4), S. Agnese (II, p. 387), S. Ciriaca (II, p. 381), and S. Sebastiano (II, pp. 363–4). Lassels (1670), II, p. 91ff, provides a detailed account of their mid-17th-century condition. The full extent of the catacombs was not explored until the mid-nineteenth century.

[2] St Peter's (Basilica di San Pietro in Vaticano) and St Paul's (San Paolo fuori le Mura) near the Via Ostiense.

[3] Santa Maria Maggiore (formerly the Basilica Liberiana), near the Piazza dell'Esquilino and San Sebastiano. The Porta Capena was a gate in the Servian Wall, marking the original starting point of the Appian Way. The site is now occupied by the Piazzi di Porta Capena.

[4] St John Lateran (San Giovanni in Laterano) on the edge of the Celian Hill, the southernmost of the Seven Hills of Rome; Santa Croce in Gerusalemme; and San Lorenzo fuori le Mura.

[5] The Piazza del Campidoglio near the Capitoline Hill. Moody is probably referring to the Palazzo del Senatore and the Palazzo dei Conservatori. See Evelyn (1645), II, pp. 220–23.

[6] The Quirinal Hill was also known as the Monte Cavallo from a striking group of horse-tamers. See Evelyn (1645), II, p. 237; and Mortoft (1659), pp. 77–8.

[7] The Vatican Palace was transformed by Pope Nicholas V (pope 1445–55) from an existing house into a palace. Pope Innocent VIII (pope 1484–92) built on the north summit of the Vatican Hill the Belvedere Pavilion. Pope Sixtus V (pope 1585–90) commissioned Domenico Fontana to build the Great Library and the block overlooking the Piazza San Pietro. See Mortoft (1659), p. 77.

[8] The Castel Sant'Angelo was originally the Mausoleum of Hadrian. intended as a sepulchre for himself and his family.

Patriarchalis Ecclefia S^{tæ} Mariæ Maioris, S. MARIA MAGGIORE. L'Eglife Patriarchale de faincte Marie Maiour, vna ex iis quæ Romæ vifitantur. l'vne des ftations de Rome

Ifrael sculp.

Fig. 41. 'S. Maria Maggiore. L'Eglise Patriarchale de saincte Marie Maiour, l'une des stations de Rome' (c. 1643–4) (Israel Silvestre). From a collection of ten engravings of views of Rome, *Les Eglises des Stations de Rome* (c. 1641–6), no. 6 (Israel Silvestre).

Eeclefia S. Ioannis Lateranenfis,
vna ex ijs quæ Romæ vifitantur.

S. GIOVANNI IN LATERANO.

L'Eglife de fainct Iean de Latran,
l'vne des ftations de Rome..

Ifrael fecalit.

Fig. 42. 'S. Giovanni in Laterano. L'Eglise de sainct Jean de Latran, l'une des stations de Rome'. From *Les Eglises des Stations de Rome* (c. 1641–6), no. 5.

Farnese, the Conselaria or Cardinall Barberin's Pallace,[1] Pallazzo Principi Pallestrino or P. Pallestrins Pallace, the Propagandafide, Il Palazzo Borgese, or the Prince of Borgese's Pallace[2] with a hunderd more. Then their is an Infinit number of the rarest Hospitalls in the world S[t] John Lateran's Hospitall,[3] S[t]. Spiritus, and S[t] James nam'd incurabili.[4] Then every Christian nation in the world has a Colledge in Rome. My Maister and all the English that were in Rome Din'd at the English Colledge on St. Thomas Day.[5]

[f. 16[v]] My Maister haveing satisfi'd his Curiosity in seing of sights at Rome as he had done before at Paris[6] and Winter over, began to think of removeing, but first went to aquaint his Holyness letting him know that he intended for Naples, Who was pleas'd to give him a letter of Recomendation to the Vice Roy and so we parted frome Rome for Naples the sixth of March 1661.

From Rome to Veletre	20
From Veletre to Sermonetta	15
To Piperno	15
To Terracina[7]	15

About 3 milles frome thence we Enter'd into the Kingdome of Naples next to Fondy[8]	}15
To Molla	15
To Cassall	15
To Capua[9]	16

Capua is a very ancient Citty and as pleasant a situation as any in the world. Haniball the great Carthagenian Generall tooke great delight in the City of Capua, and although he dy'd many hunderd Miles frome thence, yet he desir'd his body should be brought thither [f. 17[r]] to this place, and accordinglie it was and we saw his Tomb in a little Church near Capua.[10]

From Capua to the most Odoriffere Citty of Naples.[11]	}16

[1] The Palazzo Farnese, designed for Cardinal Alessandro Farnese (later Pope Paul III); and Palazzo Barberini, begun by Carlo Maderna for Pope Urban VIII in 1624.

[2] Palazzo Borghese, known from its shape as the 'harpsichord of Rome'. It was acquired by Cardinal Camillo Borghese who became Pope Paul V in 1605.

[3] The Ospedale di S. Giovanni. Evelyn (1645), II, pp. 275, 291.

[4] Evelyn also describes the hospitals di S. Spirito (II, p. 311) and di S. Giacomo degli Incurabili (II, p. 373).

[5] The English College was situated next to the church of St Thomas of Canterbury. A college of English missionaries had been established there in 1575 by Pope Gregory XIII. See F. A. Gasquet, *History of the Venerable English College*, Rome, 1920. The college buildings were rebuilt between 1670 and 1685. See Evelyn (1645), II, p. 365.

[6] 'beg' deleted.

[7] Velletri, Sermoneta, (probably) Priverno, and Terracina.

[8] Either the town of Fondi (inland) or the Lido di Fondi (along the coast).

[9] 'Molla', unidentified, Cassale and Capua.

[10] Santa Maria Cápua Vetere is situated on the site of the ancient Capua which placed itself under Hannibal's rule in 216 BC, although it was retaken in 211 BC by the Romans. In 73 BC The revolt of Spartacus broke out here in its amphitheatre. Most sources suggest that Hannibal poisoned himself in about 183 BC in the Bithynian village of Libyssa and Moody's source for his statement about Hannibal's tomb is unknown. See Evelyn (1645), II, p. 324.

[11] Naples. 'Odoriffere', odoriferous. See Evelyn (1645), II, p. 325, for the usual lodgings of foreign visitors, especially the 'Three Kings' which was popular with English visitors.

We arriv'd at Naples the 10th of March <u>1661</u>. The first thing my Maister did think on was to deliver his letter to the Vice-Roy who the next Day after sent him a present of Rich win[e]s, swet meats and some of all sorts of green fruit then in season;[1] and truely we had a many severall sortes, for I Remember we had green pease, Hartichocks, sparagrasse,[2] Cherryes and a many sorts of pretty fruits whereoff their is non growes in England. And now my Maister's letter of Recommendation went no further, and truely it was a great wonder that it went so farr, as it did, and that frome one great Prince to another, and my Maister being a stranger to them all, but as Soloman saith in his booke of Eclesiastes,[3] "That where the word of a King is their is Power", and Loyalty to his Prince being confirm'd by the Mouth of such a great Qwen as our Qwen Mother[4] was at that time, and the Letter goeing frome one great Prince to another and all Princes love Loyalty in their subjects [f. 17ᵛ] was the only cause in my opinion made my Maister and his letter be receiv'd with such great Respect.

The third Day after our arrivall in Naples we went in the company of the Prince of Brandebourg[5] who happend to be at Naples at the same time to Puzzola[6] where are many rare Antiquities of the Romain Emperors who resided much in that Place, their we saw[7] some Remnants of a Bridge which Caligula the Emperor caus'd build over an Arme of the Sea thre Milles long.[8] We saw Nerro's hunderd Prisons, the Tombe of Nero's Mother,[9] the Elizium Fields,[10] where the Heathens us'd to burry the Ashes of their dead, la Grotta de Sibille, or the Cave where one of the Sibills did study and Prophesi'd of our Saviour's birth.[11] Il Lago de Cane, a little Lake call'd the Dogg's Lake, and Just by it[12] their is a little hill and a Cave goes in under the Hill, where if a Dogg be put with his feet ty'd for a halfe quarter of an hower, he will be stark dead, and never come to life again except he be put in the said Lake, and then in a little time he will revive and live as before; this Experiment we saw tryed and prov'd true before the Prince of Bradebourgue and above sixty persons more

---

[1] 'season' added above a deletion.

[2] Artichokes and asparagus.

[3] Ecclesiastes 8:4: 'Where the word of a king *is, there is* power: and who may say unto him, What doest thou?'

[4] Queen Henrietta Maria (1609–69), who had returned to England in October 1660. After two further brief visits, she retired in 1665 to France permanently.

[5] This prince was presumably a son of Frederick William, Elector of Brandenburg (elector, 1640–88), then one of the most influential figures in continental politics. His father Elector George William (elector, 1619–40) had at first sought neutrality during the Thirty Years' War (1618–48) but this resulted only in invasion and occupation by the Swedes. Frederick William adopted a more aggressive policy and freed the electorate from the control of the Swedes. He effectively became the leading Protestant germanic prince and re-established the finances and militia of Brandenburg-Prussia.

[6] Pozzuoli, just to the west of Naples.

[7] 'saw' added above.

[8] Evelyn (1645), II, p. 344, also visited 'the Bridg of Caligula' (according to Raymond (1648), p. 157, the remnants of the mole), from where he sailed to Báia.

[9] Ibid (1645), II, p. 349: 'Passing by the shore againe we entered Bauli observable from the monstrous Murthers of Nero committed on his Mother Agrippina, her Sepulchre yet shew'd us in the rock which we enter'd, being cover'd with sundry heads & figures of beasts'. Nero's mother, Agrippina, was murdered in AD 59 and a small theatre to the north of Bacoli was tradionally claimed to be her tomb.

[10] Evelyn (1645), II, p. 351: 'Returning towards the Baiae we againe passe the Elysian Fields so celebrated by the Poets, nor unworthily for their situation & verdure, begin full of Myrtils & sweete shrubs, and having a most incomparable prospect towards the tyrrhen sea'.

[11] The Cave of the Cumaean Sybil at Cumae, where according to tradition Aeneas consulted the Sibyl.

[12] 'it' added above.

of English and Germans.[1] Haveing seen all the Rareties [f. 18ʳ] about Putzola we went back to Naples again the same night, but one thing I cannot let pass which is a way cut through a Mountain betwen Naples & Potzola about an English Mile frome one side to the Other, it is a large street and seems as if it were vaulted over head. Being arriv'd at Naples, the next day we went to see Mont-Vesuvius[2] a Mountain that alwayes burnes but some times bursts out so furiously that it throws fire Ashes and certain stones two Milles round the Mountain, and over whelms villages, spoiles vine-yards, Corne and all wher it reaches and some times throwes stones of a prodigious greatnesse into the Town of Naples which is thre long Milles distant;[3]

Another day we went to the Castle of Gaeta[4] wher the wife and two daughters of Masenelo were kept perpetuall Prisoners.

We saw the Vice-roye's Pallace within and without which is very sumptious,[5] and many other Noble Pallaces and Churches in that famous Citty which for brevities sake I ommit nameing.

And now haveing spent above a weeke in Naples we tooke our way back again to Rome the 20th of March 1661. and trod the same Path [f. 18ᵛ] which we had come before in the company of at least 20 English Gentlemen with their servants. In going back we saw a many hedds and quarters of the Banditties hanging on Trees by the way side fresh and newly hung up where with the Kingdome of Naples is much pesterd. Frome Naples to Rome it is Recon'd to be 150 miles.

Being arriv'd at Rome the 25 of March we sojourn'd their till about the Midle of May. My Maister had a mind to se the Cerimony of the Asention in[6] Venice, and that time drawing near, haveing taken his leave of all his friends and acquaintance we departed frome Rome the 15th day of May in the year of our Lord 1662.

From Rome to Prima Porta Hosteria	7
To Castelnuova Castelo	8
To Rignano Castelo	7
To Civeta castelano[7]	7
To Itricoly a Castle	9
To Narny a good hansome Citty	8
To Terny another Citty	15
To Stetura Hosteria	7
[f. 19ʳ] To spolety another Citty	8
To Fogligno Cittá[8]	12

---

[1] Commonly known as Grotto del Cane or Charon's Cave. Evelyn (1645), II, pp. 339–40, witnessed the same experiment performed on a dog.

[2] written 'Vesuius' with the second 'v' added above.

[3] Evelyn (1645), II, p. 332, provides a detailed description of his trip to Vesuvius and refers to Pliny the Younger's account of its eruption in AD 79 (*Epistolae*, VI.16). The most recent eruption had started on 15 December 1631.

[4] The citadel at Gaeta. Evelyn (1645), II, p. 323, makes no mention of this story.

[5] The Palazzo Reale was built in about 1600 for an expected visit by King Philip II of Spain. It was used exclusively as the residence of the viceroy of Naples. The building seen by Moody was extensively damaged by fire in the 1830s.

[6] deletion.

[7] Prima Porta, Castelnuovo di Porto, Rignano Flaminio, and Civita Castelana.

[8] Otricoli, Narni, Terni, Strettura, Spoleto, and Foligno.

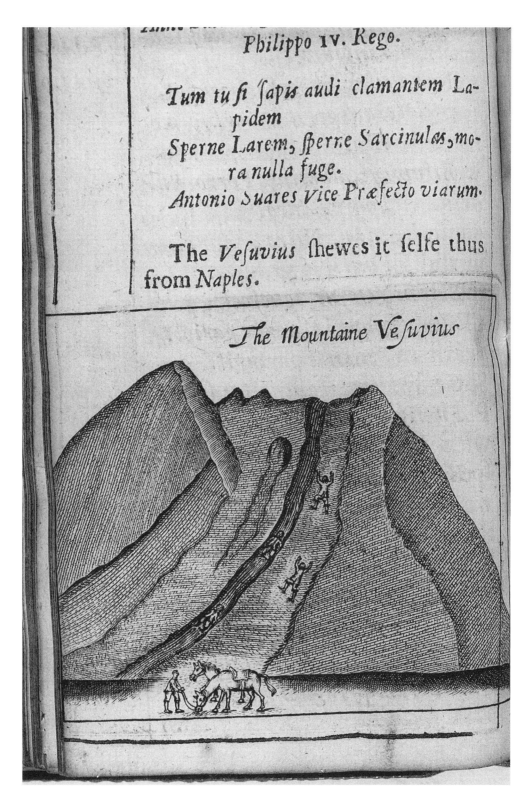

Fig. 43. 'The Mountaine Vesuvius'. From Raymond, *An Itinerary* (1648), p. 160.

To Casen Hosteria[1]	7
To Seravale Borgo	7
To la Muccia a Castle	8
To Valcimare Hosteria	8
To Tolentino Città	9
To Macerata Città	9
To Recanaty also a Citty	10
To Laureto Città[2]	3

In the midle of our Lady's Church stands as they say the Hous wherin our Saviour was borne,[3] and was brought from Bethelem thither by fower Angels. Their is a very fine Chapel built round about it; they show'd us the Dish that our Saviour eat out of, his swadleing Clouts and Severall other things and the Pickture of our B*lessed* Lady drawen by St Luke. We saw also the Treasury which is infinitly Rich, no Emperor or catholick King but sends a present thither. We saw a Heart of beaten Gould all beset with precious stons that our Qwene Mother had presented thither.[4] Their is also a famous Hospitall where all Pilgrimes are entertained 3 dayes with Meat, Drink and Lodging.

[f. 19ᵛ] The Ascension drawing neare, for feare of arriveing too late we tooke Post at Laureto for Bolgnia and so we parted the same day.

From Laureto to Ancon a noble sea Port[5]	15
To la Casa Abrugiata[6]	10
To Senegalia Citta	10
To Fano Città	15
To Pesaro Citta	7
To la Catholica	10
To Riminij Citta	15
To Savignano a fine Castle[7]	10
To Sesena Città	10
To Furgly Citta	10
To Faenza	10
To Imola Cittá	10
To St Nicollá a Castle	10
To Boglonia Città May the 22[8]	10

---

[1] 'Casen Hosteria', unidentified but perhaps either Casenove Serrone or Cesi.

[2] Seravalle di Chienti, Muccia, Valcimarra, Tolentino, Macerata, Recanati, and Loreto.

[3] The Santuario della Santa Casa near Loreto dated from the late 15th century. Legend claims that the house of the Virgin Mary (Santa Casa or Casa di Maria) was brought by angels in 1291 from Nazareth to the hill of Trsat (near Rijeka) and moved again in 1294 to the woods which surround Loreto.

[4] The Treasury at Santa Casa was despoiled in 1798 when the French took Loreto. A year earlier Pope Pius VI had sold off some of its most prized items to raise funds to pay the provisions of the Treaty of Tolentino (1797). Mortoft (1659), pp. 171–2, provides an interesting account of its contents.

[5] Ancona.

[6] 'la Casa Abrugiata', unidentified but probably in the area of the modern Falconara Maritima.

[7] Senigallia, Fano, Pesaro, Cattólica, Rimini, and Savignano sul Rubicone.

[8] Cesena, Forli, Faenza, Imola, San Nicolò, and Bologna.

Fig. 44. 'Un Entrée du port de Venize, ou l'on va espouser la mer des jours de l'Assension' (c. 1645) (Israel Silvestre).

Fig. 45. 'Veuë du pont de Realte de Venize inventé par Michel Ange. Gravé par Israel Silvestre'.

Graué par Israel Sylvestre   *P. Mariette ex*   *Auec priuilege du Roy*   12

Altra veduta del Medesima grand Piazza di S.ᵗ Marco

Fig. 46. 'Altra veduta del Medesima grand Piazza di Sᵗ. Marco. P Mariette ex. Gravé par Israel Sylvestre' (c. 1645).

We tooke water in boat from Boglonia to Venice and so went from

Frome Boglonia to Ferrara[1]	30
Frome Ferara to Venice	60

We arriv'd at Venice May the 24 1661 and[2] tooke up our Lodging at M[r]. Joanes his Hous[3] [f. 20[r]] who was then Councell of the English Merchants. A lodging and entertainment fit for the best Prince in Christendome. Two days after our arrivall was the day of the Ascension[4] where one might se shipes, Gallyes, Gallyazzos, and in numberable of Gondelo's, which are little boates whereof every Noble Venetian keepes two or thre, and Men in their own Livery to Row them. The Doge or Duke himselfe was[5] in a Rich Gally all glistering with Gould. 48 Oares on each side & 4 men at every Oare;[6] The Duke's Galley went before, and all the rest bent their Course that way till he came to the place where he Maryes the Sea, And after some turneing and winding which is a Cerimony they make, he flings a Gould Ring into the Sea;[7] upon which, all the Castles, all the shipes, and Gallyes discharge their Guns, Trumpets, Hoy-boyes[8] and Drums which Made such a noyce as if heaven and Earth had been Meeting, And to tell the truth their is not to be seen such a shew on the water as is at Venice on Ascension Day in the whole World. A day or two after M[r]. Joanes invited my Maister to his Country Hous with severall other Gentlemen, where he gave a splendid entertainement. and being come back to Venice, [f. 20[v]] my Maister employ'd the remainder of his time to se what was most remarkable as for example their are very rare Churches. St Markes Church[9] is the chiefest, Many noble Pallaces build of Marble, we saw the Arsenall where they build their Galleys,[10] The Armery which is sufficient to arme 100,000 men as they tould us.[11] Haveing spent almost a Month in Venice my Maister was resolv'd to go back to Florence to se the Cerimony of the Prince of Tuscany's Mariage who was then Mary'd to the Duke of Orleans Daughter.[12] And so we parted from Venice for Florence the 12th of June 1661. We went back again into Bolognia by Land.

---

[1] Ferrara.

[2] written 'and and'.

[3] John Evelyn and Richard Symonds stayed at the house of Signor Paolo Rodomante, Evelyn (1645), II, p. 429.

[4] Ascension Day falls on the Thursday following the 5th Sunday after Easter Day (known as Rogation Sunday).

[5] 'was' deleted.

[6] This vessel, known as the Bucentaur (It. Bucintoro), was first used in 1625 and replaced in 1728/9.

[7] The traditional ceremony of the marriage of Venice with the sea, when the Doge threw from the state barge Bucentaur a ring into the waters of the Porto di Lido (S. Niccolò), was held each year on Ascension Day. It was also described by Evelyn (1645), II, pp. 431–2, and Bargrave (1655), p. 228. The ceremony was suppressed in 1796.

[8] 'Hoy-boyes': hautboys or oboes.

[9] The 9th-century Basilica of San Marco served as the Doge's chapel. The Piazza San Marco and the Realto were the two major focal points of Venetian city life. See Evelyn (1645), II, pp. 433–42

[10] The Arsenal, protecting the entrance to the lagoon, was founded in 1104 and enlarged between the 14th and 16th centuries. See Evelyn (1645), II, p. 458.

[11] Moody is probably referring here to the Sala d'Armi del Consiglio dei Dieci, the Venetian Council's private armoury, located in the Palazzo Ducale. State arms were stored there until 1797. See Bargrave (1655), p. 229; and Lassels (1670), II, pp. 392–400.

[12] At the time of Maynard's travels, Ferdinando II (1610–70) was Grand Duke of Tuscany (from 1621). His son, later Cosimo III (1642–1723), married in 1661 Marguerite-Louise of Orléans, daughter of Gaston-Jean-Baptiste, duc d'Orléans (1608–60), the brother of King Louis XIII. This proved a dynastically ambitious but personally disastrous union and, after almost a decade of trying to prove that the marriage ceremony had been invalid, Cosimo's consort, Marguerite-Louise, abandoned him and returned to France in 1675.

From Venice to Mirvan[1]	12
To Padua Città a brave University[2]	13
To Montcelici a castle and a Bridge	10
To Rovigo Citta	15
To Ferrara Città a very larg Citty belongs to the Pope	20
To St Pietro in Casal	15
To Bolognia[3]	14
A very large Citty belongs to the Pope, their are made Choice Saseges & Bolognia Balls	} 0

From Bolognia to Florence we past the Apenin Mountains[4] which are very high and tedious
[f. 21r]

From Bolognia to Pianora	8
To Loyan[5]	8
To Scarigalafino[6]	4
To Fiorenzola	10
To Scarperia good knives made[7]	9
To the Ponte over the Mountain[8]	8
To Florence	15

We arriv'd at Florence the 17th of June 1661. And my Maister haid a lodging assign'd to him Ready furnish'd in S[r]. Bernard Gascoins Hous, where was also M[r]. Bernard Howard, and One M[r] Coventry.[9]

We saw many rare sights in that time of Solemnity, but especialy that of the Horse Dance was beyond all expression, and an Opera which was play'd severall nights one after another, and the famous Commedian Scaramuccio did sing and act in that opera.[10]

---

[1] 'Mirvan', probably either Mirano or Mira.

[2] The University of Padua was founded in 1222.

[3] Monsélice, Rovigo, Ferrara, San Pietro in Casale, and Bologna.

[4] The Apennine range of mountains, forming the backbone of peninsular Italy.

[5] Pianoro and Loiano.

[6] 'Scarigalafino', unidentified.

[7] Firenzuola and Scarperia.

[8] This was the bridge over the River Sievre at San Piero a Sieve. Evelyn (1645), II, p. 419: '... we tooke horse & supped that night at *il Ponte*, passing a dreadfull ridge of the *Appennines*, in many places cap'd with Snow, which covers them the whole summer long'.

[9] Bernard Howard (d. 1717), the youngest son of Henry Frederick Howard, Earl of Arundel, Surrey and Norfolk (d. 1652). Bernard's eldest brother, Thomas (d. 1677), was restored as 5th Duke of Norfolk in 1660. Thomas's younger brother, Henry (d. 1684), succeeded him as 6th Duke of Norfolk. Bernard Howard's great-grandson, Bernard Edward (d. 1842), became 12th Duke of Norfolk. See John Martin Robinson, *The Dukes of Norfolk. A Quincentennial History*, Oxford and New York, 1982, 'Genealogical Table II Dukes of Norfolk', between pp. 240 and 241. 'M[r] Coventry' could have been a member of the family of Sir Thomas Coventry (1578–1640), first Baron Coventry, whose son, Sir William (d. 1686), had served in Charles I's army and later withdrew to France. Another of his sons, Henry (1619–86) attended Charles II during his continental exile.

[10] Scaramouche was an unscrupulous and intriguing stock character from the *commedia dell'arte*. At this period the role was made famous by the actor Tiberio Fiorillo (1608–94) who, usually, played the role without a mask.

And as for the Horse dance, I would be too tedious to mention every particular, I will only give a hint of some few, by which you may guesse at the magnificence theroff.[1]

The Horse dance was in a Garden behind the Great Duke's Pallace, a Round place like an Amphithiater [f. 21ᵛ] about a quarter of an English Mile round, over which was fasten'd Cordes to the topes of high Poles crosse-wayes, and to those Cordes were fixt above 1,000 flamboyes or Torches. Their was at least 100 violins and base violes besides voyces which made a most pleasant Harmony. At the further side of the Amphithiater ther came from under the ground as we thought, A Troope of Horse who begun to dance to the Musick, and did keep their steps and the Cadance as well as any Christians. The first lasted for halfe and hower, and then they retir'd for a time and began again & danc'd to another sort of aire another halfe hower and so march'd all off in good order, but not without saluting the assembly.

A while after their came out frome another Corner an Atlas the most prodigious for bignesse that I think ever was seen with the world on his back. Their was under this Atlas as we were inform'd at least 100 Men by whoes help he came a very slow pace till he came to the Midle of the place, and then made a stand for some time. At last the Glob of the world split in fower partes, Resembleing the fower Quarters of the world (that is) Europe, Affrica, Asia, and America: In every Quarter their was at least twenty Persons the best voices that could be had, And [f. 22ʳ] their Clothing, Voices, and language according to that part of the world wherin they had been bred. Europe began first to sing intimating that they were come thither to congratulat and wish a happie Successe to that Nuptiall: Africa sung next on the same subject. Asia next, and last of all America: And all such Ravishing voices and all so winning and pleaseing that no man knew[2] who exceeded the other, thus they continu'd till day began to cast light upon the firmament and then broke up and every one retir'd to their severall habitations.

My Maister haveing spent above a Month at Florence in these Recreations began to think of his long Journey he had yet to make, and so haveing taken his leave of his most intimat friends We departed frome Florence on Monday Jully the 18th. 1661, and took our way back again to Bolognia and trod the same way we had gone twice before which makes 55 milles.   55

From Bolognia to Venice by the way of Mantua	
From Bolognia to Sᵗ Joan	15

To Bon-port	10
To Concordia[3] where keeps court the Duke of Mirandola.[4]	18
[f. 22ᵛ] To Castell Sᵗ Benedick[5]	6
To Mantua where the Duke of that name keeps Court	}18

---

[1] Evelyn (1645), II, p. 195: '… we went to see the Dukes Cavalerizzo, where the Prince has a stable of incomparable Horses of all Countries, Arabs, Turks, Barbs, Gennets, English &c: which are continually exercisd in the menage' (from Raymond (1648), p. 43).

[2] deletion.

[3] San Giovanni in Persiceto, Bornporto, and Concórdia sul Sécchia.

[4] Maynard's party would have passed through or near Mirandola, the seat of the Pico family, just before reaching Concórdia, which was also under their control. The family's most famous member, the Platonist philosopher Giovanni Pico della Mirandola (1463–94), was also conte di Concórdia.

[5] San Benedetto.

Mantua is Cituated in a most pleasant and fruitfull soile the ground yeilding abundance of wine and fruit and as for corne and Cattle inferiour to non. Many brave Churches & some very find Pallaces, a pleasant Lake on one side of the Citty that sends water round the Town which renders it very strong.[1]

From Mantua to Villafranka,[2] a good lodg*ing*	15
To Verona at Dinner	10

Verona is an excellent brave Citty & belongs to the Republick of Venice, It is one of the Most Ancients Cittys in all Italy.[3] Many brave Emperors has keept[4] Court their. Severall bloody Battailes has been fough[t] by Verona.[5] Their is two very strong Castles,[6] their is a brave River runs through the Citty nam'd Adice, upon which River their is thre ston Bridges.[7]
Their are very fine Church, Many ancient Pallaces and other rare Antiquities to be seen –

[f. 23ʳ] Frome Verona to Villan at night[8]	13
To Vicenza a Very fine Citty[9]	13
To Padua that famous University[10]	18

At Padua my Maister was nobly treated at the Mad Duke of Norfolke's Hous[11] for a whole weeke togither, as were all other Gentlemen of the English Nation that came thither. The City of Padua is large and strongly built and all the streets Archt, so that one May go

[1] Mantua, surrounded on three sides by the River Mincio which ultimately forms a lake in three reaches, Lago Superiore, Lago di Mezzo, and Lago Inferiore. Cultural life and the arts had flourished at Mantua under the Gonzaga family; and Charles I purchased a large part of their picture collections during the late 1620s. The city was sacked by an Imperial army in 1630 and went into a marked decline.

[2] Villafranca di Verona.

[3] Verona had placed itself under Venetian control in 1405.

[4] deletion.

[5] Moody probably derives his references to 'Battles fought by Verona' from Raymond (1648), p. 227: 'Before one side of the City lies a rich Plat Countrey; Before the other a stony Champion, or Downes, wherein *C. Marius* gave a totall overthrow to the *Cimbrians*'.

[6] Moody's reference to 'two very strong Castles' is confusing since his major source, Raymond (1648), p. 231, clearly states that there were three major castles at Verona – Castel Vecchio, Castel San Felice, and Castel San Pietro. Evelyn (1646), II, p. 486, reiterates the same point: 'It has besides 3 strong Castles, & large & noble wall'.

[7] Evelyn (1646), II, p. 485: 'The Citty is divided in the midst by the *River Athesis* [River Adige] over which passe divers stately bridges, & on its brinks many goodly Palaces' (from Raymond (1648), p. 227).

[8] Perhaps the village of Villa, just to the east of Cologna.

[9] Vicenza.

[10] Padua is still known as 'Padova la Dotta' on account of its university, founded in 1222. It attracted many notable students, including Dante and Petrarch, as well as numerous scholars from England. Galileo taught physics here from 1592 until 1610.

[11] Thomas Howard (1585–1646), Earl of Arundel, created Earl of Norfolk 6 June 1644. The Dukedom of Norfolk had recently been restored to his grandson, Thomas (1627–77) on 29 December 1660. Arundel was the most prolific of the early English aristocratic collectors at the courts of James I and Charles I. However, his extravagance led him close to bankruptcy and prompted him to explore various schemes to escape his creditors and keep his collections together. By the mid-1640s, he was determined to live abroad and established himself at a villa in Padua. See Robinson, *Dukes of Norfolk*, pp. 111–13. John Evelyn had known him in England and they explored Padua together. See Evelyn (1645), II, pp. 466–7, and p. 41.

A Delineation of the Amphitheater of Verona expressed in that forme wherein it flourished in the tyme of the Roman Monarchie, only the greatest part of the outward wall which inclosed it round about is omitted.

Gulḟ. Hole Sculp. An: Dm. 1610.

IANO SACRVM

ATHESIS FLV.

Fig. 47. 'Amphitheater of Verona'. From *Coryats Crudities* (1611), p. 308.

through the whole Town when't rains and not be Weet.[1] Their are Many brave Colledges and Academys where are some thousands of schollers.

Frome Padua to Venice   20

We arriv'd at Venice the second time Jully the 30. 1661. and tooke up our Lodging at Mr. Joanes his Hous where we had Lodg'd once before.

My Maister hyr'd fower Horses of a German and a Man to tend them at so much a Weeke and to keep them as long as he pleas'd at the rate he hyr'd them, and to send them home safe to Augsburge at last where the said German Liv'd. And so winter drawing on my Maister [f. 23ᵛ] Made the more hast of dispatching his businesse. And so haveing receiv'd Monys upon his Billes of Exchange he fill'd a large Purse with goulden Hungars[2] and haveing taken leave of all his friends at Venice he tooke his farewell of that famous Citty the 9ᵗʰ of August 1661. And so we tooke our Journey for Viena in Austria.

Frome Venice we went in a Gondella to	
Mastere which is	} 7
To Treviso at night	10
We past the Biave River in barke	
And then to Cogniari at dinner	}15
To Cecillia[3] at night	10
To sainta Bocá[4] at Dinner	10
To Spillenberge	10
We past the River Digament[5] and then	
To St Daniell Upon a Hill	} 5
To St Tomaso[6] at night	1
To Spittella[7]	10
To Venzone	3
To Ricutte at Dinner	7
To Chiusa call'd the Passe wher their is	
a strong Guard keept in Peace & warr[8]	} 5
To Ponteben[9]	5

[f. 24ʳ] At Ponteben their is a River that parts Italy and Germany and here we enter'd into the Province of Corinthia where every German Mille makes five Italian.

---

[1] Evelyn (1645), II, pp. 453, was also impressed by the covered archways in the streets of Padua: 'The Towne … is generaly built like Bolonia, on Arches, & on Brick, so as one m[a]y walke all about it dry, & in the shade, which is very convenient in these hot Countries'.

[2] 'goulden Hungars', the hungar was a gold coin from Hungary. See Somerset (1612), p. 257.

[3] Mestre, Treviso, the River Piave, Conegliano, and Sacile.

[4] 'sainta Bocá', unidentified but probably near the modern Pordenone.

[5] Spilimbergo and probably the River Tagliamento to Dignano.

[6] San Daniele del Friuli and San Tomaso.

[7] Moody's 'Spittella' is probably Ospedaletto.

[8] Venzone, Resiutta, and Chiusaforte, standing a the foot of a formerly fortified gorge.

[9] Pontebba, with a stream from the River Pontebbana running through the village, marked the old Austro-Italian frontier crossing-point.

	German Milles
From Ponteben to Malborgette at night	1
To Saves – 1 m*ile* and then to Tervis 1 m*ile* in all[1]	2
To Terle at Dinner	1
To Arnolstein 1 m*ile* and then to Villach at n*ight*	3

Villach is a pretty Market Towne and their is a famous River Runs through that Town nam'd the Drave, their is also a wooden Bridge.[2]

The next Day we past the Drave again and on our left hand we saw a noble Castle on a high Hill which belongs to the Pr*ince* van Ditterineste[3] and a little further a great Lake which reacht a Mile till we came to Felskirchen at Dinner — 3

We past a smale River & then to St Feit at night[4] — 3

The next day we saw another famous Castle on a Hill on our right hand nam'd Hochosterwits, belongs to the Grave van Hoffenhiller. We past a River by Tottenborne Castle[5] and then to Fròsach at Dinner in all — 3

We past the River Matnits,[6] [onet?] Castle [f. 24ᵛ] are warme Bathes, we past on till we came } 3

To New-mark't at night[7]

To Hounds marke at Dinner a hansome Hostesse, a Rarety in that Country[8] } 3

We past the More River, a mile and a halfe further at a Gentleman's Hous we drank Excellent purgeing water & at night To Phyles — 2

To Knedlefelt at Dinner[9] — 3

To Leuven we past a River on a bridge[10] — 4

To Brucke at night, a fine Castle on a Hill[11] — 2

To Frawleuten at Dinner[12] — 3

To Beck a River and Bridge[13] — 1

To Gratze at night — 2

Gratz is a Most pleasant Citty and the head Toun of all Stiria. Their is a most

---

[1] Malborghetto-Valbruna and Tarvísio. Moody's 'Saves' seems to be at the usual stopping point of Sella di Camporosso.

[2] Thörl (or Unterthörl), Arnoldstein, Villach, and the River Drau (or Drava).

[3] Moody is possibly referring to the fortress of Landskron, overlooking Villach to the east. During the 1620s it fell into the hands of the Catholic Dietrichstein family (perhaps Moody's 'Ditterineste', a name which clearly confused him since he first wrote 'Ditterste' and then added 'ine' above). It fell into decay in the early 19th century after being hit by lightning.

[4] The Ossiacher See, Feldkirchen in Kärten, and St Veit.

[5] The most prominent castles in this region were, just to the north-west of St Veit, the 16th-century Schloss Frauenstein, and the now ruined castles at Liebenfels and Glanegg.

[6] Friesach and the River Metnitz.

[7] Neumarkt in Steiermark.

[8] 'Hounds marke', is probably Moody's mishearing of Unzmarkt (to the west of Judenberg).

[9] The River Mur, Pöls, and Knittelfeld.

[10] Leoben, situated in the Mur Valley.

[11] Bruck an der Mur. Its Landskron fortress on the Schlossberg was largely destroyed by fire in 1792.

[12] Frohnleiten.

[13] 'Beck', unidentified. From Frohnleiten the usual route would have been via either Deutschfeistritz or Peggau.

sumptious and strong Castle upon the Top of a Hill w*hi*ch defends the Town against
their Enemyes –[1]
the Citty is also strong of it selfe. Their are many hansome Churches, the Dom, the Jesuits
Capucins and Carmelits all extraordinary fine. – – –[2]

Back againe to Brooke	6
And then to Kingberge at night	3
We past the Mirts River and Hochenbaum Castle on our left hand, and then to	
Merzustag at din*ner*[3]	3
[f. 25[r]] To Shatvien a brave Castle[4]	3
Here we went out of Stiria into Austria	
And we Marcht on to Clakenhets at night[5]	1
We past a River and then to Newstat at Diner	4

Newstate[6] is a strong Citty well fortify'd with walls and Bulworkes. The inhabitants tould
us that the Turkes lay before it a whole year and a Day and at last were forc'd to raise the
siege.[7] Their is to be seen the the Emperor's Pallace the Armery and some fine Churches[8]

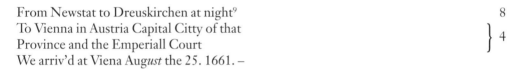

From Newstat to Dreuskirchen at night[9]   8
To Vienna in Austria Capital Citty of that
Province and the Emperiall Court   } 4
We arriv'd at Viena Aug*ust* the 25. 1661. –

Viena Lyes in a fine plane, the ground very fruitfull abundance of wine and fruite It is
waterd on one side with the Danup or Danuby River the most famous in Christendome.[10] It
yeilds rare fish, Carpe and Peake[11] in abundance. Viena is very strong well wall'd and a
prodigious large Ditch wherin the water goes round the Town.[12] Their are many brave
Churches, S[t] Stephen's is the Chiefest. [f. 25[v]] S[t] Stephen's Church has one of the highest[13]

---

[1] Graz was so named after the ancient fort (Slovene: *gradec*) which once stood on the Schlossberg. During the
16th and 17th centuries, the city was exceptionally well fortified against the threat of Turkish invasion. A huge
Arsenal was established here in 1640. Moody's 'strong Castle' is probably a reference to the Burg or Imperial
Palace.

[2] The Cathedral of St Giles dated largely from the 15th century. A university was founded at Graz in 1585 by
Archduke Karl II and was ably developed by the Jesuits.

[3] Kindberg, The River Mürts and Mürzzuschlag.

[4] Schottwien.

[5] Probably Gloggnitz.

[6] Wiener Neustadt, founded originally in the late 12th century as a frontier fortress against the Magyars. The
Burg now stands on the site of the original fortess.

[7] The Turkish army of Sultan Suleiman the Magnificent had attempted to take Wiener Neustadt and Vienna in
1529 but were heroically resisted by Count Niklas Salm and their inhabitants.

[8] Ferdinand III (Emperor, 1637–57). The most notable churches at Wiener Neustadt were the Stadtpfarrkirche
(the cathedral) and the Neuklosterkirche (the church of the Cistercian convent).

[9] Moody's 'Dreuskirchen' is probably Traiskirchen.

[10] Vienna and the River Danube.

[11] Carp and pike.

[12] Vienna's fortifications were a crucial defence for the Habsburg Empire against the threat of the Turks until the
raising of the siege of Vienna of 1683. Vienna was the imperial capital under the Habsburgs until Emperor
Rudolph II decided to move it back to Prague between 1576 and 1583.

[13] written 'f highest'.

Steeples in all Germany,[1] the Scots church is next to St Stephens, then the Jesuits, the Augustins Church, the Minerits, the Augustins without the Walles,[2] the Mint where they Coine ther money. The Emperor's Court, the Empresse's Court,[3] the favourita without *the* Walles a brave Hous and Garden; The Emperour's Gallery is both noble and Rich with Gould and precious stones and abundance of other Raretyes, and among the rest we saw six Unicorns Horns. We saw also Gustavus Adolphus King of Sweden's Buff coat that he was shot dead in with the Musket bullets.[4] My Maister while he was at Viena went to[5] visit Prince Rupert, and had the Honour to Dine with him. —--[6]

My Maister had a mind to se Presburge in Hungary[7] and so we set out frome Viena
To Newgebaw where there is a very fine
Hous and a noble Garde
and a little distance is Juersdorffe,[8] an extraordinary brave Pallace belongs to the Emperour in which place his Majesty takes great delight Most part of the summer.
[f. 26^r] To Fish[9] 2 m*iles* and then to Swech[10] 3 m*iles* in all   8
To Hainberg, out of Austria into Hungary
A brave Castle on a Hill, and frome thence went till we came to the River side and Crost over the Danup to Presbourge[11]   3

}2

Presburg is a very strong Citty well Wall'd and a brave Castle and lyes Just on the River Danube which renders it the more strong. We stay'd but one Day their, we crost the River and so came back again to Viena which makes in all   10

Being arriv'd at Viena about 3 dayes after my Maister went and tooke his leave of Prince Rupert, and some other Gentle Men who were very Civill to my Maister.

---

[1] Stephans-Dom or the Cathedral of St Stephen. It was badly damaged by fire in April 1945.

[2] Of the churches mentioned by Moody, the most interesting are the Schottenkirche, rebuilt between 1643 and 1648 but severely damaged by fire in 1683; the 14th-century Minoritenkirche of the Friars Minor; and the Jesuitenkirche, built between 1623 and 1631, with a distinctive pink and green interior. The 14th-century Augustinerkirche stood to the south of the Hofburg Palace.

[3] The imperial Hofburg Palace, begun in the 13th century and extensively added to and developed during the following centuries. The imperial apartments now mainly record the 18th- and 19th- century splendours of the emperors.

[4] Gustavus II Adolphus (1595–1632), King of Sweden (from 1611) was killed at Lützen on 6 November 1632, during a campaign in preparation for a projected capture of Vienna in the following year.

[5] 'to' added above.

[6] Prince Rupert (1619–82) of the Rhine, son of Frederick V, Elector Palatine and King Frederick I of Bohemia, and Queen Elizabeth (daughter of King James I), was the most able of the royalist commanders during the English Civil War and was created in 1644 Duke of Cumberland and Earl of Holderness. After a period of naval piracy in the Azores and West Indies (1651–2), he quarrelled with Charles II in France in 1653 and retired to Germany between 1654 and 1661. He did, however, hold English naval commands during the second (1665–7) and third (1672–4) Dutch Wars. Robert Bargrave (1656), pp. 248–9, met him at Heidelberg.

[7] Pressburg (German), now Bratislava in Czechoslovakia, where the Hungarian Diet was held from 1526. It was proclaimed as capital of Hungary in 1536 and the kings and queens of Hungary were traditionally crowned there during the next three centuries.

[8] 'Newgebaw' and 'Juersdorffe', unidentified.

[9] Fischamend Markt.

[10] 'Swech', perhaps Schwechat, although Moody would have passed through this town *before* Fischamend Markt on the way to Pressburg.

[11] Hainberg and Pressburg (Bratislava).

The Most Illustrious and High Borne Prince Rupert, Prince Electour Palatine of y Righne, Second Sonne to Fredericke King of Bohemia, Generall of y Horse of his Ma: ties Army, Knight of y Most Noble Order of the Gaster, &c

Ant: v. Dyck Pinxit.

Are to be sould by Robt: Peake at his shopp neere Holborne Conduitt.

Fig. 48. Engraving of Prince Rupert. From a portrait attributed to Sir Anthony Van Dyck.

And so we parted frome Viena for Prague in Bohemia September the 6th, <u>1661</u>.[1]

Frome Veina to Ensersdorffe[2]	}2
To Corn-warke,[3] ½ m*ile* and then to Craffendorffe[4] at Dinner	1–½
To Collbrun at night	3
to Counters-dorffe[5] a very pretty Castle	1
belongs to my Lord Devill	
[f. 26v] To Snaum Citty[6] we dinned	3
Out of Austria into Moravia and so we	
march't on till we came to Budewitz at night	3
To Bernits[7] the next day at Dinner	4
To Igeluw[8] a Castle at night	2
To Deutchbrod[9] at Dinner	3
Out of Moravia into Bohemia and so to Hubern	1
To Jenignaw at night[10]	1
To Safflaw,[11] 1 m*ile* and then to Cuttenberge[12] at din*ner*	1

A[t] Cuttenberg their is many Silver Mines belongs to the Emperor.[13] We went many fathoms under ground to se the People worke in the mines they also show'd us the way how to find out where the Mines of Silver lyes which is thus. You must take a heasell wan,[14] and hould it betwen your hand about a yard or more distance. In that manner walk over the ground, and when you[15] come over a mine where Silver is, It will pull the stick downwards towards the Earth and make it bend betwen your Hands. –

Frome Cuttenberge to Coulinat night	1
We past the Elbe River[16] & so to Bemishbrott	3
We past the Mulla River[17] and then	
To Prague Capitall Citty of Bohemia	4

[f. 27r] Prague is a noble and famous Citty, a very great River Runes through the Town,

---

[1] The usual routes for travellers from Vienna to Prague were either north from Vienna to Brno (Brünn) and then north-west to Prague (the road followed by Philip Sidney in early 1575, see Osborn, *Young Philip Sidney*, pp. 278–9); or due northwest from Vienna, via Stockerau and Horn.

[2] 'Ensersdorffe', possibly Floridsdorf.

[3] 'Corn-warke', possibly Korneuburg.

[4] 'Craffendorffe', unidentified but probably between Stockerau and Göllesdorf.

[5] Hollabrunn and Guntersdorf.

[6] Znaim in Czechoslovakia on the Dyja River, in Southern Moravia.

[7] Budejovice and 'Bernits', unidentified.

[8] Possibly Jihlava.

[9] 'Deutchbrod', possibly Havlíckúv Brod.

[10] 'Hubern' and 'Jenignaw', unidentified.

[11] Possibly Cáslav.

[12] Kutná Hora.

[13] The silver mines at Kutná Hora were discovered in the late 13th century and let to the rapid development of the town. In 1300 Wenceslas II founded a royal mint here, using Florentine expertise.

[14] A hazel wand.

[15] 'you' written above.

[16] Kolin and the River Elbe (Labe).

[17] 'Bemishbrott' and the 'Mulla River', unidentified.

and a brave Bridge.[1] Here Prince Pantin Prince Rupert's Father[2] was Crown'd King of Bohemia, and soone after fought a bloody Battle against the Emperour's forces at a place call'd Wisen-berge, or white Hill 3 English Milles from Prague, where he had a totall overthrow, 30,000 English and Scots being kill'd besides Germans, Bohemians and others that side with him. It's said that he had 80,000 men compleat, and the Emperour's Army was but 40,000. He and his Qwen with great difficulty escap'd, disguis'd themselves in poor habit, travell'd down through Germany till they arriv'd in Holland where they liv'd many years in great Penury, the Hollander not proveing kind to expectation,[3] and the King of England engag'd in a Civall Warr could not doe what he would.

My Maister had the curiosity to go and see where the Battal was fough where they show'd us abundance of Graves where hunders were throwen in one hole togither. The next day we went to se the Ireish Convent of Fraciscant Friers[4] where my Maister was receiv'd with all Imaginable Civilty by the superiour, and envited to Dinner the next day after, and accordinglie at the appointed Hower he went.

[f. 27ᵛ] Being arriv'd at the Convent, My Maister and the Governor were conducted to the head of the great Hall where a Table was Cover'd that stood Crosse the Roome, and a Table on each side of the Hall where the Fathers sat. The superiour was a very complisant Man, for after he had drank the King and Qwen of England's health, and also my Lord Maynard's, he stood up and made a smale speech to the Fathers telling them that by reason that this noble Gentleman, meaning my Maister, had honnor'd them with his company he gave them free leave to speak, and to drink to one another. Upon which their was presently such a noyce and rejoyceing among the Fathers that it seem'd to us an admiration for those Fathers are never permitted to speak to one another except at Chrissmasse, Easter, whitsontide, or some other great Solemnityes. Dinner being over the Superiour waited on my Maister home to his Lodging and so tooke his leave for that time.

Haveing the next day seen the most Eminent Churches and other Raretyes in Prague and my Maister haveing taken his leave of the superior and render'd him thankes for his great Civilty, we departed frome Prague the day after, being Sept. 15 <u>1661</u>. [f. 28ʳ] for Dresden in Saxony and so we tooke our Jorney frome Prague To Vellbrune at Dinner 3
We past the Eger River and then to Budine[5] at Night 2
To Aussich on the Elb[6] at Dinner Growes rare wine 2

---

[1] Prague stands on the River Vltava.

[2] Prince Rupert's father was Frederick V, Elector Palatine (Moody's 'Pantin') and King Frederick I of Bohemia. He had been crowned at Prague in November 1619. His forces were routed by Maximilian of Bavaria's army of the Catholic League at the Battle of White Hill or Mountain (Moody's 'Battle of Wisen-berge') near Prague on 8 November 1620.

[3] Frederick had fled to The Hague in 1622 and remained there, frugally financed by the Dutch and English for the rest of the 1620s. Prince Rupert grew up in United Provinces and visited his uncle, King Charles I, at the English royal court in 1636. When Sweden joined the anti-Habsburg coalition, Frederick joined Gustavus II Adophus's march across Germany (1630–32) but died at Mainz on 29 November 1632.

[4] Moody does not supply enough detail to make a definite identification of this Franciscan monastery but he may be referring to the former Carmelite church of Our Lady of the Snows in the New Town of Prague. It had been founded in 1347 by Emperor Charles IV to mark his coronation as King of Bohemia but it fell into serious decay during the 16th century. It was granted to the Franciscans in 1603 who immediately began a grand rebuilding and restoration programme.

[5] 'Vellbrune' and 'Budine', unidentified.

[6] 'Aussich', perhaps Aussig (Ustí nad Labem).

We past through a great wood till we came }3
To Kesseble[1] in Saxony at night
To Dresden Capitall Citty in Saxony[2]   8

In this Citty the Duke of Saxony keepes his Court. They are Lutherans by profession and the People are very Civill. The River Elb runs through the Citty. The Cunst Camer or Chamber of Rarettyes is worth seing. The Stables below and above the Wild Beasts, the Armery, the Duke's Pallace and the Mint. We went to se a famous Castle 3 miles frome Dresden belonging to the Duke cal'd Stultenaw and came back to Dresden the same day which made in all   6

We met with no acquaintance at Dresden except one English Gentleman who had a fair Daughter who was so charmeing made my Maister loath to leave Dresden, but our Churlish Governor would not stay one day longer, and so we parted frome Dresden the 21 of Sept*ember* and took our way to Meisen[3] where runs the River Elb, and their is a very fine Castle where we din'd   3
[f. 28ᵛ] To Oshats at night   4
To Worts at night   3-½
We past the Milda River and so marcht[4]
On till we came Leipsig at night   3-½

Leipsig is an University for the Lutherans. It is water'd with two Rivers the Pheise and Elster.[5] In Leipsig Sᵗ. Thomas Church, Sᵗ Nicholas Church, the Colledge Lyberary, the Castle and Phisick Garden are all worthy to be seen.

To Litzen, 2 m*iles* their is a great plain wher was fought a blody Battaile call'd the battaile of Litzen, betwen the Emperour's forces and Gustaus Adulphus King of swedland, where the King was kill'd by thre of his owne souldiours, who discharg'd their Muskets all togither and aim'd so well that everyone of them hit him which we saw in his buffcoat at Viena in the Emperour's Gallery shot through with thre Musket bullets, and yet the Sweds gain'd the Victory that Day.[6]

To Ripach at dinner[7]   1
We past the Sala River and then to Weisenfels 1 mile, and then to Naumburge 3 m*iles* in all[8]   4
Naumberg is a Pretty little Towne where Prince Maurice the Duke of Saxony's Br*other* keeps court.
[f. 29ʳ] To Austat[9] at dinner. Out of Saxony in }2
to Thuringen

[1] 'Kesseble', unidentified.
[2] Dresden.
[3] Meissen.
[4] Oschatz, Wurzen, and the River Mulde.
[5] Leipzig stands at the junction of the Pleisse, Parthe, and Weisse Elster rivers.
[6] The Battle of Lützen, at which Gustavus II Adophus, King of Sweden, was killed on 6 November 1632. See p. 276, n. 4.
[7] Probably Räpitz.
[8] River Saale, Weissenfels, and Naumburg.
[9] Auerstedt.

To Weymer a very hansome Pallace and Garden where Prince Will*iam* anoth*er* Br*other* keeps Court	} 3
To Ereforde Capitale of Thuringen,[1] their is a Scots Monastery but almost lost for lake of	} 2
Priest and students, their is a Castle GardenTo Arnstat 2 m*iles* and then to Jlminaw[2] 2 m*iles*	4
At this place is Silver, Irone and Copper Mines.	
We past through a Prodigious great wood till we came to Trawen wald at dinner	} 5
To Slessing a fine Castle[3]	1
To Remlet at night[4]	2
Out of Thuringen into Frankenland and then To Konigs-hoffen a strong place	1
To Statlawring at Dinner	2
To Sweinford a pretty large Towne[5]	2
Their Runs the River Maine, their is a Curious stone bridge the Town belongs to *the* Emperour. To swanfelt at Dinner	2
To Wirtzburge at night[6]	3

Their is a most famous Castle on the Tope of a Hill worthy to be seen.[7] The River Maine runes betwen the Town and Castle, their is a Curious Stone Bridge. At the Jesuits their is a [f. 29ᵛ] Curious Lyberary,[8] their is also a Scots Monastery of Benedictan Monkes.[9] The Abbat was Very civill, treated my Maister with wine and a Colation, and would have had him stay dinner but we went on our Journey the same day. We saw the Hous whee they cast their Cannon

From Weitzburge to Kiching on the Maine		3
To Maypern ½ mile and then to Enerhaim at dinner	½	1
To Markbiberis belongs to the B*ishop* of Ments.[10]		1
To Langfelt 1 m*ile* To newstat at night 1 m*ile* in all		2
To Furth[11] at Dinner. a good Herberg[ue?][12]		4
To Herenberge at night		1

Nerenberg is a free Citty and rul'd by Senatours. It is a very great Citty; their Runs the

---

[1] Erfurt.

[2] Arnstadt and Ilmenau.

[3] Frauenwald and Schleusingen.

[4] 'Remlet', possibly Romhild.

[5] Bad Königshofen, Stadtlauringen, and Schweinfurt.

[6] The River Main, Schwanfeld, and Würtzburg.

[7] The Marienberg Fortress was founded in the 13th century and the main body of the castle dates from the 15th century. It had been converted into a Renaissance palace but after Gustavus II Adolphus's victory over Würtzburg in 1631 it was converted back into a fortress.

[8] The present Jesuit Church of St Michael dates from the second half of the 18th century.

[9] Moody's reference to the 'Scots Monastery' may refer to the former Irish monastery in the town. Its church of St Jakob was destroyed during World War II and has been replaced by the Church of St John Bosco.

[10] Kitzingen, 'Maypern', unidentified, Markt Einersheim, and Markt Bibart.

[11] Langenfeld, Neustadt, and Fürth.

[12] 'Herberg[ue?]', meaning unclear.

River Benga,[1] their is a noble Armery able to Arme 30,000 men.[2] We parted frome
Nerenberg in the afternoon and came to Rotte at night   4

From Rotte Ellinge[3] 2 mile ½ and weisenberg at din*ner*   3
To Enstat, the is a very famous Castle on a Hill[4]   ⎫
Whe[re] the Bishope keeps his Court   ⎬ 3
To Engolstat[5] the strongest Town in Germa-   ⎫
ny. the R*iver* Danup runs by one side which adds   ⎪
to its strength. The Dom Church, the Castle and   ⎬ 3
the Armery are worthy to be seen[6]   ⎭
To Richertshoffen[7]   2
[f. 30ʳ] We past the R*iver* Stabaw[8] where is a famous   ⎫
Castle and then to Faffenhoffen[9] a[t] dinner   ⎬ 2

To Cummer[10] 2 m*iles* and then to Bruck[11] at night   3
We past the Isser River, and then to Mónechen[12] the Capitall Citty of Bavaria, and where
the Duke of that name keeps Court[13]   3

The Duke of Bavaria's Pallace is certainly the finest in Christendome. For in all our Travels
we saw nothing like it. Their is also a famous Garden and a Laberinth in it, a noble
Manage.[14]

---

[1] Nuremberg stands on the River Pegnitz (which Moody probably misheard as 'Benga').

[2] The city had been heavily fortified during the Thirty Years' War when it was occupied by Gustavus II Adolphus of Sweden. The old city arsenal courtyard stands at Bahnhofsplatz, in front of the main railway station.

[3] Roth and Ellingen.

[4] Weissenberg and Eichstatt.

[5] Ingolstadt stands on the River Donau and had been controlled by the Wittelsbach family since 1228.

[6] Moody's reference to the 'Dom Church' is probably the twin-towered Liebrauenmünster (or possibly the Franzikanerkirche). A castle had been built by Duke Ludwig the Severe in 1260 but the buildings viewed by Moody dated from a later period, with various additions made from the 15th-18th centuries. Gustavus II Adolphus of Sweden had besieged the town in 1632.

[7] Reichertshofen.

[8] 'R*iver* Stabaw', unidentified.

[9] Pfaffenhoffen.

[10] 'Cummer', probably either Hohenkammer or Kammerberg.

[11] 'Bruck', probably Fürstenfeldbrück, 22.5km west of Munich, commonly known at this period as 'Bruck'. It was a usual stopping point on the Münich-Augsburg route. Somerset (1612), p. 265, refers to it as 'Boorge'.

[12] The River Isar and Münich.

[13] Maximilian I (1573–1651) was duke from 1597. Educated by the Jesuits, he formed the defensive Catholic League in 1610 and was an opponent of the Protestant Frederick V Elector Palatine (the husband of King James I's daughter, Elizabeth). During the Thirty Years' War, during which Maxmilian I was effectively the champion of the Roman Catholic side, Münich was occupied by the Swedes in 1632 but Bavaria was liberated after the Battle of Nördlingen in 1634. By the Peace of Westphalia Maximilian I retained the electorship and the Upper Palatinate. He was succeeded as Duke of Bavaria by his son Ferdinand Maria (1636–79), who became elector in 1651 and was successful in retoring peaceful productivity to the region after the ravages of the Thirty Years' War.

[14] The Residenz or ducal palace was first built on the site in the late 15th century by the Wittelsbach family. The Old Residenz, Banqueting Hall, Antiquarium, and Old Court Chapel have survived. Between 1611 and 1619 Elector Maximilian I built the Maximilianische or Alte Residenz, adjoyning the Residenzstrasse. Reresby (1657), pp. 97–8, describes the hall, long gallery and the Antiquarium.

The Jesuits Church and Cloister is very Curious. The Minums and Augstins are also Rare.[1] The stables, the Armery, and the Mint are all Curious and well worth seing.

We departed from Munichen Oct*ober* the 9th 1661 } 3
and went back again to broock at night
To Freburg   3
To Augsburge[2]   3

In Augsburge the Jesuits Ch*urch*, the Benedictains Ch*urch* and Cloister,[3] the holly Crosse, St Anns Ch*urch*,[4] the stat Hous, the Water workes, the Port secret and the Armery al very well worth seing.[5] Their are also two Rivers, one cal'd the Lech, and the other the Werde.[6]

[f. 30ᵛ] Here at this Town we wer fo[r]c'd to quit our Horses we hir'd at Venice, by reason the Maister of the Horses and Groom liv'd at Augsburgue; My Maister haveing pay'd a good sume of Moneys for nine weeks we enjoy'd these Horses, and Hir'd others for Staesburgue. We parted from Ausburge Oct*ober* the 12. 1661.

Frome Augsburge to sumerhausen[7] belongs to } 2
the Arts-Duke of Insbruke.[8] In swaberland[9]
To Burgaw 2 m*iles*, To Gensbruge at Din*ner* 2 m*iles* in all   4
To Ulme head Town in Swabia *over* the R*iver* Danup   3
To Gersling[10] at Dinner. Many pretty de-   } 3
vices made in Ivory
To Kepring[11] at night, the Riv*er* Necar Runs   2
To Ebersbach – 1 m*ile*. To Essling on the Necar 2 m*iles* in all[12]   3
To Stuckart[13] at night here the Prince of   } 1
Wittenberge keeps Court[14]

---

[1] The church of St Michael was built for the Jesuits between 1583 and 1590. To the east is the former monastery or Augustinkirche which had been extensively enlarged between 1618 and 1621. It was deconsecrated in 1803.

[2] Fürstenfeldbrück, Freiberg, and Augsburg.

[3] The two churches, one Protestant and the other Catholic, known as the Minster of SS. Ulrich and Afra, incorporated a 15th-century Benedictine abbey (perhaps Moody's 'Benedictains Ch*urch*') which was rebuilt between 1600 and 1610.

[4] St Anne's Church (founded in 1321 and entirely rebuilt between 1602 and 1616) was formerly part of a Carmelite monastery. Luther took refuge in the monastery in 1518.

[5] The 'stat Hous' may refer to either the Rathaus or to the early-16th-century Fuggerhaus, south of the Church of St Moritz, the town house of the princes Fugger von Babenhausen. The city armoury was the west of St Anne's Church. Augsburg was renowned for its fountains, especially the Augustus Fountain (1598) near the Rathaus; and the Mercury Fountain (1599) in front of the Church of St Moritz.

[6] Augsburg stands at the junction of the Rivers Lech and Wertach.

[7] Zusmarshausen.

[8] Innsbruck had come under Habsburg control in 1363 and in 1420 Duke Friedrich IV made it his capital. Emperor Maximilian I (1459–1519) made it his imperial residence (which it remained until 1665).

[9] 'swaberland', Swabia, bordered by Austria to the south.

[10] Burgau, Günzburg, Ulm, and Geislingen.

[11] 'Kepring', probably Göppingen.

[12] Ebersbach and Esslingen.

[13] Stuttgart.

[14] Moody probably means here the dukes of Wittelsbach who ruled over Bavaria and the Rhenish Palatinate. They become electors in 1623. Wittenberg is situated on the Elbe River, south-west of Berlin, and is the city where Luther nailed his famous Ninety-five Articles on the wooden doors of the castle Church of All Saints.

To Lamberge -1 m*ile* ½ Tottenheim – 1 m*ile* – in all[1]   2 ½

To Hemsen at Dinner   1

To Mille a Castle and Diner   ½

To Troffbrune Catholicks   1

To Furtze at night Lutherans belongs to the[2]
Margraff van Durlach[3]   } 1

We past the Inse R*iver*, Nagel R*iver*, Werin R*iver* and then[4]
To Ettingebel to Graff van Baden. Catholicks[5]   } 2

[f. 31ʳ]

To Rastat the River Murke bel*ow* M. Baden[6]   2

To Higalsheim at night. M. Bade[n]   1

To Stolshoffen a pretty strong Town. M. Bad*en*   2

To Lichtenaw. Graff van Hanaw   1

To Bishopsheim am Godssteig at Diner[7]   1

We past the River Rheine on a Very
Long Wooden Bridge and the*n* Tostraesburg[8]   } 3

Straesburge is a very large Citty and at that time a free stat, but now belongs to the King of France.[9] The Dome-Church is very Curious and has a steeple the highest in all Germany.[10] Their is a Curious Armery. A Brave Hospittell in which seller we drank wine above a Hunderd years old. We drank out of one Caske Laid in the year of God. 1472. and out of another prodigious great Butt we drank laid in, in 1522. Their is two Rivers runs through the Town the Bresh and the Yeu River[11] and the River Rheine runs by one side of it.

From Straesburge to Bishopsheim   3

To Lichtenaw at night   1

To Stolshoffen 1 mile To Heiglesheim 1 mile in all[12]   2

To Ratstat at diner 1 mile To Nerret at nigh[t] 2.½ in all –   3-½

To Philipsburge a very strong Garishon Town[13]   2-½

[f. 31ᵛ] From Philipsburge to Reyneshoffen on the Rhein   ½

To Speir at night, a hansome Citty   ½

[1] 'Lamberge', probably Leonberg; and 'Tottenheim', unidentified.

[2] Heimsheim, Tiefenbronn, and Pforzheim.

[3] Durlach lies just to the south-east of Karlsruhe.

[4] Pforzheim stands at the confluence of the Rivers Enz, Nagold, and Würum.

[5] Moody's 'Ettingebel to Graff van Baden' may indicate Ettlingen under the control of the Margrave of Baden Baden.

[6] Rastatt and the River Murg. Rastatt was almost completely destroyed by the French in 1689 but was rebuilt by Margrave Ludwig Wilhelm von Baden.

[7] Hügelsheim, Stollhofen, Lichtenau, and Bishopsheim.

[8] 'Tostraesburg', perhaps Strasbourg.

[9] Strasbourg. Moody's statement that the city 'now belongs to the King of France' is a crucial piece of evidence in the dating of his account of Maynard's travels. Strasbourg had been ruled for centuries as a free city within the Holy Roman Empire by a guild of its citizens but in 1681 it was seized for France by King Louis XIV and this annexation was confirmed by the Treaty of Ryswyck (1697). Since France had not controlled the city during the 1660s, this comment would suggest that Moody's account was written up at some point after 1681.

[10] The 13th–14th-century cathedral.

[11] The old centre of Strasbourg is surrounded by branches of the River Ill, with the River Rhine to its east.

[12] Bishopsheim, Lichtenau, Stollhofen, Hügelsheim.

[13] Rastatt and Neureut, and Philippsburg.

To Franckendale at Dinner Good wine	3
To Wormes at night a hansom little Town[1]	3
To Ouersomgause[2] ½ m*ile* and then to Manheim[3] at night, here the Rheine and Necar River m*eet*s	}1
To Heidleberge at Dinner	3

At Heidleberge[4] the Prince Ellectour Pallatin did keep his Court. Their is a very strong Castle on a Hill which commands the Town.[5] In that Castle is a great Tune that houlds 5,000 Emers of wine; an Immer is more then an English Barrell. Their is a staire of 15 or 20 steps to go up to the Tope and any stranger may drink as Much as he pleases.[6] Their runs the River Necar, over which is a curious Wooden Bridge. Parted frome Heidleberge for Frankford October the 27th 1661. –

From Heidleberge to Weynen Castle[7]	2
To Lauderbach 1 m*ile* To Bensen at night 1 m*ile* in all	2
To Zwingeberg ½ m*ile* To Eberstat 1m*ile*[8]	1 ½
To Dermstat where the Prince keeps Court	1
To Allerheilige ½ To Langheim 1. ½ m*ile*s in all	2
To Langheim .1. ½ To springling.½.m*ile* in all	2
To Frankford on the Mayne[9]	1

[f. 32ʳ] Frankford is a very noble Citty, a Place of great traffick and Commerce, abundance of Jewish Merchants, their is also a synagogue.[10] It is well fortify'd with Walles and Diches, the water runs round the Town, their is a very fine ston bridge build over the Mayne River which runes through the citty. The great Dom-church belongs to Catholicks[11] but most of the Inhabitans are Lutherans. Betwen Heidleberge and Franckford one of the Horses in the Coach grew tyr'd, and the Governor step't out of the Coach and began to beat him forwards, but would not mend his pace, and at last being angrie he gave the Horse a prick or two with his sword, not thinking t'woud have done him any harme; but a day after our arrivall at Frankford, the Coachman complain'd to the Magistrats that such a Gentleman had kill'd his Horse Insomuch that my Maister was summons'd before them and was forc'd to pay for the Horse.

[1] Rheinhausen, Speyer, Franckenthal, and Worms.

[2] 'Ouersomgause', possibly Hohensachsen.

[3] Mannheim.

[4] 'Anno 1661.' added in left-hand margin.

[5] Heidelberg stands at the entrance to the Neckar Valley. The 14th-century Schloss was almost entirely destroyed by the French in 1689. In 1613 Frederick V had added a new wing for his English wife, Princess Elizabeth, daughter of King James I.

[6] The famous Heidelberg Tun, built in 1591, and capable of holding 220,000 litres of wine. The tun now at the castle dates from 1751. Evelyn (1641), II, p. 147, describes it as comparable in size with a similar tun at the Abbot's Palace, Tours. See also Coryat (1608), II, pp. 218–23, and Misson (1687), I, p. 112.

[7] The Schloss Berckheim at Weinheim.

[8] Laudenbach, Bensheim, Zwingen, and Eberstadt.

[9] Darmstadt, Arheilgen, Langen, Sprendlingen, and Frankfurt am Main.

[10] The famous Easter and Autumn Fairs at Frankfurt ensured its prominence as a major trading centre.

[11] Bargarve (1656), p. 250, noted that in the city there was 'great Confusion of Relligions: The grand Dome belongs to the Papists; no wayes worthy note, but for a litle Chapell in it, where the King of the Romans is usually cround … Lutherans have sundry Churches within the wall; but the Calvenists and Anabaptists have theyrs without'.

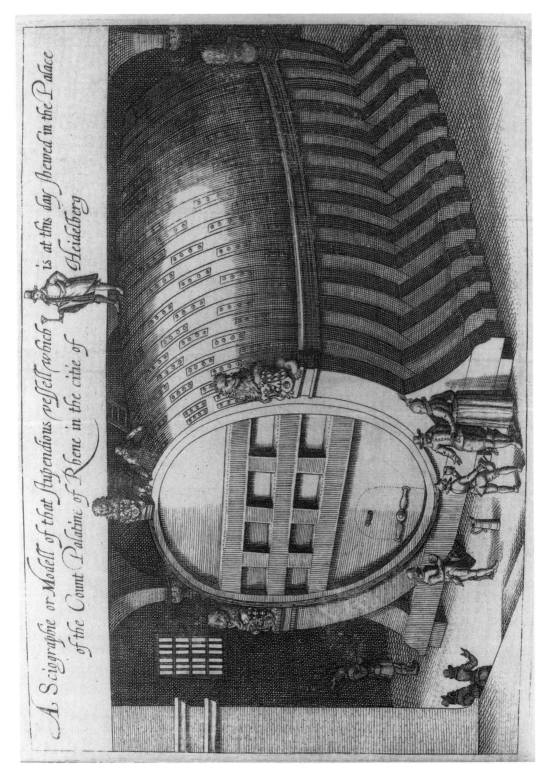

A Sciographie or Modell of that stupendious vessell which is at this day shewed in the Palace of the Count Palatine of Rhene in the citie of Heidelberg

Fig. 49. The Heidelberg Tun. From *Coryats Crudities* (1611), p. 486.

We parted frome Frankford November the first 1661. and went dirrectly to Hochstat[1]	}½
Frome Hochstat to Mentz Citty[2]	1 ½

Ments is a brave Citty and strong; It lyes on the River Rheine. The Ellector keeps his Court here.

[f. 32ᵛ] Their is to be seen the Elector's Pallace, the Cittadelle,[3] the Dome Church,[4] Our Ladye's Church, and a curious Bridge of Boates Over the Rheine.

Here my Maister's Moneys began to draw short and how to get any More till he arriv'd in Holland he knew not. I seing my Maister and his Governour concern'd tooke a knife and Rip't the headband of my Breeches, Pull'd out eighten Pisttols in Gould which I had sow'd fast in at Paris. The which, with the remainder of his owne Money, brought us Cliverly down to Holland.

Here my maister bought a boat and hyr'd two Men to Row it frome Ments to Cullen on the Rheine and so we parted frome Mentz the 4th of November 1661. –

Frome Mentz to Wall[eff?] the key of Ring[ar?]o[5]	1
To Elfelt, ½ mile Arbach and Hattenheim, ½ mile in all[6]	1
To Estrich, Millen, Vincle, and Gehaub Castle[7]	1
To Geisenheim, and then to Rittenheim[8]	1
To Noe River by Bingen, Ernefels Castle[9]	1
To Armeshausen, Fotsberge Castle, Dreks hausen on the Other sid of the Rheine[10]	}1

To Hambach, To Lurge, Tiback Castle and then to Backra,[11] their we drank the best Rhenish wine for thre half pence a Masure[?] [f. 33ʳ] which is thre pints English Measure. This Buchra is a pretty bigg Town and belong to the Ellector Pallatin, and Bachra wine is reckon'd to be the best Rhenish wine that is.

Marke, that I omit nameing neither Towne, Castle nor Village all along the Rheine frome Mentz to Cullen.

To Caw, a Castle on a Hill, a Casle in the Rheine named the Paltz, Overvessell, Schonberge Castle belongs to the Ellector of Triere in all[12]	1

---

[1] Hochstadt (to the east of Frankfurt).

[2] Mainz (lying to the south-west of Frankfurt), was the capital of the Rhine Palatinate and had been occupied by both the Swedes and the French during the Thirty Years's War.

[3] At the time of Moody's visit, building work was still in progress on a new Elector's Palace (1627–78). Much of the Schloss at Mainz dated from the 17th century.

[4] The romanesque basilica of of SS. Martin and Stephen.

[5] Both Moody's handwriting and meaning are unclear here.

[6] Eltville, Erbach, and Hattenheim.

[7] Oestrich, Mittelheim, Winkel, and 'Gehaub Castle', unidentified.

[8] Geisenheim and Rüdesheim.

[9] Bingen is situated at the confluence of the Rivers Rhine and Nahe and overshadowed by the Schloss Stahlbeck (razed in 1689).

[10] Assmannhausen and Trechtingshausen.

[11] Heimbach, Lorch, and Bacharach.

[12] Kaub and the Pfalz or Pfalzgrafenstein, a small hexagonal building, on a ledge of rock in the middle of the Rhine. Oberwesel and the Schloss Schönburg (razed 1689).

To S^t. Gerwerhausen, Casts-Castle,^{1} To sanquer^2

at night a very fine Castle on a Hill.

To Reinfelt a strong Town and Castle^3 belongs

to the Langrave van Hessen

}1

}1

To Welminach,^{4} Catzinella Castle B*ishop* of Triere   1

To Ertzinaw, Kessdorffe Triere^5 1

To Selsigh, Rottewine, Campe^6 1

To Burnehoffe Church, and two Castles built

on two Hills opposit one to the other ^{7} 1

The story is thus.

A Rich Man dy'd and left an Imense treasure of Moneys to his two sonns and a Daughter who was blind, and the Money to be parted equally amongst them, the Moneys was parted by [?] they keapt their own but strock't hers, she be being blind could not perceive it, yet she built^8 a fine Church [f. 33^v] and bought land enough sufficient to Maintain devine service for ever. But the two Brothers built each a Castle as aforesaid, Rioted and spent all their Money and at last fell at Varience, and the one kill'd the other, and the other suffer'd for his crime. The Ruines of the two Castles is yet to be seen, but the Church more splendid and glorious then ever.

Frome Burnehoffe Church to Bupport   1

To Sickhause, Spay'd, Nederspein,^{9} B. Cullen

To Rawbach,^{10} Langrave, Van Hessen, Purgemg

Water. To Raise, B*ishop* Triere, Konigstooke, Lansteine,^{11}

B*ishop* of Mentz. Capella, B*ishop* Triere, A Castle on a Hill

Lone River, and then to Hiderlanstein^{12} 2

To Ovewort. A Nuns' Cloister^{13} in an Ile in the Rheine

All Ladys and Gentlewomen and then to Coblens^{14} 1

Hermisteine Castle^{15} on a Hill over against Coblence both noble and strong belongs to the Ell*ector* of Triere

^{1} St Goarshausen, dominated by the ruined Schloss known as the Burg Katz.

^{2} 'sanquer', unidentified.

^{3} The castle of Rheinfels (razed by the French in 1797) situated above St Goar.

^{4} Wellmich.

^{5} Hirzenach and Kestert.

^{6} 'Selsigh' and 'Rottewine', unidentified; and Kamp.

^{7} Bornhofen (or Kamp-Bornhofen) is dominated by two ruined castles, reputed built by rival brothers. Its church was built in the 1430s.

^{8} 'built' added above.

^{9} Boppard, 'Sickhause', unidentified, Spay, and 'Nederspein', unidentified.

^{10} Braubach.

^{11} 'Raise', possibly Rhens; 'Konigstooke' unidentified, and Lahnstein.

^{12} Kapellen and 'Hiderlanstein', unidentified.

^{13} Moody is probably referring here to the 15th-century former monastery on an island (the Niederwerth) in the Rhine.

^{14} Koblenz. During the Thirty Years' War it was taken, successively and with considerable damage, by the French, the Spanish, the Swedes, and the imperial forces. From the late 1640s it also suffered from outbreaks of the plague.

^{15} The Ehrenbreitstein fortress was begun in the 16th century, with work still continuing at the time of Moody and Maynard's journey.

To Kesslung, Ingers, Newittigg, Erlich, Amfarr[1]
And then to Andernach a large Town   3
To Leittersdorffe[2] at night belongs D*uke* Newburge   1
To Hamerstein an old Ruin'd Cast*le* on a Hill[3] to
Niderhamerstein, Reinbrule,[4] D.N. Renock C*astle*
on a hill, Preisig, Heimigh.[5] Another Castle
D.N.B. Sternberge, belongs to the Graff van
Isseberge, Sinsige D.N.B. Lansgrave a Castle
on a Hill, whit-church[6] and then to Lents[7]   2

[f. 34ʳ] To Arbell. E: C: Renaw Cloister,[8] Apolenarysberg, then to Unkle and Kuneterf[9] under the seven Hills, Honigswinter and Millen,[10] and a little further on the same side is Cittenbergue Castle,[11] And then to the strong Citty of Bonne where the Elector of Cullen keeps Cou*r*t[12]

From Bon to Rudup a Kuns Cloister,[13] Wittich, Urbea Castle, Millande another Castle,[14] Swise, Helping, Rotkirch,[15] and then to the famous Citty of Cullen –   5

Cullen is a most noble great Citty, and lyes on *th*e River Rhein,[16] Their is abundance of faire Churches and most sumptuous Pallaces, The Dome Church is Capitall, where lyes enterr'd the thre Kings who went to visit our Saviour of Bethelem.[17] Their is also Sᵗ. Ursula's Church[18] where she with her Eleven thousand Virgins were as they say Martyr'd and lye their Enterr'd.[19] Their is a Curious Bridge of Boats over the River. It is a great place for Traffick, being the staple for Wines and all other commodities which comes down the Rhein fro*m* Germany. King Charles the second keept his Court above two years in this Citty in the time of his banishment, where he left severall prety Childern and my Maister had the curiositie to se one or two.[20] Here my Maister dismis'd the men that Row'd us down the River Rhein, he pay'd them their wages and gave them the Boat that he bought at Mants. And haveing stay'd [f. 34ᵛ] about thre dayes and haveing seene every thing the most

[1] 'Kesslung', unidentified, Engers, Neuwied, Irlich, and Fahr.
[2] Andernach and Leutesdorf.
[3] Hammerstein.
[4] Niederhammerstein and Rheinbrohl.
[5] Bad Breisig and (perhaps) Bad Hönningen.
[6] Sinzig-Bad Bodendorf has a late-13th-century romanesque church but the Schloss is now a 19th-century construction.
[7] Linz.
[8] Erpel.
[9] The Schloss Mariiensfels Apollinaris, Unkel, and 'Kuneterf', unidentified.
[10] Königswinter and Mehlem.
[11] 'Cittenbergue Castle', possibly Oberkassel.
[12] Bonn.
[13] 'Rudup', possibly Uedorf.
[14] Widdig, 'Urbea Castle, and Millande.
[15] Sürth, 'Helping', unidentified, and Rodenkirchen.
[16] Köln (Cologne). Its city centre was almost entirely destroyed during World War II.
[17] Cologne Cathedral was begun in 1248 but only completed in 1880. The Three Kings are commemorated in the stained glass windows of the choir. Their relics were formerly preserved in the Chapel of the Magi.
[18] 'Church' added above.
[19] The 13th-century church of St Ursula who was reputedly martyred with 11,000 companions. At the time of Moody's visit a new (1659) sarcophagus had been made for her supposed remains.
[20] Charles II was based at Cologne with his sister Mary Princess of Orange between October 1654 and 1656, mainly because he could easily collect from there the pension paid (erratically) to him by the Imperial Diet.

rare we departed frome Cullen November the 8th 1661 and so every mile down wards frome Cullen makes thre English

Frome Cullen to Keptdorffe D.N.B.	3
To Tunst[1] El*ector* Cullen	2
To Hewst and then to Dusseldorffe[2]	2

Their is very noble Pallace where the Duke of Hewbourgue keeps his Court; The Town is but smale but lyes upon the River Rhein.

To Keyserwart[3] El*ector* of Cullen	5
To Vurd[4] at night a good Lodging	2

We past by Angerort Castle, and then to Dure where runs the River Rue, and then to Urshy

belongs to the Duke of Brandeburgue	4
To Reinbergue the Ell*ector* of *Cullen*	1
To Vesell[5] a very strong Town, from thence to	
Beck,[6] and then to Raise all belonging to the Ell*ector* B.	}3
To Emerich we past by Ettenbourgue Cloister[7] D.N.B.	2
To skenckensconce[8] a smale but very strong	
Town belongs to the Hollanders	}1

Here we past the Tholhous and enterd into the Holland Territoryes, from thence to Huysen and the*n*

to Arnem[9] head Citty in Guilderland in all	5
To Wagening, Grupe, and Rene Citty[10]	5
[f. 35ʳ] To Amerungen, Weych,[11] and then To Utrech.	7

Utrech is a very fine Citty where their is an Academy for schoolars and a place of very good Aire

From Utrech to Amsterdame[12]	9

We arriv'd at Amsterdam November the 15 <u>1661</u>. and Lodg'd in the greatest ordinary in Holland cal'd the Heren Logement,[13] or the ordinary for Lords & great persons, non

[1] 'Keptdorffe' and 'Tunst'.

[2] 'Hewst', possibly Neuss; and Düsseldorf.

[3] Kaiserswerth.

[4] Voerde (to the north of Orsoy) seems to fit Moody's spelling of this location but, if so, is out of geographical sequence. It is possible that Moody meant Vorst to the north-west of Neuss.

[5] Duisburg on the River Ruhr, Orsoy, Rheinberg, and Wesel.

[6] 'Beck', possibly the village of Bergen (midway between Wesel and Rees). Alternatively, Moody may have confused his ordering of locations since the village of Beek lies to the east of Nijmegen and it is possible that his party headed there *after* visiting Rees and Emmerich.

[7] Rees, Emmerich, and 'Ettenbourgue Cloister', possibly Elten (to the north of Schenkenschanz).

[8] Schenkenschanz.

[9] Huissen and Arnhem.

[10] Wageninen, De Grebbe, and Rhenen.

[11] Amerongen and 'Weych', probably Zeist.

[12] Utrecht and Amsterdam. The Treaty of Munster (1648), which closed the Scheldt and ruined Antwerp, assured Amsterdam's prosperity during the second half of the 17th century.

[13] Robert Bargrave made use of the same accommodation in February 1653: 'the Heren Lodgiament: which for its statelyness neatness, and varietie of Roomes, I dare pronounce the noblest Taverne in the world: Every roome is furnishd with brave Pictures, & pav'd with black and white marble; espetially the chiefest Roome; which is like-wise hang'd with the richest Guilded Lether I have seen, & furnish'd with a glorious Organ; and here we were nobly enterteind by some English merchants', Bargrave (1653), p. 166.

dineing their for lesse then a Crowne a Male, but we stay'd their only two dayes and two nights, my Maister haveing an Eager desire to se the Hague and so we departed frome

Amsterdame to Harlem in boat	3
Fro Harlem to Leyden	5
Frome Leyden to the Hague[1]	4

Being safe arriv'd at the Hague and haveing taken a convenient Lodgin for the winter season, my Maister went to kisse the Prince's hands[2] where he was receiv'd with much respect, and was invited to dine at the Prince's Table, which he did once or twice a week dureing his aboad at the Hague and sometimes at Sr. George Downing's[3] who was his Majestie's envoy extrordinary. Where very he often went for divershion, play'd at Cards & other divertisements with Sir George and his Lady and the other Gentle women.

[f. 35v] But in November we went back again to Utrech where we stayd about a week. My Maister was civily receiv'd by a Scots Collonell who recided their. From Utrech to Amsterdame makeing in all   21

Being arriv'd the second time at Amsterdam We tooke a convenient Lodging and about two or thre dayes after my Maister came acquainted with a Gentleman one Mr Ogle[4] by whose means My Maister Receiv'd many Civilities frome severall great Merchants both English and Duch.

This Mr Ogle was the kindest, the civilest, and the Merriest Man that I ever saw. And had acquaintance in every Town with those of the best rank and had such a true kindnesse for my Maister that he never left his company till he left Holland.

One thing I cannot omit, which I shall here relate which is as fallowes. My Maister at his departure from Rome, had by a speciall friend a pretty Dogg presented him. This Dogg was of a Mouse Collour, smooth and Cleanly, long Eares, a Croocked Nose. This Dogg was by my Maister recommended to my care being resolv'd to present him to my Lady Maynard his Mother. And to tell truth, I took much pains to preserve him and thre Live Tortesses which I brought also frome Rome to Venice; frome Venice back to Florence, from Florence [f. 36r] from Florence back to Venice again, and so through all Germany till we came to the famous Citty of Amsterdame. Now as I said before, this pretty Dogg my Maister design'd all along to present him to My Lady May[n]ard which certainly made me the more carefull to preserve him but mark the Issue;

Their was at Amsterdame an English Man a Pictur drawer a good Artist and an acquaintance of Mr. Ogles, who had liv'd some considerable time in Holland. And was now design'd for England, he understanding my Maister to be of such a noble family, did insinuat himselfe

---

[1] Haarlem and Leiden, and The Hague ('s-Gravenhaage).

[2] Moody is probably referring to William, Prince of Orange, the son of Frederick Henry, Prince of Orange, and husband of Charles II's sister, Mary, Princess of Orange (1631–60), whom he had married 1641. She returned to England with King Charles II in 1660 but died there of the smallpox.

[3] Sir George Downing (c. 1623–84) had served as Cromwell's scoutmaster-general in Scotland (1650) and led a movement to offer the crown of England to Cromwell (1655). After the Restoration, he was active in securing the arrest of three of the regicides, Sir John Barkstead, Miles Corbert, and John Okey, all of whom were executed in 1662. Downing was resident at The Hague on several occasions between 1657 and 1661, and again in 1671–2.

[4] This Mr Ogle was perhaps a son or relative of Sir John Ogle (1569–1640) who had served as sergeant-major-general in the Low Countries (1591) and at Nieuport (1600). He was Governor of Utrecht from 1610 until 1618. Sir John married Elizabeth, daughter of Cornelius de Vries of Dordrecht and all of their children (four sons and seven daughters) were born in the Low Countries. Three of his sons were called John (d. 1663), Thomas (d. 1702), and Cornelius.

the more into his favour, and by M^r. Ogle's intercession get my Maister to let him draw his Pictur, which to speak truth, he did to the life. The Pictur being finish'd, his next sute was, that he might carry it for England with the Dogg[1] the Pictur for my Lord and the Dogg to be presented to my Lady, which was all graunted, and accordinglie took his leave and and shipt himselfe for England, but it being in the dead of winter, the shipe in a greivous storm was cast away. In so much, the poor Pictur drawer lost his life, My Maister lost his Pictur and his Dogg, and I for my part never had so much regret for any Dumb beast whatsoever.[2]

[f. 36^v] Haveing seen everything in Amsterdame what was most rare, as the Stat Hous, the Change,[3] all the best Churches, the Jewes synagogue, and inumberable of brave Pallaces, and to tell truth I think it to be the most famous Merchant Town in Europe except London, but for neatnesse and faire buildings it goes beyond it, Haveing stay'd about a Month at Amsterdame and Christmasse drawing neare, we took our Journey for Harlem December the 18th <u>1661</u>.

Frome Amsterdame to Harlem   3

Harlem is a good hansome Citty, their is one curious Church[4] and a Buchery before the doore, the Hollandars are generally uncivill to Gentlemen but we felt it no where so much as at Harlem, for they bringing in an extravagant Reckoning the Governor would have disputed it to know how they Reckon'd, but the Landlord tould him that it was a signe he knew not where he was. "I tell you" sayes he severall times, "you are in Holland, and here you are not to dispute Reckonings", and was so transported with rage that he call'd in some of *th*e neihgbour telling them how that he had got some English Dogs in's house who would not pay their Reckoning, upon which 3 or 4 appear'd with Clubs and staves threating to knock us down The Governor [f. 37^r] was sturdy at first but seing the fellows appear with Clubs, he was glad to tender them all their unjust demands, and so we happily scapt that brunt and tooke our way towards Leyden.   5

Leyden is a very hansome Cleanly Citty insomuch one may go with slipers in the streets the whole winter. Their is water runs through all the principall streets with curious Rowes of trees on both sides. Their is a Colledge or Academy as they call it for studdents, and a most rare Anatomy Hous[5] and the Prince of Orange has a curious Pallace in this Citty.[6]

---

[1] 'for' deleted.

[2] I have not been able to identify this English artist resident at The Hague who drowned on his way back to England in December 1661.

[3] The 'Stat Hous' was the new Koninklijk Paleis (1648–55), designed by Jacob van Campen and completed by Daniel Stalpaert. It replaced a gothic predecessor on the same site which had burnt down in 1652. It was converted into a royal palace in 1808 by Louis Bonaparte. The Burse or Exchange. Evelyn (1641), II, p. 46: 'I do not looke on the structure of this Exchange to be comparable to that of Sir Tho: Greshams in our Citty of Lond: yet in one respect it exceeds, that ships of considerable burthen ride at the very key contiguous to it'. The Amsterdam Burse (built 1608–11) and the Royal Exchange (built 1566–8 and destroyed in 1666 during the Great Fire) were often compared. The Amsterdam Burse was extensively altered in 1659–60 and demolished in the early 1840s.

[4] Haarlem. Its 'one curious Church' is the Grote Kerk or St Bavo (Bavon), built between 1400 and 1550. Evelyn (1641), II, p. 50: 'Harlem is a very delicat Towne, and hath one of the fairest Churches of the Gotique designe, I had ever seene'. Situated alongside the Grote Kerk was the Vlesshal, or meat market, in a lavish Renaissance building completed in 1602 (now used for art exhibitions); and the Grote Markt.

[5] Leiden. William the Silent founded the university at Leiden in 1575 and its members included Justus Lipsius (1547–1606), Joseph Scaliger (1540–1609), Daniel Heinsius (1580–1655), and Hugo Grotius (1583–1645). See Evelyn (1641), II, p. 52–3.

[6] Moody is probably referring here to the late-16th-century Stadhuis which was almost entirely destroyed by fire in 1929.

From Leyden to the Hague 7

Being arriv'd at the Hague we tooke Up our lodging in the Papenstraet.[1] The Hague is but a village, but the biggest and finest in Christendome where the Prince of Oranges then keept Court and also the states doe alwayes meet, and all forraigne Ambassadours recide their. We keept our Christmasse at the Hague where my Maister went some times to dine at Court, sometimes to se Balls, sometimes for divershion to se curious Duch Playes.

One day we went to Scheuelling a Village on the sea shore, before which their was a bloody sea [f. 37ᵛ] fight in Cromwell's time, Black being Admi[r]all[2] for the English gave the Dutch a great overthrow on their own Coast.[3]

Another day we[4] went to Lowsdown a village about a league frome the Hague[5] where their is a church in which lyes enterr'd 365. Children born at one birth by one woman, the one halfe Boyes and the other halfe Girles and liv'd all till they Receiv'd Baptisme. The Boyes were nam'd John and the Girles Elizabeth. We saw the two Bassons in which they were Christen'd as the people hould for a veritie, haveing been all carefully Christen'd they all dy'd the same day and the Mother with them.

The Lady's name was Margerita Hermany wife to Count of Heneberg, Daughter to Qwarles Florenti, Count of Holland and Freezland. The occation of their strange accident was as followes.

A Certain poor woman came a begging to the said Lady's doore with two Childern in her Armes. The Lady ask her if these Childern were her own, "yes" reply'd the poor woman "they are twins. I bore them both at one birth", the Lady tould her it was impossible they should be both got by one Man and that she beleevd her to be an Arren whoore; the poor woman being nettled at such an answer instead of an Alms, wish'd the Lady might have as many at one birth as their are dayes in the year.

[f. 38ʳ] The which thing fell out within a year after to the great amazement of all people that ever heard theroff. and although other nations looke on it as fabulous, yet the inhabitants their about hould it for an undoubted truth.

Another day we went to Rizick a league from the Hague where the Prince hath a very noble Pallace Richly adorn'd with Pictures and other rare furnitur. And back again to the Hague at night.[6]

The winter drawing near a Period made my Maister think of his Journey to Paris, and accordinglie went to kisse the Prince's hands, and took his leave of the rest of his friends and acquaintance, and so we departed from the Hague with Mʳ. Ogle for Rotterdame February the 7ᵗʰ. 1662.

---

[1] The Hague was the official residence of the stadholders of the province of Holland and effectively the political capital of both the province and the country.

[2] Admiral and General-at-Sea Robert Blake (1599–1657). The First English War (1652–4) was entirely naval. Blake led the English fleet and that of the United Provinces was led by Admirals Maerten, Tromp, and Michiel de Ruyter. Robert Bargrave (1653), p. 173, describes 'the late sea fight at Seae between the English and Hollanders'.

[3] Scheveningen was effectively the harbour for The Hague at this period. Charles II left from here in 1650 to accept the crown of Scotland and again in 1660 at the Restoration.

[4] written 'we we'.

[5] Loosduinen. See Stoye, *English Travellers Abroad*, p. 185, for the monument to this mother and her reputed 365 babies.

[6] Rijswijk. Evelyn (1641), p. 41: 'Risewick, a stately country house of the Prince of Orange; but for nothing more remarkable then the delicious walkes planted with Lime-trees, and the moderne paintings within'.

Frome the Hague to Delfe	2
From Delfe to Oversea & then to Rotterdame[1]	3

Rotterdame is a brave Town for Traffick, It lyes about fower Leagues up frome the Brille, & the River Maes runes by it upon which the greatest shipe in Christendome can sail to Rotterdame at a full tide.[2]

Frome Rotterdame to Islamont	1
To Lechkirchen, where liv'd a Gyant[3]	1

[f. 38ᵛ]

We past the Lech River and then to Crimp[4]	1
To Dort a very pleasant Citty	2

Dort is tearm'd the Key of Holland very profitable for Merchants,[5] for all the Rhenish wines that comes frome Germany must first come to Dort. It is a good aire, the inhabitants are more kind and Civill and better humour'd then any where else in Holland, the women are hansome and those of the best rank very Courteous. Here Mʳ. Ogle had great acquaintance, and was most kindly receiv'd by severall Merchants, but especially one Min herr Frize was kinder then all the rest who would needs have my Maister to Lodge at his Hous where for a week togither we were treated as every day had been a wedding, all sorts of wine, but especially Rhenish as plenty as watter, and at last when my Maister would stay no longer, their was a yacht fitted up with Musick and all sort of daintys, a great fresh salmont which is dear at that time of the year was bought on purpose to be Eaten in the Yacht. Mʳ Frize took his wife, his sister and severall of his relations along with him, and all this was done to Honour and convoy my Maister some part of his way

[f. 39ʳ] When we were 3 leagues above Dort they cast Anker, dinner being Just ready, Fish, Flesh, Foule, swetmeats, fruite, and as for wines you may Judge of that by the rest. This feast continu'd about 7 or 5 howers, nothing but Musick, Mirth, and drinking of healths, till it began to be dark, and then we were set ashoare at a place cal'd Werkendame,[6] and after all that rejoyceing Mʳ. Ogle, although I believe he was stout enough, yet he could not part with my Maister without sheding some tears, and I for my part was sory to part with Mʳ. Ogle, for we had many a pleasant song, many a Merry story, and to tell truth, no bodie could be Melancholy in his company. We tooke up our Lodging at Werkendame, and the next Morneing hyr'd a Coach for the Busse in Brabant and so we went from

Werkendam to Workum[7] in a little streagh	2
And then to Heusden a very strong Garishon[8]	3
From Heusden to the Busse	3

The Busse is certainly the strongest Towne which belongs to hollan[d], for the water goes 3 mile round it the whole winter, and in sumer when their is occation they can pull up the

[1] Delft, Ooverschie, and Rotterdam. Rotterdam's city centre was almost entirely destroyed by German bombing in 1940.
[2] Rotterdam stands near the outlet of the Rivers Rhine and Maas (Meuse).
[3] IJsselmonde on the River IJssel (Hollandse) and Lekkerkerk.
[4] The River Rhine (Rijn) becomes the River Lek before it reaches Rotterdam; and is then named the Nieuwe Maas as it passes through the city and the Nieuwe Waterweg as it reaches the sea.
[5] Dort (Dordrecht).
[6] Werkendam.
[7] Waardhuizen would have been the usual stopping point on the route between Werkendam and Heusden.
[8] Heusden.

sluces and get it all under water.[1] The Busse [f. 39ᵛ] was taken by the Prince of Orange frome the Spanaird in the year of God 1625. The great Church is the most ancient and finest build in Holland. Their is a strong Castle call'd by the name of Papen Brille, Or a Bridle for Papist, because most of the inhabitants are Romain Catholiques and this Castle commands them and the Town also.[2] Their is a strong sconce without the Dorter Porte, and two other stronger Sconces without the Tenchter Port[3] so that I Judge if ever the french king comes before the Busse his Bombes and Carcases will doe him but smale kindnesse for I think it Impregnable.

From the Busse to Ulymin at night	1
To sprang and then to Walwick	3
To Bungen a Catholick Village	1
To the famous Citty of Bredà [4]	2

Breda is a very pleasant Citty and extraordinary strong. It was taken by stratageme from the spainard in the year 1647.[5] In Holland the most of their fireing is Turffe, and sometimes they bring them into the Towns in prodigious great Barges. In such a one their was put in the bottom 200 stout well arm'd men, couer'd over with Turffe and this Barge was brought into the Town in the day time [f. 40ʳ] without the least suspition, and about one a Cloak after Midnight, they brak all out on a suddent, kill'd the sentrys and some of the Guards that resisted so in an hower's time, made themselves Maisters of that important Garishon with little bloodshed. About a league frome Bredà their is a wood of Fir trees, they stand so thick togither one can hardly se at noon day. The Prince of Orange has a[6] Pallace in the midst of this wood, their is also a very strong Castle in Bredà with a curious Garden.[7]

From Bredà to Rosendale a curious Village[8]	4
To Moro,[9] and then to Bergenopsome	3

Bergenopsome is a strong frontier Town. It is situated on a Hill by the sea shore by which reason it is very pleasant and delightfull. Their runs also the River some frome whence the Town takes the name.

[1] 's-Hertogenbosch (Den Bosch, Bois-le-Duc). The town was unsuccessfully besieged by Maurice of Nassau in 1601and again in 1603. It was finally taken by Prince Frederick Henry in September 1629.

[2] The 14th–16th-century gothic Sint Janskathedraal (St John's Cathedral). 'Pappen Brille' refers to its formerly heavily defended fortress. The entire town was largely Roman Catholic until its capture by the Protestants in 1629.

[3] 'Sconces', fortifications. Evelyn (1641), p. 61: 'Having viewed the Workes (which are wonderfull strong) and the Fort, built heretofore by our Country-men the English, adjacent to the Towne'. The English governed Bergen-op-Zoom from 1586 until 1596.

[4] Vlymen, Sprang, Waalwijk, 'Bungen' (probably Dongen), and Breda.

[5] Moody's historical information is not entirely accurate here. In 1625 Breda was surrendered to the Spanish under Spinola by Justin of Nassau after a gruelling siege lasting some nine months. Prince Frederick Henry retook the town in 1637 and it was finally ceded the the United Provinces in 1648. Charles II resided at Breda during his exile and the Declaration of Breda (1660) detailed the conditions on which he was willing to accept the throne of England.

[6] 'a' added above.

[7] The Kasteel at Breda (now a military academy), designed by Thomas of Bologna, was begun after 1536 by Hendrick III and Reinier of Nassau and was extensively reconstructed by William III in 1696. Its park is known as the Valkenberg.

[8] Roosendaal.

[9] The usual stopping point between Roosendaal and Bergean op Zoom would have been either Heerle or Wouw.

From Bergenopsome to sprendall[1] belongs to the
King of Spain as also Ruckenfens[2]   4
Frome thence to Antwerp   3

Antwerpe is a most famous and ancient Citty belongs to the King of Spain and lyes in the Province of Brabant. Their are many Magnificent Churches worthy to be admir'd, the great Dome cald our Lady's Church[3] is principall; but the Jesuite's is certain [f. 40ᵛ] the rarest piece of workmanshipe in the world, the Inside being all pure Marble rarely polllish'd. Their is most excellant Picturs and other ornaments, a vast Library of all sorts of Bookes.[4] Sʳ. Michels Church is also very rare, and many others which for brevitie I omit. Their is also the Hous for Merchants and the Burse or exchange, being the first exchange that ever was built in Europe but Amsterdame has deminish'd both the Trad[e] and renown of this famous citty.[5] Their is a Curious Mint where they Coyn their Money, their is also a very strong Castle guarded only by spainardes.[6] Their is an excellent stone wall goes round the Town where the water runs also rownd, their is also pleasant Rowes of trees round the Top of the wall which makes a Most delightfull Arbour in the sumer. Their is a famous River nam'd the scheld which brings any great shipe up to the walles of Antwerp[7]
We departed frome Antwerp the 28 of February towards Gent.

Frome Antwerp to Borchs a Village   1
To Heusden another great Village[8]   2
On the left hand Loore and then to Arbach   3
To Locristy a very hansome Church[9]   2
To the great Citty of Gent Capitall of all Flanders   2
[f. 41ʳ] Ghent is a vast Citty belongs also to the King of Spain. The streets are long and large, Many faire Churches and Pallaces, Many high Towers which makes it be cal'd Ghent with the Towers high and term'd one of the seven Cittyes in Christendome.[10] Their is many fair Market places and on one the great Gun of Ghent[11] which we saw and 18 score of wind Milles round the Walles.

[1] Bergen op Zoom and Sprundel, to the south-west of Breda.

[2] 'Ruckenfens', unidentified.

[3] Antwerp. The 14th–16th-century cathedral is the largest gothic church in Belgium. It was looted by the French in 1794. See Evelyn (1641), p. 64.

[4] The church of St Charles Borromeo (1615–25), designed by the Jesuit architect Pieter Huyssens and as viewed by Moody, was largely destroyed by fire in 1728. See Evelyn (1641), p. 63.

[5] The 1531 Beurs, the model for other European exchanges including Sir Thomas Gresham's at London, was destroyed by fire in 1581. The building viewed by Moody was burnt in 1858 (rebuilt, 1859–72). There was also an English Exchange at Antwerp at this period. The Oosterhuis, built between 1564 and 1568 (burnt down 1893), was the house of the Hanseatic League of merchants. Evelyn (1641), 66, mistakenly took this building to be the house of the East India Company.

[6] The Steen, originally the gatehouse and forebuilding of the main castle of Antwerp, was converted into a prison in the 13th century and later used as the seat of the Spanish Inquisition. It was restored by Charles V in 1520 and extensively rebuilt in 1890.

[7] The Scheldt River.

[8] 'Borchs', either Boechout or Berchem; 'Heusden', unidentified.

[9] Lokeren, 'Arbach', unidentified, and Locristi.

[10] Gent. Evelyn (1641), II, p. 73: 'Ghendt is an extravagant Citty of so vast a Circumference, that it is reported to be no lesse then 7 Leagues in compasse'. Bargrave (1653), p. 172; 'Gant; an old City, reported to equall Paris in Circuit'.

[11] Evelyn (1641), II, pp. 73–4, describes the 'Basilisco, or monstrous gun so much talked of' in the Vrijdagsmarkt.

Frome Ghent to Bridges also in Flanders	7

Bridges is also a great Citty many brave Churches and Pallaces, but the Town is not very strong.

Frome Bridges to Ostend.[1]	4

Ostend is Reckon'd to be the strongest Town in Christendome. It held out a siege of thre yeares both by sea and land in Qwen Elizabeth's time;[2] Sir Francis Vere being then Admirall for the English Navy,[3] and Marquis Spinola the Spanish Generall in the Low Countryes.[4]

Frome Ostend to Newport a good strength[5]	3

At Newport my Maister was Civily receiv'd by M[r]. Henry Howard afterwards Duke of Norfolke[6]

From Newport to Feurne[7]	3
Frome Feurne to Dunkerke	4

[f. 41[v]] Dunkirk is a very strong seaport Town in Flanders. It belong'd formerly to the Spainard, but at that time to the King of England.[8] My Maister was Civily receiv'd at Dunkirk by one Liuetenant collonell Horrand and Major Carris who commanded the Town in the Governour's absence who was then at the Court in England. Haveing stay'd about a week in Dunkerk, we took our way back again towards Brussells the 15th of March 1662.

From Dunkerk to Feurn	4
Frome Feurn to Newport	2
Frome Newport to Bridges	7
From Bridges to Ghent	7
From Ghent to Allest	5
From Allest to Brussels in Brabant[9]	5

In Brussells the Governour or Vice Roy keeps Court. It is a most pleasant Citty, abundance

---

[1] Bruges and Ostend.

[2] Fortified by the Prince of Orange in 1583, Ostend was the last stronghold of the Dutch in Belgium. It was captured for Spain by Ambrogio Spinola in 1604 after a siege of three years.

[3] Sir Francis Vere (1560–1609), accompanied the Earl of Leicester's expedition to the Low Countries (1585–6) and was prominent in Dutch military affairs during the next twenty years. He successfully defended Ostend from the Spanish in 1600–1602.

[4] Ambrogio di Filippo Spinola (1569–1630). After his success in taking Ostend, Spinola was appointed Commander in Chief of the Spanish armies in the Netherlands.

[5] Nieuport (Nieuwpoort).

[6] Henry Howard (1628–84), who succeeded his brother to the dukedom of Norfolk in December 1677. He was a friend of John Evelyn and, as a Catholic, lived abroad from 1678 until 1682. This reference sets the date of Moody's diary as at least after December 1677.

[7] Furnes (Veurne).

[8] Dunkirk (Dunkerque). Although Dunkirk was captured by Condé for the French in 1646, it was taken by the Spaniards in 1653. It was then retaken for the French by Turenne (1658) after the Battle of the Dunes and ceded to Cromwell in return for his military assistance. Two years after the Restoration, King Charles II sold it to King Louis XIV. Sir Edward Harley, who was governor of Dunkirk (1660–61) vigorously opposed this sale.

[9] Alost and Brussels.

of brave Churches and Pallaces. 'st er Dulle' is the Capitall Church,[1] the Jesuites is also a brave Church, the Governour's Pallace is most Magnificent and a brave Church oposit to the front of the Pallace where most of the persons of qualitie go to Masse;[2] their is a very pleasant Parke behind the Pallace with fine water workes and other rarities, their is a large and curious Market place where stands the stat hous[3] and severall [f. 42ʳ] other great buildings. Haveing stay'd about a week and seen every thing most remarkable in Brussells, we took our way fo[r] Paris the 30th of March in the year 1662.

Frome Brussells to Nostredam de Hall	3
To Lembeck, Tibys, Brain, and to soignie at night[4]	4
To Mons head Town of Hanolt	1

Mons is a very noble Citty and strong situated on the Top of a Hill. Their are many brave Churches, their is a Convent of Canonesses which are all either Princesses, Duchesses or great Ladys.[5]

From Mons to Kevern a hansom village	3
To Valencien a very strong Garishon[6]	7
and at that time belong'd to the King of Spain.	
To Hape a very brave village	4
To Cambraij[7]	3

Cambray is also a great Town and strong and the last Garishon which belong'd to the Spainard in those dayes. We had a very good Lodging at Cambray and the next morning we past out of the King of Spain's Territoryes and arriv'd at Torre in Picardy which belongs

to the King of France	4
To Perron a very strong Garishon[8]	4
[f. 42ᵛ] To le Roy in Picardy	7
To Gourney, and then to Ponte at night[9]	12
The next day we past through a great	
Wood till we came to Senlis	3
To Louvre a famous Village at night[10]	4
To the most renowned Citty of Paris	6

[1] Brussels. The Cathedral of St Michael (often simply called Ste Gudule, heard by Moody as 'st er Dulle').

[2] The Coudenberg Palace seen by Moody's party burnt down in 1731. Evelyn (1641), II, p. 70: 'I went to see the Princes Court, which is an antient confus'd building, large & irregular, not much unlike the Hofft, at the Hague'. The present Palais du Roi dates from between 1740 and 1827. Moody may be referring here to the 15th-16th-century gothic church of Notre-Dame du Sablon.

[3] The gothic Hôtel de Ville and the Maison du Roi. Evelyn (1641), II, p. 69: 'I went first to visite the State-house neere the Market-Place; being for the carving in free-stone a most laborious, & (strangely) finish'd Piece; well worth the observing'.

[4] Halle (Hal), Lembecq, Tubize, Braine-le-Comte, and Soignes.

[5] Mons, and its renowned Collégiale Sainte Waudru, founded by Ste Waudru in the 7th century. The present church dates mainly from the 16th and 17th centuries.

[6] Quiévrain and Valenciennes.

[7] Haspres and Cambrai.

[8] 'Torre', probably Ribécourt-la-Tour, and Pérrone.

[9] Roye, Gournay, and Pont-Ste-Maxence.

[10] Senlis and Louvres.

We arriv'd at this famous Citty the 3[d] day of Aprile 1662 and went streight to our old Lodging at Madam Jannos in Fauxbourge S[t]. Germains where we had left our things two years before. We found the Trunckes fast, Cloathes and Linen and everything safe and sownd as we left them.[1]

My Maister meeting with his Brother M[r]. William Maynard who was newly arrived at Paris, they continu'd togither in Madam Janos' Hous which was one of the best ordinarys in St Germans Suburb till about the Month of September, in which time my Maister went to the Danceing and fenceing Schoole, as also Carveing and other divertisment, as also M[r]. William. But one thing More, he tooke delight in the Ghitterr[2] and had a very expert Maister in which time I was not Idle, but pickt up some good tunes which I retain to this day.

[f. 43[r]] In the month of June we went to Leoncour[3] about a daye's Journey frome Paris where the King of France has a noble Pallace and the finest Gardens in France, and severall other Pallaces belonging to other Dukes and Princes. Haveing stay'd heir two dayes and seen all what was rare we came back again to Paris. Being arriv'd at Paris, my Horse being somewhat weary I was left behind, and comeing over Pontneuff or the New bridge so cal'd, I lost two good Cloackes[4] which were cut of frome behind me, the one belong'd to M[r] Henchman being a rare haire[5] Camlet Cloake worth eight or ten pound, the other was a wosted Camlet and belong'd to M[r]. William, and both were so generous as[6] to forgive the tresspasse.

In the Month of September my Maister had a mind to take a Progresse to se some Townes of France it being vintage time and the best season in the year for that purpos and so the 6th of September we departed frome Paris and lay at a Town cal'd Temple,[7] and the next day arriv'd at Orleans which is a very pleasant citty situated on the River Loire.[8] On the Bridge of Orleans their stands a rare statut of Joan of Arck cal'd the Maid of Orleans who as they say undertooke to chace the English out of France, and to tell truth did doe wonders.[9]

[f. 43[v]] We went down the River frome Orleans to Blois which is a very pleasant Town. A good Aire, the best french spoke their, their is an Academy and many expert Maisters for all sciences and learning.[10]

From Blois we went down the River till we arriv'd at Towers a very ancient Citty, where is the finest Pells mell in all France.[11]

Frome Towers still down the River till we arriv'd at Someurs also a very pleasant Citty

[1] The Faubourg Saint-Germain, on the direct route to Versailles and close to the Louvre and the Tuileries, was probably the most fashionable district of Paris in which foreign visitors found lodgings.

[2] guitar.

[3] 'Leoncour', unidentified.

[4] deletion.

[5] 'haire' written above.

[6] 'as' written above

[7] 'Temple', probably Etampes.

[8] Orléans

[9] This bridge was ruined in 1746 and replaced between 1751 and 1760. The monument to Jeanne d'Arc, erected in 1458, was vandalized by the Huguenots in 1567 and later restored. It was completely destroyed in 1792. Evelyn (1644), II, p. 137, provides a detailed description of this monument.

[10] Blois. Evelyn (1644), II, p. 142: 'Bloys is a towne where the Language is exactly spoken, the Inhabitans very courteous, the [ayre] so good that it is for that cause the ordinary nursery of the Kings Children; & the People so ingenious, that for Goldsmiths Worke, & Watches no place in France affords the like'.

[11] Tours. The alley in which the game 'pall-mall' was played. See Evelyn (1644), II, p. 145, and Lough, *France Observed*, pp. 118–19.

very plentifull of wines, we drank new wines for thre farthings an English quart, and oth*er* wine for a sous Marke which is five farthing for a quart.

Frome thence down the River to Angers[1] which is a very noble and ancient Citty many brave Churches and Pallaces and aboundance of brave Gentry and they very civill.

Frome Angiers we went to a Town call'd la Flesh[2] where the old Countesse of Sussex did then reside,[3] and a pretty young lady to her Daughter was with her. We stay'd their two dayes and the Countesse would have had my Maister to stay longer, but he took his leave. [f. 44ʳ] And so we proceeded on our Journey till we came and arriv'd at Richleiu, which is the prettyest Towne that we saw in all our Travells. A Towne built so uniforme and compact, the hows[es are] all of[4] one height that it seems to be all one fabrick, a pleasant situation and very good Air. Their is also a most noble and Magnificent Pallace, built by the Cardinall of Richleiu, many brave rareties to be seen in that noble Pallace, Excellent Gardens, most rare water workes, statutes, Pictures and other curiosites which for brevetiey I omit.[5]

From Richleiu we went back again to that ancient Citty of Towers,[6] where Charles Martell with fower score thousand Christians, encounter'd with thre hunderd[7] thousand Turkes and Saracens, over threw, beat and kill'd all most all that Huge Army not above 30 thousand escaping by flight.[8] We stay'd but one night at Towers and next morning we cross'd the River Loire, and so travell'd directly till we arriv'd at Charters.

Charters is another ancient Citty in which is a most curious Church built by the English whilest they possessed so many Towns and Provinces in France.[9]

Frome Charters we saw but little till we arriv'd at Paris, which was the 10th of octobe[r] in the year of our Lord God 1662. and arriv'd safe [f. 44ᵛ] at our old lodging Monsr. Jannos where we continu'd till after Michelmasse. And then M^r. Henchman with my Maister's consent tooke a noble Lodging in Rue de Fossé[10] not in an ordinary but a privat Hous. So when my Maister was inclin'd to Dine at home I play'd the Caterer as I had done before at Rome. But that was seeldome their being the best ordinarys at Paris in the World.

Upon the newes of my Lady Banister's death, my Maister tooke another french footman, and so we were all put in Mourning, but these two fellowes had like to have prov'd fatale to my Maister and all of us. My Maister pay'd them their board w[a]ges once a Month which was about 8 Crownes a Month. La vigne, which was one of the footman's name, whe*n* he

---

[1] Saumur and Angers.

[2] La Flèche. In memory of his parents, King Henri IV had granted the château to the Jesuits to establish a college there which officially opened in 1607 (moving to a new building in 1622).

[3] It is not clear which Dowager Countess of Sussex is meant here. Edward Radcliffe, 6th Earl of Sussex, died without an heir in July 1643. The title then passed to Thomas Savile (b. 1590), who was created Earl of Sussex in May 1644. He died between 8 November 1657 and 8 October 1659 and was succeeded by his son, James (1647–71).

[4] written 'hows all all of'.

[5] Richelieu. The Cardinal's neo-classical palace was demolished in 1805. Evelyn (1644), II, p. 151: 'About a flite-shot off the towne on the left hand is the Cardinals house, being a most princely pile, though upon an old designe, not altogether gotique, but mix'd: it has a cleare moate environing it. The roomes are stately, most richly furnishd, with Tissue, Damasque, Aras, Velevet: Pictures, Statues, Vases, & all sorts of Antiquities'.

[6] Tours.

[7] deletion.

[8] Charles Martell (c. 688–741) reunited the Frankish kingdom and halted the invasion of the Saracen Moors from Africa at Poitiers (not Tours) in 732.

[9] Chartres and its Cathedral of Notre-Dame.

[10] Probably either the Rue des Fossés-Saint-Bernard (following the line of the old city moat with the Porte Saint-Victor) or the Rue des Fossés-Saint-Jacques (in the Val de Grace district).

receiv'd his Month's wages, being very Arch wold strow his Money about the Roome and then lye down and role himselfe 20 times back and forward on the Money, and when he was over a Glasse of wine amongst his commerads would swear that he serv'd an English Lord who made him tumble in silver once a Month. But now to our purpos.

One day they haveing receiv'd their Money deserted both their Maister which they did not use to doe for the French keep them bare of money they are very good sevants. But being at that time both flush in money drank themselves drunk, and towards night [f. 45ʳ] comeing through Rue de Boushery or Bouchers street, Quarrell'd, drew their swords and wounded two or thre Boutchers, upon which in the twinkling of an eye their was thirty or forty Butchers after them, and they like fooles fled home, knock't most boysterously at the doore. The Landlord not knowing the matter open'd the door. The footmen being enter'd boulted the door, fireing two or thre Pistols within the porch, which so much enrag'd the Butchers that they forc'd and brook open the Gate for all it was very strong. The footmen Made their escape over a Wall backwards, my Maister, Mʳ. William, Mʳ. Henchman and I being above in a large Dineing Rome not thinking any hurt by a great fier, when on a suddent cames up at least twenty of these Butcherly fellowes, some with Axes, some with great knives, such as they rip open the beasts with, swearing most horrid oaths they would kill all they met. First one fearfull fellow held an axe over my Maister's head saying he would cleave him in pieces, another set on Mʳ. William threatening the like to him; Mʳ. Henchman and I endeavouring all in us lay to save me Maister and his brother frome being kill'd. and to perswad them that they were mistaken, I met with one more civill then the rest who listen'd a little to my discourse. I tould him that these Gentlemen who [f. 45ᵛ] they bent their fury against were Gentlemen and strangers and had not been out the whole day, but the Fellows that affronted them was hid somewhere below stairs, upon which he with the rest run down as if the Divill had drove them, searching every where, but as I said before they had made their escape backwards. All this while the landlord was not Idle, for he[1] slipt out and brought in the Constable with a great many wachmen with Halbords and other Weapons, and then our valiant Butchers all slunck away: and as God would have it, their was no hurt done only some smale scartches and a grieveous fright but had not the Constable come in as he did they began to come up staires again, swearing the death of somebody; one of the footmen was taken and lay along time in Prison. And at last[2] me maister was so Charitable as to pay his Fees, but would not entertain him no more in his service. Mʳ. Henchman and the landlord went to Law with the Butchers, the one for a Rijat,[3] and the other for breaking open his Hous. Much time and Money was spent, but all to no purpos. The spring being pretty far spent, my Maister resolv'd for England. And so haveing taken his leave of all his good friends, and particularly [f. 46ʳ] his Brother, Mʳ. William who stay'd in Paris about a year after before he came for England. And so we bid Paris adew the 27 day of March 1663.

From Paris to Pontois their is a famous English Nunery.[4] From Pontois to Rowen and

---

[1] 'he' added above.

[2] written 'last last'.

[3] 'Rijat': riot.

[4] It is not possible to identify this particular convent since religious houses were numerous in the region between Paris and Pontoise. Sir Charles Somerset (1611), p. 69, concisely describes the plenitude of such institutions: 'In *Pontoyse* there is a Colledge for Grammar schollars, of religious Orders there are Capucins, Cordeliers, Carmelits, Jacobins; some of them are out of the the towne. There is also out of the towne a fayre monasterie of the Order of St. Austen, which is over the river, besides some 2. other monasteries, and there is also a fayre monastery of Nunnes some halfe a league out of the towne'.

from Rowen we arriv'd at Diep[1] where we stay'd a whole week till one of the King's Men of Warr arriv'd who was sent on purpos to bring over my Maister. We went aboard the 9th of Aprile about 9 a Cloack in the Morning, and the next day about aleven we arriv'd safe at Dover. The same day we tooke Post for Canterburry where we stay'd that night, and the next day we arriv'd safe at London the 12th day of Aprile in the year of our Lord God –
<u>1663</u>.

Finis.

---

[1] Rouen and Dieppe.

BIBLIOGRAPHY

I. MANUSCRIPT SOURCES

Canterbury Cathedral, Archives
MS Lit E39a–c: John Bargrave's 'Colledge of Cardinals'.
MS U11/8: John Bargrave's travels.

Durham Cathedral, Dean and Chapter Library
MS Hunter 134: travels of Isaac Basire.

Leeds, Brotherton Collection, University of Leeds
MS Trv 2: copy of William Hammond's letters.
MS Trv.d.1: Sir William Trumbull's travels.
MS Trv.q.3: Sir Charles Somerset's travels.

London, British Library
MS Additional 19253: Philip Stanhope's travels.
MS Additional 22584: Anthony Hammond's pocket-book.
MS Additional 59785: copy of William Hammond's letters.
MS Egerton 1632: Robert Southwell's travels.
MS Egerton 1635, 1636: Richard Symond's notebooks.
MS Egerton 2148: Thomas Hoby's travels.
MS Harley 943, 1278: Richard Symond's notebooks.
MS Harley 2286: Peter Mundy's travels.
MS Harley 7007: correspondence of Henry, Prince of Wales.
MS Harley 7021: Sir Thomas Puckering's travels.
MS Lansdowne 117: correspondence of Robert Dudley, Earl of Leicester.
MS Sloane 118: Joseph Colston's travels.
MS Sloane 179: John Downes's travels.
MS Sloane 682: Sir Thomas Berkeley's(?) travels.
MS Sloane 1813: Richard Smith's travels.
MS Sloane 2142: Francis Mortoft's travels.

Maidstone, Centre for Kentish Studies
U1121: Marsham family papers.
U1475: Sidney family papers.

Nottingham, University of Nottingham Library
MSS Portland P1 E9: papers relating to Banaster Maynard.

Oxford, All Souls College Library
MS 317: Sir William Trumbull's autobiography.

Oxford, Bodleian Library
MS Additional C 173: Sir John North's travels.
MS Clarendon 137: William Edgeman's travels.
MS Doncaster c 60: Sir John Marsham's papers.
MS Lister 19: Martin Lister's travels.
MS Rawlinson A 245: Anthony Hammond's diary.
MS Rawlinson A 315: Peter Mundy's travels.
MS Rawlinson D 76: Robert Montagu's travels.
MS Rawlinson D 84: Robert Moody's diary of Banaster Maynard's travels.
MS Rawlinson D 120: anonymous travels.
MS Rawlinson D 121: Richard Symond's notebooks.
MS Rawlinson D 1150: Thomas Raymond's travels.
MS Rawlinson D 1180–1187: Richard Rawlinson's diaries.
MS Rawlinson D 1285: Thomas Abdy's(?) travels.
MS Tanner 93: Thomas Raymond's travels.
MS Tanner 309: Stephen Powle's travels.

Paris, Bibliothèque nationale de France
MSS 4611: Treasury of St-Denis.
MSS 18765: Treasury of St-Denis.

Sheffield, Public Library
MSS Wentworth Woodhouse 21, 30: Thomas Wentworth's travels.

Washington, Folger Shakespeare Library
MS V.a.428: Isaac Basire's travels.

II. PRINTED SOURCES
(Place of publication is London unless otherwise stated)

Anonymous, *A New Miscellany of Original Poems, Translations and Imitations*, 1720.
Ascham, Roger, *The Schoolmaster (1570) by Roger Ascham*, ed. Lawrence V. Ryan, Ithaca, NY, 1967.
Bacon, Sir Francis, *The Essayes or Counsels, Civill and Morall*, ed. M. Kiernan, Oxford, 1985.
Balzac, Jean-Louis, *Lettres choisies*, 1648 (rpt. 1650, 1652, 1656).
Bann, Stephen, *Under the Sign. John Bargrave as Collector, Traveler, and Witness*, Ann Arbor, 1994.
Bargrave, John, *Pope Alexander the Seventh and the College of Cardinals*, ed. James Craigie Robertson, Camden Society 92, 1867.
Bargrave, Robert, *The Travel Diary of Robert Bargrave (1647–1656)*, ed. Michael G. Brennan, The Hakluyt Society, 3rd ser., 3, 1999.
Basire, Isaac, *Travels Through France and Italy (1647–49)*, ed. Luigi Monga and C. Hassel, Geneva and Turin, 1987.

Bate, Jonathan, 'The Elizabethans in Italy', in *Travel and Drama in Shakespeare's Time*, ed. Jean-Pierre Maquerlot and Michèle Willems, Cambridge, 1996, pp. 55–74.

Beal, Mary, *Study of Richard Symonds: his Italian Notebooks and Their Relevance to 17th Century Painting Techniques*, 1984.

Bentley, G. E. 'James Shirley and a Group of Unnoted Poems on the Wedding of Thomas Stanley', *Huntington Library Quarterly*, 2, 1938–9, pp. 219–32.

Berry, William, *Pedigrees of the Families in the County of Kent*, 1830.

Birch, Thomas, *The Court and Times of James I*, ed. Robert F. Williams, 2 vols, 1848.

Birch, Thomas, *The Life of Henry Prince of Wales*, 1760.

Birch, Thomas, *The Life of the Most Reverend Dr John Tillotson* (prefacing his *The Works of the Most Reverend Dr. John Tillotson, Lord Archbishop of Canterbury*, 3 vols, 1752; revised edition, 1753).

Birch, Thomas, ed., *Miscellaneous Works of Mr John Greaves, Professor of Astronomy in the University of Oxford ... To the Which is Prefix'd, an Historical and Critical Account of the Life and Writings of the Author*, 1737.

Black, Jeremy, *The British Abroad. The Grand Tour in the Eighteenth Century*, Stroud and New York, 1992.

Black, Jeremy, *The British and the Grand Tour*, London, Sydney, Dover, New Hampshire, 1985.

Boström, Hans-Olof, 'Philipp Hainhofer and Gustavus Adolphus's *Kunstschrank* in Uppsala', in *The Origins of Museums. The Cabinet of Curiosities in Sixteenth- and Seventeenth-Century Europe*, ed. Oliver Impey and Arthur Macgregor, Oxford, 1985 (rpt. 1986), pp. 90–101.

Boucher, F., *Le Pont Neuf*, Paris, 1925.

Brennan, Michael G., 'The Exile of Two Kentish Royalists During the English Civil War', *Archaeologia Cantiana*, 120, 2000, pp. 77–105.

Brennan, Michael G., 'John Bargrave and the Jesuits', *Catholic Historical Review*, 88, 2002, pp. 655–76.

Brennan, Michael G., 'English Contact With Europe', in *The Arden Critical Companions, Shakespeare and Renaissance Europe*, ed. A. Hadfield and P. Hammond, 2004, pp. 53–97.

Brennan, Michael G. and Ortenberg, Veronica, 'Deux visiteurs anglais au trésor de l'abbaye de Saint-Denis au dix-septième siècle, *Paris et Ile-de-France Mémoires*, 42, 1991, pp. 261–71.

Brereton, Sir William, *Travels in Holland, the United Provinces, England ... 1634–1635*, ed. E. Hawkins, Chetham Society, 1, 1844.

Brown, Horatio, *Inglesi e Scozzesi all'Università di Padova*, Venice, 1922.

Browne, Edward, *Journal of a Visit to Paris in ... 1664*, ed. G. Keynes, 1923.

Browne, Sir Thomas, *Works of Sir Thomas Browne*, 4 vols, ed. S. Wilkin, 1835.

Burke, John, *A Genealogical and Heraldic History of the Commoners of Great Britain and Ireland*, 4 vols, 1834–8.

Buxton, John, and Juel-Jensen, Bent, 'Sir Philip Sidney's First Passport Rediscovered', *The Library*, 5 ser., 25, 1970, pp. 42–6.

Carter, Matthew, *Honor Redivivus: or, an Analysis of Honour*, 1655.

Chamberlain, John, *The Letters of John Chamberlain*, ed. N. E. McClure, 2 vols, Philadelphia, 1939.

Chaney, Edward, *The Evolution of the Grand Tour. Anglo-Italian Cultural Relations Since the Renaissance*, London and Portland, Oreg., 1998.

Chaney, Edward, *The Grand Tour and the Great Rebellion*, Geneva, 1985.

Chastel, André, et al., *Histoire générale des églises de France*, 5 vols, Paris, 1966–71.

Chenesseau, R. G., *Saincte-Croix d'Orléans*, Paris, 1921.

Clark, Ruth, *Sir William Trumbull in Paris 1685–1686*, Cambridge, 1938.

Cokayne, George Edward, ed., *Complete Baronetage*, 5 vols, Exeter, 1900–1909.

Collinson, Patrick, Ramsay, Nigel, and Sparks, Margaret, eds, *A History of Canterbury Cathedral*, Oxford, 1995.

Coryat, Thomas, *Coryat's Crudities Hastily Gobled up in Five Moneths Travells in France, Savoy, Italy, Rhetia ... Helvetia ... Some Parts of High Germany and the Netherlands*, 1611 (rpt. 2 vols, Glasgow, 1905).

Courthop, George, 'The Memoirs of Sir George Courthop (1616–1685)', ed. S. C. Lomas, *Camden Miscellany*, 11, 1907, pp. 91–107.

Crosby, Sumner McKnight, *The Royal Abbey of Saint-Denis from Its Beginnings to the Death of Suger, 475–1151*, ed. Pamela Z. Blum, New Haven and London, 1987.

CSPD, Calendar of State Papers, Domestic, 1547–1603, 8 vols, 1856–72.

CSPV, Calendar of State Papers and Manuscripts, Relating to English Affairs, Existing in the Archives and Collections of Venice, 40 vols, 1864–1947.

Culmer, Richard, *Cathedral News from Canterbury: Shewing, The Canterburian Cathedrall To Bee in an Abbey-Like Corrupt and Rotten Condition, Which Cals For a Speedy Reformation or Dissolution*, 1644. Wing C7478.

Darell, William, *The History of Dover Castle*, 1786.

Davies, Sir John, *Nosce Teipsum. This Oracle Expounded in Two Elegies*, 1599. STC 6355.

Denham, John, *Coopers Hill. A Poeme*, 1642 (rpt. 1643, 1647, 1650, 1655). Wing D993–6.

Dickens, A. G., ed., *The Courts of Europe. Politics, Patronage and Royalty 1400–1800*, 1977.

Doublet, J., *Histoire de l'abbaye de S. Denys en France*, Paris, 1625.

Duchesne, A., *Les Antiquitez et recherches des villes, chasteaux, et places plus remarquables de toute la France*, Paris, 1614.

Duncan-Jones, Katherine, *Sir Philip Sidney. Courtier Poet*, 1991.

Evelyn, John, *The Diary of John Evelyn*, ed. E. S. de Beer, 6 vols, Oxford, 1955 (reissued 2000).

Evelyn, John, *The Writings of John Evelyn*, ed. Guy de la Bédoyère, Woodbridge, 1995.

Faucheux, L. E., *Catalogue raisonné de toutes les estampes qui forment l'oeuvre d'Israel Silvestre, précedé d'une notice sur sa vie*, 1857 (rpt. Paris, 1969).

Félibien, M., *Histoire de l'abbaye royale de Saint-Denys en France*, Paris, 1706 (rpt. Paris, Édition du Palais Royal, 1973).

Fell, John, *The Life of the Most Learned ... Dr. H. Hammond*, 1661 (rpt. 1662). Wing F617–618.

Feltham, Owen, *Three Months Observations of the Low-Countries*, 1648.

Foster, Joseph, ed., *Alumni Oxonienses: the Members of the University of Oxford, 1500–1714*, 4 vols, Oxford and London, 1891–2.

Foster, Joseph, ed., *Men at the Bar: a Biographical Hand List of the Members of the Various Inns of Court, Including Her Majesty's Judges*, 2nd edn, 1885.

Frank, Thomas, 'An Edition of "A Discourse of HP his Travelles" (MS Rawlinson D. 83)', unpublished University of Oxford B.Litt thesis, 1954.

Fraser, Antonia, *Cromwell Our Chief of Men*, 1973 (rpt. 1974).

Fraser, Antonia, *King Charles II*, 1979.

Fréart, Roland, sieur de Chambray, *A Parallel of the Antient Architecture with the Modern ... Made English for the Benefit of Builders. In Which is Added an Account of Architects and*

Architecture ... With Leon Baptista Alberti's Treatise of Statues, by *John Evelyn*, London, 1664. Wing C1923.

Greaves, Richard L., and Zaller, Robert, *Biographical Dictionary of British Radicals in the Seventeenth Century*, 3 vols, Brighton, 1982–4.

Guibert, Michel C., *Mémoires pour servir à l'histoire de la ville de Dieppe*, 2 vols, Dieppe, Paris, and Rouen, 1878 [written 1761–4].

Gunther, R. T., *The Architecture of Sir Roger Pratt*, 1928.

Hadfield, Andrew, *Literature, Travel, and Colonial Writing in the English Renaissance 1545–1625*, Oxford, 1998.

Hainhofer, Jerome (translator): Jacques Du Bosc, *The Secretary of Ladies. Or, A New Collection of Letters and Answers*, 1638. *STC* 7267.

Hammond, Anthony, *The Gentleman's Exercise*, 1661. Wing H491A.

Hammond, Henry, *The Workes of Henry Hammond*, 4 vols, 1684. Wing H508.

Hammond, William, *Poems*, 1655. Wing H626.

Hatton, Ragnhild, 'Louis XIV At the Court of the Sun King', in *The Courts of Europe. Politics, Patronage and Royalty. 1400–1800*, ed. A. G. Dickens, 1977 (rpt. New York, 1984), pp. 233–62.

Herbert, Edward, *The Life of Edward, First Lord Herbert of Cherbury Written by Himself*, ed. J. M. Shuttleworth, London, New York and Toronto, 1976.

Heylin, Peter, *A Full Relation of Two Journeys: the One into the Mainland of France* [in 1625]. *The Other* [in 1629] *into Some of the Adjacent Islands*, 1656. Wing H1712.

Heylin, Peter, *Survey of the Estate of France*, 1656. Wing H1737.

Hiscock, W. G., *John Evelyn and his Family Circle*, 1955.

HMC Ancaster, Report on the Manuscripts of the Earl of Ancaster Preserved at Grimsthorpe, 1907.

HMC De L'Isle and Dudley, Historical Manuscripts Commission. Report on the Manuscripts of Lord De L'Isle & Dudley Preserved at Penshurst Place, 6 vols, 1925–66.

HMC Egmont, Report on the Manuscripts of the Earl of Egmont, 2 vols, 1905–9.

HMC Harley, Calendar of the Manuscripts of the Marquis of Bath Preserved at Longleat, Wiltshire [Harley Papers], 1904.

HMC Rutland, The Manuscripts of the Duke of Rutland Preserved at Belvoir Castle, 4 vols, 1888–1905.

HMC Salisbury, Calendar of the Manuscripts of the Most Hon. the Marquis of Salisbury Preserved at Hatfield House, 24 vols, 1883–1976.

Hoby, Sir Thomas, *A Booke of the Travaile and Lief of Me Thomas Hoby, with Diverse Things Woorth the Notinge*, ed. Edgar Powell, *The Camden Miscellany*, 10, 1902.

Hofmann, Theodore, Winterkorn, Joan, Harris, Francis, and Kelliher, Hilton, 'John Evelyn's Archive at the British Library', in *John Evelyn in the British Library*, London, 1995, pp. 11–73.

Holden, Henry, *Divinae fidei analysis*, Paris, 1652 (rpt. Cologne, 1655; tr. into English by 'W.G.', 1658).

Holden, Henry, *A Letter to a Friend*, Paris, 1657.

Hornblower, Simon, and Spawforth, Antony, *The Oxford Classical Dictionary. Third Edition*, Oxford and New York, 1996.

Hunter, Michael, 'The British Library and the Library of John Evelyn. With a Checklist of Evelyn Books in the British Library's Holdings', *The Book Collector*, 44, 1995, pp. 218–38.

Hutchinson, Harold F., *Sir Christopher Wren*, Newton Abbot, 1976.

Lassels, Richard, *The Voyage of Italy*, 2 vols in one, Paris, 1670.

Lauder, Sir John, *Journal of a Foreign Tour in 1665 and 1666 ... by Sir John Lauder*, ed. D. Crawford, Scottish Historical Society, 36, 1900.

Le Blanc, Charles, *Manuel de l'Amateur d'estampes 1550–1820*, 4 vols, Paris, 1854–89.

Le Neve, Peter, *A Catalogue of the ... Library Collected by Peter Le Neve* [with prices and purchasers' names in manuscript], 1731. [BL copy, 270.i.23 (3)].

Lough, John, *France Observed in the Seventeenth Century by British Travellers*, Stocksfield, 1984.

Macray, William Dunn, *Annals of the Bodleian Library, Oxford A.D. 1598–A.D. 1867*, London, Oxford, and Cambridge, 1868.

Macray, William Dunn, *Catalogi codicum Manuscriptorum Bibliothecae Bodleianae partisq Quintae fasciculus secundus. Viri munificentissimi Ricardi Rawlinson, J.C.D. codicum classis quartae partem priorem (libros sc. miscellaneos octingentos et sexaginta) complectans*, Oxford, 1893.

Mączak, Antoni, *Travel in Early Modern Europe*, translated by Ursula Phillips, Oxford and Cambridge, 1995.

Madan, Falconer, *A Summary Catalogue of Western Manuscripts in the Bodleian Library at Oxford. Volume III (Collections received during the 18th Century)*, Oxford, 1895.

Malloch, A., *Finch and Baines*, 1917.

Marsham, Sir John, *Chronicus Canon*, 1672. Wing M810.

Metcalfe, W. C., ed., *The Visitations of Essex* [1552–1634], Harleian Society 13, 1878.

Millet, S. G., *Le Trésor sacré ... de S. Denis*, Paris, 1645 edn.

Misson, François Maximilien, *A New Voyage to Italy, with a Description of the Chief Towns, Churches, Tombs, Libraries, Palaces, Statues and Antiquities*, 1695 (rpt in an enlarged edition, 1699). Wing M2254.

Moffet, Thomas, *The Silkewormes and their Flies (1599)*, ed. V. Houliston, Medieval & Renaissance Texts & Studies, Binghamton, New York, 1989.

Montagu, Edward, 2nd Earl of Manchester, *The Earl of Manchester's speech to His Majesty ... at his arrival at White-Hall, the 29th May 1660*, 1660. Wing M397.

Montagu, Edward, 2nd Earl of Manchester, *The Quarrel Between the Earl of Manchester and Oliver Cromwell: an episode of the English Civil War* [documents collected by John Bruce], ed. David Masson, Camden Society, n.s., 12, 1875.

Montagu, Henry, 1st Earl of Manchester, *Contemplatio mortis, et immortalis*, 1631. *STC* 18024.

Montagu, Henry, 1st Earl of Manchester, *Manchester al mondo contemplatio mortis, & immortalis*, 1635. *STC* 18026.5.

Montagu, Walter, *Miscellanea spiritualia: or, Devout essayes: the second part, composed by the honorable Walter Montagu Esq: Abbot of Nateul*, 1648. Wing M2473.

Montagu, William Drogo, 7th Duke of Manchester, *Court and Society from Elizabeth to Anne, edited from the papers at Kimbolton*, 2 vols, 1864.

Montesquiou-Fezensac, Blaise de and Gaborit-Chopin, Danielle, *Le Trésor de Saint-Denis*, 3 vols, Paris, 1973–7.

Mordant, John Viscount, *The Letter-Book of John Viscount Mordant, 1658–1660*, ed. Mary Coate, Camden Soc., 3rd ser., 1945.

Mortoft, Francis, *Francis Mortoft: His Book Being His Travels Through Italy 1658–1659*, ed. Malcolm Letts, Hakluyt Society, 2nd ser., 57, Cambridge, 1925.

Moryson, Fynes, *An Itinerary ... Written by Fynes Moryson Gent.*, 1617 (rpt. in 4 vols, Glasgow, 1907–8).

Mundy, Peter, *The Travels of Peter Mundy ... 1608–1667*, ed. R. C. Temple, 5 vols, Hakluyt Society, 2nd ser., 17, 35, 45–6, 55, 78, 1907–36.

Nichols, John, *The Progresses, Procession, and Magnificent Festivities of King James the First*, 4 vols, 1828.

Ogden, M., 'A Seventeenth Century Collection of Prints and Drawings', *Art Quarterly* 2, 1948, pp. 42–73.

Ollard, Richard, *Cromwell's Earl. A Life of Edward Mountagu 1st Earl of Sandwich*, 1994.

Osborn, James M., 'Thomas Stanley's Lost "Register of Friends"', *Yale University Library Gazette*, April 1958, pp. 1–26.

Osborn, James M., *Young Philip Sidney, 1572–1577*, New Haven, 1972.

Palladio, Andrea, *I quattro libri dell'architettura*, 1560. (Inigo Jones's copy in the library of Worcester College, Oxford.)

Palmer, Sir Thomas, *An Essay of ... Travels into Foreign Countries*, 1606. STC 19156.

Parry, Graham, *The Golden Age Restor'd: the Culture of the Stuart Court, 1603–1642*, Manchester, 1981.

Peacock, E., *Index to English Speaking Students ... at Leyden University*, 1883.

Peterson, Robert Torsten, *Sir Kenelm Digby, the Ornament of England, 1603–1665*, 1956.

Philip, Ian, *The Bodleian Library in the Seventeenth and Eighteenth Centuries. The Lyell Lectures, Oxford 1980–81*, Oxford, 1983.

Pope, Walter, *The Life of the Right Reverend Father in God Seth Ward, Lord Bishop of Salisbury*, 1697.

Powell, J. R., *The Navy in the English Civil War*, 1962.

Prest, Julia, 'Dancing King: Louis XIV's Roles in Molière's *Comédies-ballets*, from Court to Town', *The Seventeenth Century*, XVI, 2001, pp. 283–98.

Ray, John, *Observations ... Made in a Journey Through Part of the Low Countries, Germany, Italy, and France*, 1673. Wing R399.

Raymond, Thomas, *Autobiography of Thomas Raymond and Memoirs of the Family of Guise of Elmore, Gloucestershire*, ed. G. Davies, Camden Society, 3rd ser., 28, 1917.

Read, Conyers, *Lord Burghley and Queen Elizabeth*, 1960 (rpt. 1965).

Reresby, Sir John, *The Memoirs of Sir John Reresby ... 1634–1689*, ed. James J. Cartwright, 1875.

Reresby, Sir John, *Memoirs of Sir John Reresby. The Complete Text and a Selection from his Letters*, ed. Andrew Browning, *Second Edition with a New Preface and Notes*, ed. Mary K. Geiter and W. A. Speck, 1991.

Reresby, Sir John, *Memoirs & Travels of Sir John Reresby Bart*, ed. Albert Ivatt, 1904.

Richards, Nathaniel, *The Celestiall Publican*, 1630. STC 21010.

Roberti, G., *Disegno storico dell'ordine dei Minimi*, 3 vols, Rome, 1902–22.

Robinson, John Martin, *The Dukes of Norfolk. A Quincentennial History*, Oxford and New York, 1982.

Rowse, A. L., *Ralegh and the Throckmortons*, 1962.

Salmon, Thomas, *The Modern Gazetteer: or, A Short View of the Several Nations of the World*, 1746 (with numerous reprints until 1782).

Salusbury, Thomas, *Mathematical Collections and Translations*, 2 vols, 1661–5. Wing S517–517A.

Sandys, Sir Edwin, *A Relation of the State of Religion*, 1605 (rpt. 1629, 1632, 1637, 1638). STC 21716–22. Best known as *Europae Speculum* or *A Relation of the State of Religion: and with what hopes and pollicies it hath beene framed, and is maintained in the severall states of these westerne parts of the world* from the revised title-page of the 1629 edition.

Sandys, George, *A Relation of a Journey Begun An: Dom: 1610. Four Books. Containing a Description of the Turkish Empire, of Ægypt*, 1615 (rpt. 1621, 1627, 1632, 1637). *STC* 21726–30.

Sandys, George, *A Paraphrase upon the Psalms of David*, 1636. *STC* 21724.

Sandys, George, tr., *The First Five Books of Ovid's Metamorphosis*, 1621 (rpt. 1626, 1628, 1632, 1638, 1640). *STC* 18963.3–18968.

Sandys, George, tr., Hugo Grotius, *Christ's Passion. A Tragedy*, 1640. *STC* 12397.

Serres, Jean de, *A General Inventorie of the History of France*, tr. E. Grimeston, 1607. *STC* 22244.

Serres, Jean de, *Inventaire général de l'histoire de France*, Paris, 1600 (and rpt. in numerous later editions).

Serres, Olivier de, *La Cueillete de la soye, par la nourriture des vers*, Paris, 1599.

Serres, Olivier de, *The Perfect Use of Silk-wormes*, translated by N. Geffe, 1607. *STC* 22249.

Somerset, Sir Charles, *The Travel Diary (1611–1612) of an English Catholic, Sir Charles Somerset*, ed. M. G. Brennan, Leeds, 1993.

Springell, F., *Connoisseur and Diplomat ... The Earl of Arundel's Embassy to Germany in 1636 as recounted in William Crowne's Diary, the Earl's letters and other contemporary sources with a catalogue of the topographical drawings made on the journey by Wenceslaus Hollar*, 1963.

Stabenrath, G. de, *Le Palais de Justice de Rouen*, Rouen, 1895.

Stanley, Thomas, *Poems and Translations*, 1647 (rpt. 1651). Wing S5241–3.

Stanley, Thomas, *Psalterium Carolinum* [with musical settings by John Wilson], 1657. Wing S5243A.

Stein, Henri, *Le Palais de Justice et la Sainte-Chapelle de Paris*, Paris, 1912.

Stanley, Thomas, *The Poems and Translations of Thomas Stanley*, ed. Galbraith Miller Crump, Oxford, 1962.

Stern, Virginia F., *Sir Stephen Powle of Court and Country*, London and Toronto, 1992.

Stewart, Alan, *Philip Sidney. A Double Life*, 2000.

Stone, Nicholas, *Diary of Nicholas Stone, Junior, 1638–1640*, ed. W. L. Spiers, Walpole Society, 7, 1919.

Stoye, John Walter, *English Travellers Abroad 1604–1667. Their Influence in English Society and Politics (Revised Edition)*, 1952 (rpt. New Haven and London, 1989).

Strong, Sir Roy, *Henry Prince of Wales and England's Lost Renaissance*, 1986.

Stuart Proclamations: Stuart Royal Proclamations, Volume I, Royal Proclamations of King James I, 1603–1625, ed. J. F. Larkin and P. L. Hughes, Oxford, 1973.

Sturdy, David, and Henig, Martin, *The Gentle Traveller. John Bargrave, Canon of Canterbury, and his Collection*, Abingdon, 1985.

Swann, Marjorie, *Curiosities and Texts. The Culture of Collecting in Early Modern England*, Philadelphia, 2001.

Symonds, Richard, 'Extracts from the Note-Books of Richard Symonds. The Travels of Richard Symonds from Dover to Turin in 1649', printed as Appendix B of Mundy, 1608–67, pp. 217–35.

Thomas, William, *The Historie of Italy ... [which] Intreateth of the Astate of Many and Divers Common Weales*, 1549 (rpt. 1561). *STC* 24018–19.

Thomas, William, *Principal Rules of the Italian Grammar, with a Dictionary*, 1550 (rpt. 1562, 1567). *STC* 24020–2.

Treswell, R., *A Relation of Such Things as Were Observed to Happen in the Journey of the Earle of Nottingham to Spaine: for the Maintenance of Peace Betweene Great Brittaine and Spaine*, 1605. *STC* 24268.

Valdor, Jean, *Les Triomphes de Louis le Juste XIII. du nom, roy de France*, 1649.

Varennes, Claude de, *Le Voyage de France, dressé pour l'instruction & commodité tant des François que des estrangers* [translated by Claude de Varennes from the *Itinerarium Galliae* of Justus Zintzerling (Jodocus Sincerus)], Paris, 1639 (rpt. 1641, 1643, 1647, 1665, 1667, 1673).

Venn, J. and J. A., *Alumni Cantabrigienses. A Biographical List of All Known Students ... at the University of Cambridge, from the Earliest Times to 1900*, 4 vols, Cambridge, 1922–7.

Viatte, F., *Dessins de Stefano della Bella*, Paris, 1974.

Warcupp, Edmund, *Italy in its Original Glory* [translated from Franciscus Schottus, *Itinerario d'Italia*], 1660. Wing S891.

Ward, John, *The Lives of the Professors of Gresham College*, 1740 (rpt. 1750).

Whinny, Margaret, 'Sir Christopher Wren's Visit to Paris', *Gazette des Beaux-Arts* 51, 1958, pp. 229–42.

Whinny, Margaret, *Wren*, 1971.

Wilson, Thomas, *Thomas Wilson. The Art of Rhetoric (1560)*, ed. Peter E. Medine, University Park, Pa., 1994.

Woolfson, J. M., 'English Students at Padua 1480–1580', unpublished PhD dissertation, University of London, 1994.

Yeames, A. H. S., 'The Grand Tour of an Elizabethan', *Papers of the British School at Rome*, 7, 1914, pp. 92–113.

INDEX

Aachen, 2
Aarau, 131
Aarburg, 131
Aarwangen, 131n
Abdy, Thomas, 31
Addison, Joseph, 78
Adolf Frederick I, Duke of Mecklenburg-Schwerin, 120n
Aesop's fables, 164
Afonso VI, King of Portugal, 178n
Agincourt, 95n
Agrippa, Heinrich, 12
Aix-la-Chapelle, Peace of, 193n
Alençon, François, Duke of, 15
Aleppo, 234
Alessandria, 192, 247
Alexander III, Pope, 92n
Alexander VII, Pope, 6, 171n, 201n, 204n, 252n, 257
Algate, Captain Abraham, 69
Alise-Ste-Reine, 185
Allen, Mr, 229
Allin, Captain Thomas, 252n
Allsty, James, 212n
Alost, 297
Alps, mountains, 10, 14, 16, 18, 28, 32, 165–6, 170n, 218
Alsace, 177
Alstetten, 132
Altenstadt, 143
Altingen, 141
Amboise, 64, 108, 120, 221
Amboise, Cardinal George d', 84n
Amerongen, 290
Amsterdam , 4, 32, 41, 154–5, 222–6, 229–30, 290–92
Ancona, 264
Ancre, Marshal d', 115n
Andernach, 289

Angers, 31, 65, 116–17, 221, 300
Angerville, 106, 120
Anges, Jeanne des, 111n
Anne of Austria, Queen of France, 6, 84n, 87n, 96n, 174n, 241
Anne, Spanish infanta, 20
Antwerp, 2, 14, 20, 147, 237, 296
Archer, see Aucher and Hammond
Aren, 244
Aretino, Pietro, 11
Arheilgen, 285
Arles, 193, 195
Arnaud, Antoine, 174n
Arnhem, 222, 290
Arnoldstein, 274
Arnstadt, 281
Arpajon, 120n
Artas, 244
Artenay, 65, 106, 120
Ascham, Roger, 14n
Ashburnham, William, 35
Ashurst, Mr, 181, 184
Ashworth, Mr, 35
Assmannhausen, 287
Asti, 247
Aubonne, 130
Aubrey, John, 152
Aucher, Elizabeth, see Hammond
Aucher, Sir Anthony, 168n
Auerbach, 67, 138
Auerstedt, 280
Augsburg, 14, 43, 67–8, 119n, 134–6, 138, 147, 283
Augustinians, religious order, 94, 189
Aunis, province of, 116, 213
Aussig, 279
Auxerre, 185
Avenches, 67, 131
Avignon, 192, 197, 204

313